Britain in Europe

■ An introduction to sociology

Edited by

Tony Spybey

ROUTLEDGE

London and New York

LCR: Library

SOMERSET COLLEGE OF ARTS & TECHNOLOGY

First published 1997
by Routledge
11 New Fetter Lane, London
EC4P 4EE

Simultaneously published in the
USA and Canada
by Routledge
29 West 35th Street, New York,
NY 10001

© 1997 Tony Spybey

Typeset in Century Old Style by
Florencetype Ltd, Stoodleigh,
Devon

Printed and bound in Great
Britain by TJ International Ltd,
Padstow, Cornwall

All rights reserved. No part of
this book may be reprinted or
reproduced or utilized in any
form or by any electronic,
mechanical, or other means, now
known or hereafter invented,
including photocopying and
recording, or in any information
storage or retrieval system,
without permission in writing
from the publishers.

*British Library Cataloguing in
Publication Data*
A catalogue record for this book
is available from the British
Library

*Library of Congress Cataloging in
Publication Data*
Britain in Europe / edited by
Tony Spybey
p. cm.
Includes bibliographical
references and index.
1. Europe–Social conditions–
20th century. 2. Europe–Social
policy. 3. Europe–Economic
conditions–20th century.
4. Europe–Politics and
government–20th century. 5.
European Union–Great Britain.
I. Spybey, Tony.
HN373.5.B75 1997
306'. 094–dc21   96–45444
CIP

ISBN 0–415–11716–X (hbk)
ISBN 0–415–11717–8 (pbk)

Contents

List of figures   xi
List of tables   xiii
List of contributors   xv
Introduction   1

Part one

THE MAKING OF
MODERN EUROPE   9

1   Industrialization   11

**2   Urbanization and Urban
      Europe: the transition to
      urban lifestyles and
      contemporary urban problems**   25

**3   The State as a European
      Creation**   51

4   Reason and Modernity   69

Part two

THE MAKING OF THE
MODERN EUROPEAN   91

5   Social Stratification   93

**6   Women, Paid Employment
      and Equal Opportunity**   125

**7   Racism, Immigration and
      Migrant Labour**   147

**8   Winners and Losers: young
      people in Europe**   161

9   Old Age in Europe   173

Part three

SOCIAL PROCESSES AND
CONTEMPORARY ISSUES   199

10   Families in Europe   201

11   Education in Europe   219

12   Religion in Europe   239

**13   Work, Employment and
      Unemployment**   257

**14   European Culture and
      Ideology in Mass
      Communication**   273

Part four

THE INDIVIDUAL AND THE
STATE IN CONTEMPORARY EUROPE

295

**15 Political Participation in
Europe: theme and variation**   297

**16 Implementing Social Welfare
Policy in Europe: the
significance of social work,
social pedagogy and
community work**   317

17 Poverty and Social Security   343

**18 Health, Healthcare and
Health Inequalities**   359

**19 Crime and Penal Policy
in Europe**   379

Part five

LOOKING FORWARD:
CHALLENGES FACING EUROPE

399

**20 Urban Change and Urban
Problems**   401

**21 Peripheral Nationalism in
the European Union**   423

**22 Europe's Changing Role
in the Globalization Process**   435

CONTENTS

Sources of data	449
Bibliography	451
Index	475

Figures

2.1	Cities of the Roman Empire	28
2.2	The growth of provincial capitals, 1000–1950	29
2.3	Stocking-frame weavers in their home	37
2.4	Shanty town on the outskirts of Berlin, *c.* 1880	40
2.5	Workers' neighbourhood in central London, 1854	42
2.6	The redesigning of Paris, *c.* 1890	46
5.1	Income equality in selected countries	109
5.2	Trends in income equality	110
5.3	Regional income variations in the European Union	111
6.1	A typical inverted U-shaped curve	129
6.2	A typical M-shaped curve	130
6.3	A typical single-peak curve	130
6.4a	Women's share of service occupations	133
6.4b	Women's share of clerical occupations	133
10.1	Average age of women at first marriage and mean age at birth of their first child	214
10.2	Marriage and divorce	216
12.1	Religious divisions in Europe	243
13.1	Work calls!	259
13.2	The flexible firm	263
14.1	Silvio Berlusconi	278
14.2	Cable and satellite penetration in Europe, 1995	283
14.3	Shares of video households: European Union and world regions	285
16.1	The gap	333
16.2	Praxis – the action/reflection cycle	337
16.3	The gap (II)	338

17.1   The distribution of poverty in Europe using 'national' and
       'community' poverty lines, 1985   347
17.2   Poverty among lone mothers and pensioners in Europe, 1987/89   348
17.3   The ratio of unemployed non-EU nationals to unemployed
       EU nationals, 1987–1991   349
18.1   Health expenditure per person and infant mortality rate, 1988   362
18.2   Health expenditure and GDP per person, 1988–90   364
18.3   Health expenditure per person as a percentage of GDP, 1988–90   365
18.4   Public percentage of health expenditure, OECD and UK   366
18.5   Deaths per million children from infectious diseases, 1870–1970   375
20.1   Regional variations in population density, 1988   404
20.2   The 'Manchester to Milan' growth axis of the EC   405
20.3   A model of the Western European city   409

Tables

2.1	Fastest growing cities, in three periods, 1500–1800	30
2.2	The largest cities in Europe, 1000–1900	33
5.1	The Registrar-General's social classes	106
5.2	The Registrar-General's socio-economic groups	106
5.3	Comparative earnings	107
5.4	National differences in attitudes to dimensions of class and inequality	112
5.5	How should the economy be structured?	112
5.6	Socio-economic groups: England and Wales, 1921–91	115
5.7	Occupational transition in Europe: 'professional, technical and related workers'	115
6.1	Female percentage of the labour force in member states of the European Union, 1991	129
6.2	The percentage of women working part time, 1992	131
6.3	Female earnings as a percentage of male earnings across Europe, 1980–91	132
6.4	Percentages of mothers and fathers in employment with children aged less than 10, 1988	135
6.5	Percentage employment rates for women aged 16–39 in Europe by age of youngest child, 1988	135
6.6	Married men's preferences for a working or non-working wife, 1987	136
6.7	Female labour market activity rates across Europe, 1970–89	137
6.8	Maternity and parental leave entitlements across Europe	138
6.9	Public child-care provision across Europe	139
9.1	The ranked proportions of older people (65+) in Europe for 1993 and the projected proportions for 2025	176
11.1	The primary phase curriculum	225

11.2	Main types of qualification leading on to higher education	232
11.3	European Community initiatives to foster co-operation and innovation in higher education and training	234
12.1	Religious upbringing, importance of religion and church attendance, 1990	247
13.1	Share of economic sectors in employment in 1992	261
13.2	Usual length of the working week for full-time employees in 1992	266
13.3	Hours usually worked per week by persons in full-time employment, 1992	267
13.4	Usual length of the working week for part-time employees in 1992	268
14.1	Cable and satellite in Central/Eastern Europe	284
17.1	Retrenchments in welfare statism in five industrialized countries in the 1970s and 1980s	352
18.1	Life expectancy at birth (years) in Europe, 1960 and 1991	361
18.2	Trends in standardized mortality rates per thousand inhabitants in Europe, by gender	361
18.3	Organization of European healthcare systems	363
18.4	Infant mortality rates in Europe	367
18.5	Maternal mortality rates in Europe	368
18.6	Standardized mortality rates for cardiovascular disease in Europe, 1983 and 1990	369
18.7	Trends in the cancer standardized mortality rates by gender per thousand inhabitants in Europe	369
18.8	Standardized mortality rates for cancer of the trachea, bronchus and lung in Europe, among people aged 0–64	370
18.9	Standardized mortality rate among Swedish men aged 25–64, 1976–80	372
19.1	Figures, incidence rates and ranking of eighteen European countries for selected crime categories in 1990	384
19.2	Rates of change of officially recorded crime in sixteen European countries, 1987–92	385
19.3	Percentage of respondents victimized by crimes covered in the International Crime Survey in 1988	387
19.4	Percentage of crimes reported by victims to the police in 1988	387
19.5	European prison populations at 1 September 1990	394
19.6	Increases in prison rates	396
19.7	Decreases in prison rates	396
20.1	Proportion of the population resident in urban places, 1950–2010, for EC12 countries	403
20.2	Approximate breakdown by priority objective, billion ECU, 1994 prices	413
20.3	Targeting of Action for Cities expenditure, 1988/9 and 1989/90	417

Contributors

Pamela Abbott is Professor of Sociology and Director of the School of Social Sciences at the University of Teesside. She was formerly Principal Lecturer in Sociology at the University of Plymouth.

Louise Ackers is Lecturer and Deputy Director of the Centre for the Study of Law in Europe at the University of Leeds. She was formerly Senior Lecturer in Social Policy at the University of Plymouth.

Alison Anderson is Lecturer in Sociology at the University of Plymouth.

Doug Benson is Principal Lecturer in Sociology at the University of Plymouth.

Lyn Bryant is Principal Lecturer in Sociology and Co-ordinator of the Joint Social Sciences Scheme at the University of Plymouth.

Joan Chandler is Head of the Department of Sociology at the University of Plymouth.

David Dawson was formerly Senior Lecturer in Sociology at the University of Plymouth.

Rhys Dogan is Lecturer in Politics at the University of Plymouth.

George Giacinto Giarchi is Professor Emeritus of Social Care Studies at the University of Plymouth.

Daniel Gilling is Senior Lecturer in Social Policy at the University of Plymouth.

Eric Harrison is Lecturer in Sociology at the University of Plymouth.

Will Hay is Senior Lecturer in Social Work at the University of Plymouth.

Sue Hemmings is Lecturer in Sociology at the University of Plymouth.

Mark Hyde is Lecturer in Social Policy at the University of Plymouth.

Paul Iganski is Principal Lecturer in Social Policy at the University of Plymouth.

Sidney Jacobs is Senior Lecturer in Social Policy at the University of Plymouth.

Ann Jeffries is Head of the Department of Social Work and Social Policy at the University of Plymouth.

Ron Kirby is Principal Lecturer in Community and Youth Work at the College of St Mark and St John, Plymouth.

Werner Müller is Dean of Social Work at the Fachhochschule für Sozialwesen, Esslingen, Germany.

Geoff Payne is Professor of Social Research and Dean of the Faculty of Human Sciences at the University of Plymouth.

Keith Popple is Senior Lecturer in Social Policy at the University of Plymouth.

Tony Spybey is Professor of Sociology and Head of the Sociology Division at Staffordshire University. He was formerly Principal Lecturer in Sociology at the University of Plymouth.

Malcolm Williams is Senior Lecturer in Sociology at the University of Plymouth.

Introduction

Tony Spybey

What is Europe?   2
The formation of the European Union   2
Organization of this book   4
How to use this book   8

THIS BOOK is intended to provide students at first year undergraduate level with an innovative and comprehensive guide to the social, political and economic institutions of Britain and her European partners. Every member of British society already has some knowledge of these institutions – but here they are deliberately presented in their European context. Britain is treated in terms of both its geographic position as an off-shore part of Europe and its politico-economic situation as a member of a progressively integrating European Union.

What is Europe?

There is no hard and fast definition of Europe. It can be defined and drawn on maps as a distinct geographical or political area in a number of ways. It is possible for instance to define Europe in terms of the European Union, simply because that is the current politico-economic arrangement for co-operation and alignment between the European sovereign states. The European Union is therefore of paramount importance for the Europeans of today, including those who for various reasons have not yet become a part of the arrangement.

Throughout history there have been very different attempts to unite Europe at the hands of such powerful and charismatic figures as Charlemagne, Napoleon and Hitler for instance. Each of these aspired to an imagined community of Europe based upon particular preoccupations however misguided or perverted.

Now, however, the visionaries of a fully fledged European Union aspire to something like a 'United States of Europe' in order to provide a politico-economic power bloc capable of standing alongside the other two economic super-powers – the USA and Japan. The British government at present remains fundamentally opposed to political integration in Europe, preferring mainly economic but also political co-operation between separate sovereign states. Elsewhere, the USA has formed the North American Free Trade Area (NAFTA) which already includes Canada and Mexico and may soon be extended to Chile and possibly other Latin American countries. Japan has produced a successful economic model which other East Asian countries are emulating and Japanese leaders have frequently projected their country as the obvious leader for more concerted economic co-operation across the East Asian countries.

In the face of this trend towards three global economic concentrations there remain a variety of interpretations of the term 'Europe'. This is especially so after the break-up of the Soviet Union and the desire of its former allies in Eastern Europe to associate themselves more closely with Western Europe in general and with the European Union in particular. Most of the Western European countries are now members of the European Union and it is useful therefore to describe its formation.

The formation of the European Union

Two world wars during the twentieth century began with conflict between European countries. In the first place they could be described as more or less

European civil wars, although they grew into something much more widespread, particularly in the case of the Second World War. As a result of this in 1945 there was a general desire, both within Europe and outside, to find a way to avoid a further recurrence. In particular two Frenchmen, Jean Monnet and Robert Schuman, felt that lasting peace would only be secured by some form of arrangement that would avoid the old antagonisms between Germany and France.

The post-Second World War development of European co-operation therefore begins in 1951 with the foundation of an industrial coal and steel community involving not only Germany and France but also Italy and the Benelux countries (*Bel*gium, the *Net*herlands and *Lux*embourg). With the signing of the Treaty of Rome in 1957, these six countries extended the arrangement to include a customs union and so formed the original *European Economic Community (EEC)*. Customs union meant that each would not charge import duties on the produce of the others.

Britain at first declined to be a member, largely it is said because of its dependence on food at privileged prices from Australia and New Zealand. There was also its links with other countries outside of Europe which at that time were still British colonies. When Britain later tried to join, during the 1960s, the application was twice vetoed by the French president, Charles de Gaulle, because he thought that Britain would be a disruptive member.

The EEC of this period was primarily dedicated to economic measures, with other forms of co-operation kept largely in the background. Since then the membership has gradually been increased and Britain eventually joined in January 1973 along with Ireland and Denmark. Further enlargement came when Greece joined in January 1981 and Spain and Portugal in January 1986. The organization of this expanded EEC consisted of, as it still does, three parts: the Council of Ministers, the European Commission and the European Parliament.

The *Council of Ministers,* which meets in Brussels, is the primary decision-making body and a minister from each member country takes part. In this way government ministers from member countries come together but each country's representative is not always the same person. For instance, if agriculture is being discussed the Council will normally be made up of agriculture ministers and this changes according to the issue at hand. On issues which are considered as important the outcome has to be unanimous and therefore any country which disagrees has in effect the power of veto, although considerable lobbying and discussion will normally take place before it comes to this.

The *European Commission,* based permanently in Brussels, is a kind of civil service and the commissioners, backed up by their staffs, will draw up proposals for the Council of Ministers to consider. Each country has at least one commissioner but the larger countries, including Britain, have two. They are normally ex-politicians. For instance, at the time of writing Britain's commissioners are Leon Brittain, the former Conservative cabinet minister, and Neil Kinnock, the former Labour leader in opposition.

The *European Parliament* sits in Strasbourg and, with the addition of Austria, Finland and Sweden, has 626 members elected from member countries. Before the Council of Ministers can make its decisions they have to be discussed by the Parliament. However, many people feel that it has little say in decision-making and this forms much of the basis for fears about the power of the permanent commissioners in Brussels. Nevertheless, the deliberations of the Parliament have on a number of occasions caused the decisions of the Council of Ministers to be modified.

With increasing arrangements for co-operation during the late 1980s the EEC became known as simply the *European Community (EC)* and then during the early 1990s as the *European Union (EU)*. More specifically, in December 1991 the *Maastricht Treaty* was signed with the intention of abolishing separate currencies and having one basic interest rate. This would enormously facilitate banking and other financial transactions between European countries. It would do away with exchange rates and speculation in European currencies. It would also enable people to travel throughout Europe without having to change their money from one currency to another. However, it has since proved difficult to get the various economies into sufficiently strong condition to achieve the objective. In January 1993 the *Single Market* came into force enabling not only goods but also money and labour, that is people as workers, to pass freely between the member states. Money from British bank accounts can be invested elsewhere in the EU and people can, in principle at least, go to work wherever they choose within the Union.

In January 1995 there were further additions to the European Union when Austria, Finland and Sweden joined. This leaves Norway, whose people voted by referendum against joining, and Switzerland as the only Western European countries outside of the Union. In the future there is much further expansion in prospect mainly from the former state socialist countries of Eastern Europe. However their economies are at present significantly weaker than those of Western Europe and consequently they are likely to experience difficulty operating in the Single Market. Britain is in favour of further expansion of the Union in its present form, but it is against intensification of the arrangement particularly if it is to take the direction of a federation of states, to all intents and purposes a 'United States of Europe'.

Organization of this book

This book seeks to show the diversity of what passes for European in terms of social institutions. The institutions with which we have grown up are neither the only nor necessarily the best ways of answering society's challenges. Therefore it is useful to engage in an appraisal of what exists. The approach here will be through examination of the various European institutions. By that is meant the various forms of social, political and economic organization that have become institutionalized in European culture. It will proceed mainly by putting the British version of these institutions alongside those of its European partners, although there will be some variation chapter to chapter according to the subject matter.

The text is divided into five parts. *Part one* looks at the making of modern Europe, the most significant trends in the creation of modern European society. There are important aspects of social development which are common to the

European countries despite the cultural differences between the nation-states and regions which make up Europe.

The combination of large-scale industrialization (Chapter 1) and urbanization (Chapter 2) are features uniquely linked to the development of Europe, but of course they have since been emulated in all other parts of the world. During the eighteenth and nineteenth centuries, beginning in Britain, the people of Europe developed an innovative and progressive urban industrial culture, a style of life that has become the aspiration for people in other parts of the world. The European model of industrialization has become a global model but this does not mean that countries such as Japan cannot improve upon the industrial techniques involved. Global cultural flows are by definition global and that means that the process of change continues drawing in ever more people.

Another factor is that the Europe from which this industrial urban culture is derived was throughout its development a set of separate sovereign states (Chapter 3) and it remains so. These are commonly referred to as *nation-states*. Europe has been a collection of separate states throughout its more recent history, and the model of the European nation-state, in conjunction with the process of change to an industrialized and urbanized lifestyle, has become a universal model adopted throughout the rest of the world. The idealized model of the nation-state and its workings is not always strictly adhered to, but the most remarkable thing is the way in which all countries seek to be recognized as nation-states. To all intents and purposes the world is organized as a nation-state system, and the foundation of the United Nations Organization in 1945 was a significant confirmation of this.

The form of organization involved in the nation-state is what Max Weber labelled as 'legal–rational bureaucracy'. It is based upon rules and regulations which are seen as rational in the context of European cultural development. More broadly it is part of the rise of 'reason' in European civilization (Chapter 4), the desire to transcend 'unreasonable' forms of explanation and procedure in favour of those based upon rational analysis and the use of calculation. The quest for material progress achievable through rational or scientific explanation is what has set European civilization apart from the others and it is the basis for scientific explanation, the application of technology and the institutions of modernity in general.

Part two goes on to look at the making of the modern European. The reproduction of institutions in the development of Europe has given rise to social cleavages which we all experience in some way or other. Although one of the ideals of European culture is equality, in opportunity at least, we are not all equal and the concept of social stratification (Chapter 5) is intended to throw light on this. For a long time this was an obsession in social science, but more recently it has been recognized that gender (Chapter 6) and racial differences (Chapter 7) are at least as important. Both are related to the division of labour and the opportunities that exist for Europeans at work. In this respect income is the key to many aspirations. Age too is a significant factor in the provision of life chances, and both the young (Chapter 8) and the old (Chapter 9) have special problems in finding their place in the Europe of the late twentieth century. Changes of relative consumption or deprivation over the course of the life-cycle have relevance to many aspects of inequality that are the subject of social research.

Part three concentrates on those social processes which are constantly at issue in the review and analysis of day-to-day life in Europe. The family (Chapter 10) is arguably the most basic of all the social institutions, linking as it does the biological aspects of humanity with the social. It also provides the primary socialization encountered by human beings in their life-cycle. Therefore European family forms, in their similarities and differences, are a central pivot to social processes in Europe.

From the family the young go into education (Chapter 11), and some writers have argued that the establishment of mass education in Europe has subsequently been used as an index of progress in other parts of the world where the European model of the nation-state has been emulated. Nation-states are to some extent judged according to the extent that they provide substantive education for their citizens and educated citizens for work.

Religion (Chapter 12), however, is a social institution which cuts across both the family and education. Christianity was originally the thread by which the culture of Europe survived after the fall of Rome and in this sense it was the container of knowledge through the Middle or 'Dark' Ages to the Renaissance. The Church was responsible for scholarship throughout this period and later for much of the initial broadening of access to education.

The process of learning however became changed by the needs of industry (Chapter 13) and there emerged the more instrumental idea of 'education for work'. It has been argued that, under the social conditions of modernity, life in general has become more instrumental and oriented more specifically to achieve-ment. Educational attainment has been an effective sorting mechanism for entry into work, and mass education has taken the form of a compromise between ideals of scholarship and the necessity to obtain skills and qualifications that are valid in the workplace.

Under contemporary economic conditions, of course, work is not available for everyone whatever their aptitudes and qualifications. It is often claimed that the basis on which work is organized and allocated is in need of substantial rethink-ing. The expectation of education being followed virtually automatically by a job for life is under threat and alternative ideas of lifelong learning and work rotation or sharing have come into vogue. But it is difficult to move away from established patterns. Therefore an appreciation of the contemporary development of social processes in working life is important for an understanding of present-day Europe.

A much vaunted panacea for the decline of traditional forms of work is the electronic revolution, although the adoption of electronic techniques has also been blamed for the loss of jobs. In essence this form of technology has been largely applied to the processing and transmission of knowledge or, to put it another way, communication (Chapter 14). The communication of knowledge, human to human and human to machine, is equally an application of the new electronic technology. Communication on a global scale is another creation of Western civilization and yet by definition this could never be contained in the West. Therefore the new media of communication pose both an opportunity and a challenge to Europe.

Part four is devoted to the relationship between the individual and the state in Europe. One of the defining characteristics of modernity is political participation (Chapter 15) as developed by Europeans in the form of representative democracy. With the achievement of this form of representation in government the expectations of citizenship have gone beyond political rights to include a range of welfare benefits (Chapter 16).

A review of the ways in which these are administered across Europe is revealing of the current condition of the welfare state in the face of economic downturn. Poverty and social security (Chapter 17), health and healthcare (Chapter 18) are dimensions of this dilemma. All European countries are having to face up to the problem of trying to find appropriate levels of welfare for populations that appear to have limitless capacities for such services. Idealized notions of the levels of care that the state should provide for its citizens are characteristically European, but they must now be addressed in the face of declining public finance. The lengthening of the human life-cycle together with changes to the pattern of work mean that the costs of state welfare outstrip the means to pay for it.

It is often asserted that one outcome of unemployment and poverty is an escalation of crime and by the same token the application of punishment (Chapter 19). Dealing with this represents the hard edge of state administration and it is an area of concern particularly sensitive to public opinion in the harsh economic climate of the late twentieth century. On the one hand people demand more punishment as a response to increased levels of crime and on the other there are concerns as the percentage of the population in prison rises.

Finally, in *Part five* the focus is on the future and the challenges that face Europe. For the most part an urbanized society, Europe faces huge problems of urban renewal (Chapter 20) as a result of transformations in our desires for acceptable living space. The solutions of the 1960s for instance are simply not acceptable in the 1990s, and the reversal of outdated housing policies is often more expensive than the original schemes. This reduces significantly the capacity to bring about improvements now.

Europeans are of course also concerned about their national identity. The European Union has already begun to take over some of the functions of the nation-state, and therefore the established nation-state system – on which Europe was founded – becomes threatened. In the face of this, some groups of people seek to revive identities alternative to the accepted nationalities of the nation-states, as for instance the Basques in Spain. Others seek to exclude those who do not fit their particular definitions of nationality or belonging. Some particularly cruel demonstrations of this have been seen in the break-up of the former Yugoslavia. Peripheral or alternative nationalisms (Chapter 21), set against the existing constitution of nation-states, are a visible phenomenon virtually throughout Europe. In some cases the European Union is seen for them as a desirable alternative to the constrictions of the nation-state. If it is to survive, therefore, the European Union must find an acceptable way of accommodating the dissatisfactions of what are often minority movements in the established state structure. Moreover this has to be achieved without risking a premature disabling of the nation-state system because this is likely to be unwanted on a broader scale of public opinion.

Above all it must preserve a unity adequate for Europeans to be able to flourish in an increasingly globalized world with rival conglomerations in North America and East Asia (Chapter 22). The possibility of the Pacific supplanting the Atlantic as the hub around which the world's major economic activity takes place is more and more something that has to be addressed by contemporary Europeans.

How to use this book

This book is not intended to be read cover to cover in one sitting. Such a substantial number of pages is a daunting prospect and needs to be approached in a more calculated way. It is designed to be a resource and it is suggested that, for instance, you might study a chapter or two at a time alongside the course that you are taking or as a part of your personal studies. Key concepts appear at the beginning of each chapter and these might be used to orientate what is provided here with the syllabus that you are following, or eventually might simply be useful as revision aids. The summary that appears at the end of each chapter is a synthesis of the material that appears in it. It forms the core of what you should be drawing from it. Further reading too is suggested at the end of each chapter and amongst other things this is to help in the preparation of assessment topics or in revision for examinations. In this way the length of the book becomes less formidable and the contents more useful.

Finally, there is a format or template to each chapter. Each is consistently set out as follows:

- *Key concepts* – these are concepts that you will recognize as general social science concepts. They will help you orientate to the material which appears in the chapter.
- *Introduction* – this will relate the key concepts to the rest of the chapter and it will generally introduce you to the material that appears in it.
- *Main text* – this is the body of the chapter and in most cases it is augmented with tables, diagrams and other forms of illustration.
- *Summary* – this is a list of important points selected from the chapter and it is therefore also a handy summary of the information which you should have derived from it.
- *Further reading* – this is a short list of recommendations for further reading as provided by the authors. Other references which appear in the text have been collected in a consolidated bibliography towards the end of the book.

The making of modern Europe

PART ONE addresses the making of modern Europe through those aspects of the development of European society which set it apart from the other civilizations. Firstly, industrialization perhaps more than anything else has influenced not only the formation of European societies but their impact upon the rest of the world. Secondly, other civilizations have produced cities but the enormous growth of European trade and industrialization transformed Europeans into urban dwellers or else transformed their lifestyles to such an extent that in some respects the urban and the rural are indistinguishable. People were drawn into the towns in large numbers but agriculture was industrialized too, transforming town and countryside alike into a created environment. Thirdly, in place of the city came the nation-state as the political and administrative entity. The centralization of administration and the monopolization of power by the state have been features of European societal development but, like industrialization, they have been taken up around the world. The modern world is a world of nation-states and the model is European. Fourthly, on a more conceptual plane, the development of concepts of 'reason' in the way that people think and reflect upon the nature of society is largely due to the ascendancy of a distinctively European form of rationality. The term 'Enlightenment' denotes the historical period when this came about. European thought has been hugely influential in other cultures and only relatively recently have people begun to question whether European ways of thinking should have the primacy in the world that its progenitors, Europeans, have enjoyed during the past two hundred years or so.

Chapter 1

Industrialization

Eric Harrison

Introduction   12
Origins: Britain as pioneer   12
Enter the Europeans   16
War and industrialization   20
Reflection   22
Summary   22
Further reading   23

Key concepts

- **Industrialism**
- **Economic growth**
- **Mass production**

11

Introduction

Industrialization has a special place in the social sciences. For the sociologist, especially, it is difficult to imagine the contemporary world without the presence and consequences of industry. To many, industrialism is the very essence of what it is to be modern and 'developed'. The story of the Industrial Revolution, which changed the face of Europe, has been the staple diet of schoolchildren for decades. It evokes images of women crammed together in Lancashire mill-factories, spinning cotton on machines like Hargreaves's 'Spinning Jenny' and Crompton's 'Mule', producing goods which made fortunes for the nineteenth century's captains of industry. Nowadays historians tend to play down the 'revolutionary' element and instead portray industrialization as a gradual process which picked up speed steadily throughout the nineteenth and twentieth centuries, and which had a distinctly uneven character. The uneven nature of the European experience is a theme which emerges throughout this book and one which applies to industrialism *par excellence*. The purpose of this chapter is not to address in detail the debates in economic history about when, where and how quickly industrialization proceeded, but rather to point out a number of key characteristics of industrialism which are relevant to this book's theme – namely, the relation of Britain to its Continental neighbours. In doing so it is important to remember that, for the sociologist, the symbols and myths of industrialism are as important as the figures and trends which economic historians have reconstructed.

Origins: Britain as pioneer

Historians still argue about when and where industrialization began. Some claim to see early signs of industrial working patterns in parts of Europe from the fifteenth century onwards. However, it is still most common to associate industrialization with the movement to the towns in the later eighteenth century. To this extent, industrialism is closely related to urbanism, which is dealt with in the next chapter. Here we are concerned with the features of the emerging modern economy, though it is worth remembering that industrialization was specific to certain localities. Within a European context, it has been in parts of northern England that we usually locate the building of what Mathias (1969) called 'The First Industrial Nation'. Britain was the first, the heroic pioneer whose achievements were taken on and copied by the rest of Europe. This idea of Britain as the 'blueprint' for the European economy is somewhat misleading, but it is undeniably the case that later industrializers both mimicked British successes and learnt from experience to avoid unnecessary experimentation and speed up the process. In any case the symbolism of Britain giving industrialism to the world has continued to be culturally important. Even so, life in rural Dorset would have remained more similar to that of rural France than to that of the new mill towns of East Lancashire.

The nature of industrialism

Even if the pace of economic growth was slower and less sudden than originally believed, we must also draw attention to the genuinely revolutionary nature of the period in question. Quite simply, within the space of a generation there was an enormous increase in human ability to produce the means of existence. Many famous accounts use similar language: Kemp (1985) defines industrialization as 'A more productive use of the factors of production obtained partly by altering the proportions in which they were applied, partly by improving their efficiency, and partly by introducing new techniques.' Hobsbawm (1962) claims that 'For the first time in human history, the shackles were taken off the productive power of human societies', and Perkin (1969) talked of 'a revolution in men's access to the means of life, in control over their ecological environment, in their capacity to escape from the tyranny and niggardliness of nature'.

This emphasis upon the technical productive capacity of industrialism is what normally distinguishes it from that other driving force of modern economies; namely, capitalism. The relationship between the two has been the source of much debate. Traditionally scholars influenced by Marx have stressed the capitalist nature of modern societies, while others have been concerned to examine them first and foremost as 'industrial societies'. Theories of industrialism stress the process through which production is carried out. Theories of capitalism concentrate on the distribution and exchange of the resulting products by means of the market mechanism. The intertwining of the two is extremely complex, since it is possible to conceive both of non-capitalist industrialism (see pp. 21–2) and forms of pre- or non-industrial capitalism (see Chapter 2). From the outset of the Industrial Revolution to the First World War the two were always found together. (For a more detailed discussion of the relationship between capitalism and industrialism, see Giddens 1985: 122–47.)

Another matter on which there is disagreement is the question of just why this process should first have come to fruition in Britain. Certainly, European industrialization can only be understood in the light of British industrialization, the repercussions of which were largely negligible outside that country until the 1830s. This first phase of development was marked by businesses owned by individuals or families, and was dominated by one consumer product: cotton. Some suggest that Britain's steady and peaceful development in the seventeenth and eighteenth centuries gave it a secure environment within which profits could be pursued, a base of manufacturing skills, and easy access to capital among successful landowners and financiers. Charles Wilson (1965) has referred to this as 'England's apprenticeship', although by 1704 with the Act of Union the constitutional entity was 'Britain'. Perhaps more importantly, it also already enjoyed an active role within a world market ready to accept the fruits of its labour. Braudel (1984) has described how London took over from Amsterdam as the financial centre of a 'European world-economy' during the late seventeenth and eighteenth centuries but, whilst Amsterdam had enjoyed its primacy as a city-state, in the case of London it was as the capital city of Britain, already a properly constituted modern nation-state (see also Chapter 3 on the city-state and the making of the modern nation-state).

It is worth making the point that Britain is normally viewed as the only example of a 'spontaneous' industrialization. Elsewhere in Europe afterwards, mid-century economic expansion was far more self-conscious and state-supported. The Victorians had clear views about the role of government in the affairs of business; this was to provide minimal support by defending the realm, guaranteeing the protection of property rights, and keeping income taxes low. In this era, the idea was developed of the economy and the polity as separate 'spheres', the 'private sector and the public sector', a belief Marx ridiculed when he wrote of the (male) worker who suffered the utmost exploitation at work but was encouraged to feel like a citizen when casting his vote (though even among males, this was a privilege open to relatively few until much later).

'Yoked together with iron and steam . . .'

Let us now turn to those inputs referred to by Kemp, above. In another context these were summed up by Briggs (1959) as 'men, machines and materials' (though as we shall see, factories depended as much upon woman- as man-power). He isolated three technological advances which pushed industry forward. Firstly, there was the mechanization of the textile industry, led by the cotton sector because of its relative newness and therefore openness to change. Arkwright's 'water-frame', patented in 1769, and Crompton's 'Mule' of 1779, for instance, could not be accommodated in existing domestic workshops and so required purpose-built factories (Mathias 1969). If cotton was the key material for mass clothing, then that of mass construction was iron. The total output of 'pig iron' (iron smelted with coke) doubled between 1788 and 1796 and would remain the dominant symbol of progress until steel became cheaper in the mid-nineteenth century. Iron and coal jointly constituted the second great advance, but would not have been so valuable without the third, the development of the steam engine. Indeed steam is often seen as the key symbol of the mid-nineteenth century. Steam power meant additional motive force in production, but it also allowed factories to locate elsewhere than along waterways. Thus for the first time human production was severed from its reliance upon nature. Technology had altered not only the content of industrial production but also its geographical pattern, as will become apparent in Chapter 2.

As mentioned above, Britain already had a sound base of manufactures, and this allowed the new machinery and the new fuel to be adopted swiftly in sectors where working patterns had already developed a distinctly specialized division of labour. Thus industrial organization benefited from innovation not merely in the sphere of inanimate power but also in the way the workforce was mobilized. This specialization is described in Adam Smith's classic account of how pin-making was made more efficient by the division of labour, and this has remained a popular model right through to recent times. This combination of repetitive tasks, long hours, a noisy crowded work environment and the dictates of the new machinery meant that factory work was extremely hard, although well paid by comparison with much of agriculture. As the factory system spread the hardship of the workforce became noted by many, and reforms were passed to regulate working hours and conditions.

One of the largest contrasts with pre-industrial production was the way that the factory system imposed a highly regulated regime of surveillance and discipline on its workforce. Some observers wondered whether it was technology which was being harnessed to human desire, or whether the boot was in fact on the other foot. J. P. Kay wrote that 'whilst the engine runs, the people must work – men, women and children are yoked together with iron and steam. The animal machine . . . is chained fast to the iron machine, which knows no suffering and weariness' (quoted in Briggs 1959: 61). Indeed, women and children did form a large part of the workforce during this early period, since they either possessed small, adept fingers or were assumed to have experience of working with cloth. Women would be just as conspicuous by their later absence from the foundries; the redrawing of the sexual division of labour dates from this period.

During the first half of the nineteenth century, the changing organization of economic production gave rise to new forms of social inequality, which became expressed in terms of 'class'. Again, this is an area where there is great controversy. Many historians argue that we have been too influenced by the work of Marx and Engels and have confused much of their political sloganeering with the more measured assessments of contemporary social relations offered by others. The classic picture is of the nineteenth century as the 'bourgeois' century, the triumph of industrial capital over the traditional landed aristocracy. The relatively stable but open hierarchy of ranks and orders which characterized the eighteenth century was replaced by fewer, more clearly defined and antagonistic groups, Marx's 'bourgeois and proletarian' (see also Chapter 5 on Marx's theory of class).

A number of points need to be made here. Firstly, the rise of class was a complex uneven process, limited at first to the locations where the factory system was most conspicuous. Secondly, there continued for a long while to be a number of fine gradations within class groupings. Contemporaries spoke of the middle or working *classes* to indicate broad rather than tight boundaries. Thirdly, we need to be clear about what we mean by class in this context. The many conceptual problems involved will be dealt with in Chapter 5, but I would argue that it is more useful to think of class as a set of experiences, ideas and images shared by people of similar position within the economy. In other words, while conflict was often based on the antagonisms of the factory, and on struggles for economic resources,

> income alone . . . was never a sufficient motivation for class antagonism, or class would be as old as rent, profits and wages. What was also required was a conscious image of the class in its relation to rival classes, and of the ideal society in which it would find its rightful place.
>
> (Perkin 1969: 219)

These images did exist. The 'middle classes' increased numerically as profitable livings were made from the new production methods; they also increased their political influence, when the 1832 Reform Act made some limited adjustments to the franchise. The middle classes were not content with their role as the new producers, they also became the new consumers. By mid-century not merely the factory owners and merchants, but the shopkeepers and small business owners were gaining access to more affordable manufactured goods such as carpets, furnishings, and ornaments. They also enjoyed a more varied and exotic selection of foodstuffs, took advantage of speedier and cheaper transport to visit the seaside, read a wider assortment of books and periodicals, and increasingly relied upon domestic servants to perform their household labour. Though the landed aristocratic families retained influence, prestige and took a hundred years to enter terminal decline, it is clear that the middle classes made the principal gains from industrialization.

From the 1830s onwards, such features of British enterprise became slowly more familiar in Europe. Between 1830 and 1840 the number of steam engines in Belgium doubled. The German industrial giant Krupps installed its first steam engine. However, at this point such initiatives were not typical of the wider economies. 'The industrial landscape was thus rather like a series of lakes studded with islands' (Hobsbawm 1962: 174); that is to say, industrial centres were concentrated in localities such as Lille, Saxony and Lancashire. In 1851, when Britain staged its Great Exhibition, it was the world leader by some clear way. In the second period of industrialization this state of affairs began to be addressed by the competition.

Enter the Europeans

Only from the 1860s did industrialization become a truly European affair, as the major continental powers began to develop their economic muscle. Here we need to be concerned with two main questions: firstly, what was the relationship between European and British patterns of industrial change; secondly, what was happening to the overall nature of industrialization?

The second half of the nineteenth century changed both the relative positions of Britain and the continental powers and also the overall shape of industrialization. Hobsbawm (1987: 50–4) has defined the latter part of the nineteenth century as 'the age of empire' and sees it in terms of the following characteristics:

1   a more geographically broad world economy. World trade expanded and diversified as new countries such as Canada and Argentina were drawn into the exchange of foodstuffs. European industrialization was always determined by Europe's relationship with the rest of the world. The search for new trading opportunities and markets was one of the forces behind 'imperialism', the colonization of Africa and the Americas by the major nation-states. Many, like Lenin, believed that economic exploitation was the reason capitalism continued to flourish long after it should have reached its limits. He called imperialism 'the highest stage of capitalism' (some argue he meant latest, which suggests a slightly different emphasis).

2   a more pluralistic world economy – nation-state rivalries become stronger as other Europeans and the US become exporters and importers of the world's goods. Britain no longer had an exclusive relationship with the

undeveloped world. However in other respects Britain, or more precisely London, still dominated as a provider of financial and commercial services. Indeed in some respects industrial decline actually increased its so-called 'invisible' earnings as an international banker and investor.

3   a technological revolution – while cotton, coal and iron had been the symbolic products of early industrialization, now it was chemicals, electricity and steel which were the materials of change. Science and technology continued to make advances which both increased productive potential and offered new end-products; the telephone, telegraph and cinema all originate in this period. Moreover, the previous wave of innovations continued to be capitalized, most notably the railway boom which, having run its course in Britain, spread to the Continent. France, Germany, Switzerland and Sweden doubled their railway network in the thirty years to 1913. But chemicals, electricity and the internal combustion engine would in the future revamp and refine existing technologies.

European Industrialization summarized

The broadening out of the world economy
The diversification of the nation-states' economies
Scientific and technological advances in economic production
The growth of corporate (organized) capitalism
Mass consumer market mediated through advertising
Expansion in public and private service occupations
The extension of state intervention in economic and social affairs

4   the concentration of capital ('big business'). From the 1860s the small and medium-sized family firms which had dominated the first phase of economic change began to be joined by much larger-scale companies. Industry grew in overall size and also became more concentrated in the form that we recognize it today. The key to this was the need for larger-scale capital investment in projects like railway building and new sectors of industry. Two major developments followed from this. Firstly, new investment banks were making capital available to newly started businesses, lowering some of the barriers to entrepreneurship. Many banks made it possible for large numbers of small investors to put their savings into foreign ventures or into government-backed bonds. By the same token industrial and commercial undertakings began to spread their investment risk by developing the joint-stock company with limited liability. It is notable that there is a strong link between the state and the economy here – it was governments which introduced laws of limited liability (1862 in Britain) to facilitate greater risk-taking and larger-scale investment.

This growth and concentration is often referred to as a period of 'organized capitalism', a term coined by Kocka and developed further by Lash and Urry (1987). To most observers the best example of such a formation is Germany in the late nineteenth century. The German nation-state was founded in 1871, forged in the heat of Prussia's wars against both Austria and France. German military strength was closely related to its industrial strength. As a relative latecomer to the industrialization process, its economy was able to concentrate on the new heavy industries. The Prussian chancellor Bismarck had boasted of achieving unification of his country through 'blood and iron', indeed Lash and Urry note that by 1900 no other country had such a concentration of iron, steel and coal producers. Sweden exported most of its iron ore, France had little coal of its own, and two-fifths of Britain's top fifty campanies were involved in food-processing (Lash and Urry 1987: 18). There was indeed increasing organization and collusion among the financiers, manufacturers and suppliers. The famous German firm AEG thus forged links with mines and banks – it even controlled local electricity supplies in Genoa and Barcelona (Joll 1990: 34).

5   a new market for mass consumer goods as real incomes grew steadily for all the population, not just for the middle classes as had been the case earlier in the century. New products included the bicycle, the gas cooker, and the banana! (Hobsbawm 1987: 53). This was accompanied by a growth in distribution networks (i.e. retailers like Lipton's), and also a growth in advertising to promote the availability and desirability of the new produce. Of course both retailing and advertising were to some degree features of the modern economy long before this. It was, after all, Napoleon who dismissed the British as 'a nation of shopkeepers', and historians have identified a growth in newspaper advertising as far back as the eighteenth century. But truly national newspapers with national advertising could not exist until there was a railway network to distribute them, and there is an argument which says that modern consumerism really starts in the 1880s. Economic sociologists have tended to concentrate either on the point of production (that is, on work), or on the point of final consumption (that is, consumer culture and identities). It is important not to forget the process between these points, especially given the huge emphasis retailers give to displays and promotion. J.J. Sainsbury's dying words were reputedly 'Keep the shops well lit.' Marx himself seemed well aware of all this, devoting much attention to the issues of need, use and exchange of commodities.

Advertising helped cement the mass market by lubricating the relationship between supply and demand. The earliest mass advertising relied on the medium of the wall poster at a time when improvements in printing techniques allowed the production of such materials in high volume at low cost. Before too long commercialism's symbols were ubiquitous. 'Every gable end, every naked wall, every unblemished railway carriage, every unspoilt station surface, indeed every surface exposed to the passing public gaze was hastily covered with posters extolling the virtues of some product or some service . . . or the efficacy of some wonder pill' (Fraser 1981: 135). Many of the most famous product images which today line the walls of bistros and coffee bars originate in this period. The selling of commodities quickly took on many of the features regarded as central to today's advanced economies. Claims became wildly exaggerated; 'experts' were hired to endorse brands; advertisers became more insistent and sophisticated in their targeting of the consumer, both through slogans and, after the invention of the bicycle, through the travelling salesman.

6   the growth of the service or 'tertiary' sector in both private and public occupations. Between 1851 and 1911 commercial employment multiplied tenfold, and 17 per cent of the later figure were female. It is most important to make a distinction between an 'industrial' society and an economy dominated by heavy manufacturing processes. Some see the contemporary trend to higher proportions of service sector employment as indicative of a new stage beyond industrial society (see Chapter 13), but seen in historical context there is no particular reason why this should be the case. It was the expansion of manufacturing itself which created the need for supporting jobs in commerce and finance, as well as the new public sector.

   Where the new white-collar occupations have been significant is in altering the class structure of European nations. The first phase of industrialism had brought a new awareness of social inequalities as huge gulfs in fortunes opened up. Though many supporters of the political status quo argued that a person could always rise on the strength of their own talents, access to capital and family connections limited social mobility. With the rise of jobs which involved, as Hobsbawm (1987: 54) remarks, 'white collars and white hands', two changes took place in the division of labour. Firstly, there was the rapid creation of new middle-class groupings. The most numerous were the army of clerical workers in the new commercial and government offices. Such new occupations offered a path out of manual labour for whole families, and soon social distinctions were opening up between manual workers and the so-called 'lower middle class'. Fewer in number but no less significant were the 'new professionals' whose opportunities arose in education, health, local government and as managers of the new corporate enterprises. In time, such occupations would be the territory on which women would start the long march into labour market occupation, especially at the lower end of the earnings scale. Lacking the obvious associations with muscle, sweat and toil, office jobs could less easily be labelled as 'men's work', and thus was born the image of the mass typing pool.

7   the separation between the spheres of politics and economics described earlier became less tenable both in theory and practice. The state began to intervene both directly (through financing or provision) and indirectly (through legislation or import protection) in the economy, introducing a new element of nationalism into industrial production. Not only this, but the combined effects of industrialism and urbanism were leading to what Perkin (1969: 107) has called an overall rise 'in the scale of human organization'. We have already seen the concentration of private capital into joint-stock companies; accompanying this was a rise in the scale of public provision. As economy and society became more complex, so the state became more organized and bureaucratic. This was not an inevitable consequence of industrialization, but it was an inevitable outcome of key decisions

which were taken about the nature of modern life. For instance, introducing legislation to regulate working conditions creates a need for inspectors and a system for dealing with complaints. Passing Acts of Parliament to improve public health and education necessitated a new state system of teachers, medical professionals and a supporting bureaucracy. Thus, while there is no simple causal link between industrialization and an increased role for the state, Perkin rightly identifies them both as part of the overall rise in scale and complexity of modern life.

It is sometimes remarked that Britain was overtaken or replaced by Europe and America as the industrial leader in the late nineteenth century. It has to be remembered that both Germany and France still had a very large peasant-agriculture sector until well after the Second World War, and only then did national per capita income catch up with Britain. What is true, however, is that as 'latecomers' the Europeans did not have to slavishly adopt the 'British model' but were able to 'leap-frog' some of the stages of the process. The debate over whether Britain failed or fell behind the rest of Europe before 1914 has been the source of much debate, much of which turns on disputes about time-series analysis and definitions of growth statistics. Barnett (1972) and Wiener (1981) suggested that Britain lost its 'industrial spirit' because the ideology of the gentleman, the public school and the country elite was so resilient. This is unlikely to tell the whole story, but it is certainly the case that English literature makes many references to social snobbery between sectors of the wealthy classes. Inventors and entrepreneurs were often portrayed as rough, no-nonsense men of money with little interest in higher cultural pursuits (in Dickens's novels for instance), and many industrial millionaires actively aped the lifestyle of the landed gentry, believing this to be the true test of status. In looking at relative industrial development, however, we also need to consider more recent events, and in particular two world wars, in shaping the fortunes of Britain and Europe.

War and industrialization

European soldiers went to war in 1914 with the words 'It'll be over by Christmas' ringing in their ears. Conversely, the conflict became so protracted that it expended huge quantities of human life and both human and natural resources. The term 'total war' was first used in 1919, and later by Goebbels during the Second World War, before becoming popular in the work of Marwick and others in the 1960s. Controversy has raged over just how far the total wars of the twentieth century effected changes which would have taken place in any case. Clearly we lack 'counterfactuals', i.e. a control case where the war is removed and all other features replicated. Social scientists do not have the facility of repeat laboratory experiments. The arguments tend to focus on whether war accelerated existing trends and whether its effects were temporary or permanent. This section briefly examines some of the main evidence.

The term 'total war' does seem to capture the essence of the virtually complete mobilization of people and materials which took place twice in a thirty-year period. The organized capitalist economies now dedicated themselves to churning out the means of human destruction on a mass scale. In the fortnight prior to the battle of Passchendaele in 1917 the British army fired 4.2 million shells. During the First World War 150,000 tons of poisonous gases were used to inflict 1.2 million casualties. The battle of the Somme saw the first tanks deployed in human warfare.

In addition to the application of industry, there was also an increase in state control over production. Britain and France nationalized their mines, railways and shipbuilding capacity; strikes were banned and trade unions outlawed. It gradually became clear that in order to use resources totally and effectively, governments would have to initiate central planning. It is ironic that Germany, with much more state-led industrialization, failed in both wars to match the Allies for systematic organization of domestic resources and population. After the First World War the winning survivors were better fed and healthier. In the Second World War, despite overall reductions in civilian consumption, British infant mortality and sickness rates fell while in Nazi-occupied France, where agricultural production was high and the country was effectively non-combatant, the average weight and fitness of the population at all ages declined (Hobsbawm 1994: 47). That the war economy was planned according to equality, fairness and social justice only served to reinforce the belief that state management could bring obvious benefits.

As with other comparable events the social effects of the war economy are disputed. Some regard the experience of wartime as a 'levelling' force upon the class structure and an emancipatory force upon established ideas about gender roles. Others point to the relatively short-term impact of the war and the continuity with social changes already in motion. A number of brief observations can be made, however. The First World War was particularly destructive of the officer class and less so of working-class men, except in a few notable cases. Many working-class males were not sufficiently fit or healthy to be sent to the front. Thus the upper echelons effectively suffered a 'lost generation' (Winter 1986). Equally the middle classes found their income differentials eroded after the war and had enormous difficulty in procuring acceptable domestic servants. Most of these women had poured into wartime opportunities elsewhere in the economy, some in munitions and still more into non-industrial sectors like commerce, transport and administration. The fact that the war economy was quickly wound down and industries shed their female labour has led many to play down the war's social effects, but the symbolic importance of the female war effort was in displaying female competence (see also Chapter 6 on women and employment).

The other novel feature of industrialization in the twentieth century has been the attempt to build an industrial society on completely non-capitalist lines. One of the First World War's by-products was the collapse of Tsarist Russia and the eventual eviction of the Provisional Government from the Winter Palace by October 1917. Ravaged by the ensuing civil war and shunned by Western governments, themselves fighting off socialist uprisings, the newly formed Soviet Union set about the bold experiment of forging an industrial revolution without the world market which had facilitated their Western predecessors. Stalin, who ruled from 1924 to 1952, once remarked that 'communism is soviet power plus the electrification of the whole country'. The Soviet experiment involved the forced 'collectivization' of agriculture and the collectivization or 'liquidation' of *kulaks*, the Russian label for small-scale private farmers. In addition, Stalin set out to industrialize the country almost by sheer force of will, borrowing many of the techniques of mass production and scientific management developed earlier in the West, even to the extent of copying Ford's assembly line. The human costs of this process started to come to light fully in the 1950s, but during the 1930s many admired Stalin's USSR as a model of what could be achieved through central planning and social egalitarianism at a time when capitalist Europe was gripped by the 1930s economic depression with mass unemployment and others had turned towards the fascist state as a solution.

Reflection

This introductory survey of the industrialization process has been of necessity rather cursory, but a number of themes emerge. Firstly, it makes little sense to speak of industrialization as a single homogeneous process, even though it is tempting for sociologists to do so. In fact there were a number of phases of development:

- firstly, there was a breakthrough, slow at first, into steam-powered factory production from the 1780s onwards. This was a process pioneered in Britain and adopted in Europe;
- secondly, from the 1860s the scale and scope of industrialization increased as, with more encouragement from government, companies grew. Following this, new products emerged from chemical, electrical and motor vehicle industries, increasingly producing for an expanding mass market;
- thirdly, the twentieth century saw the consolidation of mass production and mass consumption, with the added lubrication of mass communication, and also the increasing intervention of the state as a planning and welfare agency.

The second main lesson is that industrialization before 1945 was a process confined to specific cities and regions, which sat like islands in a sea of rurality. Only towards the end of the period did economies, interconnected by roads, railways and broadcasting, begin to look remotely 'national' in the modern sense. The story of those modern European economies is taken up in Chapter 13.

Summary

- Britain was the first European country to industrialize, based on a mixture of new technologies and expanding markets.
- Other continental countries were later to industrialize, and did so in a more state-directed way.

● The consolidation of industry in the twentieth century involved mass production for mass consumer markets.

Further reading

Eric Hobsbawm's trilogy on 'the long nineteenth century' is a good place to start if you are unfamiliar with European history. His three books, *The Age of Revolution* (1962), *The Age of Capital* (1975) and *The Age of Empire* (1987), London: Weidenfeld and Nicholson, cover both the economics of industrialization and also the social consequences. While the three books will repay a complete reading, you can equally well dip into selected chapters if you prefer.

For those wanting more detail on the nature of industrialization in particular countries, **Tom Kemp's (1985)** *Industrialization in Nineteenth-century Europe* (2nd edn), London: Longman, has become a standard text which, although quite dense at times, paints a useful picture of how a general process took different national forms.

Lenard R. Berlanstein (ed.) (1993) *The Industrial Revolution and Work in Nineteenth Century Europe*, London: Routledge. This is a collection of essays which challenge aspects of the 'Industrial Revolution' orthodoxy which characterized earlier accounts of industrialization. The essay by Cannadine is an overview of this changing historiography.

Chapter 2

Urbanization and urban Europe

The transition to urban lifestyles and contemporary urban problems

Alison Anderson

Introduction   26
The rise of the West   27
Capital and industrial expansion   34
The social consequences of industrial
    urbanization   39
The age of the metropolis   43
Towards the twentieth century   48
Summary   49
Further reading   49

Key concepts

- Urbanization and urbanism
- Mercantilism and the mercantile city
- Capitalism and global cities

Introduction

Few areas of sociological investigation have sparked off such intense debate as the human consequences of European urbanization. Nineteenth-century social commentators typically viewed the rise of the industrial city with a combination of shock and fascination. Whilst they recognized that these urban centres opened up new opportunities, they were also aware that they brought many great new problems with them. For some contemporaries the industrial city was a symbol of 'progress' and 'success', whilst for others it represented all that was 'dark' and 'evil' about society. Many social commentators contrasted the new cities with a very idealized picture of what it must have been like to live in a rural setting.

Even today, people's views of urban and rural life tend to be sharply polarized. The popular myth of idyllic rural lifestyles is perpetuated in chocolate box images of a bygone age. However, many of the distinguishing characteristics of urban and rural areas have become so blurred that it makes little sense to view them as opposites. For example, rural areas suffer from many of the problems typically associated with the inner city, such as high levels of unemployment, inadequate housing and rising crime (see Chapter 20).

In order to gain a fuller understanding of contemporary urban problems, it is necessary to adopt an historical perspective. Large-scale urbanization has not only transformed our physical environment but it has changed many of our cultural habits and ways of relating to one another. Industrial *capitalism*, and the emergence of *global cities* such as London or Paris, has brought about large-scale changes to the way in which social and economic life is organized. The process of urbanization took place very gradually and its roots were laid several hundred years ago. Although there are many similarities in the experiences of different countries there are also a number of important differences. This chapter examines the history of European urbanization, concentrating upon how this has variously affected different social groupings in different countries. This involves charting the rise of *mercantilism* (an economic policy whereby the state protects against foreign competition), and the *mercantile city* (a city where rulers gain their influence from commercial interests rather than rural landownership). The chapter begins by looking at some of the problems in arriving at a definition of urbanization and industrialization.

Defining urbanization and industrialization

Narrowly defined *urbanization* is when the proportion of people living in towns increases in relation to rural areas. This usually involves the movement of people living in the countryside to the city. Urbanization does not simply refer to an increase in the number of people living in a city; it is a change in the proportion of people living in cities compared to those residing in the countryside. Urbanization takes on a wider meaning when the term is used to refer to a stage in the social development of advanced industrial societies – this is sometimes referred to as *structural urbanization*.

Urbanization is most commonly used to refer to urban lifestyles which are not necessarily found only in cities. This definition of urbanization is known as *behavioural urbanization*. Urban lifestyles may be typically characterized by isolation, individualism and calculative behaviour (de Vries 1984)

Industrialization is usually referred to as the movement away from an economy based upon agriculture (craft or cottage industry), to an economy based upon industry (for example, cotton, textiles). However, the term could also be applied to increasing productivity in modern agriculture. Although capitalism was one of the major agents of industrialization, industrialism is not the same as capitalism. Industrialization is encouraged by other agents, and capitalist systems take different forms in a variety of cultural and historical contexts. Indeed, capitalism predated large-scale industrialization (see Chapter 1).

Industrialization is usually associated with urbanism, but this is not always the case. For example, many countries in Eastern Europe have become very industrialized yet they differ significantly in their levels of urbanization. In 1980 only 42 per cent of people in Yugoslavia lived in cities compared to 76 per cent of the population in West Germany (Slattery 1985). Again, there is no clear relationship between industrialization and urbanization in the developing world, and there are considerable variations.

The rise of the West

Early cities

Cities have existed a long way back in history. More than 5,000 years ago they were usually located at cross-roads, as centres of great empires, or as centres of trading. City walls acted as a defence against unwanted intruders and emphasized the spatial division of urban and rural communities. Under the Roman Empire there was a huge network of towns and some of their remains can still be found today. As Figure 2.1 indicates, a very large number of cities founded by the Romans were concentrated along the shores of the Mediterranean Sea.

The first urban communities are believed to have developed in Mesopotamia between 4,000 BC and 3,500 BC. Whilst a great many of today's major European cities were founded a very long time ago, others were only established in the last few centuries. The ancient Greeks established a number of Mediterranean cities including Nice, Marseilles and Naples, and by the end of the Roman Empire many of today's largest West European cities had been established (White 1984). In fact nearly all of the larger cities were situated on the borders of the Mediterranean.

Cities were to play a very influential role in moulding the formation of European states, and the place of the city-state in this process is described in Chapter 3. The history of urban development is a narrative of the changing relationship between the city and the state (Tilly and Blockmans 1994). In a long tradition of literary works cities have been variously associated with civilization. For example the Greek philosopher Aristotle conceived of the city as a building block of society, and the foundation of the modern state:

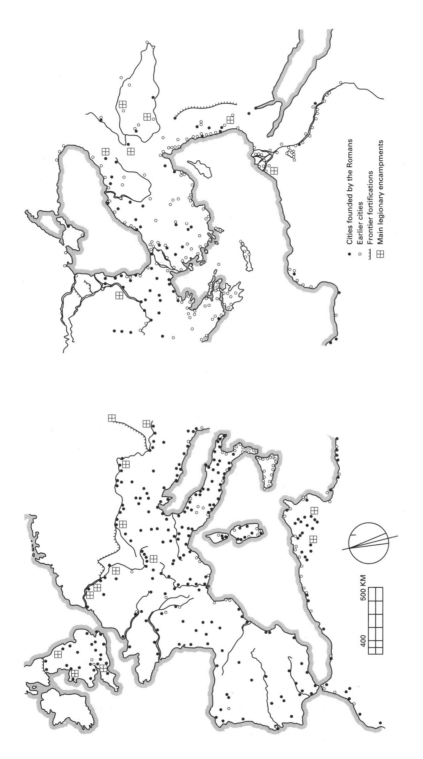

Figure 2.1 Cities of the Roman Empire

Source: Leonardo Benevolo, *The European City*, 1993, pp. 4–5. Reproduced by kind permission of Basil Blackwell Publishers.

Legend:
- Cities founded by the Romans
- Earlier cities
- Frontier fortifications
- Main legionary encampments

400 500 KM

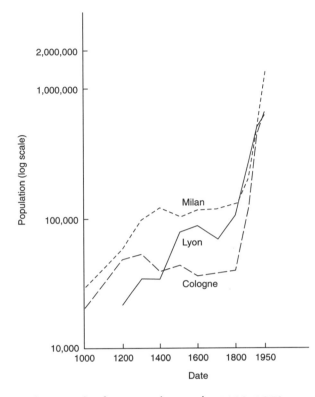

Figure 2.2 The growth of provincial capitals, 1000–1950

Source: Chandler and Fox, *3000 Years of Urban Growth*, 1974. Reproduced by kind permission of Academic Press Inc.

If all communities aim at some good, the state or political community, which is the highest of all, and which embraces all the rest, aims at a good in a greater degree than any other, and at the highest good ... When several villages are united in a single complete community, large enough to be nearly or quite self-sufficing, the state comes into existence, originating in the bare needs of life, and continuing in existence for the sake of a good life.

(cited in Benevolo 1993: 2–3)

Compared with today's standards early cities were small. Rome, in the later Empire, had 300,000 inhabitants but this was exceptional (White 1984). A more typical example is that of Babylon, one of the largest ancient cities in the Middle East, which is estimated to have had a population of only fifteen to twenty thousand. After the Roman Empire fell there was a significant decrease in the size of city populations, and even in medieval times there were few cities with over 20,000 people. The vast majority of Europe's population lived in rural areas and only a very small percentage lived in the urban centres.

TABLE 2.1 Fastest growing cities, in three periods, 1500–1800

1 Cities that at least doubled in population during each interval

1500–1600	1600–1750	1750–1800
Amsterdam	Amsterdam	Glasgow
Berlin	Berlin	Liverpool
London	London	Barcelona
Madrid	Madrid	Bath
Paris	Paris	Belfast
Turin	Turin	Birmingham
Augsburg	Brest	Dundee
Bordeaux	Bristol	Graz
Catania	Cadiz	Hull
Danzig	Clermond-Ferrand	Leeds
Haarlem	Copenhagen	Limerick
Hamburg	Cork	Magdeburg
Lecce	Dresden	Manchester
Lisbon	Dublin	Nottingham
Magdeburg	Glasgow	Plymouth
Messina	The Hague	Portsmouth
Middelburg	Leipzig	Sheffield
Seville	Königsberg	Sunderland
	Liège	Warsaw
	Liverpool	
	Livorno	
	Lyons	
	Malaga	
	Nancy	
	Nantes	
	Newcastle	
	Nîmes	
	Norwich	
	Prague	
	Rotterdam	
	Stockholm	
	Toulon	
	Versailles	
	Vienna	

2 Cities that did not double, but added at least 30,000 inhabitants to their population

1500–1600	1600–1750	1750–1800
Naples	Hamburg	Berlin
Palermo	Lille	Dublin
Rome	Lisbon	Lisbon
Rouen	Rome	London
		Madrid
		Naples
		Seville
		Vienna

	1500–1600		1600–1750		1750–1800	
	No.	Popu-lation ('000)	No.	Popu-lation ('000)	No.	Popu-lation ('000)
Urban population growth accounted for by: cities that at least doubled	18	770	34	2,253	19	1,230
cities that added at least 30,000	4	261	4	164	8	626
Total	22	1,031	38	2,417	27	1,856
% of total urban growth		41.4		80.6		56.4

Source: J. de Vries, *European Urbanization*, 1984, pp. 140–1. Reproduced by kind permission of Methuen and Co.

Early cities tended to be based near the coast or where they could be easily reached by ship. However, the spread of cities was relatively unorganized and unplanned, even the vast Roman network. There were some complex road systems that linked cities in some states but this was relatively uncommon and was mainly designed for military uses. Yet during medieval times many towns developed a service infrastructure and they began to dominate the surrounding area.

Medieval towns

During the Middle Ages the expansion of *mercantile capitalism* and long-distance trading intensified the growth of major European cities. However, the majority of the population of Western Europe still lived in rural areas in largely self-sufficient agricultural communities. Indeed, urban expansion by no means followed a smooth path and there were patches of sudden growth and periods of decline or stagnation. Urban growth was interrupted by economic factors, war and epidemics. While many cities grew in size considerably during the eleventh, twelfth and thirteenth centuries, this was generally followed by a period of decline or stunted growth until the 1800s. The population of many European cities was significantly reduced by the Black Death, an infectious plague that swept across Europe during the fourteenth century. It is estimated that in Florence, Italy, around 60 per cent of the population was wiped out (White 1984).

However, there were many individual variations and not all cities followed the same pattern. Urban growth depended upon heavy numbers of people moving into the cities, and population movements reflected the changing significance of particular European cities (see Figure 2.2).

Many cities in Northern Europe and Scandinavia did not become very important until the Middle Ages. For example, Amsterdam only seems to have been established in the second half of the 1200s. The city grew considerably during the fourteenth and fifteenth centuries, reflecting its increasing importance as a centre of trade. In fact, between the sixteenth century and the middle of the eighteenth century more European cities doubled their populations than in any other period (see Table 2.1).

The vast majority of the fastest-growing cities were capitals and/or major ports. This list of the fastest expanding cities includes almost all of the major capital cities in contemporary Western and Central Europe.

Although European urban settlements shared many similarities there was an enormous amount of variation. The large port cities of the Mediterranean, for example, had little in common with small English market towns. Whilst Florence and Milan had populations of over 50,000 (with many people living in multi-storey buildings or on the perimeters of the city walls), a typical English town had less than 5,000 inhabitants. Table 2.2 displays the shifting importance of European cities over the last thousand years.

Urban settlements did not just vary in size; they differed in political and economic organization, and in architectural styles. Cities developed their own distinct identities and Europeans increasingly expressed this through characterizing themselves as, for example, Londoners or Parisians (Benevolo 1993).

As cities expanded they became important centres of cultural activity. Gradually new rituals and festivals became associated with urban ways of life, permeating folk culture and education. Urban settlements became major centres of learning and by the sixteenth century a large number of cities had their own universities. As European countries grew in economic, political and military power they began to seek ways of extending their influence overseas by great 'civilizing' missions to areas such as Africa and Latin America. Sociologists call this process *colonialism* as it refers to the colonization of foreign lands and the subjugation of indigenous peoples.

Colonialism

The history of European expansion is inextricably bound up with imperialism. This development marked a significant new phase in the process of urbanization and was to transform the face of the globe. A small number of capitalist countries took formal political control over parts of the undeveloped world, including areas of Africa, Latin America, Asia and Australasia.

European cities formed the core of colonial political and economic systems. From the fifteenth century onwards Britain, France, Spain and Portugal engaged in large-scale colonial control. The Portuguese, for example, circumnavigated Africa and later extended their sphere of influence to include India. By the nineteenth century nearly all of Asia and Africa was dominated by colonial rule. Colonialism usually involved white people settling in those areas and/or exploiting the natural resources, although this was not always the case (see Chapter 22). Indigenous industry was often destroyed to make way for new manufacturing processes. New urban settlements were created and the new colonial towns functioned as administrative centres controlling government and trading. European urban culture was often imposed on the indigenous peoples.

TABLE 2.2 The largest cities in Europe, 1000–1900 (population in thousands)

1000		1400		1700		1900	
City	*Population*	*City*	*Population*	*City*	*Population*	*City*	*Population*
Constantinople	450	Paris	275	Constantinople	700	London	6,480
Cordoba	450	Milan	125	London	550	Paris	3,330
Seville	90	Bruges	125	Paris	530	Berlin	2,424
Palermo	75	Venice	110	Naples	207	Vienna	1,662
Kiev	45	Granada	100	Lisbon	188	St Petersburg	1,439
Venice	45	Genoa	100	Amsterdam	172	Manchester	1,255
Regensburg	40	Prague	95	Rome	149	Birmingham	1,248
Thessalonika	40	Rouen	70	Venice	144	Moscow	1,120
Amalfi	35	Seville	70	Moscow	130	Glasgow	1,072
Rome	35	Ghent	70	Milan	124	Liverpool	940

Source: Chandler and Fox, *3000 Years of Urban Growth*, 1974, pp. 11–20, 330. Reproduced by kind permission of Academic Press Inc.

Colonialism involved large-scale movements of population and transformed the shape of traditional social and cultural structures. There was a large movement of people from Africa to the Americas from the sixteenth century as the slave trade expanded. Also very large numbers of Europeans emigrated to North, Central and South America. Most developing societies experienced colonial rule. In some areas, such as Australia and North America, Europeans became the majority population and imparted numerous different ethnic influences.

By the end of the eighteenth century Britain's naval strength was such that she was able to force France from North America and India, and colonize parts of the Indian sub-continent. According to Hobsbawm (1985) three main factors made this new structural relationship possible:

1   the conquest of colonies to support European industry;
2   a growing market for mass-produced overseas products;
3   the development of economic systems to produce cheap goods in large quantities.

However, colonialism was not based upon economic supremacy alone. If there was one factor that fuelled this process it was political power, for economic strength derived from political domination. Neither did colonialism erode all social institutions since some forms of pre-colonial organization and culture continued to persist. For example, black South Africans developed their own schismatic churches and believed that blacks were fated to go to heaven, while whites were destined for hell.

Nevertheless, colonialism undoubtedly transformed the cultural and social globe. Contemporary ethnic divisions cannot be understood without reference to this major phase in the history of Western expansion. Clearly, European industrial urbanization owes a huge debt to the subjugation of the indigenous peoples of the developing world.

The control of a large, permanent military force became an increasingly fundamental factor in determining a state's economic and political position (see Chapter 3 on the absolutist state). Before the nineteenth century there was considerable variation in combinations of capital and brute force exhibited in different European states (Tilly and Blockmans 1994). Clearly, those countries such as England and France which could mobilize large amounts of capital and massive armed forces occupied a stronger position compared with smaller states.

The rise of the industrial city is central towards an understanding of modern urbanism. However, industrial growth in Europe generally followed a phase of *proto-industrial* development in the countryside. It is important to remember that at this time most people still lived in rural communities and worked in agriculture or craft-based industry. Important changes in agriculturally based communities were to precede the Industrial Revolution in Britain.

Capital and industrial expansion

The proto-industrial period

The period between approximately 1300 and 1800 is often referred to as Europe's 'Proto-industrial Age'. This was an age when capitalist productive systems began to develop. In Britain, the introduction of new agricultural machinery led many people who had previously worked on the land to migrate to the cities in search of employment in the manufacturing sector. The size and influence of cities became increasingly important. Some cities such as London or Constantinople expanded so much that they encroached on the surrounding towns. However, this reflected political influence rather than economic power (Hohenberg and Lees 1985).

Many smaller cities in Central or Southern Europe became ravaged by the effects of economic competition, war or disease. At the same time large urban centres or 'metropolises' gained increasing power, and larger market cities gained greater political influence over adjoining countryside. According to Blockmans cities fell into three broad categories (Tilly and Blockmans 1994):

1   autonomous metropoles;
2   bargaining metropoles;
3   subordinated metropoles.

Autonomous metropoles were relatively self-governing; they were either distant from imperial power bases or they integrated the interests of princes or the nobility. Many of these forms of organization could be found in Northern or Central Italy. In contrast, *bargaining metropoles* were composed of competing feudal and monarchical powers that co-existed through negotiation and compromise. These were particularly prevalent in the Southern Low Countries and in Northern France. Finally, *subordinated metropoles* were those cities where the monarchical powers retained their position of supreme power, often through conquest and territorial expansion. Much of their wealth was spent on wars and costly bureaucratic measures that actively constrained urban growth.

In the main, then, European urbanization developed in an unplanned fashion outside of the monarchic or feudal structures. By this period urban growth was no longer concentrated around the Mediterranean and a number of important political capitals rose to power in Northern and Western Europe. Significant numbers of people moved to the cities and many rural areas increased their links with urban systems as they became more heavily involved with manufacturing for export.

During the 1400s Paris was the largest city in Europe with a population of 275,000, and by the 1700s it had become a major centre of trading. While cities such as Paris flourished, the economic position of the Italian cities such as Florence and Venice became considerably weakened. By the seventeenth century they had become marginalized in the emerging world productive system. Once strong centres of mercantile enterprise, now they became increasingly inward-looking. They continued to retain a relatively strong political position, though this was largely on the basis of their past economic successes (Tilly and Blockmans 1994).

Various hierarchies of social power and control existed in different areas of Europe. Early cities were highly stratified and often very competitive. Under the European feudal system the aristocracy and gentry made up the first estate. The second estate was composed of the clergy who did not enjoy the same level of status but shared some of their privileges. Finally, the third estate was made up of 'commoners' – free peasants, serfs, artisans and merchants. Broadly speaking, southern cities tended to be dominated by the old landed aristocracy, whereas northern cities were largely controlled by merchant interests – the city *burghers* who would later form the *bourgeoisie*, the ruling class. However, it is difficult to generalize about 'feudalism' since the system varied so much from region to region. For example, within Southern Europe the city of Venice was heavily dependent upon commercial rather than feudal interests. This historical legacy aided Venice in constructing a system of government which combined elements of republicanism together with monarchical and commercial interests (White 1984). Some cities were not predominantly feudal or mercantile since they contained elements of both systems. In the Italian city of Florence, for example, wool guilds flourished alongside the traditional feudal aristocracy. During the early Middle Ages Vienna also combined elements of feudalism and mercantilism though gradually the nobility were to wield greater and greater influence (White 1984).

As well as the variations among European cities there were also major differences between social hierarchies in urban and rural communities. While countryside populations tended to be governed by personal allegiances to the lord and vassal, city inhabitants were not ruled over by a lord and they could lay some claim that it was their city (Hohenberg and Lees 1985)

As cities developed and trade increased particular urban centres emerged, providing a range of services for the surrounding locality. These networks further increased trade as markets interlinked and a wider range of products could be provided. The rise of cities was associated with three main factors:

1   centralization of power;
2   the deployment of agricultural surpluses from the countryside;
3   the emergence of a variety of new social roles associated with particular tasks.

(Giddens 1981)

Rivalry characterized the relationship between Northern and Southern Europe, whereas the relationship between Eastern and Western Europe was largely one of dominance and dependence (Hohenberg and Lees 1985). Eastern Europe was significantly less urbanized than the West, but it also experienced cycles of growth and stagnation.

However, the seeds of large-scale capitalist production were sown through proto-industrial developments in the towns and especially the countryside. The rural-based textile industries were to play an increasingly significant role in the move towards systems of centralized capitalist accumulation.

Craft-based industry

During the proto-industrial phase Europeans tended to work together in their family units in craft-based industry. Craft workers typically worked at home or in workshops (see Figure 2.3). Much of this production was based around textiles and large numbers of rural inhabitants wove linens, silks or woollen cloth. However, workshops were not confined to the rural areas; they also played a major role in the fortunes of industrial towns.

Although proto-industrial workers tended to work in family units in a community setting they experienced times of extreme hardship and insecurity. In an attempt to highlight the appalling conditions of factory-based production many authors contrast it with a nostalgic picture of a golden agricultural age. However, it is important to remember that living conditions were considerably worse *before* large-scale industrial capitalism developed. Prior to the late eighteenth century many rural labourers lived with their families in damp conditions below ground level. The contamination of water supplies and overflowing drains posed considerable health risks, and the food supplies were irregular. Workers experienced a large degree of insecurity since wages tended to be low and unemployment was common. People's living quarters were often very overcrowded, with large numbers of people living in one room. Many workers rented small rooms in large tenement blocks. For example, workers in the French town of Lille were forced to live in very overcrowded environments renting small rooms for large sums of money.

The rise of the industrial city

The period from the late eighteenth century to the mid-nineteenth century was marked by social upheaval and revolution. This stage in European history is often referred to as the age of 'dual revolutions'. In Britain the revolution was economic,

Figure 2.3 Stocking-frame weavers in their home. Proto-industrial workers commonly worked at home. The French silk-weaver's assistant, probably his wife, is winding thread onto bobbins. Invented in England during the late sixteenth century, the stocking frame was often too costly for the domestic worker to purchase. Therefore, merchant entrepreneurs might own the fixed means of production in addition to controlling the raw materials and markets

Source: Diderot, *L'Encyclopédie*. Reproduced from Hohenberg and Lees, *The Making of Urban Europe 1000–1950*, 1985, p. 124, by kind permission of Harvard University Press.

whilst in France it was political. Though these revolutions took very different forms they both served to increase the visibility of a large urban 'proletariat'.

The city of Manchester is often described as the first industrial city of the world. In his book on Victorian Cities Asa Briggs describes Manchester as a 'Symbol of a New Age', a city which by the late eighteenth century had already acquired a far-reaching reputation as a new, rapidly growing urban centre with a growing gap between the rich and poor, and filthy, squalid conditions. Manchester became a centre for the cotton industry in the late eighteenth century and its population rapidly increased over the next century. Not altogether surprisingly, Manchester was to often become the site of political agitation and uprisings.

By the 1840s a large number of books and pamphlets had been published examining the condition of the working classes in Western Europe. One such book was Friedrich Engels' *The Condition of the Working Class in England*, published in 1892. Engels, like Marx, was born in Germany but emigrated to England during his youth. Engels worked for a time in his father's factory in Manchester and developed an intense interest in the human effects of industrial capitalism. In this book he documents the existence of a highly polarized society divided into two opposing camps: a large labouring population and a small, very powerful, ruling-class or 'bourgeoisie'. These sharp social divisions were highly visible in the industrial cities since large numbers of people were concentrated into relatively small spaces. Here is an extract from Engels in which he describes life in the capital city in 1844:

> The brutal indifference, the unfeeling isolation of each in his private interest becomes the more repellent and the more offensive, the more these individuals are crowded together, within a limited space. And however one may be aware that this isolation of the individual, this narrow self-seeking is the fundamental principle of our society everywhere, it is nowhere so shamelessly barefaced, so self-conscious as just here in the crowding of the great city. The dissolution of mankind into monads of which each one has a separate principle and a separate purpose, the world of atoms, is here carried to its utmost extreme.
>
> Engels (1976: 58)

Charles Dickens also wrote of the severe conditions characterizing industrial Britain in his description of the fictional 'Coketown' in the novel aptly entitled *Hard Times*:

> It was a town of red brick, or of brick that would have been red if the smoke and ashes had allowed it . . . a town of machinery and tall chimneys, out of which interminable serpents of smoke trailed themselves for ever and ever, and never got uncoiled. It had a black canal in it, and a river that ran purple with ill-smelling dye, and vast piles of building full of windows where there was rattling and trembling all day long, and where the piston of the steam-engine worked monotonously up and down, like the head of an elephant in a state of melancholy madness.
>
> Dickens (1969: 65)

This debate about cities in England was part of a much wider discussion with different Western European countries taking their own particular perspectives. Many travellers noted, however, that the cities of England did not compare to anywhere else in Europe. One such commentator writing in 1822 observed: 'France, Germany and the Netherlands do not exhibit provincial towns to be compared to Manchester, Glasgow, Birmingham, Sheffield or Leeds' (quoted by Briggs 1968: 70). In fact some have suggested that Dickens' and Engels' descriptions were untypical of the average industrial town in nineteenth-century Europe (Hohenberg and Lees 1985).

The major difference between early cities and proto-industrial centres was the sheer size of the new industrial towns and cities. Medieval towns became closely associated with the life of the surrounding areas as they formed the centre of a local regional urban system. However, with the rise of the new city this was to change across much of Europe. Not only did towns become much larger but they became more specialized and did not enjoy such an intimate relationship with the surrounding settlements.

The effects of industrialization on European society, then, were wide-ranging, but perhaps the most important transformation concerned the structure of society. Industrial urbanization heightened the divisions between the social classes and this was reflected most acutely in living conditions and working relations.

The social consequences of industrial urbanization

Health

Large numbers of migrants were drawn into the cities in search of jobs and better wages. However, the new industrial cities were afflicted by severe overcrowding and a lack of basic sanitation. In 1884, some parts of the English city of Liverpool contained 1,200 people to one acre (Briggs 1968). Many of the migrants moving to fast growing towns were unable to be accommodated within the city and were forced to live in squalid *shanty towns* outside its walls (see Figure 2.4).

Very high densities of population aided the spread of epidemics such as cholera, typhus, typhoid and smallpox. In early nineteenth-century Paris, for example, there were instances given of thirty-two people living in a house originally intended for only one family. And during the cholera epidemics of 1831–2 the death rate in Paris increased twofold (Pounds 1985). Overcrowding and damp conditions also played a major part in the incidence of tuberculosis, flu and pneumonia.

Disease was also carried by water. Overflowing drains, cesspits and foul water supplies were common. In the large cities there were few basic amenities and large numbers of people had to share a limited supply of water. Also, air pollution filled people's lungs as factories bellowed out huge mists of smoke. The areas of factory workers' housing tended to be the worst affected, often containing large numbers of ethnic minorities. Below is a short extract from Henry Mayhew's description of Jacob's Island, an area of South London swept by the cholera epidemic:

> The water of the huge ditch in front of the houses is covered with scum almost like a cobweb, and prismatic with grease. In it float great masses of green rotting weed, and against the posts of the bridges are swollen carcasses of dead animals, almost bursting with the gases of putrefaction ... On entering the precincts of the pest island, the air has literally the smell of a graveyard and a feeling of nausea and heaviness comes over any one unaccustomed to imbibe such an atmosphere.
>
> (Mayhew, *The Morning Chronicle*, 24 September 1849)

During the early part of the century *mortality rates*, or the number of deaths per year within a particular population, were very high. Across Europe there were very pronounced differences in mortality rates for urban and rural areas. For example, in England in 1841 males born in rural Surrey could expect to live, on average, to the age of forty-four, whilst in London they could only expect to reach the age of thirty-five. In Manchester the mortality rate for males was even higher; on average men only lived to the age of twenty-four (Hohenberg and Lees 1985).

Figure 2.4 Shanty town on the outskirts of Berlin, *c.* 1880. Fast-growing towns found it hard to house the streams of in-migrating workers and their families, and hastily built settlements often sprang up outside the city. These makeshift houses will soon be replaced with enormous barracks-style apartments

Source: *Leipziger Illustrierte*, 1875. Reproduced from Hohenberg and Lees, *The Making of Urban Europe 1000–1950*, 1985, p. 254, by kind permission of Harvard University Press.

Work

If there was one aspect of life that underwent the most profound change during the nineteenth century it was the nature of work. Industrial urbanization transformed working practices and employment relations. Under the craft system workers had a personal relationship with their employers, often working together as a family unit. They owned their workplace and their tools and they sold the end-product to the consumer. In fact they were involved in each chain in the process from the first stages of producing a product to the final stages of selling it to a customer. Craft workers typically followed a long apprenticeship and possessed a large amount of control over knowledge and skills.

The factory system changed all of this. With the rise of modern industrial production craft work became less common, and in the factories the relationship between employer and employee took the form of an impersonal contract. Since there was always a plentiful supply of labour employers did not have to display any concern over their welfare. Workers became a commodity in much the same way as the goods they were producing. In *Hard Times* Charles Dickens vividly describes these conditions, and their effect on close personal relations, through the experiences of a fictional factory worker named Stephen Blackpool:

> In the hardest working part of Coketown; in the innermost fortifications of that ugly citadel, where Nature was as strongly bricked out as killing airs and gases were bricked in; at the heart of the labyrinth of narrow courts upon courts, and close streets upon streets, which had come into existence piecemeal, every piece in a violent hurry for some one man's purpose, and the whole an unnatural family, shouldering, and trampling, and pressing one another to death ... among the multitude of Coketown, generically called 'the Hands', – a race who would have found more favour with some people, if Providence had seen fit to only make them only hands, or, like the lower creatures of the seashore, only hands and stomachs – lived a certain Stephen Blackpool, forty years of age.
>
> Dickens (1969: 102–3)

Under this system workers no longer possessed control over knowledge and skills. They merely became one cog in an enormous wheel and had to comply with a rigid order of work. The way in which the day was strictly divided up by the clock must have been very alien to individuals who had been used to labouring in the fields. In order to maximize production and increase profits a strict order of work was maintained and many factories introduced their own lists of rules.

Those workers who were only able to make a living from casual labour were attacked as spendthrift, lazy and dishonest (Stedman-Jones 1992; Mayhew 1864). Writing during this period, Marx and Engels saw capitalist society divided into two great antagonistic classes, the *bourgeoisie* (those who owned property), and the *proletariat* (those who owned nothing but the skills which they brought to the labour market). For Marx and Engels it was *capitalism*, rather than industrial urbanization, which produced an alienated workforce who became isolated from the production process and their fellows.

Family

Industrialization also brought about far-reaching changes in social divisions based upon gender and age. Working-class women were increasingly forced to take on subordinate roles in factory work, domestic service or workshops. Employers often preferred to employ women or children since they were regarded as a form of cheap labour and were less likely to engage in political agitation. As mechanization was introduced some areas of work that were mainly controlled by women in pre-industrial times were taken over by men. For example, spinning had been a major source of employment for women but when new machinery was introduced men increasingly came to perform the tasks which required a higher level of skill (Bradley 1992). However, the experience of middle-class women was very

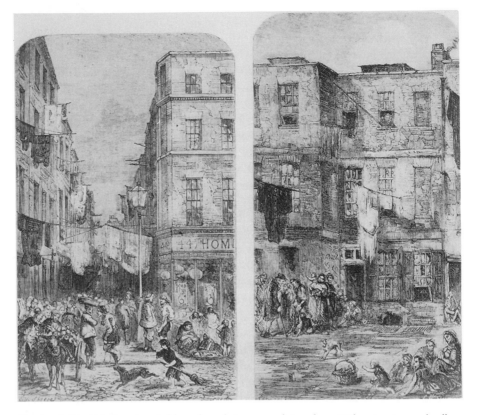

Figure 2.5 Workers' neighbourhood in central London. Side streets and alleys were among the few neighbourhood centres for crowded urban workers. Many Irish migrants lived in Wild Court and Great Wild Street, shown in this drawing from 1854. The inhabitants work, play, and congregate outside whenever possible

Source: *The Builder*, 12 November 1854. Reproduced from Hohenberg and Lees, *The Making of Urban Europe 1000–1950*, 1985, p. 268. Reproduced by kind permission of Harvard University Press.

different; generally they would have stayed at home and managed household affairs, or the more wealthy may have engaged in fashionable leisure pursuits. During this period age divisions widened too. By the end of the nineteenth century adolescence had become a socially definable stage in the life-cycle as young people delayed entering work for a longer time. And in the cut and thrust of capitalist expansion older people began to be viewed as more dispensable.

Social class and political unrest

As industrial urbanization developed, distinct class divisions became more visible within urban communities. This was by no means a sudden process and was often blurred by a range of other social divisions. Also, there were significant variations in relations between classes in different European cities and regions. Generally speaking, the capitalists and professionals formed a small elite, which Karl Marx referred to as the *bourgeoisie*; the small shopkeepers and artisans formed a fairly large intermediate class, which Marx labelled the *petite bourgeoisie*; and the mass of wage labourers formed the working class, which Marx referred to as the *proletariat*.

Within the industrial towns and cities different social groupings became concentrated in particular areas. Urban growth encouraged the development of distinctive communities since people were often living in very close cramped quarters sharing communal stairs in high-rise buildings, and using local amenities. The alleys and courtyards were full of children playing and people going to and fro about their business (see Figure 2.5). Many large European cities developed their own Polish, Jewish or Irish quarters. Jews formed a particularly significant section of the urban population in Central and Eastern Europe.

Urban industrial society provided plenty of opportunities for workers to gather together to discuss their common grievances and become an organized force to be reckoned with. And although the gap between working-class and upper-class culture narrowed during this period it still remained a very important division. However, urban cultures were also fragmented by neighbourhood, occupation, sex, age, religion, nationality and place of birth (Hohenberg and Lees 1985).

During the latter half of the century there was a significant increase in organized protest groups and political activity. Trade unions, reform societies and political parties began to be established in the urban centres. Mass political campaigns tended to originate in capital cities such as London, Paris and Berlin. Most social protest groups and trade unions were organized within sizeable cities since activists needed to be able to mobilize large numbers of people, circulate information quickly and find the necessary resources to sustain a campaign. Also, class consciousness was more developed since the sheer concentrations of people highlighted deep social divisions. This was particularly so in the new industrial cities such as Sheffield in England, or Bochum in Germany, where there were very marked divisions between the bourgeoisie and the proletariat.

The age of the metropolis

By the late nineteenth century large urban centres with extended metropolitan areas were commonplace. The metropolis, as it became known, spread out to the suburbs and acted as a major commercial centre. Britain became the first society to undergo an industrial revolution and experience large-scale movement from the countryside to the city. Other European countries became urbanized during the second half of the nineteenth century; the United States followed somewhat later. But by the middle of the century most parts of Western and Central Europe were undergoing growth, particularly cities that had already become established. This was accompanied by increased population density which covered a larger area.

Germany provides an example of a country which underwent particularly rapid urbanization. Growth after 1860 was more rapid in Germany than in any other continental European country. The capital city, Berlin, had one million inhabitants by 1880; doubling to two million by 1905. In industrial areas the large working population were housed in tenement blocks called *mietskasernen*; these became standard in the urban centres. Gradually, though, middle-class urban populations began to move out to the leafy suburbs and increasingly accessible commuter zones.

The growth of suburbia

It was not until cities became very crowded during the middle of the century that they began to spread outwards. Urban centres spread out as factories were increasingly located on the outskirts of the city close to freight transport. For example, London took in further areas to the north and east, while Paris expanded its 'red belt'. Most of the growth that occurred involved little planning and did not take into account the problems caused by congestion. The suburbs tended to be very uniform and uninspiring, though they offered a more spacious environment than the cities.

New commuting zones were created which led in turn to an increasing network of tram lines and railway tracks which connected the suburbs to the city. The middle classes were attracted to commuter towns and villages in more and more numbers as they searched for greater privacy and space. Different areas were largely segregated according to social class. Within much of Europe the highest earners lived closest to the city, whilst in the United States the more you were likely to earn the further you lived from the city centre. Parts of Northern Europe, especially Britain, more closely approached the experience of the United States. For much of Southern Europe, however, suburbs were not viewed as particularly attractive. Also, compared to Britain and the United States, the suburbs tend to be more densely populated and there is a much higher incidence of multi-family households (White 1984).

The transport revolution

The growth of suburbia was made possible, to a large extent, by a revolution in transport systems. By the middle of the century many cities formed part of an urban/regional system based upon textiles or coal. Industry needed to be able to transport large quantities of goods across a wide area as quickly and as efficiently as possible. Also, the railways and steamships provided key markets for the heavy goods industries of coal, iron and steel. Of all the developments in transportation systems it was the railways which became symbols of progress.

As industrialism gained pace towards the end of the century mass-transit systems, such as trams and railways, increased people's mobility. People were no longer forced to live in close proximity to their place of work, and the middle classes were able to enjoy holidays to nearby resorts. In Britain 6,000 miles of railway were opened between 1830 and 1850 (Hobsbawm 1985). Later on, underground railways were completed in many European capitals, including Vienna (1904), Berlin (1896) and Paris (1900). These changes led to the development of urban lifestyles increasingly based around leisure and consumption.

These transformations are particularly highlighted by the experience of Paris in the late 1800s. Paris was to undergo sweeping changes which sharpened the divisions between those who could reap the benefits of industrialization and those who merely looked on.

Haussmann's Paris

By the late nineteenth century Paris had become a great sprawling city reaching out to nearby satellite towns. Increasing numbers of people became encompassed within the city as the rings of boulevards moved outwards. New apartments were built with elaborate façades, designed to attract the wealthy *rentier* class who would move in and raise the property values. Yet within the city boundaries there were still areas of extreme poverty and insanitary conditions. Under Napoleon III a major project was established in 1853 to redesign Paris so that it could compete with London and Berlin for European leadership.

Napoleon III chose an ambitious administrator, Baron Georges Haussmann, as his new 'Seine prefect', charged with overseeing the project. The urban renewal initiatives were to be financed by a combination of public loans and direct grants. They were to transform Parisian society. However, the cost was huge and it aroused so much criticism that Haussmann was later dismissed in 1870.

By the mid-1800s over a million people lived in Paris and one of Haussmann's first projects was to establish a service infrastructure for the city. Schools, markets and hospitals were built, public transportation was developed, and areas of wasteland were cultivated into large public parks. The wealthy sections of society relaxed in street-side cafés, shopped in the fashionable boulevards, or visited the newly constructed Paris Opera building.

During Haussmann's reconstruction of Paris the centre was redesigned with an inner network of boulevards and railway stations. The historic city centre was transformed as new elegant buildings were erected and gas street lighting extended (see Figure 2.6).

The straight, wide boulevards linked the new barracks with the city centre facilitating the rapid transit and deployment of troops in the event of public disorder. Many of the new boulevards cut through the squalid back streets, alleyways and densely populated slums that had played a major part in previous uprisings. Although Haussmann was clearly moved by the squalor and overcrowding, the major purpose of the new boulevards was to minimize insurrection and control the urban masses.

Even Haussmann's measures to improve sanitation were largely designed to protect the interests of the wealthy. The ruling classes considered infectious diseases even more of a threat than social unrest, since they attacked the rich and poor alike. Before this period all of the city's sewers were directed into the Seine, and most drinking water was obtained from the same source. Under

Figure 2.6 The redesigning of Paris, c. 1890. The rebuilding of Paris relied on baroque principles of design. Major buildings or monuments served as focal points for wide, straight streets. The Avenue de l'Opéra is lined with opulent apartment houses and elegant shops. Building heights and designs were regulated by the city

Source: Personal collection of Paul Hohenberg. Reproduced from Hohenberg and Lees, *The Making of Urban Europe 1000–1950*, 1985, p. 327.

Haussmann, 260 miles of collector sewers were built to intercept the drains which flowed into the Seine. Also, hundreds of miles of aqueduct were constructed to reach the reservoirs of Paris.

Haussmann's project evoked a wide range of responses, from awe and praise, to resentment and despair. Many saw it as privileging the bourgeoisie and offering very little to the proletariat. Clearly it reinforced the spatial segregation of the rich and the poor, with the wealthiest groups being concentrated in the inner zones of the city. Many of the poor were forced to live in new shanty towns on the outskirts of the city as new streets and apartments led to a significant rise in prices. Large numbers of this new population were driven out of the city because of unemployment, taxes, high rents and poor living conditions.

The metropolis and mental life

One of the most influential essays written during this period of social upheaval was produced by the German sociologist, Georg Simmel (1858–1918). In 'The Metropolis and Mental Life', Simmel argued that a unique personality type could be identified with the modern city, in contrast to the small urban settlements of earlier historical periods. According to Simmel, this personality type was associ-ated with three major characteristics of the metropolis:

1   The sheer *size* of the metropolis tended to produce individuals who were withdrawn and isolated. In contrast to the small town, a large densely popu-lated city did not offer the sort of environment which facilitated close social interaction. In the impersonal context of the large city people no longer knew everyone they came into contact with, and social relations became fleeting and superficial. People rarely displayed emotion and they hid behind a screen of reserve.
2   A capitalist economy based upon monetary transactions was seen as producing a particularly *calculative* outlook on life. Simmel maintained that this sort of money economy produced a rational personality type who weighed up the advantages and disadvantages of a particular course of action. The emphasis on the application of scientific principles to social life, on exactness and precise timing, encouraged people to be treated in a very matter-of-fact way.
3   Simmel thought that an increasingly specialized *division of labour*, charac-terized by a multitude of social roles, led people to try to overemphasize their uniqueness in order to express their individuality. Individuals increas-ingly felt devalued in the workplace as they became merely one small cog in an enormous wheel.

Despite exaggerating the impersonality of contemporary life, Simmel's work is important for it identifies some key emergent features of *modernity*. In partic-ular it draws attention to the way in which life was becoming increasingly perceived as fragmentary and commodified. This is reflected in much of the artwork during this period. For example, artists such as Monet and Degas painted vivid scenes of street life, drawing attention to a wide range of visual symbols and signs, portraying a social life which was essentially unstable and fleeting.

The city as modernity

Nineteenth-century Paris has often been described as a 'centre of modernity' with its fashionable boulevards, cafés and shops, offering the rich a lifestyle charac-terized by overt pleasure and consumption. However, this is only one image of a society that was sharply divided by social class. For the most part, the masses were onlookers since they could not afford to engage in conspicuous consump-tion. Modern urban life was increasingly characterized by what sociologists have termed a *commodification* of time and space. This refers to the way in which modern life was perceived as fragmented and compartmentalized. The influence of the Enlightenment movement encouraged increased emphasis upon scientific logic and reasoning. As traditional religious belief declined, people turned to science in the march towards social progress. This new philosophy of scientific rationalism spread rapidly throughout Europe. It encouraged a new drive towards more efficient working practices where tasks became more and more specialized.

Also, it fostered an outlook on life which treated people in a very matter-of-fact way. For some it represented universal progress, whilst for others it simply constituted a new form of social control.

The German thinker, Walter Benjamin, has come to be regarded as one of the most important figures of the early twentieth century to subject the metropolis to detailed sociological analysis (Gilloch 1996). Although Benjamin was deeply fascinated with the city, his writings exhibit a great tension and ambivalence towards it. On the one hand he viewed the metropolis as exciting and an indispensable feature of modern life, while on the other he saw it as overcrowded, anonymous and a site of unrestrained commercialism. For Benjamin the metropolis was thought to display the *essence* of modernity. Above all, he viewed the maze-like metropolis as reflecting the dislocation and impermanence characteristic of modernity itself.

Towards the twentieth century

By the end of the century Britain could no longer be considered the 'workshop of the world', and increasingly other countries took the lead (see also Chapter 1). As economic competition increased large-scale industrial capitalism spread, first to Belgium, and later to Germany, France, the Netherlands, Scandinavia and the Alpine countries. The most rapid growth occurred in areas of Northern Europe and the United States; Southern Europe did not become industrialized until much later. By 1914 nearly half of Europe's population lived in towns; this figure was even greater for north-western Europe and Italy (Pounds 1985).

There are large variations in the historical development of cities in different parts of the globe. The historical legacy of Western European cities contrasts markedly with the experience of North America and Australasia. Western European cities have a much more lengthy historical legacy, much of it building upon imperialist domination. By contrast, North America and Australasia urbanized much later.

There can be no doubt that urbanization has had a fundamental impact upon people's habits and ways of thinking. Some present-day social commentators, echoing nineteenth-century debates, view the modern city as the site of extremes of poverty, corruption, crime and social misery. However, many rural areas have been affected by the very same problems (see Chapter 20). Moreover, it is an oversimplification to suggest that urban areas are characterized by weak community ties, whilst rural areas are held together by strong community bonds. It is important to remember that a large number of contemporary city dwellers are first-generation inhabitants and they have retained many of their rural customs and values. Gwyn Jones, for example, speaks of 'peasant villagers' who have to some extent re-created villages within city areas (Jones 1973). Today it is still possible to identify urban and rural lifestyles, but they are not confined to particular localities; and, more often than not, contemporary Europeans exhibit a mixture of these two extremes. As we shall see in Chapter 20 there is still a considerable amount of disagreement about the nature of 'urban problems', and hence possible solutions.

Summary

- Industrialization is usually associated with urbanism, but this is not always the case.
- Urbanization in Europe has not followed a linear path. Often rapid growth has been followed by stagnation or decline.
- Today, many of the distinguishing characteristics between urban and rural areas have become blurred.

Further reading

Charles Dickens (1969) *Hard Times*, Harmondsworth: Penguin. This social novel gives great insight into culture and society in industrial Britain. It provides a feel for what it must have been like to live in times of rapid social and economic change.

Paul Hohenberg and Lynne Hollen Lees (1985) *The Making of Urban Europe 1000–1950*, Cambridge, Mass.: Harvard University Press. This classic text provides an extremely useful discussion of the historical development of urban Europe. Examples are drawn from a wide range of countries.

Gareth Stedman-Jones (1992) *Outcast London: A Study of the Relationship between Classes in Victorian Society,* London: Penguin. This is a fascinating account of nineteenth-century London's casual poor and their relation to the labour market.

Chapter 3

The state as a European creation

Tony Spybey

Introduction   52
The origins of the state   52
The city-state in Europe   53
The sovereign state   55
The transition to the modern nation-state   61
The universalization of the European model
   of the state   66
Summary   67
Further reading   68

Key concepts

- The city-state
- The absolutist state
- The modern nation-state

Introduction

This chapter seeks to trace the development of the European state and the adoption globally of the European model of the state. The state function first emerged in city-states which acted as centres of political activity, belief system and the co-ordination and regulation of economic activity. Centres of 'civilization' like these became linked up to form politico-economic alliances with kings, emperors and imperial rule. Such arrangements were however based upon military power and therefore tended to be transitory, depending as they did upon the maintenance of allegiances with local rulers or 'warlords'. By contrast the absolutist kings who emerged in Europe during the sixteenth and seventeenth centuries were able to centralize power much more effectively using combinations of more efficient administration and more effective military force. The ability to concentrate the proceeds of taxation provided finance for the development of military technology and organization. In this can be discerned significant principles on which modern nation-states are based, but their full development depends also upon the onset of modernity with urbanization and industrialization giving rise to forms of emancipation which were absent in earlier forms. Emancipation drew the talents of more people into the enterprise of nation-state building. The modern nation-state, therefore, is based upon the familiar model of government by a liberal-democratic parliamentary system served by bureaucratic administration. The decisions of government are upheld by an independent judiciary and backed up where necessary by what has been described as a monopoly of the legitimate means of violence. This is normally divided into two functions, with a police force for internal order and army, navy and air force for external defence.

The origins of the state

The origins of the state lie somewhere in distinctions between tribal society and the type of society which from classical Greek times onwards has been referred to as 'civilization'. Tribal society is of course that based upon tribal or extended kinship identity. Examples of this are oral societies; that is, they characteristically have no written language, and their social organization is based upon kinship and tradition. In civilizations, although kinship and tradition are significant, the most important defining features are institutionalized forms of politics and economics with centrally maintained written records. These may be taken to constitute a simple definition of the state.

The earliest recognized civilizations are those which existed in the area which the Greeks termed Mesopotamia; that is, the land between the Tigris and Euphrates rivers which now forms part of the modern nation-state of Iraq. These have been identified as having clearly recognized administrative centres established in the form of cities. These cities typically contain the *palace*, the *temple* and the *market*. The palace is of course the centre of political rule. The temple, or some equivalent, is the centre of a belief system or religion. And the market-place is the focal point for various forms of economic exchange. The city is usually enclosed in walls for military protection and also for monitoring the passage of people and goods in and out. An important factor in the administration of these institutions was the emergence of written language for the storage of knowledge, and the earliest known example dates from about 3100 BC at the Sumerian city of Uruk. It is clear that hieroglyphics on clay tablets were not in the first instance used for the creation of literature but had the more mundane purpose of assisting in the administration of the city's growing wealth.

These then are the activities of a form of state, holding power and authority not only within the city but also in the surrounding countryside. The rulers, the priesthood, the merchants and their retainers formed only a tiny minority of the population but one that lived a privileged and cultivated urban existence within the protection of the city walls. Outside there was the great mass of the population, the peasantry, who lived on the land and worked the agriculture which was necessary for the existence of all. Their lifestyle was of course quite distinct from that of the city dwellers.

The distinction between tribal society and civilization can be set out in a simple conceptual definition. At some point in the development of human societies a section of the population encloses itself off from the rest. It does so:

- politically – by achieving recognition as rulers, usually through the exercise of military force, and thus constituting a form of government;
- spatially – by building walls and thus creating the enclosure which becomes the city;
- economically – by co-ordinating, monitoring and taxing the production and exchange of goods, with organized forms of agriculture mainly outside of the city walls and a centralized market within the city forming a nucleus to economy.

The state is the means by which the polity is organized and the economy monitored, with the city as the physical container for such activities. The city-state within its walls forms in effect a container of power (the polity), wealth (the economy), and knowledge (the written records) (see for instance Giddens 1981: 96–7).

The city-state in Europe

In the history of Europe the classical Greek city-states of antiquity, especially Athens the 'birthplace of democracy' or Sparta the model for asceticism, are connected with the northern Italian city-states of the Renaissance, such as Venice, Genoa and Florence with their reputations for cultural advances of all kinds. This forms a convenient connection between the classical foundations of European civilization and the re-birth, or Renaissance, after the so-called Dark Ages following the collapse of the Roman Empire. This is important for Europe's preferred image of itself, but Peter Burke counsels against making our examples of city-states too simplistic.

> These examples [from ancient Greece or northern Italy *c.* 1100–1500, not to say 'Athens and Florence'] present a misleadingly clear picture of the

city-state as a small but autonomous political unit, the home of liberty and democracy . . .

(Burke 1986: 137)

Undoubtedly there have been numerous different examples of the city-state throughout history and we tend to look at the more successful ones. Nevertheless the city-states of the Renaissance, not only those of what is now northern Italy but also the Flemish examples such as Antwerp, Bruges or Ghent, are crucial to European notions of developing political independence, wealth creation and broad cultural development. Their importance is both political and economic and this is indicative of a characteristic feature in the development of the European state, the combination of political *independence* within the state with economic *interdependence* between states. The Renaissance city-states were each politically independent but they were connected economically through trade and in fact formed the core of an expanding European economic system, or as Fernand Braudel (1984) has described it, a 'European world-economy'. He has emphasized as 'cores' to European world-economy, first Venice, the most successful of the northern Italian city-states in mercantile terms; then the Flemish city of Antwerp; then Genoa, Venice's great northern Italian rival; and then Amsterdam – in that historical order.

Seaborne trade between the Flemish and Hanseatic city-states of Northern Europe and Italian city-states in the Mediterranean was in fact the successor to a medieval overland trade system centred on great fairs held in the Champagne region of what is now France. There followed more widespread European economic expansion by sea, and all of this took place in the face of long-term military conflict between Christian Europe and the empires of Islam. Whilst European culture was developing in separate kingdoms and city-states, that of Islam took a different form. Vast Islamic empires stretched from Spain in the West through North Africa and the Middle East to India in the East. These were created by successive dynasties or 'caliphates': the Umayyads based in Damascus from the eighth century; the Abbasids in Baghdad after AD 750; the Seljuks and the Fatimids in Cairo from the tenth century; and from the fourteenth right up to the early twentieth century the Ottomans in Istanbul. At first Islamic culture was superior to Europe's but above all these empires posed a land blockade of overland routes to rich trading opportunities that Europeans perceived to exist in India and China. Indian spices, Chinese silks and other commodities were increasingly in demand as Europe's political, ecclesiastical and mercantile elites grew richer, but they could be obtained only via Islam. The oceanic voyages of the 'navigators' were of course attempts to circumvent this and establish direct oceanic trade routes, but they had royal sponsors and were a continuation of Christian crusades against Islam. There were large red crosses on the sails of Christopher Columbus's and Vasco da Gama's ships, and the sailors who perished on the voyages were deemed to have died as crusaders.

Before these voyages Indian and Chinese goods could only be obtained indirectly, and in the Mediterranean a virtual monopoly of this trade was held by Venice. In fact it derived much of its great wealth from acting as the commercial intermediary between Islam and Europe. Venice represents an archetypal example of the fiercely independent mercantile city-state during a crucial period in Europe's development. Its head of state was the Doge, but successful government depended upon the confidence of the rich merchants and in particular the Council of Ten from which he was elected. Their success was synonymous with that of Venice itself. In the defining terms set out earlier, the *palace* of this city-state was the Doge's Palace, now familiar to tourists visiting the Piazza San Marco. Its *temple* was the Basilica San Marco nearby. Its *market* was the core of the entrepôt trade between Islam and the rest of Europe. Regular commercial exchange had been institutionalized by the fourteenth century, and it was under the porticoes of the Rialto bridge that merchants, bankers and others met to carry out their transactions. There you could purchase shares or *partes* in the speculative trading voyages of Venetian galleys. Venice is a city 'built on water' and so it needed no protective walls. The security of the city and of its trade was assured by a fleet of armed trading galleys and an army of paid mercenary soldiers, the *condottieri*. The Venetian *Arsenale* was a state ordnance factory maintained to build and equip the galleys and manufacture other armaments. As such it was the forerunner of many ordnance factories maintained by European states during the centuries afterwards. Venice fulfils all the characteristics of a Renaissance city-state. Yet, when the Portuguese opened up a direct sea route to India upon Vasco da Gama's return in 1498, Venice soon lost its position as core to the developing European world-economy. It did so to the Flemish city-state of Antwerp and it was this city's bankers and merchants who handled much of the finance and trade stimulated by the Portuguese.

These city-states were dependent upon trade, but Vasco da Gama's voyages were undertaken for the Portuguese crown. In the long-term development of Europe, therefore, we need also to consider the sovereign states which developed from the medieval period onwards. Some of these, like Portugal, have survived and we recognize them today. Others, like Normandy, have disappeared to be swallowed up in the consolidation of larger states, England and France. We need to observe how in some examples kings became much more powerful politically but, because of the necessary military expenditure, increasingly dependent economically upon taxation. However, taxation could only be worth while if merchants were allowed the freedom to create wealth through trade. The separation but interdependence of political institutions (the sphere of government) and economic institutions (the sphere of trade and manufacturing) is therefore a key feature of the development of the European state. The outcome in modern times is the distinction between the public sector (the polity) and the private sector (the economy).

The sovereign state

The type of state administration which consists of a small urban-based elite maintaining authority over a much more numerous peasantry applies not only to the city-states but also to the kingdoms of medieval Europe. Kings maintained royal courts at urban centres as the means to administer their kingdoms. However, there is a clear distinction between the rule of kings and the independence of cities. All cities, even those within the realms of kings, usually enjoyed some measure of independence through their mercantile activities and value to the king in taxation. Set apart were the completely independent mercantile city-states like Venice and Antwerp which have been described above.

Medieval kingdoms usually contained a social structure dominated by feudal landownership or some equivalent arrangement involving a small hereditary elite with the military power to hold on to the ownership of their lands and a much more numerous but subservient peasantry. The elite was made up mainly of the ruling family and associated 'nobility', but since the area that we now refer to as Europe had a common identity in Christianity and was before 1500 generally referred to as Christendom, the higher priesthood enjoyed considerable privilege too. The Church hierarchy was, until the Reformation of the sixteenth century, entirely centred on the Pope in Rome and this meant that there were also ecclesiastical forms of 'court society'. Alongside royalty and nobility there was an ecclesiastical aristocracy ruling lands owned by the Church. Wealthy merchants became increasingly useful to kings for the creation of wealth that could be taxed and to a lesser degree to the Church for endowments, but their position was never secure during medieval times and kings frequently reneged on their debts to merchants. All three of these groups were however served in their affairs by their access to literacy and learning. By extreme contrast the vast majority of the population were peasants working the land. Under feudal arrangements they were held in 'serfdom', tied to the land and owing allegiance to 'feudal lords' who in turn owed allegiance to higher lords and ultimately to the king. The lords were of course warlords and so the whole structure fluctuated with the fortunes of war, as history books, Shakespeare's plays and many other sources tell us.

The institutions of this type of society are much more diversified than in tribal society and significant aspects such as kingship, supported by religion, are clearly urban-based symbols of state effectively separated from the day-to-day life of the great mass of the people. Only in modern societies are the majority of the population literate city dwellers. Prior to this the royal court or the city-state was integral to a class-division between a tiny minority of people living an urban lifestyle and a huge majority of rural peasants. The city walls may be seen not only as the physical embodiment of this division but also as the symbolic line of potential conflict (Giddens 1981: 237). Throughout European history such conflict erupted from time to time in the form of peasant revolts.

The absolutist state

Historians have referred to the more powerful type of kingship and attendant state which began to emerge in Europe during the fifteenth century as the 'absolutist state'. The absolutist states were those in which larger sovereign territories became ruled more effectively by monarchs using combinations of coercion and more efficient centralized administration. The two things go together. Kings and queens who could arrange for their realms to be administered more effectively collected greater revenues and so could afford better equipped standing armies. At the same time a better equipped standing army was more capable of defending a well administered state. Larger territories could be more clearly defined with permanent borders at a time when the castles of the nobility and the walls of city-states were losing their effectiveness due to the development of better artillery. By the end of the fifteenth century Europe began to consist of stronger territorial states, as for instance in the example of Spain formed through the marriage of Ferdinand of Aragon and Isabella of Castile with the combination of their royal lines and their attendant territories. France, more or less as we see it today, was formed during the fifteenth and sixteenth centuries through the drawing together of previously independent and semi-independent regions under the Bourbon kings.

Some other areas of Europe were by contrast not transformed until considerably later. The residual 'Holy Roman Empire' was the legacy of the medieval emperor Charlemagne, later ruled by the Habsburg monarchs. It was scattered about Europe and its major parts were not formed into unified states until the emergence of Prussia and then Germany, of which Prussia became a part during the nineteenth century. There was also the Austro-Hungarian Empire, which was not finally broken up until after the First World War. And there were smaller principalities, ecclesiastical landholdings and, of course, city-states like Venice, Genoa and Florence which became prey to more powerful states until Italy was unified, also during the nineteenth century.

The absolutist trend emerged with the so-called 'new monarchs' of the late fifteenth century. Ferdinand and Isabella of Spain have already been mentioned and there was also Louis XI of France, Henry VII of England and Maximilian of Austria. The archetypal examples of absolutism came later, however, with Louis XIV of France and Elizabeth I of England. England, France and Spain in particular were shaped out of centuries of bitter warfare and the process of state-building involved a reduction in the number of states across Europe. Charles Tilly (1975: 12) has counted 500 states in the Europe of 1500, reduced to only twenty-five by 1900. The hard edge of power was achieved through the patronage of improvements in weaponry and military organization. Those monarchs who could manage their affairs best, especially by finding able people to serve them, derived the highest revenues from their territories and therefore could afford the biggest and best organized standing armies equipped with the highest levels of new military technology.

The hierarchy of power in the absolutist state was steep and rigid, contrasting with the flatter and less permanent systems of allegiance during the medieval period. Absolutist monarchs relying upon greater revenues were more powerful than their predecessors. Yet the schism in society between city and countryside that was apparent in the city-states still applied. The new wealth did not touch upon the majority of the subjects of these absolutist states and they remained peasants with a way of life that changed very little. Perry Anderson (1979: 17) has described how the culture of serfdom did not disappear with the decline of feudalism. The gradual introduction of the wage bargain into agriculture did not at first change the pattern of life nor the expectations of agricultural labourers.

The most significant aspect of change was the civil administration of the absolutist states. This displaced the reliance on clerical administration hitherto provided by the clergy. The swing away from Church power can be seen at a higher level in the changes brought about by Henry VIII of England (Elizabeth I's father) and Louis XIV of France. Each firmly asserted their personal position as monarch against the Church establishment. Henry dissolved the English Church's link with Rome when the Pope refused to grant an annulment to one of his marriages. Thus was created a state religion, the Church of England, with the monarch as 'defender of the faith'. In France, Louis XIV dispensed with the counsel of priests merely by asserting that he was able to commune directly with God.

The severing of the link with Rome by Henry VIII went against the principle of pan-European Christianity centred on Rome, something that had held Western civilization together through the Dark Ages after the collapse of the Roman Empire. Yet, despite this increased concentration of political power in the person of a king, Henry VIII was recognized as maintaining a 'European court'. In fact he set out to make it the finest in Europe by attracting artists, musicians and scholars. For instance, some of the best impressions we have of Henry are from portraits painted by Hans Holbein who was from the independent city of Augsburg, now in southern Germany, but who was also associated with Erasmus in Basle. All of this gives substance to the existence of European culture at a time when the separate states of Europe were being consolidated, made more powerful, and often were in bitter conflict with each other.

A useful insight into improvements in state administration can be gained from Louis XIV's appointment of Jean-Baptiste Colbert as his foremost minister of state. Colbert was a secular figure of great ability who set about the task of modernizing France through a provincial structure of *intendants*. These replaced the local governors of the former feudal structure and may be seen as a form of civil service. Their job was routine surveillance and the collection of information for the state, but their interactions with the people created new social institutions. Colbert had more power than his equivalents in earlier reigns, such as the churchman Cardinal Richlieu, because he exercised it as the instrument of the king rather than as someone with separate power in their own right. In fact, the focus of administrative power was centralized quite literally in the person of the king so that Louis XIV could say with some justification, 'l'état, c'est moi'.

Gianfranco Poggi (1978: 68–70) observes that in the absolutist administration, the court was no longer made up just of the royal household but consisted increasingly of public offices. The king himself was a public figure and in the case of Louis XIV made to conduct even his personal and private life in public or at least in front of members of the royal court. Poggi (1978: 74–81) goes on to describe a later example, the eighteenth-century Prussian state of Frederick the Great. In contrast with Louis XIV, Frederick the Great ruled *from within* his larger state bureaucracy rather than *over* it as Louis had done. This effectively separated the office of king from the person. Prussia was the most bureaucratized of the absolutist states with something like one civil servant for every 450 inhabitants but, to keep things in perspective, Germany in 1925 had one for every forty-six of the population (Giddens 1985: 103) in the pattern of modern states.

There were other ways too in which the absolutist states were not comparable with modern state bureaucracy. For a long time the purchase of office within the state remained an accepted practice, and this was especially so in fiscal matters where officials could be expected to make personal gains in the process of tax-gathering – sometimes to the order of 300 to 400 per cent. Anderson (1979: 34) describes this practice as persisting in France, Italy, Spain, England and Holland even during the sixteenth and seventeenth centuries.

Max Weber, of course, regarded the replacement of personal roles with impersonal offices as of crucial importance in the development of 'rational–legal' authority in modern state administration. The key feature in the 'Prussian model' as identified by Weber (1978: 641–4) was 'public law' as opposed to royal commands. Michael Mann (1986: 476) confirms that the principal components of the absolutist state were law and permanent bureaucracy. Anderson (1979: 25) and Poggi (1978: 73) both see Roman law specifically, with its civil code, its property rights and its notions of contract, as a strong element against the traditions of medieval privilege. It is interesting to note that the principles of Roman law were never entirely lost during the Dark Ages largely thanks to the copying of classical texts as well as religious documents in the monasteries. With the modernization of state administration during the absolutist period those principles were recovered in practice. There was greater recourse to law and the use of professional lawyers. In this there is a reflection of the introduction of public 'notaries' in the mercantile city-states of the Renaissance. The maintenance of principles of Roman law with its enabling and constraining features relating to property was undoubtedly significant in the development of European culture.

The administrative and military infrastructure of the absolutist states was extremely expensive to maintain at a time when monarchs were already dependent on merchants for the generation of revenue and were often also in debt to bankers. A means of raising money for the state was 'mercantilism'; that is, the restricting of imports and encouragement of exports in chosen goods. For instance, in England the wool produced was of the highest quality in Europe but its export was banned so that efforts could be concentrated on exporting with greater profits the 'broad-cloth' which was produced from it. Royal charters were drawn up for trading companies of 'merchant-adventurers' and these were the forerunners of the great colonial trading companies such as the East India Company.

All duties from these monopolies could be paid directly into the state exchequer when the goods crossed borders that were more clearly defined and routinely monitored by state officials. The complicated networks of provincial excise collection from which much was lost were abolished in favour of central-ized collection arrangements. Fernand Braudel (1984: 289) describes foreign visitors to Britain during the eighteenth century expressing surprise and irritation at the thorough customs check which they received at the port of entry. But this was tempered with relief upon the discovery that there were no further checks at tolls within Britain's borders, as would have been the normal case hitherto. The collection of excise duties had clearly been taken over by a centralized state administration.

The concentration of military power in the absolutist states

There are rather obvious connections between military innovations and power of the state. The state's privileged access to the most advanced weaponry and the most efficient forms of military organization provided what has been described as 'a monopoly of the means of violence'. The state's armed forces became the only ones allowed to exist and they had advantages in equipment and organization which enabled them to enforce the restriction if necessary. The practice of kings relying on the private militias of nobles and landowners to form their armies in time of war was gradually abolished, although vestiges remained for some time in the participation of noble families in particular regiments.

Advances in warfare were connected to broader changes in society. There has consistently been interchange in technological progress between civilian and military applications. For instance, gunpowder was used for mining as well as for guns; improved metal-boring techniques were applied to cannon barrels and then to steam-engine cylinders. As the political power of absolutist states increased so did their manufacturing capabilities, and associated changes in the division of labour produced the beginnings of social changes that would later facilitate the Industrial Revolution. These were characteristically European developments. The Chinese had gunpowder by the ninth century and firearms by the eleventh, well before Europeans acquired them. Yet by the end of the fourteenth century European cannon were far superior and when mounted on ships struck terror throughout the coastal regions of the Far East during the exploratory voyages of the sixteenth century. Closer to home, the Ottoman Turks had acquired cannon as part of their rise to power in Islam but the naval battle of Lepanto in 1571 confirmed European control of the eastern Mediterranean. Islamic sea-power then presented no difficulties and the Portuguese 'caravels' which sailed into the Indian Ocean during the late fifteenth century were able to circumvent Islam's existing control of trade with India and China (Braudel 1984: 468).

Arms production tended to become concentrated in state arms manufactories, as in the prototypical case of the Venetian *Arsenale* which was mentioned earlier. The efficient organization of armies was just as important and the absolutist states set up military academies for the training of professional officers and artillery schools to ensure that European gunnery remained superior to that of its adversaries (Braudel 1984: 393–6). Significant changes in basic military organization came when standing armies began to consist of 'regular' companies, and the French *compagnies d'ordonnance* of the mid-fifteenth century were the first significant examples. They were financed, according to Perry Anderson (1979: 32), by a special tax known as the *taille royale* and this clearly links military organization with innovations in state taxation. This writer also attributes the now familiar military institution of infantry drill to the Dutch Prince Maurice of Orange; the platoon system and 'salvo' shots to King Gustav II of Sweden (Gustavus Adolphus); and the unitary vertical chain of command to Count Wallenstein of Bohemia. The latter trained mercenary groups or 'free companies' which were commonly used for military campaigns or, since they were free of local loyalties, for putting down peasant revolts. According to Robert Zaller (1984: 2), however, the last large conflict to be fought with mercenaries was the Thirty Years War of 1618–48. This was the war which heightened divisions between the Protestant states of Northern Europe and those of its Catholic South, another significant factor in the development of the European state system.

In general terms, the armies of the absolutist monarchs were permanent, more efficiently recruited, larger, better equipped and better trained. Those of their predecessors had mainly consisted of *ad hoc* arrangements for particular battles. In warfare on land, the widespread adoption of more effective artillery meant that defensive structures had to be redesigned, and the star-shaped *trace Italienne* low fortifications were characteristic of Northern Europe during the eighteenth century. At sea, regular navies were created, as for instance during the Anglo-Dutch wars of the seventeenth and eighteenth centuries. These fleets contrast sharply with practices at the time of the sixteenth-century Spanish Armada when only a small percentage of the ships actually belonged to Philip II. The rest were made up of privateers, converted merchant ships, chartered Venetian galleys, etc.

Relations between the absolutist states

The absolutist states reflect substantial changes not only in the European state but also in the pan-European state system. Charles Tilly (1992: 164) suggests that 'we can reasonably date the establishment of regular diplomatic missions within Europe to the fifteenth century practice of the Italian [city-]states'. In this, as with many things, the Renaissance was a turning point, but the principles of diplomacy developed further with the larger and more powerful absolutist states and much of this was the result of the initiatives of Louis XIV and his ministers. Dealings between the absolutist states represent the foundations of modern diplomacy with the important difference that the state's legitimacy lay in the dynasty of the monarch (Anderson 1979: 39; Poggi 1978: 68). The supreme device of alliance between absolutist states was marriage, although it did not always go to plan as the 'wars of succession' of the period indicate.

Congresses and treaties began to appear from the seventeenth century onwards, as in the example of the Congress of Westphalia. This not only brought an end to the Thirty Years War in 1648, it also set the pattern for the division of modern Europe into states – the 'Westphalian model'. Congresses mark a break from the pattern of international meetings in earlier centuries when they were normally organized through the offices of the Roman Church. The institutionalization of these meetings and the treaties which emanated from them did not prevent wars but put them on another footing. There was formal recognition of the existence of a state system and there emerged the notion of a balance of power in Europe. Any disruption of this balance and the breakdown of diplomacy provided new reasons for war.

The transition to the modern nation-state

Reference was made earlier to a sequence of city-states providing a core to a developing 'European world-economy'. By the end of the seventeenth century

Amsterdam was in this position, but during the eighteenth century London took over. At this point there is a very important difference. Whereas Amsterdam was a city-state only loosely connected with the surrounding Dutch United Provinces, London was the capital city of Britain, a nation-state which combined England and Wales with Scotland after the Act of Union in 1704. Of particular significance for present purposes is the fact that Britain had by then the hallmarks of a modern nation-state in terms of government and economy. France also was developed as a nation-state, probably more so than Britain, but lacking comparable levels of trade or innovation. By the eighteenth century the politico-military power of each was formidable, far surpassing that of any of the absolutist states, but Britain was about to embark upon the first Industrial Revolution which would augment its already considerable economic power. Certainly the age of the city-state was finally over.

It is tempting therefore to conceive of an evolutionary development in state administration leading from the city-state through the absolutist state to the modern nation-state. But this would be a mistake. There were broad disjunctures in the organization of European society during the seventeenth and eighteenth centuries, especially those connected with industrialization and urbanization. Although it may be perceived that many of its social institutions were developed from those of the city-states and the absolutist states, the nation-state is an entirely different social configuration to anything which had gone before. Industrialization and urbanization affected the lives of more people more quickly than any previous form of social change and they far exceeded any existing capacities of the state for planning and provision. The elaboration of trade and industry meant that life had to be more ordered. Time and timetables became a feature of life, and the nation-state system took responsibility for the basic regulation of these. In 1884 Greenwich Mean Time (GMT) was accepted as the international basis for the measurement of time. This impinged heavily on the organization of work, and the Industrial Revolution was a very painful experience for the majority of people. At first the state was ill-equipped to provide much comfort and this of course led to the reform movements of the nineteenth century.

One thing is clear, however: changes within the state took place against the background of an already constituted state system. Thus, even before the Industrial Revolution there existed the beginnings of the modern state system and operating alongside it there was an effective 'world-economy'. No one had consciously devised these things. They were the unanticipated consequences of Europe's history from the sixteenth century when its global role may be considered to have begun. As Gianfranco Poggi (1978: 88) has described it, the states did not 'presuppose' the system they 'generated' it. The gradual extension of European politico-economic activities into an international infrastructure, mainly through colonialism, accounts to some extent for the speed with which the industrial and commercial opportunities of the Industrial Revolution were taken up. However, whereas the British Industrial Revolution took place on the basis of *'laissez-faire'* non-interventionist economics, the governments of continental Europe shared a policy of direct participation in industrial and technological development in their haste to catch up.

As industrialization spread, drawing the population to the cities, the mechanization of agriculture made up for the shortage of labour in the countryside.

In fact, a virtual 'created environment' came to cover north-western Europe. This destroyed finally the distinctions between city and countryside which had characterized the city-states and the absolutist states. The removal of the city–countryside distinction took the feudal type of coercive compulsion out of socio-economic relationships to be replaced by what Karl Marx referred to as 'dull economic compulsion'. The scale of change was such that the wage bargain became not only an economic relationship but also the basis for social relationships too. Chapter 5 will describe how the class relationship based upon industrial work and the division of labour became a central feature of society at that time.

Two distinct social movements may be identified in the emergence of industrial capitalist society and they both impinge upon the state. There was pressure, firstly, from the emergent 'bourgeoisie' for conditions conducive to capitalist industrialization and, secondly, from reformers and mass movements for a range of citizenship rights. In this the political revolutions of the seventeenth and eighteenth centuries had enormous influence.

The English Civil War period involved the removal of the old order, symbolized by the execution of the king, and the establishment of a parliamentary republic. But it was short-lived and the crown was re-established. Therefore, perhaps, the 'Glorious Revolution' of 1688 is more important for its final and permanent abolition of the divine right of kings and assertion of parliamentary government.

Of even greater importance is the American Declaration of Independence of 1776 which marked the determination by Europeans who had settled across the Atlantic to put European traditions behind them. They devised a completely new basis for government, the first written constitution. The principle of the 'rights of man and of the citizen' on which the USA was founded emerged in Europe in 1789 with the French Revolution. The *ancien régime* of France was abolished and the aristocracy executed in the name of 'liberté, egalité et fraternité'.

These are the transformations to which attention is normally directed, but there were other important influences too such as the development of centralized bureaucracy in Prussia, referred to earlier, or the relatively early assertions of power by a free (non-feudal) peasantry in Sweden. In these ways the modernization of the state came not from within its organization but from without in the assertion by its citizens of principles which were to lead to the assertion of liberal democracy as we understand it today.

Nation, nationalism, nation-state

The most significant aspect of the nation-state is that it involves a form of administered nationality, one that is contained within its territorial boundaries. However, as many current disputes show, there is not always congruence between living within the territorial boundary of a nation-state and feelings of nationalist belonging. For instance, many Basques who currently live within Spanish territorial borders do not feel that they are Spanish at all. Even the provision of semi-autonomous government for the Basque regions has not put an end to this. See Chapter 21 for a more extended discussion of peripheral nationalism.

The most difficult term to define is 'nation'. If we go back in time far enough everyone's ancestry must converge to some extent. Yet there is a difference between provable ethnic origins and present-day feelings of nationalism. Anthony D. Smith (1986) has argued that 'ethnie' should be the proper term for ethnic origins whereas current feelings of belonging may have more to do with 'nationalism'. Ernest Gellner has gone so far as to suggest that nationalism invents nations where they do not exist.

Nationalism may take the form of identity encouraged by a nation-state. Many nation-states issue identity cards to their citizens. This practice is not universal, yet for instance everyone who lives in Great Britain and Northern Ireland is formally regarded as being of British nationality. Some people living in Northern Ireland object violently to this, as do some Scots less violently. Some Cornish people accept British identity but object to being regarded as English. The distinctions may be very fine. Taking a completely different example, the modern nation-state of Nigeria inherited its constitution from the European model when it became independent from Britain in 1960. Members of the main Hausa, Ibo and Yoruba tribes, as well as more than fifty smaller tribes, are encouraged to think of themselves as Nigerian. At one point, however, there was a bloody and extremely damaging civil war between the Yoruba and Hausa on the one side and the Ibo on the other.

The distinction between nation, nationalism and nation-state may be summarized as follows:

- Nation – ethnic origins.
- Nationalism – contemporary feelings of 'belonging' which may be conventionally attached to a nation-state but alternatively may be encouraged more forcefully by nationalistic leaders and movements. There may or may not be congruence between nationalism and nation-state.
- Nation-state – territory controlled by a constitutional government which normally grants citizenship to those who live within its borders.

Citizenship and the nation-state

The modern nation-state is an institution of social organization derived from the broad spectrum of European cultural development and it has become the universal global model. In terms of this orthodoxy, the basic elements are, in principle:

- citizenship rights of freedom and equality before the law are secured by a liberal-democratic political system – parliamentary government is formed through elections involving a secret ballot;
- government decision-making is supported by an impartial rational–legal bureaucracy;
- laws are administered by an independent judicial system;
- laws are enforced by the state's formal monopoly of the means of violence.

It is important to consider also that citizenship rights have not been awarded automatically through a process of enlightenment or social evolution. Instead they have been actively achieved by people in specific struggles and by incremental change in the more mundane reproduction of social institutions over time. The liberal-democratic state is intended to be a reflection of its citizens, rich and poor, weak and powerful. Yet as part of industrial capitalist society it must continually attempt to reach a compromise over the potential conflict between the private appropriation of profits from industry by the owners of capital and the general participation by the population as labour force. Liberal democracy implies not only the democratic citizenship rights of all but also the right of the individual to hold property even against the interests of others. This apparent contradiction may be seen as the primary conceptual location of the state in industrial capitalist society.

T. H. Marshall's (1950) summary of citizens' rights is idealistic, but nevertheless useful as a basic framework with three distinct categories:

- civil rights are sustained through the law, if necessary by recourse to the courts;
- political rights are sustained through democratic elections to representative bodies with the participation of political parties and pressure groups;
- social rights are sustained, according to Marshall, through such things as the extension of public education which constitutes society's awareness of the citizen's need and duty for self-improvement.

However, in relation to each of these three areas of citizenship the question must arise of differential access for the individual citizen in the light of such issues as for instance:

- the high cost of professional legal representation;
- the differential resources available to alternative political parties;
- the potential advantages of a privileged private education over state provision.

Additionally, the full extension of social citizenship rights would, since labour is socialized, presumably include participation in the control of work for the individual-worker-as-citizen. Yet for most people work takes place in the private sector and therefore outside of the public sector domain of state and citizenship rights. Even public sector work organizations have tended to follow the pattern of those in the private sector in that their workers have no overall rights of control. Only in a few societies, notably those of Germany, the Netherlands and the Scandinavian countries, have workers been granted some limited participation in management as a result of state legislation.

The extension of the state

As mentioned already, the development of the state in Europe has involved a separation of polity and economy. The state is the arena of politics, state administration, law and enforcement – the public sector – whilst economics and production are predominantly organized as private enterprise – the private sector. In principle the former is in public ownership and the latter in private ownership. Against this the prime examples of extension of the state have occurred in the former Soviet Union, after the 1917 Revolution, and in China, after 1949. In these two examples, what is often referred to as 'state socialism' involved the extension of state power from politics into the economy so that no significant aspect of society was outside of state control. Theda Skocpol (1979) has argued that both Russia and China were previously agrarian bureaucratic societies which found themselves confronted, and to some extent dominated, by more economically modern states abroad. In the face of this, what each revolution accomplished was the removal of a traditional landed ruling class and in its place the extreme rationalization and centralization of state institutions.

In an entirely different example, the state was extended too by means of 'nationalization' in Britain and some other European countries, particularly after the Second World War. In this case sections of industry – railways, coal mines, commercial road transport, etc. – were selected for government take-over, management and administration. This could of course only be done because the governments involved had taken a very significant swing to the left in post-war elections. Subsequently these examples of state-run industry attracted much criticism from some quarters on the grounds of their bureaucratic rigidity and general inability to deliver the levels of public service that had provided the rationale for their establishment in the first place.

Curiously, it was during the 1980s that not only did a political swing to the right throughout Europe put a virtual end to nationalized industry and bring 'privatization' into vogue, but also the Soviet Union collapsed and state socialism was dispensed with throughout Eastern Europe. Now only China remains as a really significant example of this kind of government and even there the liberalization of economic activity is having profound effects upon society.

The universalization of the European model of the state

The Second World War represents a watershed, not only in the history of Europe but also in world history. This is because it was the first truly global conflict and it resulted in radical revisions to the nation-state system and the world order, not to mention global communications and global economy. Change took place, however, against a background of existing global institutions which had been developed with the rise of Europe and the extension of Western civilization. Foremost among these was the universal adoption of the European model of the nation-state.

Nevertheless, there were considerable changes to the territorial definition of some nation-states, particularly in Europe but also in other parts of the world. The post-war dismantling of the European colonial empires had been one of the conditions for America's participation in the war, and during the 1950s and 1960s this increased the number of independent nation-states threefold. Even before the war was over the USA, the USSR and the UK had formulated plans for the

United Nations Organization, intending it to be an effective global forum for all nation-states, with the failure of the League of Nations after the First World War clearly in mind.

The establishment of the UN may be interpreted as official recognition of the European model of the nation-state and its global adoption in a nation-state system. It is a much more comprehensive organization than the League of Nations and it has benefited from the resources and participation of the USA, the most powerful of its members. This is something which the League never achieved. During the setting up of the UN there was a clear determination, mainly on the part of the USA, to maintain the capitalist system of global economy. The European countries subsequently opted for extensive state welfare but in other respects the political nation-state system has been kept separate from global economy in which private enterprise has been free to operate according to market mechanisms. This is a matter of principle. The remit of the UN's economic agencies was limited to the provision of conditions in which free enterprise capitalism could flourish. In particular the USA wanted to avoid the apparently menacing alternative of Soviet state socialism in which the state would extend its control over the economy with comprehensive state planning.

The USA was the only country to emerge from the war with sufficient resources to provide the levels of finance needed for reconstruction of the basic global economic infrastructure. There was some hesitance by the US government but it was soon realized that substantial pump-priming was necessary if private sector investment was to be attracted for full-scale economic recovery and growth. The USA therefore became the chief sponsor of the economic arrangements established under the aegis of the United Nations. These consist of the International Bank for Reconstruction and Development (IBRD), more commonly known as the World Bank, and the International Monetary Fund (IMF). They have commonly been referred to as the 'Bretton Woods arrangements' after the name of the place where they were formally drawn up. The underlying principle was that the World Bank would provide finance for infrastructure, like roads, ports, communications, etc., to encourage private sector investment. The IMF would underwrite the world's hard currencies in a set of semi-permanent exchange rates with the US dollar which itself would be linked to gold. These provisions of course represent a formal recognition of the significance of global economy in relation to the nation-state system.

Summary

- Forms of politico-military rule became centred in city-states.
- Absolutism centralized political power much more effectively, using better forms of administration and military force.
- Modernity produced the nation-state with liberal-democratic political systems and the recognition of citizenship.
- The European model of the nation-state became adopted globally.

Further reading

John A. Hall (ed.) (1986) *States in History*, Oxford: Basil Blackwell. This is a useful collection of approaches to the various forms of the state throughout history.

Charles Tilly (1992) *Coercion, Capital, and European States, AD 990–1992*, Oxford: Basil Blackwell. This is a critical approach to the emergence of European states over the past thousand years. The emphasis is on the coercive nature of the state and its facilitation of capitalism.

Anthony Giddens (1985) *The Nation-State and Violence:* Volume Two of *A Contemporary Critique of Historical Materialism*, Cambridge: Polity Press. This is an approach to the development of the modern nation-state emphasizing its capacity for the 'surveillance' of society and its members through the maintaining and use of sophisticated bureaucratic techniques. It also contains a comprehensive approach to the development of military organization and the notion of a 'monopoly of violence' held by the state.

Chapter 4

Reason and modernity

Doug Benson and David Dawson

Introduction	70
The rise of Western civilization	70
Positivism and progress	77
Modernity and certainty	83
Post-modernism	86
Summary	89
Further reading	90

Key concepts

- Modernity and modernism
- Reason and rationality
- Post-modernity and post-modernism

Introduction

Sociologically, the terms 'modernity' and 'modernism' are generally understood as referring to an approach to the generation of knowledge based upon human *reason*. Arising in early seventeenth-century Europe it can be seen to have two main characters. One, Galileo, reintroduced the importance of experimentation in coming to understand how the material world works. The other, the French philosopher René Descartes, argued that unaided human thought can provide sure and certain foundations for knowledge; that is, there is no need to rely upon a notion of God or revealed Truth. Following the writings of Descartes it was argued that human thought can provide certain knowledge of the material world if it followed certain patterns of argumentation which basically were tied to mathematics or formal logic. Over the centuries this has become the view that science, in all its forms, is the only sure foundation for knowledge and, by extension, the only rational foundation for human action. The nineteenth-century argument was between science and religion; in the twentieth century it has been between science and common sense. Post-modernism refers to the sense of implosion that has occurred in the twentieth century. The belief in science collapses with the atom bomb, and belief in human progress in the Nazi concentration camps. *Reason* is now considered to be fragmented, there being no single, unitary and universal set of procedures to arrive at truth or certain knowledge. Sociologically this entails a rejection of those theories such as Marxism which attempt to provide a grand theory of human social development.

The rise to dominance of scientific reason in Europe, and the subsequent European/Western world-wide domination in the nineteenth and twentieth centuries is central to many themes within sociology. This chapter considers the following:

- the sociological understanding of the foundations and consequences of reason is central to modernity;
- the world-view of modernity is specific to capitalist and scientific rationality and the rise of the West;
- rationality as presented in the Enlightenment of the eighteenth century and developed in the positivism of the nineteenth century has endorsed a secular belief in certainty and progress as universal features of the modern world;
- the varieties of pluralism in Europe – which inform social meanings from personal identity to those of the nation-state – calls for a sociology sensitive to the changing texture of the current social world;
- a central question for contemporary sociology is whether reason and modernity are disintegrating or whether they are being reformulated for the twenty-first century

The rise of Western civilization

The rise of the West and the flowering of European culture from the Renaissance was the product of a unique pattern of cultural and economic factors. These

> ### RATIONALITY
>
> Rationality is the belief that by using systematic reasoning and established empirical facts one can produce explanations which have general or universal application. This would give modern science, the major claimant to rationality, a privileged position in relation to such things as religion when it comes to arguments about knowledge and truth. Some regard this as being an arrogant claim, seeing in it the roots of the cultural dominance of the white, male European society in which it arose.

factors enabled Western European societies to become globally dominant in the economic, political, military and cultural spheres. This capacity for radical social change reflects the significance of two aspects of the West. First, the originality and universality of its world-view, and second, the centrality of rational calculation and technological control in its social organization.

For some writers this focus on uniqueness appears as a form of self-congratulatory Eurocentrism which seeks to justify the domination of particular institutions, ways of thinking and a particular set of moral evaluations. For others, the link between European dynamism and the ancient world of Greece and Rome appears as a form of dismissiveness towards the contributions of Afro-Asian culture (Bernal 1987). Yet these critical reservations, however important, ignore the world-wide consequences of European development and the problems this generates for modern sociology. For sociology not only has to account for this development in Europe it has also to explain itself, for it too was born in the same period.

Although sociology is still a developing discipline, it already has a long history with widely differing areas of interest. In its current form, one of its concerns is with understanding and explaining the changes which take place when a society moves from traditional to modern forms of organization and culture. This concern with *social change*, and the rise of the West, is not a romantic indulgence. Rather it is an example of sociology's hope of clarifying and demystifying social processes. In this way it captures the problems which confront sociology in its focus upon the relationship between social change, political organization, and the production of knowledge and the changes in human consciousness. It is a focus on how what we are as thinking, acting human beings is related to the wider historical changes that take place in science, industry, ideology, and the like.

During the nineteenth century and early twentieth century there were two main competing sets of ideas or *theories* which appeared to provide the boundaries of the debate regarding social change: historical materialism (associated with Karl Marx) and evolutionary theories (such as those of the founder of sociology, Auguste Comte).

Although there are many points of argument between these two approaches, both enjoy a common viewpoint – that of social determinism (that is, that there are causal laws which make certain changes inevitable). By assuming the inevitability of modernization and of various social stages, such as the move from feudalism to capitalism or from religion to science, both orientations, either by design or default, explain the past by reference to the present.

There are clear problems in explaining the past by reference to the present, not the least being that it makes everything inevitable as though humans can exercise no choice. And it produces absurdities such as the 'explanation' that the reason why our nose and ears are as they are is so that we are able to wear glasses. So sociology has rejected social determinism and instead tries to demonstrate how socially organized settings such as schools, families, legal systems are continually produced, sustained and disrupted and changed. Discussion of the rise of European eminence is not some scholastic cul-de-sac, for it is in a discussion of the role of human agency that we come to some understanding of modernity and modern life.

To describe and argue for the uniqueness of the West makes necessary an examination of the movement and interplay between the material foundations of its society and its culture and ideas. The West, understood now as Europe, has a particular geographical location, particular environmental resources, and particular cultural features and borrowings. How did these develop together? This question is inseparable from an analysis of the emergence of *modernity*. By modernity is meant:

> a historical period that began in Western Europe with a series of profound social-structural and intellectual transformations of the seventeenth century and achieved its maturity: (1) as a cultural project with the growth of the Enlightenment; (2) as a socially accomplished form of life with the growth of industrial (capitalist and later communist) society.
>
> (Bauman 1991: 4)

In order to understand the debates over the origins of modernity and the disputes in regard to post-modernism we need to explore the beginnings of capitalism, rationality and science (McNeill 1963). But before describing how 'reason' operates in modern science, both natural and social, it is necessary to indicate why this rationality was engendered in occidental rather than oriental social systems, by a comparison of Europe with China. For China, as Weber identified

---

ENLIGHTENMENT

'The Enlightenment' is a term used to describe those thinkers of the eighteenth century who established the basis of looking at society in a scientific way. In effect they established the foundations of modern social science. In rejecting a religious viewpoint they adopted a secular belief that society could be seen as the object of systematic, exact scientific enquiry. The *rationality* of this new scientific inquiry would be based on empirical facts and it would free social explanations from theological and metaphysical thought, thereby freeing people from the power of the clerics and the divine rights of kings. Their goal was to liberate people from the shackles of ignorance and the domination of aristocratic tyranny.

---

it, had many of the conditions seemingly related to the development of science and capitalism and yet singularly failed to fulfil them.

Imperial China was able to retain a relatively closed world-view either by banning influences and practices of other civilizations or by domesticating them. It achieved its stability through the supreme power of its bureaucratic class – the mandarinate. The economic and political domination of this social stratum allowed it to neutralize the dynamic factors which contributed to the disruptive changes of rationality in the West. It restricted the autonomy – and thereby the creativeness – of its cities. In the West, rather, the dynamism of the city could be equated with the emergence of capitalism. The mandarinate either incorporated and regulated trade or marginalized the 'modernizing' power of the merchant class. In contrast, trade in the West was central to the dissolution of the economic practices and social relations of feudalism. The mandarinate also sponsored and routinized a Chinese identity derived from Confucianism with its stress on harmony at the individual moral level as well as at the wider socio-political and cosmological levels. All of these factors contributed to the thwarting of the emergence of a home-grown capitalism. Finally, Imperial China was a 'capstone state' in which:

> the united Chinese elite sat atop a series of separate 'societies', which it did not wish to penetrate or mobilize; perhaps the key to its behaviour was its fear that horizontal linkages it could not see would get out of control. Its concern was less with intensifying social relationships than in seeking to prevent any linkages which might diminish its power.
>
> (Hall 1986a: 52)

The transition to modern Europe between 1500 and 1700 is characterized by the move from intensive or local power to extensive or wider power which is the hallmark of the emergence of the organic state. This period sees the routinization of mercantile capitalism, the rise of scientific rationalism and the consolidation of the organic state. Unlike the development of the capstone state, the organic state develops in the presence of the limitations imposed by the civil society – a process of development which allowed for political and cultural constraints, including religion, to impede the uninhibited exercise of central power. This move from intensive or local power to extensive or wider power occurred within the diversity of European societies. It developed within the political struggle between states and the normality of war which generated both increased production and technical invention. This was paralleled by disputes between the states and the Church, all of which coalesced in a creative tension which generated social adaptation and innovation within the ecological, normative and institutional peculiarities of Europe.

The spread of European agriculture is based upon the advantages of soil and climate of the area and the intensification of production by technological ingenuity, which produced a surplus for the market economies of the cities. This supported the principles of a market economy as they emerged in the cities. Here the emergence of a powerful merchant class required that its trade and transactions were conducted in a regulated way: within a legal framework which protected property rights and contractual exchange. All of this took place in a normative framework provided by the Church which gave to Europe a common identity in which trust could develop in economic and intellectual matters. The Church also limited autocratic political power by endorsing the significance of civil society and individual land rights as complementary to, but not interchangeable with, the state. The inertia of bureaucratic feudalism was thereby avoided. For by allowing an orderly social world the Church provided the moral code for trade between different areas and states. So the process in which Christianity 'promoted' the commercial development of European society, also aids the drift towards liberal society, with its assertion of the rights of individuals. The separation of state and society provided the framework for the ethos of individualism which from the seventeenth century onwards was central to modernity. 'So Europe also became a more orderly multi-state system in which the actors were more nearly equal, more similar in their interests, and more formally rational in their diplomacy', which 'was aimed at preventing anyone from gaining hegemony' (Mann 1978: 455). This equivalence of interest and competition not only allowed for the radical economic changes of the mercantile class, it also created an obstacle to the auto-cratic use of central power. As a result of trade, ideas – technical, artistic, cultural – crossed national boundaries. The rise of the West is therefore synonymous with the 'internationalization' of the market – the beginnings of world economy, a process facilitated by Europe's navigational innovations which allowed the sea to be used for discoveries of lands and materials which led to both military and cultural domination and commercial exploitation.

Behind the transition from medieval to modern Europe are two critical changes in consciousness which separate Europe from China: the Renaissance of the fourteenth century and the Reformation of the sixteenth century. Before enlarging upon this a crucial point needs reiteration. The social formations of the West were not the inevitable progressions indicated by determinism. In effect 'what rendered the unique passage to capitalism possible in Europe was the concatenation of antiquity and feudalism' (Anderson 1979: 420), because

> the birth of capital also saw, as we know, the rebirth of antiquity. The Renaissance remains – despite every criticism and revision – the crux of European history as a whole: the double moment of an equally unexam-pled expansion of space, and recovery of time. It is at this point, with the rediscovery of the Ancient world, and the discovery of the New World, that the European state-system acquired its full singularity. A ubiquitous global power was eventually to be the outcome of this singularity, and the end of it.
>
> (Anderson 1979: 422)

Although the Renaissance's reappropriation of Greek scientific naturalism eventually abandons its original search for essences or ends, it reorganized its concern for argument and proof in order to produce a secular logic aimed at the decipherability of the laws of nature. This revision is complemented by the Reformation where the reasoning of the informed believer progressively dispels the previous intoxication with magic (Thomas 1978). The search for regularity and uniformity replaces variability and qualitative difference. Unlike the harmonious mystical view of the world found in Chinese religion, the concern with the creation within Christianity allowed for notions central to science: causation, contradiction and certainty. It achieved this through making nature ordinary and mundane. Instead of the organic world-picture of nature as purposely intelligent, it became seen as atomistic and mechanical. As a consequence the idea of a created or constructed world had as a corollary a mechanistic world-view, a view which rapidly made connections with mathematics. The natural world is now open to analysis, manipulation and subjugation.

This move toward an empirical–rational view of the world, where measurement of actual occurring empirical phenomena is measured and combined with rational, mathematical methods of calculation and proof, did not occur in a social vacuum. It occurred within the activities and the framework of ideas which made up the stance of mercantile capitalism. Here, the forces and imperatives of the processes of exchange contributed to the metaphors of abstraction and generality, both of which are integral to scientific inquiry. In effect the independent status of merchants as people whose trading practices were based upon measurement provided a direct affinity with the compulsions of calculation in scientific reasoning (see Sohn-Rethel 1978). The break-up, then, of the organic world-view parallels the new mercantile practices and religious beliefs. This is not necessarily to equate the concepts of scientific rationality with the categories of economic rationality or reformed religion, but the acceptance of the mechanical world-view based on an insatiably progressive rationality has extreme practical implications. In effect the scientific revolution of the sixteenth century is a synthesis of attitudinal, technical and analytical factors within a distinct social world. 'Apparently a mercantile culture alone was able to do what agrarian bureaucratic civilization could not – bring to fusion point the formerly separated disciplines of mathematics and nature knowledge' (Needham 1972: 44). This fusion does not remain in isolation: it is to have profound implications for the views on progress and society which follow in the eighteenth and nineteenth centuries, and it remains at the core of the major polemics in the twentieth century. So it can be argued that this mechanization and mathematization of the facts of nature, created the preconditions of scientific progress, in that all phenomena are viewed as amenable to standardization and calculation.

In itself, the rationality of science may be dull. But its logic proved mesmerizing. For many in the late seventeenth and eighteenth centuries the seductive allure of scientific rationality over the natural world was transferred to the object of desire, *society*. If there could be an objective science of nature, then why not an objective science of social laws. It was a short journey from rendering nature mundane to taking a similar position on the social world. It was a move that had its beneficiaries, principally in the view that an objectified social world is an instrument available for manipulation. It is the routinization of these views which is to have such profound consequences for modernity.

The social orders of traditional societies, from antiquity to late medievalism, had viewed the intelligibility of the social world as mirrored in organic analogy, or metaphysical or mystical truth, or divine revelation. The newly emerging strategies of capitalism found in science when applied to society – scientism – an instrument for the advancement of their interests. It assumed that reason and observation could decipher social life. In effect it imitated the new logic of the mechanistic and mathematical world-picture by attempting to 'shape political and economic philosophy and practice according to the model of self-regulating mechanical systems, rather than as an order imposed by supreme authority' (Ben David 1971: 76–7).

The eighteenth century witnessed the origins of modern society and the capitalist world economy based on Western Europe. The economic and political movements of modernity in their hostility to traditional institutions provided a social interest supportive of the 'naturalization' of the social world. The clarity and intelligibility of the account offered by the *Enlightenment* promised an important weapon in the attack upon the *ancien régime*. But the Enlightenment had two tendencies, one 'negative' and the other 'positive', which diverge in the nineteenth century with profound implications for modernity and post-modernism.

The thinkers of the Enlightenment regarded the social world as something which could be understood in the same manner as the physical world. The progressive factual rigour of scientific method is seen as liberating knowledge from the illusions, distortions and superstitions of tradition, authority, experience and emotion. Culture contaminates knowledge; only reason is inexorably certain. This universalization makes knowledge significant and meaningful in providing the framework for practical emancipation. The stress which Descartes placed upon the unshakeable rock of individual reason produced a seemingly imperial swagger on the road to cognitive truth. For the philosophy of the Enlightenment – a fusion of French rationalism with English empiricism – its theoretical and practical significance was critical and negative. Its aim was to transcend previous knowledge, explicitly to subvert the restrictive orthodoxies of religion and state. Its focus was on the provision of an understanding which would not accommodate itself to subjugation, distortion or manipulation. This seeming irresistible claim for the unity of rational awareness and practical liberation is rapidly dissolved in the nineteenth-century separation of sociology into 'systems' and 'action' orientations. In the former, the use of a natural-scientific model of systems implies both a coercive reality, however organized, and a technical mode of cognition. In the latter, social reality is viewed interpretatively as an accomplished product of social action. This schism – initially subterranean – was to surface in the late nineteenth century as a fundamental divergence over the comprehension of modern rationality.

The consolidation of the natural-scientific model within the 'new' nineteenth-century discipline of sociology is harnessed to the aspirations of positivist logic (Giddens 1979). Here the rationalism of the eighteenth century is directed to the pursuit of human improvement, through the identification of objective social laws. This triumphant synthesis of scientific rationalism with social progress appears to relegate metaphysics to the oblivion of prehistory; but reservations and doubts remain. These anticipate reservations over treating humans as objects and societies as machines, both of which are the foundations of the instrumentalist, manipulative and controlling, approach to the social world. These criticisms inform the twentieth-century arguments over scientism and technocratic rationalism.

> ## THE SOCIOLOGY OF PROGRESS: CLAIMS AND DILEMMAS
>
> Behind the optimism of the Enlightenment in regard to improving the social conditions in which people live lay the idea of an underlying logic of social development. This is the belief in progress. Progress in the material conditions of life such as improvements in agriculture and industrial technology. Progress in the growth of knowledge both of the workings of society as well as the material world. Progress too in the development of more fully human and more fully moral people. Society and people were to be improved by the increasing use of science and scientific techniques in the organization of social life. By presenting sociology as a science of industrial society capable of understanding and explaining the social and cultural changes of industrialization and modernization certain problems arise. In particular the style of reasoning used by sociologists leads to the conclusion that sociology reveals objective social laws. It is precisely this claim to objectivity which has led to arguments as to whether sociological reasoning produces emancipation and freedom or a part of the coercive technologies of the modern bureaucratic state.

Positivism and progress

This application of objectification to social reality created an exclusively technical view of sociological cognition and explanation in its pursuit of social laws. It was produced by the need to account for the societal transformations of the French Revolution and the Industrial Revolution, and the anti-traditionalism of nationalism and capitalism. However, in observing the dislocations and the agonies as well as the improvements and potentialities of change, sociology in its aspiration for rational objectivity acquires a contradictory shape. Its perspectives are drawn from the organic societies of the past but its methods are derived from the rational empiricism of science (Nisbet 1968). In place of the fatalism of religion it introduced a secularized view of perfection: a social utopia attainable through the insights of a rational consciousness. The idea of calculation applied to society, derived from the political and moral arithmetic of the seventeenth century and elaborated in eighteenth-century 'social rationalism', is amplified into a universal rationalization of all aspects of individual and social existence in the nineteenth century. From Condorcet to Marx via Comte, progress becomes the dominant component of Western rationalism. It is the sufficiency, exclusivity and certainty of this fusion of rationalism with progress which generates a parallel dissensus in the nineteenth century. It begins with Romanticism and concludes with a plethora of criticisms of the *fin de siècle*.

For Romanticism, the commands of rational action advanced by the Enlightenment project of modernity, seemed to consign the authentic and creative human actor to simple subjection to external forces – the mere product of socially causative factors. Romanticism also saw the eulogizing of technology as a means to manipulate people. Technology did not liberate; it was simply another form of control and repression: of exploited nature and subjugated humanity. Romanticism begins as a cultural movement in Germany: economically and nationally still outside the mainstream of European social change. In its rejection of the specifically French trinity of reason, science and technology it fused aesthetic and cultural concerns into a social movement. Although partly backward looking in its origins its actual preoccupation is with an alternative social image of the future. In moving from the universal claims of the Enlightenment the Romantics embraced the significance of everyday particularities: the importance of 'the pathos of the mundane' (Gouldner 1975). The here and now, the particular objects and personages involved and the particular descriptions which may be made of them are the concern. Not some generalized account of 'mankind', but this man, this woman and what might be said of *them*.

This disengagement from the implacable logic of rational empiricism highlighted the cultural centrality of language and imagination. The identification of the salience of language raises questions of 'authenticity' and 'spontaneity' and 'self-identity' which twentieth-century reason responds to in a variety of ways. It implies that the essence of human social life is not a mechanical reflection of structural constraints found in the world. Instead the essence is to be found in the dynamics of language as exchange and transformation.

By the end of the nineteenth century, then, the solidity of reason as the theory and ideology of the social world – in progress, modernity and capitalism – is present to all intents and purposes as an accomplished fact. As modernity, or 'modernist radicalism' (Crook 1992), it has endeavoured to reach a bedrock of *certainty*. It wants to ground 'truth' upon unshakeable foundations. Its attempt at so doing results in marginalizing, if not totally ignoring, alternative accounts of reason. It vigorously aspires to a singular view of scientific reason within the universe of science. It is hostile to relativism, indifferent to scepticism and forgetful of its own origins in systematic doubt. Marx and Durkheim, two of the trinity of classic sociology – the other being Weber – are complementary and exemplary exponents of the high-water mark of Western rationality. Marx's initial synthesis of historical materialism is as a criticism of ideological distortion and mystification of the state, society and the subject person. The abolition of slavery, for example, is ascribed not to the Christian sensibilities of the reformers but to the hard-nosed economic judgement of the cost of maintaining slaves compared to that of waged labour. Through a reappraisal of Hegel's dialectic in the context of living human beings rather than in the abstract realm of ideas, and combining this with a materialist, economic specification of the route to human freedom, it aims for a radical synthesis of humanism and naturalism (see the essays in Colletti 1979). Initially this approach demonstrates how, institutionally and intellectually, humans have been coerced, dehumanized and exploited. By deciphering the contradictions of capitalism, Marx aspired to an objective which would be consonant with both scientific rationalism and Romanticism: the liberation of the human condition. This moves progressively towards a search for foundational certainty. By seeing society as coextensive with capitalism, Marx enters into reductionism: 'For him, the heterogeneous and mutually irreducible types of activities that constitute modern society (including aesthetic creation, politics, language and "spiritual reflection") are subsumed under the paradigm of production' (Rundell 1987: 197). In effect, Marx's version of modernity links emancipation to an objectified rationality derived, although modified, from Enlightenment reason.

Paradoxically, the liberating promise at the beginning of Marx's work on the potential plurality of everyday life, fishing in the morning and Shakespeare in the evening, is abandoned. The objectification of reason in Marx carries within it a restriction on alternative images for the future:

> In other words, there is an internal limit to Marx's own theorizing, and it can also be seen – even if remotely – as the intellectual–historical origin for the technocratic corruption of socialism and the levelling of the historical diversity of modernity.
>
> (Rundell 1987: 199)

But at the very stage when the social realism – however different – of Marx and Durkheim appears to dominate the field in its description, diagnosis and prescription for emancipation and change, its fundamental claims are disputed. These disputations in sociology begin with Dilthey and are developed by Simmel and Weber.

As with Romanticism and idealism, the disruption of this narrow view of reason encapsulated in positivism and realism begins in Germany. Three main currents of thought, vital to understanding twentieth-century debates, emanate from there. First, the dispute over the methods for understanding in social life – the Methodenstreit. Second, Simmel and Weber's work concerning the criticisms of modernity. Third, from Nietzsche via Spengler concerning rationality and disintegration.

In effect the Methodenstreit distinguishes between nomothetic (generalizing) and ideographic (individualizing) knowledge of social life. The former assumes the possibility of systematic explanation derived from facts and expressed in causes and laws which decipher reality. The latter accepts that the human sciences are dealing with historically and culturally specific events which are to be interpreted by understanding their meanings. As a result the unitary claims of the rationality of science for the cultural sciences remains contested throughout the twentieth century in the divide between objectivism and relativism.

Simmel and Weber are contemporaries within late nineteenth-century and early twentieth-century German sociology. Simmel's formalism or abstract approach is central because by taking interaction as crucial the generalizing tendencies of Marx and Durkheim are presented as liable to produce distorted accounts of social life. In effect, by separating the dynamics of the everyday world from the curious gaze of the sociological observer they embrace a false privilege for sociological enquiry. Their reasoning ignores direct experience, the commonsense or 'first-order' understandings and constructions of the subject. Simmel anticipates a variety of twentieth-century preoccupations: the phenomenological concern with the meanings of the mundane and the interpretation of fragmentation within the dynamics of metropolitan culture. In addition, his stress upon the insensitivity of money to individuated and qualitative differences anticipates Weber's more extensively discussed theme of rationalization. Weber's work on rationalization prefigures concerns over a technicized view of social life and a technocratic view of politics. It responds to 'a positivistic conception of science that threatened to "behaviourize" the problems of men as cultural beings' (Lash and Whimster 1987: 3). For Weber the error of the Enlightenment was found in its assumption that the individual possessed the transparency of universal reason. Instead, for Weber the devastating impetus of modernity was the appropriation of the individual's rationality by the technical reason of institutional systems: the rationalization process embedded in the logics of bureaucratic administration and empirical science. This becomes an iron cage which could trap us all.

> No one knows who will live in this cage in the future, or whether at the end of this tremendous development entirely new prophets will arise, or there will be a great rebirth of old ideas and ideals, or, if neither, mechanized petrifaction, embellished with a sort of convulsive self-importance. For of the last stage of this cultural development, it might well be said: 'specialists without spirit, sensualists without heart; this nullity imagines that it has attained a level of civilization never before achieved'.
>
> (Weber 1958: 182)

Equally for Weber the imputed logic of history, be it evolutionary or developmental, was spurious. Whether materialistic or otherwise it trivialized the texture of social existence and the varieties of social action under the emblem of a modern vision of the ultimate goal: a secular teleology. It has already been noted that the social structural milieu which produced the intellectual transformation of the Enlightenment emerged from a wide variety of causes and as a result had a wide variety of consequences, some of which conflicted. For Weber this intellectual transformation culminates in the purposive rationality of modernity: here all things are resolvable by calculation, by technique, by measurement. The new social order has its 'magic', its mystery, removed; it is a world of remorseless disenchantment.

For Weber the future of the West is based upon the connection between rationality and domination. The scale, implacability and consistency of technical reason create the preconditions for the pacification of civil society in its transference to the social world. In this, discipline and acquiescence are fundamental: themes which occur in various anti-utopian novels. Through the reification of institutional reason, for example 'measuring' education by exam results, alternative political and moral accounts are derided as unscientific, impractical, irrational. The Enlightenment dream becomes a nightmare. Within the institutions of capitalism (or whatever successor version of post-capitalism) the imperatives of technical co-ordination – from everyday social life to multinational corporations – create the *illusions* of autonomy and freedom.

For a group of scholars, including Adorno, Horkheimer and Marcuse, collectively referred to as the Frankfurt School, the agonizing theoretical and practical problems of the twentieth century is how the universal potential for liberation of the Enlightenment has become degraded into an anti-humanism: the new barbarianism. Here reason itself, whether as myth or dogma, is central to the strategic coherence of the repressive apparatus and ideology of the modern state.

This objectification becomes integral to the considerations of the Frankfurt School because it transfers quantification and measurement into the social world: reason becomes instrumental. The social subject becomes like the objects in the natural world, open to calculation and manipulation. However, the device for the pacification and domestication of the social world is not direct force or intimidation. It is rather the entire panoply of capitalism, its capacity to generate the illusion of social autonomy within a mechanized social world. Marcuse was later to call this 'repressive tolerance'. In this repressive tolerance the 'culture industry' is central and is, of course, the theme of control through pleasure to be found in Huxley's *Brave New World*. The idea of a 'culture industry' is central for critical theory because of their assumption that the rational integration of the economy and polity leaves only one problem: the management of self-identity and the homogenization of the person. The reduction of works of art to commodities of commercial exchange becomes integral to political manipulation because, as a process, it confirms orthodoxy and compliance. Dickens' critique of capitalism and industrialism in *Hard Times* becomes a vehicle for yet another costume drama of English Heritage. Whatever the ideological form of social systems of instrumental rationality, the commodification of art moves it from transcendence to simple, some would say mindless, distraction. Films, television and advertising reproduce the social relations of the existing order. In mass culture, the forms of popularization imply familiarization and normalization. Its simplistic structures of expression create a social distance and cultural amnesia in which the vocabulary of change is cosmetic. The dirt, the smell, the stink of spilled blood, upon which struggles for emancipation and change were built, get washed out to become images of quaintness over which the onward march of science and technology have effortlessly advanced. This creates an affirmation of privatization and the atomization of society in which the hedonism of the private ego is dislocated from the world of social transformation. In addition, the decline of intermediate associations within liberal capitalism, including the agency of the family, is seen as rendering individual identity as being susceptible to the homogenizing processes of rationality. As a consequence, and particularly in the hands of Marcuse, the utilitarianism of modern institutions and the ascendancy of the 'reality principle' means we have walked into the iron cage of positivism, locked the door and thrown away the key. Human potentialities have been negated because technical reason closes the domains of discussion and acts, ideologically, to the benefit of those who dispose of people and resources in society.

Habermas both extends Marcuse's argument, asserting that technical reason involves the scientization of politics and public opinion, and also endeavours to find solid ground upon which to re-establish Enlightenment concerns. For Habermas, that is, judgements about moral and political questions can be rationally grounded and differences about such questions can be rationally resolved, *in principle*. He begins his critique of positivism by arguing that its incapacity to understand its own presuppositions – *how* it is fabricated – renders it partial, parochial, specific. The central idea which Habermas uses to ground his critique is that of the *interests* of different kinds of knowledge. The first is the interest pertaining to the control and predictability of the natural world. This is the proper realm of the natural sciences with their objectifying and manipulative methodologies. The second realm of human interest is in our humanness, our understanding of ourselves and others, and in the structures and mechanisms of communicative interaction. This is Weberian *verstehen* sociology, the domain of hermeneutics or 'meaning' and the human sciences. The third interest is in that of emancipation, of freeing people from the constraints which have been imposed by others, of getting people off other people's backs. This is the domain of power, to be analysed by critical theory. Habermas's critique of positivism is that its cognitive–instrumental aspects have come to dominate the second and third realms of interests in which they are inappropriate and damaging.

Habermas is concerned to show that the pathologies of late capitalism can deform the everyday life-world – the world of symbolic reproduction. He argues that the crises in late capitalism, such as the role of the state and social welfare for example, increasingly cause the absorption of the everyday life-world into the objectifying logic of the world of material reproduction – the economic. This is termed the 'colonization of the life-world'. This colonization can be located in the formalization of conflict in the system of production through to the technicization of politics. It is expressed in the application of money values to specific, previously separate areas, including identity and sexuality.

The colonization of the life-world – its commodification and manipulation – leads to its 'cultural impoverishment' and accelerates the decline of meaning. All things are increasingly resolvable by technical reason, by expertise – from sexual identity through beliefs to social transformation. The 'legalization' and 'formalization' of the logic of expertise when combined with the impoverishment and fragmentation of the everyday culture of the life-world appears to complement Marcuse's notion of 'repressive tolerance'. This emphasis is enlarged in Habermas's detailed accounts of 'new social movements'; of the relationship between the dominance of technical reason and the exploitation of nature; of the dynamics which actualize self and subjectivity (Marcuse 1968). These examples indicate the scale of Habermas's approach which derives from his 'communicative model of reason and action'. At the back of this synthetic revision, however, is a fundamental problem for late twentieth-century reason in the human sciences: is the Enlightenment vision of authentic persons, non-repressed selves and a social future of unforced mutuality still possible?

The 'reconstructive sciences' – a title Habermas applies to his reoriented critical theory – is the late twentieth-century continuation of the aspiration of the Enlightenment aims to articulate a transparent reason within language and consciousness, actions and institutions. In rejecting the relevance of both positivism and idealism as exemplars for the human sciences, it introduces a sensitivity to the nuances of communication and culture. In incorporating radical modifications of Marxian, Weberian and Freudian insights it establishes a general claim for reason against contextual and relativistic reservations.

As a consequence some writers argue that Habermas's synthesis raises the danger of merging reason with substantive purpose or normative obligation. In his 'reconstruction', reason would become partisan rather than a device for securing the separation of reflection from practice. Habermas therefore highlights a central question: is it possible to have a meta-language which evaluates different paradigms? In effect, is the reason of foundational certainty a fading illusion along with the death of God, the dissolution of truth and the decomposition of normative universalism (see Seidman and Wagner 1992). It is to the debate over reason and certainty – within modernity – that attention must now be given.

Modernity and certainty

The basic problem in dealing with the concept of modernity is no different from the problem in dealing with any other historical period or phenomenon ... [but] the assumption of modern superiority is, of course, rooted in the idea of progress, which has dominated western thought since at least the eighteenth century. Whatever may be said for it, this view has no place within the frame of reference of the social scientist (or, for that matter, of any empirical science, including the science of history). Progress cannot be empirically verified. [Therefore] this methodological requirement has a simple but very important consequence: modernity is to be studied as a historical phenomenon – like any other historical phenomenon.

(Berger *et al.* 1974: 11)

However, the twentieth-century debate over reason has seen a divergence between certainty and agnosticism in the human sciences. For objectivism, reason and progress are able to decipher the rules of society, culture, life – immune to the blandishments and distortions of irrationalism and Romanticism, which are seen as retrograde, reactionary, decadent (see Gellner 1992). It is unnecessary, though, to become a fellow-traveller in the expeditions of irrationalism and Romanticism to realize the cogency of their reservations and criticisms over the idealization of the perfectibility of the social and moral world, because

If some ends recognised as fully human are at the same time ultimate and mutually incompatible then the idea of a golden age, a perfect society compounded of a synthesis of all the correct solutions to all the central problems of human life, is shown to be incoherent in principle. This is the service rendered by Romanticism and in particular the doctrine that forms its heart, namely, that morality is moulded by the will and that ends are created, not discovered.

(Berlin 1990: 237)

It has already been noted that modernity begins as a cultural project in the eighteenth-century Enlightenment. In these modernistic developments analytic and explanatory purposiveness is based upon the rational displacement of chaos, unpredictability, uncertainty; in effect, the clarification of the dynamics and legitimation of social order.

We can say that existence is modern in so far as it is effected and sustained by design, manipulation, management, engineering ... the typical modern practice, the substance of modern politics, of modern intellect, of modern life, is the effort to exterminate ambivalence.

(Bauman 1991: 7)

In short, the goal of modernity is to legislate for the rational foundations of the state, society and consciousness. Its approach to the state and society indicates an unease with incommensurability, contingency and ambivalence. In this the

NIETZSCHE AND MODERN SOCIAL THEORY

Until recent years the German philosopher Nietzsche (1844–1900), was probably best known for his idea of the 'superman' who was held to be the inspiration for the kind of man Hitlerian fascism promoted. A person who would break free of the bourgeois standards of morality and through the exercise of will create a new moral and social order. In the debate over understanding modern social and cultural process, however, his significance has become increasingly apparent. Unlike the views of positivism and realism which assume that scientific rationality can identify and clarify an external reality, Nietzsche assumes no foundations or external reality which correspond to truth. Instead it is the language, the will, the ideas of the subject which construct or create the world we inhabit. For Nietzsche then, scientific rationality is simply one set of ideas amongst many. It has its own vocabulary, as it were, but there are other languages and there is no privileged language amongst them. The interpretations of Nietzsche have become important in the debate over modernity and post-modernity.

logic of modernity confronts post-modernism and anti-foundationalism. Behind this are a series of developments. First, hermeneutics' concern with meaning and phenomenology's concern with intentionality and consciousness. Both object to the mechanical application of scientism to the social world. Second, the continuing debate over rationality and relativism and whether the claims of relativism decompose 'reality' and 'scientific knowledge'. Third, the arguments advanced within the framework of post-modernism which oppose general theories and 'meta-narratives' and instead turn to a radical deconstruction of all narratives. In treating modernity as a social and historical phenomenon like any other, the rest of this chapter is devoted to a basic question for reason. Do the disputes already indicated illuminate the redundancy of modernity; or does its logic anticipate and account for changes in consciousness, culture and society? At the centre of this are the notions of fragmentation and nihilism.

Nietzsche denies the main assumption of the modern view of scientific rationality: that its ascendancy, its dominance, reflects its unique privileged universality. Instead it is presented as nothing more than a belief – a metaphysical faith. Nietzsche is concerned with the re-evaluation of all morals, with the scrutiny and questioning of all assumptions. In this he continues and transforms the language of Romanticism and extends its concerns. For him all cultures, be they religious or secular, have gods, and the god of modernity is that of classical, cool, rational Apollo. The logic of modernity is predicated on the sufficiency of scientific reason for transforming the social world. It implies that rationality, when applied to social institutions and social movements will inexorably guarantee the ends of progress – whether democracy, or justice, or liberty, or equality or whatever. It will do this, moreover, without effort, or commitment, or reflection. For Nietzsche this mechanical world devoid of purpose or conflict is a denial of human authenticity. It is the 'morality of the herd animal': it makes Europe a culture of decadence. For its assumption of automatic advance concedes a decline in vitality and a devaluation of differences. These are themes which resound in the European debates of the 1990s. Modernity ushers in mediocrity. It homogenizes and flattens experience, perception and understanding. The only way forward is by the ruthless destruction of illusions – the acceptance of nihilism, both cognitively and morally. For it is because the reason of modernity is stagnant and complacent that nihilism involves a subversive logic. It requires a transcendence of the dependency of European institutions on 'scientism' and 'liberalism'. It is this abrasive and fundamental criticism of reason, progress and democracy that makes Nietzsche's work so resonant and relevant to the late twentieth-century European ideas, movements and institutions. For Nietzsche, Dionysian understanding – from Dionysius, the god of intoxication – is preferable to the Apollonian logic of modernity because when applied to the cultural sciences this scientization of reason neutralizes human will and paralyses social action. In its approach, in strong contrast to classical rationalism, there is no foundation, no essence, no certainty. Values, morality, reason are all *created*. Herein is Nietzsche's legacy to the late twentieth century: European nihilism (for a discussion see Vattimo 1988; Dreyfus and Hall 1992).

The rise of the West and the decline into decadence argued by Nietzsche has so far been described in terms of 'ideas' – the ideas of reason, rationality, scientific procedures and the like. We now need to have a brief consideration of the material situation of Europe, remembering, however, that the phenomenal significance of events and processes are not fixed. Because of this we must beware of viewing the past as a series of inevitable steps and processes which led unavoidably to present circumstances. Equally, as was noted at the beginning, we need to avoid the type of reductionism which attributes the explanation of human actions and institutions to one overriding factor. This produces 'determinism', often now 'technological determinism': the idea that particular factors inevitably lead to particular types of social and political organization. The current fashion for predicting inevitable social change through the proliferation of the computer is an example.

One feature of Europe that is often left out of consideration is that as a relatively small land mass it has a large number of states, and these states have often been at war with each other. Wars, of course, can be a vehicle for social change. Britain, which became the first industrial capitalist nation, can be seen to have risen to eminence because of the successful way in which it pursued mercantile success by waging wars, or by financing other nations to wage war on its behalf. Being an island, a naval power on the western periphery of Europe, and generally avoiding military involvement on land in continental Europe are major factors in the story of Britain's rise to power. Britain had a sound financial structure by comparison to similar countries, and its growing commercial and industrial strength and the possession of world-wide colonies enabled it to compete successfully with its major competitor of this period, France (Kennedy 1989).

By the mid-nineteenth century, Europe, with its centre on Britain, had become the hub of a global economy, a global economy that was becoming increasingly seen as integrated. Kennedy estimates that 'In the year 1800, Europeans occupied or controlled 35% of the land surface of the world; by 1878 this figure had risen to 67%, and by 1914 to over 84% (Kennedy 1989: 190). European domination of the world was not simply a rhetorical flourish.

British world power continued after the First World War, but the collapse of its economic hegemony in the financial world system was signalled by the Wall Street crisis of 1929, and the Second World War lay waste to Britain's and Europe's economic base. The balance had shifted to America, a Western nation but not European. As we come closer to our own time events move more quickly and a clamour of global changes demand our attention, from the oil crisis in the 1970s, the growth of the economies of Japan and the Pacific rim, the growing influence of Islamic nations, the explosion in computer and related information technologies, and we have still to mention the end of the cold war and the potential implications that has for European integration and world security.

The future of Europe is, of course, unknown. Just as we must beware of social determinism in accounting for the past we risk ridicule, and worse, to plot Europe's future trajectory. Post-modernists have seized upon this idea, that there is no single true 'scientific' account of social phenomena such as the rise of capitalism and European dominance. They assert that there are only a variety of different 'stories' to be told, none of which can be claimed as more authoritative than any other. This leads to further matters. First, the end of the modernist rational account of human, scientific and social development or progress. Second, to question the foundations of the social and human sciences given that all these disciplines can do is to proliferate a variety of accounts, none of which can be seriously entertained as the product of a rigorous science. Third, via a consideration of the 'stories' which society tells itself there has been a move to study, broadly, culture, and from there to emphasize, fourth, the cultural relativity of (post) modern societies. (For a discussion of these matters see Lyon 1994; Rose 1991; Turner 1990; Harvey 1990; Button 1991.)

Post-modernism

Has the Enlightenment project come to an end? The notion that the unfettered use of human reason would elevate and liberate mankind from material want and oppression by their fellows is over, because science is no longer automatically and universally accepted as a source of social meanings and social change. As well as killing and scarring thousands of people at Hiroshima and Nagasaki, the atomic bomb destroyed the notion of science as a simple boon for society. More recently, genetic engineering and pollution are other dangers blamed on science.

In addition the new communication technology based upon increasingly powerful computational machines, speeding information and media around the world has led to a fractured social order. Once homogeneous societies are now fragmented into different religious, racial, ethnic, status and stylistic sub-cultures where everything has become relativized. There is no accepted central belief system or value system around to which people can relate and integrate.

Post-modernism takes seriously the notion that sociological accounts and explanations cannot furnish the post-Enlightenment promise of a science of society. Instead sociology is inevitably enmeshed by the 'philosophical idioms' it selects, and simply mimics vernacular or common-sense accounts. This is not an entirely new argument. Indeed it has been suggested that one of the reasons why Weber became involved in *practical* issues of social policy was because he saw that sociology was unable to become a science which accumulated proven bodies of knowledge. More generally, Weber argued, social science cannot provide a basis for values, morality and action. To say, though, that this feature of the post-modernist argument is not a new observation does not undercut the force of the criticism. Alternatively, for sociology and the social sciences, there is the option of practical involvement with the sociologist as a kind of under-labourer, gathering 'facts' for others to use. Even here, though, Weber had his fears: that sociology becomes engaged with the increasing bureaucratization of society. (There are other intellectual options, however; see Garfinkel 1984.)

The role of information technology is another area of interest for sociologists concerned with the post-modern (for a discussion see Kumar 1995). In part this interest resides in the possible effects that the new technology might have on such matters as the centralizing of information, control and therefore power. The rapid speed with which large masses of information can be collated and analysed by computer has led to the argument that computers inevitably have a centralizing tendency:

> functions of regulation, and therefore of reproduction, are being and will be further withdrawn from administrators and entrusted to machines. Increasingly, the central question is becoming who will have access to the information these machines must have in storage to guarantee that the right decisions are made. Access to data is, and will continue to be, the prerogative of experts of all stripes. The ruling class is, and will continue to be the class of decision makers. Even now it is no longer composed of the traditional political class, but of a composite layer of corporate leaders, high level administrators, and the heads of the major professional, labour, political, and religious organizations.
>
> (Lyotard 1986: 14)

Lyotard's view is part of his argument concerning the changing nature of science and its position as source and legitimator of power, especially now that science is closely connected with the new informational power of the computer.

We must also be attentive to the fact that whilst much is speculated upon the manner in which computers and other recent developments in technology will impinge on our lives, there is yet to be much concerted effort to actually detail the ways in which computers are used by people in the everyday settings in which the day-to-day work of organizations and mundane activities are accomplished. Indeed such work that has been undertaken places an entirely different construction on the place of new technologies in everyday life (Button 1993). Although technologies become incorporated in everyday working practices, most sociological accounts have still to address what those working practices are in their particular details. Abstract accounts of the ways in which the 'information revolution' alters sociality and power configurations are almost always addressed to theoretical sociological concerns rather than to the particulars of technological use in actual work sites. Here again then, sociologists have much to say of interest but much more work needs to be done before we will have greater clarification of the issues of concern.

The final aspect of post-modernism to be examined is *relativity*. A central part of the post-modernist stance on relativism is the untenability of 'Grand Narratives' or the 'Truth of Science' (see Appignenes and Lawson 1989). By rejecting the truth of science it is presented as just another story, subject to the same influences that shape, if not determine, other stories and institutions. Science, in this fashion, is 'debunked' (for a summary see Woolgar 1988; Lynch 1993). As a consequence the implicit belief in progress and truth as secular icons of modernity has wavered and fractured. The fusion of reason and practice when applied to social life as a unitary logic has receded: the solidity of its reality has dissolved. What this indicates is an inextricable connection between the social, cultural and historical which itself requires respecification. Increasingly, universalization or globalization generates a concern with the 'discontents of modernity' (see Berger *et al.* 1974). The claim propounded is that the bureaucratic and technical forms of modern institutions generate a social life – including politics and religion – characterized by incomprehensibility and implausibility. Everyday social life – which includes the management of the self – becomes anomic and anonymous in the disenchanted pluralization of modernity. This is the 'homelessness' of modern social life and consciousness: the 'componentiality' of self and social relations. However, the fragmentation and transitory forms of contemporary culture are not in themselves necessarily part of a new determinism which consigns the future to inertia, despair and futility. What emerges is that whatever form of reasoning or interpretation comes from this *'fin de siècle/*millennium' debate will have to incorporate a systematic form of cultural analysis.

The other context in which relativism shakes a stick at the modernist project is in terms of ethics (see Habermas 1993; Bauman 1993; MacIntyre 1981). The fragmentation of Western societies internally, with different sub-cultures based on race and ethnicity especially, and the global 'conflict' between Western, or more specifically American, values and those of other regions, pose questions concerning the possibility of a national or international moral order. Are values such as individual freedom and tolerance 'universal'? If not, then how can unity be maintained or produced from a diversity of ethical and cultural standards? Much of the debate in these areas seems to overstate the case. The relativists have some force to their arguments. It is obvious that disagreement about fundamental ethical principles is sometimes a feature of discussions about ethics. People argue from different positions. But it is by no means always clear as to what conclusions are to be drawn from this fact. For one thing to notice about ethical/cultural debates is that argumentation does not necessarily lead to agreement in the manner of scientific arguments. There is no 'evidence' to settle the matter under dispute. The evidence indeed may not only be seen differently by the alternative sides but can also be used by the various positions as part of their argument. On the other hand this does not necessarily mean that people are unable to come to an 'agreed solution' (Winch 1987). Habermas's discussion of power-free relationships is one attempt to formulate a context within which agreement might be obtained. Debates about what ought or ought not to be taught in curricula are similarly often couched in oppositional terms, with the picture presented being one of irresolvable opposition. The actuality is, however, often more complex, with areas of common ground often established. In many ways the sociological contribution to this area of debate with its picture of collapse of moral authority is, as was noticed earlier, dependent on an idealized past or rather a past which has often been idealized in certain sociological accounts. That the world, and Europe, at the end of the twentieth century has not turned into the rather monolithic conception of a Westernized capitalist set of democracies perhaps speaks more to the failure of certain kinds of theorizing – as the post-modernists point out. But that does not necessarily lead to a profound despair nor to wild dreams. The need for political debate and action over a wide range of issues, both within and between nations, will continue.

This takes us to the end of this discussion over reason and the rise of the West and its implications for the modernity/post-modernity debate. Much of the criticism of 'deconstruction' and 'post-structuralism has focused on the fallacy of modernity in viewing Western reason as transcendent and universal. These arguments are elaborated by writers such as Lacan, Derrida and Foucault (see Heckman 1986). They are summarized in the exchanges between Foucault and Habermas. They provide a focus for a fundamental question over reason. If reason is to be understood as embedded in interests which are themselves located in, and explicable by, culture and society then the future debate will have to clarify questions over history, society, culture and agency for the human sciences. Within this the prospect revolves around three possibilities: 'continuation', 'reconstruction' and 'transgression'. For the first, the human sciences can continue by a process of internal adjustments; for the second, they need a radical solution to replace or reconstruct their existing paradigms; whereas for the third the present commitment to the reason of modernity is fraudulent – it needs abandoning, transgressing. In conclusion, therefore, it can be seen that just as history has not ended, then nor has the need to develop and extend sociology's conception of itself and its subject matter.

Summary

- The rise of the West refers to that period in history when a small part of the world, small enough to be a mere ancillary of Asia, rose to intellectual, military and economic dominance of the world. Europe rose to pre-eminence for a variety of reasons. Geographical location, military developments, the location of mineral resources, the development of its cities, its intellectual reincorporation of the ideas of antiquity and aspects of its religious beliefs all contributed to its rapid expansion.
- Reason and science, until recently seen as the highest embodiments of human development and the sure engines of progress, have come under sustained attack in the twentieth century. From diverse areas such as linguistic philosophy, phenomenology and post-modernism the notion of a unitary and universal form of reason has been undermined. Despite these debates the world remains resolutely as it is.

● The question for the contemporary human sciences is whether their modes of reasoning and explanation are sufficient for deciphering and informing current social transformations or whether they need to reformulate their approaches.

Further reading

Anthony Giddens (1990) *The Consequences of Modernity*, Cambridge: Polity Press. Modernity is analysed, with the main focus being institutional change. Epistemological concerns are kept in the background.

Paul Kennedy (1989) *The Rise and Fall of the Great Powers*, London: Fontana. A grand study of recent world history. Notable for bringing geography back into the picture of the development of nations. Instructive to pundits: despite its astounding breadth of knowledge Kennedy's last chapter fails to foresee the collapse of the Soviet Union.

David Lyon (1994) *Postmodernity*, Milton Keynes: Open University Press. Provides a good guide to the debate around post-modernism and post-modernity. Endeavours to give a balanced view.

Max Weber (1958) *The Protestant Ethic and the Spirit of Capitalism*, New York: Scribners. This is one of the classic texts of sociology. It links the development of capitalism to the contemporary forms of protestantism, in particular Calvinism.

The making of the modern European

PART TWO addresses those aspects of European society which have produced cleavages within it. Although we all go to make up that which is referred to as society, the experience of individuals and groups varies according to their particular identity or the way that the rest of society views them. Clearly, there are differences of class, gender, race and age which affect people's positions in society and their access to its rewards and benefits. Historically, social stratification – as Max Weber put it, class, status and power – has been of particular importance to the development of sociological analysis and it remains important. But gender, race and age have become much more significant during the contemporary period as women have pressed for equality, European society in general has become much more cosmopolitan and, with the development of 'youth culture' and an extended human life-cycle, society has become much more aware of the young and the old. Gender, race and age have physical characteristics – there are differences between men and women, between blacks and whites and between the young and the old – but the social identity of people with these characteristics is a social construction. That is, interpretations which are often mistaken or malicious, or both, become ingrained, or in sociological terms institutionalized, over time and are difficult to reverse. Therefore there is a pressing need to examine further all of these processes in the European context.

Chapter 5

Social stratification

Doug Benson and Geoff Payne

Introduction	94
Social class as sociological theory	97
Class in European history	100
Social class in contemporary society	103
European attitudes to class and inequality	110
Class dynamics in contemporary society	113
Alternative interpretations of social stratification	118
Reflection	122
Summary	122
Further reading	123

Key concepts

- Social class
- Status groups
- Power relationships
- Social mobility

93

Introduction

Social inequality

One of the most striking features of all human societies is not that people are different from *each other*, but that large *groups* of people have distinctive levels of wealth, power, and honour. Consequently, sociologists have always taken a major interest in these *social inequalities*, trying to identify the different forms of inequality, to explain what causes them, to understand why they are socially acceptable, and to explore their consequences. Patterns of inequality are interesting in themselves, but they also form the basis of group identity and collective behaviour. It is this that makes them sociologically relevant.

Although all societies display systematic social inequalities, these are not everywhere the same. For example, in simple tribal societies, which depended on hunting and gathering or basic farming for their existence, nobody could be very rich, and almost everybody worked at the same basic tasks. However, even in such *subsistence economies*, men and women, and adults and children, were clearly differentiated, and played separate roles. In some of these societies, people were grouped into *age-sets* which had particular tasks at each stage of their lives. Although each age-set was treated with greater respect as it gained seniority, an individual could never move out of the one age-set into which he or she had been born.

These small societies were displaced in most parts of the world, including Europe, by larger social systems. Many of these kingdoms, city-states and federations developed military technologies, complex artistic cultures, and writing. They also had more specialized occupations and crafts, and their rulers amassed great riches through warfare and monopoly control of trade. However, even great empires were still mainly based on agriculture and, except for the ruling elite, most people shared very similar experiences of life. The majority were poor and politically powerless, and often confined for life to their social station as slave or serf. This restriction to a social position determined at birth was reinforced by custom, religion, and even in some cases by the legal system. One particularly well-defined case was the Indian caste system, in which the relationships between the four main castes were rigidly reinforced by religious ritual for maintaining the purity of the Brahmin ruling caste.

Contemporary European societies, although containing rural areas, are largely industrialized. They depend on advanced technology for the production of the goods that they consume, and the wealth they create. The production tasks (the jobs) to be performed are more differentiated and specialized, so that the members of any one society do not all share the same experiences of work or living conditions. People come together in a variety of political parties, or trade unions, or social movements, in which they combine with others with similar experiences and views to advance their own interests. The competition for wealth and power takes place through these groups, as well as between individuals, and people's lives are not settled from the moment of their birth.

These examples of three types of society – tribal, pre-industrial, and modern – show that inequality is related to the economic circumstances of a society.

Earlier societies were not just poorer but also simpler, sharply differentiated and more rigid, in that people were born into a social position from which it was often almost impossible to move. Such societies also display clearer associations between wealth and power than in our current, more fragmented and complex societies.

We can therefore think about social inequality in several ways. First, there is the dimension in which social inequality shows itself. We have already talked about differences in wealth, in political power and in social honour. We can look at how extreme is the variation between people in each of these dimensions, and whether the same people who do well in one dimension also do well in all the others. Third, we can consider how fixed are these differences: can individuals move between levels of inequality? And fourth, we can ask what is the basis for allocating people to levels of social inequality? We have mentioned age, birth, military power, control of trade, the law, and jobs. Other important principles of stratification include gender (see Chapter 6) and ethnicity (see Chapter 7), while some writers have championed individual ability as the real explanation.

Social stratification

When systematic study of social inequality began in the eighteenth and nineteenth centuries, social differences were very clear. If we contrast the lifestyles of the aristocrats in France with their peasants just before the French Revolution, or the great textile mill owners with the children who worked their mills in early Victorian England, it is easy to think of society as consisting of separate layers. Those at the top generally had most, and those at the bottom least, of wealth, power, prestige, and any other aspect of advantage in human society. Relatively few individuals could move from one layer to another. The layers in such a social hierarchy were like the layers of different rocks in geological formations. These patterns have been described using the metaphor of *social stratification*. While today's large industrialized societies consist of many more groups and levels of wealth and power, and more people move between them, the metaphor of social stratification remains a powerful one.

Given this complexity of modern societies, an alternative view is to think of wealth, power and honour (or 'prestige') as each being a continuous gradation, with everybody arranged from high to low in tiny, subtle degrees of difference. Most sociologists have argued that while this may be a valid view, in practice there are clusters where groups of people clump together in a shared condition of inequality. On the one hand, there are 'natural breaks' in the gradations as well as points on the 'scale' where we find more people. On the other hand, the dimensions of inequality are connected, with rich people usually having the power to hold onto property, and powerful people the ability to obtain property and be respected. They achieve this through using their wealth to influence the legal system, and to legitimate their position of advantage by promoting their own values more effectively than those in less advantaged positions in society. A picture of society that emphasizes only subtle gradations of difference cannot do this justice.

Social class

This is one of the reasons why so many sociologists have used the idea of *social class* – or often 'class' as a shorthand – to describe the key form of stratification in contemporary society. A social class is a collection of people who share similar economic circumstances. In contemporary society, if we know a person's occupation, we can make a pretty good estimation of that person's income, educational qualifications, lifestyle, etc., including housing, holidays and fashions, and even political and religious affiliation.

It will of course only be a rough and ready approximation. In the first place, sociologists are not so naive as to believe that all people in a particular job are identical. At the very least they differ in age, gender and locality, and their various previous experiences will mark them out as people with differences in attitudes and personality. Our approximation is intended to show what most people have in common, or their most probable shared features, rather than their differences. We are not trying to account for every single person.

In the second place, the precision of the approximation will reflect how detailed we wish to make our categories. If we talk about 'white-collar workers' or 'the middle class', we include a wide range of occupations from managers of large companies, through doctors, lawyers and lecturers, to clerks and receptionists. The range of incomes, qualifications, lifestyles, etc. would be very wide, compared with a single occupational group, and so be more of an approximation. What matters is that the level of approximation that we employ fits our needs.

While sociologists have all accepted the importance of *social inequality*, there has been a considerable debate about its precise form and causes, not least about the concept of *social class*. Part of this has addressed the problem of how exactly we should define and measure class, and whether it is too rough an approximation. A second strand of the debate has been over the causes and consequences of class, with arguments between several schools of thought over what produces social classes, the best way to think about them, and what role various classes have played in history. There has been disagreement about whether we need class as a concept at all, with some more-recent writers seeking to account for social inequality using different models. If we are to understand the complexities of both inequality and the debate over class in sociology, we need to begin by exploring the two key contributions to our understanding: the work of Karl Marx and Max Weber. This will give us a more systematic basis on which to proceed.

CONCEPTS FROM THE INTRODUCTION

- social inequality
- age-set
- social stratification
- social class

Social class as sociological theory

Developing the idea of social classes: Marx

The idea of using people's economic circumstances as a way of constructing categories for social analysis has its intellectual roots in the work of Marx, and much of the later sociological debate over class has been in response to his writings. We therefore need to explore some of the main features of his ideas, both as a reflection on the previous section and in connection with our later discussion of class in contemporary society. Marx saw social stratification as an outcome of the central human activity of material production; that is, the production of food, shelter, clothes and other requirements for physical survival. People's identity was determined by their place in the social organization that was needed for production, or in Marx's term, by their *relationship to the means of production*.

In human history, there were always two main groups, or social classes in the social organization of production. There was one social class that owned property (land, factories, equipment, even other people as slaves) and who hired other people as labour; and a second social class of those who owned no productive property and had to sell themselves as labour to the owners. Class is defined by property ownership and production, and it is these that create differences in income and lifestyle. Power over others is only a result of class, rather than a way of defining it. The new industrializing societies of his time were run by the *bourgeoisie* of capitalist industrialists who exploited the labour of the industrial workers, the *proletariat*.

Capitalism as a system is central to Marx's writing, and in one sense his account of class is only a by-product. *Capitalism* entails the application of capital (land, finance, equipment) with labour, to produce the maximum profit. What distinguishes it from earlier systems is its use of cash and markets, and its organized relentless competition between capitalists, and between capitalists and workers in pursuit of profit. This is why Marx addresses so much of his attention to the bourgeoisie and the proletariat.

Marx also talks about other smaller classes or fragments of classes, such as white-collar workers, managers, professionals, peasants, small farmers and shopkeepers. Such groups were distinctive not because of their occupations *per se*, but because of how they occupied a particular relationship to the production process. The small farmers and shopkeepers who made up the *petite bourgeoisie* occupied a temporary position between capitalists and workers, while below the proletariat were an even lower category, the *lumpenproletariat* of criminals and others. He believed that these sub-classes were either a hangover from pre-capitalist days, or that as capitalism developed, they would be swallowed up into one or other of the main social classes. Advancing capitalism contained the seeds of its own defeat, as the endless search for profit would increasingly polarize society into a few very rich and an ever more impoverished mass of workers. Eventually the proletariat would rise up and overthrow the bourgeoisie in the 'proletarian revolution'. This was an inevitable outcome: the proletariat would be the ultimate great winners in history. It is in this respect that Marx's theory of class is inherently political, as well as social and economic.

The key to understanding Marx is that he saw the people in each economic situation as having the potential to generate a sense of shared identity. Each class, on achieving this true consciousness of its own identity would recognize that its best self-interests were in conflict with those of other classes. In turn, this would lead to collective (political) action: the people would act together as a group. Until this happened, the ruling class could succeed in imposing its own values and beliefs on others, by creating an ideology that led to other classes having a false consciousness about themselves.

There are several problems with Marxism as a theory of social stratification. It is based on a very simplistic view of pre-industrial societies, while as a political theory of history – predicting the inevitable 'proletarian revolution' – it is either incorrect, or has to be cast in a much longer time-span than he intended. There are subtleties of position that do not fit neatly into the two great social classes, and people manifestly do not simply act in terms of their class position.

Marx could not foresee the way that the social organization of production would actually evolve under twentieth-century capitalism. First, ownership was modified by the 'joint-stock company'. This legal and financial arrangement enabled capitalists to own an enterprise without directly managing it themselves. This created a new class of managers, who serviced the needs of the capitalists by running their companies for them, but who were not themselves members of the capitalist class. Second, as production became more complex, new specialist functions evolved, expanding the intermediate white-collar occupational classes that Marx had predicted would wither away. Third, a new governmental apparatus of economic support, co-ordination, and regulation grew up, staffed by professionals and bureaucrats, the managers of the state. Rather than a polarization between bourgeoisie and proletariat, there was a multiplication of social classes, and new chances for people to move between classes.

Moreover, the electoral politics adopted by most European countries, under the influence of these new classes, introduced reforms that blurred the conflict of interests between the two social classes. Whether one sees the welfare state of education, housing, health, and social security as *won* by the workers, or as crumbs dropped from the rich man's table to *pacify* the lower orders, the great

---

CONCEPTS FROM MARX'S VIEW OF CLASS

- material production
- lumpenproletariat
- relationship to the means of production
- social class
- bourgeoisie
- proletariat
- capitalism
- petite bourgeoisie
- class consciousness
- false consciousness
- ideology

mass of society has not been progressively impoverished and down-trodden. A different social order has replaced Victorian England, both in this country and elsewhere in Europe, although by no means uniformly in either time or extent.

Developing the idea of social classes: Weber

The other major contribution to understanding social stratification was that of Max Weber. We can think of Weber as differing from Marx in three ways. First, although Weber was mainly interested in power, his theories are non-political. They make no claims for the inevitable overthrow of capitalism by the proletarian revolution.

Weber also recognized that there are other forms of group identity related to stratification, such as membership of a political movement or a non-class group (based for example on ethnicity, kinship or education) with a distinctive lifestyle. Rather than treating these as merely sub-sets of class, Weber saw these as discrete dimensions that *could* be related to class, but which should be analysed separately. He talks about *social strata* as occurring where people's situations on several dimensions tend to coincide. However, if membership of these *status groups* does not coincide with class membership, then it is unlikely that class identity will develop.

For example, class-determined life-chances can lead to distinctive lifestyles such as where people live, their habits, manners, speech, and dress. Before the Second World War, the British 'working man' typically wore a cloth cap and muffler – a scarf that covered up his neck in place of a collar – whereas male clerks and other non-manual workers wore a collar and tie. These 'badges' marked off the difference in status or social honour associated with one group rather than another. By using the same patterns of speech or dress, members of a group could feel a greater sense of mutual identity, even if they were in a lower status group.

Although Weber had originally applied his idea of status group to distinctions of birth or ethnicity (to explain features of China, India and medieval Europe) it also provided a way of describing what he saw in Germany and other European countries at the turn of the century. Whereas Marx regarded differences between other property-less groups as temporary or relatively unimportant, Weber saw this important distinction between manual workers and white-collar workers, particularly in their possession of educational qualifications. Education placed them in a better position to market themselves.

On the other hand, Weber like Marx does place great emphasis on the possession and non-possession of property, seeing that this largely determines material aspects of life-chances. He defines a class as made up of people who share the same *class position*; that is, have the same opportunities to use their property (or lack of it) to create income in any given economic circumstances (i.e. a *market*). Property may be land that can be rented out, or capital (money) that can be invested. In predominantly agricultural societies, ownership of land by a traditional aristocracy is likely to be the significant factor, whereas in more industrialized societies ownership of capital is more important.

In most European countries, the political history of the last century has been marked by the displacing of the landed class by the capitalist class, although through intermarriage the division has been blurred. The industrialists have married to obtain titles and the prestige of 'old money', while the aristocrats have married to replace their flagging fortunes with 'new money'. In contemporary Britain, more than in most other European societies, a newer division has emerged between the industrialists, who are involved in manufacturing and production, and the financiers, whose capital is invested in the banking, insurance, stocks and commodities markets which make up the City of London.

Weber therefore introduced a way out of seeing stratification as just about two great opposing classes. He shows there are several kinds of property and marketable skill, and that group identities are more likely to be based on status than on class, at least in the way Marx talks about class. Weber can thus more easily talk about how people come together in a variety of political movements to further their shared interests arising from status group membership. His writing on this is often translated as political 'party' but this should not be taken to mean political parties like Labour or the Conservatives. He means any collective action for political ends, so that a pressure group, a club, or a social movement of a much looser kind is just as important in explaining social processes or historical changes.

CONCEPTS FROM WEBER'S VIEW OF SOCIAL STRATIFICATION

- class position
- life-chances
- lifestyle
- status
- status group
- political movement
- social strata

Class in European history

Feudalism

While we will not be constantly referring to the connections between these two writers and the events described in this section, their influence on the way we cover (in a very short space) the broad sweep of more than a thousand years of European history will be apparent. The idea of classes as approximations, reflecting economic interests, and sometimes acting collectively, also provides a framework for this analysis. Although terms like 'social class' will be used very sparingly, the historical review is intended to demonstrate how the economic circumstances of different groups (or classes) shaped their experiences and the political events of their times, and how our contemporary systems evolved. It will be important to remember that until the nineteenth century much of Europe did not fully function with a monetary economy. Certainly *capitalism*, a money-based system in which economic life is organized around the consistent maximization of profit, is in historical terms a recent development.

As we saw in Chapter 3, the Middle Ages in Europe were characterized by a pre-capitalist social order, the *feudal*, or as it is sometimes called, the *estate system*. Feudal society was a response to the centuries of attacks that had taken place on the Christian Romano-Germanic world that had arisen after the collapse of the Roman Empire in the early fifth century. From the south the expansionary forces of Islam threatened and at times dominated two major regions – southern Italy and Spain. At times they crossed the Pyrenees into France, and in the ninth century held the Camargue and made attacks up the Rhône as far as Poitiers and Tours. From the east the Magyars or Hungarians raided from the Asian steppes into Europe and, although they became territorially settled in contrast to their previously nomadic existence, they made constant expeditions into the areas of the Rhine, Burgundy in France, and northern Italy too. From the north came the Northmen of Scandinavia who, from the beginning of the ninth century and continuing for about a century and a half thereafter, harassed and attacked the British Isles and France as well as making forays south to the Mediterranean. Those who settled in northern France became known as Normans.

Military organization was necessary to defend against these attacks and, in place of the professionally organized Roman army which had defended the territory before, a system of 'military vassalage' developed that has come to be known as feudalism. Warriors were granted control over large tracts of land in return for an oath to fight for their lord. Armies required economic support and this was provided by the great mass of the population through agriculture. The estate or manorial system tied peasants or, more specifically in feudal terms, 'serfs' into labouring for a class of soldiers. The inherent military instability, the lack of an economy based on money and a workable taxation system, together with poor transport meant that kings were slow to emerge as powerful monarchs of nation-states. The ruling landed class was defined both by its control (but initially not, in a strict sense, ownership) of land and by its military power.

The decline of feudalism

As described in Chapter 2, the following centuries saw a gradual and often spasmodic growth of towns and cities; the improvement of roads for transportation; the more widespread adoption of a money economy; the use of accounting practices such as double entry book-keeping; improvements in agricultural methods; and of course the increasing role of markets and the commodification of goods. These developments began to change the intricate relationships which had flourished in feudal society. On the one hand, new craft skills and the need for merchants to market their products created a new urban 'middle class' who owed no political allegiances to local lords. On the other hand, the development of market towns with improved communications between them and the generation of profit through the increased sale of commodities meant that estates became a site of conflict between landowners, tenants and serfs who worked the land.

More output meant that more profit was made. This surplus which would previously have been merely overproduction for local needs now became commodities for exchange. Equally, the maintenance of the serf by the lord or landowner became in times of shortage a burden, and a barrier to agricultural innovation.

The 'day labourer' and even payment by the hour developed, not without struggle of course. One of the striking images called to attention by Thompson (1968) is the clock on the village church tower. He suggests that their rapid spread evidenced a practical concern with measured time, making it possible to regulate the number of hours a worker spent in the fields. He also notes that this new measurement of agricultural labourers' work also became an arena of conflict with struggles over hours to be worked and rates to be paid. Other breakthroughs brought improvements in agriculture with superior crop varieties and breeds of cattle and sheep. In England people had to adjust to the enclosure of land for the new forms of agriculture and this added to movement towards the towns.

These are only a few of the changes that took place over a considerable period of time. The growth of science and a rational outlook on the material world led to a collapse of religious explanations of both the physical world and the social order. Continuing technological developments led to the spread of factories for industrial manufacturing, drawing people into rapidly expanding towns and cities.

There was also widespread emigration from Europe with the settling of the Americas and Australasia. European colonialism was extended and new markets opened to the East. The decline of powerful Renaissance city-states, principally Venice, Genoa and Florence in the south of Europe and Antwerp in the north, coincided with the rise of the Dutch operating from Amsterdam and the surrounding United Provinces. Britain and France competed with each other as the first of the new nation-states.

These changes did not take place uniformly. Ireland had never been feudal in the sense employed here, while in England feudalism did not develop from within the society but was rather imposed from above through the Norman Conquest. There were also backwaters where older practices lingered on: lands on the periphery such as Brittany for example were not drawn into the major post-feudal advances.

More significantly, the concentration of politico-economic activity in north-western Europe had a reverse impact characterized as a 'second serfdom' in Eastern Europe. The landlords there had failed to modernize and their crops served mainly to increase the profits of the emerging grain-dealers in the north-west. The free peasants of Eastern Europe saw their lives drastically altered, losing their rights to move geographically, to marry whom they pleased, and to use cash payment instead of dues fixed in kind. In Poland the number of days of compulsory labour was 'insignificant' in 1500, but by 1600 it had by stages increased to six days a week, and likewise in Hungary it increased from one day a week in 1514 until eventually all the laws governing labour were put in abeyance and compulsory labour was left to the determination of the landlord.

There was thus no seamless line of progression from feudalism to industrialism across the whole of Europe. Indeed MacFarland argues that the notion of a simple transition from feudalism to capitalism is inappropriate when applied to England. By the thirteenth century people were not tied to the land, the land was bought and sold, women were quite commonly the landowners – not surprising given the earlier deaths of men – and labour was geographically mobile. One of the factors contributing to England becoming the site of the first full development of capitalism is that its population was already geographically mobile and consisting of small family units, thus facilitating the development of an economic order which could take advantage of these facets.

The first flourishing of European capitalism is usually located in the second half of the 1700s, in the towns and new cities. Although the eighteenth century became 'a period when commercial and administrative bureaucracy grew up in nations side by side with the persistence of feudal privileges' (Sennett 1977: 47), the merchants or 'burghers' (i.e. the bourgeoisie) came to dominance, displaying an attitude to wealth creation that differed fundamentally from that of the landowners. Braudel (1981: 514) goes so far as to make the claim that 'capitalism and towns were the same thing in the West', and so it was in the towns that the first two oppositional classes of capitalism came into conflict.

We have already referred in this chapter to the highly stratified order of the early industrialized period, with its disparities of wealth and advantage between factory owners and the labouring masses (see also Chapter 1). In addition to the classes of landowner and burgher, the new industrial working class – the proletariat – first largely replaced the peasantry as a significant force. The political history of that era, whether it is the struggles for political power through voting rights or the wars between nation-states, is largely the history of the changing social division of labour. Later in the nineteenth century, craft skills and occupational specialization increasingly fragmented the working class into competing occupational interests. We shall return to more recent economic and occupational changes, and their historical significance, later.

CONCEPTS FROM CLASS IN EUROPEAN HISTORY

- feudal society
- serf
- industrialization

Social class in contemporary society

Fragmentation and political change

There is always a risk of treating historical change, as well as the current social order of European countries, at too general a level. Thus while it is true that contemporary societies are more like each other than they are like feudal ones, and do indeed share many common features, there are still wide national and regional variations. For example, agriculture employs less than 2 per cent of British workers: as recently as the 1970s, agricultural employment, with its continuing emphasis on landownership rather than on occupations *per se*, ranged from 30 per cent to 57 per cent of the economically active populations of Ireland, Greece, Poland, Portugal, Spain and what was then Yugoslavia.

Such countries have a greater potential for *rural to urban migration*, with its typical association with under-employment. Archer and Giner describe this as creating

> a double pattern: that of advanced industrialized societies where a new working class has already emerged with a distinctive lifestyle and that of less developed economies in which the working class is a proletariat, a 'dwindling stratum of totally unskilled labourers who are characteristically either newcomers to industry (beginners, former agricultural labourers, immigrants) or semi-unemployables'. While rural migrants swell this proletariat, only the older age group, which is in the minority, is never absorbed by the 'established' working class.
>
> Archer and Giner (1971: 29)

The two situations can co-exist in the same country – the Southern European countries are a good example – so that the 'working class', already fragmented by a growing variety of work tasks, specializations and lifestyles, is even less cohesive. Nor is the 'middle class' homogeneous, so class politics become replaced by less coherent political attitudes and movements (including a lack of interest in politics). Parties cease to represent a whole class, and support is found from a mixture of groups.

In Britain, Germany and Scandinavia these coalitions took the form of social democratic parties that built up a new state welfare apparatus. The old ruling class had to share its power with other groups in the economic field with the rise of the managerial class, and now had to accept new taxation and state-owned enterprises. The ruling class was in most cases replaced by several independent *elites*, each with power in a limited sphere: political, military, industrial, financial, public sector, scientific, intellectual and media. However, Greece, Portugal and Spain had military dictatorships in the 1970s, while in the communist countries the old order was replaced by a new party cadre more unified than in the capitalist nations. The former communist countries have yet to establish a new, stable social order.

Occupational differentiation

Up to this point we have looked at how class has been used in the analysis of social and political history, stressing the dynamics of inequality and that out of economic circumstances arise the forces for political action. However, much of modern sociology has been concerned with a more detailed and less ambitious approach, in which class is treated as one among other measures of difference between people's social characteristics. In addressing specific issues (such as explaining why some schools have better exam results than others, or how people vote), in a systematic way, using careful measurements, sociologists have recognized the limitations of, and progressively abandoned, the broad-brush definitions of class inherited from Marx. Instead, 'class' has come to be defined in terms of *occupational category*: what we referred to as 'economic circumstances' has been operationalized as 'type of *employment*'. The approximations we spoke of in the introduction – middle class, working class – become more refined.

While it is still sometimes useful as a shorthand to talk about these large classes, we find ourselves increasingly using smaller occupational class groupings because we need our approximations to be more accurate. We might for example distinguish between skilled manual workers, semi-skilled manual workers, and unskilled manual workers – not least if we were interested in studying industrial training. If we were looking at the composition of leisure activity clubs, we might need to differentiate between, say, office workers and self-employed professionals. *Occupation is not class, but it serves as a good indicator of it*, and in its own right is a valuable means of analysing inequality. There is a considerable choice of schemes which classify occupational groups in slightly different ways.

One of the oldest British classifications, the 'Registrar-General's Social Classes' which (with minor modifications) dates from 1921, was devised originally as a means of investigating rates of illness and death. Although lots of people die before retirement age, and some babies are born with low birth weights, these and many medical conditions were found to be related to social class. It was and still is much healthier to be born into a family where the head of the household is a white-collar worker than into one where the head is an unskilled manual worker. These findings illustrate the power of social class as a means of analysis because disease and mortality, normally thought of in terms of biology and chemistry rather than sociology, are also found to be patterned by socio-economic factors.

The Registrar-General's classification has been widely used in official statistical reports such as the Population Census. It builds social classes out of similar groups of occupations on the basis of their 'general standing within the community', a measure that correlates closely with education and 'economic environment' but less well with income or wealth. At first based on five classes, the Registrar-General's classification currently subdivides one of its original classes into two, as shown in Table 5.1. It is no coincidence that for the most recent Census in 1991, the original term 'social class' was officially changed to 'social class based on occupation'.

The Registrar-General (RG) also uses a set of seventeen *Socio-economic groups* (SEGs) in which each category consists of people whose occupation and employment status (i.e. manager, foreman, employee, self-employed) suggest that their 'social, cultural and recreational standards and behaviour are similar'. These seventeen SEGs can be used when we need greater detail, or in combinations to create another set of social classes, as in Table 5.2 (more details of each SEG can be found in Table 5.6, see p. 115).

An illustration of the way the SEGs can be used is given in the section on labour market changes later in this chapter (see pp. 113–16). In this section we are for the moment not discussing several other key elements of class and occupational classification. For example, gender and ethnicity interact with

TABLE 5.1 The Registrar-General's social classes

Class	Title	Examples of occupations in each class
I	Professionals, etc.	Accountants, doctors, solicitors, etc.
I	Managerial and technical	Nurses, teachers, managers, lab assistants, etc.
III(N)	Skilled non-manual	Cashier, estate agent, secretary, shop worker, etc.
III(M)	Skilled manual	Bricklayer, driver, electrician, fireman, etc.
IV	Partly skilled manual	Barman, postman, telephone operator, etc.
V	Unskilled manual	Cleaner, driver's mate, labourer, etc.

TABLE 5.2 The Registrar-General's socio-economic groups

Socio-economic class	Socio-economic groups	Descriptive titles of classes
1	3, 4	Professional
2	1, 2, 13	Employers and managers
3	5, 6	Intermediate and junior non-manual
4	8, 9, 12, 14	Skilled manual and junior self-employed
5	7, 10, 15	Semi-skilled manual and personal services
6	11	Unskilled manual

employment and status group formation processes, as Chapters 6 and 7 demonstrate in proper detail.

These two schemes by no means exhaust the range of classification systems available to the sociologist. One of the most systematic accounts can be found in Ivan Reid's *Social Class Differences in Britain* (1989). For the purposes of most of this chapter, what matters is that each schema has its own advantages for exploring social stratification. When we seek data to make international comparisons, we often have to make do with whatever classification is available.

More sociologically sophisticated occupational class schemas tend to draw on Weber's ideas, or rather Lockwood's reworking of them into two elements: market and work situations. The former is self-explanatory in the light of our earlier discussion of Weber. The idea of 'work situation' is that people's experiences at work influence their class behaviour. For example, some people manage others; some have more control over their own pace and method of work; some people work in large organizations whereas others are self-employed. One of the more widely used classifications, the Hope–Goldthorpe class schema, was constructed with this distinction in mind.

Class differences and inequality

In an era when lucky individuals can win £8 million pounds in the Lottery, our sense of the scale of differences in income and wealth becomes dulled. This has

TABLE 5.3 Comparative earnings

Salary component	Managing Director		Chauffeur	
	Per year	Over 6 years	Per year	Over 6 years
Signing-on fee	£500,000	£500,000	–	–
Basic salary	£600,000	£3,600,000	£20,000	£120,000
Annual bonus (max.)	£300,000	£1,800,000	–	–
Share options	–	£2,400,000	–	–
Long-term bonus (max.)	–	£2,400,000	–	–
Pension (max.)	£620,000	£3,720,000	–	–
Car plus chauffeur	£70,000	£420,000	–	–
Total		**£14,840,000**		**£120,000**

not however stifled the protests about the huge salaries paid to senior managers on the decisions of very-well-remunerated company directors. A recent British case was that of the managing director of GEC. The *Guardian*'s report on 25 August 1996 enables us to calculate that if Mr George Simpson works the six years of his contract to his retirement, he will receive nearly £15 million in wages and benefits. Table 5.3 compares his earnings with those estimated for his chauffeur.

The pre-tax benefits to the managing director are nearly 125 times more than his chauffeur's, even if we do not allow for any other minor benefits (other 'free' travel or hospitality) or for his earnings being invested and earning interest during the six years.

While this may seem an extreme example, differences in income and wealth are extensive. Wealth is what people own, and income is what they earn, wealth being distributed more unequally than income. The richest 5 per cent of Britons earn 17 per cent of all income, but own 37 per cent of all wealth. Their share of the wealth declined from about 80 per cent in the 1920s to 53 per cent in the 1970s. Since the 1980s they have held on to their share, and may even have increased it.

As far as income goes, a TUC survey of 1,247 companies showed that by 1994 an average worker's gross annual pay was just under £17,000. The average pay of the higher-paid directors was over £211,000. This excludes any share options or the other benefits shown for the managing director in Table 5.3.

A recent extensive inquiry by the Joseph Rowntree Foundation (1995) found that, using 1993 prices, those households making up the one-fifth of highest earners received more than £342 per week, with common examples of more than twice this amount. The poorest one-fifth of households on the other hand earned less than £126 per week, and nearly two-thirds of households fell below the average British household's net weekly income of £254.

At the extremes, of course, the difference is much greater. The household of GEC's managing director – if he were the sole breadwinner – will have an average pre-tax income over the six years, of just under £40,000 every week. A pensioner couple living in council housing might be on a gross income of £92 per week, while £84 would be the state benefit for a small family with both parents unemployed.

The same report updates the metaphor of the Dutch economist, Jan Pen, of an hour-long parade of people whose heights are matched to their incomes. For more than twenty minutes we would see the toddlers and dwarves go by. It would be nearly forty-five minutes before we saw people of average height or taller. But by the last minute the walkers would be ten times taller, twenty metres or more; in the final seconds, in Britain as in Holland twenty years ago, the scene is dominated by colossal figures: 'their heads disappear into the clouds and probably they themselves do not know how tall they are' (Hills 1995: 9). Each group of marchers can be identified by their occupational circumstances, by their capacity or incapacity to use property in the market to raise income (i.e. by their social class).

With such a wide range of income and wealth (see also Chapter 17 on poverty) it would be surprising if there were not other differences between social classes. We do not need to labour this point with a long list of statistical facts about Britain. Three examples will suffice as illustrations.

We have already referred to health as being socio-economically patterned. For example, twice as many women in RG Class V suffer from high blood pressure as do women in RG Class I (Benzeval *et al.* 1995: 16; see also Townsend *et al.* 1992 on health and poverty). Classes have distinctive family sizes: RG Class V families on average are nearly 'half a child' bigger than families in RG Classes I and II (Reid 1989: 236). And among newspaper readers, less than 5 per cent of the manual working class read a 'quality' newspaper – the *Guardian*, *Financial Times*, *Independent*, *Telegraph*, or *Times*. The equivalent figure for the professional, managerial and technical classes is around 55 per cent (Reid 1989: 374). Other examples can be found throughout the later chapters of this book.

Is Britain like other countries in having this range of inequality and social class differences? We can compare the British income and wealth overall position with several countries. As Figure 5.1 shows, all the countries had marked income inequality in the 1980s. The *Gini coefficient* measures differences in income: if all incomes were the same, it would be zero per cent, so that the higher the score, the greater the inequality. Finland and Sweden had much less than Italy, with Britain lying just above the middle of the range.

If instead of the average figures, we compare the earnings of the richest 20 per cent with the poorest 20 per cent, the difference in Britain is greater than in any other Western industrial nation. An OECD report places us on an inequality par with Nigeria and Singapore, some way in type from our European partners. The ratio of rich to poor incomes is 6:1 in Germany, 7:1 in Italy, 8:1 in France, and 10:1 in Britain (*The Economist*, 10 August 1996, p. 25).

Income inequality has been falling in Italy (and in Finland, Denmark, Ireland, Portugal and Spain) but has increased elsewhere, most notably in Britain. In 1979, Britons living in households with less than half the average net income (after housing costs) numbered five million. This figure had risen to fourteen million by 1993 (*The Economist*, 1 June 1996, p. 18). Among European nations, it is those in the north-west that have the greater increases, as Figure 5.2 shows.

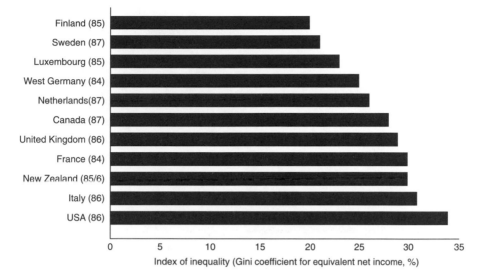

Figure 5.1 Income equality in selected countries

Source: Hills, J., 1995, p. 64.

It is interesting to note that not only does Britain have the fastest growing inequality of the north-western European countries, its profile of change in the last twenty-five years is more typical of the English-speaking world (United States, Canada, Australia, New Zealand – and Japan) than the European Union or Scandinavian nations (Atkinson 1994: 3–6).

Of course, not all nations have the same levels of material well-being. If a country is poorer than other countries, and income differentials are higher, then the lower classes are likely to be particularly worse off. The national pattern for the European Union is given in Figure 5.3.

We can conclude from these comparisons that Britain is not unique in having material inequalities. However, it is marked in recent years as having an unusually high difference between the richest and poorest. These differences have been increasing at a high rate during a period when many other countries have been moving in the opposite direction. The British and comparative figures in this section help to explain the moral outrage many people feel about inequality and class.

CONCEPTS FROM CLASS IN CONTEMPORARY SOCIETY

- urban migration
- elites
- occupational categories
- socio-economic groups
- social inequality
- Gini coefficient

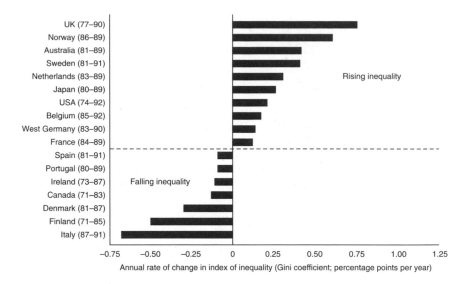

Figure 5.2 Trends in income inequality

Source: Joseph Rowntree Foundation, 1995, p. 15.

European attitudes to class and inequality

How much does class matter?

Despite the empirical evidence illustrated in the previous section, sociologists are often accused of being too obsessed with social class. As we will later see, this is in part a technical criticism about the accuracy of what we earlier called our 'approximations'. However, the complaint also comes from those with a vested interest in playing down inequality. For example, it is often said by Conservative politicians and directors of big companies that British people in general 'are obsessed with class'. Those editions of the annual British Social Attitudes series that deal with international comparisons show that this is untrue. When asked if they believed there were strong conflicts between the working and middle class, and the poor and the rich, people sampled in five countries gave the answers shown in Table 5.4. Britain does not come out top, but rather lowest but one on both counts.

A similar result is given in the third question, with the British less likely to blame the rich and powerful for continuing inequality. Two separate surveys show the British more willing to accept large differences in income as being necessary for national prosperity (although there is little difference between Britain, Hungary, the former West Germany, and Austria in this respect). Britain is like Hungary and the former West Germany in wanting less inequality (Question 6), but more Austrians and fewer Swiss take this view.

Another source of data on attitudes to class and inequality is the surveys of the European Values Systems Study Group (Ashford and Timms 1992). People

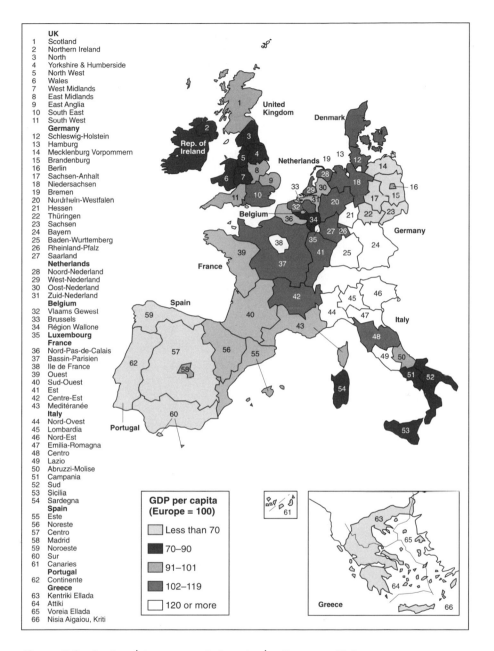

Figure 5.3 Regional income variations in the European Union

Source: Joseph Rowntree Foundation, 1995, p. 75

TABLE 5.4 National differences in attitudes to dimensions of class and inequality (%)

Questions	GB	Hung.	Italy	Neth.	W.Ger.*	Aust.	Switz.
1 Perceiving strong conflicts between working class and middle class	20	37	45	22	13	n/a	n/a
2 Perceiving strong conflicts between rich and poor	52	54	59	77	36	n/a	n/a
3 Agreeing inequality continues to exist because it benefits the rich and powerful	59	36	74	58	63	n/a	n/a
4 Agreeing large differences in income are necessary for own country's prosperity: 1989	26	25	18	16	24	n/a	n/a
5 Agreeing large differences in income are necessary for own country's prosperity: 1994	26	24	n/a	15	24	25	16
6 Agreeing there is too much inequality	74	73	n/a	64	72	87	65

Sources: Questions 1–4, Jowell *et al., 6th British Social Attitudes Report,* 1989, pp. 70–1, Aldershot: Gower. Questions 5 & 6, *10th British Social Attitudes Report,* 1993, pp. 132, 128, Aldershot: Dartmouth.

* The former West Germany

TABLE 5.5 How should the economy be structured?

	Total	GB	NI	RI	WG*	N	B	F	I	S	P
Incomes should be made more equal/ should be greater incentives for individual effort	5.4	6.1	6.5	5.9	5.6	6.0	5.4	4.8	5.3	4.7	4.5
Private ownership of business and industry should be increased/government ownership should be increased	4.3	4.7	4.7	4.1	3.7	4.3	4.0	4.3	4.3	4.9	4.2
Individuals should take more responsibility to provide for themselves/state should take more responsibility	5.0	5.2	5.3	4.9	4.2	4.7	4.8	4.1	5.5	5.9	5.0
In the long run hard work usually brings a better life/it's more a matter of luck and connections	4.8	4.8	4.3	4.6	4.3	5.3	4.8	4.5	5.1	5.3	5.9
People can only accumulate wealth at the expense of others/wealth can grow so there's enough for everyone	6.3	6.0	6.2	6.1	6.5	6.9	6.5	6.0	7.0	5.7	5.7

Source: Ashford and Timms 1992: 105.

Key: GB Great Britain; NI Northern Ireland; RI Republic of Ireland; WG West Germany; N Netherlands; B Belgium; F France; I Italy; S Spain; P Portugal.

* The former West Germany

were asked to choose between a series of paired contradictory statements, giving a national result that could lie between one and seven. A low score means agreement with the first statement in the pair, a high score indicates more agreement with the second statement. For example, the EVSSG equivalent of Question 6 in Table 5.4 was a choice between 'Incomes should be made more equal' and 'There should be greater incentives for effort'. On this pair, the average for ten countries was 5.4, and Britain scored 6.1 (less in favour of more equality), the second least egalitarian country. Other results showing a tougher line on unemployment, more tolerance of other people's wealth, and lower antagonism towards private ownership, can be compared with nine other nations in Table 5.5.

Other examples can be found in the 1993 European Commission's research into how people see poverty (Room 1995). While being intolerant of the unemployed, the British are more likely than most to say that this is the major cause of poverty. They are also more likely to blame cuts in welfare and family breakdown.

What this section demonstrates is that there is widespread awareness of and concern about social inequalities among the people of Europe. It is not only the British who take this view; indeed, by most measures other Europeans are even *more* concerned despite having *less* inequality than in Britain. As sociologists we have ample reason to continue to study class and inequality.

Class dynamics in contemporary society

Industrial change and occupational transition

Although in the earlier part of this chapter we talked about class and social change, our later discussion of class as occupation and social inequality has treated social stratification as a more static and fixed structure. In fact, if we think of class defined in terms of occupations, then changes in employment – of which we have experienced many in recent years – must also imply changes in how we see class. There are two particular changes that we need to consider, and they are related. The first is changes to the number and types of jobs, and the second is the process by which individuals come to fill those jobs and so take up their occupational class identities – *social mobility*.

Patterns of employment consist of two main features, the industry in which they are based and the type of work done within any given industry. As societies modernize, fewer people work in agriculture and more in manufacturing. At a later stage, more employment shifts out of manufacturing and into service industry. Bell (1973) has suggested that in *post-industrial society*, the process goes on, with employment becoming more dependent on ideas and knowledge, and those sub-sets of the services like finance and leisure. This process of shifts between industrial sectors has been called *industrial transition*.

In class terms, the traditional, predominantly male, working class of the steel foundry, the coal mine, and even the car plant is replaced by the technician, the office worker, and the retailer. The new jobs are in different physical settings and smaller work groups, carrying different rewards and opportunities for group formation. For older workers the new order has little to offer. Alternative employment is likely to be in different localities, part-time and short-contract rather than full-time and permanent, and in offices and shops (conventionally considered 'women's work'). Industrial transition is not a neutral process which just involves creating brand new types of employment in the service sector. It also involves the destruction of older jobs and people's livelihoods through automation and by competition from countries with lower wage levels.

As well as industries growing and shrinking, the types of tasks within them also change. The number of hands-on production jobs declines, and new specialisms in marketing, accounting, personnel, law and management increase. This process has been called *occupational transition*. Expressed in class terms, occupational transition reduces the size and power of the working class, it reorganizes manual work into different settings, and creates new middle classes. Some idea of the scale of this is given by Table 5.6.

In England and Wales, core manual work (SEGs 9, 10 and 11) has fallen from 54 per cent to 29 per cent since the First World War. Middle-class occupations have risen from 23 per cent to 52 per cent: each of the component SEGs has grown (a change in the classification schemes slightly underestimates the 1991 growth in SEG 6). The middle classes grow to outnumber the old working class, and the dynamics of class politics changes.

This process has been repeated across Europe, although, as we earlier noted, most countries have started with a larger agricultural population, and others like Germany have retained a stronger manufacturing base. An indication of the new European occupational class structures is given in Table 5.7. 'Professional, technical and related workers' is an International Labour Organization occupational class which includes traditional professions, engineers, educators, scientists, journalists, social workers, medical staff, and similar occupational groups. On this indicator a clear north-west/south division is evident. Sulkunen also notes the connection between agriculture's decline and the growth of the new middle classes in other industrial sectors:

> Among Western European countries, Finland probably represents an extreme, although not a unique case, where change has occurred rapidly and where the rise of the new middle class has been spectacular. The share of the economically active population in agriculture was forty-six per cent in 1950, only thirteen per cent in 1980, and it had dropped to nine per cent in 1988. The fastest growing group had been managers, supervisors and clerical staff (from sixteen per cent to thirty-nine per cent).
>
> (Sulkunen, 1992: 26)

Although the extent and the rate of the expansion of the new middle classes vary, expansion is a universal feature of all European societies, including those that were formerly communist.

In an early discussion of these changes, Dahrendorf (1959) attempted to shift our frame of reference away from class. He accepted the past significance of social class, but argued that the economic circumstances of various groups of people in Western Europe were becoming radically different from those of the

TABLE 5.6 Socio-economic groups: England and Wales, 1921–91 (economically active)

SEG/Year	1921	1961	1991
Employers and managers	6.6	7.6	14.6
Self-employed professionals	0.5	0.5	0.9
Employed professionals	0.9	2.2	3.6
Technicians	2.9	5.8	12.5
Junior non-manual	11.8	20.2	20.0
Personal service	8.1	4.7	4.4
Manual supervisors	1.2	2.3	1.9
Skilled manual	30.8	23.7	12.7
Semi-skilled manual	15.3	15.0	10.7
Unskilled manual	8.3	7.8	5.4
Non-professional self-employed	5.1	3.1	6.3
Farmers and farm managers	1.7	1.4	0.7
Agricultural workers	4.3	1.8	0.7
*Other	2.3	3.8	5.6
Total	17,178,050	22,296,010	23,895,910

*Other – Armed forces, Government Training Scheme (1991) and not stated.

Source: OPCS, Population Census Reports.

TABLE 5.7 Occupational transition in Europe: 'professional, technical and related workers' (% of economically active population)

Country	1960	1990
Sweden	12.9	31.8
Finland	8.2	23.8
Denmark	7.8	22.9
Norway	8.0	22.3
Netherlands	9.2	22.0
France	9.1	18.0*
Britain	8.6	17.0*
W. Germany†	7.6	15.0
Ireland	7.1	14.3
Austria	6.8	14.2
Greece	3.4	11.7
Spain	4.1	9.6
Portugal	2.7	8.5

Source: Adapted from Sulkunen, 1992: 26.

Note: *Authors' own estimate.

† The former West Germany

previous century. New groups were emerging – scientists, technocrats, managers – with new personal and political agendas. The new political systems had changed who held power. Class and inequality were not irrelevant, but were taking new forms which in turn required a fresh analysis.

Other writers commented on the 'fragmentation' of the old classes. In part this was another way of describing occupation transition, but with the emphasis on how new specialist occupational groups ceased to behave as classic members of the old working or middle classes. The increased material well-being, or affluence, of the working class was propounded as a source of changing class attitudes and identities. Studies in the 1960s of this *embourgeoisement* of British workers found only moderate evidence of change: new working-class patterns were emerging, but the workers were not adopting established middle-class behaviour or attitudes.

Social mobility

It will be clear from the previous section that industrial and occupational transition change the working lives and opportunities for work of whole populations. If the size and boundaries of classes change, individuals have to adjust in order to take up the new roles that are being created. Throughout Europe there has been an expansion of white-collar work, creating fresh chances for the children of manual and agricultural workers to move up the occupational scale. In this respect, the class system is not rigid and the social mobility of people from one occupational origin to another occupational destination tends to break down any sense of being trapped at one level of social inequality for generations to come.

On the other hand, it is not the case that these changes affect everybody in the same way. There is no level playing-field on which everyone can compete for the new opportunities or those that already existed. If there were equality of opportunity, then the sons of professionals, for example, would be no more likely to become professionals themselves than would the sons of manual workers. In practice, the sons of professionals in England and Wales have been found to be about three times more likely to be members of the professional class than their manual counterparts. It is not only the children of the working class who enter the new employment: the offspring of the existing middle classes also benefit. That they do so to such an extent suggests that there has to be some other process influencing social mobility than the structural transitions alone.

Contrasting the characteristics of those who are upwardly mobile, or who have retained their advantage, with those who are immobile helps to identify the dimensions through which such inequality processes work. Thus if the upwardly mobile have better educational qualifications than the immobile, we might look to the schools as being a mechanism of opening up or closing off prospects of advancement to certain groups. The identification of such processes is one of several ways in which social mobility is central to an understanding of inequality.

Indeed, mobility is itself a measurement of inequality. A society with a great deal of movement between classes – an *open society* – has a less rigid, less all-pervading and less oppressive system of inequality than one with low rates of mobility. Mobility also helps to show where classes begin and end. Westergaard has suggested that there is a 'threshold', that is, more of a break, between the manual and non-manual classes than at other points. Parkin sees the middle occupational range of technician and routine white-collar work as a buffer zone with low mobility that separates the professionals and managers from the less-skilled manual workers. Others have written about the upper middle classes as a self-contained elite (Payne 1989).

A fourth use of mobility in stratification theory is to account for levels of class conflict. Where there is mobility, there is less chance of a group developing a fixed set of values, lifestyle or a sense of self-identity. The mobile dilute class consciousness. They also dilute political opposition: as Marx wrote more than a hundred years ago, 'The more a ruling class is able to assimilate the most prominent men of the ruled class the more solid and dangerous is its rule' (Marx 1959: 706).

Unfortunately, measuring social mobility is an extremely complicated process. What we count as mobility depends on the number of classes we count, and whether we see the classes as a hierarchy. The Nuffield Mobility Study dealt mainly with movements to and from the *service class* of professionals and managers, and the manual working class, because of this uncertainty about the middle range (Goldthorpe 1987). It also measured mobility in a complicated way that combined the chances of reaching the top with the chances of ending up at the bottom. As we have seen, the manual classes are contracting, so the chances of ending up there are unlikely to improve. It is therefore harder for this combined chances measurement (the 'odds ratio') to show the high and increasing levels of mobility that the data actually demonstrate. It follows that the study's emphasis on odds ratios, 'relative mobility' and lack of hierarchy means that it can be misunderstood as minimizing the amount of reported mobility. Not surprisingly, several introductory texts inadvertently misrepresent current patterns.

We can summarize the main British patterns of male 'absolute' mobility (the social mobility of women has been less studied) as follows. There is a lot of general movement after a single generation – *intergenerational mobility* – with about half of all sons entering different classes from those of their fathers. There is also a considerable degree of long-range mobility, with 40 per cent of the service class children being downwardly mobile, and 45 per cent of manual workers' children going in the other direction. Measured over seven classes, the top class has at least 10 per cent of its members drawn from each of the other six possible origins. There is neither a mid-range barrier nor a closure protecting the professional/managerial class (Payne 1989).

Other European societies seem to have similar patterns. Counting across three classes, France and the former West Germany have the same upward mobility rate at about one in three, but less downward mobility. Hungary and Poland show a little more upward movement, Ireland less, and Sweden is markedly more open at 42 per cent upward mobility, though with no greater downward mobility (Erikson and Goldthorpe 1992: 195). Most sociologists tend to emphasize the distance these results fall short of an entirely open society with full equality of opportunity. Others have argued that this interpretation misses the large scale of movements that are taking place, even if this is not anything like equality.

Recently Saunders has been something of a lone sociological voice in championing this view of the openness of contemporary society for individuals with ability. In several careful analyses of other studies, he extracts evidence to support his view that Britain is in fact something approaching a *meritocracy*, a society in

---

CONCEPTS FROM CLASS DYNAMICS IN CONTEMPORARY SOCIETY

- social mobility
- post-industrial society
- embourgeoisement
- industrial transition
- occupational transition

- open society
- service class
- intergenerational mobility
- meritocracy

---

which the best rise to the top: 'Occupational selection, by and large, is not rigged . . . The game is worth playing, even for those born into the poorest social conditions . . . All that is needed is the ability and the will to start climbing' (Saunders 1996: 91).

He is not claiming that a perfectly meritocratic system is in operation, only that sociologists and others with left of centre political views have refused to treat differences in individual ability as a significant factor. His doubts lead us neatly into our final section, which deals with some radically different interpretations of social stratification from the ones we have offered so far.

Alternative interpretations of social stratification

What is the significance of social inequality?

Saunders' argument is that the disparities of family background, educational opportunity, occupational selection and career promotion are real but that, except for gender and ethnicity, they do not have a great impact on social mobility. Individual ability is more important, and sociologists have been wrong to pay so little attention to it. In reply, most other sociologists, like Marshall for instance, would point to the kinds of inequality documented in this chapter. Others such as Payne have argued something of a middle ground, criticizing the conventional sociological overemphasis on social immobility but calling for new ways of understanding emerging patterns of inequality, class, and the upward mobility created by occupational transition.

It is true that most sociologists do see inequality as undesirable. There are, however, two schools of thought that reject such a starting point. The first is usually called the *functionalist theory of stratification* because it draws on a set of ideas called Structural Functionalism, which explains the existence of all social phenomena by their function (or contribution) in maintaining the social structure in being. Thus it can be argued that some demanding tasks necessary for society to exist would not be filled simply by altruistic volunteers: greater rewards are needed to recruit members of society to do them, and so inequality is both inevitable and necessary. All occupational tasks are necessary, but some are more necessary than others: some tasks only a few people can do (being managing director of GEC) whereas lots of people have the talents to carry out other tasks (being a chauffeur, for instance).

This functionalist view is considered by most British sociologists not to provide a fully satisfactory account of stratification. It may go some way to justify salary differentials, but not to explain why the managing director of GEC is 125 times more valuable to society than his chauffeur or, as our weekly income example showed, 430 times more than a pensioner couple. Nor does it explain the extensive and highly patterned variations that we have been describing elsewhere in this chapter. These seem to require notions of power, control, exploitation and conscious action to account for them.

A second similar school of thought attributes inequality to the outcome of market forces. As this view regards the market as the key mechanism of human existence, which must not be interfered with in any way, then those who are rewarded by the market must have a moral right to their wealth and power. Governmental interference in the market should be removed. Entrepreneurs should be encouraged by financial benefits because only entrepreneurs can 'create' wealth. Whereas in a functionalist view, it is the need to carry out *tasks* that is central, in this extreme '*liberal*' or 'monetarist' interpretation there is a greater emphasis both on the *market* and on the inherent *superiority* of those people who are 'successful'. Some critics of this view would point to the results of British government economic and social policies between 1979 and 1997 as evidence that this view of the market and inequality is no more than an ideological cover for the rich and powerful to benefit themselves at the expense of poorer and weaker people. This may be going too far: a more sympathetic – and in some ways the best – introductory discussion of these two now largely discredited schools is to be found in Saunders (1990: 41–67).

Social stratification or social class?

The fragmentation of the old classes undermined the confidence of many sociologists in the very idea of class. At the same time, new and technically more sophisticated ways of measuring inequality were being developed, which cast doubt on the quality of the 'approximations' provided by previous social or occupational class schemas. One resulting view has been that inequalities can be better explored by simple numerical categories, comparing for instance the top 20 per cent (the 'upper quintile') with the bottom 20 per cent (the 'lower quintile') on any component of social inequality. While some of these measures do indeed offer enhanced precision and new understanding, there is a danger that the conceptual insights of the class analysis 'baby' get thrown out with the looser approximations of the older class schema 'bath water'.

In a key debate over class analysis in the pages of the British Sociological Association's journal, *Sociology*, Pahl responded to a call for a new empirical and less theoretical programme of class analysis by accepting that there are 'lumps' of distinctive work and market situation, but then asks:

> But *why* do the lumps endure? It is not convincing for Goldthorpe and Marshall to claim that they do so because of class, because they make no commitment to any theory of class in their programme. They simply

> construct certain demographic categories ... in the absence of any well-articulated theory by the authors, why should readers assume that these lumps or categories are anything more than proxy indicators of highly complex processes ...
>
> Pahl (1993: 255, 257)

It is these 'highly complex processes' that should be the focus of study. Pahl's observations show that class and levels of inequality are not simply technical measurements; they only make sense themselves, and help to make sense of society, as part of a coherent framework of sociological theory.

Because of this theoretical dimension, ideas and measurements of stratification cannot exist in a vacuum. Theories of class have been cross-fertilized by other ideas, such as new work on labour markets, methods of management, welfare policy, and migration. Social events in contemporary society such as high rates of unemployment, ethnic relations, and not least the changing role of women have had even more impact on how we now think of class. The feminist critique of employment practices and indeed of the concept of work itself, has fundamentally altered the sociology of class.

As Chapter 6 on gender demonstrates, recognition that there is *gender segregation of occupations* into 'women's jobs' and 'men's jobs' immediately means that their economic circumstances are different, and the stratification processes they experience must be different. As Crompton writes in one of the best current discussions of class analysis:

> Women have been concentrated in less well-paid, sex-typed occupations; disadvantaged in the labour market as a consequence of their domestic and childrearing obligations; and, until relatively recently, excluded by men from access to many of the better-paying and more prestigious occupational roles.
>
> (Crompton 1993: 101)

It follows that the convention of coding households to the class of the male head of household becomes problematic for *any* household, let alone for those containing women in paid employment, or those with no male adults in them. Closer inspection of occupational classifications has also shown how poorly differentiated are 'women's jobs' like SEG 6, junior or routine non-manual work, compared with 'men's jobs'.

The impact of feminism on class analysis is not just a technical matter. Women, particularly those who have participated in campaigns around rights to abortion and nursery provision, or against marital violence and rape, have an altered sense of identity. Their political actions are as likely to be based on their gender as on their class.

A parallel argument applies to minority ethnic groups, where colour, religion, culture and shared economic hardships provide a strong basis for mutual solidarity. Despite the common element of antagonism from parts of the white population, not all minority ethnic groups share the same difficulties. For example, in general the children of families formerly from India, Pakistan and Bangladesh out-perform their white contemporaries at school, whereas the Afro-Caribbean experience in Britain has been a particularly marked one of under-achievement in education and extremely high levels of unemployment, especially amongst young males. In parts of Provence and the Languedoc in France racial tension exists for the Arabs from France's colonial past. In Germany Turks who were brought in to do low grade and dirty work are now on the wrong side of an economic and social divide. Ethnicity is both a source of identity and strongly associated with economic circumstances and political action.

Other 'events' in contemporary society that have been influential include the visibility of, on the one hand, a more affluent working class and, on the other, an impoverished non-working class of unemployed people. People in secure and fairly well-paid jobs, it has been claimed, begin to consume new products and services that they buy for themselves. They own a car, buy a house, save for a personal pension, even possibly purchase private medical care or education for their children. As they are spending their own money directly, they resent paying taxes for public transport, social housing, the National Health Service and schools, both because they no longer consume these public services, and because taxation leaves them less available personal income to go on purchasing for their private needs. This resentment extends to antagonism towards the old and the unemployed who are seen as a drain on the newly affluent. Identity and political action thus reflect the *consumption sector* in which people are to be found, rather than their class.

As with many quasi-political theories, the consumption sector idea has some elements of truth in it. The 'Essex Man' supporter of right-wing British government policies in the 1980s would seem to be a concrete example of consumption sector behaviour. However, as our earlier section on attitudes to class and inequality showed, both in Britain and elsewhere in Europe, there is no strong sign of the attitude or consciousness shift that should be evident if this were a substantial effect.

On the other hand, our inequality data do suggest that many people live in poverty. We shall leave discussion of the social significance of poverty to Chapter 17, but it is worth mentioning that some critics of welfare provision and government action to reduce poverty have described the unemployed urban estate residents as an *underclass* of potentially criminal, dangerous, and certainly undesirable people. While it may be useful to highlight the plight of the disadvantaged, it does not help to make sweeping generalizations about what are quite complex processes and situations. The terms 'class' or 'underclass', in the singular, do not fit well with the phenomena that need to be analysed, and few British sociologists have adopted the underclass perspective.

This section demonstrates three things. The traditional approach which saw class in a fairly simple way, with people taking *all* of their cues for identity and action from their membership of a very large, economically similar social class, has had to be modified. Second, class and inequality therefore do not consist of bodies of fact and ideas that are uncontested: even after many years, there is still active debate. Third, these are not just academic debates, isolated from the 'real world'. Not only do the debates respond to real life events, but the issues they address are central to the political struggles that determine our everyday lives.

CONCEPTS FROM ALTERNATIVE INTERPRETATIONS OF STRATIFICATION

- functionalist theories
- liberal theories
- consumption sectors

- underclass
- gender segregation of occupations

Reflection

It is no coincidence that this is one of the longest chapters in the book. Stratification is not only a topic of central importance (both in sociology and in the outside world) but it is one with a long history and a track record of adaptation and change. The debate continues, both at a conceptual and a technical level, with class still being redefined and respecified, as the work of E. O. Wright, the American sociologist, demonstrates (Marshall *et al.* 1989).

Following this evolution of research is a demanding task. We have tried to show several faces of social stratification: statistical patterns of social inequality; conceptual frameworks to explain these in terms of people's economic circumstances; a historical overview of economic and political history in which class interests have played a central part; technical matters of classification; how Europeans see class; the occupational fragmentation of classes; and the dynamic changes and social processes of contemporary society. We have moved backwards and forwards between levels of generalization and specificity, dealing with broad areas of Europe and whole classes, and national regions and smaller occupational groups. We have seen that Britain in most respects resembles its north-western European neighbours, while having some characteristics of its own, such as early industrialization and higher levels of inequality.

Despite this wide-ranging discussion, there has been a central strand about social inequality, and the capacity of class to explain it. Because sociologists use the term 'class' in so many different ways (as a result of their theoretical orientations), and because the ideas have had to evolve to match the changing patterns that need to be understood, that theme may not have always been apparent. Class may not now be the only or even the first principle that people invoke when it comes to expressing their identities and deciding on political action, but the core experience of work and occupation, wealth and income, and property and the need for employment remain. The 'classless society' may serve as a political slogan, but it will not do as a foundation for rigorous sociology.

Summary

- Social inequality is found in all societies, but it takes many forms: Britain's pattern of social inequality is broadly similar to that of our European neighbours.
- Social class has provided a powerful tool to explore and explain social inequality.

- Social change has fragmented classes, and new sources of identity and political action have emerged: occupation, gender and ethnicity are particularly important.
- Ideas of class and inequality have had to adapt, and remain hotly contested topics of central importance for a sociological explanation of contemporary society.

Further reading

Peter Saunders (1990) *Social Class and Stratification*, London: Routledge. This is the most accessible introduction currently available. It takes an unconventionally generous view of some topics and makes a good balance to Crompton (1993).

Rosemary Crompton (1993) *Class and Stratification*, Cambridge: Polity Press. A thorough and lively defence of the class analysis approach which incorporates a wide range of recent thinking and critiques of the traditional approach, this reflects much of the current mainstream sociology of stratification.

Peter Saunders (1996) *Unequal but Fair?*, London: IEA. A short fire-cracker of polemic against the conventional wisdom about social mobility.

Chapter 6

Women, paid employment and equal opportunity

Pamela Abbott and Louise Ackers

Introduction	126
Understanding women's position	126
Women and paid employment	128
Women and labour market segmentation	131
Women, children and employment	134
Explanations of gender inequality in the labour market	136
The European Union and the promotion of gender equality	142
Summary	145
Further reading	145

Key concepts

- Public and private patriarchy
- Welfare regimes
- The male breadwinning model
- Labour market participation and segmentation

125

Introduction

> One of the major objectives of the European Community (EC) is to improve the living and working conditions of all people. The main problem facing women in the European Community has been identified as that of equality with men at work and equal opportunities in society.
>
> (CEC 1991)

This chapter will demonstrate, via documentary evidence, the persistence of gender inequalities in Europe. In particular it focuses on the position of women in European labour markets, identifying key similarities and differences in experience between countries. It then considers explanations of gender inequality, including: the importance of cultural differences and social attitudes on gender roles; the impact of caring responsibilities and family 'obligations' on women's labour market participation; and the role of the state in regulating the relationship between paid and unpaid work. Finally we outline the scope of Community competence in the area of gender relations.

The Treaty of Rome provides for equal pay for men and women, and the European Union has adopted five directives to create Community rights against sex discrimination which can be enforced in national courts and employment tribunals. However, this does not mean that men and women are treated equally in paid employment or in society more generally. Indeed, it could be argued that introducing legislation for equal treatment and equal opportunity does little to improve the situation for women – that social inequalities between men and women cannot be changed fundamentally by giving women equal opportunities at work. This is in part because these legal changes do not alter the relationships between men and women in the family, where women are expected to provide care for children and elderly relatives, nor do they provide help for women in carrying out the informal care for which they are seen as responsible. Even legislation for paid parental leave does not mean that fathers will take a larger share in 'family work', as has been demonstrated in Sweden, where parental leave, available to either sex, is mainly taken up by mothers. Nor does legislation for equal pay for work of equal value mean that the average wages of men and women become the same, or even that the differences narrow.

Understanding women's position

Ostner (1994) has argued that in order to understand the position of women in Western European society we need to explore the relationship between dependence and independence for women, the relationships within the public and the private spheres and the interface between women's paid and unpaid work. She suggests that the emergence of welfare states in Western Europe has resulted in a decline in women's dependence on men for economic support; they can receive support from the welfare state. As Pateman (1988: 250) suggests, 'The Welfare State has . . . brought challenges to patriarchal power and helped provide a basis for women's autonomous citizenship. Women have seen the welfare state as one of their major means of support' (see also McIntosh 1984; Abbott and Wallace 1992). However, Walby (1990) has argued that during the twentieth century there has been a move from women being controlled by private patriarchy (men in the home) to increasing control by public patriarchy (the state and the labour market), rather than towards becoming equal with men. This process, she argues, is discernible in all Western societies but has developed most fully in the Scandinavian countries. Ostner goes on to suggest that women can become equal with men only when their role in the private sphere and the expectation that they will take on the unpaid work of caring for children and elderly relatives is fundamentally changed: 'equal opportunities for women require changes in employment patterns, an increase in child-care facilities and men ready to share family responsibilities more equally' (Ostner 1994: 37).

All Western European welfare states were built on the assumption that a woman's prime responsibility is caring in the private sphere and that men are the breadwinners. However, there is considerable variation between them. Jane Lewis (1992) distinguishes between strong, moderate and weak 'male breadwinner states'. Britain, the Netherlands and Germany are examples of 'strong' male breadwinner states, where wives are assumed for purposes of social entitlement to be entirely dependent. There is strong reliance in these countries on women's unpaid care work (Sjerps 1988; Abbott and Wallace 1992). France and Belgium are examples of 'moderate' states; women's rights have been recognized as both mothers and workers and policies have been developed to support the working family unit (Schultheis 1988; Hantrais 1993). In both countries there are well developed and comprehensive child-care facilities (Moss 1990; Glasner 1992) as well as a child-care allowance for those who prefer to pay for children to be cared for in their own homes. However, there are few services to support the elderly either in their own homes or in residential care (Jamieson 1990); older people have to rely very much on kin. Denmark (like Norway and Sweden) is a 'weak' male breadwinner state. Women are seen as workers and as independent of their male partners. Welfare rights are tied to individual labour market participation – widows' pensions are low, there are no statutory family obligations and 50 per cent of children under the age of three (and 85 per cent over that age) are in state-provided child-care. Most older people requiring social care have this provided by the state as a right of citizenship (Jamieson 1991).

It is therefore necessary, in order to understand women's position in Western European societies, to understand the relationship between their positions as carers, workers and citizens. Feminists have argued that the welfare state is not gender-neutral but, through its public policies, political ideologies and organizational principles, has helped to produce and reproduce a sexual division of labour and male domination (Pateman 1987; Abbott and Wallace 1992). Welfare states have been built on the assumption of familial ideology that the nuclear family, with man as breadwinner and wife as dependent carer, is not only how people do organize their lives but how they ought to do so; woman's primary role is as wife and mother (Wilson 1977). This ideology may be stronger and more structurally embedded in some Western European states than in others, but it underpins all of them. Women are, thereby, excluded from the central areas of decision-making – that is, from membership of powerful economic and political elites – and tend to be concentrated in lowly paid, low-status work. When women, especially single mothers and older women, do not have a male partner on whom to depend, they tend to exchange private dependency for the public dependency of the state. In sum, women's caring work in the family tends to be a major barrier to their achieving the full social and economic citizenship enjoyed by men.

It is not only that state welfare benefits are related to paid employment, but that those in marginal jobs or not in paid employment at all are excluded from occupationally based benefits. In all Western European countries welfare entitlement is based on a blend of two elements – employment-funded provision and state provision. Women do not have access to paid work on the same basis as men, not only because of their assumed and actual domestic responsibilities but also because of labour market segmentation resulting in their concentration in a narrow range of lowly paid, low-status jobs (Martin and Roberts 1984; Sutherland 1990). Even solo women are far from equal with men (Abbott and Sapsford 1987; Miller 1990). Thus women now make up nearly two-fifths of the European Union's workforce, but the majority are still in low-paid jobs, and mostly working with other women. The trend is towards more part-time work for women, which serves to reinforce segregation and segmentation of the labour market, and there is little evidence that women are achieving equality with men in employment:

> Women's lack of opportunities for personal and career development is a serious stumbling block to the achievement of equal opportunities between men and women and a gross waste of talent, skills and abilities and helps to maintain men's perception of women's traditional role.
>
> (Deshormes LaValle 1991: 9)

Furthermore, there is little evidence that men are taking on more responsibility in the private sphere. Women who have paid employment as well as domestic responsibilities are still expected to take on the burden of both, with the associated costs (Martin and Roberts 1984; Arber 1990; Benigni 1989). To the extent that men do take on a greater share of work in the private sphere, it tends to be those aspects of child-care that women find most rewarding and enjoyable, not the routine drudgery of domestic cleaning (Edgell 1980; Langberg 1994).

Women and paid employment

Participation rates for women in paid employment increased in all Western European countries between the 1970s and the 1990s. This is especially true for married women. In the 1960s, 30 per cent of the working population in EU countries was female; by 1991 the figure had risen to over 40 per cent, but with considerable variation between countries (see Table 6.1). This is about the same as the female contribution to the Japanese labour market, but lower than the United States (45 per cent) and the EFTA countries (44 per cent). The labour force participation of younger women – married and single – increasingly resem-

TABLE 6.1 Female percentage of the labour force in member states of the European Union, 1991

Member state	Percentage of labour force
Belgium	41
Denmark	47
France	45
Germany	42
Greece	37
Ireland	34
Luxembourg	40
Netherlands	40
Portugal	44
Spain	36
UK	48

Source: Derived from CEC (1993: 145).

Note: Women make up between a third and a half of the labour force in EU countries. Figures vary from a low of only 34 per cent in Ireland to a high of 47 per cent in Denmark.

bles that of men. The participation rate of women of working age in EU countries in 1989 was highest in Sweden (where 85 per cent of women were engaged in paid work in 1988) and lowest in Ireland (around 38 per cent).

The changes in women's participation rates and the differences between Western European countries can best be considered by examining the three types of activity curves (across the life-span) that mirror women's participation: see Figures 6.1, 6.2 and 6.3.

1   The inverted U-shaped activity curve (Figure 6.1) is typical of countries such as Denmark and Portugal where the majority of women participate continuously, without career breaks for child-rearing.

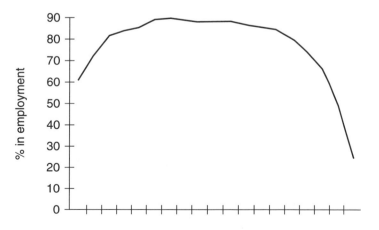

Figure 6.1 A typical inverted U-shaped curve

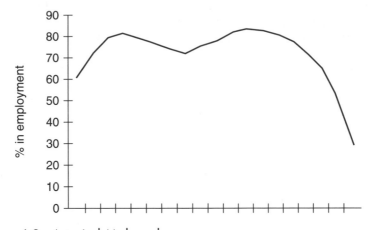

Figure 6.2 A typical M-shaped curve

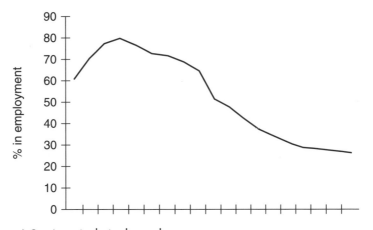

Figure 6.3 A typical single-peak curve

2   The M-shaped activity curve (Figure 6.2) is typical of countries such as France, the United Kingdom, Germany and the Netherlands where women's labour market participation is generally high but where a majority take a career break while they have and rear children.

3   The single-peak curve (Figure 6.3) represents those countries where high rates of activity are found only amongst young, mostly single women with high rates of withdrawal on marriage or when they have children. This is typical of countries such as Italy, Spain, Greece, Ireland, Luxembourg and Belgium where, despite the increase in female economic activity rates, there continues to be a peak in female employment at about age 25 and a decline thereafter.

The major area of growth in female employment in Western Europe has been in activity among women aged 24–49 – that is, women of child-bearing age. In 1991, over the European Union as a whole, 84 per cent of single childless women in this age group were economically active (in paid employment or actively seeking it), compared with 67 per cent of married childless women in the same age-range. Indeed, bearing children seems to have less effect on women's participation rates than marriage; only in the UK and Germany did having children as opposed to being married have a significant effect. (Having more than two children, however, did decrease the likelihood that a woman would be in paid employment – especially in France and the UK.)

However, whereas women represented just over 40 per cent of the total labour force in the European Union in 1991, they accounted for under 35 per cent of the total hours worked. This is because women work, on average, less overtime than men and because many more women are in part-time employment. In 1991 over 28 per cent of women worked part time, but only 4 per cent of men. Women also account for the majority of part-time workers; between 76 and 90 per cent of all part-time employees in the European Union are women (CEC 1993). In the Northern European states part-time work is more important for women than in the Southern ones (Table 6.2). These figures must be interpreted with some caution, however, as high levels of part-time work in Scandinavian countries reflects the number of women exercising their right to work reduced hours during periods of family formation whilst retaining full employment rights. Married women and women with children are more likely to work part time.

Women and labour market segmentation

Feminists have pointed out that the labour market is segmented horizontally and vertically (see for example Hakim 1979; Abbott and Tyler 1995). Women tend to be concentrated in lowly paid, low-status occupations and into work done only by women. Within each occupational stratum women also tend to be concentrated

TABLE 6.2 The percentage of women working part time, 1992

Member state	%	Member state	%
Belgium	28.1	Italy	11.5
Denmark	36.7	Luxembourg	16.6
France	24.5	Netherlands	63.8
Germany	30.7	Portugal	11.3
Greece	8.4	Spain	13.7
Ireland	18.6	UK	45.0

Source: Derived from CEC (Commission of the European Communities) (1995).

Note: These figures illustrate the variation, across EU member states, in the proportion of women working part time. Of those women engaged in paid work, lowest levels of part-time working are found in Greece, Italy and Portugal and highest in the Netherlands and the UK. These figures should be interpreted with some caution given the importance of the 'informal economy' and unpaid family work in Southern European countries.

TABLE 6.3 Female earnings as a percentage of male earnings across Europe, 1980–91

	Manual workers		Non-manual workers	
	1980	1991	1980	1991
Belgium	70.2	75.6	61.9	65.2
Denmark	86.0	84.5	n/a	n/a
Germany	72.4	73.4	66.0	67.1
France	78.3	80.2	61.1	67.2
Greece	67.5	79.2	n/a	68.5
Ireland	68.7	69.5	n/a	n/a
Italy	83.2	79.3	n/a	n/a
Luxembourg	64.7	68.0	49.7	55.2
Netherlands	73.0	76.2	59.1	64.8
Spain	n/a	72.2	n/a	60.9
Portugal	n/a	70.8	n/a	70.7
UK	69.8	67.2	54.5	58.3

Source: Derived from European Commission (1994: 8)

Note: The '1991' figure is in fact from 1990 for Netherlands and Luxembourg and 1989 from Italy; n/a indicates data not available. Data for Germany before 1989 is for the Federal Republic only.

Pay differentials are greatest in non-manual occupations. For those countries with available data, non-manual employees in Luxembourg and the UK fared the worst. Female manual workers in Denmark have achieved the highest level of 'equality' in relation to earnings levels.

Figures 6.4a and 6.4b evidence high levels of job segregation in clerical and service occupations across Europe. Around 70 per cent of employees in service occupations in Denmark, the UK, France, the Netherlands and Luxembourg are women.

at the lower levels (Martin and Roberts 1984; Payne and Abbott 1990; Siim 1987). Furthermore, the work that women do is less likely to be classified as skilled than the work men do (Phillips and Taylor 1980). The gender pay gap has not narrowed significantly in the last ten years; while some women have secured employment in the higher-paid professional employment categories, women are still over-represented in lowly paid jobs (see Table 6.3). The pay gap varies from country to country and is on the whole wider for non-manual than manual work – probably reflecting women's concentration in routine non-manual (clerical and secretarial) work.

In all community countries, irrespective of women's participation rate in paid employment, most women are concentrated in a narrow range of occupational sectors and in a small number of jobs. They have also made few inroads into the higher-level jobs. The growth in part-time employment reinforces job segregation; where part-time employment develops, women become confined to an even more limited range of jobs, especially in service work, where jobs have often been created as 'women's work' (Figures 6.4a and 6.4b).

Although women are heavily concentrated in the service sector, particularly in health, education and catering, they are becoming better educated and increasing their proportion of senior positions. However, they remain concentrated in public-sector professional jobs such as teaching. While some women are gaining more senior posts, there has also been a substantial increase in the number of

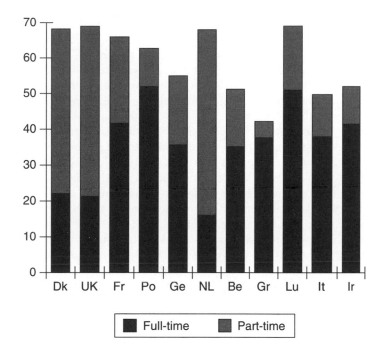

Figure 6.4a Women's share of service occupations

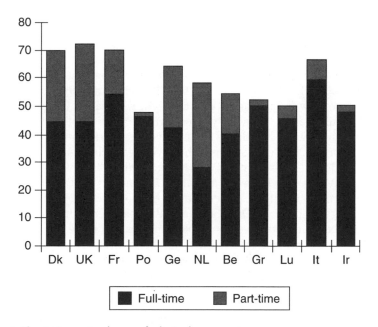

Figure 6.4b Women's share of clerical occupations

women employed in lower-level clerical and service jobs. This means a widening gulf between women at different levels of the labour market. For those with high educational credentials and professional jobs, the pattern of activity rates and occupational participation across the life course is becoming more like men's (Abbott forthcoming). Less educated and qualified women are more likely to have periods of withdrawal from the labour market or to withdraw permanently on marriage or the birth of children.

However, even women in professional occupations tend to experience labour market segregation, with the women concentrated in lower-status and less well paid jobs than men. An example is education (which accounts for 10 per cent of female employment), where, except in the Netherlands, a majority of employees are female. Nursing and kindergarten teaching is almost exclusively female, primary-school teaching is also predominantly undertaken by women – about 65 per cent in most countries, but as high as 80 per cent in Italy and Portugal. Secondary-school teaching is shared about equally between men and women, although over 60 per cent of secondary teachers in Italy and Portugal are women, while fewer than 30 per cent are in the Netherlands. Higher education, by contrast, is a male preserve; only about a quarter of jobs are filled by women in this sector.

Women, children and employment

The arrival of children has a profound impact on mothers' labour market participation – and virtually no impact on that of fathers (Table 6.4). Some 44 per cent of mothers with young children are in employment, compared with 92 per cent of fathers (European Commission 1990). The highest levels of mothers' employment are found in Denmark, Portugal and France and the lowest in Spain and Ireland.

The age of the youngest child notably affects employment rates for mothers in some but not all EU countries (Table 6.5). In Ireland and Spain, for example, activity rates are low for all women with children, whereas in Denmark they are high. In the United Kingdom activity rates increase significantly with the age of the youngest child: while less than a third of mothers work whose youngest child is younger than 3, 70 per cent of those whose youngest child is 7 or older do so.

Two-thirds of employed mothers have part-time jobs. Over 50 per cent do so in Germany, the Netherlands and the UK and a significant minority in Denmark; however, less than 15 per cent of employed mothers do so in Italy, Greece, Portugal and Spain. Over 50 per cent of mothers who work part time work twenty hours or more a week – 14 per cent working more than thirty hours. Only 14 per cent work less than ten hours a week. Mothers working part time in the Netherlands and the UK tend to work short hours – over 20 per cent less than ten hours and the majority less than twenty. In contrast, over 25 per cent of part-time working mothers in France, Italy, Denmark and Greece work longer than thirty hours a week.

Employed mothers are concentrated in an even narrower range of occupations than women in general. They are to be found in large numbers in three

TABLE 6.4 Percentages of mothers and fathers in employment with children aged less than 10, 1988

	Men with children aged less than 10	Women with children aged less than 10
Belgium	94 (1)	60 (22)
Denmark	92 (2)	85 (28)
France	92 (1)	59 (16)
Germany	94 (1)	55 (24)
Greece	96 (1)	41 (3)
Ireland	81 (2)	30 (9)
Italy	95 (2)	42 (5)
Luxembourg	97 (–)	40 (13)
Netherlands	92 (8)	40 (35)
Portugal	96 (1)	69 (6)
Spain	91 (7)	33 (4)
United Kingdom	88 (1)	51 (35)

Source: Derived from Roll (1992).

Note: Figures in parentheses are those in part-time work.

This table shows the impact of having young children on parents' employment. For men, the presence of children has little impact on their employment. For women, highest levels of employment of mothers with young children are found in Denmark, Portugal and Belgium. Women are far more likely to work part time when their children are young. This is particularly marked in the UK and the Netherlands.

TABLE 6.5 Percentage employment rates for women aged 16-39 in Europe by age of youngest child, 1988

	Women aged 16–39			
	With no child	Age of youngest child		
		Up to 2	3–6	7–15
Belgium	68	52	57	53
Denmark	84	74	79	85
France	78	50	42	44
Germany	83	31	41	50
Greece	56	39	40	44
Ireland	75	27	22	24
Italy	54	40	42	44
Luxembourg	78	33	39	40
Netherlands	78	28	33	41
Portugal	64	58	64	64
Spain	52	28	28	28
United Kingdom	83	33	51	70

Source: Derived from Joshi and Davies (1994: Table 2.1). Data for Germany is for the Federal Republic only.

The presence of children has a marked effect on women's labour market participation, with employment rates falling in every case. Employment rates generally pick up a little as the youngest child reaches the age of 7. This effect is not seen in France, however, where rates fall back as the child reaches school age.

main types of economic activity: 45 per cent in 'other services', 20 per cent in 'distributive trades', and 11 per cent in 'other manufacturing'.

Explanations of gender inequality in the labour market

Attitudes to women holding paid employment

Attitudes in European Union countries to the roles of men and women in the home and paid employment may, however, be changing. In a comparatively recent study of attitudes in Europe (Deshormes LaValle 1987), 41 per cent of those interviewed said that men and women should have equal roles in the home and in paid employment (39 per cent of men and 41 per cent of women – see Table 6.6). Of married men 47 per cent said they would prefer a working to a non-working wife. However, there are clear variations between countries. In some (Germany, Ireland and Luxembourg) a majority of married men would prefer to have a *non-working* wife, whilst in others (Denmark, France, Italy, the UK, Greece, Spain and Portugal) the majority of men would prefer their wives to work. Of course, wanting to enjoy the benefits of having a wife in paid employment does not necessarily indicate that these men share (or would be prepared to share) unpaid labour in the private sphere equally with their wives. Nevertheless, in those countries where married men prefer a working wife, there is some evidence of a desire for shared roles. However, Denmark is the only EU country where a majority (53 per cent) think that men and women should have equal, shared

TABLE 6.6 Married men's preferences for a working or non-working wife, 1987

	Prefer wives not to work (% of all men)	Prefer wives to work
Belgium	43	50
Denmark	35	58
Germany	58	31
France	41	53
Ireland	53	34
Italy	43	51
Luxembourg	59	29
Netherlands	40	42
United Kingdom	40	50
Greece	28	63
Spain	35	50
Portugal	41	52

Source: Derived from Deshormes LaValle (1987: 24). Data for Germany is for the Federal Republic only.

Married men's attitudes towards the employment of their wives varies between countries, with most positive attitudes recorded in Greece and Denmark and highest levels of resistance in Luxembourg and Germany.

roles, and in Ireland and Luxembourg nearly 40 per cent believe that women should stay at home and not go out to work.

Demographic explanations

A number of broad trends can be discerned across Europe which have an impact on the lives of men, women and families and influence women's ability to participate in the labour market. There is a declining fertility rate in all Western European countries. This means that women are spending less time pregnant and caring for young children. At the same time there is an increase in the number of elderly people – especially the very old – who need care. In most EU countries families are expected to care for the frail elderly. There has also been an increase in the divorce rate and in the rate of illegitimate births, suggesting an increasing number of female-headed households. In addition there has been an increase in the number of women, especially married women, who are in paid employment (Table 6.7).

The role of the welfare state

Children have a very large effect on women's ability to participate in the labour market – although child-care is clearly not the only factor and clearly interacts with cultural attitudes to married women having paid employment. Maternity leave is a universal right for all employed women in the European Union, although the length of time and degree of income entitlement vary significantly from country to country (Table 6.8). Only Denmark and Sweden have statutory paid

TABLE 6.7 Female labour market activity rates across Europe, 1970–89

	All women		Married women	
	1970	1989	1984	1988
	(% of women of working age in employment)			
Denmark	58.0	77.3	63.8	66.7
France	48.5	48.3	50.2	50.8
Germany	48.1	54.8	41.9	42.4
Ireland	34.3	37.5	24.2	29.1
Italy	33.5	44.3	32.4	34.7
UK	50.7	65.4	51.0	55.6
Norway	38.8	71.2	61.0	66.0
Sweden	59.4	80.5	68.9	82.9

Source: Derived from Lewis (1993b: Tables 1.4 and 1.5).

Note: The '1989' figure for Germany is in fact from 1988. Data for Germany before 1989 is for the Federal Republic only.

Female labour market activity rates have increased right across Europe, but most markedly in Denmark, Sweden and Norway. Married women, in the main, have slightly depressed employment rates.

TABLE 6.8 Maternity and parental leave entitlements across Europe

	Maternity leave	*Parental leave, etc.*
Belgium	75 per cent of earnings. 8 weeks before birth and 6 weeks before or after (14 weeks in total)	None but workers can take a 6–12 months career break from employment for personal/family reasons. Paid at a flat rate – a higher rate if taken within six years of birth of second or third child. Unpaid for first child.
Denmark	90 per cent of earnings. 4 weeks before birth and 18 weeks after birth (18 weeks in total)	90 per cent of earnings for 10 weeks. In addition, with employer's consent, can take 13–35 weeks' leave paid at flat rate. Unpaid for first/second child
France	84 per cent of earnings. 6 weeks before birth and 10 weeks after birth (10 weeks in total)	Payment for third and subsequent children (low flat rate) until child is 3
Germany	100 per cent of earnings. 6 weeks before birth and 8 weeks after birth (14 weeks in total)	Low flat-rate payment for 6 months, then means-tested payment for 18 months, then 12 months unpaid
Greece	100 per cent of earnings. 16 weeks taken before or after birth	Three months' unpaid leave per parent. (Not transferable from one parent to the other)
Ireland	70 per cent of earnings (tax-free). 4 weeks before birth, 4 weeks after and 6 weeks before or after (total 14). An additional 4 weeks' unpaid leave can be taken	None
Italy	80 per cent of earnings. 2 months before birth and 3 months after birth (5 months in total)	30 per cent of earnings. 6 months
Luxembourg	100 per cent of earnings. 6 weeks before birth and 8 weeks after birth (14 weeks in total)	None
Netherlands	100 per cent of earnings. 4–6 weeks before birth, 10–12 weeks after birth (16 weeks in total)	6 months per parent of reduced hours (min. 20 hours per week). Not transferable between parents
Portugal	100 per cent of earnings. 60 days after birth and 30 days before or after (90 days in total)	24 months, unpaid
Spain	75 per cent of earnings. 10 weeks after birth and 6 weeks before or after (16 weeks in total)	12 months, unpaid
UK	90 per cent of earnings for 6 weeks. Low flat-rate payment for 12 weeks. No payment for remainder. 11 weeks before birth and 29 weeks after birth (30 weeks in total)	None

Sources: Moss (1990) and European Commission (1993).

TABLE 6.9 Public child-care provision across Europe

	Percentage of children under 3	Percentage of children aged 3 to school entry	Age of school entry (years)	Length of school day (hours)
Belgium	20	95	6	7
Denmark	48	85	7	3–5.5
France	20	95+	6	8
Germany	3	65–70	6–7	4–5
Greece	4	65–70	5.5	4–5
Ireland	2	55	6	4.5–6.5
Italy	5	85+	6	4
Luxembourg	2	55–60	5	4–8
Netherlands	2	50–55	5	6–7
Portugal	6	35	6	6.5
Spain	n/a	65–70	6	8
UK	2	35–40	5	6.5

Source: Derived from Maruani (1992: Table 4).

Note: Data are for 1988 except for Italy (1986), Germany (1987), and Netherlands, Luxembourg and Denmark (1989). Data for Germany before 1989 is for the Federal Republic only.

Only Belgium, Denmark and France provide public child-care facilities for more than 20 per cent of under 3s. Public provision for children aged 3 and over increases considerably, with the majority of countries providing places for over half of all children. Portugal and the UK provide the lowest levels of publicly funded child-care.

paternity leave, but seven countries have parental leave entitlement (leave which can be taken by either parent), and Belgium offers more general leave that can be used in connection with children. The length of parental leave varies from ten weeks in Denmark to nearly three years in France. Four EU countries – Luxembourg, Belgium, France and Portugal – provide for some tax relief for child-care costs, while Germany gives tax relief on the cost of buying private domestic help.

All the EU countries with the exception of the UK and Portugal provide publicly funded child-care for over 50 per cent of children aged from 3 to the compulsory age of school entry (Table 6.9). Only Denmark provides a significant amount of publicly funded child-care for children under the age of 3 or out-of-school care for those of primary-school age. Although the availability of child-care is clearly a factor in explaining women's varied participation in paid employment, it is not by itself a sufficient explanation. France and Belgium, for example, have places in publicly funded care for 95 per cent of children aged from 3 years to school entry age, but the activity rate of women aged 25–49 is only 66 per cent in Belgium, compared with 73 per cent in France. Ireland and the Netherlands have significantly more places for pre-school children in publicly funded care than the UK, but much lower employment rates for women aged twenty-five to forty-nine – 45 and 58 per cent respectively, compared with 73 per cent (Maruani 1992). Maruani suggests that 'female activity rates are influenced less by the number of children or availability of child-care than by the strategies for coping with family obligations. This is where the European countries exhibit the greatest diversity' (1992: 9).

However, it is clear that the availability of child-care is a significant factor in enabling women to participate in the labour market. In France, for example, the almost universal availability of pre-school publicly funded child-care, combined with long school hours, has enabled French mothers to work full time. By contrast, in Britain the low level of pre-school provision and a relatively short school day account both for the continuing M-shaped pattern of the female activity rate curve and for the high level of part-time employment of women with children. It is also likely that the provision or not of child-care by the state interacts with cultural attitudes to whether married women or women with children should participate in paid employment.

The interaction of cultural and structural factors: the Swedish and German experience

The ways in which these factors interact is clearly illustrated by the contrasting situation of women in the Federal Republic of Germany (West Germany) and the German Democratic Republic (East Germany) prior to unification. In West Germany it was assumed that married women would not have paid employment, whereas in East Germany it was assumed that all women of working age would be in paid employment. In the GDR there was almost universal provision of pre-school places for children in heavily subsidized day care. In West Germany pre-school places rarely met 20 per cent of the demand and there was no state subsidy (Senftleben 1992: 85). The welfare system in West Germany assumed that married women's main responsibility was to care for their husbands and children. Both parties had an obligation to work for their own and their family's mutual interest – the man by being the breadwinner, the wife by fulfilling their domestic and care responsibilities (Flamm 1993). In East Germany, by contrast, it was an obligation for all adults to participate in paid employment: 91 per cent of women were in paid employment before unification in East Germany, compared with 50 per cent in the Federal Republic (Perree and Young 1992: 4). In the GDR women were expected to take on the dual role of paid employment and domestic care, supported by the state, whereas in the FRG emphasis was placed on women's domestic obligations, with little or no support provided to enable them to participate in the labour market (Wilson 1993). In the GDR, despite the emphasis on formal equality, women were excluded from the more highly paid jobs because of the ideology that meant that wages were higher in heavy industry than in white-collar occupations. There is also no evidence that domestic tasks were shared between men and women, and there was a high level of single female-headed families – in 1989 over a third of births were to unmarried mothers. The welfare system made this possible because of the high level of support given to working mothers (Perree and Young 1992: 4). In contrast, the FRG gave a heavy subsidy to marriage through its tax system, and women's pensions and other social security benefits were tied to their husbands' earnings.

On the unification of East and West Germany, East German women lost sub-sidized child-care, legal abortion rights, affirmative action for women entering male jobs and their paid maternity leave. Their parental loan rights and subsidies for children were withdrawn, youth clubs were closed and subsidies for kindergarten withdrawn, as well as free community care services. At the same time as these welfare rights were withdrawn, the East German economy collapsed, and women were employed in occupations even more vulnerable to unemployment than those occupied by men. 'The consequence is that, with reunification, traditional gender roles have re-emerged. It has become expected that men have primacy in finding employment and that a woman's place is in the home' (Karger 1992).

Sweden provides an example of a Western European country with a high level of female participation in the labour market and state support for this partici-pation. Women's activity rates approach those of men in paid employment, there is liberal abortion legislation, extensive statutory parental leave and publicly funded day care. Parents are entitled to eighteen months' leave at 90 per cent of gross earnings. In addition, women are entitled to fifty days' pregnancy leave and men to ten days' parental leave. Parents are also entitled to ninety days per year, per child under the age of 12, to care for sick children or to care for a child if the normal care-giver is ill, and two days per year to visit the child's nursery school (Rappaport and Moss 1989: 11). In addition, parents have the right to work a six-hour day until the child is 8 years old. In 1987, 34 per cent of children under the age of 3 were cared for by a paid childminder or a municipal nursery, while the vast majority of children aged 3–7 were cared for part or full time (Broberg and Hwang 1991). Parents are expected to cover between 10 and 15 per cent of the cost of child-care organized by the local authority – nurseries and child-minding schemes. The services are more used by middle-class than working-class parents.

Despite this position of formal gender equality, however, women are much more likely than men to take parental or other paid leave. On any given day, about 20 per cent of female workers are on paid leave – 30 per cent in the public sector – and as many as 47 per cent of those with children under the age of 5 (Esping-Anderson 1990). Women are also more likely to be unemployed than men (Vogel 1987) and likely to earn less (Ruggie 1988). Women are also concen-trated in certain occupations – 89 per cent of secretaries, 94 per cent of nursing auxiliaries, 78 per cent of shop assistants and 90 per cent of cleaners are women (Scriven 1984). Esping-Anderson (1990) suggests that over 50 per cent of Swedish women are in typical female jobs. Women in part-time employment are heavily concentrated in lowly paid, low-status work (Ruggie 1988). Hernes (1987) has suggested that the Swedish welfare state has reconstituted patriarchy. Women are more dependent on the welfare state than men for income maintenance (single parents, older women) and for employment. Women are also more heavily depen-dent than men on the services and benefits provided, because of their greater responsibility for unpaid domestic and care work. Yet the control and adminis-tration of the welfare state remains in the hands of men. 'One can describe the Scandinavian state form as a tutelary state for women, since they have a minimal role in the actual decision-making processes concerning distribution' (Hernes 1987: 76). Borchurst and Siim (1987 – see also Siim 1987) argue that while the

Scandinavian welfare state has swept away some of the traditional patriarchal assumptions about women's primary role being as unpaid workers in the private sphere, it has elaborated a new form of patriarchal citizenship for women, where women are controlled by the welfare state as both employer and provider.

The example of the two Germanys and the changes brought about in the situation of women in East Germany by unification, and the case of Sweden, clearly demonstrate that while equal opportunity legislation and the provision of state services for children and other dependent groups facilitates the greater participation of women in paid employment, by itself this does not bring about equality with men. Not only do women tend to end up in 'women's jobs', with lower pay on average than men's, but they exchange dependency on the income of their male partners for dependency on the patriarchal state – for employment, child-care, maternity and other paid leave, provisions which can be reduced or withdrawn by government decisions. Not only that, but the majority of employed married women, especially those with children or other dependants, continue to do the double shift – paid employment at work and unpaid labour in the domestic sphere.

The European Union and the promotion of gender equality

The following section considers the competence and achievements of the European Union in the area of gender inequality.

The Treaty of Rome was fundamentally an economic treaty seeking to promote an area of free trade. The only measure dealing explicitly with gender equality is the Equal Pay Principle (Article 19), which states simply that men and women should receive 'equal pay for equal work'; in other words, it applies only to cases where a woman is in receipt of lower wages than a man doing exactly the same job in the same organization. The concept of pay, however, includes not just wages but also other occupational benefits such as employer pensions, redundancy payments, etc. The Equal Pay Directive of 1975 introduced the concept of 'equal value' into the legislation, enabling women to take action in cases where they were doing work of equal value to that of their male counterparts but receiving lower wages or other benefits. While overcoming some of the problems of finding a male doing exactly the same job, given the high levels of job segregation, this Directive has still not solved all the problems of comparison. A woman may now compare herself to a man who previously held her job – though the temporal scope of such comparisons will be limited – and she is no longer restricted to finding a comparator in the same place of work. The comparator male must still be employed by the same company or under the same collective agreement, however, and women cannot compare themselves to a 'hypothetical' male.

The legislation is therefore likely to have only limited impact, given the concentration of women in certain areas of employment. We have seen above that a key cause of gender inequality lies in the concentration of women in part-time work and the association of this form of work with low pay and poor working conditions. The ability of the Equal Pay legislation to have any impact on this area of discrimination has been tested in the European Court of Justice (ECJ), with mixed results. On the one hand the Court has found that whilst the payment of lower wages to part-time women workers may form the basis of a sex discrimination case, it is open to the employer to justify the lower rate of pay 'objectively' on grounds other than sex. One such ground may be that the lower rates of pay correspond to 'a genuine need of the enterprise' (Bilka Kaufaus, Case 170/84). A firm may therefore argue that payment of lower wages to part-time workers is essential in order to remain profitable. As such, it is not actionable as a form of sex discrimination.

The Equal Pay Programme was complemented by the introduction of four new Directives covering equal treatment in employment, and state and occupational social security for the self-employed. The first of these introduced the principle of equal treatment of men and women as regards access to employment, vocational training, promotion and working conditions. A substantial amount of litigation under this Directive has been concerned with discriminatory retirement ages. It is important to note, however, that these Directives are not about the promotion of women's interests as such but about securing equal opportunities; indeed, many of the pension cases have been taken by men. The results of these cases may actually worsen the position of women if member states are permitted to raise women's retirement age to 65.

We have looked, above, at the impact of welfare systems on gendered dependency. The Equal Treatment in Social Security Directive (Council Directive 79/7) sought to reduce the extent of discrimination in national social security systems. It states that there shall be 'no reference in particular to marital or family status' and covers the scope of and access to social security schemes and the calculation of benefits. It has been used in Ireland to prevent the payment to married women of lower rates of unemployment benefit for shorter periods (*McDermott and Cotter v. The Minister for Social Welfare and the Attorney General*, Case 286/85) and to challenge the UK social security arrangements which required married women to prove they were incapable of performing normal household duties in order to qualify for its non-contributory invalidity pension (a requirement not applied to married men).

In terms of its broader equal opportunities strategy the European Commission (and the Equal Opportunities Unit in particular) has endeavoured to step beyond a narrowly defined 'public' world of work and extend Community competence into the 'private' world of domestic responsibilities and familial roles, in recognition of the fact that women's position in the labour market cannot be improved by measures which focus exclusively on equal pay and equal treatment in employment (see Pillinger 1992; Meehan 1993; Edwards and McKie 1993/4). This concern to reconcile women's position within the family with their role in caring for dependants has been reflected in the development of a variety of initiatives. The European Commission has, for example, proposed three further Directives covering parental leave, part-time work and the reversal of the burden of proof in equal treatment cases. The last of these would create a presumption of discrimination, thus requiring the employer to prove that they had not infringed the principle of equality; at present the burden rests on the claimant to prove discrimination. The Resolution on Sexual Harassment and Recommendation on

Child-Care, similarly, demonstrate a commitment to go beyond the strict remit of the single market. The fact that the majority of these initiatives have either taken the form of non-binding measures or have failed to get beyond the Council of Ministers and remained 'in draft stage' for over a decade does not reflect the commitment of the Commission or the wider Community as such. Indeed, the European Commission set up a Network for Child-Care and other measures to reconcile working and family responsibilities which has sought to promote the use of European structural funds for child-care purposes. In particular the NOW (New Opportunities for Women) programme recognized that 'lack of adequate child-care provision formed one of the principal causes of women's disadvantaged position in the labour market' (European Commision 1992).

The lack of progress on equal opportunities at EU level reflects the weak legal base for social policy in general and a lack of political consensus across member states. The requirement for unanimity in voting procedures, in particular, has meant that individual member states (notably the UK) have been able effectively to block initiatives in this area. Despite the lack of legislative progress, the Third Community Action Programme on Equal Opportunities (1991–5) and its proposals for legislative action suggest a commitment to a strategy which locates women's labour market position within a broader analysis of gender inequality.

The future position is uncertain. The Community Charter of the Fundamental Social Rights of Workers (1989) reaffirms the commitment to equal treatment for men and women and talks of the development of measures 'enabling men and women to reconcile their occupational and family obligations' (Article 16). Disagreement over the inclusion of the Charter in the Maastricht Treaty, however, resulted in the adoption of a separate, watered-down version known as the Protocol on Social Policy, appended to the Treaty but signed by only eleven member states (excluding the UK). In September 1994 the UK, for the first time, used its 'right' to opt out of EU social policy under the Maastricht Treaty, thus leaving the other eleven member states to draw up laws, under the Protocol, without Britain. The issue here concerned planned legislation on paternity leave giving fathers the right to a statutory three months' unpaid leave after the birth of a child. The UK opposed the legislation on the grounds that it would add extra costs to industry.

As a result of limited legal competence in the social field generally, and political conflict between member states over the direction of sex equality legislation, the impact of EU policy on women has been largely restricted to measures to improve their position in the labour market. Both the Equal Pay and the Free Movement Provisions strengthen the association between occupational status and social entitlement. This, coupled with the trend across all member states for a shifting emphasis within the mixed economy of welfare in favour of informal, largely unpaid care provided primarily by women, has clear implications for women's labour-force participation and, as a consequence, their access to social rights (Cochrane 1993; Glasner 1992; Lewis 1992). Janet Finch concludes her analysis of the position of European women by expressing concern that the impact of the EU will 'lead to pressure for strengthening the welfare benefits associated with being employed . . . [which] is certainly bad news for women' (Finch 1990: 4).

Summary

- Modern welfare systems have played an important role in modifying women's relationship with both paid and unpaid work.
- Any attempt to promote gender equality via measures to increase women's participation in the labour market needs to take full account of the sexual division of unpaid work – particularly child-care and care of the elderly.
- The restricted competence of the European Union – confining it largely to forms of labour market regulation – seriously restricts its ability to advance gender equality.

Further reading

Linda Hantrais (1995) *Social Policy in the European Union*, London: Macmillan. This book examines the development of the social policy role of the EU and the impact of the EU on the domestic social policies of member states. Three chapters focus on aspects of gender inequality, family policies and citizenship.

Allan Cochrane and John Clarke (1993) *Comparing Welfare States: Britain in the International Context*, London: Sage. This textbook, written as part of an Open University course, provides a very clear and accessible introduction to comparative social policy and in particular focuses on family policies in a range of welfare systems.

Jane Pillinger (1992) *Feminising the Market*, London: Macmillan. Jane Pillinger's book concentrates on the role of the EU in relation to women's pay and employment policies in Europe to assess the impact of the EU on women's labour market opportunities.

Diane Sainsbury (1996) *Gendering Welfare States*, London: Sage. For those students interested in developing their expertise in the area of comparative social policy, this edited collection includes a variety of chapters on aspects of welfare of particular concern to women – such as child-care, pensions and single parenting. At a more general level, it questions existing theoretical approaches to comparative social policy analysis from feminist perspectives and asks whether new forms of classification are required.

Chapter 7

Racism, immigration and migrant labour

Paul Iganski and Sidney Jacobs

Introduction: migrant labour and Europe   148
Capitalism and migrant labour: 1945–73   151
A rising tide of racism across Europe?:
   the 1980s and 1990s   155
European policy   158
Summary   160
Further reading   160

Key concepts

- Migrant labour
- Racist violence
- Cultural racism

Introduction: migrant labour and Europe

Pre-Second World War Central and Eastern Europe were essentially multicultural societies. Certainly the large cities and towns were highly cosmopolitan. However, historic enmities were nurtured by the growth of nineteenth-century nationalism, associated with the development of the contemporary nation-state system (see Chapter 3). These were ever present, casting a shadow of insecurity over the many minorities which co-existed throughout Europe. Violence sometimes erupted and it was usually directed against Jews – anti-Semitism was endemic to the region. It resulted in the mass migration of Jews from Eastern to Western Europe and from Europe to the Americas. Thus, for instance, some three million Russian Jews emigrated to the United States between 1881 and 1924. Gypsies too suffered terribly and were, then as now, the focus throughout Europe of constant discrimination. Nevertheless, for the most part, Germans, Poles, Lithuanians, Russians, Czechs, Hungarians, southern Slavs, Jews, gypsies and many more besides managed to live relatively peacefully together. Despite these growing ethnic tensions, it was also an intellectually exciting, artistically and culturally vibrant world in which new ideas, political passions and egalitarian dreams abounded.

After 1939, this was all brutally unscrambled and destroyed. The link between 'race', racism and nationalism, leading to the rise of right-wing movements espousing a 'one nation, one state', ideology is, as Hobsbawm (1993) notes, largely a late nineteenth-century phenomenon. It led directly to fascism and the horrors of the Second World War and its aftermath. 'Mass murder and mass expulsion', Hobsbawm (1993: 157) writes, 'did drastically simplify the ethnic map of Europe ... yet the movement of peoples has since restored the ethnic complexity which barbarism sought to eliminate.'

Europe emerged from war in 1945 with many of its cities and much of its industrial infrastructure in ruins. Tens of millions were killed, mostly civilians, including the murder of almost all of the Jews of occupied Europe. Millions more were on the move: survivors of the Nazi death camps, freed slave labourers, refugees, de-mobbed soldiers, deserters and whole populations of expelled ethnic Germans. They were trudging in every direction, returning home, emigrating, fleeing retribution or the advance of the Soviet empire, either seeking to build a new life or desperately searching for the old.

During the war, Enzensberger (1994: 128) writes, 'nearly ten million forced labourers, a third of them women, were abducted to Germany from all over Europe'. Thus in Nazi Germany 30 per cent of all jobs, and in the armaments industry more than half, were filled by foreigners. Many, of course, would not have survived the war but, between 1945 and 1950, it is estimated that a further twelve million refugees entered Germany, although 'only a very few of them remained' (Enzensberger 1994: 128–9). However, the post-war Federal Republic of Germany, which was West Germany until 1989, did absorb during these early post-war years some nine million Germans expelled *en masse* mostly from Poland and Czechoslovakia. Further, an average of 200,000 East Germans annually fled to the West until numbers drastically declined with the building of the Berlin Wall in 1961.

West Germany was thus provided with a massive internal supply of labour, largely comprised of German refugees expelled from Eastern Europe. For this reason and because post-war economic recovery in Germany started later than elsewhere, foreign workers were not imported in significant numbers until the late 1950s. West German industry then turned to Italy, Yugoslavia, Turkey, Greece and Spain for its migrant labour. In 1956 there were only 95,000 migrant workers in Germany, but numbers rose rapidly thereafter to 507,000 in 1961, 1.3 million in 1966, and 2.6 million in 1973. German policy towards foreign labour was, as Castles *et al.* (1984: 72) note, 'shaped by the view that migrant workers were temporary mobile units which could be recruited, utilized and disposed of according to market requirements'. There are now in the 1990s more than 5 million 'foreigners' resident in Germany.

In contrast to Germany, there were 1.6 million foreign-born people living in Britain in 1951, rising to 3.4 million in 1981 (Castles *et al.* 1984: 41). Having avoided Nazi occupation, Britain was able to begin the process of post-war reconstruction relatively early but progress was hampered by chronic labour shortages. It was thus to Europe that Britain initially turned for a solution. Kushner (1994: 413) quotes from the 1940s Royal Commission on Population which advised that 'immigration on a large scale ... could only be welcomed ... if [they] were of good human stock and were not prevented by their religion or race from inter-marrying with the host population and becoming merged in it'. By 1947, an estimated 120,000 Poles, mostly ex-servicemen and women were recruited for work in Britain. An additional 90,000 displaced persons, the so-called European Voluntary Workers (EVWs), were imported and employed under stringent migrant labour laws. While roughly a quarter of displaced persons in Europe were Jews, less than 1 per cent of the EVWs who came to Britain were Jewish. As explained by a senior Foreign Office official, the recruitment of Jews would excite 'opposition from public opinion' (Kushner 1994: 420). A further 100,000 Europeans, mainly Italians, were granted work permits and were subsequently allowed to remain in the country.

The Irish, Britain's traditional supplier of cheap labour, remained the largest immigrant group. In 1966 there were 739,000 people born in the Irish Republic resident in the United Kingdom. However, by the late 1940s, Britain increasingly drew upon her colonies in the Caribbean and, later, from the newly independent Commonwealth countries within the Indian sub-continent to supply her growing labour needs during the boom years of the 1950s. But Britain turned to black and Asian labour only very reluctantly. As Joshi and Carter (1985) show, serious misgivings were privately expressed within top government circles by politicians and senior civil servants about the importation of 'coloured colonials' as they were then called. These immigrants were, under the 1948 Nationality Act, British and Commonwealth citizens and like the Irish were granted rights of entry and settlement.

In Switzerland, the largest group of migrant workers was drawn from Italy: 522,000 in 1969; followed by Germans (116,000) and Spaniards (98,000). France and the Netherlands, like Britain, drew labour from their colonies and ex-colonies. In consequence, by the mid-twentieth century the exploitation of colonial labour in Asia, Africa, and the Caribbean had transferred to Europe with the establishment of a new 'internal colonialism' (Nikolinakos 1973: 378). In addition to labour from Spain, Italy and Portugal, nearly a third of immigrants in France by the late 1960s were from the North African countries of Algeria, Morocco, and Tunisia, and from the West Indies. The Netherlands drew labour from her former colonies of Indonesia and Surinam.

Between 1945 and 1975, it is estimated that about 30 million workers and their dependants entered Western Europe, making it 'one of the greatest migratory movements in human history' (Castles *et al.* 1984: 1). Yet, as Enzensberger (1994: 112) suggests, the flow in the opposite direction from Europe to the 'New World' during the nineteenth and early twentieth centuries was of even greater importance and magnitude. Thus, he points out, between 1810 and 1921, 34 million people, mainly from Europe, emigrated to the United States alone. Indeed Europeans in their tens of millions flowed to the Americas, Australia, New Zealand, South Africa and elsewhere. They created new nation-states largely by killing or enslaving the indigenous populations: the American Indians, the Aborigines, the Maoris, etc., and expropriating their land, wealth and resources.

Simultaneously, mass migrations occurred within Europe. In particular, from the latter half of the nineteenth century migrant workers were essential to the progress of industrialization throughout Western Europe. The ready availability of labour was vital to the continuing creation of wealth and accumulation of capital. The indigenous labour force in European nation-states met the growing demand for qualified labour generated by technological progress (Nikolinakos 1973: 378), whilst migrant workers were commonly recruited as a replacement population at the bottom of the jobs ladder. There were 800,000 foreign workers in the German Reich in 1907. More than a third of the Ruhr miners were Poles. Switzerland had half a million foreigners in 1910, accounting for 15 per cent of her total population. French heavy industry was highly dependent on immigrant labour right up to the Second World War, and Irish workers played a vital part in British industrialization.

In Britain, during the late nineteenth century, 'alien' immigrants, mainly Eastern European Jews, were the focus of bitter agitation. As a result the 1905 Aliens Act was passed, primarily designed to restrict Jewish entry to Britain. In 1919 further restrictive legislation was enacted in response to a growing xenophobic campaign conducted by the press which combined anti-Semitism with anti-Bolshevism and anti-German feeling, and in which 'the alien' stood for all three (Cesarani 1987). During the inter-war years, aliens were largely excluded from state welfare provision. Thus as Cohen (1985) shows, anti-black racism, which became so pervasive within the institutions of the post-war British welfare state, was part of an unbroken racist tradition already deeply embedded and originating from the anti-Semitism of the early twentieth century. This linked state welfare benefits with nationality and immigration control. 'The relationships of welfare throughout the entire twentieth century', Cohen (1985: 92) argues, 'have been premised on national chauvinism.' In these terms, after 1945 'the welfare state never failed the black population; it was never, in the first place, intended to apply to them' (Jacobs 1985: 12).

Capitalism and migrant labour: 1945–73

After 1945, as Castles *et al.* (1984: 1) observe, 'the import of labour was a marked feature of all advanced capitalist countries'. Capitalism from its very beginnings has always been dependent upon migrant labour. Indeed, Enzensberger (1994: 104) argues that the history of humanity is characterized by 'conquest and pillage, expulsion and exile, slavery and abduction, colonization and captivity. A considerable proportion of humanity has always been in motion.' It was the Atlantic Slave Trade, the involuntary movement of millions of people from Africa to the Americas, which provided essential commercial preconditions for industrial take-off in Europe. Britain had increasingly captured control of the slave trade so that 'by the early 1780s, more than half of all slaves exported from Africa made profits for British slavers . . . our industries and economy grew out of our commerce and especially our commerce with the underdeveloped world' (Hobsbawm 1983: 54).

By the mid-nineteenth century Britain was established as the 'workshop of the world'. The new industrial order was fed by a seemingly endless supply of cheap labour. The rural poor migrated *en masse* to the newly formed slums of Britain's rapidly growing industrial towns and cities. There they competed for both work and living space with tens of thousands of Irish migrants who, desperately escaping from famine and starvation at home, were super-exploited, abused and seemingly despised by all classes. It was Irish labourers who, at incredible cost to themselves, were largely responsible for building Britain's industrial infrastructure and communications network, especially the railways, so necessary for successful industrialization. The benefits that accrued were immense, due not only to the cheapness of Irish labour but equally to the disunity within the working class caused by the prevalence of anti-Irish prejudice which turned worker against worker. As Marx then observed:

> Every industrial and commercial centre in England now possesses a working-class divided into two hostile camps. English proletarians and Irish proletarians. The ordinary English worker hates the Irish worker as a competitor who lowers his standard of life. In relation to the Irish worker he feels himself a member of the ruling nation and so turns himself into a tool of the aristocrats and capitalists of his country against Ireland, thus strengthening their domination over himself. He cherishes religious, social and national prejudices against the Irish worker. His attitude toward him is much the same as that of the 'poor whites' to the 'niggers' in the former slave states of the USA. The Irishman pays him back with interest in his own money. He sees in the English worker at once the accomplice and the stupid tool of the English domination over Ireland. This antagonism is artificially kept alive and intensified by the press, the pulpit, the comic papers, in short, by all the means at the disposal of the ruling classes. This antagonism is the secret of the impotence of the English working-class, despite its organization. It is the secret by which the capitalist class maintains its power. And that class is fully aware of it.
>
> (Marx and Engels 1962: 551–2)

Marx's analysis is adopted by Gorz to explain the enormous benefits derived from post-Second World War migrant labour to Western Europe. He argues that the political advantages even outweigh the economic 'since massive reliance on immigrant labour enables a basic modification in the social and political structure of the population to be artificially produced' (Gorz 1970: 28). To illustrate what he means by 'massive reliance', Gorz quotes figures which show that in 1970 immigrant and migrant workers comprised almost 14 per cent of manual workers in both Germany and Britain, from 20 per cent to 25 per cent in Belgium, 25 per cent in France and 35 per cent in Switzerland. Given that in most of Europe, but not in Britain prior to 1971, immigrant workers were largely deprived of political, trade union and civil rights, the advantages of excluding up to 35 per cent of the working class from active participation in politics and trade unions is very obvious. As Gorz explains (1970: 28), it leads to 'a considerable decrease in the political and electoral weight of the working class [and] a still more considerable weakening of its ideological force and cohesion'. In fact Gorz (1970: 30) even suggests that the very survival of capitalism depends on its excluding 'a decisive fraction of the working class'. The ideal form is a reservoir of foreign workers, in classical Marxist terms constituting a 'reserve army' who, outside of organized labour, can be used against it. Because of the vulnerable legal–political status accorded to migrant workers, together with intense racism found everywhere in Europe, it is possible for employers to treat migrant workers as individual wage-earners whereas it is forced to deal with the indigenous working class collectively through the organized labour movement. As explained by Castells in his seminal paper (1975: 52), 'the utility of immigrant labour to capital derives primarily from the fact that it can act towards it as though the labour movement did not exist . . . a twenty-first century capital and nineteenth century proletariat'.

Castells points out that since foreign workers are commonly concentrated in key industries their significance for the economies of Western Europe are even greater than is suggested by the mere size of foreign populations. Thus, for instance, in 1972, while foreign workers represented 10.8 per cent of all wage-earners in Germany, they constituted 25 per cent of workers in building and public works. In France they represented 27 per cent of all such workers, rising to 90 per cent on building sites in the Paris region. Significantly, there were over half a million 'foreign' workers in the automobile industry. Similarly, 40 per cent of all workers in Swiss factories were foreign. In Belgium in the 1970s they were concentrated in the mining, building and metallurgic industries. From these and other similar data Castells (1975: 38–9) concludes that 'immigrant labour is thus a fundamental element in the economic structure of European capitalism and not simply an extra source of labour in conditions of rapid growth'.

To suggest that it was the post-war economic recovery and boom which attracted these immigrants to Europe is, as Castells (1975: 36) further argues 'completely tautological, since migrant labour is in fact one of the motors of this growth, rather than simply a result'. In these terms foreign workers are clearly central rather than, as is sometimes supposed, marginal to European labour markets. The centrality of their role, and the scale of their contribution in ensuring post-war prosperity, needs to be unequivocally acknowledged by both the EU and the governments of the member states.

MIGRANT LABOUR

After 1945 during the period of post-war reconstruction in Europe, the migration of foreign workers to the industrialized West occurred on a massive scale. An estimated 30 million migrant workers and their dependants entered Western Europe between 1945 and 1973, when the first wave of migration ceased. Britain, and to a lesser extent France and the Netherlands, drew labour from their colonies and former colonies. These workers generally had rights of settlement, family reunion, and most, if not always in practice all, civil, social, and political rights of citizenship enjoyed by native-born populations. Most colonial immigrants intended to settle permanently in Europe. On the other hand, migrants, or guest workers as they were often euphemistically known, were recruited as a temporary workforce without rights of entry, work, or settlement in the receiving countries. They were expected to leave after completion of their work contracts to be replaced on a rotation basis by other temporary workers. Most were single, and were not entitled to family reunion or permanent settlement. However, since the 1970s the difference between immigrants and migrant workers has been considerably eroded. Thus, for instance, in Britain, former colonial migrants have lost the right of entry and settlement, while migrant workers in Western Europe have generally acquired many of these rights. But full citizenship rights are all too often denied, most notably in Germany where the German-born children of migrant workers are regarded as foreigners.

The savings in social costs from the importation of 'ready made' workers has also been quite considerable, constituting in effect a subsidy paid by the underdeveloped world to Europe. It was healthy, fit young adults, educated and trained in their home countries who were commonly recruited for work in Europe. Accommodated with minimum cost to the host country, sometimes in appalling conditions in hostels or multi-occupied slums, typically having to share cooking and washing facilities and, in some instances, even beds. In short, through the importation of migrant workers Europe planned largely to avoid the costs of reproducing the labour power of substantial sections of its workforce. Although only expected to remain in Europe on a temporary basis, migrants were increasingly joined by their families and, through the 1960s, permanent settlements were established in virtually all the major industrial and commercial centres of Western Europe, where their living and working conditions were characterized by discrimination and disadvantage.

However, the welfare needs of Europe's new ethnic minorities were only reluctantly, if at all, encompassed within welfare state provision. Thus, Ward (1975: 29) quotes a 1970s report (*Der Spiegel*, 19 October 1970) which suggests that 'an astonishingly high percentage of migratory workers' children – 20 to 50 per cent in West Germany – do not attend school at all'. In addition, as Leitner (1987: 79) notes, German policy creates obstacles which make 'the complete reunion of foreign workers' families difficult, expensive and risky'. She quotes a 1984 survey which estimates that at least 274,000 children who were eligible for family reunion were still living in sending countries.

It is not only a matter of citizenship rights or lack of them, for these, even if achieved, do not always translate into welfare benefits in practice. Thus, the Roma, or gypsies, who after 500 years in Europe surely by now are native Europeans, are still largely excluded from European society. This situation continues even though, as Fraser (1992: 309) states, in Europe 'sedentary Gypsies are now in the majority'. Hawes and Perez (1995) estimate that only between 30 and 40 per cent of gypsy children in the European Union attend school with any regularity; over half have never attended school and only a tiny percentage ever get into secondary education. Much of the neo-fascist violence directed against immigrants and refugees has been targeted on Eastern European gypsies fleeing to the West.

In Britain immigrants from the Commonwealth who entered before the 1971 Immigration Act, and were entitled to full citizenship rights, have in practice found that these were often curtailed. The experience of migrant workers in this period cannot simply be reduced to the workings of the 'invisible hand' of the labour market. Discrimination was a key factor. Research for the Political and Economic Planning broadsheet series in 1966–7 (PEP 1968), carried out before employment discrimination on the basis of 'race' was outlawed in Britain in 1968, showed that minority ethnic workers were steered away from the more desirable jobs. It revealed processes pushing and restricting them to the bottom of the jobs ladder.

Migrant workers, especially black women, made a significant contribution to the British National Health Service. They were recruited to fill a shortfall of indigenous labour, due chiefly to the low wages paid to Health Service workers and the subsequent competition from the private sector which offered more attractive pay and conditions. The employment of migrant labour enabled wages to be held at low levels, thus minimizing the drain of resources into the National Health Service, which has provided an important element in the continuing reproduction of the labour force. If costs are kept to a minimum, the drain on resources is also minimized. A source of labour was required which would be receptive to low-paid servile work. For Ramdin (1987: 310), for instance, black women were especially suited to this servile role, for nursing has not only traditionally been the function of women in their domestic labour of caring for men and their children but black women in particular have been associated with service work during slavery and colonialism. Likewise, the Black Women's Group in Britain observe that:

> The relationship between black women and nursing, of other people's children and other people's husbands and wives, dates from before any National Health Service ... in the head of the black nurse from the Caribbean is the echo of slavery: in the head of the Asian nurse is the servitude to Sahib and Memsahib.
>
> (Black Women's Group 1974: 226)

Many migrant women in the Health Service were subject to exclusionary processes which maintained their disadvantage. Some were channelled to the bottom of the nursing hierarchy where they served as cheap labour. Some were steered into lower grade training. Others were channelled into less popular specialities and less prestigious training schools. Such discrimination goes a long way to explain why in Britain migrant workers found themselves located and trapped at the bottom of the jobs ladder. The implications were profound. As the House of Commons Home Affairs Committee noted in 1981, 'Disadvantage in employment leads to many other disadvantages, because in our society the job that someone has determines or influences so many other things' (House of Commons 1981). Quality of housing, standard of health, enjoyment of leisure activities, and indirectly the educational opportunities of children are all dependent upon employment opportunities. It was argued that this set in motion a 'cycle of cumulative disadvantage' (House of Commons 1975: para. 11) whereby the disadvantage of the first generation inhibited the opportunities of the next.

A 'rising tide of racism' across Europe?: the 1980s and 1990s

The import of migrant labour laid down a legacy of tensions which now reverberate across Europe. One of the most extreme legacies has been the incidence of racist violence against migrants and their descendants, particularly directed at the visible minorities. Such violence has characterized Europe for centuries. But there has been a strong belief that the late 1980s and early 1990s have been characterized by a period of escalating violence, indicative of a rise of 'racism'. The Commission of the European Communities, for instance, observed in 1992 that, 'Nearly all countries report increased numbers of racist incidents and attacks on foreigners and individuals belonging to ethnic, racial or linguistic minorities' (CEC 1992: 7).

Despite these claims, however, we must be circumspect about the alleged rise in racist violence. As Miles (1994: 554) warns, a rise in incidents of racist violence recorded in official statistics might not simply represent an actual increase in violence, as they might also represent a greater willingness on the part of victims to report incidents. They may even represent a greater willingness by the authorities to record incidents. In the same way we must be circumspect about the 'rise of racism' across Europe, for as Miles argues, there is 'no unitary, homogeneous "rise of racism" throughout Europe: rather, there is very considerable uneven development, and explanation must retain a reference to national specificity' (Miles 1994: 552).

The 'national specificity' of racism and racist violence is evident by comparing Germany and Britain in the late 1980s and early 1990s. In Germany, according to the Commission of the European Communities, there was a tenfold increase in the number of racist attacks between 1990 and 1991, and in the month of October alone 900 attacks were recorded (CEC 1992: 9). The Commission noted that the Turkish population 'bears the brunt' of racist violence, a strong degree of anti-Semitism persists, and other groups such as the Sinti and Roma community (the gypsies) are also subject to discrimination and harassment. Extreme right-wing groups have additionally been linked to at least some of the violence (European Parliament 1990: 53–4). The racist attacks in Germany during this period occurred in the context of rapidly increasing migration; by the late 1980s and early 1990s Germany had again become the foremost country of immigration in Europe. Following the collapse of communism, Germans from the former DDR, Poland, Romania and the Soviet Union began to move west. Applications for asylum from Eastern Europe increased. In a unification boom in 1990 and 1991, West German industry once again needed additional labour supplies. Migrants from Turkey and elsewhere entered Germany on the basis of family unification. Short-term labour schemes – especially in the construction industry – were established for workers from Poland, Czechoslovakia, and other Eastern countries. All told, in 1989 and 1990, migrants numbered approximately one million each year (Thränhardt 1995).

Repercussions emerged when the new immigrants were seen to be given priority treatment for public housing. But a *de facto* quota system has operated in Germany since 1993 and government-sponsored campaigns emphasizing the German origin of many of the migrants appeared to dissolve the fermenting discontent. This was not the case, though, for the increasing numbers of asylum seekers and refugees. The backlog of asylum applications grew as the bureaucracy became even more protracted. In elections the 'race-card' was allegedly played by government against opposition. As Thränhardt observes,

> [it] created an explosive situation, particularly in East Germany, where the people were unprepared for such a sudden inflow of strangers. Administrative negligence led to large groups of refugees being left in a central area of Rostock and caused more hysteria. The first violent riots occurred in the East, and subsequently spread to West Germany. Skinhead gangs took to the streets, and the resulting wave of violence spanned three years, coinciding with the media and leading government party's campaigns on the issue and only dying down approximately a year after the campaign ended.
>
> (Thränhardt 1995: 32)

In Britain racist attacks persisted – and some believe increased – without the huge inflow of migrants or a rise in asylum applications of the magnitude experienced in Germany. Certainly, on the basis of official statistics the number of racist attacks increased. But as data were not collected prior to 1981 – when there was arguably the first government recognition of the problem of racist violence – it is impossible to confirm the increase. Britain has a long history of racist violence, including serious race riots in 1919 in Cardiff, Liverpool and elsewhere; fascist violence in the East End of London during the 1930s; and race riots in Notting Hill and Nottingham in 1958. Police records in England and Wales in the late 1980s, though, represented a rise of racist incidents. They almost doubled between 1989 and 1993 from 4,682 to 8,700 incidents (*The Runnymede Bulletin*, 7 April 1994). They included at least three deaths of black teenagers. In 1993 alone, there was a 13 per cent rise in racist incidents compared to the previous year, and in one incident an 18-year-old black teenager – Stephen Lawrence – was stabbed and killed in a street attack (*Observer*, 16 May 1993). Anti-racist campaigners believe that the apparently increasing number of racist attacks has been encouraged by the activities of the far-right British National Party, a view supported by the House of Commons Home Affairs Committee which concluded that such organizations are 'creating an atmosphere of hatred' (House of Commons 1994: para. 69, xxv). In the Isle of Dogs in London, where the British National Party won their first local council seat in 1993, there was subsequently a rise of nearly 300 per cent in the number of racist incidents recorded by the police.

RACIST VIOLENCE

In its narrowest sense the term 'racist violence' refers to physical attacks against persons, which are motivated by a hostility towards their ascribed ethnic or 'racial' characteristics. In a broader sense racist violence may be conceptualized as any display of hostility against persons because of their ascribed ethnic or 'racial' characteristics. This broader conceptualization would include acts of physical violence and other acts of harassment and intimidation, such as verbal abuse, damage to property, graffiti, and threats of physical attack.

But the number of reported incidents in Britain – as in other European countries – severely understates the real extent of racist violence. Even the British Home Office has estimated – on the basis of the British Crime Survey (Aye Maung and Mirrlees Black 1994) – that there could have been as many as 130,000 racist incidents in 1991. Notably, their research concluded, though, that there was no 'firm evidence' despite the police statistics of an increase in racially motivated incidents overall experienced by Britain's black and Asian minority ethnic groups.

In France there was also an escalation in racist violence in 1989, in the view of the European Commission, when 2,237 incidents were reported (CEC 1992: 7). The Commission observed that the majority of victims have been of North African origin. But anti-Semitism has again surfaced, and one of the most notorious recent incidents occurred on the 9th and 10th of May 1990 in Carpentras where Jewish tombstones were desecrated and a corpse disinterred and mutilated. As in Germany, extreme right-wing groups have orchestrated some of the violence, including members of the extreme-right police union Fédération Professionnelle Indépendante de la Police (European Parliament 1990: 56–60).

In other European countries the extent of racist violence has also seemingly been on the increase, although again caution must be exercised about the data. A wave of racist violence spread across Italy in February and March 1990, including the fire-bombing of immigrant reception centres (European Parliament 1990: 61). In Denmark attacks against immigrants and refugees escalated in 1985 and 1986 accompanying the arrival of an increasing number of asylum seekers (European Parliament 1990: 50).

The racist violence across Europe in the 1980s and 1990s occurred in the context of a growing articulation of cultural racism which has superseded the pseudo-scientific racism formulated in the mid-nineteenth century, which reached its zenith in the Holocaust but was discredited after 1945 with the defeat of the Nazi regime. This supposed 'new' racism (Barker 1981) has been characterized by the reduction of 'race' to culture, and the boundaries of cultures equated with national boundaries. Cultural racism has provided the axis for both the intermittent emergence of historical animosities between European nation-states, and for 'racial' animosity within states. Migrant workers and their descendants have been regarded by some as illegitimate competitors for the share of jobs, income, housing, welfare, and in general the standard of living enjoyed by white European workers. In Britain, for instance, the distinctiveness of African, Caribbean, and Asian cultures has been regarded by some as an alien presence which must be restricted and controlled because of the assumed threat of cultural dilution. Black and Asian cultures and 'British-ness' have been seen as being incompatible (Gilroy 1987: 45–6). There was similarly an upsurge in cultural racism in Germany in political, academic, and media circles in the early 1980s. As Thränhardt observed:

> Quality newspapers, conservative as well as liberal ones, printed academic articles arguing for the 'repatriation of all non-central Europeans' or 'Asians' . . . They argued that people with different cultural or regional backgrounds could not live together . . . The tabloids paralleled the anti-Turkish sentiments in the established media. Their sensational reports about Turks especially stressed crime, exoticism, and cultural difference.
>
> (Thränhardt 1995: 27)

Barnor Hesse has recently added a further dimension to culture-based theories of racial hostility by conceptualizing racism as 'spacism'. He argues that racist violence and harassment involve:

> a civil and political struggle over the spatial dominance and representation of British identity as white identity . . . If we take the question of racial harassment seriously as a pattern, what you begin to see when some people say, 'Our country is being swamped' or 'go back to your own country', is a struggle among everyday people in the spaces that surround and define them; the areas, regions, locations, designations which constitute Britain
>
> (Hesse 1993: 15)

Racist violence and harassment might therefore be regarded as a struggle over territory, and not just the spatial dimension, but also the material and ideological resources that constitute that territory.

European policy

Over the last three decades there has been a growing convergence of policy in European Union member states affecting migrant workers, their descendants, and minority ethnic groups in general. Potential immigrants have faced increasingly restrictive immigration controls (Hammar 1984). In the same period, by the 1980s, most member states had enacted liberal equal opportunities legislation outlawing 'race' discrimination. But as Solomos has argued in the case of the British Race Relations Acts, for instance, their enactment was 'based as much on

> **CULTURAL RACISM**
>
> The term 'cultural racism' is used above to refer to the antipathy directed against persons on the basis of their ascribed cultural characteristics. Such characteristics may be the same as, or may transcend, social group boundaries associated with ethnicity and nationality. Cultural racism is a process whereby persons who see themselves as belonging to a locality, neighbourhood, city, region, or nation-state, classify others as outsiders on the basis of cultural difference. The outsiders are seen to pose a threat to the way of life, identity, and culture of those persons who believe that only they legitimately belong in the neighbourhood, city, region, or nation-state.

political expediency as on any commitment to justice and equality' (Solomos 1989: 68). From this view, therefore, the Acts have been expeditiously used to manage potential social conflict arising from 'the negative response of the majority white population to the competition of black workers in the housing and labour markets' and 'the frustration of black workers who felt themselves excluded from equal participation in British society' (Solomos 1989: 71).

By the early 1990s four countries – France, Britain, the Netherlands, and Germany – stood out from the rest of Europe in terms of the scope of their measures (Forbes and Mead 1992: 71). But the anti-discrimination measures are to a large extent ineffectual. A common limitation is presented by the difficulty for victims of discrimination in actually realizing that discrimination has occurred in the first place, and then producing evidence. The experience of 'race' discrimination in Britain demonstrates the point. Experimental tests between the late 1960s and mid-1980s using bogus job applications have provided firm evidence of substantial direct discrimination, despite the enactment of the Race Relations Acts.

The European Union has been characterized by a singular lack of action on 'race' discrimination and racist violence, in marked contrast, for instance, to its initiatives for gender equality. There have as yet been no Directives requiring member states to harmonize their 'race' discrimination legislation, or to establish legislation outlawing racist violence and harassment. Policy intervention has largely been at the level of rhetoric.

One of the strongest measures was the adoption of a Joint Declaration against Racism and Xenophobia in June 1986. It 'vigorously' condemns 'all forms of intolerance, hostility and use of force against persons or groups of persons on grounds of racial, religious, cultural, social or national differences' (CEC 1992: 83). But the impact of the Declaration has been limited. It has no binding force, as it is a 'declaration of principle' only and not a recipe for policy intervention. The European Parliament's Consultative Commission on Racism and Xenophobia (1995) has recently made comprehensive policy proposals for action by European Parliament institutions and member states, involving a holistic policy approach to racist violence and harassment in the areas of education, employment, and criminal justice. But without a requirement for action, they too will remain at the level of rhetoric.

Even worse, for some commentators, the establishment of the Single European Market, with the strengthening of external frontiers, both reflects and will potentially exacerbate racism and xenophobia within Europe. As Gordon argues:

> it will fuel hostility towards black people already in the EC by conveying the message that black people and other Third World people are a problem, on a par with drug smuggling, terrorism and rabies, with which they are frequently grouped in official statements and discussions. They are a problem which must be kept out and against which the combined forces of EC states must be mobilized. Black people, refugees and others – deemed not only not to be European but probably also illegal immigrants – will find their security, already precarious, increasingly threatened.
>
> (Gordon 1989: 26)

Gordon's predictions do not seem overly pessimistic when seen within the wider context of ethnic conflicts in the former Yugoslavia, Chechnia and elsewhere in Eastern Europe. The UN's and EU's intervention in Bosnia, albeit largely ineffectual, was, it seems, motivated as much by military and strategic objectives to confine the conflict to the Balkans, and, by the desire to stem the flow of refugees to the West, as it was by humanitarian concerns to halt the bloodshed. Clearly, it is the exclusive, racist ideology of 'one nation, one state', embodied in the brutal *de facto* creation of 'Greater Serbia', which has been allowed to triumph. In the process, the prime casualty has been the liberal ideal of a democratic, secular and multicultural state in Bosnia. So the twentieth century ends in Europe almost as it began: with the rise of extreme right-wing nationalism.

Summary

- Migrant workers have been central to the growth of capital.
- The use of migrant labour has generated tensions within European working classes, manifest in the most extreme form by racist violence.
- Racist violence appears to be escalating.
- There has been an inadequate policy response, especially by the European Union.

Further reading

Robin Cohen (1994) *Frontiers of Identity: The British and the Other*, London: Longman. This original work shows how British identity has been shaped, defined, and redefined, by interaction with peoples defined as the 'other'.

Robert Miles (1993) *Racism after 'Race Relations'*, London: Routledge. This book evaluates shifting definitions of the concept of racism in relation to the history of nation formation in Europe.

John Wrench and John Solomos (1993) *Racism and Migration in Western Europe*, Oxford: Berg. This edited collection presents a critical analysis of the links between racism and migration, contributed by some of the leading authorities in the field.

Chapter 8

Winners and losers: young people in Europe

Keith Popple and Ron Kirby

Introduction	162
Young people in history	162
Europeanization?	163
Youth and inequality in Britain	165
Youth and inequality in the rest of Europe	166
Cultural responses	167
Young people, nationalism and racism	169
Reflection	171
Summary	172
Further reading	172

Key concepts

- Europeanization and young people
- Youth and inequality
- Youth culture
- Young people, nationalism and racism

Introduction

The purpose of this chapter is to consider and analyse the different trends effecting young people in Europe, with particular focus on British young people. After a brief historical consideration of young people we will be examining what it is to be a young person in contemporary Europe. What are the advantages and disadvantages of being young and European? For example, a young educated multi-lingual European has opportunities of working and studying in different countries in the Union and to travel and experience a number of cultures. On the downside the majority of young Europeans do not have such chances because they are not skilled in the employment that is in demand; or they lack the necessary qualifications to work outside their own country; or they cannot finance visits to regions outside their own. The central question we pose therefore is whether we are witnessing the creation of a two-tier Europe that will lead to different outcomes and different responses for young people. The evidence presented here leads one to believe that Europeanization is of benefit to a small number of young people, while many young Europeans are becoming increasingly alienated and disenchanted and are turning to ideologies that support nationalism and racism.

Young people in history

Youth has been a focus for attention, often negative, from the rest of society throughout history. For example, Plato, writing two thousand years ago, viewed youth as the political force most likely to challenge the status quo. In Elizabethan times, Shakespeare touched on another favourite theme when he declared that the young were more likely to be 'wronging the ancientry' and 'getting wenches with child' than doing anything useful (Coleman and Warren-Adanson 1992: 9). 'Youth as a threat' remains a consistent theme in the analysis of young people as Pearson notes in his 'history of respectable fears' which demonstrates how each generation sees itself as having most to fear from uncontrollable youth (Pearson 1983).

Whilst the idea of the 'generation gap' is as old as history, there is some debate in the literature over the degree to which present notions of youth as an essentially separate age category are products of industrialization. The French historian, Philippe Aries, writing on pre-industrial society in what Bruce Leslie describes as his path-breaking *Centuries of Childhood*, asserts that 'as soon as the child could live without the constant solicitude of his mother, his nanny, or his rocking chair, he belonged to adult society' (Leslie 1984: 49).

The theme of the 'generation gap' is picked up by Griffin when she states, 'Pre-industrial European societies made no clear distinction between childhood and other pre-adult phases of life. There was no concept of adolescence, nor any clear physiological boundary at puberty' (Griffin 1993: 12). The distinction is blurred, however, with groups like the French 'Abbayes de la Jeunesse' and the German Bruderschaften cited as examples of non-institutionalized youth (Leslie 1984). In Tudor England the period of 'youth' could be extended well into the twenties as young men wandered the land in search of a place in a limited economy. In the context of a short life expectation, youth represented a significant proportion of the male population.

Whilst industrialization itself did not mark a sharp break with previous perceptions of youth, in time with the gradual decline in child labour, and the lengthening of periods of education, the idea of 'adolescence' was created. The idea of adolescence as a special stage of development was introduced by the American writer G. Stanley Hall and, as the historian J. Springhall (1983) suggests, owes much to the context of America in the 1890s. Hall contrasted what he perceived as the degeneration of modern, urban industrial society with an idealized version of an earlier, rural, simpler and purer American society. Hall must take some responsibility for constructing the myth of adolescent 'storm and stress'. As Coleman outlines, the theme of 'storm or stress' has tended to dominate both psychoanalytical and sociological accounts of adolescent behaviour, but 'broadly speaking, research provides little support for these traditional theories' (Coleman and Warren-Adamson 1992: 16). The reality for the vast majority of contemporary young people is that they do not experience a crisis of identity and have a good relationship with their parents in a smooth transition to adulthood. This, of course, does not make headline news.

Europeanization?

Moving to contemporary concerns we note that the glossy output from the Office for Official Publications of the European Communities reveals an upbeat assessment of Community programmes for the young. Both the quantity and quality of the programmes receive plaudits. Achievements include the enhanced mobility of more than 25,000 students and the weaving of 'a whole fabric of networks linking universities, schools, firms and specialist training institutions ... throughout Europe' (O'Dwyer 1994: 14).The success of the 'first generation' of Community programmes has, it is claimed, broadened the horizons and increased the learning opportunities for young Europeans, 'giving them an opportunity of familiarizing themselves with Europe in all its diversity, learning to be tolerant and developing a sense of being part of a major endeavour' (from the European Union brochure, *A Young People's Europe* 1991).

The various European Community learning skills initiatives have spawned a range of acronyms: Erasmus, Commett, Lingua, Tempus, Eurotecnet, Force, Iris, Petra, Arion, and Youth for Europe. Thankfully, since 1995 these have been organized and developed under three headings: 'Socrates' for education, 'Leonardo' for training and 'Youth for Europe III'. The choice of these is significant in so far as the name 'Socrates' for an education programme denotes the fundamental aim of stimulating personal development, whilst that of 'Leonardo' for the vocational training programme highlights the role of training in both the artistic and technical domains, with the accent on creativity.

The popularity of schemes which encourage the mobility of young people is not in doubt. 'Erasmus', which is concerned with the inter-mobility of students, has made a significant impact in every subject and in more than two hundred institutions in the United Kingdom. Numbers of students involved in Erasmus increased by 70 per cent in Britain between 1991 and 1994, and 100,000 students were involved in 1993/4 according to *The Times Higher Education Supplement*. The vast majority of students involved in the scheme speak highly of their experience, describing it as 'the best way to learn a language'; 'the chance to study subjects from a European angle'; 'a fantastic opportunity to meet new people, to see different lifestyles and cultures ... to feel independent and self confident'; 'the chance to completely integrate into the language and culture of a country completely different from my own and to experience different styles of lecturing and education' (from *The Times Higher Education Supplement*).

Whilst the importance of the English language ensures that Britain is a highly popular destination for European students, the downside of the apparent euphoria surrounding this contact with Europe is that the numbers involved remain a very small proportion of the population of young people. Only 4–5 per cent of students in Britain were able to take advantage of schemes in 1993/4, and despite the increase in student numbers they remain a minority, relatively privileged group. For the majority of young people foreign travel may not be a possibility or, where it does occur, may simply reinforce existing prejudices. Mobility of itself does not increase understanding. The rejection of what is foreign and different is a deep-seated trait amongst some young people. This rejection starts at home, and in the British context has been encouraged by the individualist and protective philosophy of the Thatcherite 1980s. Such attitudes fit badly with a notion of an open and multicultural Europe. Genuine cultural exchange demands an inner readiness to accept the new, to examine ourselves in relation to others, to ask why and how we perceive things and how we form our opinions.

The Youth for Europe exchange programme and the 'Priority Actions in the Youth Field' are attempts to engage in intercultural youth work. This is especially true when they are not limited to a one-off youth exchange programme, but placed in a broader spectrum of youth work as a systematic preparation for intercultural contacts and active participation in the life of society. Young people on exchanges get to meet others of the same age and learn something of the culture of the other country. Exchanges can promote an openness to being part of a wider multicultural Europe. Encounters amongst young people from different countries often give rise to statements like this from a young Irish person at the end of a multilateral youth meeting with immigrants living in the United Kingdom, France and Germany.

> We have experienced what it means when others treat you like human beings. We've felt for the first time what a great feeling it is when you are treated with respect. And we'll do all we can to avoid contributing to discrimination against others through indifference.
>
> (Editorial in *Le Magazine* 1994: 6)

One of the aims of the Youth for Europe schemes has been to give priority access to young people who may be disadvantaged on social, economic or geographical grounds. Evidence from south-west Britain suggests that it is very difficult to meet such aims. Young people joining exchanges are recommended by full-time youth workers and this excludes many in rural areas where youth work, if it exists at all, is on a part-time basis. In France exchanges are only available to larger registered youth groups. The contraction of youth work provision in the British context makes it more difficult for youth workers to undertake the detailed and sensitive planning needed to take disadvantaged groups abroad.

Between 1988 and 1993, 160,000 young people and youth workers took part in the Youth for Europe programme. Out of a total of 70 million young people in the Community the figure does not sound so impressive. Youth for Europe III plans the expansion of these programmes, partly through improving the information base available. One strand in further development is to use youth exchanges as an instrument to overcome racism and xenophobia. But experience suggests such strategies need to be carefully thought through. One black young person from south-west England needed a police escort whilst on an exchange to Germany. This hardly encouraged others.

There is clearly a strong intent expressed by the new Community programmes to make the best aspects of international exchange available to a larger range of young people. One highly significant aspect of Socrates is the proposal to involve schools, making them the basis for exchange at the Community level. Such a move could widen the base and shift the balance between winners and losers. However, as we will now discover, young people as a social group in both Britain and the rest of Europe have been victims of the economic restructuring that has taken place in the last fifteen years. The outcome is that their position is one of disadvantage and inequality.

Youth and inequality in Britain

The most influential feature of recent and contemporary British economic, social and political life has been the influence of Thatcherite or New Right policies. Named after the British Conservative Prime Minister (1979–90) Margaret Thatcher, Thatcherism in Britain, which has parallels in the rest of Europe, has come to mean the primacy of wealth creation; the regulation of distribution through market mechanisms, accompanied by the notion of individual rather than public choice; redistribution based upon the theory of 'trickle down'; an attack on, and a restructuring of, large areas of public and private activity; an assault on the influence of the trade union movement; and the notion of poverty as being absolute as opposed to relative. In Britain however the Conservatives did not perform the economic miracle they promised and the rise of the New Right was accompanied by an economic recession borne disproportionately by the poor. Statistics for 1991/2 show that real disposable income – that is, cash left over after taxes, National Insurance and pension contributions – was almost 80 per cent higher than in 1971. However, the increasing wealth is far from evenly distributed. The share of income for the poorest fifth of the population has fallen from 10 per cent when the Conservatives took power in 1979, to 6 per cent in 1990/1. In contrast, the richest fifth of the population has increased its share of income from 35 per cent to 43 per cent (Central Statistical Office 1994).

The increasing divide between the rich and the poor in Britain has also been reflected in the unemployment rate. In March 1996 Britain's official unemployment rate stood at 2.2 million. However, it has been estimated by the Unemployment Unit that the thirty changes in the methods of counting unemployed people since 1979 have disguised a much higher figure of about one million more people (Unemployment Unit 1990). Unemployment is not random, however. People's age, gender, occupation and race are all features in the shaping of unemployment. For instance, in the years 1967 to 1989 the unemployment rate for young people from minority ethnic groups was almost double that for the young white population. Of the minority ethnic 16–24 age group, 21 per cent were unemployed compared with 12 per cent of whites of the same age. There are differences among minority ethnic groups, with 27 per cent of Pakistanis and Bangladeshis unemployed and 25 per cent from the West Indian/Guyanese group (Department of Employment 1991).

British young people in general have suffered a disproportionate level of social, economic and political inequality in the last fifteen years. As well as being affected by unemployment young people receive lower salaries compared to the rest of the population, with 18- to 20-year-olds earning only 53 per cent of average earnings. This compares with 61 per cent in 1979 (British Youth Council 1993). Furthermore, 16- and 17-year-olds are not automatically entitled to Income Support if unemployed. Those young people in receipt of Income Support find their benefits lower than older recipients. Unemployed people aged 25 and over receive 66 per cent more in Income Support than 16- and 17-year-olds and 26 per cent more than those aged 18–24. Similarly, homelessness among the young is increasing due to their declining ability to pay for rents, and the reducing stock of satisfactory accommodation (Hutson and Liddiard 1994).

Youth and inequality in the rest of Europe

The situation in the rest of Europe is mixed. Until the mid-1980s youth unemployment in nearly all European countries was very high. For example, in Spain the youth unemployment rate was 45 per cent and in Italy it was 34 per cent (OECD 1986). There are signs that the situation is improving in many, but not all, EU countries, with the overall unemployment rates still high. Together with Britain the countries with high youth unemployment rates are France, Portugal, Belgium, Italy, Spain and Greece, whereas Luxembourg, the Netherlands and the former West Germany have the lowest youth unemployment rates in the EU. Closer scrutiny of the data indicates that youth unemployment rates also vary across macro regions, with unemployment concentrated amongst those from disadvantaged backgrounds and from minority ethnic backgrounds.

The main response in all European countries to the high levels of youth unemployment has been an extension and reform of training opportunities for young people. The situation now is that young people are required or expected to extend their schooling and to undertake longer vocational courses. However, these increased rates of extended educational participation have coincided with cutbacks in public expenditure and social benefits and this has created different patterns of family units and dependence and independence between parents and their offspring. Historically families in Southern Europe have acted as the primary source of economic and social support for young people, whereas in Northern European countries, where their welfare states have become restructured, the family has regained its importance as an institution that assists the young.

Cultural responses

The changed socio-economic circumstances for young people in Britain has had a profound impact on their cultural life and, in turn, on academic approaches to the study of youth culture. The 1950s heralded a 'cult of youth' which identified and focused on youth as a special age. In a fast-growing economy young people were viewed, not least by media hype, as the new consumers and social trend-setters. Academics arguably fuelled this process by concentrating on the more exotic male youth sub-cultures (Mods, Rockers, Skinheads, etc.). Whilst some of the earlier youth cultural forms were portrayed as threatening, in the 1960s and early 1970s the idea of the 'counter-culture' was born stressing the notion of the positive energy of youth for change. To that extent the portrayal of youth in Britain has been a mirror of the national mood. Since the economic crisis of the 1970s, and with it the rise of a New Right philosophy, especially in its authoritarian form during the Thatcher administration, the image of youth has been largely negative and characterized by a series of moral panics. Thus the spotlight shifts from football hooligans to teenage pregnancy, joy riders, and ravers as each in turn gets picked up in the media glare.

One of the major strands of New Right thinking in Britain has been the celebration of the individual and the denigration of collective approaches. This phenomenon is not confined to Britain, as Gill Jones and Claire Wallace indicate in quoting the German sociologist Ulrich Beck's 'individualization thesis' (Jones and Wallace 1992: 15). Beck argues that there has been a fragmentation of the established structures of reproduction in society, in terms of education, work and family forms, and a breakdown of traditional institutions, with the result that individual roles are no longer clear. This fragmentation results in a world where individuals must compete to create the best situation for themselves. In doing so they turn their back on old class cultures and the traditional networks of the family. It is difficult to sustain an argument concerning the degree to which this is the case in Europe. As Chisholm suggests 'we cannot presently draw a comprehensive, useful and above all meaningful picture of young people's circumstances and orientations across the Community' (Chisholm 1993: 49). There is great diversity. In Greece, for example, housing policies and kinship networks lead to a radically different cultural environment for the young than that experienced in Britain or Germany (Chisholm 1993: 54).

Whilst young people in Britain have been subject to 'a new authoritarianism' which it could be argued is designed to control the consequences of the very processes Beck has described (Jeffs and Smith 1994), in other member states there has been a range of political responses (Chisholm 1993: 54). Other European nations have however experienced a period of intense cultural and economic change, and common themes do emerge. The retreat from the collective and the celebration of individualism is echoed in Jan Hazekamp's comments on the Netherlands:

> Young people are having to cope with a climate of individualism and the promotion of self. Collective organizations such as trade unions, churches, youth organizations and political parties hardly have influence now. Young people are not embedded in larger collectives and they do not share collective opinions. Moreover, politics is seen as irrelevant to young people's personal lives. This has led to what I consider to be a dangerous state of affairs where young people are prone to act negatively towards foreigners.
>
> (Popple 1993: 65)

Likewise, many of the themes that might apply to British young people can be found in Germany:

> Perhaps the major issue that exists in relation to young Germans is the lack of orientation. Changing family structures, together with dominant forces and an ideology of a society they do not subscribe to, has left young people feeling unconnected with German culture and life ... The ability to plan and calculate their lives seems to be out of the reach of many young people.
>
> (Popple 1993: 64)

Many young people in Europe would therefore appear to live in a 'risk society' (Giddens 1991: 28). Life becomes a constant calculation to better one's position, and the stakes are high as those on the edge are at risk. One response to the risk society is to seek solace in the comfort of the past, and in Britain in the 1990s nostalgia is rife and the heritage industry is booming. Thus a major part of youth culture takes the form of recycling that of the past.

> Platform shoes, flared trousers, love beads – they are all back with a vengeance. Abba is in and Abba-esque abounds! Top of the Pops features endless cover versions, re-releases and re-mixes, with new bands desperately turning out old songs in an attempt to achieve popularity and success. Who would have imagined a cover version of a Barry Manilow song would be the trendy hip sound of 1993?!!
>
> (Johnston 1993: 70)

Laura Johnston, in examining what she calls 'Post-Punk Nostalgia' argues that the shift from collectivism to individualism and change in cultural mood brought about by the advent of Thatcherism has led to the current obsession with the past and the lack of vision and optimism that goes along with it (Johnston 1993: 70). Youth culture, always the subject of commercial exploitation, has like other areas of the arts become an eclectic re-vamp of the past. Acid House and Rave represent a collage of anything from 1960s beat to classical music. Rave, however, has its defenders, who believe it is something distinct from its youth cultural predecessors and has some very positive attributes (Merchant and MacDonald 1994). Rave, it is claimed, appeals to a wide range of young people and this appeal crosses the boundaries of class and race. Further, in contrast to much-cited earlier youth cultures, it is not essentially a masculine affair but 'the more egalitarian gender relations and lack of sexual threat at Raves make them virtually unique' (Merchant and MacDonald 1994: 16). The authors acknowledge, however, the limitations of Rave:

> Rave culture is essentially hedonistic: it is about fun and feeling good. It does not seek to change the status quo but to allow room for young people to enjoy dance music and to take drugs like Ecstasy.
> (Merchant and MacDonald 1994: 32)

'Thatcher's children', it could be argued, are a product of their times. In the 'risk' society you conform and seek a good time when you can. This is an essentially inward looking position and not a good embarkation point for the European project.

One specific concern that has evolved in the last few years is the development among certain sections of Europe's young people of virulent nationalism and racism. This is also described in Chapter 7, along with the broader ramifications of race and racism. The cult of the individual and the protecting of one's self has transcended to the level of communities and nations looking inwards and after themselves. Outsiders are viewed with suspicion and mistrust, particularly amongst those young people who are the losers in Europeanization. We now examine this worrying trend.

Young people, nationalism and racism

Firstly a brief note on nationalism, which is addressed more extensively in Chapters 3 and 21. Nationalism in Europe is not a new phenomenon, having developed during the seventeenth and eighteenth centuries as the Western European states emerged and consolidated themselves (see particularly Chapter 3). These new states created nationalism as a means of securing their political identity and power in fast-changing political and economic conditions. The socialists of this period hoped that nationalism would prove to be a temporary step on the way to internationalism. This was not to be the case and in both wartime and peacetime conditions during the twentieth century we have witnessed the powerful role of nationalism as a response by heterogeneous societies to feel a collective identity; to reflect a nation's economic interests; and to influence the relations with other nations. In recent years the growth of large-scale unemployment, the deterioration of living standards for the poorest members of society, and the increasing insecurities for countless other sectors within Europe have led to the harnessing, by both the New Right and far right groups, of nationalism and popular racism. This is well expressed by Ford:

> There is no doubt that the re-structuring of European industrial societies with its attendant social strains – de-industrialization, unemployment, the labour

movement's loss of its traditional working-class constituency – coupled with the collapse and de-stabilization of the former Communist bloc have created new anxieties whose profundity democracy has not yet fully grasped. One product has been a gravitational shift rightwards on a continental scale.

In the five short years since Evrigenis (the Final Report of the European Parliament's Committee of Inquiry into the Rise of Racism and Fascism in Europe), France and West Germany, in particular, have witnessed the spectacular re-habilitation of the extreme right and its appearance on the mainstream political stage, through exploitation of the deep-rooted social worries and via the legitimation of racism.

(Ford 1992: xii)

One of the major target groups for recruitment by the far right groups has been young people, particularly those most affected by the trend towards a modern Europe. In Britain, for example, there are three significant ultra-right-wing movements: the National Front, the British Movement, and the British National Party. Each movement has fostered racial hatred and violence and inspired fascist thuggery. The most prominent of these organizations is the British National Party (BNP), which is also active in the arena of local council elections.

Developing since the mid-1980s, the BNP has a national membership of around 2,000. This is supplemented by some 10,000 members and supporters of the skinhead Nazi 'Blood and Honour' group which is now under BNP control (Platt 1992). According to Ford (1992), the leaders of the increasingly active BNP have serious criminal convictions ranging from organizing illegal paramilitary groups, possession of firearms and the making of bombs, and a number of convictions centred on race relations and public order. The BNP sees the influencing of young people as one of its key roles, and much of its racist material is directed at school students and the unemployed. It has a strategy of 'educating' the young with a range of racist and anti-Semitic books and videos and audiotapes, which are sold through a book club and therefore avoid prosecution under the law. The BNP also publishes a monthly magazine called *Spearhead*, and *British Nationalist*, a monthly newspaper. Both are sold in public places, often where young people (particularly males) meet – for instance outside league football grounds on match days.

Like other racist and nationalistic movements the BNP has tapped into young people's fears and anxieties for their future. We have noted above the contemporary economic difficulties Britain is experiencing. These are likely to remain in the foreseeable future, and with young people continuing to face problems in obtaining worthwhile and well-paid employment they are increasingly likely to look for political explanations of their predicament. In the face of economic deprivation, and the failure of the mainstream political parties to respond effectively to the problem, the BNP provides a simple and apparently logical explanation. 'Get rid of the blacks and the Jews and you will be better off.' To quote Ray Hill, a fascist turned anti-fascist:

I became a fascist because the fascists got their first . . . It acts as a magnet to many rebellious and disaffected white youths who see everything they are interested in, from football matches to raves, criminalized by the state and derided by many in the middle class. The youth who join the fascist movement are as much victims of its ideology as those they persecute, because they are used by the middle-class leadership and will either end up in jail or with poisoned minds.

(Youngs 1994)

In September 1993 the BNP won its first-ever local council seat, only to lose it at the local elections in May 1994. Whether the BNP will have any further success in elections is uncertain. What we do know is that the BNP, with its 'rights for whites' slogan, has a strategy of targeting areas where poor whites perceive their communities as being 'taken over' by minority ethnic groups. In such a strategy the negative feelings of young people are harnessed and exploited.

To counter this trend two significant anti-racist groups have emerged in Britain. The Anti-Racist Alliance and the Anti-Nazi League are well supported by both black and white young people who take exception to the activity of racists. Both groups have been active in street demonstrations, organizing petitions, holding meetings and countering the propaganda distributed by the racists. This is a positive move and it is hoped that similar groups in the rest of Europe will have success at raising the profile of anti-racism.

Reflection

With particular reference to British youth, we have discussed the way in which European young people have experienced social change over the last fifteen years. The evidence we have presented is full of paradoxes. On the one hand the European movement has appeared to benefit a small minority of young people who are able to taste the life of studying and working in another European country. However the numbers involved are small, and the time most spend away from home is short. At the same time, the cultural responses of many young people to their increasing inequality is to be engaged in hedonistic movements or to wallow in the nostalgia of a previous 'golden age'. We have noted that the changes that are taking place across Europe are not uniform and the experience of its young people is not exactly the same. Nevertheless there is evidence that young people in the EU are spending longer in full-time education and/or in vocational training, which is having an impact upon family structures. The most worrying trend however is the increase in nationalism of the most reactionary kind. The fostering of racial hatred is a dangerous activity that threatens to damage the commitment to a harmonious Europe. The task is to ensure the gap between the winners and losers is reduced, and to implement measures to outlaw the menace of covert and overt discrimination against all European young people.

Summary

- Whilst a small minority of young Europeans have benefited directly from the European movement, the majority have not.
- The experiences of young people in Europe are not uniform; overall, however, there is evidence that young Europeans are spending longer in full-time education and/or vocational training.
- Cultural responses of many young people to their increasing inequality is to engage in hedonistic movements or wallow in the nostalgia of a previous 'golden age'.
- Increasing nationalism and racism among the young threatens a harmonious Europe.

Further reading

Alessandro Cavalli and Olivier Galland (eds) (1995) *Youth In Europe: Social Change in Western Europe*, London: Pinter. This edited book contains a range of useful, interesting and accessible articles by sociologists which address issues affecting young people in the United Kingdom, the Czech Republic, France, Germany, Italy, the Netherlands, and Spain. One of the most significant points made by the collection is the radical and relatively recent changes in the transition from adolescence to adulthood affecting young people in all the European countries studied.

Jan Hazekamp and Keith Popple (eds) (1997) *Racism in Europe: A Challenge for Youth Policy and Youth Work*, London: UCL Press. This timely work examines the rise of racism in Europe and its impact on young people in selected countries including the United Kingdom, Germany, the Netherlands, Belgium and Spain. The theme of the essays is to improve the understanding and awareness of racism and nationalism, while examining and comparing strategies and policies that affect young people. Its purpose is to examine the development of suitable and effective youth policy and youth work practice.

Chapter 9

Old age in Europe

George Giacinto Giarchi
and Pamela Abbott

Introduction	174
The severe demands made upon welfare provisions by the significant increase of older Europeans	175
Negative stereotypes of old age constructed in European history	177
Diminishing and contrasting living standards and patchy leisure pursuits of the retired in Europe	184
Reflection	196
Summary	197
Further reading	197

Key concepts

- 'Old age'
- Ageism
- The social construction of old age
- The regulation of the older body

Introduction

No continent has as high a proportion of older people as Europe (see UN 1991; Eurostat 1991; Giarchi 1996). Clearly the demographic impact will have implications for the state, for the household, and for older people throughout the Continent and not merely in the EU. The implications must also be set against the negative stereotypes of 'old age' that have developed over time in wider Europe and which persist today (Bytheway 1995). In addition the current problems and needs that older people are dealing with may also escalate, affecting their living standards and lifestyle. However, before proceeding with any discussion suggested by these points, four key interrelated concepts need to be examined because they are central and pivotal to any analysis of the ageing experience in contemporary Europe.

'Old age'

When is somebody old? 'Old age' is an imprecise term and is highly subjective. 'To be old' has more to do with people's perceptions than with the state of our arteries, or the healthy functioning of the brain or how sound our heart might be. The ageing process and the social construction of ageing are interrelated. Chronological age is often used in society to exclude or include people from activities or benefits. For example, 'under-age drinking', the 'age of consent' and 'retirement age' are well-known examples. However, the cut-off point and determinant of maturity and ability are not primarily age-related. Stage of development and achievement, not age, is what really counts. In Western society 'old' is also a pejorative term, which will shortly be further explored.

Ageism

Ageism is being biased against others and behaving negatively towards them on the grounds of age, either regarding them as either too young or too old. Here, in this chapter, we are dealing with adopting, conserving and passing on to others negative and stereotypical images about being old. The retired person may therefore be regarded as 'past it' or 'on the shelf'. Prejudice (which really means to pre-judge) builds up distorted images of the aged by means of negative stereotypes, which label and stigmatize the older people in society. 'Being old' is also described as a 'jeopardy', meaning that it puts the older person in danger of being discriminated against. When the older person is also a black woman, she may be described as having to cope with 'triple jeopardy' – not only ageism, but sexism and racism (see Norman 1985).

The social construction of 'old age'

The regard persons have of older people is determined by the way they construct 'being old' in their minds, and this determines attitudes towards older people. Attitudes are determined by our perceptions. But where do they come from? Social perceptions are primarily based upon salient views established over the years in particular societies, which greatly condition people's definition of reality (see Berger and Luckmann 1967). Ageing is not only a *natural* process, it is also a *social* process. By this we mean that because of age older people's way of life and the way they are treated is largely determined by *social* expectations. For example, they are told 'to act their age'. The conformity to societal attitudes is established by societal constructs, and has a long European history, as this chapter will demonstrate. On the basis of these observations, this text does not use the term 'old', instead it refers to 'older people', which is in keeping with the preference of Europeans themselves (Walker 1993; Walker and Maltby 1996).

The regulation of the older body

Just as 'old age' is a construct in the mind, so too are older bodies. Ageism leads not only to negative behaviour, it also engenders pejorative ways of viewing and treating older bodies (see Turner 1992; Featherstone and Wernick 1995). The weaker the group is in society, the more it is exposed to control and bureaucracy. Exclusion and marginalization of older bodies are established by regulations, which could constitute legal, medical and welfare modes of control, as this chapter will show.

Keeping these concepts and notions in mind, the following concerns will be discussed. Older Europeans have mixed experiences because of three challenging factors:

1   the severe demands made upon welfare provisions by the significant demographic increase in their numbers;
2   the negative stereotypes constructed of 'old age' within the Continent, which have persisted throughout the development of European society; and
3   diminishing and contrasting living standards and patchy leisure pursuits.

The severe demands made upon welfare provisions by the significant increase of older Europeans

Table 9.1 presents the comparative proportions of older people in most of Europe and the predicted increases. Predictions for the new nations are not available. UN predictions (1994) have indicated that in 2025 the proportion of the populations made up of older Europeans (65+) will probably be 19.8 per cent, whereas that of the world will be 9.8 per cent, that of Africa 4.2 per cent, that of Asia 9.3 per cent, that of Latin America 9.7 per cent, and that of Oceania 13.7 per

TABLE 9.1 The ranked proportions of older people (65+) in Europe for 1993, and the projected proportions for 2025

Country	1993 (%)	Country	2025 (est. %)	% differences 1993–2025
Sweden	18.6	Italy	25.1	9.2
Norway	16.1	Greece	23.9	9.1
Italy	15.9	Germany	22.9	7.8
UK	15.8	Spain	22.6	9.3
Denmark	15.5	Switzerland	22.4	7.4
Belgium	15.5	Netherlands	22.2	9.4
Germany	15.1	Norway	22.0	5.9
Switzerland	15.0	Austria	21.3	6.4
Austria	14.9	France	21.3	6.7
Greece	14.8	Sweden	21.2	2.6
France	14.6	Luxembourg	21.2	7.5
Hungary	13.9	Finland	21.2	8.0
Bulgaria	13.9	Denmark	20.9	5.4
Luxembourg	13.7	Slovenia	20.1	8.3
Spain	13.3	Portugal	19.4	6.3
Finland	13.2	Croatia	19.2	7.5
Portugal	13.1	UK	19.0	3.2
Latvia	13.1	Malta	19.0	8.4
Czech Republic	12.9	Russian Federation	18.0	7.2
Netherlands	12.8	Estonia	17.8	5.0
Estonia	12.8	Bosnia-Hercegovina	17.6	10.7
Ukraine	12.3	Ukraine	17.6	5.3
Slovenia	11.8	Belgium	17.5	2.0
Croatia	11.7	Hungary	17.5	3.6
Romania	11.6	Latvia	17.3	4.2
Ireland	11.3	Romania	17.1	5.5
Lithuania	11.2	Belarus	17.1	6.0
Belarus	11.1	Iceland	16.6	5.7
Iceland	10.9	Ireland	16.5	5.2
Russia	10.8	Poland	16.4	5.7
Poland	10.7	Cyprus	16.3	6.3
Malta	10.6	Lithuania	16.1	4.9
Slovakia	10.5	Czech Republic	15.9	3.0
Cyprus	10.0	Slovakia	14.9	4.4
Bosnia-Hercegovina	6.9	Bulgaria	12.0	−1.9
Albania	5.4	Albania	9.8	4.4
Turkey	4.4	Turkey	9.2	4.8

Sources: CPA (1989), Eurostat (1995), UN (1994)*

* The UN projection (1994) does not include the statistics for Moldova, Liechtenstein and Macedonia.

Note: With the sole exception of Bulgaria, all European countries will have significant increases in the proportions of older people. The greatest changes in the proportions of older people will particularly affect Bosnia-Hercegovina (10.7%), Spain (9.3%), Italy (9.3%) and Greece (9.1%).

cent. In addition, life expectancy in Europe, currently at 73 years and at least 77 by the year 2025, contrasts with that of all the major world societies (see CPA 1989: 2–3). Never in the history of the world have there been so many older Europeans.

It is true that older people are now fitter and healthier and are an asset in society, but they also have needs and social and health problems. Older Europeans occupy a disproportionate number of beds and places in institutions. On the basis of present needs a modest conservative estimate indicates that at least a 5–10 per cent dependent population will exist in the next fifty years in Europe. With the rise in extended lives there will be a corresponding rise in terms of need, although breakthroughs in care and cure could cut down the numbers in need. There is also financial need. In fact medical breakthroughs may add to the costs of cure and so may also add to the problems for significant numbers of poorer older Europeans. Some will probably have one of the dementias, or other life-limiting disorders or chronic conditions that statistically occur in the over-eighties especially. For example, by the turn of the century it is expected that about a million older people in the UK alone may suffer from Alzheimer's Disease (see Jones and Miesen 1992; Woods 1989). Without being alarmist, given the significant increase of the over-eighties the costs are expected to be enormous in terms of formal and informal care and the increasing costs of living, leisure, social and health care.

Inequalities in income will affect the lives of older people – that factor will not go away in a capitalist Europe. Recessions and set-backs arise. Europe is made up of poorer and richer nations, and the fate of older people is inextricably tied to such economies. For example, as can be seen from Table 9.1, the Western European demographies contrast with those of the former Eastern Bloc countries. The contrast is especially significant with regard to mortality and morbidity. Laczko (1994: 34–41) points out that in Hungary only 61 per cent, and in Poland 63 per cent, reach 65. Between 1970 and 1985 the death rate for middle-aged men decreased in Western Europe by 25 per cent, whereas that of their counterparts increased by 25 per cent in Poland, Hungary and the former Czechoslovakia. In Poland, the crude disability rate rose from fifty-five to eighty per 1,000 persons, the majority being people over 60 (see Laczko 1994: 35).

The concern is not only for the increase in the demands of the well-established populations, but also for an increase in services for the growing numbers of mobile populations in a Europe without frontiers, of which further mention will be made later (see pp. 182–4). Given the new challenge to the welfare, health and social systems, how prepared is Europe to meet the increased demands of the older Euro-society? As the next section will show an ancient, persistent and intractable ageism may get in the way of a fair deal for European older people, especially when resources are scarce or too expensive.

Negative stereotypes of old age constructed in European history

Stereotypical notions about ageing create prejudices and distortions which are referred to as 'ageism' (McEwan 1990; Bytheway 1995). The resultant modes of discrimination and regulation go back centuries. The past is in the present and long histories of established biases seldom abate, usually endure and often increase.

Ageism in pre-industrial Europe

Ageism goes back to Greece, which has often been described as the cradle of European civilization. By the fifth century BC, all older people were eliminated from the halls of power in Athens. The elderly (along with women who did not have a vote) were later to have little sway or say within the constitution. Although there was a counter-reaction, when Plutarch (AD 125) extolled the merits of being older, by the year 200 BC ageism had taken root within European civilization everywhere.

In the mythology of the Hellenist culture, all the wicked Olympian gods were represented as having older bodies and most of the good and the popular ones had younger bodies. Minois (1987: 44) refers to the ancient temple to 'old age' in Athens, where longevity was depicted as an aged female body dressed in black, leaning on a stick by a water clock that had almost run dry. In the ancient Homeric epics, the elders were often described as nothing more than over-garrulous advisers. Homer's Aphrodite declares, 'The gods hate old age.' Homer later refers to the 'accursed threshold of old age'. In addition, the ancient writers refer to the ugliness of old bodies, the rejection, the uselessness, the boring talk, and the decrepitude associated with being old. Indeed, 'old age' was the final curse of the gods visited upon lonesome people.

Hippocrates referred to the seasons of life in which old age was depicted as the winter of life and youth as the summer. Plato's idealist positive remarks in the *Republic*, about being aged, were to be eclipsed by the morbid ageist ideas put forward by Aristotle, whose influence dominated pre-modern Europe.

Roman civilization was to take up where Greece left off. The negative Graeco-Latin constructs of 'old age' and of crippled older frail bodies were to be widely disseminated throughout most of Europe for more than eight centuries (Minois 1987: 77). Later, the influential Galen, born in Greece but a Roman citizen by adoption, the founder of medicine in Europe, held out no hope for the older organism in his *Gerocomica* (de Beauvoir 1977: 22). There is evidence that the Romans probably drowned their unwanted elders, throwing them from the bridges of the Tiber: they were sent '*ad pontem*' (de Beauvoir 1977: 127). The Roman plays and literature ridiculed the older women in particular, often describing them as 'bawds' (see de Beauvoir 1977: 129–32). The positive views of ageing by Cicero's *De Senectute* and of Seneca's defence of older people were nullified by the contrary views expressed by Pliny, Horace, Ovid, and Juvenal, and by the satirical poets and later comic authors.

In the early Middle Ages, known as the Dark Ages, the young warrior was eulogized and older people were regarded as the obsolete fighters. During these years 'old age' was often presented as an image of sin (Minois 1987: 118–20), or a curse and a punishment (Minois 1987: 120–3), or as a state of sinfulness and the hotbed of vice (Minois 1987: 123–8).

The Christian writers, under the cultural influences of the Graeco-Roman world, departed from the earlier Middle East biblical reverence shown older people and were generally as critical of older people as their contemporary unbelievers. Minois (1987: 128) sums up the situation when he comments, 'Seen as a whole, Christian literature provides a very negative view of old age. This being the case, it is in direct line with Graeco-Roman thought.'

During the period from the eleventh to the thirteenth century being old was likened in many writings and in popular imagery to the shrivelling of the world. Contemporary writers and commentators referred to Saturn, the coldest and slowest planet, as the astrological symbol of senility and death. Significantly, it was also represented as an old man leaning on a crutch. The writers also spoke of old age as the loss of reason, decrepitude, clumsiness and ruination (Minois 1987: 200).

During the European bubonic plague of the fourteenth century a third of the population of Europe was destroyed within three years (1348–41). However, the young comprised a high proportion and in the later epidemics from 1350 onwards nearly all were children and younger people (see Minois 1987: 210). As a result, a disproportionate number of the survivors were older people. Younger populations felt cheated by fate and were to resent the status enjoyed by older people. Waves of criticism and caricatures of 'being old' were to abound. Chaucer summed up the bad feelings at this period: 'youth and age are often in debate' ('The Miller's Tale'). His characters reflect the negative comments of his day: 'old dotard crow', 'old traitor', 'old barrelful of lies', 'old beef', 'old and hoar', 'wretched crone' and 'old fool'.

The sixteenth century was a period when the cult of youth damned 'old age', particularly in the centres of the Renaissance. The paintings of older women's bodies in this period were amongst the worst portrayals in existence of women on canvas (see de Beauvoir 1977: 182). The humanists and the courtiers attacked 'old age' as life's spoiler. Scholars such as Erasmus joined in the ageist onslaught. It was at this time that the well-known ageist Dutch proverb probably emerged, 'The older a Dutchman the stupider' (see Minois 1987: 260). Shakespeare in *As You Like It*, was to describe 'old age' as 'second childhood and mere oblivion, sans teeth, sans eyes, sans taste, sans everything'.

It might be pointed out that being old was not then the norm, since life was generally short and brutish, but as stated at the outset chronological age is not the sovereign factor and old age has always been, and continues to be, relative. People in their fifties were labelled as 'old' and senile. Whatever the lifespan, those who were weakest and entering upon the last chapter of life, like old clothes, were of little use and therefore discarded by society. The enduring negative imagery about old age was to be carried forward into the nineteenth century, in spite of the noble sentiments of the Enlightenment about freedom, equality and social justice. De Beauvoir (1977: 214–17) cites many novels that reflected the harshness and neglect suffered during the exploitation of Europe's peasantry. Older people in France were often fed with rotten food and even buried alive by their offspring (she describes the offspring as parasites). Having taken over their bodies their desire was to take over their property.

Modern ageism in industrial Europe

These negative notions of 'being old' continued to be constructed and perpetuated in modern Europe, but, they were given a new twist because older people in industrial Europe were regraded as redundant (Hugman 1994). Elsewhere this book has identified the change over to mass production and standardization of industrial output that accompanied modernity, often referred to as 'Fordism' (see Spybey 1992: 76–8). In a Fordist Europe an ordered and regulatory system dominated people's everyday lives from the first to the last factory hooter (Giddens 1991; Hall *et al.* 1992: 8–9). Older people were to be excluded from the division of new labour. Along with children, they were also the first casualties in Britain's polluted cities. Their care within workhouse institutions tended to follow the assembly-line Fordist process of production and they were treated as objects in a society that extolled steel and iron and put capital before people. The weaker the body, the greater the danger of it being treated as an object and the older person as a 'geriatric case' and non-producer. Industrialization created the retired non-active citizens who no longer had the right to work. Compulsory retirement brought about an increased loss of personal status. The age of retirement in effect constituted the older workers' 'sell-by date' after which their lives were to be progressively devalued.

The regulation of the older body was to be tightened further by the legal–rational construction of 'old age' within new laws which further objectified older people in line with Foucault's (1977) analysis of the power relations of bureaucrats. The all-pervasive model at that time was of the 'body as a machine' – old bodies were simply obsolete like discarded gadgets and clapped-out motor engines.

Along with the marginalization and objectification which accompanied industrialization throughout the modern era, there were also the medicalization and welfarization processes. Ironically these beneficent measures and curative systems have often deepened the hurt suffered by the older populations and controlled their bodies. The care and cure of older people's bodies were increasingly governed and controlled by the new experts, which was an extension of the control exercised and regulated by professionals which Foucault described as the 'panopticon' factor. Incarcerated behind locked doors, their minds also were often subjected to regulatory medications and a surveillant nursing system within custodial and oppressive asylums, exposed in the many inquiries in Western Europe into the mental health institutions prior to the general switch to community-based care (see Mangen 1985; Basaglia 1968).

The pre-modern medical construct of 'old age' as an inevitable, metabolic decline was carried forward well into the modern era. The medicalization process created the 'geriatric patient'. 'Geriatric' and its equivalents became pejorative labels in most European languages. The needs of the body were defined and imposed upon the frail, bedfast and housebound older populations, who perceived 'old age' as decline and disengagement. In fact, these negative notions were given academic respectability with 'disengagement theory' in the 1960s (Cummings and Henry 1961).

The professionalization of healthcare in Northern and Western Europe particularly, propagated the notion of 'the authority of the expert' (the *subject*) whilst the older person was expected to be passive (the *object*) within the provision of medical, nursing and medical social work intervention within a power relationship which Foucault (1984: 283) describes as 'medicalization and hygienist intervention'. An unintended consequence was the diminution of self-determination, of human dignity and often of human rights, especially when older people were 'put away', reflected in Foucault's (1984) references to the 'great confinement' of the docile body and the birth of the asylum. Thousands of older Europeans over the years have been 'put away', which Brearley (1990: 99) describes as an 'experience of compulsion' and Parker (1988) as pervasive 'social control'. Estimates of the proportion of those residents in the Northern and Western countries, who were 'put away by compulsion' in the heyday of the welfare state in the post-war years, vary between 15 and 20 per cent of older populations (Giarchi 1996).

Admittedly, the public health and national health schemes in Europe were of enormous benefits to older Europeans, but at a price. The older patients were addressed as passive clients, subservient to the authority of professionals, who were mandated to prescribe care, keep secret records and files on their older patients, supervise their every action, monitor their thoughts in psycho-geriatric units, regulate their bowels and even incarcerate them for the remainder of their lives. These mandatory and prescriptive powers were exercised from the vantage point of the panopticon of the experts, shielded behind their surveillant systems (Foucault 1977).

The needs of the European 'pensioners and the welfare claimants' were also produced and constructed by welfarization. Needs were defined for them and welfare models were imposed upon them by the social work professionals of Europe, who 'knew what was best' for older persons and the disabled. With welfarization, legal–rational bureaucracy turned older people into 'cases' and their presenting problems into 'assessments' where the accredited experts told older people what their 'real problems' were.

In addition, de Beauvoir (1977: 247) refers to the modern exploitation of care, which enriched the professional and turned caring into profitable businesses. This was to reach a high point in Northern and Western Europe with the establishment of thousands of residential and nursing homes, whose patrons became the *'nouveaux riches'*, particularly in Western and Northern Europe, especially during the aftermath of the Second World War (Giarchi 1996).

More recent ageism in the post-industrial technological era

So much for the pre-modern and modern societal context of ageism; what of ageing within the third context of the emergent technological European society? Does ageism still exist? Before answering these questions, so as to pin-point the context of ageing in contemporary Europe, a few words about post-modernity are necessary which should be considered together with what has been stated elsewhere in this book. Post-modernity accompanies the shift to technology (referred to elsewhere in this text as post-Fordist), which has been described by Toffler

(1980) as 'the third wave'. A more pluralist and flexible society is said to have emerged in the wake of socio-economic changes brought about by new technologies (see Bauman 1992), and former dogmas and mega-beliefs, as well as divisions of labour, are being deconstructed and a reconstructed emphasis upon diversity and life-choices is emerging. However, current debate around the existence of a post-modern order does not allow us to fully explore the relevance of the 'third wave' upon the social construction of older Europeans. Suffice it here to make a few observations about the contemporary European scene.

Alongside the blurring of the sharp divisions of the industrial Fordist era between the sexes, between professionals, between the Churches, between the disciplines alongside the collapse of the older divisions of labour, the sharp divisions and significance of age-bands are also being questioned (see Hockey and James 1993). The modern constructions about ageing are being challenged (deconstructed) and replaced by other views about what constitutes being an older European (reconstructed). The differences between older and younger adults and the phases attributed to life-cycle stages (see Hockey and James 1993) are now being rejected (de-differentiation) (see Featherstone 1991). Put simply, many older people are 'doing their thing' by departing from the traditional modes of behaviour, ways of dressing and pastimes, and by reconstructing their lives according to personal choice rather than 'acting their age' as society wishes them to. Gubrium (1986) beckons older Europeans to remove the mask of 'old age' and be liberated. Has ageism decreased because of these ideas and shifts in behaviour? Texts such as that of Bytheway (1995) would indicate that the ancient warped constructs of old age abound in contemporary Europe.

Firstly, what new liberties are granted the older people of Europe and have they taken advantage of the new trends? It costs money 'to do your thing' in terms of fashion and a liberated lifestyle and high-quality living. The Joan Collins option is out of the question for millions of older Europeans. Is choice affordable for vast numbers of older Europeans? The sight of the liberated, holidaying, well-heeled, older groups frustrates the underclass of older Europeans managing to survive on wretched pensions, who psychologically may be caught in the time-warp of earlier modernity and in remoter rural areas even in that of pre-modernity. For them both time and benefits have stood still.

Other factors such as the emergence in Europe of a singles liberated culture and alternative living have to be considered in the context of ageing. Younger liberated youths in bed-sits may become older solitary people. Wall (1989: 135) states that there is a recent trend towards smaller less complex households in Europe as a whole. This latter comment is of considerable importance to the future welfare policies for older Europeans. There are also the widowed who live alone, especially women, some of whom enjoy independence and others languish. Living alone may mean that some die alone. For example, as reported in the *Guardian* (1994: 3), in 1993 a 69-year-old man lay dead in west London for almost four years before he was found by a plumber. In February 1994, an 88-year-old woman was found dead in her chair in north London, having been dead for about six months. In April 1994, a man aged 80 was found dead in Neasden, Brent, having been dead for several months. The facts about people dying alone in Europe have yet to be surveyed. Vast numbers of older Europeans are out of sight and out of mind. Day care and other outreach programmes hardly serve the majority of older European people living at home (Giarchi 1996). Nor can assumptions be made about the care enjoyed by older people cared for at home, even in the Latin countries, as Giarchi's European studies (1996) demonstrate.

The impact of an ageist society and the rationing of care in Europe act against older women more than against older men (for example, see Arber and Ginn 1991, 1995). On the basis of the most recent available statistics and studies, it appears that older women, within Europe as a whole, are usually in greater need than older men. Firstly, they live longer and so the married women are more likely to be widowed sooner and at a younger age. Secondly, there are two common features about the elderly in Europe which result from these factors as described by Potter and Zill (1992):

1   more older men are likely to live at home and are less likely to live alone;
2   more older women are likely to be in care and those who are at home to be alone.

Apart from this common trend, there are significant differences between the elderly in Northern, Western and Central European countries and those of the Southern and Eastern countries. Firstly, in Northern, Western and Central Europe, more elderly couples are likely to be on their own, especially in Germany, where virtually every second older person lives alone (see Potter and Zill 1992: 119). The women are more likely:

1   to be in homes for the aged and other institutions;
2   to be widowed sooner and at a younger age.

Secondly, in Southern and Eastern Europe, women and men are less likely to be on their own and both women and men are less likely to be in institutions. As cited by Potter and Zill (1992: 121), the largest proportions of older people living in extended households are in the southern countries. The top countries with older people in extended households in rank order consist of Portugal, Italy, Greece, Ireland, Spain, and France follows close behind.

The need for companionship and the struggle to combat loneliness are major issues for older Europeans. Sally Greengross (1988: 2) has identified the various forms of isolation generally facing older people in Europe. She refers to the many older Europeans who are:

1   isolated from their families due to the greater mobility of their offspring;
2   isolated from their neighbourhood within inward-looking households;
3   isolated from the younger generations with their own networks;
4   isolated from social interaction, entertainment and leisure pursuits;
5   isolated from the provision of health and social services;
6   isolated from local forums for discussion.

A disproportionate number of European women over 75 are living alone, often suffering from multiple loss and a lack of contact with neighbours, particularly in the rebuilt post-war localities (Wall 1989). According to Walker and van Craeynest (1993: 35), recent Euro-barometer studies indicate that 20 per cent or more of Portuguese and Greek older people often feel lonely. Other figures are 15–19 per cent in Italy; 10–14 per cent in Spain, Belgium, Ireland, France and Luxembourg; 5–9 per cent in the UK, Germany and the Netherlands; and less than 5 per cent in Denmark. So much for the assumption that older Latins enjoy more family support and companionship, also brought out by Giarchi (1987) in Italy. In general, one in eight EU older people state that they feel lonely often, and one in three state that they experience loneliness occasionally (Walker and van Craeynest 1993: 35). Of note is Pilkington's observation (1994: 2), when commenting upon data regarding lone deaths in the UK, that 'With a population that is ageing and with the mountains of broken families and fractured communities, loneliness has become a new British disease.' Might it not also be a European disease?

The hoped-for liberation of post-modern older people is also blocked by the racism that continues to discriminate against black and white ethnic minority groups. Here there is a widespread lack of awareness of discrimination against older immigrants and scant research. Amongst Europe's 8 million migrants are the increasing numbers of older migrants from countries outside Europe, such as Turkey, Morocco, the new Commonwealth countries and Algeria. The number of rootless older people in Europe is growing, but the size of the problem is unknown (Giarchi 1996). This is especially so in Russia and in the territories of former Yugoslavia after the wars. In mainland Europe many older migrants are without rights and benefits. Squires (1991) and Fenton (1987) have pointed to the unmet special needs of older black and white ethnic minorities.

Diminishing and contrasting living standards and patchy leisure pursuits of the retired in Europe

The following overview within five clusters of European countries provides an overall impression of older people's standards of living and pursuits. The data is based upon Giarchi's (1996) trawl of various research findings carried out in twenty-nine European countries which provides the various sources on the basis of which the ensuing snapshots can be checked out (see Giarchi 1996, sections 4 and 11 on leisure pursuits and education in Chapters 1–29).

The snapshots indicate that the grass on the other side of the English Channel is not always greener. They often focus upon the extent of the lower income of older Europeans in most countries and their constrained lifestyle. Lower incomes constrain leisure choices on both sides of the Channel.

Retirement snapshots in Northern Europe

In Northern Europe the welfare state has been the major provider of services and of pensions or benefits for its elderly populations. In the Scandinavian countries it is generally assumed that older people are amongst the most secure, comfortable and liberated citizens of Europe. But do the beneficiaries constitute a majority? The bleak realities facing significant numbers of older European people in retirement indicate they do not.

Norway

In spite of a much-vaunted state pension scheme, disparities in incomes exist, curtailing enjoyment of leisure pursuits. State housing bank loans provide excellent terms to maintain excellent housing provision. About 34 per cent of those aged 60-plus continue to work. Indeed, 82 per cent of the older people do not attend leisure or educational centres. Older people enjoy 50 per cent travel concessions, which compares badly with the poorer country of the Republic of Ireland where at 66 years of age all people travel free by bus or train (see Giarchi 1996: 65–7, 72).

Sweden

There has been a rising inequality in incomes for well over a decade (see Joseph Rowntree Foundation 1995: 14). Also, one out of every five pensioners is financially hard pressed and 20 per cent believe that their income is insufficient to maintain a decent standard of living. Those aged 75-plus have a lower average income than their counterparts in the UK, Germany, France, Belgium, Italy, Luxembourg and the Netherlands. More than half of older people own their own house – 2 percent are in sheltered housing. Food is costly for pensioners, being 20–30 per cent above the EU average (see Giarchi 1996: 77–9, 88).

Denmark

Two-thirds of the retired in Denmark have an average annual income of between 40 and 50 per cent of their original earnings. However, about half of the pensioners have no other source of income than the state pension which is regarded by some as inadequate. The purchasing power of Danish 'old age' benefits only ranks as seventh in the EU. About a third are fortunate in having between 75 and 90 per cent of their former income. However, there is some concern about the housing for older urban people where about one-fifth are below urban standards. About 13 per cent participate in educational activities and there is a 50 per cent reduction in admission to galleries/ museums, plus subsidized holidays (see Giarchi 1996: 93–5, 103).

Iceland

The pension is very comprehensive and flexible in that it can be deferred for five years to allow older people to continue working. Housing is of the highest quality with 80 per cent owning their own houses. Only 3 per cent of older people live in sheltered accommodation. The evidence to date indicates that state leisure agencies are scant. None the less, the older populations are very active – swimming in heated pools being a popular option. There are only two major organizations, the first has under 200 members (0.8 per cent of older population); the second, with forty-three branches, is service-orientated and is limited to providing conferences and lectures (see Giarchi 1996: 42–3, 46).

Finland

The inequality and gross disparities of disposable income in Finland are greater amongst older people than amongst other social groups. Also, the housing standards lag behind those of the other Scandinavian countries. Older people in the remoter forested 'extreme peripheries' experience the worst conditions in the Scandinavian countries. There are five times more older persons living alone than thirty years ago. Although this may mean they enjoy greater independence, a significant numbers of these reside in the remoter poorly resourced rural areas. The neighbourhood clubs are a nation-wide feature, offering social as well as self-help centres. Subsidized educational courses for older people flourish in the summer season (see Giarchi 1996: 51–3, 59).

Retirement snapshots in Western Europe

In spite of the fact that there has been an increase in numbers, older people appear to be enjoying greater latitude and leisure pursuits within society particularly in Belgium and France. Yet modern and pre-modern attitudes still abound (see Hugman 1994; Bytheway 1995). At present, entrenched traditionalism, poverty and deprivation slow down any significant shift to better quality of life and more leisure pursuits in most parts of Western Europe. The 'leotard hype' projected by the media with regard to new 'post-modern liberated living' for older Europeans relates only to a minority of older Europeans. It is too expensive for most to engage in the advertised leisure pursuits. The downturn in state provision and the upturn in private provision caters for the relatively superannuated privileged few.

The Republic of Ireland

Older people are seldom involved in the nation's economic, social and political life. The net replacement ratio of the state pension is only 42 per cent, the second lowest in Western Europe. There is a sharp distinction between the 'have much pensioners' and the 'have less pensioners'. None the less, older people aged 65-plus are now a low-risk poverty group in comparison with other age bands. Also, the relative lack of social benefits for older people is counterbalanced by the benefits in kind such as heating tokens and free phone rentals. The travel concessions have already been referred to. The 17.5 per cent who live alone are a matter of concern for state and Church. But Ireland has come a long way since Power's (1980) report on the isolated and marginalized lone older Irish (see Giarchi 1996: 108–11, 121–2).

The UK

Older people generally have less money to spend than their counterparts do in most Northern, Western and Central European countries. More than half derive three-quarters of their income from the state pension, which is less generous than most EU pensions. The Luxembourg Income Studies data file indicates that older UK citizens have lower average incomes than their counterparts in Belgium, France, Luxembourg, Germany and the Netherlands. Thirty-three per cent of pensioner couples and 42 per cent of solo pensioners have incomes that are below half of the average disposable income; 58 per cent have at least three-quarters of their income from state benefits. Two-thirds of older people (5.9 million) in the UK live on the margins of poverty, whereas only one-fifth of the non-elderly are within the same category (see Hills 1995: 19). About a third live alone and 43 per cent are living in rented accommodation. Contrary to assumptions most do not own their own homes. Only 2 per cent participate in educational courses (see Giarchi 1996: 129–34).

The Netherlands

Social expenditure protection as a percentage of GDP is the highest in Europe. The housing stock is impressive – 35 per cent has been provided by 840 housing associations offering cheap rents. However, there is much concern about the social isolation and loneliness of many older people. The vast majority do not indulge in sport or socialize in clubs. Also, large numbers of older women have not acquired adequate pensions due to their short periods in employment. One out of every six households with older people relies upon an income at the level of the social minimum, and so too do a quarter of those older people who are living alone (see Giarchi 1996: 161–4, 176).

Belgium

The full pension is equivalent to 60 per cent of average earnings. The poverty rate amongst those aged 75-plus has dropped by 6.1 per cent, in contrast with that of 3.3 per cent amongst the EU general population, and there is an emergence of retired people within mutual societies and municipal advisory committees. Housing is least impressive. About 20 per cent live in houses built before 1915 and they often lack amenities. Eighteen per cent do not meet the housing needs of older people. However, social integration in families and the involvement of older people in clubs are impressive. But the variety of pursuits is limited and less liberating, as dictated in a more traditional society (see Giarchi 1996: 180–3, 190–1).

Luxembourg

The pension is one of the most generous in Europe, providing almost 85 per cent of the final salary. Sixty-seven per cent of older people are owner-occupiers; 97 per cent have indoor toilets; and 83 per cent have baths/showers. Surprisingly, there are no Universities of the Third Age, nor state educational facilities provided for older people. Considerable pollution may explain why the life expectancy at 65 for women is ranked sixteenth in Europe and that for men is ranked eighteenth (see Giarchi 1996: 215–17, 222–3).

France

In contrast with the other countries in Western Europe, the replacement rate of wages by pensions has reached 80 per cent. It remains to be seen whether the nation can cope with the generous level of state pensions and benefits, given the impact of the recent long recession and the costs of unemployment to the taxpayers. The housing of older people is a matter of concern: 22 per cent of the houses were built before 1871 and 53 per cent before 1962. One in four does not have an indoor toilet. France is the home of the University of the Third Age, with over forty universities providing outward-bound-type trips, yoga, science updates, the humanities and the arts. There are 20,000 clubs. The fees are nominal. These inter-age groups are self-managed. There is also another similar educational agency, the MGEN (Le Club de Retraites de la Mutuelle Générale de l'Education Nationale) (see Giarchi 1996: 195–8, 209). In spite of these facilities, the domestic culture traps most grandparents within the home in line with Dominelli's (1991) features of trapped patriarchal conjugality.

Retirement snapshots in Central Europe

The standard of living of the retired in each of the three countries in Central Europe, particularly in Austria, is impressive generally, but the eastern regions of Germany are currently lagging behind (Laczko 1994). As stated elsewhere (Giarchi 1996), the Czech Republic should be included with the Central European countries, and others make a case for including Hungary and Poland (sometimes described as East Central Euro-countries), but as yet these countries are not liberated or stable enough to be bracketed with the affluent centre of Europe.

Germany

In Germany, the net replacement ratio of the compulsory pension is 77 per cent of the previous employment income: one of the highest in Europe. However, up to 50 per cent of older people in Germany do not claim their state benefits. Almost half of the older people live in the oldest housing, 14.3 per cent have no bath, and 6 per cent have no inside WC. Self-help potential and social integration are salient features of social policies regarding older people. The conditions in the eastern *Länder* lag behind those of the more affluent western regions of Germany, but data is in short supply. The older German populations are increasingly involved in politics, but they constitute small minorities of several hundred activists out of a population of almost 9 million persons (65-plus). None the less, the Grey Party (Die Graunen), set up in 1980 to voice the interests and champion the rights of older people, has had considerable intergenerational support, but falls far short of the United States counterpart. The older population has been slower to take up interests in sport and educational programmes, but this is changing in the western *Länder* (see Giarchi 1996: 251–5, 268).

Austria

In Austria, many older people have the means to buy their way into a fuller involvement in the life of the community. The full pension (after forty-five years of contributions) is almost equivalent to 80 per cent of earnings. Widows are paid 60 per cent of the insured's basic pension (Giarchi 1996). There are about 250 housing associations, and the modernization of housing stock within a scheme of generous subsidies for low income older people is a major feature. In addition, leisure and educational interests of older Austrians appear to be significant. Increasing numbers attend 350 adult education colleges and 3,400 local institutions, but the vast majority of the 1 million or so older people (65-plus) are still under-educated and most stay away (see Giarchi 1996: 238–9, 247).

Switzerland

Switzerland provides higher old-age insurance (contributory) benefits than the USA, Belgium, France, Austria, the Netherlands, the UK and Germany. None the less, women and second generation immigrants make up a significant number of the 10 per cent of the poorest older people because they have had less employment. The non-contributory supplementary pension is means-tested. Housing provision for low income older people and the coverage of installation costs (often up to 90 per cent) is one of the most generous in Europe. Universities of the Third Age exist in most cantons. Many older people in the urban areas attend the Gymnastic Federation facilities, but these are in largely traditionalized centres. However, the gap in income between the retired in the industrial or confederate states and of those in the poor rural areas has become greater recently. Many older people keep to themselves – 54 per cent of older people in the urban areas are not involved in the life of the community (see Giarchi 1996: 228–9, 234).

Retirement snapshots in Eastern Europe

The former Eastern bloc European countries are in sharp contrast with the rest of Europe. Laczko (1994) and Giarchi (1996) have provided overviews of the lifestyle of older Eastern Europeans, which illustrate abundantly that pre-modern as well as modern factors block any likelihood that older people in eastern countries might begin to live within a post-modern society. Many remoter parts of the former Eastern bloc countries were never really serviced by their communist regimes – in accordance with Leninist ideology poverty could not exist.

Bulgaria

Bulgaria has the highest proportion of older people within the former socialist states. Rose (1991: 16) points out that probably around 76 per cent of the Bulgarians depend upon a 'shadow economy' for survival. The future looks bleak for the older population with the astronomical rates of inflation (the increase of the price of bread can be as high as 600 per cent and food prices have risen at times by 700 per cent). It is not surprising that over a quarter of older people aged 65–69 are working, one of the highest proportions in Europe. The housing for older people, especially in the rural areas, is amongst the worst in Europe (see Giarchi 1996: 285–7, 289).

Czech Republic and Slovakia

Older people in the former Czechoslovakia, according to the United Nations (1991) and Eurostat (1991), have the lowest life expectation at 65 for men and the second lowest for women on the Continent. Pensions are low and not inflation proof in a country where about two-thirds have not subscribed towards a pension. About 6 per cent of Czechs and 2 per cent of Slovakians continue to work after 65 to make ends meet. On the positive side, special/social housing in Bohemia and Moravia is impressive, but in a country where 23 per cent have no running water and about 43 per cent have no integral bath suite older people occupy the oldest out-dated dwellings. There are about 1,100 clubs for older people. There are also highly subsidized cinema and leisure tickets and cheap transport for older people (see Giarchi 1996: 275–6, 281).

Poland

In Poland, ironically, many older people are a great deal worse off than they were under the old communist regime, because of the headlong rush into unregulated market systems. Older Polish people retire early to collect their pension and add to it by work. A third of the total expenditure on pensions is devoted to women under 60 and men under 65. Over the past five years, Poland has had the highest proportion of older workers in Europe. Housing deprivation is amongst the worst in Europe: 57.9 per cent of older urban residents have no flush toilet; in the rural areas it is 84 per cent. In the urban areas 15.5 per cent have no running water; in the rural areas it is 60.1 per cent. Only 12 per cent of older people have had a basic primary education. For some, the monotony of their work is alleviated to some degree by the senior clubs, of which there are about 1,700, which are mostly organized by local people's co-operatives (see Giarchi 1996: 307–8, 320).

Hungary

In Hungary, the basic pension did not cover everyone under the communist regime. This and a tight control on benefits and a means-tested approach have embittered the older population. The basic pension was not index related, except for those aged 70-plus, until the mid-1990s. Also, 56 per cent of men and 66 per cent of women, aged 60-plus, state that they have a lasting or chronic illness. The housing improvements and provision of social housing have almost been exclusively for the young – housing for older people has been at a standstill since the early 1980s. Hungarian people are beginning to attend the 'third stage of life' educational programmes, but in relatively small numbers. Many older people are isolated, which is not helped by the fact that the proportion of telephones in Hungary is one of the lowest in Europe, with many older persons on waiting lists for twenty-five years (see Giarchi 1996: 325–8, 337).

Romania

In Romania, the veneer of democracy is thin. There is also a marked difference in the standard of life between the rural and urban older people, and between the Bucharest older people and the rest of urban Romanians. Those over 60 are more than four times as likely to be on a low income as middle-aged and younger households. Significant numbers of rural older people, in fact, have no pension. More than half of Romanians are caught between pre-modern and modern worlds in a world where television sets appear incongruously within semi-primitive rural dwellings or in urban flats where the supply of water and electricity is confined to set time-bands. The plan to create 300–400 agro-industrial centres in rural areas under the Ceauşescu regime halted major urban housing developments. The oldest city residents occupy the oldest city houses (see Giarchi 1996: 341–2, 346).

Russia

The data for the new Russia, with its several distinctive cultures and histories, is scant. In most of the countries of the former USSR, stretching from the Baltic to the Ural Mountains, cultural and religious splits fragment the people (see Edwards 1990). In Russia today, there are some 60 million older people, 10 million of whom are single unmarried persons or widowed, who are mostly women. Russia has been burdened with an enormous task – for example, older people constituted about one-fifth of persons below the poverty line in the former USSR. Currently many older people in these areas experience 'food poverty'. Bad housing conditions are amongst the worst in Europe. For example, in a sample of older people in Russia and the Ukraine, 30 per cent of the urban elderly and 58 per cent of the rural older population have no running water; about 87 per cent had no phone, and 57 per cent in the towns had no central heating in one of the coldest regions in Europe (see Giarchi 1996: 294–6, 301).

Retirement snapshots in Southern Europe

Many of the older people in the southern countries live largely in rural settlements. As is the case within the eastern countries, there are more marked inequalities in income amongst the pensioners themselves and between the pensioned and the working populations. With regard to the intergenerational gap, the high hopes of the EU 1993 'European Year of Older People and Solidarity between Generations' have not easily been established in a capitalist society where the socio-economic gap between the deprived and the privileged older people has never been greater. The wide diversity of goods and the wide latitude in lifestyle are not available for the deprived populations.

Spain

Spain has one of the youngest population profiles in Europe. However, its aged dependency ratio, which is now one of the lowest in Europe, will become one of the highest in the next century. The income of the older people is more generous than it is in most southern countries and, after Germany, Spain spends more on the older population than any other country within the EU. Since 1990 pensions have been index-related. Between 1982 and 1991 pensions have increased by 30 per cent in real terms. Spain's stock of sheltered housing lags behind that of most EU countries. It has the second highest percentage of owner-occupied houses, but these are disproportionately rural and in very bad repair. The urban apartments compare badly with those in Italy, France and the German western *Länder* in terms of lifts and quality of accommodation. Together with Greece the Spanish older people spend the least amount on leisure out of all the OECD countries (see Giarchi 1996: 379–80, 386).

Portugal

Thirty-three per cent of pensioner couples and 42 per cent of solo older people have incomes below half of the average national disposable income. The privileged stock of houses under the Salazar regime contrasts with the slum dwellings in which a disproportionate number of older people reside, often in crowded conditions. Forty-two per cent of Portuguese houses have no bath/shower; 42.3 per cent have no internal WC. For persons aged 65-plus, a 'Gold Card' provides half fare on most rail journeys, and older persons on low income are provided with exemptions from radio and television licences. The high degree of illiteracy amongst the older people is one of the worst in the EU (see Giarchi 1996: 391–3, 398).

Italy

In Italy, the pension was one of the most generous in Europe until the financial crises of 1994. It had been the largest single item in the country's social expenditure. However, almost a fifth of people on 'low income' in Italy are older citizens. Their largest expenditures are on food and travel. Leisure activities and educational pursuits vary considerably between the regions. Housing for older people has suffered in the past from the lack of government planning. The high quality of houses in the north contrasts with the low-quality housing south of Rome. However, the state's control of rents, special low income loans and reduced taxes and grants for social housing projects have benefited older people. Free Open University courses are available. There are at least 176 Golden Age Universities, a counterpart educational facility to that of the University of the Third Age, but in a country with 7.5 million persons aged 65-plus. In response to the alternative lifestyle of the younger generations, older Italians often react by becoming even more traditionalist, especially in the rural areas, and older women are still the victims of flagrant pre-modern, sexist discrimination (see Giarchi 1996: 353–8, 386).

Malta

In Malta, persons retired before 1978 receive considerably less in pensions than those who have retired since the significant amendment of the Universal Pension Scheme in 1979. Those who retired before 1959 are the worst off. Older people's housing tends to be in need of repair and often has restricted sanitation. In the late 1980s the government provided local centres and independent sheltered flats to tempt older people out of one of the oldest stocks of houses in Europe. Most own their houses, and the rent for the non-owners is controlled by the authorities. Leisure and educational pursuits are limited in a home-centred Latin society in a conservative island where older people are still constrained by the traditions of one of the most ancient pre-modern European cultures (see Giarchi 1996: 440–1, 449).

The former Yugoslavia

In what was Yugoslavia life for older people is one of massive deprivation. The wars have inflicted homelessness, ethnic cleansing programmes and multiple losses for the older people. The historic pre-modern divisions between Serbs and Croats and unholy conflicts between Christians of the Orthodox Churches and Islamic groups have hindered solidarity and make a mockery of the former proclamation of a national brotherhood and civic unity (*bratsvo-jedinstvo*). Numerous older people have been caught in the crossfire – their numbers are yet to be counted. Even before the massive destruction of houses the government and the builders fell behind with their provision of houses. Many older people have been left behind by their younger progeny in under-occupied houses which were customarily built for ten to twenty persons. Previous residential municipal units in Macedonia for older people only provided for 1,188 older people. The people have tended to build their own houses, the older, more affluent, family members providing the money for materials and the younger members providing the workforce. Obviously, relatively few older people could be part of this collective effort. Previously there were many leisure centres and a University of the Third Age in Belgrade. There are at least 325 leisure and educational centres in Slovenia, with some 461 sports circles. Some 2,780 health education Red Cross courses were run in the mid-1980s (see Giarchi 1996: 417–18, 429).

Albania

The post-war non-contributory universal pension was relatively generous, but has now lost its value in a volatile market economy. Thousands of Albanians who emigrated to Italy and Greece left many destitute elderly behind in the remote mountains of the interior. Housing is poor, but rents are cheap. Traditionalism and tribal allegiances conserve many pre-modern values, mainly amongst older Albanians. Vast numbers of older people are semi-literate – only in 1946 was education made compulsory (see Giarchi 1996: 433, 435–6).

Greece

The insurance schemes are fragmented. There are as many as 327 social insurance schemes in Greece and glaring disparities between urban and rural pensioners. A bleak situation faces large numbers of older people, whose standard of living has worsened recently. Eighteen per cent of older men and 10.7 per cent of older women aged 65–69 have had to remain in employment, as well as 12.6 per cent of older men and 6.5 per cent of women aged 70-plus. Many older people in rural areas have been employed for a pittance over the years and depend upon the Church and charity for survival. On the positive side, a 'Third Age Card' entitles older people to half-fares. The KAPI (Open Care Day Centres) provide older users with cheaper holidays as well as educational programmes. Such facilities, however, have to be set against the research evidence of widespread discrimination against many older retired people in Greece, even within their families, simply because they are non-producers (see Giarchi 1996: 402–4, 410).

Turkey

Turkey's pension is adjusted every two years in accordance with wages and prices nationally. Agricultural workers are not eligible for welfare payments, unless they can demonstrate that they have no means of support. The non-contributory and means-tested social assistance programme provides for a quarter of the retired population. Many older people live in shanty towns (60 per cent of the population in the urban areas resided in them as late as the 1980s) or in the near-primitive rural dwellings. Many Turkish older people have never been to school, and thousands are illiterate. Educational courses and leisure pursuit centres are few (see Giarchi 1996: 453–5, 458).

Cyprus

The housing programme was set back years by the Turkish invasion, and pensions were only introduced in 1980. Older people are captives in their homes, especially the women, within one of the most traditionalist domestic cultures in Europe. They also live in an insecure setting with the constant danger of conflict between the Greek and Turkish Cypriot populations (see Giarchi 1996: 463, 467–8).

It is clear from the album of snapshots taken of the income, housing, educational and leisure interests/pursuits of older Europeans, that the liberated and more affluent lifestyle heralded by the theorists is as yet only available to minorities of European older people, even at times in the more affluent countries of Europe. The 'unrecognised discrimination' (McEwan 1990) perpetuated by the survival of ageism engendered in ancient Europe right down to modern times continues to create a bleak winter in retirement for majorities of older people throughout Europe and penetrates the so-called advanced conditions of Europe's emergent technological society. The ageist notions of 'old age' still survive. On the basis of present conditions and the increasing demands made upon social and healthcare services by the growing numbers of older Europeans, within economies which are dismantling the welfare states of Europe, the prospect of a 'second spring' in retirement seems to be remote for majorities of older Europeans, even in the Scandinavian and Western countries.

Reflection

The demographic expansion of older people well into the next century, together with the eclipse of the European welfare state, the contraction of the availability of carers, the demise of traditional European families, the increasing gap between the poorer and more affluent older Europeans, the contrast between minimal or nominal pensions and those that are index-linked, and the shift from collectivism to individualism present enormous problems for the planners and households as Europe moves into the next millennium.

When assessing what constitutes the construction of 'old age' in the context of 'Britain in Europe', three key points emerge which are dictated by realism based upon the emerging data and not by a mindless pessimism or empty optimism:

Summary

- There will be a massive increase in the burden of social care and welfare provision as Europe moves into the next millennium.
- Ageism within the British Isles is but part of a historic build-up of negative stereotypes which continue to transcend the geographic and social boundaries of Europe.
- The inequalities and contrasting lifestyles between upper and lower socio-economic groups of older people, within whatever European nations, will diverge yet more.

Further reading

Bill Bytheway (1995) *Ageism*, Buckingham: Open University Press. This text introduces the concept of 'ageism' and explores what it is, whom it affects and how it relates to services for older people. It utilizes readily available printed material such as newspapers and biographies. It also includes case studies plus adverts and other helpful illustrations.

Jennifer L. Hockey and Allison James (1993) *Growing Up and Growing Old*, London: Sage. This book focuses upon dependency in the life course. It shows how older people are treated as children (infantilization) and how negative notions about gender and the life course are embedded within social contexts and culture. It explores the stigmatizing role of ageist stereotypes.

George Giacinto Giarchi (1996) *Caring for Older Europeans*, Aldershot: Arena Books. This book focuses upon formal and informal care in twenty-nine European countries. It begins with a discussion of the impact of the age explosion in Europe. It presents the administrative and political contexts of the state's provision for older Europeans and the types of services that are available. This very large study (over 560 pages) presents the most complete review to date of European research into formal and informal European care within the continent of Europe, rather than simply the EU countries. The snapshots presented in this chapter are made up of the data collated and referenced in this volume of sources from hundreds of authors and research programmes.

Alan Walker and Tony Maltby (1996) *Ageing Europe*, Buckingham: Open University Press. This book presents the key findings from recent policy-orientated research undertaken on behalf of the Commission of the European Communities through the EU's 'Observatory on Ageing and Older People' chaired by Alan Walker. Together they represent the most definitive account to date of socio-economic policies affecting older people and their social integration into European society. This book also presents the results from a specially commissioned Euro-barometer survey of public attitudes to ageing and older people conducted in twelve European Union countries. It thus provides a unique insight, as well as the first comprehensive EU portrait, of how older people are perceived and how they perceive themselves and the ageing process.

Social processes and contemporary issues

PART THREE looks at those social processes which form a key part of European society. These are contemporary issues too in that they are seldom absent from conversations, newspapers and news broadcasts, political debate and other forms of discourse. Therefore they are crucial to sociological analysis. The family, in some form or other, is present in all societies. It is possible to detect differences in family patterns between the European countries but, at the same time, there are similarities because all European countries have to some extent passed through processes of industrialization, urbanization, etc. These form central threads to the 'modernization' process and a further aspect is the establishment of mass education – education for all. This was in the first place a European development, but it is one that has been emulated elsewhere and levels of education are often taken as a measure of a society's 'modernity'. From the bosom of the family children normally proceed into education, as arguably the second great influence in their 'socialization' into the norms of society, but religion is important for many as well. Much of Europe is regarded as secular society in that only a minority of people are regular churchgoers, but, broadly speaking, religion is more important in the poorer fringe areas, especially in Southern and Eastern Europe, and amongst immigrant groups too. In addition there is something of a revival of spiritual beliefs quite separate from the orthodox religions. In terms of the life-cycle people are expected to pass from education to work, but the economic problems of the late twentieth century have made this problematic right across Europe. The sociological study of work has therefore taken on a whole new area which is perhaps best described as 'non-work' especially in relation to men, the traditional breadwinners. There is also part-time and temporary work which now applies to a much larger proportion of the total workforce, but particularly involves women. Finally, in this part of the book, there is the quintessential late twentieth-century phenomenon, mass communication. All aspects of contemporary European society are communicated through the mass media and by the same token the mass media have come to form an essential part of European life. The media converge as television, video and computers increasingly share the same developments in electronic technology, and the compact disk, which is capable of carrying several forms of data, is perhaps the best illustration of this.

Chapter 10

Families in Europe

Lyn Bryant and Joan Chandler

Introduction	202
Terms and definitions	202
Families and social reproduction	203
The process of industrialization and family forms	204
Family life and labour	206
Private and public spheres	208
Contemporary families and family relationships	209
Changing family structures	213
Changing family values	216
Summary	217
Further reading	217

Key concepts

- Kinship and household
- Social reproduction
- Public and private domains
- Domestic division of labour

Introduction

In all societies most people live in a network of family relationships and obligations. The ways in which these families are constituted and which people are counted as members of the family or kin group vary widely between cultures, but across Europe family roles have both a high degree of social recognition and far-reaching behavioural effects. That is, even though ideas about the detailed nature of relationships may vary, terms like 'mother', 'father', 'daughter', 'aunt', are both widely recognized and understood and are important in influencing not just expectations about the behaviour of people holding these titles but more general expectations about social activities. Furthermore these networks of family relationships must be conceptually distinguished from units of living, usually termed 'households'.

Family life locates the individual in a set of personal relationships which are complex and multidimensional. These relationships are at once emotional, economic and political. Family life is seen as a personal and private domain removed from the world of public affairs. Families and households are also vehicles for property transfer and sites for the consumption and production of goods and services. As families rear the next generation they act as agents of social and cultural reproduction and as such attract state interest and frequently state regulation. These contrasting aspects of family life, evident in both family organization and family values, are the central concern of this chapter.

Terms and definitions

Family forms in Europe varied in the past and differ in the present. Such variations, both in Europe and world-wide, have made it notoriously difficult to formulate definitions of the family. Indeed Diana Gittins (1985) has argued that 'there is no such thing as the family, only families'. It is, however, important to describe some of the structures and forms of organization which have characterized families in order to examine systematic variations in family structures and to understand the ways in which theorists and social commentators have described and explained families. Some of the important terms are described below.

Marriage refers to a form of formalized relationship marked by a public ceremony, which recognizes a sexual relationship between the partners and places the children of the marriage formally in the society. Marriage creates wider relationships with other families and kin groups who are not necessarily related by blood. Different forms of marriage are found in different parts of the world, with the possible number of partners and the expected duration of the relationship varying. Some societies expect marriage to be life-long, while others allow divorce under certain circumstances. The social expectations about marriage also affect the unmarried. For example, in the UK, people who cohabit may be referred to as 'living as man and wife'.

Forms of the family circle also vary widely, but a general distinction is usually made between *nuclear* and *extended* families. The nuclear family consists of the married (or cohabiting) partners and their children. This form of the family is also referred to as conjugal, immediate or simple in the literature. Extended families of various types exist throughout the world and the rules about their make-up are often very formalized. In *patriarchal extended families* authority tends to be vested in the (older) males and descent reckoned through the male line (*patrilineal*). *Matriarchal/matrilineal* families, where the female line is most important in reckoning descent and handing on property, are less common. In European societies the term 'extended family' tends to be applied to a number of different groupings; for example, three-generation families or households containing a number of people related to each other by ties of blood or marriage. The terms 'extended family' and 'kinship' or 'kin group' are often used interchangeably, both in everyday speech and in the literature. This is partly because recognition of kin in contemporary societies is a matter of choice and chance as much as of formal rules.

The *household* is an important focus of attention for sociologists and historians, as one of the features of family life has been seen as the sharing of a common home or household. However, empirical studies have demonstrated that households may contain single individuals, married couples, couples and their children, more extended groups and other relatives and lodgers. We often think of households as having a single 'head', with the implication that there is some coherent or even single source of authority within the unit; this is often the case even in fairly large groups. Households, however, may also contain members who would ideally prefer to form separate units and those who do not necessarily consider themselves 'part of the family'.

In Europe, historically, family authority has been patriarchal and members took the father's name, although large patriarchal groups, such as the *zadruggas* found in Serbia, which include a number of families living and working together under the authority of one head man, were relatively rare. In general both male and female lines were, and are, recognized in kin groupings and in the reckoning of descent.

Families and social reproduction

While family forms and relationships vary, families have always been involved in biological reproduction and the care of children. Families, indeed, have a crucial role to play in the socialization of the young and the physical and emotional maintenance of adults, and this is recognized by both sociologists and social commentators. The processes of socialization are important in attempting to ensure that new generations are fitted into the wider social order that is, in the reproduction of culture and society. New members of society have to learn the appropriate ways of behaving and to have the 'right' feelings and attitudes. Family processes are pivotal both in the construction of individual identity and the placing of individuals into the wider society.

Sociologists have emphasized the role played by families in social reproduction, although they frequently view the political implications of the process differently. The work of Parsons (1951) influenced the way in which post-war sociologists

viewed the organization of family relationships in the West. He stressed the importance of the nuclear family in maintaining central social values and argued that the
family's role in reproducing gender and age role differences was beneficial for the
social system as a whole. His approach assumed both a consensus of social values
and that the nuclear family was a 'good fit' for industrial society.

Marx, on the other hand, considered the role of families in the reproduction of capitalism to be problematic for families and their members. The authority
relationships within the nuclear family he saw as reflecting the authority
relationships in the wider society, with women and children being particularly
exploited. Feminist writers more recently have furthered this debate, describing
the ways in which the reproduction of gender roles within the family reflect and
maintain traditional values and relationships – at the expense of women and to
the benefit of men.

The importance of families in maintaining control and passing on social
values has meant that quite frequently both sociological and social commentary
have had a strong moral and political content. Indeed, families are the frequent
subjects of political debate and directives. Concerns about the relationship
between families, the economy and social values are very clear in the ways in
which changes in family organization and activities during the processes of industrialization and urbanization have been described.

The process of industrialization and family forms

One early theorist who was influential in the debate about the relationship between
family organization and industrialization was Frédéric Le Play (1855). He
describes three main family forms:

1   The large patriarchal family, which was stable and traditional and a feature
     of agrarian societies. The eldest male was the authority figure and head of
     the family. Sons when they married brought their wives to the family home-
     stead. Family members could receive continuous support at all stages of
     their lives within this large grouping.
2   The stem family, *la famille souche*, which was a variant of the patriarchal
     family. Here, one son would inherit the farm, or other property, and the
     stem of the family would thus be maintained over generations. Younger
     children might look to the core family for help and support over the years.
3   The nuclear family, *la famille instable*, which he saw as the family most
     characteristic of industrial societies. Not rooted in a joint enterprise, this
     family was founded at marriage, grew in size with offspring, and declined
     once more when the children grew up and left home to start their own
     families. This small group was seen as highly vulnerable to external pres-
     sures and inclined to drift 'upon the tide of circumstance', unable to protect
     or secure a stable future for its members.

This general model had great influence over much sociological writing about
the family. Indeed an assumption that in the agrarian past of Europe families had

generally been both larger in size and more complex in structure held considerable sway in the literature. Families, it was argued, were extended, both horizontally and vertically, and were often engaged in family farms or in domestic industry. The large numbers of people involved in the household and economic activities were able to cater for the needs of individual members as they arose. As in Le Play's model, industrialization together with population growth, which contributed to an increasingly complex division of labour and high rates of geographical and social mobility, were seen as having encouraged the proliferation of nuclear families living separate and independent lives: a family form much more suited to the needs of both individuals and the state. The changes in size and structure were also seen as having an influence upon the activities carried out by modern families, their capacity to support their members and their ability to exert control over these members.

The empirical evidence, however, does not support this view of almost unilinear change in family structures running together with economic change. Rather, there is evidence of the existence of a variety of family forms across Europe and within its constituent states.

Macfarlane (1978), contrasting England with the rest of Europe, argues both for the greater independence of English nuclear families and for smaller household size. His evidence coincides with that of Peter Laslett (1972) as far as England is concerned, who demonstrates that prior to industrialization the majority of English children lived in households constituted of nuclear families. Diana Gittins also points out that

> Prior to industrialism most people lived in relatively small households – the average being about 4.75 persons. Most of these households – but by no means all – correspond to nuclear families. A substantial proportion never married at all and either lived with other kin or with other single people or, in some cases, alone.
>
> (Gittins 1985: 6)

Macfarlane saw the English difference as related to a number of factors, including the system of inheritance – people were free to will their property to whoever they wished – and the fact that most parcels of land were small. Although his argument is focused on England, even in the Celtic areas the country was marked by landowners with tenants and hired workers rather than by peasants owning their own pieces of land. Households were also more likely to be enlarged by servants and lodgers than by family members, and Tilly and Scott (1978) point out that between 1574 and 1821 approximately 60 per cent of the population of England and Wales were servants and that in pre-industrial England a half of all young people would have experienced living in other households.

Laslett argues that continental Europe was also marked by small households which, it might be inferred, contained nuclear families. The evidence, however, shows a much more varied picture. While clan types of groupings, where families grouped together under one male head to farm relatively large plots of land, were infrequent, Martine Segalen (1980) found in Finisterre, for example, that the mean size of the household was high, with numbers of complex households. On the other hand, Dupaquier and Jadin (1972) found the proportion of the households containing only nuclear families to be high in Corsica, with few patriarchal extended families and few servants. In Tuscany household size tended to increase with wealth, numbers being swollen by both family members and servants (Klapisch 1972). Similarly, van de Woude (1972) reports that in the United Provinces of the Netherlands in the seventeenth and eighteenth centuries there were wide variations in patterns of family and household structures depending upon region and socio-economic status. Three-generation families were more common in certain agricultural areas, while pauper families were the most likely to live in simple nuclear families.

There were, then, variations in household size and family structure across Europe prior to industrialization. As O'Day points out, 'race, ethnicity, class and geography acted separately and in varying combinations to determine the family experience' (1994: 15). While size of household varied across Europe, complexity was also often introduced into households by the presence of servants, lodgers and single adult family members. The numbers of children born to a family tended to be generally high, but so were mortality rates. For example, the average life expectancy at birth in England in 1860 was 40 for men and 42 for women, and between 1821 and 1831 in the small town of Redruth in Cornwall 49 per cent of boys and 41 per cent of girls had died before they reached the age of 10. Families were frequently broken by death, and the chances of children knowing their grandparents and even great grandparents are greater now than ever before.

Family life and labour

The examination of the historical aspects of family size and household structure also prompted a questioning of assertions that families in the past supported their members more effectively or that family life was in some way better both prior to, and even in the early stages of, industrialism. Ronald Fletcher (1962) has attacked such notions strongly, arguing that families in the second half of the twentieth century were better able to provide for the material, educational and emotional well-being of their members than had ever been the case. While he considers that for the well-off, or the farmers who could provide for their families, life, if lacking modern amenities, was reasonably comfortable in the past, for labourers the poor conditions were frequently intolerable.

In examining the conditions in the eighteenth century, Fletcher quotes from a report by the steward of the Marquis of Bath who wrote: 'Humanity shudders at the idea of the industrious labourer, with a wife and five or six children, being obliged to live, or rather to exist, in a wretched, damp, gloomy room, of ten or twelve feet square, and that room without a floor' (1962: 76). The Commissioners of Inquiry into the Mines also found children as young as 4 working underground; indeed, John Locke argued that no family should be eligible for poor relief unless all the children over the age of 3 were working (see also Chapters 1 and 2 for further descriptions of the effects of early industrialization and urbanization).

Tilly and Scott (1978), while recognizing the hardship suffered by many families in agriculture and domestic industry, point out that there was a family economy in rural societies, with labour tending to be family labour and all members contributing. Lodgers and apprentices who expanded the size of the household may also have contributed to the joint economic enterprise. Once farming began to be capitalized, wage labour became increasingly common, with all members of the family contributing to the wage packet. It must be recognized, however, that there was no assumption that the children of the poor should remain with their parents. Apprenticeship into agriculture or domestic service was common, and Laslett (1972) suggests that the poor child was likely to have left home to go into service by the age of 10, while in some areas in both France and England some would have left home by the age of 6.

As factory work increased, workers in domestic industry, like their agricultural counterparts, became hirelings, and members of the family worked to support the unit or went into service where conditions were frequently harsh and some employers cruel. Anderson and Zinsser quote from the story of Lucy, born in 1848, who in one post in service was 'treated like a dog – forbidden to sit down for her meals' (1990: 228).

While the worst conditions were suffered by poor families, through Europe death rates were high and widowhood and orphanhood were common for all social groups. The frequently harsh treatment of children, together with the frequent experience of death, has sometimes been interpreted as meaning that family life was less caring as well as less comfortable than in the past. Fletcher, for example, epitomizes the contemporary family as child-centred, contrasting the favourable situation of most modern children with the lack of concern demonstrated for their counterparts in former times.

Childhood did not have a special status in the past and children, as part of the labour force in agriculture, domestic industry and the factories, were often treated harshly. Children of wealthier parents were often left in the care of servants and, in nineteenth-century England, to the sometimes cruel regimes of boarding schools. However, it should also be recognized that frequent child deaths could only be met with stoicism by the family and acceptance did not necessarily indicate a lack of concern. Elizabeth Gaskell, the nineteenth-century writer and wife of a clergyman who lived a comfortable middle-class life, wrote of the death of her little son: 'That wound will never heal on earth' (quoted in Anderson and Zinsser 1990: 137). Similarly, Lucy, a working-class woman, having lost one of her three children writes, after just moving to London with her husband and other children, 'I think I cried most of the time, for my husband was on night work, and I amongst strangers and thinking of my poor child I had so recently buried.'

Certainly there was child cruelty and neglect and even infanticide, but as Anderson and Zinsser point out, most poor mothers across Europe fought to look after their children and neglect and cruelty were frequently the results of economic hardship and despair. Unmarried women in particular would have found it almost impossible to support children when pregnancy meant instant dismissal from service.

Private and public spheres

The notion of a division into private and public spheres developed alongside the processes of industrialization. The division has both behavioural and ideological significance. It relates to the exercise of power and authority in the family and society, and to employment and the domestic division of labour.

Authority in the family in most of Europe was patriarchal, with men having extensive powers over women and children. In many cases the rights of the father were legally recognized, although the period of this right varied. In Brittany, for example, a man remained dependent upon his father until the age of 60 if he remained unmarried, whereas in Beri, also in France, all children became independent at the age of 25. Twenty or 21 were the ages to be achieved in other areas, whilst in England patriarchal control over children was 'a matter of precept and pragmatism rather than law' (O'Day 1994: 59).

Women's situations in the family were also very varied. Whilst as we have seen women in the past were frequently part of joint family labour and in wealthier families, at least into the nineteenth century, frequently maintained roles in the home and in the family enterprise, the actual rights of women within families varied across Europe and over time. Women in medieval England, for example, had legal recognition and rights to property, inheritance and occupation (Macfarlane 1986). Goody, in examining the Germanic tradition, argues that historically women appear to have been able to play a public role and to have some political authority. Goody points out that the 'position [of women] clearly differed in the various regions of Europe as in the rest of the world' (1983: 26). For example, in Provence, Gascony and Languedoc, women were kept out of the fields because their presence would threaten the honour of the men. However, in the Basque region, where the heir to land was the oldest child of either sex, women traditionally had access to more economic power; in the north women worked in the fields side by side with the men, and in Brittany and Lorraine both men and women participated in village affairs.

In spite of these differences, it has been argued that a more distinct division between the public spheres of work and politics and the private domestic sphere of hearth and home gradually became increasingly apparent across Europe: the public sphere became almost exclusively the domain of men; the private the province of women. This dichotomy is crucial to our discussion of family life as it underpins the definitions and expectations of gender roles within families.

Much of the discussion relating to this dichotomy has been concerned with the changes taking place during industrialization. Tilly and Scott (1978), for example, emphasize the impact of the increasing number of factories using machines and bringing the workforce together under one roof. Factories were seen by some as destroying female morals and the maternal instinct and it was widely thought that women should be kept out of the work sphere in order to preserve family life. Certainly, once home became separated from work the care of young children became more obviously problematic and although factory work was undertaken by children from a very early age the care of young babies was more difficult.

In spite of the fact that high death rates meant that many families were dependent on female wage earners women were gradually increasingly associated with the domestic sphere and men with the public and wage earning sphere. Women's wages were low in general and the 'ideal' of the male breadwinner increasingly became an economic necessity. The changes were gradual and affected different parts of Europe and different classes at different times. Abbott and Wallace (1990) argue that in England middle-class women had largely accepted the housewife role by the beginning of the nineteenth century. For working-class women the process was slower, but Roberts (1982) has shown that by about 1900 most working-class English women thought that 'ideally' women should stay at home to look after their husbands and children.

The economic basis for this increasing differentiation of spheres of activity was, as we have seen, founded in industrialism. The ideological basis was more strongly rooted in custom in some areas of Europe than in others, but across the Continent the religious beliefs relating to marriage and family life certainly gave some legitimation to notions of separation. Christian doctrine stressed monogamy and women were to obey their husbands to whom they owed service. Marriage rules in general had been laid down by the Church and even in 'Protestant' England marriage was seen as a sacrament. Divorce and annulment of marriage across Europe in the past was both rare and expensive. The rules have changed slowly up until the present day with changes being dependent both on the changing attitudes of the religious establishment and the civil order; attitudes therefore remain different in the separate states of Europe.

Contemporary families and family relationships

It is argued, then, that the family as an economic unit was changing as industrialization progressed. By the twentieth century some of the harshest conditions had been alleviated and children in Europe were being gradually removed from the workforce and increasingly received a minimum period of compulsory schooling. After the Second World War material standards gradually, although not uniformly, improved for much of the population of Europe and greater emphasis was placed upon the quality of relationships within families and the home.

European families have experienced both changing structures and changing values. These changes reflect the response of family relationships to other aspects of social life, particularly the economy. Mitterauer and Sieder (1982) argued that in pre-industrial Europe individuals were more economically dependent on their families, but that in mature capitalism people are employed and consume as individuals. Whether those employed were men, women, children or the elderly alters the dynamics of family life and, with the twentieth century, there has been the disappearance of legal and economic obstacles to marriage and increased opportunities for divorce. The declining demands of a family economy have introduced more choice about marriage partner and style of conjugal life, fewer children and a longer life expectancy. There are strong themes of individualism in family life and greater emphasis on the relational aspects of 'family'.

Marriage, particularly, has come to be seen in psychological terms where individuals are concerned about the quality of marriage as an emotional relationship. Mansfield and Collard (1988) found that young people wanted to achieve both self-realization and togetherness in their partnerships, and in a tide of rising expectations about marriage and partnerships there is more stress on companionship, self-disclosure and sexual fulfilment. Furthermore, emotional shortfalls and dissatisfaction threaten family life and provide a rationale to rescind family ties.

A survey of European values (Barker *et al.* 1992) found that the quality of interpersonal relationships was seen to be the key ingredient for a successful marriage, with at least 80 per cent emphasizing being faithful, tolerant and respectful. There was less emphasis on material factors such as income and housing, and even less on the organization of household chores; only a third of those interviewed thought sharing household chores important to a successful marriage. And those in the younger age group regarded sexual satisfaction as essential to a happy marriage. Furthermore, in northern countries the focus for marriage was seen as the relationship between the couple, while those in Roman Catholic countries were much more likely to see children as an important adjunct to marriage.

Family life has a strong economic aspect. Kinship networks provide mechanisms for the transfer of property and the exchange of goods and services, and households provide the setting for the organization of domestic consumption and labour. Property transfer and inheritance are increasingly important aspects of kinship connection where larger proportions of homes are privately owned. Family and kinship are economic networks through which economic support may flow. This includes gifts and loans, particularly for deposits on property and school fees, and are especially common in parent and grandparent relationships. Family ties remain important in finding work as only half the jobs available are ever advertised and personal introductions and informal contacts and information are valued by employers. Migrant groups are particularly reliant on families for work and accommodation. Family businesses are still common and many of these are established by family capital and staffed by family labour.

Macfarlane (1978) has argued that since the thirteenth century English family values have stressed individualism and independence; marriage was delayed as the new couple were expected to form a separate household and live economically independent lives. These values are just as important today. Finch and Mason's study of family responsibilities (1993) found that individuals are not seen as having an automatic right to claim support from families. Support-givers are concerned not to undermine family members by rendering them dependent, and support-receivers are anxious not to become beholden. In Britain the moral pressure is to limit support and ensure that it is reciprocal and negotiated. Responsibilities and obligations are built up over time and these processes in part explain the pattern of informal care; parent–child relations were particularly strong because of their longevity and continuity with patterns set from childhood.

Smigielska and Czynczyk (1994) have also explored the ways in which family support and obligation operate in Poland. As in Britain, support and resources tend to flow down the generations and Polish parents and grandparents felt financially responsible for children. However, the nature of families in Poland was particularly important in countering the problems of shortage and rationing of food, goods and accommodation. Polish families were important in the 'permanent hunt for necessary and basic supplies', for queuing and providing information about what had arrived in what shops. Also, in Poland more families lived in flats and accommodation tended to be smaller than in, for example, Britain; in 1984 only 7 per cent of the Polish population had a room of their own. Unlike in Western Europe, it is not assumed that establishing your own family meant acquiring you own accommodation. Although such shared accommodation increased family tension it also meant more support for child-care.

FAMILY ACCOMMODATION IN POLAND

Seven of us share a floor area of forty-three square metres: two rooms, a kitchen and a bathroom for my parents and brother, my husband, our two children and myself. It's worse in the mornings when we're all in a hurry to get ready to go to work, and the children must be taken to kindergarten. We have to prepare a schedule of visits to the bathroom. I make my face up at work. We haven't the ghost of a chance of our own flat. My brother's moving out soon though: he's getting married and he'll live with his wife's parents . . .

(quoted in Smigielska and Czynczyk 1994: 81).

Housework can be seen as part of domestic labour, essential but unpaid work largely undertaken by women as wives and mothers. Women have increased their participation in the labour force, but this has not altered the gendered division of labour in the home. On average women do about fifty hours of housework a week and women who are in employment do less housework but have a longer working day. A desire to increase family resources has encouraged women to remain in paid employment, but this raises questions about their continuing responsibilities for family care and the compatibility of paid and unpaid work.

National policy and the legitimacy of women's employment outside the home shape the experience of combining paid employment with family responsibility. However, long hours and the acceptance of women's economic contribution to the household budget does not necessarily alter their traditional responsibility for housework or providing a homely atmosphere for family life.

The EVSSG survey also revealed considerable conflict about the roles of men and women; paid employment was endorsed as important for the fulfilment of women and as a contribution to household income, but was seen to create problems for child-rearing. The tension was most apparent in the responses from West Germany where it was felt by 38 per cent that working mothers could not establish satisfactory relationships with their children. The contradictions between family responsibility and individualism seemed most keenly felt here.

The management of household budgets is central to the economic life of families. Although it is often assumed that all members of the household have equal access to its resources, their distribution within the household may

---

DOMESTIC LABOUR IN FRANCE AND BRITAIN

Grimler and Roy used national budget studies to identify the amount of time French men and women spent on household chores in 1985 and how much this had changed. They found that men in paid employment spent an average of two hours and forty-eight minutes performing household tasks, compared with four hours and fifty minutes for women in paid employment. Over the past decade men's involvement had increased by twenty-one minutes and women's fallen by four minutes. Men's involvement has increased in child-care and shopping rather than in cleaning, washing or the care of elderly relatives. A similar situation is found in Britain, although French women spend more time in housework than their British counterparts; whatever their work pattern they have less free time and fewer domestic appliances. In France there appears to be a larger gap between theory and practice, with more men claiming to share household tasks than actually performing them. Although French women experience more time pressure and a sense of greater domestic overload, they had a greater sense of legitimacy about combining family and work than their British counterparts.

Sources: Grimler and Roy (1987), Hantrais (1990).

---

disadvantage women and children (Wilson 1987). Men and women have different attitudes to money in the household. Women are more likely to manage the day-to-day budgets, and to regard money as housekeeping and something separate from personal expenditure. This attitude persists even when they are the main earner. Men see themselves as having a greater personal claim on household income, legitimated by their breadwinning status. There are links between money and power in marriage, and greater equality in household financial arrangements appears to depend both on women's full-time participation in paid employment and their willingness to challenge the traditional status of the husband as bread-winner.

There is also a political dimension to family life and this operates at the micro-level between individual family members and at the macro-level in national debates and policies. Families are political in their operation, as individuals use power to pursue vested interests and this political dimension is present whether we are talking about families as sources of support or agents of abuse. The feminist critique of family relations emphasizes patterns of subordination and dominance within families and the reduced power of women and children. This gender- and age-based pattern of power shapes the politics of caring and means that women and children are more likely to be the targets of violence and abuse within the family.

Kellerhals *et al.* (1990) noted the importance of the family as a 'relation-ship' and explored the logic of decision-making within Swiss family relationships. Those in higher socio-economic groups made family decisions in relation to ideas of 'contract, where fairness depended on how it was negotiated and agreed upon'. Families operating with this logic were regarded as *association* families, where cohesion is based on personal autonomy and the importance of individual difference and liberty. Families in lower socio-economic groups made decisions in terms of 'status', where legitimacy depended on what was proper for age, gender and kin relationship. Kellerhals *et al.* saw this logic as producing *shelter* families which emphasize consensus and are more rigidly organized. A third type found throughout Swiss society was the logic of 'effect', where decisions were assessed on the extent to which they maximized the welfare of all family members, balancing the welfare of the individuals with the welfare of others. This logic underpins *companionship* families where domestic organization is flexible and couples are cohesive but maintain strong links with the wider social environment.

At a national level all political parties claim some affiliation with 'family values'. In particular, right-wing parties claim to support traditional families as a defence against social permissiveness and moral decay. Family values also shape public policy and family law in Europe. Maclean and Kurczewski (1994) have suggested that family obligations and individual rights are differently conceived in Eastern and Western Europe. In the East there has been a post-war tradition of state involvement in child support and the facilitation of women's involvement in the workforce. In the West there is greater emphasis on the rights of individuals and non-interference in the private lives of patriarchal families.

There have been moves to 're-privatize' the family in both Eastern and Western Europe, with the rejection of state involvement and greater emphasis on liberal values. After Stalin's death in 1953 each Communist Party was freer to decide national policy and this introduced considerable diversity; in Romania large families were encouraged, pregnancy was heavily monitored and abortion criminalized, unlike, in Poland and East Germany where laws were liberalized. More recently in Poland de-sovietization has been associated with a new emphasis on religious precepts, which seeks to strengthen the traditional family, reinforce differences in gender roles and limit access to divorce and abortion. Change and diversity continue; in the reunification of Germany the West German approach to family matters prevailed, with restrictions on child-care and the criminalization of abortion.

In the West recent moves to the right in politics have led to a rolling back of welfare provision and individual self-sufficiency within the context of the patriarchal family. But within the West there is also variation. Hantrais's (1990) comparative study of French and British women in professional occupations describes the greater political and cultural support for French women to remain in full-time paid employment and to have children. These supports include more generous child allowances, more pressure on employers to provide child-care facilities, and the provision of cheaper child-care and after-school facilities.

Changing family structures

Since the 1960s there have been a number of changes in the shape of the European family. There have also been questions about the extent to which traditional and patriarchal family values are in decline and the extent to which the growth of individualism threatens family obligation. Major family trends are described below.

1   Households have become smaller. The average number of persons living
     in a household has fallen during the past decade and there has been an
     increase in the proportion of the population who live alone. This trend has
     been particularly marked in Denmark, Germany, France and the United
     Kingdom. In the United Kingdom in 1991 27 per cent of households
     contained only one person, whereas in 1961 the figure was 14 per cent.
     Individuals are much less likely to live alone in Portugal, Spain and Greece,
     where 3 to 5 per cent of the population live in single-person households. A
     number of factors contribute to the drop in household size: lower birth
     rates, fewer mature children living with their parents, and an increase in
     the elderly (and largely female) population.

2   Fertility rates have declined across Europe since the 1960s but there has
     been some variation within this overall trend. In Northern Europe national
     birth rates have reached a low plateau which is below generational replace-
     ment. In Southern Europe post-war birth rates started from a much higher
     level, but there has been a swifter and steeper drop in birth rates in recent
     years which is now slowing down. One of the surest indicators of declining
     fertility is completed family size; looking at the cohort of women born in
     1950, Irish women had the largest families (averaging 3.0 children) and
     those in Luxembourg and Germany the smallest (averaging 1.7). Not only
     are European women having fewer children, they are also delaying child-
     birth; in 1975 the average European woman had her first child when she
     was 24, compared to 26 in 1990 (see Figure 10.1).

          Fertility rates were slightly higher in Eastern than in Western Europe.
     Bodrova and Anker (1985) explored the extent to which this may be the
     result of socialist population programmes which attempt to reduce conflict
     between the roles of mother and worker; 2.5 per cent of national income

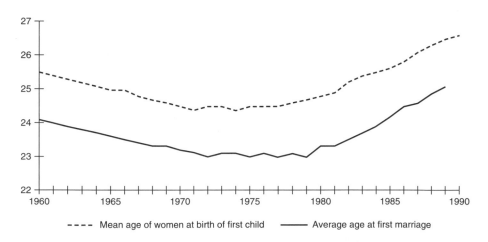

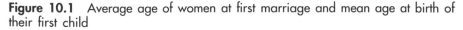

Figure 10.1 Average age of women at first marriage and mean age at birth of
their first child

Source: *Demographic Statistics*, Eurostat, Bruxelles-Luxembourg, 1993

in the form of family allowances was available in Bulgaria, Czechoslovakia and Hungary, and these allowances were cumulative with increased numbers of children. For families with five or more children in Czechoslovakia child allowance could amount to 30 per cent of family income. However, despite strong state incentives, the authors conclude that population policies influenced the timing of births but had little impact on the overall numbers of children born.

3   Marriage rates have declined since the 1960s; fewer people are getting married and those that are marry later; in 1990 the average age for a first marriage in the European Union was 27.6 years for men and 25.1 years for women. This decline has been partially balanced by the growth of cohabitation. These trends developed first in Scandinavia (Popenhoe 1987), but today characterize much of Northern Europe. In the UK 18 per cent of unmarried men and women aged 16–59 were living with a partner in 1992. Cohabitation is particularly prevalent as a prelude to marriage and in the aftermath of divorce.

There is a question about whether cohabitation marks the development of a new type of domestic relationship with more tenuous connection to 'family'. Bejin (1985) notes the prevalence of living together among the young and regards this 'juvenile cohabitation' as an attempt to maintain a more negotiated personal commitment and to emphasize the emotional aspects of the relationship. There is some debate about whether cohabitation is marriage by another name or an attempt to resist conjugality.

4   The divorce rate has risen everywhere in Europe except Eire, where divorce remains illegal. The UK now heads the European league table of marital dissolution, with 2.9 divorces per thousand population in 1991 (see Figure 10.2). At the other end of the scale Italy and Greece have the lowest rates of divorce with 0.5 and 0.6 per thousand population. At current rates one in three marriages will break down within fifteen years and, for every two marriages currently being contracted, there is one divorce. Furthermore, over half the divorces involve dependent children, and as the average time between a first marriage and divorce is shortening the age of children involved in divorce proceedings is declining.

Over the past few years those countries where divorce has become increasingly prevalent, the UK, Denmark, Belgium and Luxembourg, have seen some stability or slight decline in the divorce rates. Again the popularity of cohabitation may mask the numbers of dissolving partnerships as it reduces the numbers of officially recorded dissolutions.

5   The growth of remarriage and reconstituted families. In 1991, 15 per cent of marriages for both men and women were second or subsequent marriages, compared with 9 per cent of marriages for men and 7 per cent of marriages for women in 1960. The growing prevalence of divorce and remarriages has been seen to add a greater turbulence to contemporary kinship relations and flux to family living arrangements.

6   The growing numbers of children born outside marriage. Since 1975 this has increased threefold to reach 19 per cent of births in the European Union in 1991. However, figures vary widely from 47 per cent of Danish births

and 30 per cent of UK and French births to 2 per cent of Greek and 6 per cent of Italian births. However, it cannot be assumed that these children are living in lone parent households or outside stable relationships as three-quarters of these children are jointly registered by both parents.

7   The growth of four generational families. As life expectancy has increased, so generational ties have been extended. As a result elder care is being received and delivered by older age groups, and elderly parents are more likely to be pre-deceased by their children.

8   The growth of gay families and partnerships. Homosexual men and women may live in couples as if married and seek to adopt, foster and, in the case of women, have children through AID. Gay partners may also wish to be recognized as next of kin and prime carers. Danish law recognizes marriage between homosexual partners.

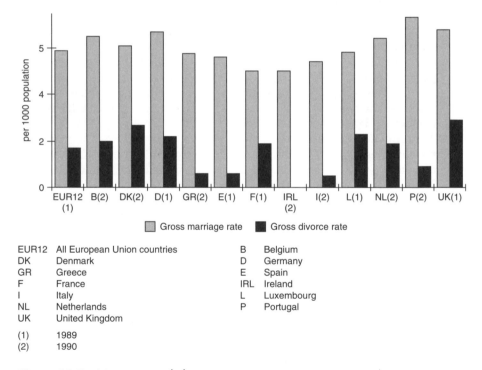

EUR12	All European Union countries	B	Belgium
DK	Denmark	D	Germany
GR	Greece	E	Spain
F	France	IRL	Ireland
I	Italy	L	Luxembourg
NL	Netherlands	P	Portugal
UK	United Kingdom		
(1)	1989		
(2)	1990		

Figure 10.2 Marriage and divorce

Source: *Demographic Statistics*, Eurostat, Bruxelles-Luxembourg, 1993

Changing family values

The EVSSG examined popular attitudes towards the family and the changing assumptions of family life. Europeans were surveyed in 1981 and again in 1990 and in this time period there appeared to have been some reassertion of traditional family values; in 1990 eight out of ten Europeans identified the family as very important in their lives and despite the changing forms of family life fewer thought marriage was an outdated institution in 1990 (21 per cent) than in 1981 (25 per cent). Although people declared a commitment to traditional families, the study also identified the growth of liberalism and permissiveness in relation to abortion, divorce and sexual morality, except in the context of sex below the age of consent.

Respondents from Great Britain and Eire seemed the most family-orientated and those from Germany the least. In Europe the ideal family size was two or three children, although this was smaller in West Germany and larger in Eire and Northern Ireland. There was also less support for the notion that parents should be self-sacrificing for their children in Germany and the Netherlands. The EVSSG also identified a tension between commitment to family responsibility and the pursuit of individual freedom. This was found in the contradiction between the public perception of the needs of children and the rights of adults and was particularly marked in the younger age groups; 48 per cent of those aged 25 to 34 endorsed the rights of single women to have children, whilst 84 per cent agreed that children needed to be brought up in a home with two parents.

This suggests that the idea of family is strongly embedded in European culture. Irrespective of the form of particular families 'the family' has considerable ideological force, firmly identifying family life with the patriarchal, nuclear family, and heterosexual couples, organized as breadwinning husbands and home-making wives and their dependent children. Even where domestic arrangements were looser and more transitory in people's lives, this remained the model for family life.

Summary

- Family relationships are shaped by the nature of economy and polity.
- In post-war Europe there has been an overall movement towards smaller households and fewer children.
- Traditional family structures and values are more apparent in Southern and Catholic Europe.
- Europeans today place greater emphasis on relational aspects of the family, particularly marriage and partnerships.
- Families play a crucial role in the socialization of family members and in social reproduction, especially the reproduction of gender roles.

Further reading

Diana Gittins (1996) *The Family in Question* (2nd edn), London: Macmillan. This book provides an accessible but critical look at 'the family', examining its variability as an ideology and as a set of living arrangements. It includes material on families in different cultural and historical settings.

Rosemary O'Day (1994) *The Family and Family Relationships, 1500–1900: England, France and the United States of America*, London: Macmillan. This book takes a detailed historical look at family relationships in England, France and the United States of America. It provides rich detail on the relationships between parents and children and husbands and wives, and insight into how family relationships are linked to the world of work, the state and the Church.

Chapter 11

Education in Europe

Sue Hemmings and Lyn Bryant

Introduction	220
Educational traditions	220
Educational provision	223
Sociological interpretations	233
Standardization and co-operation	235
Summary	236
Further reading	237

Key concepts

- **European educational traditions**
- **Political repertoires**
- **Social and cultural reproduction**

Introduction

A common feature of all advanced industrial societies is that they have a system of mass education. European systems differ in the ways in which they are organized and administered, in the content of their curricula and in the organization of the teaching and learning processes. Indeed, within Britain alone there are two distinct and different systems: those of Scotland and of England and Wales. Throughout Europe 'education' has formed a key battleground in debates about national economic competitiveness, national identity and social justice, being variously seen as a conservative force which protects the social status quo and the key to personal growth and social transformation.

For the most part these systems were established in the mid-nineteenth century and have continued to expand to the present day. Education, originally established for a small social elite, has been transformed to encompass members of more social groups, for an increasing proportion of their lives. Despite the differences between the systems, all perform the same roles of transmitting knowledge and values which reproduce a society's structures and culture over time and of sorting children to fit into future adult social roles as citizens, workers and members of families and other social groups.

In this chapter we look at some of the social and cultural factors which have shaped Europe's national education systems. In doing this we recognize both the importance of forces common across countries which shape the institutions of the modern world and the diversity of ways in which these link with national cultures, political agendas and traditions as nations move through their own histories.

Educational traditions

Historical sociologists have asked the question: why did mass education appear in so many places at around the same time? Using comparative methods they have sought to isolate the factors which triggered the development of mass systems of education. There is no agreement over whether it is possible to point to one causal factor, and what that might be, or if many factors coming together caused this development (Green 1990). The nineteenth century was a time of great social upheaval across Europe and saw the coming to maturity of a number of the processes associated with the development of modernity: urbanization, industrialization, the consolidation of bourgeois capitalism and the drawing of the boundaries of the modern nation-states of Western Europe (see also Chapters 1, 2 and 3). These underlying processes affected all parts of Europe but to different extents, at different rates and in different ways as they interacted with the unique histories and cultures of these societies.

These issues are not just of historical interest. All of the countries of the European Union operate within the constantly moving and transforming economic, technological and ideological structures of advanced capitalism. Both political and economic processes are more than ever before manifested in supranational forums as countries jostle to establish their places within the Union and the Single European Market. Beyond that, educational ideas and practices are no respecters of national borders: both educationalists and policy-makers have drawn from educational traditions other than their own, looking not only to other practices within Europe but also beyond to the United States and Japan.

The development of national education systems has been shaped by both educational traditions and philosophies and the broader political and ideological concerns of the day. Four broad traditions can be identified within European educational thought: Encyclopaedism, Humanism, Vocationalism and Naturalism. These traditions had very real influences in establishing the forms of education upon which today's systems are built (McLean 1990). Beyond that, they provide a useful tool for those interested in thinking about the role and purpose of education and we will be using them in that way in the following sections.

During the eighteenth century a major philosophical movement known as the Enlightenment spread across Europe changing the ways in which people thought and the things they believed. Enlightenment thinkers saw the key to human progress as lying in the overthrow of tradition and superstition and their replacement with rational, scientific forms of enquiry. Some thinkers set about collecting and ordering all of this new knowledge about the world into one great encyclopaedia. *Encyclopaedism* in educational thought is a direct inheritor of the ideas of the Enlightenment and has been particularly influential in countries such as France and Scotland which were major sites of Enlightenment activity. This view holds that it is possible to identify a body of valid knowledge which should be ordered, codified and learnt. Beyond that education should pass on the ability to think rationally, to create abstract models and to reason as this leads to better people and ultimately to a better society. The usefulness of education derives from the ability to transfer knowledge and the analytical skills of reasoning to all situations in life as they present themselves.

This system tends towards the rigid division of knowledge into separate subjects and an emphasis upon formal academic knowledge over the practical or vocational, which are seen as simply sites where reason and knowledge can be applied.

In contrast ancient philosophy provides the roots of the approach known as *Humanism* which was developed in its purest form in the English public school and university system of the mid-nineteenth century. This approach emphasizes the role of education in producing a 'virtuous individual' who will have a highly developed sense of morality and an appreciation of the arts and elegance in thought and the construction of arguments. This approach closely links the academic and pastoral roles of the tutor who is seen as a guide for individuals following their paths towards becoming fully rounded individuals. Subject specialization is possible as individuals develop their own interests, but as a whole the system privileges the appreciation of art and literature over the scientific and practical which are seen to offer little to individual moral improvement.

Vocationalism is a view that education should be directly targeted to meet the needs of a national economy for skilled labour and the inculcation in young people of appropriate attitudes towards work. All education systems to some extent contain vocational elements but vocationalism is distinctive in its reference to the Platonic tradition which holds that different types of education should be offered to different categories of people. As a result vocationalism tends to form the basis of the education of the masses in systems where Humanism dominates for the elite.

The chronologically most recent philosophy of education is that of *Naturalism* which is rooted in developmental psychology and sociology as well as philosophy. It emphasizes the importance of starting from the knowledge, abilities and needs of the individual child and the social world in which that child is located rather than from bodies of abstract knowledge. It is a skills- rather than knowledge-based approach which emphasizes the skill of 'learning how to learn'. In different settings it has been variously expressed through child-centred learning strategies, education throughout life, strong school–community links and the organization of the school as a mini-community. There is not a strong distinction between academic skills and more practical and vocational skills as the acquisition of all of these elements is seen as part of the integrated process of developing a whole person.

EUROPEAN EDUCATIONAL TRADITIONS

Encyclopaedism
Key principles: core of shared knowledge, rationality and reason, usefulness.
Main influence in: France, Belgium, Luxembourg, Italy, Spain, Portugal and
   Scotland
Humanism
Key principles: morality, individualism and specialization.
Main influence in: England, Wales, Ireland and Greece
Vocationalism
Key principles: economic need, usefulness and specialization.
Main influence in: England and Wales
Naturalism
Key principles: developmentalism, holism, application.
Main influence in: Germany, the Netherlands and Denmark
Main source: McLean (1990).

These philosophical positions are the products of the various social conditions which gave rise to them. Today they operate in two ways: as part of the 'taken for granted' structures and cultures of the societies in which they are embedded and as more formally discussed positions within educational debates across cultures. In addition to questions of educational philosophy, education systems form one arm of the activities of the political system. Political concerns about the economy, nationhood, sexualities, families, law and order and so on are expressed across policy areas and find expression within education policy. Individual political parties form policy platforms not on the basis of coherent philosophical or ideological systems of thought but by linking together issues and ideas in a way which appeals to the electorate. Thus the same party may draw on a range of political repertoires in establishing its educational policies and different parties will link together the same repertoires in different ways. These repertoires all contain elements which depict in different ways the nature of the individual, the relationship between the individual and society, the relationship between education and citizenship and the relationship between education and the economy. Within contemporary Europe it is possible to distinguish four broad political repertoires which members of political groups draw upon in discussing education: neo-liberalism, neo-conservatism, social reformism and social transformation.

POLITICAL REPERTOIRES

Neo-liberalism stresses individualism and education as a marketplace where individuals can invest time and effort in their own development which will later be rewarded in the labour market. Society will benefit from individuals operating out of self-interest.

Neo-conservatism stresses the importance of education in maintaining national traditions and cultures through the transmission of a common cultural heritage. The individual is a member of a national community and education equips the individual with economically and socially useful skills.

Social reformism stresses social equality and education as a political right of citizenship. Individual and societal interests are essentially the same. Education is a mechanism for maximizing the human resources of an individual and of a society for the common good.

Social transformation. Education is a mechanism by which the existing social order can be challenged. Institutional barriers to equality may be overcome by the promotion of anti-racist and anti-sexist strategies. Education seeks to develop a critical and questioning intelligence which fundamentally challenges the power of dominant groups.

The education systems which exist within Europe today can be seen as the products of broad changes in economic and political conditions. Beyond that, the specific forms they take represent the outcomes of long processes of social struggle where these conditions are shaped through educational and political debates. We will now go on to look at some of these outcomes.

Educational provision

Pre-school and primary education

Across the European Union children begin compulsory schooling somewhere between the ages of 4 and 7, most commonly at the age of 6. Before starting formal schooling many children will have experienced some kind of pre-school education, although the dividing line between child-care provision and pre-school education is far from clear cut and is managed differently in different countries.

In Sweden and Finland pre-school education is treated as part of the public child-care sector. Elsewhere what distinguishes pre-school education from what follows is the nature of the curriculum. Pre-school education is largely a time of play, sometimes freely entered into and controlled by the child and sometimes used as a means to pursue teacher-determined goals. In Denmark some pre-school provision is located within the social affairs sector, but recent reforms have also brought together into single units pre-school classes and the early years of compulsory education. This has caused teachers from two different educational cultures, one emphasizing play and the other teaching, to work together. France is the only system in which the formal teaching of school subjects occurs at this level, with reading, writing and calculating skills being introduced at the age of 5. In the earlier years of the French system, and across the other states providing pre-school education, the emphasis is placed in differing amounts upon the twin aims of Naturalism – the development of the individual's personality, creativity and intellect and the socialization of children to act as members of a group outside of the family. Luxembourg is the only country where pre-school education is compulsory and begins at the age of 5. In the Netherlands, where compulsory schooling starts at the age of 4, there is no formally recognized pre-school system although some crèches and play groups do exist. In practice similar situations exist in Ireland and the United Kingdom where compulsory schooling starts at the ages of 6 and 5 respectively, but large numbers of 4- and 5-year-olds are entered voluntarily into state-run primary schools. Elsewhere in Europe pre-school education is optional, formally organized and widely taken up, with participation rates rising as children near school age. High levels of participation are found in Belgium, France and Denmark. In Belgium all pre-school provision is free of charge and 95 per cent of 3-year-olds and 100 per cent of 5-year-olds participate. In France, 85 per cent of pre-school education is state funded and free of charge and 15 per cent is state subsidized but fee paying; 35 per cent of 2-year-olds, 99 per cent of 3-year-olds and 100 per cent of 5-year-olds participate. In Denmark where, depending upon their level of income, parents may be asked to contribute up to 35 per cent of the cost, 35 per cent of 3-year-olds and 90 per cent of 5- to 6-year-olds participate.

Once children enter formal schooling the Naturalist consensus of the pre-school years breaks down and the impact of different educational traditions becomes more apparent. Yet there remain similarities.

All children in Europe can expect at the primary stage to cover work with their own language, mathematics or arithmetic, physical activity, some sort of natural or environmental science and art and craft. All will cover at least one of history, geography, social studies or civics. Most will have some experience of music. Table 11.1 illustrates these similarities. It is compiled from information given by member states to the European Commission (EURYDICE and CEDEFOP 1995) and shows some of the problems of a comparative sociology of education. The table starts from the authors' own experiences of the education system in England. We have fitted the experiences of other countries into our framework of subjects. For example, German children would be surprised to be told that they study History, Geography, Movement/PE, Science and Social Studies as they experience a single 'subject' called Sachundterricht designed to

TABLE 11.1 The primary phase curriculum

	Fr.	Belg.	Lux.	It.	Sp.	Port.	Eng. & W.	Ire.	Gr.	Ger.	Neth.	Den.
Own language	S	S	S	T	T	T	S	S	S	S	S	S
Maths/Arithmetic	S	S	S	T	S	T	S	S	S	S	S	S
History	S	S	–	T	T	T	S	T	S	I	S	S
Geography	S	S	S	T	T	T	S	T	–	I	S	S
Civics/ Social Studies	S	S	S	T	T	T	–	T	S	I	S	–
Art/Craft	S	S	S	T	T	T	S	S	S	S	S	S
Movement/PE	S	S	S	T	S	T	S	S	S	I	S	S
Science/ Environment	S	S	S	T	T	T	S	T	S	I	S	S
Music	S	S	–	–	T	T	S	S	–	S	S	S
RE	–	S	–	T	T	T	S	S	–	S	S	S
Second language	S	S	S	T	–	–	*	S	–	S	S	–

S = separate subject.

T = within thematically linked curriculum.

I = within fully integrated curriculum.

* = Welsh is taught in some schools.

Note: In some countries subjects are introduced at different ages within the primary phase.

lay the groundwork for these separate subjects when they are introduced at secondary level. Reflected through this integrated curriculum is the holistic emphasis of the German form of Naturalism.

Missing from the table are what, from the standpoint of England, look like national idiosyncrasies but from within the countries concerned are key parts of the educational process. Thus in Greece the Humanist tradition is upheld in the naming of school subjects, as the children in the first two years of primary school receive 'aesthetic education'. In Denmark a particularly Danish version of Naturalism is expressed through the specification of 'free class discussion' as part of a common compulsory curriculum.

In addition the table shows that in many countries a second language is taught. The amount of language teaching has increased in many countries in the light of the perceived growth in importance of trade and commerce across European boundaries, but the implications of learning a second language vary considerably with the national context. Luxembourg has three national languages. Letzeburgesch is the language spoken in most homes and is widely used in private life, but the teaching language for practically all subjects becomes German which is the language used most widely in the print media. In addition French, which is the language of parliament and the legal system, is introduced to the school curriculum from the age of seven. In Finland children are taught in their mother tongue with each school typically employing only one language. Schools thus deliver education in Finnish, Swedish or Sámi, with the teaching also of a second language which may be a foreign language or one of the other two national languages. Belgium has three separate school systems based upon the division of the country into three different linguistic communities: Dutch-speaking, French-speaking and German-speaking. In Ireland, Wales and the Friesland province of the Netherlands the teaching of two languages is part of a defence of a traditional language against the onslaught of the 'national' language.

By stressing the similarities of subject content it is also possible to over-look the way differences in the underlying philosophies shape the actual educational experience of children. It is possible to learn the same skills and knowledge within vastly different types of classroom practice. These differences can be seen by comparing English and French primary schooling.

The history of primary education in England and Wales in many ways starts with the publication of the Hadow Reports of 1931 and 1933. Up until then prepara-tory education very much in the Humanist tradition had been available to the fee-paying few whilst, since the 1880s, the majority of children had received a free state elementary education designed to transmit basic skills and values to the children of the labouring classes. The Hadow Reports recommended a trans-formation of this state provision into primary and secondary sectors. Primary schooling, organized around the principles of developmental psychology, would form the basis for children to enter into a highly differentiated secondary school system. These proposals formed part of the basis of the 1944 Education Act. In the period of post-war reconstruction from 1945 through to the late 1960s, a time of broadly social reformist political culture, child-centred learning became the professional ideology of English primary school teachers.

By the mid-1970s it had become fashionable to blame teachers for all aspects of national decline and in October 1976 Prime Minister James Callaghan, in a speech at Ruskin College, Oxford, launched a national 'great debate' on education. This relocating of economic issues into the education forum had implications for all sectors of education, in the primary sector it resulted in an attack upon the child-centred movement which became associated in the press and parliamentary debate with the 'loony left' and allegedly inefficient local government.

These attacks greatly influenced the Education Reform Act, 1988, intro-duced by a government drawing upon both neo-liberal and neo-conservative educational repertoires. With this Act, for the first time in Britain the national government imposed a National Curriculum, although only upon maintained schools in England and Wales. The National Curriculum and the testing proce-dures associated with it have formed the site of a major struggle between schoolteachers and the government. The curriculum can be seen to introduce a strong Encyclopaedist strand into the English and Welsh system and also to limit the teachers' ability to apply their professional judgement. The logic of the reforms is to move teachers towards being the deliverers of a curriculum to passive learners, a long way from the professional aspirations of teachers committed to the philosophy of child-centredness. In Scotland the period since 1988 has also seen curricula change. Whilst there is no legally imposed curriculum and schools retain a degree of freedom in determining their curriculum, the 5–14 Development Programme includes government guidelines on broad curricular areas.

During the same period the French education system also faced reforms. The primary system in France shares a similar history to that of England, having been first established in the late nineteenth century as an elementary education for the working classes to prepare them for the practical world of work. Debates around the reform of the teaching profession in the early 1990s show a strong distinction being drawn at the rhetorical level of political debate between the work of the primary and the secondary teacher. The secondary teacher was seen to require little in the way of teaching skills but rather to be the transmitter of a cultural tradition. The primary teacher was seen to be following a calling requiring dedication, self-denial and resilience 'in the service of the development of the children' (Greaves and Shaw 1992: 204).

The distinctions between the English and French systems are perhaps, there-fore, not as marked as they are traditionally presented. Both profess a commitment to the development of the child; both are structured by the demands of a nation-ally prescribed curriculum. The French commitment to the development of the child is, however, conceived of very differently from the child-centred approach. French political traditions view equality as requiring that all citizens be treated in the same way. Developmentalism, then, is expressed in a highly structured learn-ing programme requiring all students to move through the same stages at the same rate. Teachers are thus committed to getting children through the stages as efficiently as possible and, unlike their British counterparts, they do not view their professional role as involving curriculum development. This view of equality has also shaped English and French responses to living in a multicultural society. In England multicultural and anti-racist approaches stress that children from differ-ent social groups need to be treated differently if they are to have equal oppor-tunities, and their cultures are to be seen to be equally valid. The French response has been far more assimilationist, stressing the equal opportunity of all children to participate in what is conceived of as a single national culture.

In an ethnographic study of two French primary schools located in socially different areas of the same city, Sharpe (1992) found the school buildings to be rather dull and uniform and in a poor state of repair. In the classrooms individual desks were ordered in straight rows facing the blackboard. A great deal of use was made of chalk and talk methods, along with photocopied worksheets taken from books used widely throughout the French system. There was little oppor-tunity for the children to display individuality or creativity and little evidence of children's work on display.

In contrast, child-centredness as an approach to teaching continues to inform English and Welsh practice in the delivery of the National Curriculum. Its main influence remains as a series of techniques such as topic work; classroom org-anization strategies, such as children working in groups around tables, domestic play corners, the display of children's work around the classroom; and in the fabric of the primary school buildings of the suburban expansions and inner city redevelopments of the post-war era. These schools were designed for child-centred learning: built on a single level, with large windows and flexible rooms, often set in playing fields.

The political attack upon child-centred education in Britain has not ended. In 1991 the then Secretary of State for Education, Kenneth Clarke, ordered a report from Her Majesty's Inspectorate on the French education system. The report identified, and was approving of, the extensive use of whole class and didactic teaching, a fact which Mr Clarke used to order a report into primary teaching methods and classroom organization in British schools. It is possible, therefore, that the British systems may come to resemble the French even more closely. Paradoxically, this would be through direct government intervention in teaching practices whereas in France the adherence to these 'traditional' methods is an element of the teachers' professional culture rather than the result of government directive (McLean 1993).

A move in the opposite direction, from the Encyclopaedic tradition to a more Naturalistic philosophy is evident in the policy statements of the recently reformed systems of Italy, Spain and Portugal (EURYDICE and CEDEFOP 1991). Here we see the language of Naturalism with emphasis upon the child's role in the education process, the introduction of more integrated curricula and the idea of meeting the developmental needs of the child. Again, though, much lies beneath the surface of these national documents. In Italy there are great regional variations within a broad national framework. In Spain authorities at national and local level work together within the framework of a national curriculum introduced to counter the teacher autonomy of the late Franco years which had in practice produced a highly traditional and socially divisive curriculum (McLean 1993).

Secondary education

Secondary education begins somewhere between the ages of 10 and 12 and is marked by the transition to a new school. In many European countries the first two years of secondary education is known as an orientation or observation phase during which young people continue to follow a broad curriculum before being separated into distinct educational streams for the rest of their education.

Patterns of secondary school provision differ across Europe, and indeed within countries. At various stages of secondary schooling, in-school provision may see pupils separated into different schools emphasizing varying types of academic, technical and vocational education, or children may concentrate on different types of education within the same school.

The system in England and Wales today is a complicated one reflecting successive waves of educational reform. The 1944 Education Act established a system of grammar, secondary modern and technical schools. The Humanist tradition was retained in the grammar school, whilst versions of Naturalism informed the notion that the needs of different types of children were best met by different types of schools. In fact few areas established technical schools and despite the official pronouncements that these different types of school had equal status and simply offered different types of education it became increasingly clear that those who went to grammar school would have the opportunity to go on to higher education whilst the secondary modern's emphasis was to prepare pupils for direct entry into the labour market. In the social reformist culture of the times this situation was seen to be socially divisive and a waste of talent, particularly working-class talent, and as a result in 1966 the then Labour government issued an instruction encouraging local authorities to establish comprehensive schools. Most authorities complied, although there are still areas where the tripartite system remains. Comprehensive education provided an opportunity for the child-centred philosophy of the day to find a home in the secondary sector, but many comprehensives retain within them banding and streaming strategies which maintain social divisions within a single institution. Comprehensive reorganization also led to the creation of middle schools, sixth-form colleges and tertiary colleges which combined the work of Further Education colleges and sixth forms. Since the 1988 Education Act further reorganizations have occurred in England and Wales. Some schools have left local authority control and opted for Grant Maintained Status whilst others under the Local Management of Schools remain within the LEA but compete separately with other schools for pupils. In addition a new category of school – the City Technology College – has been established. There have also been developments in the school curriculum, with the introduction of TVEI in some schools aimed at increasing the amount of technical and vocational education within compulsory education and the apparently contradictory introduction of a traditionally subject-based National Curriculum. Assessment patterns have also changed with the introduction of National Curriculum Tests and the abolition of the old CSE and O-levels and the introduction of GCSE, the invention of the 'half A-level', the AS level, and the introduction of National Vocational Qualifications and General National Vocational Qualifications set at five levels from foundation to professional and designed to bring into a national framework the bewildering array of vocational and technical qualifications.

In practice, of those children attending state secondary schools 90 per cent in England, 100 per cent in Wales and 99 per cent in Scotland attend comprehensives, but nevertheless the schools produce a highly streamed output of children variously destined to enter higher education, vocational education, vocational training schemes or the labour market.

The situation in many other European countries is just as complicated, as various systems of organizing both compulsory and post-compulsory secondary education are in operation.

Denmark provides a useful comparison here as it too has witnessed major educational reform in recent years (Winther-Jensen 1994). Whilst many of the issues and debates in Denmark were similar to those in Britain the final national outcomes can be seen as shaped by forces specific to the educational traditions of the particular countries. In 1982 a Social Democratic government committed to social reformist and social transformative policies stressing late specialization, the erosion of subject boundaries and the promotion of topic-based and socially relevant studies, was replaced by a Liberal government committed to the reduction of both state expenditure and the power of educational institutions, shorter vocationally relevant courses and an emphasis upon separate subjects. Political debates at the time also emphasized the role of education in revitalizing the economy at a time of structural economic change and the need to develop a common core of skills and knowledge allied with the introduction of testable educational objectives as a curricular framework. So far, then, the debates in Britain and Denmark seem very similar; indeed, in 1989 Her Majesty's Chief Inspector of Schools was invited to visit Denmark to pass on the British experience. In the reforms that followed, however, the deeply embedded importance of the Naturalist consensus in Danish educational thought is clear. The idea of the 'folk school' was first developed in the nineteenth century and forms one element of what is known as the Grundtvigian element in Danish education. Named after a Danish priest, poet and writer this tradition stresses not only a single comprehensive institution covering the whole of the compulsory years of education but also a strong commitment towards educational experiences which develop the whole personality, teaching practices which are highly child-centred and a preference for history and literature in the curriculum. Thus whereas a 'return to basics' in British, especially English, political debates marks a looking backwards to an elitist, selective and content-driven curriculum, in Denmark the same appeal to tradition has very different implications. The changes impacted upon the *folkeskole* mainly in the form of a strengthening of guidelines on the content of Danish history and a return to the older classics of Danish literature. Foreign language and science curricula were also strengthened in a slight move towards Encyclopaedism. In the upper secondary schools, which prepare 16- to 20-year-olds for higher education, the single subject approach was strengthened rather than topic based study. The curriculum here, however, remains much more broadly based than the English equivalent with all students following a broad common core of subjects, together with subjects specific to their chosen area of specialization and subjects chosen from a range of options. Danish classrooms remain among the noisiest and most informal in Europe, as regardless of curriculum content the commitment to student-centred experiential learning remains strong. In 1993 Denmark elected a new coalition government led by the Social Democrats, and social reformism again came into play within educational policy as multiculturalism and environmentalism found their way into curricular guidelines and streaming and setting within the *folkeskole* was forbidden.

In the German system local variations exist but generally, after a two-year orientation stage, at the age of 12 students will enter into a highly differentiated system comprised of the Gymnasium (which prepares students for entry to university), the Realschule (which prepares students for higher level vocational courses) and the Hauptschule (which prepares students for vocational training). There have been some limited experiments with comprehensivization with the Gesamtschule. France has a similar 'observation cycle' for the first two years of secondary schooling. At the age of 13 students may attend a College or Vocational Lycée in preparation for transfer at 15 to a Lycée General or Technical or a Vocational Lycée. The General and Technical Lycées prepare students for the General or Technical Baccalaureate examination which provides qualification for university entrance. The Vocational Lycée is primarily concerned with preparing students for entry to the labour market but since 1989 a Vocational Baccalaureate has been available; this qualifies students to enter a further year of education to upgrade the qualification to a Technical Baccalaureate and thus be able to enter university.

The Italian system is based upon a common school for 11- to 14-year-olds, the Scuola Media. At post-compulsory level students enter a highly differentiated system of schools for the 14–19 age group: the Classical, Scientific and Artistic Liceos which prepare students for higher education; direct entry to primary or nursery teacher training; Art Schools preparing students mainly for skilled entry to the labour market; Technical Schools where courses are divided into nine occupational categories and prepare students for labour market entry or further higher level training. In addition Vocational Schools for the 14–17 age group offer vocational training in five occupational streams.

In all countries of Western Europe the last ten years have seen a trend towards increased participation in both further and secondary education after the compulsory period of schooling, together with more vocational training being included as part of both school curricula and post-school provision. There are differences, however, in school-leaving ages, and Belgium, Germany, Spain and the Netherlands stipulate an element of educational attendance after compulsory schooling has finished, coupled often with vocational training.

The variation in types of training and levels of participation makes it difficult to make definitive statements about vocational training in Europe, which has been described by one author as 'a crazy quilt' of provision (Chisholm 1992). There have been specific moves by the Community to encourage member states to 'train a better-skilled labour force and to create more equal opportunities for the regions' (Eurostat 1992). Such demands for education systems to supply skilled workers for the labour market are not new, but they have become more widespread.

The differences existing in the vocational elements of education certainly relate to the history of educational provision generally and to the level of economic development in particular societies. The more developed economies, on the whole, have more prolonged periods of general education and more complex systems of training. The rhetoric of a 'skills-led recovery' is often deployed as the cure for economic ills, as the blame for them is located by policy-makers in the education and training systems. The link between education and national economic well-being is far from clear (Finegold and Soskis 1990). Clearer is the link between the expansion of training schemes and the need to control large numbers of unemployed young people and the need for governments to be seen to be doing something about unemployment (Finn 1987). However, it has been demonstrated that there is a relationship between lack of educational qualifications and the likelihood of being unemployed (Coleman and Hendry 1990). Hence it might be argued that the drive to increase vocationalism in education and to provide more training schemes is of benefit to young people as well as employers.

In recent years just as the number of young people participating in post-school further education and training has increased so have the proportions entering higher education.

Higher education

Higher education is defined in the International Standard Classification of Education (ISCED) handbook as more specialized study normally undertaken after successful completion of a good basic education lasting for at least eleven years. Within higher education three subdivisions are recognized. Level five is below degree level and is frequently vocational; in Britain level five would include Dip. HE, BTEC and SCOTVEC. Higher National Level six is first degree or equivalent; level seven is postgraduate.

TABLE 11.2 Main types of qualification leading on to higher education

Country	Examination	Description
Belgium	Maturitie	A three-subject examination
Germany	Arbitur	Two main subjects plus one option with written exams, oral exam in an additional subject
Italy	Maturita	Exam in four subjects
Netherlands	Leaving exam	Seven subjects taken in a pre-university school
Spain	Bachillerato	Six compulsory subjects plus three options, plus one-year university orientation course
Britain	A-levels/Highers	Two or more subjects, mainly written examinations
Denmark	State exam	State-controlled exam in a range of subjects
France	Baccalaureate	Divided into a number of series, written and oral exams in about seven subjects; distinct tracks, some vocational

Unlike schooling, higher education in Europe is neither compulsory nor open to all. Students must usually obtain a standard qualification, or, in the case of older adults, prove that they are capable of completing the course. The main qualifying examinations are shown in Table 11.2. Their content is academic in the main, although alternative more vocationally orientated qualifications are increasingly being accepted by universities in most European states. Across Europe the majority of entrants are aged 18–21, although increasing numbers of older people are entering courses – in Germany, for example, a certain number of places are reserved for them.

Looking at recent figures, Eurostat reports that 7.2 million students across the EU participated in tertiary-level courses in 1988/9 as compared with 5.5 million in 1980/1. While the highest participation rates (1986 figures) in level five courses were recorded in the Netherlands and Belgium, these proportions are lower than those for Sweden and do not compare favourably with those for the USA and Japan. The numbers of people obtaining the necessary qualifications for university entrance also vary, and obtaining the qualification may not guarantee a place. For example, in the UK two A-level passes together with specified GCSE passes is usually the minimum stipulated, but an applicant with two A-level passes at grade E may not be offered a place at all and probably not at the university or course of her or his choice. The universities also differ in age and prestige, with the oldest and most prestigious being able to restrict entry most effectively. Thus in spite of increased numbers of places and qualified candidates university education is still elitist in nature.

There are marked differences in the participation rates in higher education between countries. There are also many patterns of full-time and part-time provision in degree programmes which variously take between three and seven years to complete.

Access to higher education for both mature and younger people may also be affected by the ability of the would-be candidate to pay. Even in those countries where students have mainly been supported by grants, loans are increasingly being introduced to supplement or supersede grants, and students are increasingly being asked to contribute to tuition fees. For example, in 1994 Portugal attempted to increase the fees paid by students at state universities from, to use British equivalents, £8 per year, a figure set in 1941, to £280. Portuguese students, like their counterparts in Britain (Leon 1994), have protested, but moves to reduce government funding are widespread. A recent survey in Britain has shown that some school-leavers have been discouraged from applying to university because of their fears of accumulating debts. Debt has certainly become a much more prominent feature of university life in Britain since the introduction of the loan schemes and the scaling down of grants. Differences in participation rates, which are already very varied, could increase further if, in some areas, the ability to pay becomes an increasingly important factor in obtaining a university education.

Although there are differences between the systems of higher education there are also moves at national as well as at a Europe-wide level to standardize some of the patterns in higher education. Germany and the Netherlands, for example, are both attempting to shorten the length of time students take to complete their degrees. The Dutch government is also seeking to devolve more management responsibility to the universities and to look at the problems of accessibility and selection. Within the EU there have been a number of initiatives to improve student mobility between member states and to encourage research and the learning of languages; indeed, a new programme initially worth ECU 12 billion was launched in 1994 and over 100,000 students will have studied in universities outside of their own countries during 1993/4. Programmes have been instituted to try to improve technical and vocational training and to encourage co-operation in higher education. These programmes are summarized in Table 11.3.

In spite of, or perhaps because of, the variations across Europe, a Memorandum on Higher Education in the European Community (Task Force Human Resources 1991) advocated that the Community and its member states should respond to the challenge of science, technology and global competition increasingly within a Community structure, together with EFTA and other Central European structures. Higher education was seen as of strategic importance in meeting labour market demands for 'more people with higher levels of knowledge and skill'. The Memorandum calls for much greater levels of participation in higher education and a major initiative to increase the numbers of people who have the 'capability to operate across national and cultural boundaries'. Much, in fact, is expected from higher education in meeting technological and knowledge demands, contributing to regional development and 'safeguarding and developing the European cultural heritage' while, at the same time, 'helping to equalize educational opportunity'.

Sociological interpretations

We started this chapter by noting a similarity: that all advanced industrial societies have a system of mass education. We then went on to consider the different philosophical traditions which shape educational practices in Europe today and the

TABLE 11.3 European Community initiatives to foster co-operation and innovation in higher education and training

Initiative	Description
SOCRATES	This programme is scheduled to run until 1999 and has three main strands: two relating to HE by increasing and reinforcing the existing ERASMUS and LINGUA programmes
ERASMUS	Launched in 1987, designed to increase the numbers of students spending a period of study (3–12 months) in another EU state. Aim is for 10 per cent to do this. Staff exchanges are included. EFTA countries were admitted in 1992/3
LINGUA	Launched 1989, main objective to improve language competence across Europe and to improve communication skills
TEMPUS	Launched 1990. Main objective is helping countries of Eastern and Central Europe to restructure their higher education systems
LEONARDO	Announced in 1993, this replaces a number of initiatives to do with vocational training. Aims to encourage mobility and to promote new learning methods
FORCE	Established 1990, aims to improve vocational training schemes, make better use of training resources, improve strategies for training, encourage investment
EUROTECHNET	Launched 1990, aims to promote innovation in basic and continuing vocational training; especially relates to technological changes
IRIS	Launched 1987, aims to increase the accessibility of vocational training to women

wider political debates within which educational reforms have been located. By looking in some detail at the various education systems we have noted degrees of both similarity and difference between them. That analysis is itself 'doing sociology', but as sociologists what else are we to make of all of this?

It is clear that all of the education systems we have considered produce a differentiated output. This is a stronger statement than saying that schools produce people who have individual differences. What emerges from education systems is a highly sorted and stratified potential labour force, differentially trained and qualified to fill professional, technical and semi-skilled occupations across the range of primary, manufacturing and service industries. This potential labour force is also gendered, with boys and girls emerging as young men and women destined for the most part to enter occupations where most of their colleagues will be of the same gender as themselves. This potential labour force, in addition to the occupational skills they have acquired, also holds values and attitudes which enable them to play adult roles in the family and community. In its broadest sense they are equipped to keep a society going into the next generation. They are the bearers of economic skills, political attitudes and cultural values, all of which are in part a reflection of the internationally shared experiences of capitalism and liberal democracy and in part a reflection of the particular histories of their nation. The distribution of these skills and attitudes is not random throughout the population but shows a marked trend for the children of higher-class parents to gain higher levels of qualification and for young women and young men to be differentially qualified. Sociologically, these processes are known as 'social and cultural reproduction'.

SOCIAL AND CULTURAL REPRODUCTION

Social reproduction
The processes by which a society maintains its social structures, patterns of inequality and division of labour from one generation to the next.
Cultural reproduction
The processes by which a society transmits dominant knowledge, values and beliefs which support the existing social order from one generation to the next.

Many sociologists have stressed the role of education systems in meeting the needs of the capitalist economy for a disciplined and differentially skilled labour force. They have noticed that the structure of schools corresponds to the structure of the workplace with its demands for time discipline, obeying and accepting the authority of superiors and not expecting the work to be intrinsically interesting but rather to be carried out as a means to an end (Bowles and Gintis 1976). However, as we have seen education systems and educational experiences do vary, so a simple correspondence does not occur. In explaining this, Weberian sociologists stress the strategies that different social groups use to maintain their social advantages by ensuring that members of other social groups do not have access to the same educational opportunities (Collins 1977). Alternatively, these processes can be seen as the coming together in unique ways of different ideologies in specific socio-historical settings. Dale (1989) argues that a wide variety of school forms can exist, but nevertheless the boundaries of the possible are determined by the logic of a capitalist state which has to perform the balancing act of securing the conditions for capital accumulation and meeting the demands generated by liberal democracy.

Sociologists have also looked in great detail at the ways in which social and cultural reproduction take place at the level of classroom interaction. Processes as different as child-centred and didactic teaching have been seen to contribute to the reproduction of both class advantage and gender difference. Further, what actually goes on in a classroom is as much a product of the cultural resources the pupils bring to it as the school system. Thus Willis (1977) and Griffin (1985) have shown how young men and young women, even when resisting the authority of the school, can act as agents in the reproduction of class and gender inequality.

Standardization and co-operation

In the early years of the European Community education policy did not feature as a key element in Community strategies, these being concerned primarily with limited labour market objectives and thus acting only in the area of post-school vocational training. However, the harmonization of qualifications and the content of schooling is provided for by Article 126 of the Maastricht Treaty. We have noted above some convergence between national education systems as formerly Encyclopaedist nations adopt elements of Naturalism and Vocationalism, and formerly Humanist and Naturalist systems adopt elements of Encyclopaedism. It is possible that as the nations of Europe move economically and politically closer together some further convergence will occur. It could be argued, however, that this mixing and matching of educational approaches is indicative of the impending death of the old grand narratives of rationality, economic improvement and personal growth which have inspired, justified and shaped educational change.

Education systems remain key elements in the transmission of national cultures. Thus whilst it is possible to argue that the approach of British National Curriculum history is encyclopaedist (and thus borrows from a continental tradition) its content is very much about placing a particular version of Britishness at the core of history (Whitty 1992; Ball 1993). Until such time as a European identity emerges the 'European dimension' in the curriculum of all European national systems will remain difficult to identify. Some see the development of this European identity as vital to the consolidation of the political and economic structures of Europe, whilst others warn against the replacement of narrowly nationalistic histories with a narrowly Eurocentric one.

At the beginning of this chapter we suggested that the processes of urbanization, industrialization, the maturation of capitalism and the formation of the modern nation-state had all influenced the emergence of systems of mass education. As European states approach the end of the millennium all of these processes are clearly moving through a period of accelerated change. The role of cities is changing, service industries are becoming more important both as employers and as financial forces, and the membership of bodies such as the European Union affects the operation of the nation-states themselves. The impact of these processes upon education systems has so far been uneven and unpredictable, reflecting both a looking forward to the future and a nostalgia for the systems of the past. The key question for both educationalists and sociologists remains, however, the extent to which education is a force for personal and social transformation or a mechanism of regulation and control.

Summary

- Education systems develop within the context of broader social, political and economic changes.
- The philosophical and cultural traditions of societies are transmitted through their education systems.
- Governments use education policy as a tool of economic and social policy.
- There are both similarities and differences between Europe's education systems and there have been moves towards a standardization of provision.

Further reading

Andy Green (1990) *Education and State Formation*, London: Macmillan. This book addresses macro sociological questions about the forces in societies which lead to the formation of state systems of education. He uses a historical and comparative approach which looks at these developments in nineteenth-century Europe. He argues that whilst other theorists have tried to explain the development of education systems in terms of the growth of popular democracy, urbanization, industrialization and the influence of national and religious cultures, the key factor he has identified is the process of political state formation.

Roger Dale (1989) *The State and Education Policy*, Buckingham: Open University Press. This book examined the role of the state in the formation of educational policy and provision. This classic text takes a historical overview and also traces specific case studies, including the introduction of vocationalism into the secondary curriculum.

Ali Rattansi and D. Reeder (eds) (1992) *Rethinking Radical Education*, London: Lawrence and Wishart. In this collection a number of leading contemporary sociologists critically evaluate the radical traditions within education. The contributions include treatments of feminism, anti-racism, developments in the curriculum, educational provision and learning and teaching.

Chapter 12

Religion in Europe

Joan Chandler

Introduction	240
Key concepts in the analysis of religion in contemporary Europe	241
Mapping religion in Europe	242
Patterns of belief and participation	245
Church and state	250
Islam in Europe	252
Summary	255
Further reading	255

Key concepts

- Secularization of society
- Privatization of religion
- Globalization and religious pluralism
- Religiosity

239

Introduction

Sociologists have a long-standing interest in religion as an area of social activity that attempts to provide an ultimate meaning for existence and a programme of common values and collective action for its adherents. Classical sociologists, writing in the nineteenth century, saw religion as central to the social fabric of a traditional society and important in understanding the development of modernity. Durkheim examined the way in which religious belief and practice expressed and sustained communities; Marx examined the use made of religious beliefs in class domination; and Weber explored the contribution of religious ethics to the creation of capitalist values and the consequences of the rise of science and rational calculation for the disenchantment of the world. These founders of sociology were concerned with the moral impact of modernity, but their endeavours present us with the first of our problems.

Sociology was itself a product of the intellectual and social change that it was describing. Its part in the move to modernity shaped the way in which it approached religion. In its development, sociology absorbed the values of the Enlightenment, the assumption of social progress and allied itself to the growing dominance of science. In this framework religion was closely associated with what was seen as the superstition and irrationality of traditional society and it was assumed that religious influence would diminish as society was restructured and tradition faded.

Sociology's association with modernity continues to shape the ways in which it approaches the study of religion. It is not concerned with the ultimate truth or falsity of religious beliefs but their *social* reality and their consequences for social life. In sociological analysis religious activities are examined in relation to the material interests of individuals and groups and religious beliefs are seen as the ever-changing product of a particular culture. Thus sociological analysis inevitably adopts the perspective of methodological atheism.

A second problem is encountered in attempts to define religion. Durkheim provided one of the most comprehensive definitions where religion is 'a unified system of beliefs and practices relative to sacred things, that is to say, things set apart and forbidden – beliefs and practices which unite into one single moral community, called a church, all who share them'. For Durkheim, religious activity is organized around 'the sacred' which inspires reverence, provides a focus for meaning which transcends the mundane and acts as a source of social solidarity. However, empirical problems about how the sacred is identified remain.

In the debate about definition, there are disputes about the boundaries between religious and non-religious belief and practice. For instance should 'televangelism', socialism or psychotherapy be treated as religious phenomena? There are also difficulties in establishing universal criteria for religion that would encompass Eastern and Western faiths and traditional institutional religions as well as newer more diffuse forms of spirituality. Furthermore, there is the problem of whose religion is being discussed; even within one creed there are differences between the religious leaders and the ordinary populace, and there is often a considerable gap between orthodoxy and folk religion.

These definitions have some implications for speculation about the future of religion in modern Europe; narrower and institutional approaches to religion suggest some decline while broader existential definitions suggest the more permanent presence of religious expression in human society.

Finally, there are different levels of social analysis and each is important to our understanding of religion in modern Europe. One level is concerned with the place of religion in the lives of individuals – their religiosity. This is not a single attribute but composed of different expressions of religion, each of which may be regarded as an independent dimension or measure of religiosity. These dimensions tend to divide between those that refer to institutional participation such as practice, membership and religious knowledge and those that focus on the experiential, including belief and spirituality. Here there are questions about the contemporary European pattern of beliefs and practices and what, if anything, is treated as sacred. Another more macro level of analysis examines the relationship between religious organizations and wider society. In Europe there are particular questions about the relationship between Church and state and the impact of religious thinking on public policy.

Before these questions about the relationship of religion to the individual and society can be tackled, it is useful to pause and outline key themes in the social analysis of religion and sketch in the religious map of Europe.

Key concepts in the analysis of religion in contemporary Europe

Three connected issues inform any discussion of the place of religion in contemporary society: secularization, privatization and globalization.

One approach to *secularization* suggests that there is a fundamental incompatibility between religion and modernity. Here secularization describes the process whereby society has become more socially differentiated and 'Religion has lost its presidency over other institutions' (Wilson 1985: 15). In a secular society the social significance of religious symbolism is diminished, the public influence of religious organizations is reduced and there are falling levels of religious participation. The Church has lost its moral authority and its capacity to shape the rules of other organizations or the consciences and behaviour of individuals. In modern society religion can no longer be imposed on people – it must be marketed, and in the marketplace religion is commodified in a competition for followers and commitment. Secularization also suggests that religion has lost its inspirational power in a world of rational calculation and technological control where less and less is sacred.

However, for Martin (1978, 1991) secularization is neither inevitable nor irreversible. As a general theory it often makes false comparisons, constructing a past 'golden age' of religious life that is largely unsupported by historical research. Instead, secularization for Martin is the product of particular historical circumstances and best approached as an *empirical* question to be answered in the detailed examination of the relationship between religion and nation.

As religion has become more marginal in society, it has become *privatized*. Here faith and practice become matters of personal choice, activities which confirm spiritual autonomy and are devoid of public significance. Privatized religiosity is associated with a new type of spirituality that places a premium on religious experience and commitment. It is less socially visible and less amenable to sociological study. The privatization of religion also suggests a change in personal morality, the decline in a popular endorsement of traditional values and the growth of individualism and permissiveness.

Globalization has added a new dynamic to the existing processes of secularization and privatization. In globalization the world has become a single place, where communication has broken through geographical barriers and distinct and culturally bounded societies no longer exist. Globalization is part of recent European experience, part of the search for economic, political and cultural unity and linked to the removal of internal boundaries, the collapse of the Soviet Empire in Eastern Europe and the post-colonial immigration of an Islamic population.

Beyer (1994) argues that globalization produces a strange contradiction for religious experience and identity; cultural differences are blunted by being placed in a common context where each faith loses any ultimate claim to truth and appears relative and arbitrary; but cultural clash is made more possible by increased communication which makes individuals and groups more aware of religious differences. In pre-modern society the close association between morality, religion and group membership structured inter-group and inter-societal conflict. In justifying conflict religion promoted the survival or expansion of the group in question. But in global society there are now no outsiders and the nature of evil has become contested and less clear. In this global context religion faces some dilemmas: how can it provide ultimate meaning and moral solutions for people whose lives are very different from one another – how can it integrate diversity? And how should individuals and groups, firm in their own faith, relate to those whose religious beliefs and practices may not only be viewed as different but also as unacceptable?

Beyer suggests that globalization provokes two very different cultural reactions. One leads to the further privatization of faith and values, a tolerant acceptance of religious pluralism and a religious life that is personally undemanding. The other solution asserts the certainty of the sacred where the world is seen as heading in an evil direction from which it must be turned. It seeks to make religion a visible and vital force in the world, opposing religious compromise and pluralism and restating the divine legitimacy of religious action. This latter solution is an attractive option to the traditional, communally orientated society faced with globalization and its social consequences. Hence globalization leads in two directions at once. It supports the privatization of belief and practice and provides fertile ground for the renewed public influence of religion.

Mapping religion in Europe

The religious map of Europe (Figure 12.1) can be read in a number of ways. It charts both the spread and the fragmentation of Christianity and its relationship to other value systems. It also maps the range of religious expression and

Figure 12.1 Religious divisions in Europe

The legend for Figure 12.1:

- • • • • • The divide between the Eastern Orthodox and the Western Latin Church
- ——— The Reformation divide between the Protestant and the Roman Catholic Churches
- – – – The divide between the former communist and the non-communist regimes
- (shaded) Islamic populations and enclaves

symbolism, the variable relationship between peoples and their Churches, points of religious commonality and division.

Beginning as a small Middle Eastern cult, Christianity spread west, through missionary activities and the foundation of religious communities, to become the dominant religion of Europe. One can pick out some landmark events in Christianity's contribution to the making of European society.

1   A vital factor was the conversion of the Roman Emperor Constantine in the early fourth century. He was keen to use Christian symbolism and divine justification for his powers, and under his influence Christianity spread quickly. The tradition continued following the collapse of Rome and Charlemagne was crowned Holy Roman Emperor by Pope Leo III on Christmas Day in 800. He was styled as the defender of Christendom and sought unity through the imposition of a single Christian faith throughout the vast territories he controlled in Western Europe. Christianity provided some common values, religious communities, places of learning and sacred symbols, and a distinctively European relationship developed between Church and state.

2   The legacy of the Emperor Diocletian's division of the Roman Empire in AD 284 had been the split between the Western Roman and the Eastern Orthodox Churches. The Emperor Constantine's subsequent emphasis on the eastern half of the empire left Rome for a while as the poorer half in this division of Christianity. A series of doctrinal disagreements led eventually to formal schism in the eleventh century. On each side of the divide the potential relationship between national identity and religion is different. Eastern Orthodoxy is organized into thirteen independent Churches, each with a patriarch who is head of a national Church. Hence there is a Greek Orthodox, Russian Orthodox and Serbian Orthodox Church. By contrast, the Western Latin Church was centred on the Papacy in Rome and was supranational.

3   The Western Church itself divided in the sixteenth century, creating a number of national Protestant Churches in north-west Europe and leaving Southern and Central Europe predominantly Roman Catholic. The Reformation of the Western Church was also associated with the Enlightenment and the Renaissance, making modernity an enterprise not so much of Europe but of Western Europe. The new Protestant Churches were organized on a national or regional basis. European unity continues to present a greater challenge to Protestantism as it lacks the supranational structure and remit of Roman Catholicism, and the lower proportion of the EU population are Protestant, 16 per cent, in contrast to the 63 per cent who are Roman Catholic (Willaime 1994).

4   Christendom was constructed as a single faith within a single community to be defended against infidels and heretics. In this construction, although Jewish and Islamic populations had themselves made a significant contribution to the development of European art and science, they were targeted as outsiders. Anti-Semitism has been an undercurrent in European history, with the Jewish population denied civil rights and confined to ghettos in

many cities, the object of attacks in 'pogroms' and, in the twentieth century, decimated in the Holocaust or Shoah, instigated by the Nazi regime. Azria (1994) argues that the Holocaust has disrupted the continuity of Jewish culture in Europe as it has swept away the Ashkenazi population and traditions. It has left the European Jewry struggling for a new cultural identity which is being shaped by non-European factors in the establishment of the state of Israel, the influence of American Jewry and the arrival of non-European Jews, especially in France from North Africa. The Crusades were waged between the eleventh and the fifteenth centuries and were authorized by a Papacy intent on rescuing Jerusalem from the Muslims. In Eastern Europe the diversity of religious groups is a cultural reminder of the rise and fall of old empires. For example, the Ottoman Empire advanced to reach the gates of Vienna and then receded, leaving pockets of Islam in Eastern Europe, especially in Bosnia-Hercegovina, Albania, Romania and Bulgaria.

5   The end of the Second World War in Europe brought a new religious divide as an 'Iron Curtain' was drawn between the communist Warsaw Pact countries and the Nato Alliance. This was also a religious divide as the new communist states took firm control of public life and set about the abolition of religious thinking and influence. In most countries there were efforts to *enforce* a privatization of belief and practice. Albania, the most dramatic example, officially abolished religion, outlawing all religious organizations and forbidding all public ritual.

Although the divide was one between atheism and freedom of worship, it produced different climates for religiosity and some ironic consequences. Since the Second World War religious activity has declined in the tolerant regimes of the West and flourished in some former communist countries, most notably Poland. Furthermore, religious identity became a vehicle for opposition to Soviet control and communist organization. In the formerly communist East, *glasnost* has been accompanied by new laws guaranteeing freedom of conscience and worship. There has been an upsurge in religious expression and a new warmth in Church–state relations as governments seek new value bases for national integrity.

Religion has been both a source of unity and of division in past and present Europe. The lines of religious cleavage are particularly evident in the case of the former Yugoslavia, historically known as the Balkans.

How religion maps onto other social divisions – nation-states, ethnic and language groups and classes – is an essential part of the social texture of Europe (Davie 1994a). It is influential in shaping patterns of religiosity and the relationships between Church and state.

Patterns of belief and participation

A major source of information on European religious beliefs and practices is available in surveys carried out in 1981 and 1990 by the European Values Systems Study Group (EVSSG) (Barker *et al.* 1993; Ashford and Timms 1992). The study

CASE STUDY 1: RELIGIOUS DIVISION AND THE BALKANS

Complex religious divisions run through the area of Europe traditionally known as the Balkans. Slovenia and Croatia are Catholic, Serbia and Macedonia are Eastern Orthodox; and although 3.5 million Muslims live throughout this region, nearly half of these live in Bosnia-Hercegovina where they account for 40 per cent of the population. Historic tensions between these religious groups were held in check in post-war Europe by the former communist regime, but political liberalization has unleashed civil war between socially and religiously divided groups.

The Muslim populations are associated with alien invaders from the East, and past battles between Muslims and Serbs are seen as part of the war between good and evil. These battles are the basis of epic stories and nationalistic folk songs. For instance the Battle of Kosovo in 1389, in which a Turkish-Islamic army defeated the Christian Serbs, remains today emblematic of Serbian misfortune and martyrdom and an inspiration for vengeance. Although religious affiliation has become inseparable from old scores and national aspirations, there are two important caveats. Firstly, there is little difference between the day-to-day religion of Muslims and Christians in the region. Breakaway religious movements often drew on elements of Christianity and Islam, and the Islam of the Balkans has become distinctively European, detached from scriptural doctrine and accepting of local saints and practices. Secondly, Islam spread as much by conversion as by conquest. In Bosnia, as Muslims were more likely to be landowners and Christians serfs and peasants, social betterment was associated with conversion to Islam.

Sources: Norris (1993), Nitzova (1994).

group had both scientific and ideological objectives. It was inspired by the desire to contribute to the building of a European consensus which retained Christianity at its core. It also wanted to assess the extent to which Western Europe shared a common Christian value system and the ways in which this might be changing. The study involved large questionnaire surveys, with over 1,000 individuals interviewed in each Western European country, and has provided some bench-mark measures of beliefs, attitudes and practices. But it also has its limitations: as it sums individual responses it does not tell us how religious institutions are operating or the meaning of the religious ideas that lie behind people's responses; as its religious starting point is Christian orthodox belief and practice there are questions about its treatment of new and non-Christian forms of religiosity; as an international study it encounters methodological problems of translation and meaning; and there are also difficulties in interpreting trend data as the study draws on a time period when the definition of Europe changed so much – for instance the 1990 survey continued to collect data on West Germany only.

The EVSSG found an overall decline in religious participation and belief and the continued strength of a general, although institutionally unattached, faith. The steepest religious decline occurred in the late 1960s and early 1970s, and in recent years this decline has been sharpest in predominantly Catholic countries.

TABLE 12.1 Religious upbringing, importance of religion and church attendance, 1990 (%)

	Religious upbringing	*Religion important*	*Monthly attendance*	*Unchurched*	*Belief in God*	*Life after death*
European average	73	48	33	–	70	43
Catholic countries						
Belgium	84	45	31	32	63	37
France	71	42	17	39	57	38
Ireland	94	84	87	4	96	77
Italy	94	70	53	15	83	54
Portugal	79	56	41	28	80	31
Spain	93	54	43	13	81	42
Mixed countries						
Great Britain	59	45	23	42	71	44
West Germany	63	36	34	11	63	38
Netherlands	71	44	30	49	61	39
Northern Ireland	84	67	68	10	95	70
Lutheran countries						
Denmark	43	31	11	8	58[*]	26[*]
Iceland	75	56	9	2	–	–
Norway	45	40	13	10	–	–
Sweden	30	27	10	19	–	–

Source: Harding *et al.* 1986; Ashford and Timms 1992.

Note: [*] Figures refers to 1981.

The religious population of Europe is predominantly female, older and more likely to subscribe to a more traditional and less permissive morality. However, there is considerable variation within this pattern both between regions and on the different dimensions of religiosity. Table 12.1 suggests that there are bands of secularity within Europe. Although the trend data is focused on Western Europe the 1990 survey examined parts of Eastern Europe. Here it found that the levels of religiosity are very variable, with 90 per cent of the Polish population regarding themselves as religious compared to 19 per cent in Estonia.

Church membership

Although three-quarters of those surveyed in 1990 claimed membership of a particular Christian denomination, the proportion not claiming such a member-ship had doubled since 1981. This trend was particularly pronounced in Belgium, France, Great Britain and the Netherlands, countries that already had relatively low denominational affiliation. However, it is worth noting that religious affiliation has different implications for individuals in different countries. In the former West Germany, where religious affiliation has a civic significance, nearly 90 per cent of people interviewed claimed membership of a religious denomination, although just over half identified themselves as religious people.

Church attendance

This reflects the denominational map of Europe. The highest attendance is found in the Mediterranean Catholic countries and the lowest in Lutheran Scandinavia. However, within the regional pattern, there are some notable exceptions; Northern Ireland has the highest weekly attendance (81 per cent) and France the lowest (10 per cent).

Since 1981, although there had been only a small decline in attendance and in core membership, the numbers of marginal and irregular attenders has dropped and there has been a significant increase in the proportion of the population who are 'unchurched'. This trend is clearest in Britain, with the unchurched increasing from 9 to 42 per cent, and in the Netherlands which is increasingly divided between an active and religiously committed minority and a large and growing section of the population which is entirely estranged from its Churches.

The level of *orthodox beliefs* was also examined by the EVSSG and, although there has been some slight decline in this aspect of religiosity in the last 10 years, the majority claimed a religious faith and only 10 per cent of the population described themselves as atheists. The strongest belief was belief in God (70 per cent) and the existence of the soul (61 per cent) and the weakest in Hell (23 per cent) and the Devil (25 per cent), indicating a qualitative shift in European religiosity towards the more positive elements of faith.

Furthermore, God is seen as important in the personal lives of only one in five of those surveyed and Barker and his colleagues suggest that Europeans are increasingly expressing a 'diluted' form of Christianity. Here the Churches 'may have more to do with authenticating personal life than authorizing doctrine', marking 'a decline at the personal level in religious ways of being in the world' (Ashford and Timms 1992: 43, 47). In Scandinavia Church membership is a civic matter, an experience largely devoid of religious meaning; their orientation is summed by the phrase 'belonging without believing' and contrasts sharply with that of England where there are much higher levels of belief than institutional participation (see Case Study 2). Although strong belief may survive outside the Church, without institutional process to shape it, religion is likely to become not only more personal but also more unorthodox.

The work of the EVSSG supports arguments for the growing privatization of faith and individualism of European values. Although the Church was seen as having some right to pronounce on general topics of social justice, people, including those who were core Church members, were more guarded in their support for the right of the Church to comment on sexual morality or government policy. People were also more satisfied with the guidance that the Church was offering on specifically spiritual matters rather than with religious comment on social or national policy. There were general moves towards more permissive values, both amongst those who described themselves as religious and those who did not, although those who were religious continued to support a more traditional viewpoint.

There is some debate about the future of belief as the religiosity of young adults is recorded as half that of those over 50, suggesting that as the more

CASE STUDY 2: BRITAIN

In Britain 71 per cent of the population claim nominal allegiance to a religion, 64 per cent being Christian (predominantly Anglican) and 7 per cent non-Christian. However, when active membership is considered, the proportion drops to 14.4 per cent and the denominational picture changes; the Roman Catholic, independent and ethnic Churches have higher numbers of active members than the Church of England. Although there has been an overall decline in British religiosity, there has been a growth in Orthodox, Afro-Caribbean and Islamic congregations, and in independent Churches and religious activity – most notably the House Church Movement. There is also considerable regional variation in Britain with higher levels of religiosity in Wales, Scotland and particularly Northern Ireland. England is characterized as 'believing without belonging'; 10 per cent of the population attend church each week, but 76 per cent report that they believe in God and 58 per cent describe themselves as religious. This trend has affected all the mainstream Churches and denominations and there has been a change in religious relationships. For instance in English Catholicism there has been a decrease in priestly authority, a sharp decline in those taking confession and accepting habitual forms of religious obedience, an increase in lay spirituality and greater scope claimed for personal conscience.

In Northern Ireland religion has a very different history and standing in the community. The population is divided between Protestants, who are mostly Presbyterians (60 per cent of the population), and Catholics (40 per cent), and this division developed as British foreign policy tried to subdue Catholic Ireland by encouraging Protestant settlement. These religious divisions coincided with class differences and became the basis for regional politics and community conflict. There are high levels of religiosity in Northern Ireland; 76 per cent of the population are members of a church, 95 per cent believe in God and there is strong support for the Church's voice in public affairs and private morality. Although religion reinforces other social divisions and provides rich symbolism, there is also a fundamentally religious dimension to the conflict in the region. Presbyterianism is one of the best surviving examples of ascetic Calvinism, where the world is characterized as a struggle between good and evil and community threat is given religious affirmation in biblical images derived from the Old Testament.

Sources: Davie (1994b), Bruce (1986), Hornsby-Smith (1987), Brierley (1991)

religious generations pass away, orthodox and institutional religion may decline further. Only a quarter of those surveyed thought a religious upbringing important for their children, again indicating the slow but widespread disengagement of the population from Church life.

However, the focus on institutional and traditional religiosity provides a limited perspective. It ignores newer religious forms and misses the subtler reorganization of the expression of religious feeling. Hervieu-Leger (1990, 1994) identified sources of religious renewal amid the continuing decline of Catholicism

LCR: Library
SOMERSET COLLEGE OF ARTS & TECHNOLOGY

and its parochial structure in France. These include the growth of new religious movements, the development of ideological and religious communities and the resilience of 'popular religion' with its pilgrimages, prayers and healing practices.

The EVSSG suggested commitment to unorthodox belief; in 1981 21 per cent of those surveyed believed in reincarnation. Also, Heelas (1988) has argued that the religious impulse in Europe is being redirected to feed the growth of 'self-religions'. These address not a transcendent religiosity but 'the God within', and they reflect the strong influence of Eastern philosophies and spiritualized psychology and ecology. Heelas cites early European examples such as Psychosynthesis and the Institute for the Harmonious Development of Man, both formed in the 1920s. Today there is a vast array of self-religions, including Transcendental Meditation, Scientology, Re-birthing and Primal Therapy. They offer personal improvement and spiritual awakening to the world population. Although numbers of core members are small, thousands of people have at least dabbled in this new type of spirituality, and their influence has seeped into wider culture through their educational programmes and their extensive literature. Both Hervieu-Leger and Heelas conclude that these new forms of religion are not a sign of decline but of religion reorganizing itself in Europe to address and counter strains and uncertainties engendered by modernity.

Church and state

Another aspect of secularization is the extent and the ways in which religion is keyed into and influential in other areas of social life. Particularly important here is the relationship between Church and state. Martin suggested that European culture was shaped by the mix of Christianity, Greek rationalism and Roman organization and sought unity through the possession of one God and one Caesar (1978). Today this historical unity overlays a diversity of peoples and nation-states. As political power and allegiances shift, older religious identities and antagonisms surface to shape new political alliances and movements. 'After all, religion is not bound in with intimacies and with ethnic identities but also has reference points across the conventional frontiers. Indeed, religion is one reason why older maps exist like older paintings underneath contemporary configurations' (Martin 1994: 14). The presence of these older politico-religious maps is a major point of contrast between religion in Europe and the USA.

De Tocqueville, writing in the aftermath of the French Revolution, noted that in Europe, religion and politics were historically entwined. State apparatus was used to disenfranchise religious minorities and political opposition was expressed through religious dissent. Although with secularization there has been some disengagement of Church and state, Caplow (1985) suggests there are remaining links in constitutional arrangements, religiously allied pressure groups and political parties. Britain is a good example of these constitutional arrangements. The Church of England is an Established Church where the Head of State is also Head of the Church, bishops sit in the Lords and state ceremonies are enveloped in religious symbolism. By contrast France has a fiercely secular state and educational system, and there is a strong theme of anti-clericalism in French thinking. Yet another type of relationship is found in Germany where the state authorities collect Church membership subscriptions and distribute them to the relevant denominations.

Furthermore, Caplow restates de Tocqueville's conclusion that religion in America, in contrast to Europe, has retained its vitality because its independent religious organizations have been free to pursue popular religiosity; in the USA over 40 per cent of the population attend church regularly and 41 per cent identify themselves as core members of a church.

Kokosalakis identifies the dynamic links between religion and ethnicity and the connection between religious group/groups and the state. He argues that globalization increases the importance of religion as a means of expressing national and ethnic identity, for instance in Ireland, Poland and Cyprus, and in promoting the religious factor in both European integrity and division. It provides rich symbols which generate emotion and sustain commitment, linking peoples to historic missions and sanctifying their relationship to the land. This helps us to explain why 'the process of secularization has been very different from one European country to another and this cannot be explained by reference to industrialization and the changes in the social structure alone' (1992).

Kokosalakis's arguments support those of David Martin who suggests that the relevance of the religious factor depends on how it keys into other social divisions. How it is allied to or cross-cut by ethnic and national identity, language differences and class relations will determine its public and political relevance. The religious factor is, then, not automatically important and its prominence depends on the part it plays in any particular social and cultural mix. For instance religion provides some integrity in an Italy economically and politically divided between North and South; in the Netherlands the divisions between Protestants and Catholics are cross-cut by class difference and in the twentieth century have been friction free. By contrast in Northern Ireland religious affiliation expresses a community divide that runs through housing, education, political parties and class relations (see Case Study 2).

Eastern Europe provides yet another picture. Under communism the Church in Poland, Czechoslovakia and Hungary aimed to ensure its own survival, to provide support for individual rights and to 'de-sovietize' the nation-state (Michel 1991, 1994). The quest for national self-realization led to the emergence of practising non-believers and increased participation in saints' festivals as acts of resistance. Either in the public stance of Polish Catholicism or the underground churches of Czechoslovakia, religious organizations spearheaded the collapse of the Soviet regimes in 1989 and 1990.

Religion's contribution to integrity and division can also be examined on a more global scale. The religious factor has assisted Eire's integration with Europe and its Catholic heritage, and affiliation provides a cultural connection to the heartland of Europe. By contrast Britain's global religious links reflect an imperial past which is embedded in the Commonwealth and the international, but essentially non-European, Anglican communion (Davie 1994a). Finally the possibility of Turkey's membership of the EU raises a new question about European unity as Turkey will be the first Muslim state, albeit a highly secularized one, to join. It reinforces the multi-faith dimension to European culture and may alter

> ### CASE STUDY 3: POLAND
>
> Poland is predominantly Roman Catholic and the church was closely involved with Solidarity, a Trade Union movement for popular democracy, in its resistance to Soviet control and in its efforts to delegitimize the communist state. The Catholic Church was seen as the guardian of Polish identity, suffering down through the ages and latterly subjugated by Soviet Russian imperialism. In this allegory the cult of the Virgin Mary flourished and the icon of the Black Virgin of Czestochowa was the symbol of the nation. This feeling was strengthened by the election of a Polish Pope and his visit to Poland in 1979.
>
> In Poland religion maintained a strong public profile and, as an organization that appeared to transcend politics, it bound together divergent interests, both secular and religious, in their opposition to communism. In the period before liberalization there was a significant fall in atheism, from 17 per cent in 1977 to 5 per cent in 1988, and a rise in 'non-believing adherents' – people who used religion explicitly for non-religious ends.
>
> However, a long history of resistance to totalitarianism has also shielded Roman Catholicism in Poland from modernity and pluralism. This raises questions about how it will reorganize itself in a Europe that is more open and democratic and in a state that is seeking new sources of social stability. The efforts of the Church to re-Catholicize the Polish state are likely to be less successful than its opposition to communism.
>
> Sources: Michel (1991, 1994).

Europe's identity in any global conflict between the Christian and the Islamic world. The religious pluralism of Europe is also increased by the presence of a relatively new Islamic population as is discussed in the next section.

Islam in Europe

Islam in Europe has a long history but, since the 1950s, it has had a renewed presence, brought to Europe this time by economic migrants. Overall, 3 per cent of Europe's population is Muslim and Islam is now a significant minority religion in many European countries; for instance there are approximately 1 million Muslims in England and 3 million in France. It is also a metropolitan population; 6.5 per cent of West Berliners are Muslim (Thoma-Venske 1988).

The migration of Islamic groups to Europe illustrates one aspect of globalization and the new Islamic presence raises a number of sociological questions about the migratory experience, the expression and redefinition of religious identity and the role of religion in local and national politics. Religious migration has also been the focus for moral debate about development of religious pluralism and multi-faith communities and the focus for fears about fundamentalism.

A key feature of Islam in Europe is its own diversity and the variable ways it relates to national politics and local communities. This variability has a number of sources:

- Each country has tended to attract an Islamic population from a different part of the globe, often reflecting past colonial connections. British Muslims are predominantly from Pakistan, French from North Africa, German from Turkey and in Netherlands the Muslim population has come from Morocco, Surinam and Turkey. Each Muslim group has its own homeland community and its own ethnic interpretation of Islam.
- As within Christianity, Islam contains different sects and creeds. The Muslims of Europe are predominantly Sunni, who tend not to be politically radical and see Islam as helping to produce the good citizen. In addition, there are non-practising Muslims where Islam is a more distant cultural heritage.
- Their political status varies; the Islamic population of Britain has more permanent rights of settlement than in Germany, where they are seen as 'guest workers'.
- The particular relationship between Church and state influences the religious expression of Islam. France has the strictest separation of Church and state and a strong secular culture. For Modood (1994), where secularism is the privileged ideology there is greater religious friction as secularism problematizes public expression of religiosity and denies the rights of religious minorities to shape public debate or national policy. At a local level a commitment by councils to multiculturalism does not necessarily satisfy an Islamic population, as Muslims may support welfare programmes but be very uncomfortable with policies which promote personal and sexual liberalism.
- In places of settlement new religious organizations such as the Muslim Liaison Committee of Birmingham and the Bradford Council of Mosques have developed. These play an important part in the participation of Muslims in local politics and in the expression of Islamic interests.
- Although the Muslim population has historic allegiances to countries of origin they also have links to other Islamic nations, particularly those in the Middle East, as these provide financial and educational support for Islamic activities.

Religious values are embedded in civic organization. Europe runs on a calendar of the Christian year and a Christian week and disprivileges religious groups with other cycles of festivals and other holy days. Although Sunday may no longer be a religious day for the bulk of the population it is still a different day, distinguished from the working week. There are numerous points of religious tension in the field of education, including religious and sex education, single-sex schooling and state support for Islamic schools, dress codes and the organization of physical education for girls as well as the provision of *halal* (religiously pure) food. Although Western education is valued, elements may be resisted if they undermine a Muslim way of life and an Islamic view of marriage and family relationships. The expression of religious identity may also lead to local tension and conflict over the control of public space in the metropolis and this is illustrated in the case study of Sweden (Case Study 4).

The meaning of religion to the individual and the nature of their spirituality is also altered by the migratory experience. Here Schiffauer (1988) compares the

---

CASE STUDY 4: ISLAM IN SWEDEN

The first duty of a Muslim is to establish a place for public prayers, a mosque. However, an application to build a mosque in a Gothenburg suburb provoked public demonstrations. Although Sweden is a highly secularized society, a freedom of religion act was only recently passed in 1951 and Sweden continues to be built on the formula of one nation, one people and one (Christian) religion. In the local debate about the mosque, Swedish organizations and Churches identified Islam as a danger to the Swedish way of life. The Muslim desire for *public space* for the expression of religiosity sharpened the religious divide, where Islam was constructed as a threat to a nominally Christian but, more particularly, secular culture. The mosque was also resisted as it symbolized the firmer planting of cultural roots, signalling a more permanent settlement and changing the identity of a metropolitan district to that of a Muslim area.

Source: Kuusela (1993).

---

religious experience and practice of Turks in their home village to that of migrants to Germany from the same village. He found that in the village there was less choice about religious participation as beliefs and practices integrated all the households, the rhythm of village life and the turning of the seasons into a sacred cycle. In Germany religion became a separate and distinctive sphere of life, no longer coterminous with other social relationships. Membership of a religious community became a private affair, unconnected with local status, and there was greater choice about which religious group to join and which practice to follow. Islam came to provide a haven which, in Germany, was self-consciously both Turkish and Islamic.

The future of Islam in Europe offers a range of possibilities:

1   It may absorb a new individualism and adopt the cultural characteristics of European faith.

2   Local Muslim groups may continue to show few signs of radicalism and to pragmatically pursue the local defence of a Muslim way of life.

3   As ethnic diversity subsides in subsequent generations of Muslims, there will be a greater homogeneity of European Islam which may become more closely associated with a more singular ethnic identity. This single identity may provide a link to the rest of the world; in global relations, there may develop a distinct European Islam which will provide a bridge between new power blocs in the world and particularly between European and Arab states. Alternatively it may be the basis of new division as, like all religions of a diaspora, Islam may become a vehicle for protest and the assertion of minority identity. Leveau (1988) found that young Muslims born and brought up in France no longer followed Islamic practice but had strong emotional ties with an Islamic identity and global Muslim causes.

Summary

- The role of religion in Europe and its sociological analysis has been deeply influenced by the development of modernity.
- How we define religion shapes what is seen as its present and future status in Europe.
- There has been a widespread decline in institutional and orthodox forms of religiosity.
- There has been a growth of more permissive and personalized religion, especially among younger age groups in Europe.
- The prominence of a religious factor in European regional and local politics depends on how religious identity maps onto other social divisions.
- There is a growing religious pluralism in Europe, which is the product of migration and the popularity of new religious movements.

Further reading

Steve Bruce (1995) *Religion in Modern Britain*, Oxford: Oxford University Press. This is a very readable account of the place of religion in contemporary Britain. It provides a comprehensive picture of the overall place of religion in Britain and the variation between regions and religious orientations in one state.

John Fulton and Peter Gee (1994) *Religion in Contemporary Europe*, Lampeter: Edward Mellen Press. This is an interesting collection of papers which examines different aspects of religion in Eastern and Western Europe.

Grace Davie (1994) 'The Religious Factor in the Emergence of Europe as a Global Region', *Social Compass*, 41, 1: 95–112. Grace Davie provides an excellent discussion of the place of religion in contemporary Europe and the contribution that the religious factor makes to European unity and to social conflict within Europe.

Chapter 13

Work, employment and unemployment

Eric Harrison

Introduction	258
The evolving occupational structure	260
The experience of work: flexibility for whom?	262
Working time in Europe	265
Getting on and getting along: management–worker relations	267
The forgotten workers: Europe's unemployment problem	269
Summary	270
Further reading	270

Key concepts

- Occupational structure
- Flexibility
- Unemployment

Introduction

We saw back in Chapter 1 that industrialization involved a reorganization of working life, and that this entailed a number of social consequences. In the opinion of many, the advanced Western economies are undergoing a series of long-term changes of similar magnitude to that of the nineteenth century. Again there will be social upheavals as a result. It is impossible here to do full justice to the multiple debates which surround the idea of 'work' defined in a broad way. Sociologists currently regard work and economic life as rather less central to the discipline than they once did. The reasons for this are complex though in part it is a reflection of a growing recognition of non-economic issues as a basis for identity and political activity. What remains true, however, is that work and matters relating to economic life remain central to the daily lives of most Europeans. Figures show that within the fifteen countries which constitute the European Union there were more than 165.1 million people registered as 'economically active'. Whether engaged in it, actively seeking it, avoiding it or simply worrying about it, work still looms sufficiently large for talk of 'the end of work' (Rifkin 1996) to be regarded as premature (see Figure 13.1).

From the perspective of Britain in the 1990s it often seems as though the European question was about economics to the exclusion of all else, as debates have run and run about the European economies and increasingly about the prospects for a single European economy with a single unit of currency controlled by an independent European bank. In the run up to the creation of the single market at the end of 1992 there was endless speculation about the ferment this would create. Freed from the shackles of border controls on people and goods Europe would see huge competitive forces unleashed with implications for national industries. In the event the changes have been less apocalyptic than some might have thought, but for those opposed to greater European integration the signs are evident. To simplify somewhat, plans for Economic and Monetary Union (EMU) are predicated upon European economies going through a process of convergence until they reach a point of sufficient parity with one another for their currencies to be linked at a particular level of exchange for a foreseeable period. In order to be accepted each economy has to achieve certain targets for inflation, public borrowing and so on. Many argue that such stringent discipline removes national autonomy and is partially responsible for the rising levels of unemployment which characterize the European Union in the mid-1990s. The above sketch can give only a flavour of the arguments. It is not intended here to discuss macroeconomic policy, but rather to give a portrait of the nature of employment in Europe: the way work is organized, negotiated and performed in the paid economy. The gendered nature of labour markets has already been examined at length in Chapter 6, so we will not dwell on labour segmentation here. Rather the following sections set out to do the following: firstly outline the occupational structure of the European workforce to answer the question, 'Who does what where?'; secondly it will look in more detail at working arrangements throughout the EU, and in particular the notion of 'flexibility'; thirdly we examine the controversy over the length of the working week in Europe;

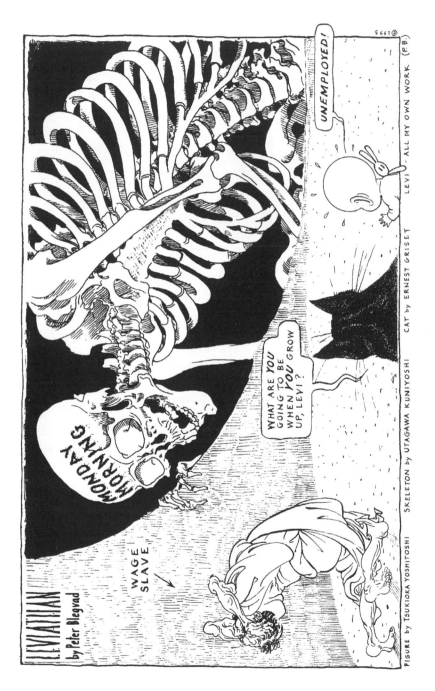

Figure 13.1 Work calls! 'Leviathan' by Peter Blegvad by courtesy of *The Independent on Sunday*, 15 January 1995.

Note: Sociologists have played down the centrality of work, but for most of us it refuses to go away.

fourthly we tackle the problem of workplace relations between management and workers. The last (but by no means least significant) section discusses the enormous problem of mass unemployment which faces Europe in the years to come.

The evolving occupational structure

The most commonly noted feature of modern economies is a tendency for the composition of their employment base to alter over time. We saw in Chapters 1 and 2 that the period of industrialization transformed what were primarily agrarian rural communities into industrial urban societies. In the late twentieth century many have argued that the more advanced Western economies have moved on again, this time to become *post-industrial*. During this latest phase, the argument runs, the emphasis in terms of both output and employment shifts from the manufacture of goods to the provision of services. The industrial era is dominated by the machine as a form of mass production and as a source of profit. By contrast the post-industrial era has as its core not physical capital but human capital. Profits are now to be accumulated through control and exploitation of knowledge or information. For this reason many accounts use the expression the 'information society'. Some versions of post-industrial theory argue that all societies pass inevitably through a number of stages as they modernize, from agricultural to industrial to post-industrial. It is customary to refer to a number of *sectors* within the economy. In the UK the Standard Industrial Classification (SIC) system distributes all jobs within a complex system of categories and sub-categories in order to keep a track of the make-up of the economy.

SECTORAL MODEL OF THE ECONOMIC STRUCTURE	
Primary sector	Extraction, mining, agriculture
Secondary sector	Manufacturing industries
Tertiary sector	Services
Quaternary sector	Information and knowledge processing

To what extent can Europe be portrayed as a post-industrial continent? The picture is complex; there is much internal variety both between and within nations and regions, and also a number of conceptual difficulties involved in classifying different types of economic activity. If we examine Table 13.1 it is possible to discern an overall pattern even amongst the variations. Every country in the EU relies on 'services' for the majority of its employment. What is less clear is that there is a correlation between a high percentage of service employment and economic advancement. Yet one of the most striking features of the table is that Germany, arguably the strongest economy in Europe, is also the most industrial with a lower proportion of service employment than Finland and Ireland.

Other observations can be made. It should come as no surprise that the UK, the industrial pioneer, should have the smallest agricultural sector. By the same token it remains clear that Greece, Portugal and Ireland remain very

TABLE 13.1 Share of economic sectors in employment in 1992

	Agriculture		Industry		Services		Total	
	000s	%	000s	%	000s	%	000s	%
EUR15	8,705	5.8	48,718	32.6	92,205	61.6	149,628	100
Belgium	109	2.9	1,164	30.9	2,498	66.2	3,770	100
Denmark	136	5.2	715	27.2	1,780	67.7	2,637	100
Germany	1,368	3.7	14,273	39.1	20,887	57.2	36,528	100
Greece	804	21.9	933	25.4	1,942	52.8	3,680	100
Spain	1,257	10.1	4,075	32.7	7,126	57.2	12,458	100
France	1,301	5.9	6,497	29.6	14,187	64.5	22,021	100
Ireland	157	13.7	322	28.1	667	58.2	1,149	100
Italy	1,657	7.9	6,962	33.1	12,396	59.0	21,015	100
Luxembourg	5	3.3	47	29.5	107	67.1	165	100
Netherlands	247	3.9	1,571	24.9	4,503	71.2	6,614	100
Austria	250	7.1	1,261	35.5	2,036	57.4	3,547	100
Portugal	517	11.5	1,468	32.6	2,523	56.0	4,509	100
Finland	187	8.6	602	27.7	1,382	63.7	2,171	100
Sweden	140	3.3	1,112	26.5	2,935	69.9	4,195	100
UK	569	2.2	7,715	30.2	17,237	67.5	25,630	100

Source: Eurostat (1996).

Note: Data for Austria refers only to persons working more than 12 hours per week.

reliant on working the land. It is also worth remarking that for all the talk of manufacturing giving way to services, the most significant story since the Second World War is the decline of agriculture, especially in France and Spain – it was only the period after 1945 which saw them fully modernized. Fernando Caballero, director of a retraining centre for unemployed people in Orcasitas, Spain, was recently quoted as saying that 'Spain was a rural society until 20 years ago. The country has moved from a pre-industrial to a post-industrial society within a generation' (Nash 1995).

This is not to say that many economies have not experienced a period of de-industrialization. The UK underwent a massive process of restructuring from the late 1970s onwards. Two factors were influential. Firstly, new technologies and developments in working practices meant that output was greatly enhanced with fewer workers. Secondly, in the early 1980s a radical Conservative administration embarked upon an economic policy which involved a harshly deflationary fiscal policy, the removal of subsidies to key industries and a strong currency which made UK exports relatively expensive abroad. It has been estimated that something like a third of the country's manufacturing base disappeared during this period.

One of the problems for the sociologist is to interpret what such changes mean. Firstly, Table 13.1 shows us that there is nothing inevitable about a shift from manufacturing to services. It is to some extent a reflection of conscious choices by government and investors. While the UK has embraced the service economy wholeheartedly, with a thriving financial services sector and a highly advanced food retailing market, countries like Germany have fought to preserve manufacturing industry, unconvinced that service employment was of as much value. An illustration of this contrast came with the opening in September 1996 of the 'mega-mall', 'CentrO'. Built on the site of a defunct steel mill, CentrO is the largest shopping centre in Europe, lying as it does in the heart of North Rhine-Westphalia and hopes to attract 30 million visitors per year. However, no developer in Germany appeared willing to take the project on. In the event the DM1.1 billion investment was provided by P&O and Eddie Healey of the Stadium Group (responsible for Sheffield's Meadowhall Centre). Enthusiasm for the 3,500 new jobs is tempered by fears about the effects of the mall on existing towns (see Chapter 20) and concern about pay and conditions.

The other point of note is that the 'service sector' is a term which conceals enormous variety in the nature and quality of employment within it. The 'service' economy and the 'knowledge' or 'information' economy are not synonymous. For a start, many services are so-called 'producer services', provided to firms in the course of their manufacturing activities. Professionals such as accountants, personnel officers and designers may be integral to the success of a manufacturing process, but technically it is service employment. More clear-cut cases of services are those which have a direct link with the public, 'consumer services'. Retailing is the most obvious one here, though one can think of cases where the line between manufacturing and service is blurred. For instance, a visit to the opticians will begin with a sight test and advice on frame-size and style (service) but will end with the grinding of lenses and their fitting into the selected frame (a product manufacture). Such anomalies do not matter too much as long as we do not read too much causal power into the 'changing occupational structure'. What matters more for individuals perhaps, is the way their work is organized and controlled.

The experience of work: flexibility for whom?

So much for the *content* of the employment in contemporary Europe. In the last twenty years the major issue of interest to academics and practitioners has been the tendency for new patterns of working arrangements to emerge. One word can sum up this whole area of debate – 'flexibility'. The term has become like a mantra, intoned by labour market analysts and senior managers as the key to commercial success. But what does it mean? Broadly speaking 'flexibility' is an umbrella term for a variety of ways in which human resource managers deploy their workers. It takes three major forms: functional, numerical and temporal.

Functional flexibility refers to the redesign of jobs away from the highly specialized division of labour associated with F.W. Taylor and Henry Ford. While task division and subdivision proved to be highly efficient in producing various types of product, it was also found to limit overall performance as it discouraged employees from using their initiative and left firms vulnerable to turnover of specialized staff. It was also accompanied by the growth of trade unions based upon particular crafts or trades, and in the 1960s it was common for firms to encounter 'demarcation disputes' as unionized workers refused to perform tasks

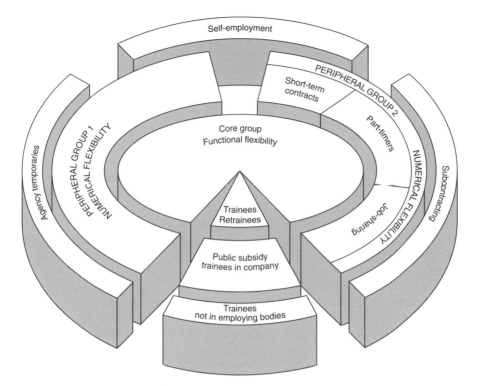

Figure 13.2 The flexible firm

Source: The Institute of Manpower Studies, 1986.

which were the remit of a worker in a different union. Satirists have referred to this attitude as the 'jobsworth' tendency, based on the apocryphal employee who when instructed to carry out a task, shakes his head sagely and says, 'I'm sorry, mate. I can't do that – it's more than me job's worth.' By contrast functionally flexible workers are not tied to one set of responsibilities, but have the skills to move between areas of the firm's operations. The advantage to the employer is the ability to 'cover' for sickness absence and vacancies. The advantage to the employee is that multi-skilling usually enhances their labour market value, and such workers are often described as the 'core' (see Figure 13.2).

Outside the 'core' workforce, firms have increasingly sought to employ *numerical flexibility*; that is to 'flex' their labour budget in time with peaks and troughs of demand. By their nature these jobs tend to be ones where less training is required to achieve the appropriate skill level. The types of arrangements involved here would depend on the cycle of demand for the firm's product or service. Where demand is seasonal or predictable in some way, the use of the short-term temporary contract is most suitable for the employer. In parts of the educational sector employers use 'term-time only' contracts to concentrate their resources on the period when their customers are most conspicuous! This may also be attractive to parents of school-age children who either wish or need to perform child-care during school holidays. Another form of numerical flexibility is the 'contracting out' of time-limited jobs to outside firms. The advantage here is that the firm does not 'carry' the burden of labour and other fixed costs itself. It will simply advertise the details of a contract and invite interested parties to bid, often at a fixed price for the job. If the contractor fails to meet the completion dates the firm will not have to worry about paying the workers overtime rates, nor does it have the headache of worrying which contract will keep its employees in work when the current one ends. In the UK this process swept through local government in the 1980s, particularly in cleaning, catering and building maintenance services. However, it has since spread to a wide range of professional services, and has long been part of the landscape for academic researchers.

Sitting somewhere between these two forms of flexibility is a third, more general one, *temporal flexibility*. In short this refers to any situation where there is flexibility in either the number or arrangement of working hours. The most traditional of these is of course overtime, where full-time employees are paid at premium rates if they work longer than their agreed maximum. Also well established in the public sector is the flexitime system, where workers can arrive and leave within a 'band' of time provided that they are present within a core period during the day. However, what is new about flexible time in the 1980s and 1990s is that it exists within the context of a substantial growth in part-time working. Although most countries in Europe have no legal definition of what constitutes 'part-time' a useful rule of thumb might be anyone working fewer than thirty hours in a week. Employers have increasingly found that, rather than employing someone for two days a week, or for five mornings a week, they may need to expand their workforce during very specific and limited periods. This need has largely been stimulated by the extension of opening hours, particularly in a sector like food retailing. A part-time worker might now be asked to work five 3-hour shifts during a week in order to provide extra staffing when superstores are busiest (i.e. between 5.00 and 8.00 p.m. on weekdays as people do their shopping after leaving work). An additional advantage of part-time working is that in order to solve the jigsaw of staff rosters, employees can be asked to work different hours or offered a few extra hours at their normal hourly rate, rather than having to incur overtime costs. At the extreme end of this policy, the restaurant Burger King was reportedly instructing its young counter staff to 'clock off' when they were not actually serving customers, hence only receiving wages for part of their period of employment. Other retailers have operated with so-called 'zero hours' contracts, where the employees simply wait to hear whether they are required to attend for a particular day or week. For the employer this represents the ultimate temporal flexibility – for critics it represents a return to the worst exploitative practices of nineteenth-century capitalism.

It is not possible here to give more than an indication of some of the new working practices. The main features of 'flexibility' are summarized in Figure 13.2. What remains in dispute throughout Europe is the desirability of such practices and the effect they have on economy and society more generally. Some see a flexible labour market as more competitive and indeed more fulfilling for employees, as they will learn a greater variety of skills and change careers two or three times during their working life. For others, such notions rest on a view of the world skewed towards the experience of the highly qualified, highly mobile middle classes. For individuals in this fortunate position there is the chance to rethink their organization of work, leisure, and family. Many have become 'time pioneers' (Hörning *et al.* 1995), seizing the chance to break away from the nine-to-five model of working life which has been dominant in the twentieth century. By contrast those lower down the labour market ladder do not experience flexibility as a liberation but as an opportunity to work longer for less. At the margins of the labour market, peripheral employment shades into the grey economy, where payment is in cash and there are no employment rights.

CHAPUZA: SPAIN'S HIDDEN ECONOMY

In Spanish this means 'botched work', and represents the marginal economy where products are produced at low costs by those outside the structures of formal employment. A recent report highlighted the impact of flexibility on a group of out-of-work kitchen fitters. 'Santiago, 30, who lives with his mother, has been unemployed for five years. But, he says to general laughter, he has never been out of work. "There's always something, a contract for a couple of days here and there, sometimes by the hour, building work, loading, seasonal work." Payment in cash, no insurance, no questions asked. A law passed last year to create more jobs produced only exploitative short-term *contratos basura* (rubbish contracts) and less security, the kitchen-fitters say' (Nash 1995).

In the following section we look more closely at an apparent paradox; namely, that in a Europe where unemployment is rising and part-time work is lauded as the new orthodoxy in a leisure-driven society, the average working week seems to be getting longer.

Working time in Europe

During the economic restructuring of the 1980s, as jobs were shed and full-time work gave way to more part-time employment, many speculated on the decline of work, the rise of a leisure society and the need for job sharing to spread job opportunities to all. It came as something of a surprise to learn in the late 1980s that average working time was on the increase. The popularizer, Charles Handy, has written of a paradox of underwork and overwork, and explains it through an equation which, he argues, encapsulates the way in which firms have made productivity gains. His '1/2 × 2 × 3' equation expresses his claim that in order to maintain profit margins, in addition to employing the kind of marginal flexible workers already discussed, companies have been expecting more of their remaining core workers. As a rule of thumb Handy suggests most are paying half as many people double the money to work three times as hard.

This also needs to be viewed within the context of wider socio-economic change. While the UK has moved towards a more deregulated market with evening and Sunday trading, Germany continues to restrict retailers to some of the shortest hours in the Union. In August 1995 when the German car giant Volkswagen proposed the introduction of Saturday working, the union IG Metall organized stoppages in protest. One banner on a march in Hamburg showed a caricatured boss holding the severed head of a worker, proclaiming 'Dein Papa gehört Samstags Mir!!', an inversion of the traditional German slogan where a little boy says 'Daddy belongs to me on Saturdays' (von Waldersee 1995). The enormous battle by business interests to achieve limited extensions of retail opening hours from November 1996 reveals a climate very different from the '24-hour economy' associated with the US which has been embraced in the UK.

If we examine the figures across Europe there are a number of interesting variations. Table 13.2 shows a breakdown between each economic sector for the twelve countries in the EU at 1992 and refers only to full-time employees. It shows that in virtually every area the UK had the longest working week in Europe. The overall European average of 40.3 hours was some three hours shorter than the UK's 43.4 hours. The longest working week in Europe was to be found in Irish agriculture where a 50-hour week was deemed to be the usual. Agriculture was also the sector where there was the most variation between countries, French farmers averaging just under 41 hours. Despite some unevenness the figures for industry and services appear to cohere more firmly around the 40-hour orthodoxy. This is not surprising given the historical development of trade unions in these sectors and their focus on reducing the working week.

Table 13.3 gives us an additional insight by clustering workers into groups depending on their usual length of working week. This shows that despite the spread of non-standard working patterns there is still an overwhelming majority (just under three-quarters of European employees) who work between 36 and 40 hours a week. What is especially marked, however, is the way that Greece,

TABLE 13.2 Usual length of the working week for full-time employees in 1992

	Average			Agriculture			Industry			Services		
	All	M	F	All	M	F	All	M	F	All	M	F
EUR12	40.3	41.1	38.8	43.0	43.7	40.9	40.5	40.8	39.5	40.1	41.2	38.6
Belg.	38.2	38.7	37.0	40.2	40.5	n/a	38.8	38.9	38.4	37.8	38.5	36.6
Den.	38.8	39.5	37.7	42.2	42.9	38.9	38.3	38.6	37.4	38.9	40.1	37.7
Ger.	39.9	40.1	39.4	42.1	42.1	42.0	39.4	39.5	38.9	40.2	40.8	39.6
Gr.	40.5	41.3	39.0	46.4	47.5	43.8	41.3	41.5	40.7	40.0	41.1	38.4
Sp.	40.6	41.0	39.6	44.3	44.9	41.1	40.5	40.5	40.2	40.3	41.0	39.4
Fr.	39.7	40.4	38.5	40.9	41.4	39.3	40.0	40.2	39.4	39.5	40.6	38.3
Ire.	40.4	41.9	37.9	51.1	51.9	n/a	40.8	41.5	38.8	39.7	41.5	37.6
It.	38.2	39.5	35.6	40.6	41.5	39.0	40.1	40.4	39.4	37.1	38.9	34.1
Lux.	39.7	40.5	38.2	47.9	48.1	n/a	40.2	40.5	38.3	39.4	40.4	38.1
Neth.	39.4	39.5	39.1	41.0	41.2	38.7	39.1	39.2	38.8	39.5	39.7	39.1
Port.	41.3	42.8	39.5	48.2	49.7	44.6	43.0	43.3	42.3	40.0	41.8	38.1
UK	43.4	45.1	40.2	49.5	50.4	45.4	43.8	44.8	39.9	43.1	45.2	40.2

Source: Eurostat (1996).

TABLE 13.3 Hours usually worked per week by persons in full-time employment, 1992 (%)

Hours	EUR12	Belg.	Den.	Ger.	Gr.	Sp.	Fr.	Ire.	It.	Lux.	Neth.	Port.	UK
< 36	7.8	8.9	5.3	1.4	10.3	5.8	14.0	19.7	10.5	–	0.7	19.5	10.1
36–39	40.5	65.1	74.3	55.1	15.3	9.0	61.0	28.9	26.4	–	37.8	5.3	27.9
40	32.1	21.3	6.0	33.2	52.8	72.8	9.8	33.3	48.1	–	58.4	26.2	13.7
41–44	6.2	0.4	2.4	3.1	4.1	2.7	4.8	1.8	3.9	–	1.0	26.8	15.4
45–48	6.0	1.5	5.3	2.3	10.8	4.6	4.5	5.4	7.4	–	0.9	15.1	13.1
> 48	7.4	2.8	6.4	4.9	6.7	5.1	6.0	9.8	3.7	–	1.3	7.2	19.8

Source: Eurostat (1996).

Portugal and the UK stand out as long hours nations. Almost half Portugal's workers labour for more than 40 hours a week, and more than a fifth for more than 44 hours. It seems likely that in the case of Portugal and Greece the largely agricultural base of the economy helps produce such outcomes. This seems a less adequate explanation in the case of Britain where, according to these figures, almost a fifth of the workforce were putting in more than 48 hours a week. This statistic has taken on increased significance in the 1990s as the European Commission's Working Time directive has attempted to place a ceiling of 48 hours on the weekly hours which employees shall work. The tension between, on the one hand, labour market deregulation in the UK and, on the other, EU legislation on convergent standards of employment rights has proved to be an enduring theme of the 1990s and promises to be so for the foreseeable future.

By contrast, when one examines the hours of part-timers (Table 13.4) the UK has the lowest figure in the Union, while male part-timers in Portugal may work more than 30 hours. Overall these figures suggest that there is still a major distinction between full- and part-time work in terms of its status and purpose. Part-time workers are still seen in the majority of cases as 'fillers' who help iron out fluctuations in the demand for labour. However, European directives have forced the British firms to award the same rights and privileges to both full- and part-time employees, and in 1996 Marks and Spencer announced it was ending the distinction between the two groups, thereby at a stroke making all workers potentially 'flexible'.

Getting on and getting along: management–worker relations

Another way in which the world of work has changed greatly since the 1970s is the decreased emphasis upon trade unions within economic life. There are academics and practitioners who now dismiss the whole subject of industrial relations as a relic of a bygone era. There have certainly been changes in the framework of workplace relations between workers and management. Many of the traditional manufacturing activities which were heavily unionized have either disappeared altogether or scaled down their level of employment. Many service sector organizations have little or no history of collective organization, and the demise of the vast industrial location means that union officials now have a more difficult

TABLE 13.4 Usual length of the working week for part-time employees in 1992

	Total	*Men*	*Women*
EUR12	19.6	19.2	19.6
Belg.	20.7	21.3	20.6
Den.	18.7	12.2	20.7
Ger.	20.0	17.3	20.2
Gr.	25.5	28.8	23.1
Sp.	18.5	20.0	18.1
Fr.	22.1	22.3	22.0
Ire.	18.5	20.2	18.0
It.	28.0	33.0	25.8
Lux.	20.0	26.8	19.2
Neth.	18.7	19.0	18.6
Port.	24.5	30.7	22.8
UK	17.4	15.5	17.7

Source: Eurostat (1996)

job in communicating with and recruiting potential membership. The increase in part-time employment also adds to these logistical problems.

On top of these structural changes, which were pronounced in Britain but by no means unique to it, a sequence of right-wing governments passed legislation to restrict the activities of trade unions. In the UK limitations were placed upon the ability of unions to picket workplaces or to take industrial action, and union leaderships were made more accountable to their memberships, most notably in terms of holding ballots prior to taking strike action. The end result has been a severe reduction in the influence of unions on economic management and on the shape of employment policy.

However, it would be unwise to infer from this that trade unionism has become redundant, or that work in advanced capitalist economies no longer involves conflicts over resources or procedures. Fewer days are now lost through strikes than was the case twenty years ago, but periodically a major dispute acts as a reminder that all is far from harmonious in the contemporary workplace. The balance of power has shifted a long way back towards employers and yet many features of workplace relations remain familiar. A text on industrial relations written in the late 1970s described a 1976 walk-out by staff at 'Kitchenco', a pseudonym for a major manufacturer of kitchen furniture. The cause of this was management's failure to consult over buying in parts to meet unexpected demand, and this combined with resentment over poor heating facilities in the factory to provoke a walk-out (Marchington 1981).

In September 1996 the joinery group Magnet, which manufactures kitchen furniture, sacked up to 300 workers after a two-week strike over pay and conditions. Every week the UK's conciliation service ACAS is called in for either advice or even arbitration in response to a breakdown of talks within the workplace. Large public sector unions have organized periodic days of protest over either pay restraint or wider political issues around public services. At the time of writing France's primary, secondary and high-school teachers were planning a national strike to protest at education cuts made by Prime Minister Alain Juppé's administration in order to meet the economic criteria for economic union which were mentioned in the introduction to this chapter. In the Autumn of 1995 France had been severely disrupted by a series of strikes by public sector workers, most notably the railway workers. Industrial relations has changed only in so far as the rules of engagement have shifted; the root causes of industrial conflict have barely altered.

The forgotten workers: Europe's unemployment problem

Hitherto all the discussion has concerned the 150 million or so Europeans in paid employment. However, in the mid-1990s unemployment – so often a problem in the early 1980s – was again high, rising and subject to large variation. In 1993 the average rate of unemployment within the Union was 10.7 per cent but those for Ireland and Spain were almost double and more than double respectively. One of the most difficult problems for the politicians of the Union is that with many large firms now operating plants in a number of locations jobs are relatively 'footloose'. The implications of this are spelt out in more detail in Chapter 20 but one example of this is Italy's now defunct Law 64 under which the state offered subsidies to industries wishing to set up in the Mezzogiorno, the poorest region of the country. The famous scooter manufacturer Vespa announced in 1993 its plans to build four new plants in the southern region, investing £260 million in the process. This enraged Tuscan workers who saw the spectre of their jobs being transferred to a new subsidized location (Glover 1993). Add to this the fact that many companies operate across nation-states as well as regions and the problem of co-ordinating policies to tackle unemployment grows ever larger.

One of the major obstacles to effective measures against unemployment is a lack of consensus as to its main causes. There is much enthusiasm within Europe for measures to improve education and training and to give aid to areas of greatest distress. At the same time most member states have now resigned themselves to restrictive economic regimes which are deflationary and contribute towards a downturn in economic activity.

As we shall see in Chapter 20, unemployment is one of the major contributors to urban deprivation and decline. The case of Rotterdam is one very representative of the European trends discussed in this chapter. As with Europe generally Rotterdam's economic structure has undergone great change. Between 1977 and 1987 employment in the manufacturing sector fell by 29 per cent and the 18 per cent rise in service employment failed to compensate for this loss. In 1990 Rotterdam's unemployment rate was four times that of the Netherlands as a whole and was concentrated among the young.

Since 1991 employment policy in the Netherlands has been in the hands of twenty-eight regional employment boards (RBAs) with 'tripartite' representation from local authorities, employers' federations and employees' organizations. These have seven major aims:

- to fill three-quarters of vacancies of the Employment Service with unemployed persons, including women returners;

- to reduce significantly the level of long-term unemployment;
- to reduce significantly unemployment among ethnic minorities;
- to provide equal opportunities for women;
- to bring about a sharp reduction in youth unemployment;
- to rehabilitate those partially incapable of work;
- to have more preventative policing by promoting education more tailored to the needs of the labour market (Symes 1995: 109).

To aid the pursuit of these there is a whole raft of schemes and benefits to assist an active labour market policy. Vocational Training Centres (CVs) provide supplementary courses for the unemployed and those who feel vulnerable in their current employment. Unemployed participants retain their benefits during training. Eighty per cent of those who complete a course find employment subsequently. Such schemes are buttressed by other measures, such as 'Jobclubs', and schemes directed at the long-term unemployed, such as the Re-orientation Interview (HOG) and the Integration into Working Life (KRA) initiative (Symes 1995: 112–16).

Summary

- The future of work and associated economic activity remains far from settled. Issues still to be settled as the 1990s drew on were the degree to which national labour market policies would be constrained by directives and then court rulings from Europe.
- In 1996 two of the main economic controversies, over working time and a minimum wage, both had a strong European dimension to them. While those in secure 'core employment' maintain their demanding schedules in order to increase their living standards, those out on the margins of economic life, those reliant on a succession of *contratos basura*, seem destined also to work longer hours to compensate for their poor rates of pay.
- The post-war settlement has on the whole brought prosperity to European populations but continues also to bring inequality, insecurity and conflict.

Further reading

Phillip Brown and Rosemary Crompton (eds) (1994) *A New Europe?: Economic Restructuring and Social Exclusion*, London: UCL Press. A good overview of the economic and social changes taking place in Europe. Chapter 1 by Kennett is a good way in to some of the debates about regulation theory, post-Fordism and patterns of exclusion.

Richard Hyman and Anthony Ferner (eds) (1994) *New Frontiers in European Industrial Relations*, Oxford: Blackwell. This collection of essays tackles a number of trends and issues arising from increasing European economic integration.

Valerie Symes (1995) *Unemployment in Europe*, London: Routledge. A well-researched treatment of the unemployment problem in Europe. The core of the book is a collection of case studies looking at labour market trends and policy responses in five European cities. In this regard the book can also be read in conjunction with Chapter 20 of this book.

Chapter 14

European culture and ideology in mass communication

Alison Anderson

Introduction	274
Bias and objectivity	274
Ideology	275
Theoretical perspectives	277
Mass society, commercialism and the world information order	279
New media technologies	282
Ownership and control	286
Culture and power	288
Summary	292
Further reading	293

Key concepts

- **Bias and objectivity**
- **Ideology and culture**
- **Mass consumption and media imperialism**

Introduction

The study of the mass media raises fundamental questions about the relationship between the individual and the state in European society. During the last two decades enormous changes have taken place; so much so that many commentators talk about the emergence of a new World Information Order. With the development of satellite, cable and video technologies the boundaries between nations are, to some extent, closing. These new technologies have profoundly changed political behaviour and the nature of political negotiation.

The European media stage tends to be dominated by a small number of immensely powerful tycoons – Murdoch, Berlusconi, Hersant – to name but a few. These media moguls have established major empires stretching their interests across national boundaries and seeking out global markets. They have a particularly high profile in Europe and North America. The concentration of multi-media ownership highlights some important issues concerning the role of mass communications in modern society. To what extent does the transmission of Western values and lifestyles threaten the culture and identity of indigenous peoples in developing countries? Have new media technologies ushered in an age of increased freedom of choice? Or do they merely serve to heighten divisions between the information 'haves' and 'have nots'? And how far are social attitudes and behaviour shaped by the mass media?

The term 'mass media' is commonly used to refer to television, cinema, radio, newspapers and magazines. The media have become an increasingly pervasive part of the lives of contemporary Europeans. They are all around us – at home, school, work, and leisure – offering us an increasing proliferation of news and entertainment facilities. The media constitute key arenas in which national and international public affairs are staged. However, the media do not simply mirror current political events; they provide us with particular constructions of reality.

Bias and objectivity

Politicians from all points of the political spectrum have denounced the media for bias. Clearly, it is not difficult to find instances of bias and partiality in the modern age of mass communications. Bias may be conveyed in a multitude of different ways from the subtleties of language, to the positioning of camera angles, to the juxtaposition of images, to choice of background sound. Or there may be intentional omission of items which do not fit in with the chosen story angle. There may be intended or unintended forms of bias.

However, we need to be cautious in our use of the term 'bias'. An item of news can only be considered to be biased in relation to some preconceived notion of objectivity. In other words, bias is deviation from an objective norm. There are several grounds, however, for concluding that complete objectivity in news-reporting is an impossible ideal.

The production of news involves a complex process of selection and assimilation of competing records of events and viewpoints. Journalists rely heavily upon their routine *news sources*, such as government, industry or interest groups, for story material. These sources themselves engage in selective activity through the sifting and processing of information for press releases. Thus, even before journalists piece together a report the material has been framed in various ways.

Media professionals have their own particular values, interests and prejudices too. They are continually making decisions about what can be regarded as the most newsworthy stories of the day. Consider, for example, the judgements that might be made about two competing stories. The first is a long-running story on a famine in Africa which has claimed the lives of thousands of people. It may be considered 'old' news, too dull, or too far removed from our everyday lives. By contrast a national feature story about a celebrity female who is reunited with her new-born kidnapped baby may be perceived to possess much wider appeal. Both items contain emotive overtones, yet the latter may be more likely to be interpreted as conforming to established *news values*: it involves a well-known personality, it is considered to be of national interest – something that can be widely identified with – and it contains an element of drama and immediacy. These judgements, of course, are likely to vary depending upon the type of newspaper (tabloid or broadsheet), or the category of broadcast news programme.

News processing is inevitably *selective*. News values tell us something about the political and cultural assumptions concerning the acceptability of particular views or forms of action within a particular society. This is reflected in the relationship between journalists and their sources, and in the framing of issues and events. The use of the term 'terrorist', for example, carries remarkably different connotations compared to, let us say, 'freedom-fighter' or 'political activist'. News sources such as government departments, industry or pressure groups enjoy differing levels of access to the news media; while some sources are regularly over-accessed others may be routinely under-accessed, or fail to get into the news. This hierarchy of source access may be influenced by the perception that an organization is challenging the consensual foundations of society.

Notions of *impartiality*, like objectivity, are often invoked in liberal–pluralist arguments about the freedom of the press. Impartiality may be defined as the reporting of news events without taking sides, or promoting particular interests. The idea that journalists report the news in a neutral, balanced fashion forms a central part of their professional ideology. Yet even here we may question the extent to which balance and fairness is achieved.

But the suggestion that impartiality may not be attainable does not absolve media professionals of their responsibilities. Although objectivity and impartiality are ideals journalists still have a duty to strive to report news as fairly and as accurately as possible.

Ideology

The selective character of news reporting raises questions about the centrality of *ideology* in the study of mass communications. The media are often viewed as major tools of ideological state control through censorship and propaganda. From a common-sense perspective governments seek to manipulate the media in order to maintain their position and protect their own vested interests. Thus a one-sided or 'partial' view of reality is favoured under conditions of peace as well as war.

The concept of 'ideology' has long been associated with the work of Karl Marx. For Marx, ideology was used to refer to the dominant ideas representing the interests of the ruling class. In *The German Ideology* he wrote: 'The ideas of the ruling class are in every epoch the ruling ideas, i.e. the class which is the ruling material force within society is at the same time its ruling intellectual force.'

Thus Marx maintained that bourgeois ideology becomes the accepted way of making sense of the world disseminated throughout the whole of society. However, the ruling ideas may be reproduced by a number of different groupings within society such as academics, teachers and media practitioners. In this way ideology is transmitted relatively *autonomously* from the state.

According to the French Marxist philosopher, Louis Althusser, we can identify a number of what he labels '*Ideological State Apparatuses*', or ISAs (Althusser 1971). These ISAs are the social institutions, independent of the state, which reproduce the dominant ideology. They include the education system, religion, the family, the legal system, party politics, cultural activities and mass communications. These institutions are compelled to uphold these ideologies in order to further their own interests rather than through state coercion. Finally, ISAs conceal privileged interests in capitalist society through presenting class-based divisions as natural.

If, as Althusser maintains, the mass media play a pivotal role in this process it is not surprising that mass communication theorists have devoted so much attention to the question of ideology. Althusser was right to point out that there are a multitude of competing forces that determine our lives – cultural as well as economic and political. In a more general sense we may talk about *all* language and models of society as underpinned by particular ideological positionings. However, Althusser assumes that the state is mainly a vehicle through which class power is maintained. Many aspects of the state cannot simply be reduced to the interplay of class interests.

More recently theorists have sought to rethink the relationship between ideology and the mass media. Thompson (1992), for example, talks of a critical conception of ideology that re-analyses the relationship between meaning and power. According to this approach the mass media are seen as playing a *central* role in 'cultural transmission' – the process through which ideas and symbols are produced and disseminated. Indeed, cultural transmission may be seen as one of the major distinguishing characteristics of modern society. Increasingly, the advent of new media technologies such as cable and satellite has meant that Western European news 'events' are simultaneously beamed around the globe. Thompson maintains that the dominant ideology thesis represents an overly simplistic account of the transmission of ideology in contemporary society. It makes the assumption that a common set of values and attitudes binds people together. Also, it fails to take account of the ways in which different social groupings make sense of ideology in different ways, and how the social context may influence power relations. It overplays the importance of class and obscures other power differentials based on, for example, ethnicity, gender or age.

Theoretical perspectives

Liberal pluralism

There is a long tradition in Western European society which holds that the press sustains the principles of freedom and democracy. In contrast to the totalitarian regimes of the former Eastern bloc countries, Western society is heralded for its openness and accountability. The press is seen as possessing a special watchdog role akin to a fourth branch of government, the other three branches comprising the legislature, the executive and the judiciary. Independent of the state, newspapers can provide the public with access to sensitive information and highlight wrongdoings carried out by representatives of the state through investigative journalism. Also, it provides a mechanism for ensuring that the government responds to public opinion.

In contrast, there is much less support for the notion that broadcasting is bound by a free-market public watchdog role. Before the most recent developments the Western European broadcasting systems were generally influenced by a philosophy which emphasized public service and accountability. The liberal–pluralist position makes a number of basic assumptions. First, the theory suggests that we have a free press which is not controlled by the state. Private ownership of newspapers is seen as guaranteeing editorial independence. Second, it assumes that a diverse range of newspapers and broadcasting outlets ensures that different points of view can be given adequate representation. However, the assumption that all interests can be adequately represented has long ceased to stand up to critical scrutiny. Third, it maintains that consumers have ultimate sovereignty since they can always switch to another channel or purchase a different newspaper. If a particular point of view is not represented in the press this is seen as reflecting the fact that it does not have enough support among the public. Finally, it overplays the extent to which public opinion is formed through a rational process.

In recent years this traditional perspective has come under increasing attack. According to the radical critique it fails to recognize the ideological character of the informational role of the media. A number of social and political groups are competing with one another to influence media agendas. Some versions of reality privilege the interests of one section of society over another. James Curran observes:

> Different ways of interpreting and making sense of society, different linguistic codes and conceptual categories, different chains of association and versions of 'common sense' privilege the interests of some while disadvantaging others. The media's informational role is never purely informational: it is also a way of arbitrating between the discursive frameworks of organized groups in ways that can potentially affect the distribution of resources and rewards in society.
>
> (Curran 1996: 101)

Figure 14.1 Silvio Berlusconi
Source: Popperfoto. Copyright Paul Popper Limited.

The mass-manipulative model

In contrast to the pluralist model, mass-manipulative theories maintain that the state works alongside capitalist interests to ensure the media represent the interests of the dominant class. At its crudest, this view suggests that the media and the state collude in a conspiracy to protect the status quo. The notion of conspiracy implies that a small, powerful elite have secretly plotted among themselves to protect their own interests. The masses are diverted away from thinking about the important political issues of the day by the continual emphasis placed upon lotteries and game shows, the rich and famous, sexual scandal, and sport.

There are indeed plenty of examples of close ties between media tycoons and government. Perhaps one of the most striking cases in recent times is that of the former Italian prime minister, Silvio Berlusconi, who controlled the Finnivest Group (see Figure 14.1). This huge media enterprise runs twenty-seven Italian television channels (three of Italy's six national channels) and possesses television holdings in France (Channel 5), Germany (Telefunf), Spain (Telecino), and Canada. Often referred to in Italy as '*Sua Emittenza*' or 'His Transmittance', Berlusconi has blatantly used his media interests to further his own political career. During the mid-1990s his television channels gave free advertising for his political campaigns. Also, in his climb to power he developed a close friendship with Bettino Craxi (leader of the Socialist Party and prime minister between 1983 and 1987) (Mazzoleni and Palmer 1992). These strong links with the establishment enabled him to flout legislation which was designed to limit multi- or cross-media ownership.

Similarly, Australian-born Rupert Murdoch, controller of the giant News International Corporation, built up a close relationship with the former president of the USA, Ronald Reagan, and the former prime minister of Britain, Margaret Thatcher. He managed to get around foreign ownership restrictions in the United States by becoming a US citizen, which allowed him to obtain major stakes in television.

Heads of state continually attempt to use the media in order to strengthen their positions. In a recent *News of the World* feature article the British prime minister, John Major, celebrated a very politically unstable year by pointing to a string of 'successes'. In the same edition, the opposition leader Tony Blair is derided as too young, idealistic and inexperienced to run the country, in an article headlined

'BOY BLUNDER BLAIR'S NO MATCH FOR MAJOR'.

Similarly, it is not difficult to point to instances whereby media magnates exert considerable influence in the day-to-day running of their empires. For example, Rupert Murdoch removed Stafford Somerfield, editor of the *News of the World*, and Harold Evans, editor of the *Times*, when their views clashed. Clearly, proprietors have close involvements with the world of politics and their position opens up a large degree of opportunity to manipulate and control the media.

However, popular notions of a conspiracy between the state and the media are difficult to substantiate given the sheer volume and complexity of the modern system of mass communications. Political elites and media moguls operate under particular constraints. Though they have the ability to influence the news agenda they are not always able to do so (Golding and Murdock 1996). Competing interests among key players is a major factor that works against conspiratorial control. Another concerns the deep divisions within the upper classes themselves. So although it would be a mistake to dismiss conspiracy theory out of hand, it offers us very little in terms of an understanding of the general mechanisms of news production.

Mass society, commercialism and the world information order

Mass society

The early development of the communications industry took place at a time of great social upheaval and change. As we saw in Chapter 2, nineteenth-century urbanization heightened divisions between the great two classes: the bourgeoisie and the proletariat. *Mass society theory* reflected a climate of increased fear and anxiety among European elites. The old order was crumbling and a new popular culture was beginning to emerge. Although mass society theory has greatly influenced modern European social and political thought, it was based upon a simplistic view of the audience. Typically, people were seen as a homogeneous mass of damp sponges, uniformly soaking up messages from the media. It failed to account for the sheer diversity of interpretations which could be drawn by different sub-sections of the population.

Modern communications theory can also be traced back to another major influence; that of the *hypodermic model* which became popular in the United States during the early part of the twentieth century. This approach saw the audience as essentially passive; the media simply inject messages syringe-like, into the audience and individuals respond in a predictable way.

Both mass society theory and the hypodermic model were challenged during the 1940s by the rise of a new commercially orientated approach to the media in the USA. This became known as the *uses and gratifications* approach. In contrast to earlier theories, it focused upon the ways in which people *use* the media. It suggested that people use the media in different ways and for different reasons. Rather than viewing the audience as a mass of atomized individuals, it recognized that individuals were members of social groups, and that responses to the media are mediated through these networks. For example, Katz and Lazarsfeld's (1955) 'Two-step Flow' model implied that the effects of the media on the audience were limited, while the social and cultural context in which communication took place was of great importance.

Mass production and mass consumption

As suggested above, the origins of mass society lie within the USA. With the declaration of Independence in 1776, the USA was established as a nation of European emigrants who wanted to sever ties with the European establishment and its 'old order'. During the twentieth century the 'American dream' has involved the raising of material standards of living for the mass of the population through the development of mass production and mass consumption. Mass production and its consequences are often referred to as 'Fordism' after Henry Ford, the principal pioneer of the assembly line in manufacturing during the early twentieth century. His success is attributable to the introduction of 'super rationality' into manufacturing industry. At a time when manufacturing was still individualized and engineering had hardly progressed from craft production in this respect, he standardized the components, the working practices and the financial calculations involved in the manufacture of the motor car. Before this manufactured goods had been only for the well-off, but he introduced the principle of producing for a mass market and of paying the workers sufficiently for them to form part of that market too. Assembly line production has also attracted, quite deservedly, a reputation for 'de-skilling' and for the exploitation of workers, but, undoubtedly, without mass production mass consumption would not be possible. The Fordist formula has been highly successful and companies like Ford have become manufacturers to the world.

A similar kind of rationality was also developed for service industries in the USA and probably the best-known example of this is McDonald's fast food restaurants. Here again, the components, the working practices and the financial calculations are standardized to produce a certain quality of product that everyone can afford. Today, the principles contained in the McDonald's formula can be perceived in all kind of commercial and non-commercial activities, from package holidays to the system building of housing, to the provision in some state services (such as, for instance, in modular courses in education). The standardization of procedures has become the cornerstone of many organized activities during the twentieth century.

By contrast the success of Japan in manufacturing industry during the late twentieth century can be attributed to the maintenance of principles of standardization whilst introducing more flexibility into the finished product and the way that it is manufactured. In the first place Henry Ford is reputed to have said: 'You can have a Ford car in any colour as long as it is in black', reflecting his obsession with standardization. Consumers now expect and take for granted much more choice, and Japanese companies in particular were quick to recognize and develop the need for this. Moreover, they achieved greater flexibility with reduced capital investment through the use of horizontal rather than vertical structures. Stated simply, the principle is that large companies and the departments within them, together with their outside component suppliers, work with great co-ordination and with increased co-operation between management and workers. This has come to be referred to as 'post-Fordist' manufacturing. Increased flexibility of products has fitted in very well with contemporary desires for greater personal freedoms and with suspicions over bureaucratic inflexibilities in society. This is perhaps characteristic of mass society during the late twentieth century.

Mass communication

It can easily be appreciated that mass communication provides a kind of 'lubrication' for mass production and mass consumption. Products and services are intentionally advertised but in addition images of a mass culture are projected in all kinds of other ways, intentional and unintentional. It was the Europeans who emigrated to the USA and subsequently developed the idea of mass participation society, involving at first political participation through liberal democracy and then economic participation through mass production, mass communication and mass consumption. Since then the Europeans have become, so to speak, the recipients of their own Western culture transformed by Americans into the universalized forms of a mass society. Nowadays, however, the 'Americanization of the world' not only affects Europe but has become a global phenomenon and, above all, the Japanese have taken full advantage of globalization in order to further their own forms of industrialization and global marketing. Particularly with the development of electronic communications technologies in forms available for mass consumption, the Japanese more than any other manufacturing nation have made it easier for people to participate in the global culture. The mass media of communication bring the world into virtually everyone's living space, whilst additionally, mass travel, including emigration and tourism, has taken many more people to different parts of the world. Yet through this process the global media have remained dominated by the English language as computer technology, with its 85 per cent use of English demonstrates.

New media technologies

Cable and satellite

Since the early 1980s many Western European countries have experienced phenomenal growth in the uptake of new media technologies. Europe has been strongly influenced by developments in the USA, particularly the rapid penetration of cable television. The USA has also led the way in the spread of satellite television. Rupert Murdoch's Sky Channel was launched in 1982 and to begin with could only be beamed to households with cable television. By 1985 Sky Channel reached 5 million homes. In 1988 the advent of direct broadcasting by satellite (DBS) did away with the need to relay satellite channels by the cable network.

Rates of satellite uptake have been much greater than cable because of lower financial costs. When Sky Channel was first launched there was only one other satellite service available in Europe. Yet by 1991 there were seventy-one services available, mainly in English, French or German (Negrine 1994). Britain, Germany and France were particularly unprepared since their cable systems were outdated and thinly spread. During the last decade the highest take-up rates for cable were in countries like Belgium, the Netherlands, Switzerland and Canada where people could obtain access, relatively inexpensively, to better-funded television services relayed from a nearby country in a language that can be understood (Collins 1992). In 1984, for example, 81 per cent of homes in Belgium and 74 per cent of homes in the Netherlands subscribed to cable television networks (Collins 1992: 22). In comparison take-up rates for Britain, West Germany and France were less than 10 per cent.

However, by 1994 almost a third of households in Western Europe had access to satellite or multi-channel cable networks. Estimates suggest that by the year 2000 cable and satellite television will have been installed in 50 per cent of homes (*Screen Digest*, August 1994). Figure 14.2 illustrates huge variations in take-up rates for cable and satellite across Western Europe.

At present, Belgium, Luxembourg, Monaco and the Netherlands have the highest cable penetration rates in Western Europe. But cable television has still failed to make a significant impact in countries such as Spain and Italy. However, there are signs that even here major expansion could occur with increased numbers of people subscribing to new cable telephone services. Indeed, in the UK British Telecom and Mercury are likely to invest as much as cable television in the future 'information superhighway'.

Satellite television has had the most impact in countries where the provision of entertainment programmes by the existing broadcasting structures has been weak, for example Germany (Collins 1992). In 1995, Germany, Denmark and Norway had the highest penetration rates: 25.8 per cent, 21.9 per cent and 16.9 per cent respectively. However, the UK and Sweden also have relatively high numbers of satellite subscribers: 15.9 per cent and 13.0 per cent respectively. Satellite television generally has had little impact in France, Greece, Italy and Finland. In December 1994 the Italian government announced that it was giving the go-ahead for SAT2000, its first media initiative to boost satellite penetration.

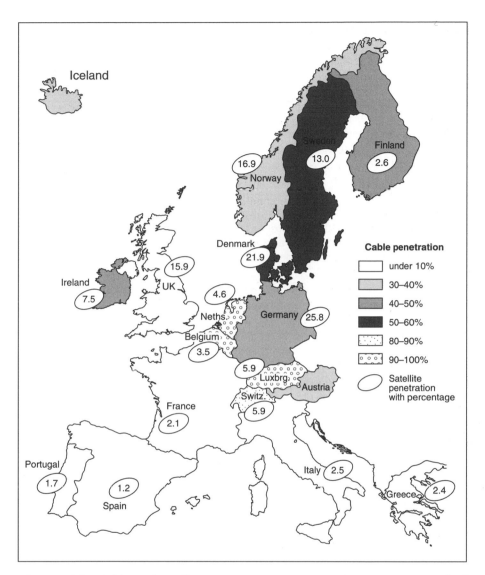

Figure 14.2 Cable and satellite penetration in Europe, 1995, percentage of all households with TV

Source: Reproduced by kind permission of *Screen Digest*.

As for Central and Eastern Europe, cable and satellite have generally had a low impact (see Table 14.1). Hungary, however, enjoyed a relatively high penetration rate for cable television with 15.9 per cent of homes connected in 1993. Also, there is evidence of the beginnings of significant growth in Poland, Serbia and the Czech Republic. The greatest numbers of satellite dishes in 1993 were also to be found in Poland, Hungary and Serbia.

TABLE 14.1 Cable and satellite in Central/Eastern Europe

	Cable connections (000s)		Satellite dishes (000s)		Cable penetration (%)		Satellite penetration (%)	
	1991	1993	1991	1993	1991	1993	1991	1993
Bulgaria	1.0	n/a	1	70	0.0	n/a	0.0	2.8
Croatia	n/a	13.0	n/a	40	n/a	1.5	n/a	4.5
Czech Republic	n/a	70.0	n/a	60	n/a	2.3	n/a	2.0
Czechoslovakia	20.0	–	75	–	0.4	–	1.7	–
Hungary	500.0	700.0	50	150	12.2	15.9	1.2	3.4
Poland	200.0	220.0	250	360	1.9	2.0	2.4	3.3
Romania	–	20.0	4	10	–	0.5	0.1	0.2
Serbia	n/a	40.0	n/a	120	n/a	2.0	n/a	6.0
Slovakia	n/a	30.0	n/a	40	n/a	2.1	n/a	2.8
Slovenia	n/a	22.0	n/a	50	n/a	3.4	n/a	7.8
USSR/CIS	5,000.0	[*1]	–	–	5.1	–	–	–
Yugoslavia	380.0	[*2]	7	–	8.6	–	0.2	–

[*1] Satelite estimates for former Soviet republic: Belarus 20,000 (0.7%), Estonia 10,000 (2.0%), Moldova 10,000 (2.5%), Russian Federation 50,000 (0.1%), Ukraine 20,000 (0.1%). [*2] Former Yugoslavia republic of Macedonia 10,000 (2.5%). See also Croatia and Slovenia.

Source: *Screen Digest* from national agency and other data. Reproduced by kind permission of *Screen Digest*.

Video

There are also great variations in video cassette recorder (VCR) ownership across Europe. In 1993 VCR sales in Europe were highest in Germany, the UK and France (see Figure 14.3). On average almost 8 per cent of households in Western Europe had two or more VCRs in 1993. However, the VCR market is still heavily dominated by the USA. In fact, in 1994 the US accounted for over 25 per cent of total VCR sales. By contrast, parts of the developing world such as Singapore, Ecuador and Uruguay had very low rates of VCR ownership.

In much of Europe a new multi-channel environment has been created by the advent of VCRs and cable and satellite television. Governments have had difficulty in regulating the content of these new media. It is hard to make predictions about future trends since this is a constantly changing field and statistics on current penetration rates are not always very reliable and have to be treated cautiously.

Future developments

Forecasts differ as to the likely impact of these changes. Curran and Seaton (1991) group these into two major categories: the 'neophiliacs' and the 'cultural pessimists'. The neophiliacs, such as Anthony Smith (1987), are very optimistic about the future. They argue that the information revolution will result in the

European Union

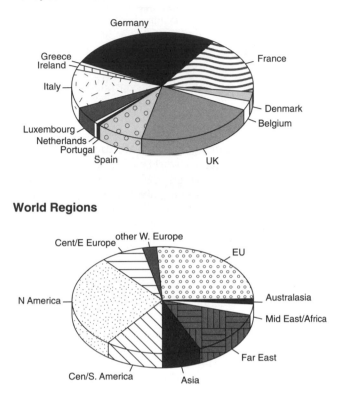

World Regions

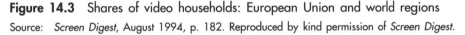

Figure 14.3 Shares of video households: European Union and world regions

Source: *Screen Digest*, August 1994, p. 182. Reproduced by kind permission of *Screen Digest*.

disappearance of traditional forms of work and a major expansion of the service sector (this includes occupations that provide public services such as banking or teaching). The growth of the 'knowledge industries' will lead, they suggest, to a major shift towards home-based work using computer terminals. Alongside this, they predict that ultimately the production process will be relocated to developing countries. Moreover, they conclude that traditional divisions based upon social class will be virtually eliminated.

By contrast cultural pessimists, such as Collins *et al.* (1987), believe that the revolution will threaten standards and actually serve to heighten social inequalities. They are concerned about the *de-skilling* of the workforce – the continual lowering of workers' skills – brought about by the expansion of computer technology. They see a society sharply divided between the information 'haves' and the information 'have nots'. An alternative view is provided by Bernard Woods (1993), who argues that the information revolution contains a great democratizing potential for people in the developing world through the spread of education and the development of new skills. How far this potential is actualized, given the existing power structure, remains to be seen.

Ownership and control

Globalization is the process by which increasing numbers of people throughout the world are affected by the same cultural influences (see Chapter 22). A physical consequence of this is the growth in the number of transnational corporations which provide products and services for global mass consumption. The Ford Motor Company was founded upon Henry Ford's dream of a single product, the Model T Ford, as a world product – a 'world car' for everyone. Within a few years of the establishment of the original assembly line in the USA there were Ford plants in Britain, Germany, France and many other parts of the world. The formula has been copied many times and there are now many hundred large transnational corporations. Most of them are still American in origin, but the Japanese have moved into second position in a relatively short time and the European countries trail behind in this respect. Nevertheless, there are many large European transnational corporations.

The provision of the various media services through mass communications has also lent itself to the formation of transnational corporations, and the application of advanced electronic technology has furthered the process. However, despite tendencies towards absolute globalization, the contemporary world has three discernible 'cores' in North America, Europe and East Asia. This is especially apparent in communications. The electronic technologies themselves tend to converge with, for instance, the use of fibre optic cabling which nowadays has the capacity for hundreds of thousands of relayed messages at the same time. Mainly, this operates along the so-called 'information superhighway' which stretches between the cores of the global system in North America, Europe and East Asia. Other parts of the world are relatively neglected by this front-line technology but have nevertheless been accommodated by the alternative use of satellites. With these, the high cost of fibre optic cabling is avoided because satellites operate regardless of the distance which has to be covered. Satellite transmission is therefore the ideal medium for less-developed countries and in India, for instance, the take-up has been phenomenal given the apparent poverty of the country.

There has tended to be a process of conglomeration in global mass communications and this chapter will conclude with descriptions of some systems which are probably familiar.

Rupert Murdoch's News Corporation

Murdoch's extensive communications empire provides us with a useful illustration of the tendency towards transnational media enterprises. Like multinational companies, transnational companies are capitalist ventures which spread their interests across national boundaries and orientate themselves towards global markets. However, unlike multinationals, transnationals do not have a clearly identifiable home base. Murdoch's News Corporation has holdings in cable and satellite television in the USA, Latin America, the UK, Germany, Australia and Asia. The company owns a number of satellite channels transmitted by BSkyB in Europe, satellite companies in Australia and Twentieth-Century Fox Cable Corporation in the USA. In addition to this, there is his huge newspaper empire with major titles in Britain and Australia (he controls a third of daily newspaper sales in Britain), and he is increasingly moving into books and magazines (his company owns HarperCollins publishing house).

News Corporation is also expanding its links with the telecommunications industry through a planned deal with MCI Corporation, the second largest telecommunications company in the USA. As part of this deal MCI Corporation will invest up to $2 billion in the Murdoch empire and, in return, telephone subscribers will be able to sample products such as pay-TV or newspapers. Another major trend is for media enterprises to diversify their interests by expanding into other economic areas. Murdoch's News Corporation now has interests in, for example, airlines, oil and minerals.

Bertelsmann Group

Based in Germany, this is a key European-based conglomerate with huge stakes in film, television, radio and magazines. It includes Germany's largest cable TV company and the RTL Plus television channel. Also, it holds interests in the US book and record companies, RCA and Bantam.

Maxwell Communications Corporation

This was controlled by the late Robert Maxwell and is based in Britain. It controls a major group of newspapers which span an area from the US to Eastern Europe, and is heavily involved in the publishing industry. In Britain 21 per cent of daily newspaper sales are controlled by the Maxwell owned Mirror Group. Also, Maxwell Communications has television interests in Britain, France and Spain. For example, the Maxwell Group has a 20 per cent interest in the DBS satellite TDF 1 in France.

Ted Turner's CNN global channel

CNN is the original global news channel. It owes much of its success to the fact that it was installed in international hotels so that travellers of many kinds were introduced to a new channel that drew news from the world and transmitted it in a similar fashion for twenty-four hours every day. During the Gulf War of 1990–1 CNN reporters made a name for themselves by remaining in Baghdad throughout the hostilities and providing continuous transmissions by satellite. They used a kind of upturned umbrella transmission device to bounce their pictures off the satellites and then on to the CNN world system. Cruise missiles launched by the armed forces and targeted on Baghdad were virtually filmed as they arrived!

Culture and power

The concentration of ownership into relatively few hands effectively limits public access to the full spectrum of political thought. But 'transnationalization' may also constrain cultural autonomy – this is what is known as media imperialism, or 'cultural imperialism' as it is sometimes referred to. Media imperialism is part of the broader process of imperialism described in Chapter 22. The media imperialism thesis suggests that developing countries have become increasingly reliant upon exported media products from the West (particularly the USA and Western European countries) and that this is threatening their traditional culture (for example, Schiller 1985). According to Fejes' broad definition it is: 'the process by which modern communication media have operated to create, maintain and expand systems of dominance and dependence on a world scale' (1981: 281).

So media imperialism refers to a cultural imbalance in the transmission of media messages between nation-states in the global capitalist economy. This privileges the interests (political, economic and cultural) of world powers such as the USA, Germany, Britain and Japan. In turn it tends to disadvantage economically less powerful nations in Asia, Africa and South America. The development of global communications systems now means it is much easier for media to cross cultural and national boundaries. Indeed, transnationalization has taken place on such a scale that many theorists talk about moves towards a 'new world information order' (MacBride 1980). The media imperialism thesis reflects deep-seated anxieties about local cultures being invaded by foreign influences, and a standardization or homogenization of values, styles and products. Also, it maintains that developing countries are increasingly reliant upon Western communications technologies and technical skills.

Annabelle Sreberny-Mohammadi (1996) identifies two general processes which are at work together in the modern communications environment. The first trend is towards globalization: in this context it is taken to mean the flow of information from wealthy northern countries, which some argue is creating a homogeneous world culture. The second is towards media localization: the production of indigenous cultural forms such as folk music or locally produced soap operas. Often localization occurs in direct response to the pressures of globalization. However, it is important to remember that much of this localized material is produced by large companies and is a part of the network of consumer capitalism. In many cases it is produced at the national level rather than the truly local.

Hollywood globalization

Since the early part of this century Hollywood has dominated film culture. For a considerable time European countries have deferred to this powerful commercial enterprise (Tunstall and Palmer 1993). By the 1980s more and more foreign companies were attracted to owning a share in this hugely successful money-spinning empire. Australian, European and Japanese corporations bought into the American broadcasting system:

- Twentieth-Century Fox was purchased by the Australia-based Murdoch corporation.
- MGM/United Artists was purchased by the Italian company PatheSA.
- MCA Inc. (including Universal Studios, Universal Pictures and MCA Records) was taken over by the Japanese Matsushita company.
- Columbia Pictures, together with Tri-Star Pictures and CBS Music, was purchased by the Japanese firm, Sony.

News is distributed around the world by a variety of news agencies which provide different services. Western news agencies such as the US-based CNN or the London-based Worldwide Television News (WTN) television news agency tend to dominate news distribution and favour a Western outlook. Reuters has become the largest distributor of computerized information and has offices in some eighty countries (Tunstall and Palmer 1993). Additionally, the European news exchange body, Eurovision, which is limited to members of the European Union, circulates news around Europe.

Western news agencies tend to be dominated by the professional ideologies of objectivity and impartiality. Broadcast news exchange organizations are often based upon the assumption that pictures cannot distort the truth in the way that words can. Though news agencies clearly exert a considerable influence, recent studies suggest that modern news exchange systems tend to be characterized by a degree of interdependency, rather than the complete subordination of those of less-developed countries (Gurevitch 1996). Regional news exchange mechanisms have taken on greater significance as agencies have increasingly cooperated to form more powerful influences in various parts of the world.

Western values and ideology

Media imperialism has long been associated with the influence of the USA, particularly the Hollywood film industry. Many perceive 'Americanization' as responsible for creating a bland, homogeneous culture. Over recent years there has been a surge of mass marketed media products promoting Western values, identities and lifestyles. The soft drink 'Coca-Cola' campaigns provide a classic example of a heavily advertised product designed to appeal to the 'American way of life'. Through Coca-Cola advertising campaigns, images of Western lifestyles have been transported across the world. What was new about the 1980s 'Coca-Cola is it' campaign was that it was based upon particular cultural appeals through featuring US national symbols such as leisure and powerful social ties. These sorts of cultural signs do not appear by accident; they are designed to promote a particular image or way of life which becomes associated with the product.

Dallas

Similar sorts of national symbols and lifestyle appeals can be found in the popular US-produced television serial, *Dallas*. This serial became so successful it was the most popular programme in the world during the 1980s. A study conducted by Ien Ang in 1985 found that the serial was being shown in ninety countries worldwide. Ang wanted to explore why this serial about a rich, Texan oil family enjoyed such enormous popularity, particularly among women. She found that a large part of its appeal lay in the way it was based on universal themes. Many Dutch viewers were found to relate with what Ang calls the 'tragic structure of feeling'; in other words the emotional realism of the serial reflecting transitory moments of happiness and sorrow. Though the characters and the plot are far removed from most women's everyday lives, some individuals relate to more universal human experiences involving the family, personal relationships and work. Other viewers enjoyed watching the serial but used humour as a way of distancing themselves from it. Another study of *Dallas* by Herzog-Massing (1986) suggests that German, in contrast to Dutch, viewers tended to see the appeal of the programme in terms of an escapist fantasy which allowed them to look at taboo subjects.

A later study of *Dallas* by Liebes and Katz (1993) further underlines the multiple ways in which viewers make sense of media texts. The notion that texts may be open to more than one possible reading is known as *polysemy*. Liebes and Katz's ethnographic audience analysis reveals that the programme is open to multiple interpretations influenced by the viewer's cultural identity and ethnic background. For example, different ethnic groups varied in the extent to which they identified with the programme in 'real' or 'abstract' terms. Liebes and Katz found that non-Americans were more likely to view the programme as a 'realistic' portrayal of US life than were Americans. However, we cannot simply lump all 'Americans' together and assume that members of such a diverse range of communities will all interpret it in the same way. In general, however, viewers were found to identify with the melodramatic features of the story line rather than with underlying messages about consumption and capitalism.

The active audience

Towards the beginning of this chapter it was noted that early effects models conceived of the audience as highly susceptible to media influences. Current approaches to the audience view the process of media persuasion as much more complex. There has been a movement away from the notion that mass media influence can be conceptualized simply in terms of unidirectional flows from the media to the mass audience. Emphasis is increasingly placed upon how individuals construct their own meanings, in the diversity of readings and responses, and how this then influences the communication process.

An interesting study by Greg Philo (1993) provides an example of recent research in the tradition of the Glasgow University Media Group. In *Seeing and*

Believing Philo explores the ways in which different social groupings were influenced by the television portrayal of the 1984/5 UK miners' strike. Philo asked the respondents, who were recruited from different areas of Britain, to construct their own news stories as though they were journalists basing them upon the original news photographs. Though responses were mediated by social class and cultural differences Philo concluded that, where people had no direct experience of the picketing, television pictures tended to stick in their minds. In other words, at least for some sections of the public, seeing *was* believing.

Some qualifications to the media imperialism thesis

Recent studies suggest that the media imperialism thesis should be accompanied by a number of qualifications if it is to reflect the sheer complexity of the modern communications environment.

Firstly, reception theory indicates that the audience cannot be taken as a homogeneous 'mass'. Images of Western lifestyles, for example, are likely to impact on individuals in different ways depending upon their cultural and ethnic background, and their gender and social class position.

Secondly, over recent years there has been a significant increase in flows of material from southern countries such as India (a country which produced over 900 films in 1985), Brazil and Mexico. In certain instances we can see a reversal of the traditional power equation. For example, Brazil exports a substantial amount of material to Portugal without any proportionate reciprocation.

A third qualification concerns the ability of imported products and traditional culture to co-exist together. Many theorists point to the existence of *hybrids*, or mixtures of foreign and indigenous culture, as evidence of much-watered-down influence. The production of 'hybrid' cultural forms can be seen with the influence of US and British broadcast media on Indian cinema, such as the new category of film which has attracted the label 'curry eastern' (Sreberny-Mohammadi 1996). Also, it can be seen in the way that US ghetto rap music has been appropriated across the world in the 1990s.

Fourthly, on occasion indigenous cultural forms can be actively resistive. Consider, for example, the hugely successful Indian soap opera, *Ramayana*. This series was so popular during the 1980s that people would come together on a Sunday morning to watch it beamed into the rural villages via satellite. *Ramayana* was based around mythical gods representing forces of good and evil in Hinduism. The programme is acknowledged as contributing to a revival of Hindu fundamentalism, and is believed to have played a part in the fall of the Rajiv Gandhi government (Lull 1995). Some members of the cast were even encouraged to stand for parliament in the Indian general election, even though they had very little political experience

The Indian satellite television audience is subjected to competition between the Hong Kong-based Star TV, controlled by Murdoch's News International Corporation, and the popular local Hindi language station, Zee TV, which uses the same satellite relaying system. The electronic media are certainly reaching some of the poor people in India and it is having a cultural effect. Star TV transmits a diet of mainly Western 'soaps' and pop music, but the Indian alternative combines Hindi films with programmes about controversial issues in Indian politics and society. Most surprising of all Indian state TV, Doordashan, easily outdoes the two satellite stations when it comes to audience figures. It is not so much that India is swept by Western culture in the form of television programmes, but rather that it has adopted the media of Western culture to provide a diet of mixed Western programmes, Asian-origin versions of the Western television diet and specifically Indian-culture transformations of the pattern. Whatever the format, Western lifestyles and aspirations are an important part of the message.

A final difficulty with some versions of the media imperialism theory is that 'Western ideology' cannot be reduced to any one coherent set of norms and values. Media organizations embrace different conflicting ideologies and contradictions. Though they are governed by particular professional norms these vary within and between media. We cannot simply assume that there is a US message in the text which is decoded by the audience and then interpreted similarly by viewers in different countries.

Future trends

The European Union has brought in a number of initiatives to market the EU broadcasting industry and foster the 'cultural uniqueness of member states'. After several years of discussion the European broadcasting policy, detailed in the 'Television without Frontiers' directive, was finalized in 1989. 'Television without Frontiers' proposed a maximum quota of 50 per cent on imported programming (this was mainly intended to include television series and feature films) by October 1992. However, it was only a voluntary agreement and lacked any binding force. The directive reflected French broadcasting policy more than any other European country and established France as the leading policy mover at the time (Tunstall and Palmer 1993). This period saw an increase in co-productions between American and European broadcasting industries, a trend likely to continue in the foreseeable future. It did little to break the cycle of dependency affecting a large part of the developing world.

Summary

- The European media are owned and controlled by a small number of very powerful tycoons.
- There are large variations in new media technology take-up rates across Europe.
- The effects of the media are varied and not always as might be expected.

Further reading

James Curran and Michael Gurevitch (eds) (1996) *Mass Media and Society* (2nd edn), London: Edward Arnold. A collection of stimulating essays which represent the diversity of existing perspectives on the role of the media in European society. This text contains particularly useful essays by Annabelle Sreberny-Mohammadi and Michael Gurevitch on the globalization of international communications.

James Lull (1995) *Media, Communication, Culture: A Global Approach*, Cambridge: Polity Press. An accessible introduction to culture and communication drawing upon examples from around the world.

Jeremy Tunstall and Michael Palmer (eds) (1993) *Media Moguls*, London: Routledge. An interesting discussion of the emergence of the 'media tycoon' in Western Europe and the USA. Draws examples from France, Germany, Britain and Italy in addition to the USA.

The individual and the state in contemporary Europe

PART FOUR examines the relationship between the individual and the state. Throughout this book, and especially in Chapter 3, it has been emphasized that Europe, after Charlemagne, developed as a collection of independent states. This distinguishes it from the contemporaneous civilizations of Islam and China which were single imperial hierarchies. Although some parts of Europe continued to be styled as empires and were often quite powerful, in the long term they fitted into the European state system. The Habsburg and Austro-Hungarian Empires were such examples within the European sphere. The distinction between Europe and the rest of the world meant that the relationship between ruler and ruled developed differently. Until modern times the links between the mass of the population in Europe and their rulers would not have been very different from anywhere else. It is in the way that European states developed that the distinction increased. With the absolutist states of the fifteenth to eighteenth centuries there came improved arrangements for the administration of the state and this meant that the state could enter into the affairs of its citizens in a much more intensive way. Earlier monarchs may have had great physical power over their subjects but they lacked efficient means of routine administration. However, the administrative capacity of the absolutist states does not compare with that of modern states which use forms of Weber's rational–legal bureaucracy enhanced by the modern technology of computers. The modern state can enter into our lives in ways undreamed of by the kings and emperors of old. The registration of births, marriages and deaths; taxation; the registering of voters; means tests for the dispensing of welfare benefits; and criminal records are all varied examples of ways in which the state keeps us all on file – but there are many more. The relationship between the individual and the state in political participation, social care, social security, healthcare and the penal system are covered in this part of the book.

Chapter 15

Political participation in Europe

Theme and Variation

Rhys Dogan

Introduction	298
The variety of political participation	298
Political culture	298
Political value formation	300
Political socialization	302
Social cleavages	303
De-alignment, post-materialism and 'catch-all parties'	305
Interest group mediation	306
Institutional structures	312
Summary	316
Further reading	316

Key concepts

- Political values and political culture
- Social cleavages and de-alignment
- Impact of institutional structures on political behaviour

Introduction

This chapter considers the variety of mechanisms through which the people of the European Union (EU) participate in the political process. It identifies three distinctive and parallel processes – structural socialization, individual interest articulation and institutional dynamics – which operate in all member states and together help to explain both the differences and similarities between the democratic experiences of modern Europeans.

The variety of political participation

People in modern Europe participate in the political process in a complex variety of ways. They vote and thereby determine the actual composition of governments. They join interest groups which lobby the many individuals and institutions involved in making political decisions. They take to the streets and demonstrate about particular issues. Their views and attitudes help to determine the policies developed by political parties. These general mechanisms of political participation can be observed in all the nations of the European Union (EU), and they are known collectively as liberal political processes (Macpherson 1977).

Despite the common themes which can be found in the means by which Europeans seek to influence the political process, it is important to appreciate that the pattern of political participation varies between the member states. Thus, whilst people across the EU vote, join interest groups, participate in demonstrations and express opinions which influence political parties, they do all these things in slightly different ways. Germany and Sweden have very different voting systems. Interest groups in Austria, Ireland and Italy have quite distinctive relationships with each other and their respective governments. People in France march through the boulevards of Paris much more frequently than the people of Britain march through the streets of London (Macridis 1990).

Political culture

Within this range of diverse political activities, it is nevertheless possible to identify a common theme which enables us to claim that the EU offers a more or less coherent process of political participation. This lies in the liberal notion that social attitudes should direct the course of government action (Holden 1993). Indeed, virtually the only similarity between the multitude of political mechanisms found within the EU is that they all reflect a belief that citizens and society 'own' the government. Attitudes to the fundamental relationship between the citizen and the state, together with the associated concepts of power, authority and legitimacy, are known as political culture (Kavanagh 1972). The point to be made about liberal democracy, and all other political cultures, is that the basic values about the citizen and the state they express can be satisfied through a variety of institutional mechanisms, or political systems. Thus, European politics becomes coherent when viewed as a common political culture expressed through a variety of political systems.

One of the most interesting dimensions of politics is the process by which guidelines are set for the acceptable exercise of power. These rules of the political game concern the type of things governments do and how they do them. Should governments provide universal health care, should they imprison fishmongers, is it appropriate for them to finance the worship of the Devil? Should governments fund industrial development by throwing money in the air on Wednesday afternoons? British governments have imprisoned gays, German governments have persecuted entire ethnic groups, the Emperors of Rome decided policy by examining the entrails of a goat. When these actions and policy processes occurred they were tolerated by the bulk of the population. They were considered normal, ordinary and uncontroversial. Discrimination against Jews, gypsies, the disabled, blacks, even fishmongers, continued for centuries without major protest, and whilst the soothsayers have gone from the European political scene, the Lords Spiritual still play a role in the legislative process of the United Kingdom. How can we make sense of this enormous range and variety of political action? Why do certain types of government behaviour become, or cease to be, acceptable?

Ultimately, we explain the changing nature of the politically acceptable in terms of popular attitudes or values (Gellner 1987). If everyone consults the soothsayer on important decisions – marriage, travel, national lottery numbers – then it is likely we would expect the government to do the same. If we habitually abandon underweight babies on mountain tops, then it is unlikely we would support an expensive programme of disability benefits. In other words, there is a connection between political legitimacy and commonly held social attitudes.

Social values shape and influence our attitudes about politics and political institutions. They determine what we consider it appropriate for governments to do, and how they should operate. It is the relationship between social and political values which lies at the core of the concept of political culture (Gibbins 1989). The box labelled 'Political Culture' provides a very basic account of the connection between certain social values and the political values they tend to generate to create individual political cultures.

Societies which place a premium on individualism and freedom generally demand political institutions based on democracy and equality because they limit the state and empower the citizen (Dunleavy and O'Leary 1987). If most people believe they have a right to do pretty much whatever they like, as long as they do not interfere with other people, then they are unlikely to wish to see the state intrude into the daily lifestyle of the citizen. In this situation, there is simply no demand for laws which regulate attendance at religious services, or the length of a man's hair, or the type of sexual act committed between consenting adults. However, societies which admire order, stability, or a particular way of life, may wish to ensure that the state is able to protect these particular values by constraining the private activities of citizens (Avis 1987). If most people believe in a vengeful God, likely at any moment to visit plagues and brimstone on a godless people, then they might quite sensibly demand that the state uses the full force of the law to seek and destroy the ungodly (Williams and Houck 1993).

POLITICAL CULTURE

The diagram below indicates the connection between particular social values and the political values associated with them. People who value individualism in their social life tend to favour democracy in politics (every individual's view is legitimate and should be represented in the political process). Likewise, those who believe in freedom usually support political equality (we should all be equally free). However, other people who believe in the social value of order, community or obedience may have very different views about the proper exercise of state power. These people could well prize political values such as the rule of law, tradition or hierarchy above those of democracy and equality, particularly if they view democracy and equality as a threat to their economic security, religious and moral views, ethnic or language group.

POLITICAL CULTURE

SOCIAL VALUES	and their associated	POLITICAL VALUES
Individualism		Democracy
Freedom		Equality
Order		Rule of Law
Community		Tradition
Obedience		Hierarchy

A nation recently exposed to the chaos of radical democracy, civil disorder and hyper-inflation, might equally sensibly turn to a strong, authoritarian leader and very consciously trade freedom for prosperity (Brown 1984). Finally, a people proud of their traditions and history might well demand respect for authority and hierarchical government. To the committed monarchist, it appears right and proper that the king and nobles rule, whilst the artisan and labourer toil.

The notion that governments do, or do not, have the right to use the power of the state to control particular aspects of citizens' lives is a matter about the way in which we define concepts like power, authority and legitimacy. In short, authority is the legitimate exercise of state power where legitimacy is defined as governmental behaviour which reflects social values. These fundamental political values are described by the collective term 'political culture' which is used to explain the nature of legitimate power and authority in individual political systems.

Political value formation

The concept of political culture provides an important element in the study of politics. It enables us to identify the fundamental values and principles which inspire the type of political institutions found in different political systems (Almond and Verba 1965). However, a deeper question concerns the nature of social values themselves. If social values direct political institutions, the attempt to explain politics must also include an explanation of the social values by which they are shaped. We need to know where social values come from and how they change.

The answer to this question has puzzled philosophers for centuries. Indeed, the process of value formation remains a highly contentious issue in the social sciences. Whilst all commentators agree that the experience of individual human beings plays an important role in value formation, they disagree over how these experiences are processed into distinctive beliefs (Held and Thompson 1989). Some social scientists – the structuralists – contend that values and attitudes develop through interaction between individuals. They explain the social world in terms of the structure of this interaction and assume that individuals exposed to similar social environments will have similar social experiences and develop similar, and predictable, social and political values (Parsons 1969). Thus, people with similar class backgrounds, or members of the same religious or language group, are deemed *necessarily* to share certain social and political values. Other social scientists - the individualists – contend that our values and attitudes result from complex psychological, as well as social, processes which are unique to each individual. They explain the social world in terms of individuals' responses to common forms of interaction and, like structuralists, assume that individuals exposed to similar social environments will have similar social experiences. However, unlike structuralists, those who accept the individualist approach (also known as the agency approach) do not assume that all people who share common experiences will necessarily develop similar, let alone predictable, social and political values. Different people react to the same event in different ways. Thus, structuralists believe that shared values are created by participation in common social groups, whereas individualists believe that common social groups are created by people who have shared values.

Ultimately, we do not know whether all people act on the basis of group values, personal values or a combination of both. One working-class child will grow up to join the Labour Party and revel in proletarian culture; another will despise the poverty in which they live, change their accent and adopt the value systems of the middle classes. The historical record provides support for both approaches to social explanation. There is evidence to suggest that many people in similar social situations behave in similar ways, but there is also evidence to suggest that not all people in similar social situations follow the general trend.

This debate has important implications for attempts to explain the cause of social and political behaviour. Structuralists would explain political events in terms of class systems, language and ethnicity, or even patterns of religious affiliation. (The work of Lipset and Rokkan, to be considered below, rests on this structural approach.) By contrast, individualists would explain the same political events in terms of the psychological, spiritual, cultural, even financial, interests and commitments of the individuals who participate in these various social groups. (The work of Crewe, also to be considered below, rests on the agency approach.) Whilst the academic debate has not been resolved, and continues to rage through the learned journals, the student of contemporary political science needs merely to recognize that the different approaches to social explanation are reflected in the type of explanation offered by different political scientists.

Political socialization

Despite this important philosophical debate, there is a certain consensus that social values are derived from our social environment. It is generally accepted that political behaviour is deeply affected by group values and mores, regardless of whether these are viewed as independent structures or as mere reflections of the views held by collectives of like-minded individuals. We have the beliefs and values that we do because of the environment in which we live and the experiences we have as a result of living the way that we do. The habits of consulting soothsayers or abandoning underweight babies on mountain tops are learned during the course of our interaction with other people. These patterns of behaviour reflect the requirements and conditions of life under particular circumstances – level of scientific knowledge, availability of medical technology, degrees of physical security – and they change with the social circumstances associated with them. The process of learning through social interaction is called socialization, and the process of learning about politics is called political socialization (Stacey 1978). Whilst structuralists contend that we are forced to accept these views and individualists contend that we are free to reject them, both accept that socialization takes place and has a great impact on social and political values and behaviour.

How then do we actually learn political values, and what are the processes of political socialization? We learn about the political world through the family, education, work and leisure activities. We are taught political principles in childhood in indirect, but powerful ways (Stevens 1982). Five-year-olds do not normally receive lectures on equal opportunity from their mothers, but they are taught to share the cake at their birthday parties. Few 7-year-olds are taught the principles of democracy in primary school, but they experience it through decisions about how to select 'treats' for a group – shall we go to the zoo or the cinema, let's vote!

However, social values do not always reflect a concern with freedom, individualism or democracy (Avis 1987). Indeed, the social values traditionally learned in childhood generated political values that were antithetical to liberal democracy. The emphasis placed on freedom and individualism in contemporary European child-rearing was once enjoyed by the values of obedience, order and community. Eight-year-olds were rarely taught to despise individualism, but they were probably punished for being selfish. Six-year-olds did not understand the perils of social fragmentation, but they learned to associate free thought with disobedience, and radical demonstrators or gypsies with 'bad men'. This pattern of socialization encourages people to perceive the world in terms of a conflict between good and evil in which the important values of tradition, nation, stability, religion and truth need to be protected against the chaos of radical subversion. These social attitudes easily translate into support for authoritarian political values, law and order, strong government and respect for hierarchy.

The process of political socialization continues throughout our lives and occurs through our participation in the social world. All our experiences can affect our social attitudes and political views, but probably the greatest influences are derived from our participation in social institutions like schools, firms, voluntary associations and religious groups (Scott 1991). The activities and experiences to which we are exposed in various social environments greatly influence our attitude to a multitude of political issues. This socialization can be the result of individual level considerations: a person who has experienced prolonged periods of unemployment, or poverty, is likely to support extensive programmes of social welfare; a member of a drug-smuggling cartel is unlikely to demand strong measures against the narcotics trade. Alternatively, values can develop through the process of mixing with other people in groups: an apprentice gas-fitter will probably join a trade union, mix with people who have particular views about the importance of workers' rights, and might well be socialized to accept and identify with those views. These processes of socialization can be seen to operate in most social environments. We generally learn to adopt particular attitudes and modes of behaviour either because they are accepted by our friends and colleagues, or because we come to acquire them as a result of our personal experiences.

The extent to which a society will tolerate certain categories of political action will depend on the nature of the attitudes ordinary people acquire through their social interaction. Thus the question of legitimacy cannot be determined in absolute ethical terms but must be viewed as a function of political socialization. A process which produces different social values as social environments change over time.

Social cleavages

Even though liberal democratic systems enjoy high levels of stability and legitimacy, the stuff of politics remains competition over the authoritative allocation of limited resources. Simply because people agree on how conflicts should be resolved does not mean they have no conflicts. We have already seen that our political views are greatly influenced by our social environment. This suggests that political conflict probably reflects the different types of social and political values generated by different social environments. If all of these assumptions are correct, it follows that we should be able to explain the pattern of political conflict by examining the overall structure of the social environment – political divisions reflect social divisions. Because these social divisions – known as social cleavages – represent clusters of shared values and common socialization patterns, many political scientists believe they provide reliable indicators of the type of attitudes and values which will be articulated by individuals who have been subjected to their formative influence. The concept of social cleavage developed by Lipset and Rokkan provides the key to traditional explanation of political behaviour. Their work rests squarely on a structural approach to social explanation, and relies on the assumption that the vast majority of individuals acquire their social and political values through the process of political socialization in groups (Lipset and Rokkan 1967).

The Lipset and Rokkan analysis identified a number of fundamental social cleavages which they claim have dominated politics in Western Europe: the centre–periphery, the Church–state, the rural–urban, linguistic and class cleavages (Gallagher *et al.* 1995). Most people in England instinctively view political behaviour in terms of the class cleavage – the working class votes Labour, the middle classes vote Conservative (Butler and Stokes 1974). However, whilst this

SOCIAL CLEAVAGES AND POLITICAL BEHAVIOUR

People who live in the country generally need to co-operate with each other in order to guarantee many of the community services which are provided by the ratepayers, or private companies, in urban communities. Country people have to pull together to deal with floods, fires and other natural disasters, and to provide their own entertainments such as the village dance or bingo nights, because the resources and facilities found in urban concentrations simply do not exist in thinly populated areas. It therefore makes sense for rural parents to encourage their children to participate in community life, and to see neighbours as friends on whom they can rely. This pattern of socialization contrasts with the tendency of urban parents to warn their children about strangers, to view their neighbours as potential murderers or child-molesters, and to keep themselves to themselves. It is not that urban parents are intrinsically more suspicious than rural parents, merely that urban life and its associated dangers are very different to those presented by life in the country, and that these environmental differences produce quite distinctive patterns of socialization.

We would expect these differences of social values to be reflected in differences of political values, and to produce distinctive political interests and voting behaviour. For instance, country people may be much more relaxed about juvenile crime than city people – they may view young offenders as whippersnappers or scallywags, rather than drug-crazed 'Rambos' or thugs. They may also be much more inclined to accept the notion of community responsibility and welfare provision than people who live in urban fortresses and view homeless beggars and buskers as riders of the apocalypse threateningly stationed at the gates of the Paris Metro. Thus, a country midwife may believe in subsidies for food, housing and transport, and vote Peasant Party; whereas the beleaguered urbanite could well rebel against funding the menace of 'welfare criminals' and vote for the Low Tax Alliance.

is the dominant cleavage in most European countries, a little reflection soon identifies the operation of the other major cleavages. For instance, the people who vote for the Scottish National Party (SNP) are not expressing values which derive from their class experience but from their identification as Scottish patriots. People who vote for Plaid Cymru may do so because of their experiences as Welsh-speakers in an English-speaking state (Steed 1986). In many European countries there are significant political divisions based on the different social attitudes towards religion. The various Christian Democratic parties seek to represent Christian, particularly Catholic, social values within the political system (Daalder 1987). A number of member states also possess agrarian, or peasant parties which seek to articulate the particular values of rural communities. The 'Social Cleavages and Political Behaviour' box provides a description of the way in which our social and political attitudes might be affected by living in rural and urban communities.

This basic pattern of social cleavages only provides a starting point for the explanation of political behaviour. In reality, people invariably participate in a number of social institutions and are subject to various channels of socialization.

This raises the problem of identifying which of several social cleavages is most likely to inspire political action. How would a working-class Flemish nationalist, who is a devout Catholic, living in a rural community actually determine their vote? According to the class cleavage they would vote for the socialist party, but the Church–state cleavage suggests they should vote for the Christian Democrats, the centre–periphery cleavage demands they vote for the Flemish nationalists, and the urban–rural cleavage indicates they are likely to vote for the agrarian party. This problem is captured by the notion of cross-cutting cleavages which is usually resolved in one of two ways. Either one cleavage dominates the others and thereby excludes them from mainstream politics, or the party system itself reflects the various combinations of mutually consistent social cleavages. The following examples should clarify the situation.

In Britain, the class cleavage dominates the party system. Most of the population either vote for the Labour or Conservative parties. However, a relatively small proportion of the population has placed a greater premium on the political values generated by the other types of socialization to which they have been subjected. These people join and vote for the much less popular regional nationalist parties: the SNP, Plaid Cymru and Mebyon Kernow (the Cornish Nationalists). Thus, the range of social cleavages present in British society is represented in the party system (Stevenson 1993), but the conflicts generated by cross-cutting cleavages are usually resolved by a simple and uniform choice between them – most people appear to vote on the basis of the class cleavage. The alternative solution is apparent in the party systems of Belgium and the Netherlands, where voters are confronted with a bewildering array of parties which reflect different combinations of logically consistent social cleavages (Daalder and Mair 1983). The middle-class, Catholic, Flemish nationalists can vote for the Flemish Christian Democrats, and their agnostic nationalist friends can vote for the secular Flemish liberals. Whatever their background, Belgian and Dutch voters are quite likely to find a political party which reflects the particular combination of social interests to which they are attached. The exact way in which the tensions between cross-cutting cleavages are resolved in different political systems is largely a function of the particular electoral laws employed, and these are considered in detail below (see pp. 312–14).

De-alignment, post-materialism and 'catch-all parties'

The structuralist approach of social cleavage analysis has provided the major traditional explanations of political behaviour. However, since the 1960s two phenomena have emerged which tend to weaken the connection between social cleavages and political parties. The first concerns the alleged breakdown of traditional social cleavages, known as de-alignment. The second concerns the emergence of new social values which are unrelated to social cleavage, known as post-materialism. These explanations of political behaviour concentrate on the factors which shape individuals' decisions about social and political values.

The proponents of de-alignment claim that class has become diluted by changes in the relationship between income and social status (plumbers now earn more than professors), and also by a general increase in prosperity which has made class an issue of relative wealth rather than absolute poverty (even low income earners can afford to buy their own home, travel abroad and purchase the latest consumer durables) (Crewe and Denner 1985). This dilution or de-alignment can also be seen in other social cleavages, the massive decline in religiosity has reduced the impact of the Church–state cleavage, continued urbanization and rural depopulation has dramatically reduced the number of people whose lives are closely associated with agriculture and rural communities.

In parallel with this alleged process of de-alignment, new values like feminism, anti-racism, environmentalism and pacifism have entered the political debate which are apparently unrelated to membership of particular social groups (Inglehart 1977). The women who demonstrated on Greenham Common against nuclear weapons came from all classes of the social spectrum; similarly those who march against racism, the export of live sheep and calves, and the members of Greenpeace or Friends of the Earth do not appear to have anything in common other than their shared ideals. These values are called 'post-materialist' because they are not usually associated with the particular material well-being of the individuals who hold them – men can support the women's movement simply because they believe it is right, not through any vested interest. Similarly, the distress of a dumb animal has no direct impact on the life experience of a retired astro-physicist.

Together these two processes have resulted in a significant increase in issue-based voting. All political parties have been forced to address the new concerns of an increasingly volatile electorate: de-alignment has reduced voters' loyalty to cleavage-based political parties; they are now inclined to shop among political parties, and to vote on the basis of personal interests and values. The emergence of post-materialist values has forced political parties to include environmental protection, equal opportunities, and anti-racist policies within their official programmes. The combined effect of de-alignment and post-materialism has been to transform the major political parties into 'catch-all' parties whose policies are increasingly driven by the perceived needs and desires of the electorate at large, rather than particular elements within it (Kirchheimer 1966).

Indeed, virtually all mainstream political parties are now committed to the support of post-materialist values in one form or another, and most seek to gain electoral success by moulding their policy programmes to popular attitudes rather than appealing to class, or other cleavage, loyalties. Thus, whilst European party systems do still reflect past patterns of social cleavage, they are no longer mere expressions of the social cleavages found in contemporary society. It is important to remember that whilst the structure of the party systems may remain intact, the substance of individual parties' programmes can develop away from their traditional cleavage basis (Mair 1990).

Interest group mediation

Social cleavage analysis and the various proponents of de-alignment and post-materialism provide important insights into the nature of political participation in Europe. They help to explain the electoral process which is the most obvious way in which society controls the state – individual prime ministers, cabinet ministers and city councillors retain office only as long as the electorate allows (Meny 1993). However, elections are themselves relatively 'blunt', if powerful, mechanisms of control, because the voter is presented with very limited choices: the entire Tory manifesto competes with the entire Labour manifesto; voters cannot pick and choose between the components of each.

The detailed and subtle control of the state requires much more sophisticated methods which allow society to inform the government of what it wants in relation to highly specialized questions: a by-pass at Twyford Down, or a nuclear power-station in Schleswig-Holstein. This day-to-day social control is undertaken by a wide range of so-called interest groups which mediate between society and the state. There are three main ways in which interest groups operate in the EU: pluralist competition, corporatist negotiation and consociational accommodation. Whilst each allows social values to flow through to political decision-makers, they offer very different means of achieving this liberal goal.

Pluralism

Despite the presence of other forms of interest group mediation in several member states, all the political systems of the EU have *pluralist* competition. Indeed, pluralism is one of the abiding characteristics of politics in Europe. It represents the most basic mechanism by which citizens seek to exercise their right to influence and direct government. Indeed, the freedom of people to form groups to campaign against taxes on beer, expenditure cuts in education and health care, or sleep-deprivation of battery hens, lies at the heart of liberal democracy (Dahl 1961).

The basic notion of pluralism is most simply expressed by the activities of non-governmental organizations of two types: interest groups and pressure groups. Interest groups tend to represent the attitudes of particular sections of society: Greenpeace represents environmentalists, the Automobile Association speaks on behalf of motorists, the British Surfing Association articulates the concerns of surfers. The mechanisms through which trade unions, firms and voluntary interest groups like the National Union of Students or the Consumers' Association influence the political system are reasonably straightforward and obvious (Ball and Millard 1986). They speak to politicians and civil servants, they conduct public advertising campaigns, they hold demonstrations and they lobby the individuals and groups involved in making political decisions. Whilst pressure groups also lobby decision-makers, they are usually formed to address a single issue and they seem to arise from the almost instinctive reaction of people in similar situations faced with similar problems (Richardson and Jordan 1985). These *ad hoc* groups may champion causes as diverse as local garbage collection, the Newbury by-pass or vegetarian meals in the staff canteen. The range is limited only by the imagination of the citizen. Once established they operate in much the same way as specialized interest groups, although they generally have much fewer resources and do not usually survive any longer than it takes to resolve the problem they were formed to address (Jordan 1991).

The explosion of pluralist lobbying since the 1970s resonates with the notions of de-alignment and post-materialism. As society becomes increasingly classless, urban, multicultural, secular and post-materialist political programmes and ideologies based on traditional social cleavages become increasingly irrelevant to ordinary citizens. If most people define their political interests on the basis of their particular personal experiences – as joggers, home-owners, dog-lovers, lesbians or victims of the tabloid press – and not on the basis of their membership of large social groups, then no political party or sectoral interest group could possibly hope to reflect the attitudes of more than a very small section of society. Indeed, in a society composed of millions of individuals each with their own unique collection of diverse political and social interests, the only viable mechanism of interest articulation is one driven by the frenzied self-representation of pluralist competition.

Despite the undeniable growth of lobbying within political systems of the EU, European society still retains considerable evidence of structural socialization. Whilst it is relatively easy to understand the manner in which individuals and groups of individuals participate in pluralist activity, it is less obvious how social institutions like the family, schools or universities 'direct' the conduct of public policy (Macpherson 1962). In the first instance, political parties and the media try to 'give the punters what they want' in the expectation of obtaining votes, newspaper sales, radio or television ratings. Of course, political parties do try to convince individuals of the validity of their own political philosophy and policies, but they have nevertheless to address the concerns of the general public if they wish to win elections (Kirchheimer 1966). Likewise, the media's near monopoly of information gives it enormous influence over the formation of public opinion; however, media moguls need the punters to buy their newspapers and tune to their radio and television stations before they can attempt to influence them (Whale 1977). Both politicians and journalists listen to the particular concerns and attitudes of people with young children and mortgages, the elderly, the homeless, students and people with new and important views on economics, technology, education and social policy. This enables these 'social institutions' to indirectly influence decision-makers and opinion-makers.

Finally, it is important to remember that politicians, civil servants and judges are themselves participants in social institutions and are subjected to exactly the same types of political socialization as the rest of the population. They also have private personas as wives, vegetarians, fathers, trade unionists and landowners which inform the values they bring to public office.

Corporatism

The corporatist variety of interest-group mediation essentially involves negotiation between the government, employers and labour – the social partners. It has been used extensively in Scandinavia, Germany, Austria, and Luxembourg, but has occasionally been utilized in other member states (Lehmbruch and Schmitter 1982). The focus of corporatist decision-making has traditionally been economic policy, although this has usually been taken to include all those issues which affect workers and employers, such as social security, industrial development, education and training. The keywords used in corporatist arrangements are 'social contract', 'tripartite' and 'concertation'. These terms indicate the important idea of negotiation and agreement between the social partners. Indeed, the most famous example of corporatist negotiation – the Luxembourg Model – granted each participant in the tripartite arrangement a veto over all decisions (Hirsch 1986). Whatever the formal nature of corporatist structures, they invariably involve the government, trade unions and employer groups undertaking quite detailed consideration of national economic questions.

In terms of the substance of corporatist interest group mediation, the core issues relate to wages, productivity, investment, inflation and interest rates – labour offers industrial peace and productivity increases, employers offer agreed wage increases and investment commitments, the government offers agreed levels of public expenditure and taxation, and appropriate inflation and interest rate targets. The idea behind corporatism is that all the social partners need each other, and need to compromise with each other, if the nation is to enjoy high levels of economic prosperity. There is no point in workers demanding wages which will bankrupt their employers, nor can firms hope to maintain their share of the market and secure the jobs of their employees unless they invest in new technologies and plant. The task of economic management requires that governments occasionally be able to regulate the level of wages and investment in order to control inflation and ensure economic growth. The corporatist model allows all parties to the economic activity to consider the overall, long-term interests of the nation as a whole, and to reach agreement about the short-term sacrifices and trade-offs which need to be made in order to achieve these common interests.

The corporatist approach to interest-group mediation has suffered from a number of problems, primarily because it rests on contradictory notions of social explanation. On the one hand, it expects 'labour' and 'employers' to participate on the basis of individual-level self-interest – an agency approach. However, the success of the overall undertaking requires that the individuals subject to these agreements will abide by them on the basis of group solidarity – a structural approach. The term 'labour' includes virtually every conceivable occupation, level of income and education. Lawyers, garbage collectors, parliamentarians, train drivers, company directors, gas-fitters and merchant bankers are all found in waged and salaried positions; they all have trade unions. But they are subject to very different patterns of socialization, and also have very different types of interest. Likewise, the range of interests and opinions held by employers varies enormously. Individual firms may be small or large, strong or weak, public or private. Thus, corporatism is confronted with two major difficulties. In the first instance, each social partner suffers internal disagreement over what constitutes their own best interest, so any policy proposed by either 'labour' or 'employers' cannot represent the totality of each group's membership. Secondly, neither social partner has any sociological means of gaining internal support for the necessarily controversial agreements they make with each other – why should the merchant bankers care what the lorry drivers think. These tensions have been exacerbated by the processes of de-alignment and post-materialism which generate even more diversity within each group, but have always made corporatism a difficult and unsatisfactory approach to interest-group mediation. Indeed, the historical record of corporatism strongly suggests that it is only likely to succeed in small countries, like Sweden or Austria, when potential external disruptions – Soviet military pressure and EU trade policy – provide everyone with an incentive to co-operate sufficiently to overcome the sociological contradictions of the system itself.

Consociationalism

Consociationalism refers to a complex pattern of interest-group negotiation designed to ensure stability in societies which are divided by deep social cleavages. It is usually associated with social conflicts over religion, language, ideology and ethnicity. Where individual countries encompass groups with very different cultural values, stable government depends on the provision of guarantees to the various groups that their essential beliefs and lifestyles will be protected by the state (Lijphart 1969). Unfortunately, the antagonism associated with fundamental cultural differences tends to produce mutual distrust and suspicion which make the simple majoritarian systems used in most member states inappropriate, as each community fears a dictatorship of the other minorities combined. In order to ensure against this threat, consociational systems operate strict 'rules of the game' designed to protect the interests of the component groups which are themselves recognized in law and constitutional practice. Thus, consociational countries bestow rights and privileges on groups of individuals, as well as on individual citizens themselves.

This system of government was first identified by Arend Lijphart in his study of communal negotiation in the Netherlands (Lijphart 1968), and has since been applied to the political systems of Belgium, Austria and Switzerland. The consociational political system rests on a profound fragmentation of national social life. In the typical consociation, individuals spend their entire lives within social environments arranged on religious, ideological, ethnic or linguistic lines. A Catholic would be born in a Catholic hospital, attend Catholic schools, play and support Catholic sporting teams, read Catholic newspapers, listen to Catholic television and radio stations, study at a Catholic university, work in a Catholic-run business and vote for a Catholic political party (Lorwin 1971). Individual Catholics and Protestants may well live next door to each other, or a French-speaker next to Flemish or Arabic speakers, but the array of communal social institutions would mean that they need never actually meet in any ongoing social environment. These distinctive 'pillars' of national society have a number of important consequences for consociational politics. In the first instance, they generate strong channels of socialization which serve to maintain and support the various communities within society – they perpetuate cultural fragmentation. Secondly, they provide an institutional structure for negotiation between the separate communities. Each community is composed of a number of clearly identifiable organizations which can both articulate and represent the demands of the communities (Lustick 1979). Third, the strength of socialization engendered by these social institutions creates a degree of discipline within each community because their members are socialized to accept the compromises forged by their leaders in negotiations with the other communities.

These characteristics of consociational society enable the political elites to manage the potential tensions, anxieties and conflicts associated with cultural fragmentation. The politics of accommodation involves the explicit guarantee of each community's vital interests. Whilst these guarantees will almost invariably concern specific public policies which affect the particular interests of the various communities – language rights, religious freedom, communal education – the more significant guarantee concerns the right of each community to equal influence over the decision-making process. The protection offered to minority groups in a society of minorities is the right to direct participation by the community authorities in the process of government. The essential characteristic of consociational democracy is that government should be conducted by representatives of the communities, as well as by representatives of the nation as a whole. Thus, Belgium has a French-speaking Community Council, a Flemish-speaking Community Council and a German-speaking Community Council which operate in association with the Belgian Parliament (Witte 1992).

In addition to the formal representation of the communities within the structure of government, decisions tend to be the product of agreements and compromises among the communities – no one group should constantly win or lose, the vital concerns of all must be reconciled, and everyone should compromise. In particular, no community should be excluded from the decision-making process. The actual task of compromise is facilitated by the grant of a veto over decisions to each community (Lijphart 1968). This reassures each group, but also makes compromise an essential ingredient of successful decision-making. Finally, consociations generally operate a law of strict proportionality which means that the various communities are represented in the major institutions of the state: the civil service, the police, the armed forces and the judiciary. These quotas ensure that the laws and compromises struck at the political level are not subverted during the course of implementation. It also means that the diversity of values represented by the different communities are reflected throughout the full apparatus of the state – the Flemish lifestyle is not only protected by law but also by Flemish-speaking police and judges.

The consociational system is very much the creature of structural political socialization. In the first instance, it developed in the attempt to resolve the potential problems and conflicts created by the presence of deep and hostile patterns of socialization. Secondly, it utilizes the group coherence and discipline provided by strong patterns of socialization to manage these problems and conflicts successfully. It is not, therefore, surprising to discover that the process of class de-alignment, post-materialism and the decline in religiosity experienced by all societies within the European Union have served to remove both the problem which lies at the heart of the consociational system as well as the means of its solution. Thus, none of the classic cases of European consociation – the Netherlands, Belgium, Austria and Switzerland – are today considered to operate on this basis. There are certain residual consociational features within the Belgian and Swiss constitutions, and the Austrian and Dutch party systems. Nevertheless, consociational democracy remains an important model of interest-group mediation which has proved to be highly effective in dealing with political societies marked by deep social cleavages. Indeed, it could yet play a part in the reconciliation of the cleavages which continue to produce war and civil war on the eastern borders of the Union today.

Institutional structures

The numerous processes and political phenomena described in the preceding sections of this chapter represent the basic mechanisms, themes and variations to be found within the liberal democracies of the European Union. They represent the collection of phenomena which constitute political participation in Europe. It remains, however, to highlight the important impact of the institutional structures of individual member states on the manner in which these mechanisms or techniques of participation can be used. There are two major institutional factors which shape the particular operation of these many socio-political phenomena: electoral laws and constitutional frameworks. In the first instance, the extent to which cross-cutting cleavage patterns or complex individual and post-materialist interests can be represented within the party system depends on the structure of choice allowed by the electoral rules. Secondly, just as there is no point complaining to the local education authority about treatment received at the local hospital, the process through which society seeks to direct the course of government activity is greatly affected by the structure of government itself – participation takes place within an established institutional framework which determines the utility, relevance and impact of particular forms of participation. It is important to know what type of state society is attempting to control – federal, regional or unitary – in order to understand the subtle operation of social cleavages and interest-group mediation.

Electoral and party systems

Electoral laws shape party systems to the extent that they determine the type of choices which confront the voter. These choice structures are primarily a function of the number of representatives elected by each constituency, although important variations are introduced by the voting procedure itself. The range of electoral systems in operation in the various member states are outlined in the box labelled 'Electoral Systems Used within the European Union'.

If voters are asked to choose three representatives for a single locality, they have a number of options. They can vote for three candidates from a single party, they can vote for two candidates from one party and one candidate from another, or they can vote for a single candidate from each of three parties. They are prepared to exercise the second and third options because the possibility exists that these votes could be translated into their preferred electoral outcomes – three representatives will be elected, and they could each come from different parties. It follows that voters in this situation are free to support the values and attitudes they acquire from at least three channels of socialization: the working class, Welsh-speaking, anti-European could vote for the Labour Party, Plaid Cymru and the Anti-European Party. Alternatively, a complex de-aligned or post-

ELECTORAL SYSTEMS USED WITHIN THE EUROPEAN UNION

Plurality is an extremely simple voting procedure which involves the election of the candidate who receives the greatest number of votes, regardless of whether any candidate receives an absolute majority. In Europe, this procedure is only ever used in single member constituencies. However, it could conceivably be used in multi-member constituencies, with the rank order of candidates' votes being the basis for election to the first, second and other parliamentary vacancies. There is also a two-ballot plurality system. If no candidate gains an absolute majority at the initial ballot, a second is held between the two highest polling candidates from the first round. Plurality is associated with two-party dominant systems.

Single transferable votes involve the allocation of preferences by the voter to each candidate. Where no candidate receives an absolute majority of first preference votes, the number of second preference votes received by each candidate is added to their respective tallies. The allocation of preferences continues until one candidate emerges with an absolute majority of the total number of votes counted (a function of the number of preferences allocated). This system can operate in either single- or multi-member constituencies. Where it is used in multi-member constituencies the threshold for election will be a certain percentage of the total number of votes counted based on the number of representatives to be elected. Single transferable votes are associated with limited multi-party systems.

Proportional representation is a system which allocates seats to political parties on the basis of the proportion of the vote they receive in multi-member constituencies. The units of representation are usually very large, either regions or the nation as a whole. Whilst 'pure' proportional representation demands that votes be cast for political parties, rather than for individual candidates, it is more commonly the case that voters are presented with lists of candidates arranged by political party. Proportional representation is associated with multi party systems.

materialist individual is free to vote for the Gay Rights Alliance, the Green Party and the Anti-Racist League. Furthermore, it follows that each major social cleavage, major individual and post-materialist interest groups are likely to generate viable political parties and that the party system will contain several moderately sized political parties. This situation tends to prevail under proportional representation and multi-member constituency single transferable voting systems.

This situation is in marked contrast to that in single-member constituencies where the voter can only vote for a single candidate or party. The fact that only one candidate can be elected obviously means that the voter must cast their vote, or first preference vote, for a single candidate (Duverger 1964). It also means they have to decide between the various social cleavages and post-materialist values represented by the different candidates. However, this choice is more complex than a simple determination of primary values. Because few voters wish to support candidates with virtually no chance of election – they do not want to waste their vote – their choice is usually influenced by their perception of how other people are going to vote. This characteristic of single-member constituencies has three important implications for the party system. In the first instance, most people in modern Europe have traditionally placed their class interest – money – above all other interests when forced to choose. This accounts for the dominance of the class cleavage in the party systems of those member states with single-member constituencies. Secondly, whatever the outcome of the enforced choice, it tends to be reasonably uniform throughout the nation. If people are not inspired by their class interest, it is probably because they are fired by a major battle over language rights (a burning issue in Belgium), or the perceived resurgence of racism (an issue in contemporary Germany). This uniform pattern of choice probably accounts for the strong association between plurality electoral systems and two-party dominant party systems. Thirdly, because variations from the national pattern require strong voter perception of the popularity of the deviation – in order to overcome their fear of wasting a vote – these variations usually have a regional basis. This occurs because issues big enough to displace the dominant national choice pattern are invariably bigger than a single constituency. Indeed, they are based on distinctive regional political cultures – the historical voting behaviour of the South West of England (Liberal); the language issue in Wales; the religious, nationalist and unionist issues in Northern Ireland – which all serve to shape regional party systems in this way.

Constitutional structures

The member states of the European Union possess a wide variety of constitutional structures. There are unitary states in which the legislative, bureaucratic and judicial functions are concentrated within a single set of national institutions. There are federations which are permanent unions between a number of smaller territorial states. In federal systems, there is a national legislature, bureaucracy and judiciary responsible for a number of defined areas of governmental activity, but the constituent territories retain their own legislatures, bureaucracies and judiciaries which exercise jurisdiction over other areas of government activity. In addition, several member states operate systems which lie between the extremes of unitary and federal states, these countries possess central governments which have a primary responsibility for determining the overall structure of government, but they also have regional governments and legislatures which are able to operate autonomously within the framework established by the central government.

The diversity of constitutional structures within the European Union is complex. Each member state operates in slightly different ways, and it is not really very helpful to do more than outline the three basic systems – unitary, federal and regional – because a more detailed statement about any one of these structures would be bound to contradict a particular idiosyncrasy to be found in one of the member states. Nevertheless, the point needs to be made that just as different liberal democracies may be subject to different forms of liberal political participation, diversity can also be found within individual member states, both in relation to different regions and issues. The following speculations serve to highlight exactly how important constitutional structures are to the manner in which liberal democratic processes operate.

Let's start with social cleavages and the probability that different regions could well have different patterns of socialization. For example, the class cleavage might well explain general trends in political behaviour across the United Kingdom, but not in South Kensington (where the dominant cleavage may be a post-materialist debate over the cost of environmental protection), or in Wales (where it increasingly concerns language). This regional variation in social cleavages is not particularly significant because Britain is a unitary state, and what matters is the national trend – only a very small proportion of the national electorate lives in either South Kensington or Wales. However, the situation would be considerably different were Britain to have a constitutional structure similar to that of Germany where a place like Wales could be expected to have its own state government, making laws for Wales and sending delegates to the upper house of a federal Britain. Furthermore, Germany has a number of city states, such as Hamburg and Bremen, and it is not entirely impossible that a similar structure in Britain might see Westminster/Chelsea and Kensington emerge with its own state government, legislature and a stake in the upper house. Under this arrangement, the nature and explanation of politics in Wales, South Kensington and Britain as a whole would be radically transformed, even though the underlying pattern of socialization, de-alignment and post-materialism would remain the same. What this means is that issues associated with the newly empowered and articulated social attitudes would enter mainstream politics – Britain's official language, let alone languages, is not currently on the political agenda, but it would be under these different institutional arrangements. In other words, a new institutional structure would liberate, or bring to the surface, issues which currently exist but are smothered by the class issue.

A federal or regional system also allows the possibility that a single member state may actually operate a number of different electoral systems: proportional representation at one level (elections to the European Parliament); single transferable vote in multi-member constituencies at a second level (elections to regional assemblies); and plurality at a third level (elections to the national parliament). Or, to make analysis even more complicated, the various levels of government may be responsible for their own electoral laws and, whilst the federal government might select proportional representation, some regional governments might choose plurality, others a single transferable vote – some with single-member constituencies, others with multi-member constituencies. This diverse structure of electoral rules and procedures would mean that different parts of the country would be subjected to different structures of electoral choice; this could be expected to lead to a variety of national and regional party systems: those elections fought under plurality would tend to produce two-party dominant systems, those under proportional representation multi-party systems. This would mean that a relatively small political party, such as the Greens, or even the British Liberal Democrats, would succeed or fail in some regions and not others, or at certain levels of government and not others, purely on the basis of the particular electoral system – even in the face of equivalent support. Thus, the process of political participation depends not only on the constitutional structure but also on the particular electoral systems used within particular constitutional structures – the bottom line being that Green issues are heard under some systems but not under others, even though they exist in all.

Summary

- Politics within the European Union is the result of liberal democratic political values which dictate that society directs the actions of the state.
- Individual citizens acquire their social and political values through socialization in social groups (structuralism), or on the basis of the psychological response to their personal experience of social interaction (agency).
- The exact manner in which these general processes of political participation are expressed in individual member states will depend on the type of interest-group mediation, electoral laws and constitutional structure.

Further reading

Michael Gallagher, Michael Laver and Peter Mair (1995) *Representation in Modern Europe* (2nd edn), London: McGraw-Hill. An extremely useful text which combines a thorough account of the detailed operation of contemporary European political systems with an accessible description of the sociological theories associated with political participation.

Seymour M. Lipset and Stein Rokkan (1967) 'Cleavage Structures, Party Systems and Voter Alignments: An Introduction', in Seymour M. Lipset and Stein Rokkan (eds) *Party Systems and Voter Alignments: Cross-National Perspectives*, New York: The Free Press, 1–64. This is the classic work on social cleavage analysis. It analyses the development of the European party system in terms of historical patterns of political socialization in all major EU countries. Whilst rather complex, it is essential reading.

Ivor Crewe and David Denner (eds) (1985) *Electoral Change in Western Democracies: Patterns and Sources of Electoral Volatility*, London: Croom Helm. This is the major work on de-alignment. Although much more recent than Lipset and Rokkan, it provides an equally broad treatment of trends in political behaviour throughout the EU.

Vernon Bogdanor and David Butler (eds) (1983) *Democracy and Elections: Electoral Systems and their Political Consequences*, Cambridge: Cambridge University Press. This book tells you all you need to know about the political consequences of various electoral systems. Even though it is now reasonably old, its concentration on the basic dynamics associated with different systems makes it an extremely useful source.

Chapter 16

Implementing social welfare policy in Europe

The significance of social work, social pedagogy and community work

Ann Jeffries and Werner Müller

Introduction   318
Aims of this chapter   320
The social policy framework for social welfare
   services in Germany and Britain   321
Role and education of professionals providing
   social support services   325
Issues in the provision of social services   329
The contribution made by social practitioners
   to policy implementation   331
Summary   342
Further reading   342

Key concepts

- The importance of implementation processes for policy outcomes
- The importance of social/political context for policy outcomes
- Subsidiarity and solidarity
- Pluralism
- Praxis
- Empowerment

Introduction

Social work and allied helping professions have expanded vastly since the end of the Second World War and now have an established role in the field of welfare provision across Western Europe. Nevertheless, little attempt has been made to undertake cross country comparisons of their place in the implementation of social policy in Europe (see box 'Comparing Social Welfare Policies and Practices' for elaboration). The importance of this task is suggested by the intensity of debate in all Western societies around issues of the appropriateness for the next millennium of welfare provision in the form developed since the end of the Second World War and the competencies required to implement its various dimensions.

Such comparisons are complicated, however, by the fact that the responsibilities and organizational structures relating to social welfare vary considerably even within the European Union. They include a broad spectrum of practice from statutory intervention by social workers to protect people being abused, to support for community development groups. Furthermore, while this range of work may be forthcoming in each country, it will be undertaken by professionals with various titles, such as social worker, specialist educator, social pedagogue, or community and/or youth worker.

This chapter aims, therefore, to identify key common elements in the roles of such practitioners in EU countries, regardless of their official titles, in order to identify the essence and significance of this work. We will discuss the varying responsibilities of these practitioners within their particular social and political systems and the various ways in which they are organized, financed and educated. We will contextualize this by considering the place of these services in the implementation of social policy, using Germany and Britain as case studies.

It is important to remember that Britain and Germany represent very different types of political decision-making systems, with a strong central government on the one hand (Britain) and a wide distribution of power in a federal and pluralistic structure on the other (Germany). This has considerable influence on concepts, organization, budgets, staffing and outcomes for the users of the services in question. We will explain the German model in more detail and bring the British situation in by way of additional commentary.

Our interest is to encourage a unifying and reciprocal approach to research and analysis by linking practice to policy. This broad concept of social policy (see 'The Scope of Social Policy' box) complicates comparisons of social welfare provision for it points to the importance of considering not only the policy but its implementation, the outcomes of the nature and degree of support as well as the nature of partnership between professionals and citizens, and thus the qualitative impact of social policies. In other words, while monetary transfers or staffing costs in two systems might be similar, the effects both for users and for professionals can be very different depending on whether the system is based on local autonomy or on central decision-making. Without clarity in these regards, analysts can misunderstand the true nature of social support in a given country. Consequently an additional aim for this chapter is to illustrate the importance of understanding different social systems before attempting to make comparisons.

COMPARING SOCIAL WELFARE POLICIES AND PRACTICES: ISSUES AND IMPLICATIONS

Comparative studies in this field tend to concentrate on single aspects of social support services without considering the broader complex of social provision in the countries studied (Brauns and Kramer 1986); or they focus on services for special groups such as older people (see the contribution of Giarchi and Abbott in Chapter 9) and invariably they are descriptive (e.g. Cannan *et al.* 1992). Three over-lapping reasons for this tendency can be identified:

1   Until recently a widespread neglect of research by the majority of people responsible for education and the practice of social and community work. Often because of the pressure of circumstances (heavy teaching/work load), they have tended to define themselves as 'doers' rather than as 'investigators' (Jones 1994).

2   Thus, with some notable exceptions, research in the field of social welfare provision has been undertaken by social scientists who have no direct experience of practice. This is particularly the case in Germany. The tendency has been to concentrate on obviously 'big topics' such as national insurance and benefits. More recently however the general concern with equal opportunities has generated studies in areas such as child-care provision or care for older people.

3   The organization of social support activities in Western European countries is so varied and dispersed that it is confusing and hard to categorize, particularly for comparative purposes. Work of a similar nature is organized under different names and is the responsibility of different organizations. These may be statutory in one country, voluntary non-profit in another, or provision may be reliant on self-help in a third.

Implications: This gap has provided an opening for politicians to debate social welfare under the banner of cost effectiveness and with the instruments of 'new managerialism'. This has meant that in Britain, for example, under the guise of the identification of specific competencies required to perform narrowly defined functions, the multi-dimensionality of social work is being devalued in favour of a task-orientated approach for which less broadly qualified workers can be employed. Considering that in Germany, for example 10 per cent of the 'social budget' is used to employ people to operate the welfare state, it would seem essential that professionals familiar with this work contribute to the debate. Yet, when the Council of Europe set up a study group to review the definition of social work, it was not even willing to talk to the International Federation of Social Workers in the process of developing its report (Paul 1995).

> **THE SCOPE OF SOCIAL POLICY**
>
> We consider that social policy should aim to promote social welfare and social justice in a regulated market economy system that is democratic in practice as well as in theory. Thus social policy will include but should not be limited to:
>
> - monetary transfers from insurance funds and state budgets to recipients of contributional or non-contributional benefits; *plus*
> - provision of protective rights for at-risk groups (children, people with disabilities, etc.) in the workplace, the home and in the community; *but should also ensure*
> - the provision of professional support in a way that facilitates empowerment on a personal and group basis from a range of social and community workers in agency, residential and community settings;
> - the creation and maintenance of an institutional and physical environment which helps individuals, families and groups to lead a creative, independent and social life and to receive support as needed to cope with transitions and crises.

With these aims in mind, we will continue this chapter by providing a more detailed examination of the German social policy framework, particularly in terms of social support services, with some summary points of comparison to Britain. We will then build on this with an overview of the varying roles community and social workers assume across the European Union. The purpose is to identify key elements of the broad social work task in whichever country it is undertaken and then clarify *how* social and community workers approach such multi-dimensional work. This is often left unstated. Despite the different titles and organizational structures, we see a commonality which unites practitioners regardless of the differences in tradition, legislation and administration. Indeed awareness of the diverse work seen as essential for social welfare in other European countries could help British policy-makers reassess not only the potential of the full range of practice that falls under the social work umbrella but also its importance in terms of social policy outcomes.

Aims of this chapter

- To illustrate the importance, in order to be able to make valid comparisons, of a comprehensive understanding of different social systems in terms of both policy development and implementation practices.
- To develop an appreciation of the link between policy-making and its implementation and thus for the full scope of social policy.
- To increase understanding of the similarities and differences in the responsibilities of those charged with providing and/or enabling social support within the European Union.

- To identify the commonalities in their practice and thereby to develop an appreciation of the potential contribution of social and community work to social well-being in Europe.

The social policy framework for social welfare services in Germany and Britain

Traditionally social policy in Germany, *Sozialpolitik*, has been defined as a responsibility of the central state. Central government in Berlin or Bonn was seen, and sometimes still is seen, as the social policy-maker in that it provides the legal framework (and in some areas the budget too) for social insurance and social benefits. In reality the field of *Sozialpolitik* is much wider and embraces other levels of policy-making, especially regional and local government.

In Germany, as in Britain and most other European industrial states, provision for social security and welfare was introduced in the second half of the nineteenth century in the following four areas:

1   Insurance against the risks of old age, sickness and industrial accidents. Unemployment insurance was added in Germany in 1927.
2   Public maintenance for veterans and other especially designated categories of people.
3   Local provision of benefits for the poor (initially this was combined with rigorous controls and loss of civil rights).
4   Local provision of social support services for people in more or less deprived situations. Initially this was delivered in day centres and residential homes run by voluntary organizations. In Germany these were run predominantly by the Protestant and Catholic churches. Since the beginning of this century, local government also has become more involved in service provision.

In Germany the first two categories were considered to be legitimate areas for state intervention and were subsumed under the traditional concept of *Sozialpolitik*. In the 1920s, with the widening of the classes of recipients, benefits for the poor were included under central government legislation, but it was left to local authorities to provide the funds for these benefits. Social support services (point 4 above) were not considered to be an area for political policy-making. This division has meant that the provision of social welfare and social support services in Germany is still both more multi-dimensional and less uniform than it has been in Britain since the development of the welfare state following the Second World War.

The Beveridge proposals, which provided the foundation for the British welfare state, grew out of the conditions of war which both necessitated and engendered confidence in a strong central government and uniformity in the allocation of scarce resources. After the war the Germans, on the other hand, were resistant to changing their long-standing pluralistic approach to social welfare. Given their disastrous experience of an autocratic central power, this is hardly surprising. Their focus was on the social state (*Sozialstaat*) in contrast to the welfare state (*Wohlfahrsstaat*). Their concern was to ensure that ultimately the state was responsible for fostering a social environment in which people could exercise choice in meeting their needs.

Developments in the 1970s and 1980s have meant that, though coming from these different policy perspectives, most EU countries ended up with a similar range of welfare provision, but nevertheless these deep-seated orientational differences remain. For example, as we will illustrate, they are clearly visible in the pattern of employment of social workers.

The philosophy behind the emphasis on the local level for welfare provision in Germany is found first in the historically accepted principle of local self-government, secured by the constitutions of the *Länder* and in the federal constitution (*Grundgesetz*) and, secondly, in the principle of 'subsidiarity'. Subsidiarity means that the smaller public or civil unit in society shall have the right and the means to regulate its own affairs as much as possible.

Praising the German state from a British perspective, A.J. Ogus (1990) stresses the dual function of the 'social state' principle in Germany's constitution. This is, on the one hand, a legitimizing and a legally binding function which 'allows government and parliament the power to follow social welfare goals' and, on the other, 'commits politicians to protect individuals and groups whose personal or social development has been damaged by their individual life circumstances or by social disadvantage' (Ogus 1990: 78). The British government's reluctance in this area is clearly illustrated by the refusal of the Conservative government to sign up to the EU Social Chapter. The European Court has had to play a major role in ensuring British citizens some of the environmental and social justice rights that are taken for granted in some other EU countries. These differences draw attention to the way British social policy has developed so that the focus now is more on assessing individual entitlement to welfare and personal social services and less on social action to ensure that the social and community context promotes societal well-being (Cannan *et al.* 1992).

The principle of subsidiarity or 'opting out' tends to have currency in countries that retained a major role for Church involvement in social service provision with the concomitant sense of mutual responsibility for the well-being of the community. This results in a plethora of non-governmental organizations, all of which employ social workers to fulfil various roles. However, it is doubtful if such non-profit provision by itself would be adequate. It should not be forgotten that the British welfare state arose in part because of the woeful inadequacy of voluntary provision to tackle poverty.

Pleas for choice and private insurance tend to be associated with a powerful middle class. To temper tendencies to disregard the needs of the less fortunate there needs to be a sense of mutual responsibility between the state and its citizens. Thus in Germany if voluntary provision is unable to meet needs, there is an expectation that the state will step in. German pluralism is founded on principles of a socially responsible state as well as on the principle of subsidiarity. Furthermore, subsidiarity does not mean that the financial burden simply is jettisoned to the lowest possible level. Nevertheless voluntary organizations in Germany are expected to generate a certain portion of their funds themselves – *Eigenbeitrag*. Thus they do partly rely on collections, donations and, where they are denominational, on Church taxes. The latter equals 8 per cent of income tax and is automatically collected by employers.

In short, unlike more centralized countries such as Britain and Sweden, central government in Germany does not have the power to shape the entire social security and social welfare system. Furthermore, whereas in Britain children's services, welfare and psychological services were merged after the 1968 Seebohm Report, in Germany these offices are distinct and still form the basis of local administration today. Only the Health Office became part of central administration in Nazi Germany and after the war it remained there for the most part. Multifarious levels and types of provision are typical also of EU countries such as Austria, the Netherlands, Spain (after Franco) and Italy.

THE NATURE OF SOCIAL SUPPORT SERVICES IN GERMANY

The following overview of legislative reforms from the early 1920s illustrates how Germany maintained such diversity in the provision of social services.

After several years of public discussion the order of the Reich on Income Support (*Reichsfursor-gepflicht- Verordnung* 1924), and the Youth Welfare Act (*Jugendwohlfahrtsgesetz* 1926), helped to abolish the Poor Law, which had driven social policy for so long in Germany, as of course it had in Britain. In Germany the provision of personal support services and the budgets for income support and family centred youth welfare support remained the responsibility of local government. Today the rural or metropolitan districts (*Landkreis* or *Stadtkreis*) still have to provide the money for social assistance. It is taken from local rates and from the local government share of income tax. This is collected by the *Länder* and partly distributed to the municipalities according to the number of inhabitants.

Legislative reforms by the Bonn government after the war did not change this traditional structure. Under the Social Assistance Act of 1967 entitled *Bundessozialhilfegesetz* (abbreviated to BSHG), social assistance remained a means-tested, non-contributory benefit, but it became an entitlement. The revision of the Youth Welfare Act in 1970 and again in 1990 under the title of *Kinder-und Jugendhilfe-Gesetz* (KJHG), i.e. Children and Youth Assistance Act, also left the levels of responsibility unchanged. If anything the influence of local family and youth welfare offices was strengthened by the requirement that not only should there be plans at the local level for the well-being of children and their families but that these should include evaluation of their living conditions (e.g. housing, leisure and sports facilities, etc.).

The consequence of the German-type system is that the focus of attention is on the provincial level. While pluralism is intended to enable choice, it also can result in a lack of uniformity in provision across the country. Sometimes there is a splintering of work between the provincial and local level and a lack of regional co-operation. There also are obvious advantages to this approach. Generally social workers do not have to wait for national policy changes to start a service. *Länder*, local authorities and independent institutions can experiment and try to find their own way to solve local problems. As a result many social problems have been tackled in different ways all over the country.

THE ROLE OF LOCAL GOVERNMENT IN PROVIDING SOCIAL WELFARE IN GERMANY

The provision of monetary support traditionally has been the responsibility of local government in Germany, whilst Church-affiliated and other non-profit welfare organizations are the providers of a wide spectrum of personal support services from family advice centres to all kinds of part-time and residential care services. Local authorities are the providers, nevertheless, when non-profit voluntary organization provision is not enough to cover needs or is non-existent. Thus the public sector provided day care for children when the Church did not offer this service because of their conviction that mothers should stay at home with their young children. Local authorities have also provided youth centres when Churches were interested in promoting more Church-orientated work.

Since the end of the 1960s, earmarked grants from the *Länder* have stimulated an enormous growth in the local social infrastructure. These grants were offered to both local authorities and voluntary organizations and helped to finance the expansion of child and youth care, youth work, counselling work for families in crisis, work with drug addicts and those with special needs because of mental or physical disability, and residential accommodation for older people. In the 1970s the growth rate of staff in personal support services in West Germany was one of the highest of all professions and trades.

Outside the services of local and voluntary social welfare institutions, social workers are only employed and financed on the *Länder* level in health services, probation and affiliated services and in some of the *Länder* for social work in schools. Additionally there is a small commercial sector which offers personal support services, especially for care of older people.

The trend in British social policy since the 1987 reforms has been to devolve detailed budgetary decisions increasingly to the district level and to engage the voluntary and private sector more fully in the provision of social welfare services. It is to the point, however, that the long-established and well-knit web of dispersed responsibility in Germany (see 'The Role of Local Government in Providing Social Welfare in Germany' box for more detail) can only function properly when institutions on a more central level do not mop up the lower level's financial resources. This incidentally was one reason many doubted the capacity of British social services to ensure the provision of adequate community care. Separating purchasing from provision could be beside the point if local budgets are capped and/or cut nationally.

It should be clear by now that getting the policy balance right is extremely complex. This is where the implementation process itself becomes such an important factor.

Role and education of professionals providing social support services

Role

The extent to which social and community workers are employed in a pro-active and pro-social way (see the last two points in 'The Scope of Social Policy' box on p. 320) rather than being limited to the statutory focus, varies considerably within Europe. Likewise the nomenclature and organization of those employed to implement social welfare policies is far from uniform.

British social work is rooted in a broad role definition so that, in theory, much of the work referred to in our 'Scope' box could be undertaken by social workers (with more or less involvement of youth and community workers). However, in practice British social work increasingly has become much more narrowly focused on child protection, control of deviance and the purchase or provision of social care. Indeed the title 'social worker' is being increasingly replaced by more job-specific titles, such as 'care management', 'social care' or 'child protection'. Other aspects of social work have suffered. The provision of school social workers, for example, is now minimal, while the funding of community workers remains spasmodic across the UK.

In much of the rest of Western and Central Europe, however, an intermediary and well-organized profession has developed which takes up much of the slack between statutory, protective social work and more radical community work. In Germany and much of Northern Europe these well-trained professionals are called 'social pedagogues', while in France and much of Southern Europe similar work is undertaken by *'animateurs Sozio-Culturels'* or 'specialist educators'. As Jones points out (1994) this latter specialization developed out of the closing of children's homes with the child care staff following their charges out into the community. Thus social pedagogues are situated between teachers and social workers and their focus these days is the promotion of support in all facets of community life in order to promote social well-being. In keeping with the principles of Paulo Freire, they seek to empower people to develop their capacities to take action to improve their situation.

While the work of social pedagogues may be far removed from the radical community action that typified community work in the UK in the late 1960s and early 1970s, it encompasses the sort of work that would be familiar to most youth and community workers today and to those social workers in Britain who can still pursue a community social work approach. The difference is that in the rest of EU Europe such work is seen to be as important as the protective, crisis aspects of social work.

In Britain the employment of youth and community workers by Community Education Departments declined significantly in the later part of the Thatcher years, though there is now an increasing interest in community health development work. In Holland such workers are called *'socialagoges'*, meaning social leaders, and the Danish have developed the concept of *'milieu pedagogues'* who are charged specifically with the planning and administration of urban areas for the well-being of their inhabitants. If British policy-makers want to develop a more pluralist approach to social services, the importance attached to such work in the rest of EU Europe needs to be given very serious consideration.

In Germany, then, there are two main branches to social work: *Sozialarbeit* and *Sozial Paedagogik*. While there is some interchangeability between the two, child protection work is more likely to be the responsibility of social pedagogues, alongside residential and community-based youth work. Financial assistance, probation and public health work tend to be the responsibility of state-based *Sozialarbeit*. In voluntary organizations *Sozialarbeit* tends to focus on general social services to specific groups of people, such as older people or families.

Education

In Germany since the end of the 1960s there has been a clear two-level structure for the education and training of social welfare practitioners:

1   At the Further Education level 'educators' and 'professional carers' who work in residential homes for children, older people and people with disabilities, are trained for two years in *Fachschulen* with an additional supervised placement;
2   At the Higher Education level social workers and social pedagogues undertake a four-year course in *Fachhochschulen* (comparable to the old British polytechnic). This includes placements which total a minimum of one year.

Both levels lead to state certificates and both *Fachschulen* and *Fachhochschulen* can be run either by the *Länder* or by trusts. Thus the *Länder* (together with the welfare organizations) have control over the length and content of the courses (Brauns and Kramer 1986) – another example of the principle of subsidiarity in operation. This is a marked difference to the UK where decisions about professional education are the responsibility of central government via the Central Council for the Education and Training of Social Workers (CCETSW). The aim is to ensure comparability of qualification.

In Britain the two-year Diploma in Social Work (Dip.SW) includes 130 days on placement, and practice learning is rigorously assessed. Dip.SW programmes are provided by local partnerships between universities (particularly the former polytechnics), some colleges of further and higher education, social services departments and independent sector agencies. The resultant programmes are approved and monitored by CCETSW to ensure they meet nationally set requirements. They lead normally to an academic award of a Level Two Diploma in Higher Education as well as the professional Dip.SW, but the latter is sometimes delivered in conjunction with a degree or a higher degree in Social Work and/or Social Policy.

There is still no national award for community work specifically, but Youth and Community Work courses are nationally validated. Again these are rarely offered with a degree. In Germany all candidates with the requisite academic qualifications are entitled to enrol on social work programmes. In the UK students are subject to interview and usually only those with some relevant experience, as well as the requisite academic background, are accepted.

Only a few German universities offer undergraduate and, very occasionally, graduate studies in either branch of social work. Normally these lead to the Diploma in Social Pedagogics and qualify people to pursue careers in social education, as distinct from primary and secondary education.

Graduates from the *Fachhochschulen* concentrate on the provision of services, while administrative staff have responsibility for the budgets, thus ensuring separation of purchase and provision within a single agency. In social work promotion depends on skilled specialist work with clients. They are not eligible for management positions except perhaps of a residential or day-care institution, alongside a director of finance. In public agencies in Germany there are normally no directors of social welfare who were trained as social workers or social pedagogues. The 1990 Children and Youth Assistance Act actually strengthened the non-administrative profile for social support professionals in public agencies. The Act sees them as empowering partners with their clients, separated from budget-orientated decision-making. Thus in disputes with their finance divisions over the cost of care plans, reaction by social welfare workers can be based solely on promoting the needs of their clients.

While the philosophy of separating the purchase from the provision of care is present in the British National Health Service and Community Care Act of 1990, the difference is that care managers, who assess need and purchase suitable services, normally would have at least a basic social care qualification (though not necessarily the full Diploma in Social Work) as well as some minimal financial and administrative/management experience and/or training. Thus while both countries now seek to separate the purchase of packages of care from the provision of that care, Germany has stressed the need for quite distinct qualifications in each sphere. In Britain, by focusing on the competencies needed for specific tasks, some local authorities are adopting a minimalist approach to the qualifications required.

In Britain it is more usual for senior managers of both social services departments and major non-profit welfare organizations to have social work experience before they acquire additional management qualifications. Nevertheless the gulf between administrative, budget-holding staff and client-orientated professionals is a common tension. However this is a particular characteristic of the situation in Germany (for more details see the 'Factors Contributing to the Management/ Practitioner Gulf in Germany' box).

The barrier to management for German social workers diminishes job satisfaction, creates a deficit in applied research undertaken by professionals with direct practice experience (the range and rigour reflected in British social work journals are cited with envy by other Europeans) and latent conflict between professional and administrative staff within the same welfare agency. The social costs of this ceiling in German social services have been ignored. Even the massive changes brought about with German reunification did not lead to the discussion of alternative ways to organize professional education and practice in the social welfare field. Rather the divisions were simply taken over by the new East German *Länder*.

FACTORS CONTRIBUTING TO THE MANAGEMENT/PRACTITIONER GULF IN GERMANY

1   As in Britain, the majority of practitioners in the helping professions are women, whilst the majority of the management and administrative staff are men. This not only reinforces the difference between the management and caring cultures but in Germany it combines with a second factor, namely a 'ceiling'.

2   A 'ceiling' is put on the promotion of professional staff because, in the vast majority of cases, their diplomas are awarded by *Fachhochschulen,* whereas upper middle and senior management posts are, by state regulation, only open to university graduates. Most ministers of higher education do their utmost to keep *Fachhochschulen* on a lower level to universities. This means that *Fachhochschule* professors have higher teaching loads, very limited research resources and there are no post-diploma awards available for students. Employing agencies, whether statutory, non-profit or profit, seem to be content with this as it helps to keep staffing costs down. On-the-job training opportunities are provided, which do not entitle participants to university graduate scale salaries.

This is significantly different to the situation in Britain. Although the huge majority of social services senior managers have been men since the post-Seebohm (1968) amalgamation of Children's Services (which had traditionally been managed by women) with welfare departments, both men and women with professional social work qualifications *can* move into management. It is to the point that, although Britain refused to enforce the EU directive for three-year social work training, there are now a few social work degree programmes linked to the Dip.SW. Also it is now national policy to encourage post-qualifying professional education for social workers who have the two-year Diploma in Social Work. This can be achieved by working towards a degree and/or a nationally recognized post-qualifying professional social work award, an advanced social work award and/or a postgraduate award – for example an MSW or equivalent or an MBA. Despite the commitment to the four-year initial professional qualification, there are no postgraduate social work or social administration courses in German institutions of higher education.

However the pressure of the economic crisis of the *Sozialstaat* has led now to controversy about the level of social welfare provision united Germany can afford, along with calls for devolved budgets and lean management structures. The establishment of lower-level training for work as a 'social assistant', 'education assistant' or 'care assistant' under the supervision of a social worker (or equivalent) is being considered. This would be roughly equivalent to the British Higher National Diploma in Social Care and could result in a German equivalent of community care workers, handling basic assessment and care planning for less complex cases. The appeal of reduced staffing costs is expected to be as enticing in Germany as it is in the UK.

Issues in the provision of social services

Though there is no dispute in Germany as to the importance and standing of professional social welfare work, controversy abounds over what kind and what level of social welfare provision a united Germany can afford. Many of these issues are prevalent in other EU countries.

There are six main areas of contention:

1   the cost of health services and of residential and nursing care for older people;
2   the cost of day care for children under 3 and between 3 and 6;
3   the cost of provision for refugees and asylum seekers;
4   the cost of unemployment generally, particularly in regard to young people and women;
5   the cost of funding the recovery in East Germany;
6   the cost of finding a solution to social housing policy problems, especially in light of a deficit of nearly two million flats for the poorer segment of the population.

Invariably German central government will be on one side of the issue and the *Länder* and/or local government on the other side. For an example see the box 'Assistance to Refugees'.

ASSISTANCE TO REFUGEES

In the 1980s central government dispersed the growing number of asylum seekers and refugees (at first mostly of Vietnamese and African origin, then from Yugoslavia) evenly across the country in proportion to the size of the population. It was left to the *Länder* and, above all, local communities to provide accommodation, income benefit and personal social services for them. This was based on the legal obligation of local authorities to help any person in need who lives within their borders. Certainly it meant an enormous drain on local welfare budgets and consequently on local taxes. This had predictable consequences in terms of attitudes of community residents to immigrants. Local authorities argued, on the basis of their constitutional rights of self-government, that funnelling this burden down to them was undermining that right. The pressure on central government was increased by a swing to right-wing parties in local and *Länder* elections, fuelled by racist attitudes and arguments. The outcome was legal changes limiting the number of asylum seekers and closing borders. Welfare provision for asylum seekers was regulated on a smaller scale and separately from the general social welfare account.

Some disputes about social welfare provision serve to consolidate the position of local government and of voluntary organizations in the German welfare system. Also, given the shift to assist people to live at home, they can increase the demand for professional community based workers. One area in which local government in Germany has been partly successful is in reducing the costs of social welfare with regard to nursing care for disabled and older people. Up until March 1995, the rising costs of personal services and accommodation fell on local *Sozialhilfe* budgets (i.e. social assistance) which had to be financed by local taxes plus a contribution of a 15 per cent share of income tax if an individual's pensions and savings were not sufficient and/or the person was not entitled to some health insurance benefits. However Health Insurance insisted that it had to provide only medical assistance and not care for older people. The solution has been the development of a new national and contributional Nursing Insurance, which has helped to cover the cost of home-care from April 1995 and residential care one year later. Though there is a ceiling on its contributions to the costs of care, it is expected to bring three advantages:

1   reduced strain on local welfare budgets;
2   expansion in the labour market for home-care and day-care provision;
3   pay for family members and other private carers who engage in caring for disabled family members in their homes.

In Britain, as forecast, the societal cost of decreased institutional care without a concomitant increase in community support services is now beginning to be realized. Not only has the autonomy of local authorities to decide that they need to raise increased monies in order to adequately fund social services been undermined, but also, because 'care in the community' has coincided with drastic cuts by central government in local authority budgets, it has led to cuts in the employment of professional social workers and even of home helps, forcing people to rely more on family members or to become increasingly isolated and needy.

In Germany, too, in other areas of dispute the outcome might be diffcrent. As far as unemployment is concerned, for example, by limiting benefits paid by unemployment assistance, central government can shift the cost of long-term unemployment to local government, who will have to provide *Sozialhilfe* (social assistance). Central government expects that a higher burden on local shoulders might induce local and *Länder* governments to agree with cuts in the level of benefits. This would widen the difference between *Sozialhilfe* pay and the lowest wage rates in industry. It reflects the coalition parties' arguments in the last national election that the social net in Germany is too cosy, pampering people who rely on *Sozialhilfe* rather than work. Such debates doubtless will have a familiar ring to British and other European readers.

Tensions, such as those engendered over the distribution of the public costs of German unity, signal a deepening controversy over the level and nature of social supports and welfare benefits in Germany – that is, the role of the welfare state and the nature of social support specialists needed to purchase and provide such services.

In Britain when there is talk of reducing the number of qualified social workers employed by social services departments, it is suggested that voluntary and private organizations and institutions will need to employ more social workers. The reader might question how realistic this is given that:

1   Britain, particularly since the start of the welfare state, has a minimal tradition of private and voluntary sector provision;
2   that the development of the welfare state was in part a consequence of the inability of the voluntary and private sector to meet basic support needs in society; and
3   that even other European countries, such as Germany, which have maintained a wider base of responsibility for the provision of social support, are now seeing the resources in the voluntary sector shrinking and commitment to the principle of solidarity teetering as the cost of social support has risen.

Perhaps it would seem more likely that services will disappear or take advantage of less qualified workers rather than meet the costs of professional salaries. This should give the social work profession cause to pause. We need much greater clarity about the importance, or the 'added value', of the contribution of social work professionals, in the broadest sense of a spectrum which includes social protection, social control and social care as well as work to create a supportive infrastructure that promotes individual and community capacity.

In other words what do social workers, social pedagogues and community workers uniquely contribute to society? Next, this chapter will develop an analysis of key characteristics of this work which is undertaken throughout the EU to varying degrees, and which we maintain would be discarded at considerable loss and long-term cost to society.

The contribution made by social practitioners to policy implementation

Compounding uncertainties as to the nature of social provision possible in the next millennium are uncertainties about society itself. For example, how will we respond to the impact of globalization, not only economic globalization but the fundamental transformation of local experience by computerization and instantaneous communication? As Anthony Giddens pointed out in a lecture at the British Association of Canadian Studies Conference at Cambridge University in March 1993, globalization impacts not only on local life but on the intimacies of personal life. It leads to fracturing and creates new conflicts. We can no longer hide, for example, from the legitimate claims of people with other traditions. While this can be positive if it frees us to acknowledge difference and the partiality of our particular experience, people tend to experience it as threatening, as the German examples illustrate. The tendency is to resort to fundamentalism or violence, which is, of course, an increasing hallmark of these times.

The way popular culture has stepped into the void left by the old certainties of religion and science, capitalism and Marxism, is reflected in post-modernism. While this may not do justice to the seriousness of the changes confronting us today, it does capture the confusion and incoherence in our experience of space and time (other worlds, other times jump back and forth before our eyes). This cannot help but contribute to a sense of not being rooted in either space or time; of being outside history and outside tradition; of having little sense of connectedness within a family let alone to an extended community; no clear frame of reference within which to form one's identity and little sense of belonging. In Germany discussion in this regard focuses on 'individualization' and 'value pluralization in society'. In such an environment, instead of welcoming the potential of diversity, we tend to cling to old symbols (virulent expressions of local nationalism, 'Little Englanders' and Neo-Nazism, etc. People become indifferent and socially incapacitated, neglecting their democratic rights which are the cornerstone of a just society.

When one recognizes that this is the context within which the job of providing social support, let alone empowerment, must take place, the enormity and complexity of the task before us is clear. Is social and community work up to it? One of the outcomes of forming links with social work programmes in other European countries has been the clarification of the way social work in its broadest sense can contribute to our society at this time. In order to assess the strengths and unique features of such work, Butler and Jeffries (1994) concluded that we needed first to attempt, in feminist and post-modern terms, to deconstruct social work. It seems logical, therefore, to start our search for the core elements of social work in EU Europe by exploring the common and, incidentally, often contradictory criticisms that have been levelled and which seem relevant to social work in both Germany and the UK. These were nicely summed up by Ian Sinclair in a 1992 paper in *Issues in Social Work Education*:

- Firstly, that social work goals are too grandiose, too vague and too ambitious and therefore unattainable.

It is partly this concern, of course, that is behind the drive in the UK to specify competencies and expected outcomes. However, it is not simply a matter of being more circumspect in our claims or specific in our goals. Furthermore, there is an obvious link between this first criticism and two of the other criticisms Sinclair lists, namely that:

- social work is ineffective, and that
- aims of client and social worker are at cross-purposes.

At one level of analysis, if goals are unrealistic or at cross-purposes, concerns about effectiveness are hardly surprising. Nevertheless research shows that social workers and those with whom they work can negotiate mutually acceptable and realistic goals and effectively meet them. Indeed good social work practice has always meant this (cf. Sinclair 1992 and Cheetham 1992). There is plenty of research to demonstrate the effectiveness of various social work interventions, so it is ironic that social work so often appears to collude in creating a sense of its own ineffectiveness.

The explanation probably lies in the fundamentally contradictory nature of social work, which is epitomized by the long-standing tension between traditional and radical orientations to practice. While the former stresses a professional responsibility to work within the system to fulfil legal responsibilities, the latter stresses the justice and equality value base of social work and thus the responsibility of social workers to address structural oppression.

In Germany it seems the resolution of such a contradiction has been the separation of functions into social work and social pedagogy. However, the problem is perhaps precisely that the tendency to juxtapose the two, as all too often happens in Britain in regard to social and community work, presents a false dichotomy. One without the other would be an incomplete portrayal of the broad social work task. In Germany the trap is perhaps avoided by stressing the importance of both forms of practice. Not only does society need skilled practitioners to work from within the system to perform statutory, protective roles but a democratic society also needs this to be undertaken from a value base that commits us to ensure social justice and promote individual and community capacity in order to enable societal well-being. It is to the point that in Germany qualification in one branch of social work does not preclude subsequent work in the other (Cannan *et al.* 1992), whereas in the UK the education and training of social workers and community workers is separate.

In a 1986 paper, Jennifer Sayer captured the problematic nature of such contradictions with an illustration of the gap between the day-to-day reality of practice and theory in regard to addressing the root causes of need (see Figure 16.1). Ann Jeffries has modified and extended this to illustrate aspects of this division and the contribution social and community workers can make to bridging the gap.

For the worker caught up in the pressing needs of people, which require immediate attention, the task of working for structural change that addresses the roots of their problems can seem impossibly idealistic and unrealistic. Conversely students going on placement full of theories about working to bring about social

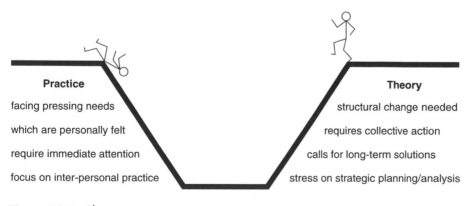

Figure 16.1 The gap

well-being, for example, could soon be tumbling head-first into the abyss when confronted with the demands of the day-to-day reality of clients' lives.

In practice, of course, we have to 'start where the people are' (Freire 1985: xxi) struggling with pressing personal problems. The social worker's immediate task is both to help people manage these pressing problems and their related feelings *and* to empower them in the process. Community workers and social pedagogues aim to develop an environment that prevents personal problems becoming crises, by building supportive community networks, social and political awareness and the commitment to work collectively for social and economic change. Thus well-developed interpersonal, problem-posing/problem-solving skills are essential for community workers as well as for social workers (Freire 1985: 39, 40).

Furthermore, as Paulo Freire again stresses (1985: xvii) and Lawrence Shulman's research indicates, 'other factors must be considered as influencing outcomes' (Shulman 1993: 96). These variables relate not only to the particular people involved in the interaction, but to the context of the problem and the context within which the working relationship is developed. In other words, if we are concerned about outcomes, we need social workers to be informed and concerned about the context in which people live their lives, not just because of our social justice value base or because the wider context is so often the root of personal problems, but because of the impact the context has on a person's ability and motivation to work on the presenting problems (Freire 1985: xx); that is, context-related work has a crucial bearing on the interpersonal practice outcome.

To return to Figure 16.1, it is essential then that social workers too are committed to long-term work for a social environment that promotes well-being and social justice (shown on the right). In order to work effectively with pressing personal problems (on the other side of the diagram), they need to be involved, either directly or indirectly, with the immediate context in which their clients live their lives, while still fulfilling their statutory obligations. All too often the tendency is to present this multi-dimensional social work task as discrete pieces, with the latter aspect being treated as an optional extra. This has dire implications for long-term effectiveness, as Shulman's research suggests.

Our conclusion is that, regardless of the particular professional distinctions and organizational structures developed in a given country, it is essential to hold both in dynamic and effective tension. The social workers' professional responsibility is not solely aligned to the control/protection aspects, but neither can these statutory responsibilities, nor the resource limits on practice, be ignored. Social workers must continually seek to ensure that the potential gap between the various aspects of this multi-dimensional task is bridged at least by more collaborative, multi-professional approaches to social policy implementation.

As our brief discussion of the role of social pedagogues in many EU countries illustrated, one way of doing this is to break down the tasks and assign them to different professional groups. However, the danger with this is that:

1   Crucial elements get left out. This is happening increasingly in the UK with no one taking responsibility for developing some basic aspects of social support essential for the success of care in the community, for example.

2 Antagonism develops between different professional groups, as has happened in the UK between some community workers and social workers; or between different aspects of the work (e.g. between purchase and provision, or management and practice, functions as in Germany).

On the other hand, if one profession tries to maintain responsibility for the full range of the work, the danger then is that, in trying to be everything to everyone, we fall into the trap reflected in Sinclair's (1992) fourth common criticism of social work, which incidentally also has been levelled at community work:

● Social work equals tokenism, in that at best it serves to quieten the public conscience by 'cooling out' clients; at worst it reinforces oppression.

There is a strong theoretical basis for that claim. Freire (1985: 39), for example, saw this as an obvious pitfall for social work. Michel Foucault also cautioned us to look very closely at the way social work knowledge and practice has been used, in collusion with other powerful disciplines and mechanisms of society, as a means of control (Skinner 1990: 9). Dorothy Smith is more direct, 'The organization of professional knowledge is more than a guarantee of standards, more than a monopoly of knowledge and skill, it is a monopolization of control within a dominant class' (1987: 217).

Foucault, on the other hand, has praise for those who challenge the norm-creating, dominant discourses in society; for those who empower people to resist such imposed identities in order to speak for themselves. As people take upon themselves the right and the responsibility for self-definition, they create the means for a more expansive democracy to emerge.

Despite the constraints outlined by Dorothy Smith (1987: 218–19), this also has been an ongoing thread in the history of social work in Northern Europe (Cannan *et al.* 1992: 30). It certainly is evident in community social work practice and is eloquently addressed by Mike Oliver (1992) in regard to policy-making, practice and research as they relate to people with disabilities.

While the desire to be taken seriously as a profession did lead to social work's wholesale adoption of the white, 'male-stream' and middle-class-orientated social sciences and research practices that are part of the problem (Oliver 1992: 106), the development of a clear professional identity for social workers, particularly in Britain, paradoxically is also a legacy from which our practice has derived strength and recognition. This has meant that our views and recommendations are given more weight by other professionals, which should be to the benefit of consumers. Certainly research shows that the input of social workers in Britain has been crucial, for example, in returning older people successfully from hospital to their homes rather than into institutions (Sinclair 1992: 71). The problem is that no sooner is a positive contribution by social workers identified than one has to acknowledge that, under certain circumstances, that very strength can be problematic.

Particularly in Britain, with our high profile legal requirements with regard to child abuse for example, social work is ridden with contradictions. The child protection role could be considered to impede the requirement to work with parents to promote family functioning, for example. There is also a contradiction

335

between the desire to care for people in the community and the burden this can put on the diminishing pool of unpaid home carers – particularly women and people over 65 years of age. The German solution of Nursing Insurance is a note-worthy development in this regard. (See earlier section, on 'Issues in the Provision of Social Services'.)

The point is that, as a profession we have not flinched from the challenge of working with such contradictions. Jeffries has suggested that it is perhaps precisely this that points us to the unique and paradoxical strength of social work, namely that:

> social work is about living with contradiction in such a way that the outcome is creative at best and good enough practice at least ... Our success in managing this tension, in embracing paradox, actually has put us at the cutting edge of a renewed discourse for our times. A discourse that points to the way to move beyond the paralysis which it has been suggested is inherent in post-modernist analysis.
>
> (Jeffries 1992)

The challenge, posed by Foucault, is to live with uncertainty (Skinner 1990: 78–80). Social workers have become very good at doing that! One of the earliest concepts social work students are expected to understand is that of ambivalence; the capacity of human beings to feel conflicting emotions at the same time. They are expected to learn skills in communicating in a way which acknowledges these conflicts, both within individuals and between individuals and others. In family work, group work, multi-disciplinary as well as individual work, social workers have to negotiate a way through ambivalence. Like social workers, feminists have consistently had to act in less than perfect circumstances, where confusion and competing needs have required a radical challenge to the way we perceive reality and the way to respond to it:

> This has produced a capacity for creativity and discipline, honed by the harsh reality of limited resources and the low status of women, which has clear parallels in social work. Feminism is a theory in which praxis – simul-taneous action and reflection – allows the coexistence of contradiction without the consequence of immobilization.
>
> (Butler and Jeffries 1994)

It is important to be clear that the problem is not so much the delineation of the dichotomies, e.g. the maintenance/medical model as compared to the empowerment model, but how we deal with or respond to our recognition of the inherent contradictions. It is the recognition of this process that has led post-modernists to reject grand theory or 'meta-narratives'. But what feminists have realized (because of the way our values required us to recognize and accommo-date the multi-dimensionality of truth resulting from the variety in women's experience) is that the way forward is to embrace the paradoxical nature of discourse. It is not a matter of either/or but a case of both/and.

Thus it can be said that social work *is* about care *and* control; about main-tenance *and* empowerment. By living with such contradictions, rather than

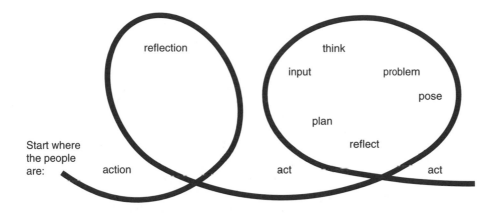

Figure 16.2 Praxis – the action/reflection cycle

choosing between them, by embracing rather than seeking to resolve the tension between the vigorous, apparently opposing poles between which our work is stretched, we have some hope of realizing the paradoxical possibility of individual and societal transformation.

At its best that is what social work is about, and it is this ability to think and practise on a multi-dimensional level that is the added value of such work. Thus social and community workers must be accountable *both* to their employing agency *and* to their professional value base; social workers must develop inter-personal problem-solving skills and knowledge, juxtaposed with analytical, organizational and management abilities. A focus on problem-solving in isolation from variables such as the context in which the problem occurs and the context in which it is being addressed would diminish the potential contribution social work can make (Shulman 1993).

The question remains, on a day-to-day basis how do we hold all these facets of the broad social work task in creative tension? How do we bridge the apparent contradictions and dichotomies? This is where praxis comes in (Freire 1972: 41). At its best, in whichever country it is undertaken, because of its complexity, social and community work must be reflexive disciplines which encompass theoretical knowledge on the one hand, practical experience and innovation on the other, and make the demand that each constantly informs the other. Praxis is illustrated in Figure 16.2.

Giving a vital indication of the strength of social work in recent years are the attempts that have been made to develop and sustain a creative tension between the dichotomies that constantly confront us. In Britain the demand for a partnership ideology in the planning and delivery of social and community services helps to ensure that this tension remains dynamic (see the 'Partnership Ideology in Practice' box for examples).

The challenge, then, is to look more closely at the contradictions in our work and consider whether they could not be, paradoxically, strengths. To

> **PARTNERSHIP IDEOLOGY IN PRACTICE**
>
> Examples of creative partnership can be found in:
>
> 1 The mandatory inter-agency collaborations, such as the Area Child Protection Committees, joint Social Services and Health Authority planning groups, etc., which effectively increase the accessibility of voluntary and private sector provision, encourage a greater sense of partnership amongst the caring profession, and augur well for a more person-focused and co-ordinated experience for the service user.
> 2 The academic/field partnership that is required by the Central Council for the Education and Training of Social Workers (CCETSW) in social work education and training.
> 3 The demand in recent legislation for consultation and involvement of local communities and 'consumers' as partners in social services planning and decision-making regarding their needs.
> 4 The partnership in Plymouth between local authority departments, government and independent sector agencies and community groups to enable maximum participation in, and coherent development of, the city's communities.

illustrate how this can work, let's return now to our poor workers poised on the brink of the abyss (see Figure 16.3).

If we apply the logic of praxis (Freire 1985: xxii) and start with the pressing needs of people in the context of their community, informed by theory and

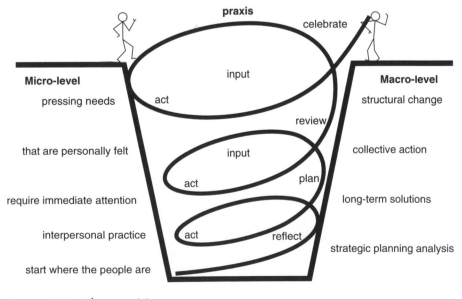

Figure 16.3 The gap (II)

drawing upon all we and the people with whom we work know and are committed to, you can see how praxis becomes the means for transforming contradiction into paradox, for drawing together the apparently contradictory elements so that they inform each other, and for doing this in a way that empowers people to act for themselves, thus strengthening the likelihood of positive outcomes. (See the 'Practice Examples' box for examples of good practice in the UK which illustrate the way apparent conflicts have been embraced to produce a high-quality reflexive practice.)

PRACTICE EXAMPLES: EMBRACING THE PARADOXICAL NATURE OF SOCIAL WORK:

1   In the field of juvenile justice and diversion from care and custody, the emphasis by social workers on criminal proceedings and sentencing tariffs has, paradoxically, offered young people better care than when their behaviour was explained socially and avoided. In the current climate which stresses punishment and control, this is particularly significant.

2   Social workers in fostering and adoption have confronted the difficulty of placing many of the children in care in 'normal' family situations. The recognition that all children have the right to family experience has led to social workers challenging the stereotypical notions of what constitutes a 'normal family'. Rather than admitting defeat, or placing children in unsatisfactory, second-best situations, social workers have acknowledged the needs of children beyond the physical, extending the notion of normal family to include different race, sexuality, marital status and culture.

3   Services for people with a learning disability where, paradoxically, the provision of a service has often reinforced the process of labelling and creating dependency. Rather than simply continuing or withdrawing, social workers have developed ways of working alongside individuals and groups so as to politicize their claim for full citizenship rather than patronage, and empower them to speak for themselves.

4   In the field of child protection, when confronted with competing interests of children and families, social workers have contributed to an analysis of child abuse beyond the individual pathology of the abusing individual(s). They have developed skills in working with families to both listen to and protect children through prevention and statutory intervention.

5   Community social work has confronted a similar dilemma for workers who have to act as agents of statutory control even as they are offering active support to individuals and groups in the same community. Their practice has been more visible, open to public scrutiny and comment, and more accountable to the consumers. The paradox here is that the very investment of the statutory power in a known 'local' individual serves to reduce the power imbalance between the local authority and the community.

> 6   Community development workers, instead of giving up as the societal effects of the pervasive Thatcherite years trickled down to magnify the deprivation of poor communities, have co-opted the self-help and enter-prise ethic to promote grassroots development of co-operatives and community-run enterprises. These range from fruit and vegetable co-ops and credit unions to tenant-managed council housing and city-wide part-nerships between local authority departments, government and independent sector agencies and community groups. While making at least some tangible impact on the immediate economic and social conditions of communities (the pressing felt needs), this work brings people together to develop individual and collective skill capacity and self-esteem, to begin to raise awareness of the connection between personal problems and political action, thus taking the first steps towards structural change.
>
> 7   Finally, the way social work has developed the field of mediation. In rejecting the notion that competing claims have to be fought over with one side winning, social workers have been able to establish ways in which conflict can become the means to build conciliation. It is this skill in mediation, demanding tolerance of ambiguity, conflict and uncertainty between individuals, groups and institutions, which distinguishes social work and is evident in all the examples. It epitomizes the professional social worker's ability to cross boundaries of discipline and function.

The elements of the complex task presented in the 'Practice Examples' box can be summarized as follows:

- A political analysis which recognizes the fundamentally unequal nature of society.
- A recognition of the scope and limitations of the social or community worker's role, given their agency mandate and the political structure, and an ability to work in partnership to maximize the likelihood of positive outcomes.
- A recognition of the processes of both individual functioning – physical, social, emotional, intellectual and spiritual – and group dynamics; as well as the skills to enable problem-solving and capacity-building.
- A recognition of the importance of, and ability to work in, partnership in order to bring about improvements in the socio-economic and political context in which people live and work.
- The use of research and theoretical frameworks to inform assessment and action.
- The centrality of a value base which informs and directs the whole of a worker's practice.

In order to manage this complex task, it is inevitable and necessary that agencies will need to identify different elements of the work which may need specific training and expertise. Equally, it is not surprising that some workers find it helpful to define their work in terms of content specialization (e.g. child-protection or mental health, advocacy or community development), or in terms of specific skills such as management or family therapy, social work or social pedagogy. However, in light of the analysis developed here about the nature of social work, the above could be self-defeating if it contributes to the separation and dislocation of the elements of social work which are effective because of the way these different elements interact. In short, a social or a community worker

> is not someone who merely acts like a motor mechanic assessing, taking action, and (hopefully) curing the problem. She is one who in addition, recognises the contribution made by the intervention to the specific process of transformation ... She can build from small activity to small activity on a dialectical model of reflection and action.
>
> (Sayer 1986: 300)

Thus praxis and partnership become the mediating mechanisms for social workers and the people with whom they work. Their importance for our polarized society cannot be overestimated.

To conclude, whether one stresses a generic or specialist orientation to practice, or whether one isolates particular aspects of the broad social work task and gives them to specified practitioners such as social pedagogues or care managers, or community workers, is not so important so long as we hold on to this appreciation of *the importance of a reflexive interaction between the different elements of the broad social work task*. And so long as *the full range is recognized as crucial* for the well-being of society *and*, therefore, is *adequately resourced*.

This analysis points to the conclusion that social work will only be effective if, at a practical and policy level, we maintain the tension between the poles of, for example, care and control, prevention and protection, empowerment and adjudication. Whatever the function, specialist or generic, and regardless of the organizational arrangements adopted, all these practitioners need a fundamental ability to recognize and build bridges between the apparent contradictions in the social policies they are required, collectively, to implement. They must, for example, point out and work with the connection between people's personal problems *and* the context in which they occur. This is what social and community work education is intended to equip these students uniquely to do.

This multi-dimensional work calls for highly skilled, committed, knowledgeable and well-trained practitioners. We strongly contend that this is an orientation and a way of practising that is needed now, across Europe, more than ever. Indeed, perhaps the added value of social work (in its broadest sense) in relation to social policy is that social workers, with their unique education, quite simply 'hold it all together'. They do this while also fostering some vision of how micro-level practice here today, with a particular person's pressing individual problem, can be part of a macro-level transformation of the wider society. Furthermore, the social worker's understanding of, and involvement in, that socio-political context, maximizes the likelihood that the helping relationship established with a particular consumer will be effective.

Summary

- By looking at the various forms this multi-dimensional profession assumes in Europe, the gaps in and threats to social welfare provision in any one country become clear.
- Also, the essential characteristics and the importance of this work in terms of the outcomes of social policies are apparent.
- One danger is that, at a critical point in our rapidly changing society, we will undermine the very aspect of social work that is the particular contribution the profession can make to the welfare of society.
- Another danger is that a fragmented service, developed in the name of efficiency, will be self-defeating, resulting in higher levels of need and demand for social work but in a shrinking economy.

Further reading

With regard to the place of social work within the social agenda of the European Union, more detail on the forms that social work assumes in other European countries and the relevance of issues such as citizenship, participation and marginalization to social work, see the following books.

Cresy Cannan, Lynne Berry and Karen Lyons (1992) *Social Work and Europe*, London: Macmillan.

Walter Lorenz (1994) *Social Work in a Changing Europe*, London: Routledge.

Chapter 17

Poverty and social security

Mark Hyde and Louise Ackers

Introduction	344
Definitions of poverty	344
The incidence of poverty	345
Explanations of poverty	349
The 'social dimension' of the European Union	352
The Social Chapter and EU social policy	355
The future	356
Summary	357
Further reading	357

Key concepts

- Poverty and social deprivation
- The 'underclass'
- Economic and social restructuring

Introduction

For the first time since the 1930s, poverty is growing, but there is considerable disagreement about the causes of this problem.

Many conservatives blame poor people for the circumstances in which they find themselves. In this view, contemporary poverty is caused by a growing 'under-class' of people who have rejected society's main customs including marriage and employment. Alternatively, it has been argued that economic and social restructuring are at the heart of the problem. Unemployment has led to a loss of income for some households while part-time working has led to low pay. These trends have affected Europe as a whole and have thus led to growing poverty in all of the member states of the European Union.

A consideration of these issues illustrates why it is important to look at Britain in terms of the broader European picture. However, Britain also has a distinctiveness that can be established by a review of factors that are peculiar to this country. The most important is the decisive influence of New Right ideas on welfare. Poverty in the UK is influenced by cross-European trends and by the distinctive approach of recent Conservative governments to social policy. As far as welfare is concerned, Britain is a part of, but also apart from, Europe.

Definitions of poverty

Before we can measure the incidence of poverty we first have to define it. Poverty as a concept can be defined in a number of different ways with important implications for the degree and nature of poverty identified. This section compares two contrasting definitions of poverty: absolute and relative.

Absolute poverty is a measure that seeks to identify the minimum level of resources required by a family or individual in order to survive. 'Survival' is equated with the concept of subsistence. The concept is not concerned with broader 'quality of life' issues nor with the overall level of inequality in society. Absolute poverty would therefore include those individuals and families who lack certain basic resources such as adequate nutrition, shelter and warmth. However, it would not include those who possess these basic resources but maintain a very poor quality of life relative to their peers in a given community or society. As a basis for social policy, absolute poverty identifies a role for the state in the provision of basic necessities required for subsistence, and no more. Absolute poverty implies a residual welfare state (Alcock 1993).

Not surprisingly, the concept has been heavily criticized, and on a number of grounds. For example, in order to make the most of their meagre resources, the poor would have to have an expert knowledge of nutrition, which is unlikely. Of greatest importance, however, absolute poverty fails to recognize that individuals are members of communities that have important conventions and customs. The concept therefore fails to recognize that individuals have important social and cultural needs.

This problem was instrumental in prompting the development of another concept: relative poverty (Alcock 1993). Unlike absolute poverty, relative poverty is concerned with the overall distribution of household incomes. It is concerned with income inequalities, and not just the incomes of the poor. People are poor if they fall below prevailing standards of living.

Relative poverty has also been highly influential. It has framed empirical research into the prevalence of poverty, including Townsend's (1979) acclaimed study during the 1970s. Following this example, Mack and Lansley (1985) developed a consensual approach to measuring poverty. Their poverty standard was established by asking individuals what they considered to be the necessities of an acceptable standard of living. Those without the necessities were deemed to be poor.

An important criticism of both concepts is that they are largely concerned with income. Inadequacy of income, whilst in itself an important indicator of poverty, is not an adequate means of measuring or quantifying social deprivation. Inadequate housing, poor diet, lack of access to education, inability to travel, inability to be taken seriously by those in authority or those with the power to assist can lead to a loss of human dignity.

Clearly, poverty has many dimensions. However, the main measure used by many studies of the incidence of poverty is household income. Most available evidence therefore restricts researchers to the problem of income deprivation. The next section adopts one particular definition of income deprivation: relative poverty.

The incidence of poverty

There are considerable difficulties in establishing evidence of cross-national differences in the incidence of poverty in Europe. National estimates of poverty are often not directly comparable, as they are based on surveys that employ different definitions and measurements of deprivation (Alcock 1993). This may lead to a variety of inconsistent conclusions about the distribution of poverty. For example, some international comparisons have shown that poverty is more extensive in France than in the UK, and others the reverse. The main problem with establishing reliable evidence, then, is one of comparability. Do different national estimates measure the same thing?

A number of recent studies have taken steps to facilitate greater comparability and, whilst problems remain, they provide the best evidence available on the incidence of poverty in EU member states. These studies are summarized in the 'Measuring and Comparing Poverty in the EU' box.

The 'Poverty in Figures' study (Eurostat 1990) adopts two approaches to measuring relative poverty in EU member states – one which uses national poverty lines to compare countries, the other using an EU poverty line. Both measure relative poverty; in the former, poverty is measured relative to prevailing standards in member states, whilst in the latter, poverty in member states is measured against prevailing standards in the European Union as a whole.

The distribution of poverty in Europe using national poverty lines is represented in Figure 17.1. This evidence refers to persons 'whose resources are so limited as to exclude them from the minimum acceptable way of life in the member state in which they live' (Oppenheim 1993: 157). The black bars represent poverty

---

MEASURING AND COMPARING POVERTY IN THE EU

It is very difficult to obtain up-to-date data that compares poverty in different EU member states. Existing comparative data such as that presented in Figure 17.1 is based on the findings of different national household income surveys. For example, the British government regularly collects information on family incomes which can then be used to establish the extent of poverty amongst the UK population. The national studies are collated by the EU's statistical department Eurostat and are made available in two forms: 'Poverty in Figures' compares income poverty for 1980 and 1985 whilst 'Poverty Statistics', compares income poverty for 1988. There are also 'one-off' studies which have compared countries by looking at indicators of lifestyle rather than income. The indicators include housing conditions and the possession of consumer durables such as a washing machine, a colour TV and a car. Households without the consumer durables are deemed to be poor. In one recent study people in different member states were also asked to provide a self-assessment of their lifestyle, and this was used to compare 'subjective poverty' in EU member states. The data available in these 'one-off' studies is also confined to the mid- to late 1980s. In spite of the range of definitions and indicators of poverty used, the different studies tend to show broadly similar trends for a similar period of time. Thus the data presented in Figure 17.1 provides a fairly good picture of national differences in poverty, based on some of the most up-to-date information available.

Further reading: H. Deleeck, K. van den Bosch and L. de Lathouwer (1992) *Poverty and the Adequacy of Social Security in the EC*, Aldershot: Avebury.

---

according to national poverty lines. They suggest clear differences between member states in the incidence of poverty. More than a third of Portugal's population were living in poverty in 1985, compared to 10 per cent for the Federal Republic of Germany. Of the relatively prosperous member states, the UK had the highest rate of poverty at 18 per cent.

It is arguable that poverty only has significance in the context of prevailing styles of living in particular societies (Mack and Lansley 1985; Townsend 1993). However, the use of national poverty lines to compare countries can result in anomalies. For example, many of those deemed to be poor in relatively prosperous countries such as Germany may be better off than average earners in countries with a lower GDP per capita – for example, Portugal (Oppenheim 1993). In view of this, it is also important to establish differences between countries using a common standard of poverty or a standard that measures the incidence of poverty within member states according to the average standard of living within Europe as a whole.

The distribution of poverty in Europe using a single EU poverty line is represented by the white bars in Figure 17.1. Poverty is defined as less than 50 per cent of average household expenditure throughout the EU.

Not surprisingly, this approach generates different results. Over two-thirds of Portugal's population were living in poverty in 1985 compared to very small

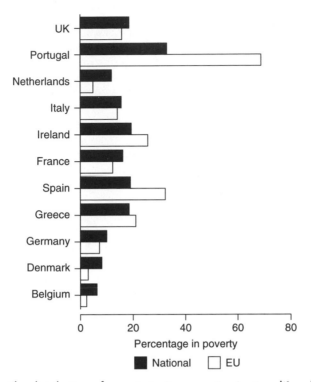

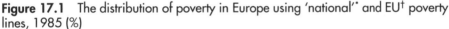

Figure 17.1 The distribution of poverty in Europe using 'national'* and EU† poverty lines, 1985 (%)

Source: Eurostat, 1990.

Notes: * The poverty line used is 50 per cent of national average household expenditure adjusted for family size. Luxembourg is not included in the Eurostat figures.

† The poverty line used is 50 per cent of community average household expenditure adjusted for family size.

proportions for countries of the centre and the north of Europe, Germany, Netherlands and Denmark.

The levels of poverty reflected in Figure 17.1 are not randomly distributed across the population, however, but disproportionately affect particular social groups. Owing to discrimination in employment, women in Europe are much more likely to be found in part-time work on low wages and with little job security. Moreover, European welfare states tend to reinforce women's exclusion from adequate employment opportunities. Many require women to take responsibility for unpaid work in the home, but those that do 'permit' paid employment encourage women to take up jobs that mirror their roles in the home. These jobs are usually low paid. In consequence, women as a group are much more likely to be excluded from acceptable standards of living. Lone mothers are at particular risk of falling onto the breadline.

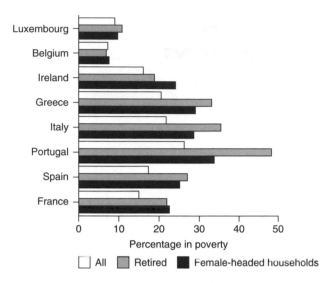

Figure 17.2 Poverty among lone mothers and pensioners in Europe, 1987/89 (%)

Source: Various national household budget surveys (see Ramprakash 1994).

Note: The poverty line used is 50 per cent of national average household expenditure adjusted for family size. The countries were selected because of the relative comparability of their surveys. The UK is not included here because data were not available. However, the patterns of inequality shown here are significant features of British society.

Figure 17.2 is based on data taken from household budget surveys in eight European countries between 1987 and 1989 (Ramprakash 1994). It represents the percentage of persons falling below 50 per cent of average household expenditure in each country, or relative poverty. The white bar represents the poverty average in each country and the black bar represents poverty among female-headed households. In all countries female-headed households experience higher than average poverty.

Age is also a good indicator of poverty. Research shows that older workers are routinely discriminated against by employers, leading to poor work prospects and higher than average unemployment. The onset of retirement increases the likelihood of economic disadvantage. There are two nations among pensioners in Europe; those with savings from a lifetime of employment and generous occupational pensions and those who are entirely dependent on state support. The grey bars in Figure 17.2 represent poverty among persons of retirement age. In most countries, poverty is significantly higher than the national average. Because of interrupted lifetime earnings and longer life expectancy, women form the majority of poor pensioners. The problem of poverty among Europe's pensioners and its causes are discussed at greater length by Giarchi and Abbott in Chapter 9 of this volume.

Ethnic minorities are considerably disadvantaged in Europe's labour market. They face discrimination and they tend to live in areas of economic decline, leading to high unemployment (Cross 1993). Non-EU nationals have fared the worst. Figure 17.3 shows the ratio of unemployed non-EU nationals to unemployed EU

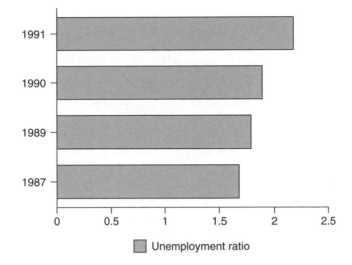

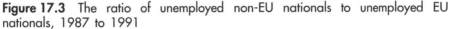

Figure 17.3 The ratio of unemployed non-EU nationals to unemployed EU nationals, 1987 to 1991

Source: European Labour Force Surveys.

Note: The bars represent the ratio of non-EU nationals that are employed for every EU national that is unemployed, for four particular years. They also provide an indirect measure of the effect of racial discrimination on patterns of unemployment.

nationals. It presents a stark image of restricted opportunities. For example, in 1991 there were more than two unemployed non-EU nationals for every one EU national out of work. This translates into higher than average levels of poverty.

Perhaps the highest levels of disadvantage are experienced by disabled people (Hyde 1996). In Britain, for example, they are two and a half times more likely to be discriminated against when applying for a job, even when their skills and qualifications are identical to those of a non-disabled applicant. Disabled people are routinely excluded from professional occupations and those in employment are often overlooked for promotion. A similar picture applies across Europe, although discrimination is less of a problem in France and Germany, because both countries apply swift legal penalties for discriminating employers. Disabled people across Europe experience profound economic disadvantage, suggesting that they are a 'dependent underclass'.

Explanations of poverty

Poverty in Europe has grown over the last fifteen years, but there is no universal agreement on the causes. However, an increasingly popular view among conservatives explains at least part of this growing poverty in terms of the rise of an underclass.

In the view of one leading exponent, Charles Murray (1990), the underclass is concentrated in 'lower working class neighbourhoods', where unmarried mothers constitute a 'hefty' majority of all households. In Murray's view, the absence of a male parent means that young men will grow into adulthood with no clear understanding of what it means to be a good father, leading to another generation of children ill-prepared to take advantage of opportunities.

The main culprit behind the rise of an underclass for Murray is the 'generous' welfare programmes that were promoted during the post-war years. Murray complains that social security benefits are enough to get by on without a male partner. Local authorities make lone parenting a viable option by prioritizing the housing needs of single mothers. Overall, the solution is simple. The underclass problem can be resolved through a combination of significant reductions in benefit programmes and tough prison sentences for violent offenders.

Murray's argument is based on the idea that a group of the poor are essentially different from the rest of society in terms of their values and behaviour. They do not place any importance on personal achievement, leading to failure at school and work and, ultimately, a life of poverty. Moreover, they make inadequate parents who fail to prepare their children for success as adults. Poverty is transmitted from generation to generation.

This argument is not new. In 1972, Sir Keith Joseph, Secretary of State for Social Services, announced that a minority of parents fail to prepare their children for success in the adult world, leading to a 'cycle of deprivation'. However, a massive research programme contradicted this view. The overall conclusion was that more than half of children born into disadvantage are not disadvantaged as adults. In other words, cultural transmission is not an adequate explanation of poverty.

Another explanation focuses on recent labour market trends (Hyde and Armstrong 1995). The fortunes of national economies have been increasingly dependent on investment decisions of transnational corporations. There is considerable competition for this investment, not just between EU member states but also between Europe and the countries of the Pacific Rim (see Chapter 22). Increasingly, transnational corporations have invested in global regions where labour organization and costs are low, leading to growing unemployment in the West. More recently, unemployment has fallen, but this has not translated into satisfactory employment opportunities.

European employers have attempted to attain greater labour market flexibility by promoting non-standard employment or temporary part-time work and self-employment. Non-standard employment has grown steadily over the last two decades and now accounts for a large proportion of labour market opportunities. Those in non-standard employment are typically paid less than other workers and they are more likely to experience unemployment and, therefore, a loss of earnings. In addition, they often receive a lower income when out of work because they don't qualify for social security benefits if their partners are working.

Growing poverty in Europe is also a consequence of national policies that have reduced employment and social protection in order to retain or attract capital investment. A study of five capitalist countries found that public debate has increasingly focused on the 'problem' of high labour costs (Pfaller *et al.* 1991). In Germany, employers have complained about what they see as excessive social contributions, and in France declining national competitiveness was blamed on rising unit labour costs. These fears translated into demands to strengthen national competitiveness in the international marketplace by reducing employment and social protection.

A coherent policy programme to achieve this aim was carried out in the UK only. An important feature of Conservative social policy during the 1980s was its aim to deregulate the labour market. This involved restrictions on the power of trade unions, significant reductions in employment rights, the promotion of 'less eligibility' in social security provision, and the development of employer-led training programmes for young adults and the long-term unemployed. British labour market policy during the 1980s represented a cohesive and far-reaching exercise in social engineering that met with considerable success.

Table 17.1 indicates that other member states also promoted similar measures, albeit without the same degree of ideological coherence and commitment. Most countries have abandoned a commitment to growing social expenditure, viewing it as harmful to national economic performance. Other evidence (Cross 1993) shows that spending on social protection as a proportion of gross domestic product fell consistently in all EU member states with the exception of Denmark. These problems of deindustrialization and welfare retrenchment have been referred to by the EU as examples of 'social dumping', a problem which is discussed further in the box.

SOCIAL DUMPING

A central feature of capitalism as an economic system is 'competition'. At its most basic level, individual workers compete for jobs by promoting their attractiveness to potential employers; for example, by acquiring skills and qualifications or by offering their labour to employers for less pay than other workers. At a broader level, nation-states compete to attract and retain investment in employment from multinational firms. They might do this by investing in education to improve the quality of the workforce or, alternatively, by reducing social security provision in order to drive down the price of labour. These competitive pressures were intensified by the Maastricht Treaty which created an internal market where there is free movement of capital, goods and labour. The threat of social dumping is a major problem associated with this trend. In 1993, 'Hoover Europe' announced the closure of its factory at Longvic in France, involving the loss of 600 out of 700 jobs. Production was relocated to the Hoover factory at Cambuslang in Scotland where workers had previously agreed to an effective reduction in pay and other conditions of employment. The Conservative government claimed this as a success of its policy of labour market deregulation because, in their view, firms are more likely to invest in geographical areas within Europe where employment and social protection are lower. A problem arises when other EU member states start to reduce their employment and social protection in order to compete effectively for investment. Social dumping results in unemployment, low pay, welfare retrenchment and therefore growing poverty.

Further reading: A. Amin and J. Tomaney (eds) (1995) *Behind the Myth of European Union*, London: Routledge.

TABLE 17.1 Retrenchments in welfare statism in five industrialized countries in the 1970s and 1980s

	USA	Britain	France	Germany	Sweden
Tax cuts	*	*	(*)	(*)	
Regressive shifts in the tax load	*	*	(*)	*	(*)
Reduced benefits for recipients of state transfers	*	(*)	(*)	(*)	(*)†
Reduced eligibility for state transfers	*	*	(*)		
Reduced social services		*			
Residualization of benefits and services to the poor	(*)	*		(*)	
Reduced formation of social capital		*	*	(*)	
Reduced coverage of occupational benefits	*				
Reduction of public in favour of private provision		*			
Rising unemployment		*	*	*	
Rising inequality	*	*	(*)	(*)	

* Indicates a policy shift.

(*) Indicates a policy move of minor importance.

A blank space indicates that the policy did not apply or that the opposite policy was carried out.

† Temporary measure.

Overall, it is labour market change and welfare retrenchment that have led to growing poverty – not the rise of an underclass as suggested by Charles Murray and the New Right. Poverty is primarily a consequence of the operation of labour markets, but it is also associated with recent changes in social policy across Europe including the reduction of employment and social protection.

The 'social dimension' of the European Union

In order to understand the impact of the European Union on poverty in Europe we need to be aware of certain constraints restricting its ability to develop and implement anti-poverty programmes (Amin and Tomaney 1995). In particular, we must consider its limited legal competence in the 'social field' and the lack of political consensus between member states on social policy.

The Treaty of Rome in 1957 set up an essentially economic, market-orientated union whose central objective was to secure a common market and area of free trade. It envisaged limited intervention in the area of social policy principally as a means of securing a level economic playing field and to facilitate the free movement of workers. Improvements in living standards – and reductions in poverty – were seen to be a by-product of economic expansion and therefore left largely to market forces.

Article 119 on the principle of equal pay is perhaps the most powerful piece of legislation affecting the living standards of EU citizens. Concerned with reducing a key cause of poverty amongst women employees and their families, it seeks to reduce the ability of employers to exploit women employees through discriminatory wage settlements. However, the legislation is limited by the requirement for a woman to identify a comparator male employed by the same organization or covered by the same collective agreement in order to prove discrimination. This has restricted the ability of the legislation to tackle a major cause of gender inequality – namely occupational segregation (where men and women are concentrated into different occupational groups).

The lack of progress in reducing sex discrimination does not reflect a lack of commitment on the part of the EU as such; indeed the European Commission and the Women's Rights Committee of the European Parliament have campaigned actively for the introduction of further measures to improve the position of women in the labour market. Limited progress is due to a combination of the weak legal base for social policy in general and a lack of political consensus across member states. The requirement for unanimity in voting procedures, in particular, has meant that individual member states (notably the UK) have been able to effectively block initiatives in this area.

The only area in which it could be said that the EU had begun to develop a coherent policy in relation to social rights is in relation to the rights of migrant workers under the Free Movement of Persons Provisions (Article 48 EEC). The free movement provisions were included in the founding Treaty in order to promote the free movement of labour and secure the wider objectives of the internal market. They do not provide a common floor of social protection but seek to prevent discrimination on grounds of nationality. Entitlement to such rights is, however, dependent upon employment status. The families and spouses of migrant workers also have a right to accompany the worker but they have no independent rights to social assistance; their rights are derived from the migrant worker.

In addition to the development of social rights through legislation, the EU also has a limited role in the funding of social policy through its structural funds. The structural funds are EU budgets that are used to provide financial support for initiatives in member states and include the European Social Fund (ESF), the European Regional Development Fund (ERDF) and the Common Agricultural Policy (CAP). Together these funds account for only 3 per cent of the gross domestic product of the Union (European Commission 1992). An evaluation of their impact must therefore be seen in the context of their limited size.

The ESF is geared primarily to the retraining of workers and improvements in labour supply, whilst the ERDF focuses on capital investment in regional development to promote industrial expansion and labour demand. Both of these measures have also been used as a means of regulating labour mobility. Indeed when the ESF became operational in 1962 initial allocations were used to promote the skills training of migrant workers in order to facilitate the free movement of labour (as a means of overcoming unemployment). The ERDF, on the other hand, has been seen as a means of preventing the depopulation and decline of peripheral regions through regional development. Rather than encouraging workers to leave areas of high unemployment by providing them with the skills to migrate the policy emphasis has shifted to the improvement of employment prospects in declining regions themselves. In practice these funds now work closely together as the main focus of EU regional policy. The CAP, which accounts for some 60 per cent of EU funding, is not specifically concerned with poverty but with the regulation of agricultural production through direct income subsidies to farmers.

The scope of the structural funds, as a means of reducing poverty in Europe is, at present, clearly limited. They serve essentially as compensatory devices to facilitate the achievement of broader economic objectives (such as the restructuring of major industries) through regional regeneration and local economic development – apart from the CAP, which provides a form of income support albeit to many who could not be defined as 'poor' – as such, they are, once again, primarily labour market initiatives.

In addition to the structural funds and legal developments under Articles 48 and 119 of the Treaty of Rome, the European Commission has run three research-based programmes concerned directly with the issue of social exclusion (known as Poverty One, Two and Three). These programmes were essentially 'task orientated', in that they involved action research projects working with the poor to identify routes out of poverty. The most recent to be completed, Poverty Three, aimed to foster the social integration of the most excluded groups in the Union. In a pioneering role, a small number of projects aimed to develop prototype models of intervention that could subsequently be adopted by public authorities across Europe (Alcock 1993).

There is little doubt that the three Poverty programmes have raised the public profile of poverty in Europe. Moreover, they pioneered grassroots modes of intervention that could be used to complement formal income maintenance systems in the fight against social exclusion. However, there are problems.

First is the problem of seriously limited funding. Poverty One, for example, operated on a shoestring budget that amounted to only 2 per cent of the European Social Fund. Poverty Two was similarly funded to the tune of 0.2 ECUs per head of Europe's poor. Measured in terms of financial resources, then, the scope of the Poverty programmes was negligible (Alcock 1993).

Second is their limited influence. They aimed to set examples of intervention which could then be followed in more substantial terms by member states, but they have largely been ignored. Although a small number of local authorities in Europe have developed anti-poverty work, most national anti-poverty regimes in Europe experienced retrenchment. The Poverty programmes have had a limited impact on poverty in member states due to their essentially persuasive and symbolic role. They illustrate well the limitations of EU action in an area of limited legal competency and during a period of economic crisis and ideological conflict.

The Social Chapter and EU social policy

Political conflict over Union competence in the social field came to a head in the debate surrounding the inclusion of the Social Chapter in the Treaty on European Union 1992 (the Maastricht Treaty). The Social Chapter itself is concerned largely with industrial relations issues and the promotion of dialogue and consultation between the two sides of industry. It also reiterates Union commitment to improve living standards, promote the health and safety of workers, combat social exclusion through labour market integration, and equal pay. Article 2.3 is more ambitious in its scope and talks of action on social security and social protection for workers and the conditions of employment of third-country nationals. It is significant, however, that the requirement of unanimity is retained for these last two measures thus reducing their potential for promoting opportunities.

The UK was opposed to the inclusion of the Social Chapter in the Treaty on European Union, partly because of ideological conflict over the measures themselves but also because of its view that the introduction of qualified majority voting for many of the measures would amount to a further loss in sovereignty (in other words a single member state would no longer be able to veto a proposal). As a result of political compromise the Social Chapter became a separate 'Protocol on Social Policy' annexed to the Treaty but signed by only eleven member states (with the UK excluded). The precise implication of this for EU action to combat poverty is uncertain; the eleven member states who have signed the Protocol may now have a freer hand to steer the direction of social policy by taking measures under the Protocol and avoiding UK opposition. The recent Works Council Directive was the first to be taken through this route. There are two key reasons why this may not happen, however: firstly it could result in a two-tier Europe and consequent 'social dumping' as industry chooses to locate in the UK as a result of its lower social costs and, secondly, because vigorous action in the social field under the Protocol may contravene the principle of subsidiarity embedded within the Maastricht Treaty (Article 3b).

The debate about subsidiarity is essentially about establishing the appropriate level of decision-making in the EU. It concerns all aspects of EU policy, but has been invoked particularly in relation to social policy to curb EU intervention in domestic social policy. This can be expected to restrict the ability of the Union to develop a coherent anti-poverty programme at European level.

The Green Paper on Social Policy published by the European Commission in 1994 marked the beginning of a consultation exercise on the future social policy role of the EU. The document identified a series of 'social challenges' facing Europe and a set of possible policy responses including, for example, the idea of minimum income provision and the provision of a job, training or 'activity' for all those seeking work. A more recent White Paper on Social Policy resisted pressure for further dilution of social protection, offering additional protection for part-time workers, stronger health and safety provisions, a new look at equal opportunities and possible extension of rights under the free movement provisions to non-Union nationals.

It can be seen from the preceding discussion that the social policy role of the EU is largely restricted to employment-related issues with member states retaining exclusive competence in other areas of social policy. The equal pay legislation and the extension of rights under the free movement provisions primarily benefit workers as do the opportunities for retraining under the Social Fund. In so far as it has a role to play in reducing poverty and social inequality EU intervention can thus be expected to increase the relationship between paid employment and social citizenship, thereby marginalizing those citizens outside of the formal labour market.

The future

As far as poverty and welfare policy are concerned, Britain shares a number of common experiences with the rest of the EU while also remaining quite distinct. The emergence of 'social dumping' as an issue and the rise of Europe as an economic and political entity are clear examples.

Labour market flexibility, unemployment and low pay have led to an intensification of poverty throughout the member states of the EU. Reference has already been made to the economic imperatives that have prompted welfare retrenchment in Europe. In addition, mass welfare is increasingly losing popular support. Offe (1996) explains how the European labour force has experienced a process of 'de-massification', causing a growing polarization between a skilled employed core, a partially employed periphery and the unemployed. Growing occupational diversity has undermined the post-war welfare consensus which favoured limited redistribution through state welfare provision. Instead, large sections of Europe's population routinely support political parties that aim to promote reductions in personal taxation and an expansion of private welfare. Declining levels of national social provision will make the position of Europe's poor even more precarious causing some observers to speculate about the rise of a European 'underclass'.

Whilst these problems affect the EU as whole, they have been particularly marked in Britain which has been enthusiastically committed to a policy of labour market deregulation and reductions in state welfare provision. Driven by the free market policies of the New Right, inequality and poverty grew more rapidly than in any other EU member state. In this sense, Britain has more in common with the US than with the EU. Both have similar approaches to welfare policy informed by the New Right and both are prepared to endorse growing inequalities as an acceptable price to pay for economic growth.

EU membership is also an experience that the UK shares with many other countries, but the benefits are less than certain. The EU is largely an economic enterprise, informed by monetarist ideas about economic activity and involving the creation of a free internal market. Economic union on its own would almost certainly lead to unemployment, low pay and rapidly growing social inequalities, as recognized in the important EU policy document *Growth, Competitiveness and Employment*. It is this recognition that has prompted the development of the notion 'Social Europe', to emphazise that European integration is also about convergence around adequate social minima. However, this is a far cry from the reality of EU social policy. The EU has developed some important initiatives, but its scope and competence in the field of social policy is, for the present at least, limited.

Britain is a part of the internal market, which means that it shares with other EU member states the increased risk of social dumping that this brings. However, the UK has also opted out of certain aspects of EU membership, which means that its citizens have even less protection from European social policy. Low pay and poverty seem to be a likely consequence of this unique position *vis-à-vis* the EU.

Fifty years after the creation of the welfare state, poverty in the UK is on the increase. This partly results from factors that are affecting the EU as a whole, but it also reflects the UK government's distinct approach to social policy. Where the New Right is a challenge to the EU, it has been actively embraced by Conservative governments in this country. On the issue of social welfare Britain is clearly in, but also apart from, Europe.

Summary

- Unemployment, low pay and job insecurity have increased throughout Europe, leading to rising inequalities and poverty.
- Governments have reduced employment and social protection in order to attract investment from multinational firms. This is a trend that is likely to continue.
- The European Union has developed a number of social policy programmes and proposals, but they have limited powers and resources. EU social policy will not be sufficient to make significant inroads into European poverty.

Further reading

Pete Alcock (1993) *Understanding Poverty*, London: Macmillan. Written by the most respected UK author on poverty and social security, this book covers the full range of issues including the definition and measurement of poverty, its explanation and the experiences of specific social groups including women, ethnic minorities, disabled people and older people. It also looks at the development and structure of the UK social security system. There is something for everyone in this book.

Phillip Brown and Rosemary Crompton (eds) (1994) *A New Europe?: Economic Restructuring and Social Exclusion*, London: UCL Press. This book examines the relationship between recent changes in the labour market and the growth of poverty in Europe. Separate chapters look at unemployment, part-time employment, women's work and discrimination against ethnic minorities. The book provides evidence that poverty in the countries of the European Union is rapidly becoming a serious problem.

Ash Amin and John Tomaney (eds) (1995) *Behind the Myth of the European Union*, London: Routledge. This book is one of the most authoritative of recent works on the effects of European integration on patterns of inequality. Although it tends to focus on the difficulties that EU member states are experiencing, it ends on an optimistic note. It outlines a promising alternative to the 'free-market' scenario of deregulation, welfare retrenchment and poverty.

Chapter 18

Health, healthcare and health inequalities

Pamela Abbott and
George Giacinto Giarchi

Introduction	360
Health in Europe	360
Formal healthcare	363
Health and healthcare	365
Healthcare and health inequalities	371
The power of medicine	373
Reflection	377
Summary	377
Further reading	377

Key concepts

- **Health inequalities**
- **Structural explanations**
- **Material deprivation**
- **The new public health**

Introduction

In this chapter we are going to consider some of the issues that are of interest to sociologists of health. In the last twenty years or so sociologists have become increasingly interested in developing explanations for health inequalities. Following the reasoning of the nineteenth-century sociologist Emile Durkheim they have argued that the pattern of health inequalities in Western societies cannot adequately be explained either by biological differences between people or individual behaviour. Instead they have argued it is necessary to develop sociological explanations that take account of social inequalities between groups. These inequalities, sociologists argue, are structural – that is, they are caused by the way in which society is organized and, consequently, reductions in health inequalities can only come about by social intervention not by changing individual behaviour. Thus the most powerful determinants of health are social, economic and cultural circumstances and improvements in health will only come about from a reduction in social disadvantage and inegalitarian economic, social and health policies. The New Public Health is the development of health promotion strategies that explicitly recognize that health is affected by social and economic factors and not purely by individual decisions. Sociological research indicates that the major determinant of health inequalities is material deprivation – low income, poor housing, deprived environments – and that reductions in health inequalities are achieved by raising the living standard of the poorest members of a society.

Health in Europe

The populations of European Union countries are comparatively healthy, especially when compared to those of less industrialized countries. Life expectancy (the number of years a person can expect to live from birth) is high and increasing (Table 18.1). Standardized general mortality rates (death rates corrected to allow for the demographic structure of the population) and infant mortality rates (the rate of deaths of people aged less than a year per thousand live births) are comparatively low and continuing to decline (see Table 18.2). Indeed, the populations of the EU countries are the healthiest in the world, except for the Japanese. However, while the overall health of the population is good, there remains a considerable 'health divide', with those who are materially deprived having poor health as measured by morbidity (illness) and mortality (death). Sociologists have argued that this health divide arises not so much from inequalities in access to healthcare (although this may well be a factor) as from wider social and economic inequalities. Furthermore, it is evident that medical science can do little to cure people of the major killer diseases and that preventive strategies may be more productive. Sociologists have also suggested, looking back to the public health movement of the nineteenth century, that strategies aimed at populations are more likely to be effective than individualized health education campaigns. Nevertheless, demands for healthcare continue to grow both as a result of the ageing of the population and because of the development of new, high-cost

TABLE 18.1 Life expectancy at birth (years) in Europe, 1960 and 1991

	Men		Women	
	1960	*1991*	*1960*	*1991*
EUR 12	67.3	72.9	72.7	79.5
Austria	n/a	72.6	n/a	79.1
Belgium	67.7	72.8	73.5	79.5
Denmark	70.4	72.5	74.4	78.0
Finland	n/a	71.3	n/a	79.3
France	66.9	72.9	73.6	80.1
Germany*	n/a	72.1	n/a	79.1
Greece	67.3	74.6	70.4	79.8
Ireland	68.1	72.2	71.9	77.7
Italy	67.2	73.6	72.3	80.3
Luxembourg	66.5	72.3	72.2	79.1
Netherlands	71.5	74.0	75.3	80.1
Norway	n/a	74.0	n/a	80.1
Portugal	61.2	70.2	66.9	77.5
Spain	67.4	73.3	72.2	80.5
Sweden	n/a	74.9	n/a	80.5
UK	67.9	73.2	73.7	78.6

Sources: EC (1992: 85) and EU (1996: 10).

Note: * Figures for 1991 are for the unified Germany.

TABLE 18.2 Trends in standardized mortality rates per thousand inhabitants in Europe, by gender

	Men		Women	
	1960–4	*1980–4*	*1960–4*	*1980–4**
Belgium	14.44	12.54	9.71	7.41
Denmark	11.98	11.48	n/a	7.66
France	14.42	11.21	8.84	6.01
Germany (West)	14.50	12.31	10.06	7.36
Greece	11.08	9.62	8.71	6.91
Ireland	14.01	13.19	10.67	8.51
Italy	13.47	11.48	9.56	6.89
Luxembourg	n/a	13.42	n/a	8.14
Netherlands	11.24	10.65	8.24	5.98
Portugal	15.79	13.01	11.31	8.16
Spain	13.02	10.06	9.61	8.17
UK	14.71	12.22	9.39	7.48

Source: EC (1992).

Note: * Most recent data available.

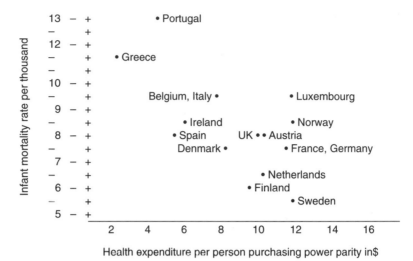

Figure 18.1 Health expenditure per person and infant mortality rate, 1988
Source: Derived from OECD 1991.

technologies and treatments. All the countries of the EU spend a comparatively high proportion of their GNP (gross national product) on healthcare, and especially on curative medical sciences.

However, there is no evidence that there is a causal relationship between increased healthcare spending and improved health, at the higher levels of spending. Health expenditure in the United States is greater than that of Europe, as a proportion of GNP, but the health record of the United States is not as good as that of Europe in terms of life expectancy and infant mortality (Wennemo 1993). An OECD report in 1981 indicated only a weak relationship between spending on formal healthcare and standardized mortality rates in Western European countries (see Figure 18.1).

With the election to power of New Right governments in some countries of Western Europe and the desire by a majority to reduce public expenditure, there have been attempts to contain the costs of formal healthcare provision in many countries. A number – including the United Kingdom, Finland, Sweden, the Netherlands and Germany (see Aslund 1990; Blee 1991; te Maarssen and Janssen 1994) – have attempted to introduce competition into healthcare provision, arguing that this will ensure that medical care is provided more effectively and efficiently. However, the market system of healthcare provision in use in the United States appears to be both less effective and less efficient than the social healthcare systems of Western Europe. Not only is healthcare expenditure greater in the USA, but an estimated 17 per cent of the population have no health insurance cover at all (D'Intignano 1993) and there are much greater health inequalities than in Western Europe.

TABLE 18.3 Organization of European healthcare systems

	'System 1'	'System 2'
Countries	Denmark, Ireland, Italy, Greece, Norway, Portugal, Spain, Sweden, UK	Belgium, France, Germany, Luxembourg, Netherlands
Decision-maker	Government	Sickness fund
Financing	Taxes	Contributions
Benefits in kind	Denmark, Ireland, Italy, Greece, Norway, Portugal, Spain, Sweden, UK	Germany
Recompense for healthcare expenditure	–	France, Luxembourg, Netherlands
Service providers	Mainly public	Mainly private

Formal healthcare

Western European nations all have formal systems of healthcare providing more or less comprehensive coverage – although in all of them the emphasis is on curative rather than preventive healthcare. The state plays a major role in ensuring that all citizens have comprehensive healthcare coverage, but there are two different ways in which this is achieved. The first is the system of, for example, the UK, where there is a state-provided National Health Service funded mainly out of taxation. The second is the system of, for example, Germany, where every employee has to be a member of a sickness fund or to opt out of the statutory system and join a private scheme. The differences are illustrated in Table 18.3.

In all Western European states a majority of healthcare is funded by taxation and/or compulsory contributions. However, private insurance and out-of-pocket expenses amount to a third of expenditure in Switzerland, 27 per cent in the Netherlands and 23 per cent in France. By contrast only 8 per cent of health spending is private in Sweden and 7 per cent in Britain (Maxwell 1981).

Thus in all Western European countries medical care cover is compulsory for the vast majority of citizens – whether the payments are derived mainly from general taxation, from state insurance earmarked for healthcare or from other insurance schemes. The main sources of private funding are voluntary insurance schemes and direct or 'out-of-pocket' payments by individuals, such as the over-the-counter purchase of drugs or charges for a particular service or treatment. Philanthropic organizations often provide care without formal payment, and consequently their contribution to healthcare is often under-calculated. They do, however, continue to play a significant role in many countries. In the United Kingdom, for example, it has been estimated that voluntary help to hospitals is equivalent to about 300,000 full-time workers. These volunteers spent most of their time on administrative tasks and fund-raising (CIPFA 1984: 33).

The contribution to healthcare spending by the public sector has risen considerably since the 1960s. However, since the 1980s governments have been concerned to reduce public expenditure, including public expenditure on healthcare. A number of governments in Western Europe have introduced health service reforms aimed at increasing efficiency and thus reducing the cost of healthcare. In Britain, for example, the 1990 National Health Service and Community Care Act introduced managed markets, the argument being that the ensuing element of competition would result in increasing emphasis on providing care in the community – especially for older people. This would reduce costs to the state not only because caring for people in their own homes is less costly than providing residential care but because it relies to a considerable extent on the unpaid care of kin, especially women.

Healthcare spending remains relatively high, however, in all Western European countries and continues to grow. Although there arc differences between European countries in the amount spent, the gulf between Northern and Southern – rich and poor – is much greater than that between Western European countries. Using a stable conversion rate between currencies in order to make them comparable in terms of the price of goods and services within different countries – purchasing power parity (PPP) – it is possible to see that while many less industrialized countries spent less than a thousand units per person on healthcare in 1990, Greece, the lowest-spending EU country, spent just under 8,000 units (OECD 1991: Tables 4, 8 and 29). The differences between EU countries are nevertheless fairly large, with the Northern European countries generally spending more than the Southern ones. France, for example, spends nearly twice as much on formal healthcare per person as Ireland. Greece spends the least per person of the EU countries; Germany spends four times as much. Germany also spends three times as much as Portugal and twice as much as Spain.

The major reason for the variation in healthcare spending per person is variation in level of national income. Broadly, the higher the level of national income, the higher the spending per person on formal healthcare (Figure 18.2).

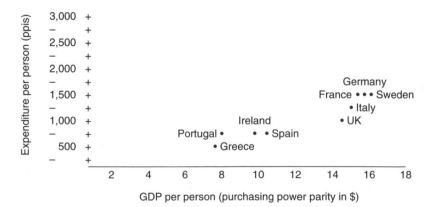

Figure 18.2 Health expenditure and GDP per person, 1988–90
Source: Derived from OECD 1991, Tables 4, 8 and 29.

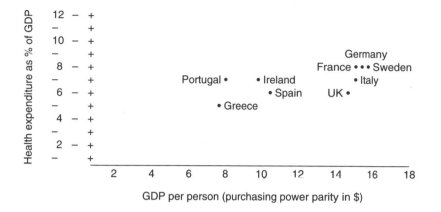

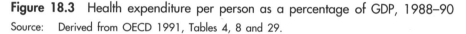

Figure 18.3 Health expenditure per person as a percentage of GDP, 1988–90
Source: Derived from OECD 1991, Tables 4, 8 and 29.

However, higher-income countries also seem systematically to devote a larger and larger proportion of their income to formal healthcare. Broadly, countries with a higher GDP per person also devote a larger share of their national income to formal healthcare. The UK is somewhat of an exception to this rule, having the same GDP per person as Italy but spending less per person on healthcare (Figure 18.3). It seems that the richer a country is, the more it tends to spend on health.

This is borne out not only by the differences in spending on healthcare comparing rich and poor countries but also, as we have seen, if we compare richer and poorer countries within Europe. It is also the case that spending on healthcare as a proportion of GDP has increased steadily in all Western European societies as they have become wealthier – although spending has increased at a faster rate in some than in others. In 1960 the OECD average was 4 per cent of GDP, as was the UK's. In 1990 the OECD average had nearly doubled to over 7.5 per cent of GDP, while that of the UK stood at just over 6 per cent (OECD 1991). However, the rate of increase has declined in recent years and the public share of healthcare expenditure has also declined – the decline being more marked in the UK than the OECD average, although the proportion of total health-care spending contributed by the public sector remains higher in the UK than in the OECD as a whole (Figure 18.4).

Health and healthcare

All Western European societies have a relatively high standard of living, good healthcare systems and a reasonably healthy population when compared with less industrialized countries. None the less, there is variety in spending on health-care (as we have seen) which correlates highly with the GDP of the country. However, whether there is a causal relationship between increased health

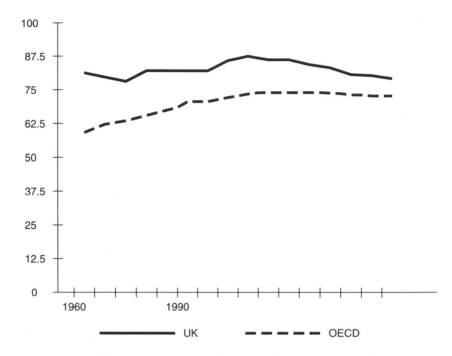

Figure 18.4 Public percentage of health expenditure, OECD and UK

expenditure and improved health at the highest level of spending is debatable. The United States, for example, spends considerably more on health than Western European countries but has on average poorer health, while Japan spends less than Sweden, France or Germany and about the same as Italy but has a better health record (Gray and Davey 1993). Nevertheless, using mortality (death) data it is possible to demonstrate that the general health of the populations in European Union countries has been improving. Arguably one of the most sensitive indicators of the general health of a country is its infant mortality rate. Table 18.4 shows that the infant mortality rate for the European WHO region as a whole in the early 1980s was 36.05 per thousand births, but this average included countries such as Turkey, Albania, Yugoslavia and Romania. All the European Union countries had lower rates than this average: Portugal was the highest with a rate of 16.7 and Finland the lowest with 6.1: Portugal was the highest with a rate of 16.7 and Finland the lowest with 6.1). By the 1990s Portugal's IMR had declined to 9.3, Sweden's to 5.3 and Finland's to 5.1. The industrialized nation with the lowest infant mortality rate in the world is Japan, with a rate of less than 5.

There appears to be some relationship (correlation) between health spending and infant mortality rate (IMR) (see Figure 18.1) – countries with a lower level of healthcare spending tend to have higher IMRs – but the relationship is a weak one. Greece spends the least on healthcare per person of all European Union countries but has a lower infant mortality rate than Portugal.

TABLE 18.4 Infant mortality rates in Europe

	1970s data: rate per thousand live births	Year of data	1980s data: rate per thousand live births	1992 data: rate per thousand live births
European region	49.34	1982	36.05	n/a
Austria	25.90	1983	11.90	7.5
Belgium	21.10	1984	10.10	8.0
Denmark	14.20	1983	7.71	6.6
Finland	13.20	1982	6.10	5.2
France	18.20	1982	9.40	6.8
Germany (E)	18.50	1984	10.00	}6.2
Germany (W)	23.60	1983	10.20	
Greece	29.60	1982	15.10	8.4
Ireland	19.50	1984	10.10	6.7
Italy	29.60	1982	13.00	8.3
Luxembourg	24.90	1984	10.00	8.5
Netherlands	12.70	1983	8.40	6.3
Norway	12.70	1983	7.90	5.8
Portugal	58.00	1984	16.70	9.3
Spain	26.30	1982	9.60	7.4
Sweden	11.00	1983	7.00	5.3
Switzerland	15.10	1983	7.60	6.4
United Kingdom	18.50	1983	10.00	6.6

Source: WHO data, derived from Towers (1992; Table 10.4), and EU (1996: 16).

Similarly, Ireland and Spain spend less than Belgium, Italy and Luxembourg and yet have lower infant mortality rates.

The maternal mortality rate has also declined in EU countries during the last twenty to thirty years (Table 18.5). Portugal had the highest level of maternal mortality of EU countries in the 1980s, along with the highest infant mortality rate; indeed, its maternal mortality rate was higher than the average for the European WHO region as a whole. The lowest rates were in Luxembourg and Norway, which both had no maternal deaths in the relevant year. (While these figures undoubtedly reflect these countries' low maternal mortality rate they also reflect their low population, and to gain a true picture it would be necessary to average maternal mortality rate over a number of years.)

The major 'killers' in the European Union are accidents – despite a decline in deaths and injuries on the roads – and the so-called diseases of affluence. (In the less industrialized countries, contagious diseases remain the major killers – as they were in the West until this century.) Death rates from many of these illnesses have declined in EU countries in the last thirty years, with the steepest decline, on average, in those countries with the highest levels of healthcare spending. All EU countries have experienced a decline in the mortality rate for cardiovascular disease, but there are considerable differences between countries. Finland, despite showing a 30 per cent decline in mortality rate for cardiovascular disease between 1971 and 1981, from 192.6 to 133.6, still had the highest rate in

TABLE 18.5 Maternal mortality rates in Europe

	1970s data		1980s data	
	Year of data	Rate per thousand live births	Year of data*	Rate per thousand live births
European region	1971	36.93	1982	19.75
Austria	1970	25.82	1983	11.10
Belgium	1973	12.40	1982	7.21
Denmark	1972	4.00	1981	3.80
Finland	1971	8.20	1981	4.73
France	1970	28.10	1981	15.50
Germany (E)	1970	43.00	1981	14.73
Germany (W)	1973	45.90	1984	10.78
Greece	1972	29.80	1981	11.40
Ireland	1971	25.20	1981	4.16
Italy	1970	54.50	1979	12.20
Luxembourg	1973	52.60	1984	0.00
Netherlands	1973	10.30	1983	5.29
Norway	1973	3.30	1982	0.00
Portugal	1971	54.50	1982	22.51
Spain	1970	33.10	1979	10.40
Sweden	1970	9.90	1981	4.30
Switzerland	1972	21.90	1981	6.80
United Kingdom	1972	15.52	1982	6.95

Source: WHO data, derived from Towers (1992: Table 10.5).

Note: * Most recent data available.

Europe in the 1980s; the risk of dying of cardiovascular disease in Finland was more than twice the risk in France, for example (Towers 1992: Table 10.1). The United Kingdom also had a comparatively high death rate from cardiovascular disease. The decline has continued into the 1990s, with a few notable exceptions, women having a lower mortality rate than men (Table 18.6). Deaths from cancer have tended to increase, especially for men (Table 18.7); for women there is no clear trend, with some countries showing a marginal increase and others a slight decrease. Deaths from cervical cancer have declined significantly in most European countries in the late twentieth century, although Spain and Greece have shown an increase. Again there appears to be no clear relationship between the mortality rate from cancer and healthcare spending.

Notable examples where the mortality rates have increased are cancer of the trachea, bronchus and lungs and AIDS-related deaths. Cancer of the respiratory system is highly correlated with cigarette smoking, and the link is likely to be causal. Only two European countries – Finland and the United Kingdom – showed a decline in deaths from cancer of the respiratory system between the 1970s and 1980s (Table 18.8), although the death rate in the UK in 1983 was still well above the European average and higher than the rate in most EU countries. More recent statistics (EU 1996: 30) indicate that by the early 1990s the death

TABLE 18.6 Standardized mortality rates for cardiovascular disease in Europe, 1983 and 1990, men and women

	1983		1990*	
	Men	Women	Men	Women
Austria	169	134	117	88
Belgium	115	96	80	67
Denmark	85	69	104	89
Finland	120	100	78	66
France	102	74	71	48
Germany (unified)	134	106	101	80
Greece	144	155	136	133
Ireland	126	116	96	80
Italy	141	109	110	82
Luxembourg	195	155	151	117
Netherlands	84	68	77	62
Norway	104	83	92	77
Portugal	287	217	223	194
Spain	133	115	102	83
Sweden	80	67	72	64
Switzerland	88	70	66	51
United Kingdom	110	99	97	84

Source: WHO data, derived from EU (1996: 26).

Note: * The '1990' Belgian data are in fact for 1989.

TABLE 18.7 Trends in the cancer standardized mortality rates by gender per thousand inhabitants in Europe

	Men		Women	
	1960–4	1991*	1960–4	1991*
Belgium	2.62	3.13	1.84	1.60
Denmark	2.47	2.79	2.09	2.01
France	2.57	2.98	1.55	1.29
Germany	2.53	2.69	1.80	1.60
Greece	1.71	2.17	1.05	1.11
Ireland	2.02	2.68	1.62	1.82
Italy	2.11	2.85	1.45	1.45
Luxembourg	n/a	3.01	n/a	1.70
Netherlands	2.51	2.96	1.79	1.62
Portugal	1.57	2.28	1.17	1.30
Spain	1.90	2.53	1.30	1.18
UK	2.67	2.76	1.68	1.86

Source: EU (1996: 143).

Note: * The '1991' Belgian data are in fact for 1989.

TABLE 18.8 Standardized mortality rates for cancer of the trachea, bronchus and lung in Europe, among people aged 0–64

	1970s data		1980s data	
	Year of data	Rate per thousand live births	Year of data	Rate per thousand live births
European region	1972	16.68	1981	19.90
Austria	1973	15.50	1983	16.92
Belgium	1973	24.30	1983	28.32
Denmark	1972	20.60	1983	25.50
Finland	1971	22.90	1981	20.90
France	1972	13.30	1981	16.90
Germany (E)	1973	15.80	1982	16.64
Germany (W)	1973	13.90	1982	16.40
Greece	1972	13.50	1981	17.10
Ireland	1971	20.80	1981	22.03
Italy	1970	16.20	1979	21.70
Luxembourg	1973	20.70	1982	29.30
Netherlands	1973	23.90	1983	22.70
Norway	1973	8.90	1982	13.70
Portugal	1971	6.60	1979	8.60
Spain	1970	9.40	1979	12.76
Sweden	1973	8.60	1982	10.80
Switzerland	1972	16.90	1981	18.60
United Kingdom	1972	30.10	1983	26.27

Source: WHO data, derived from Towers (1992: Table 10.2).

rate from lung cancer among men was declining in the United Kingdom, Luxembourg, the Netherlands, Belgium, Austria, Finland, Denmark and Ireland, but that it was continuing to rise for women in all EU countries with the exceptions of Spain and Ireland. The decline, where it has occurred, is likely to be linked to the series of health education campaigns and government measures designed to reduce the amount of smoking.

The major exception to the decline in the importance of infectious diseases as a cause of mortality in Western countries is AIDS, which has been described as a global epidemic. The numbers of reported AIDS cases have increased during the 1980s and 1990s in all EU countries. Despite widespread health education and governmental concern there does not seem to be a real decline in the rate of increase (EU 1996: 20). At this time medical science can offer little in the way of treatment to victims of the disease, and the only preventive measures are those individuals can take to reduce the risk of being contaminated by infected blood. However, despite all the concern about AIDS, the mortality rate from AIDS-related deaths is still considerably lower than that from cardiovascular disease.

Healthcare and health inequalities

There are vast inequalities in health experience and standard of health between the rich and the poor, between First World and less industrialized countries. In the industrialized countries the main killers, as we have seen, are the so-called diseases of affluence – heart disease and cancers – while in the less industrialized countries the major killers are infectious diseases. Life expectancy and quality of life is much higher in the North than in the South. However, there are also inequalities in health within the rich countries of the North. Not only do those in managerial occupations experience better health and have a longer life expectancy than those in manual occupations, but they also tend to receive better healthcare even in socialized healthcare systems. Tudor Hart (1971) called this 'the inverse care law': the groups in the population with the poorest health also receive the poorest healthcare. In France, the Netherlands and the United Kingdom there is clear evidence of regional health inequalities in provision (Maynard and Ludbrook 1981: 62), with the narrowest gap in the United Kingdom, where the best-endowed region was +13 from a fair share of expenditure and the least endowed –9; the comparable figures for France are +31 and –57.

Inequalities in health (as measured by morbidity and mortality rates) exist in all Western European countries. They are lowest in the Scandinavian countries and the Netherlands and most marked in the countries of Southern Europe. Health inequalities mirror class inequalities (income and job opportunities) and countries with less class division in general have higher life expectancies (Wilkinson 1992; Wennemo 1993). The risk of men dying in the lowest occupational group is 1.2 or 1.5 times the risk in the highest occupational group in a number of Scandinavian countries (excluding Finland) and 2.0 in England and Wales and in Finland (Mackenback 1992). There are similar, if less marked, differences in the ratio of age-standardized prevalence of self-reported chronic illness, when the lowest and the highest income quartiles are compared; the lowest is 1.07 times larger than the highest in Denmark, 1.25 in the Netherlands, 1.26 in Norway, 1.28 in Sweden and 1.75 in Finland (Mackenback 1992).

Sweden, for example, despite the fact that it has overall one of the best health records in the world, still has inequalities in health. Mortality statistics show a moderate social gradient between major occupational groups, with those in manual occupations having higher mortality rates on average than the non-manual rates. Men in service industries, seamen, miners and commercial travellers have high mortality in all Scandinavian countries (see Table 18.9). In terms of morbidity (ill health) there are also clear differences: the unemployed, those in lowly paid occupations and those who are very poorly educated are more likely to suffer from chronic illness than other groups in the population. There is also a clear correlation between sick leave and occupation, although women take less sick leave than men, and between occupation and in-patient hospital treatment. Unskilled and skilled workers have more sick leave and are more likely to receive hospital care than higher civil servants, salaried employees, farmers and entrepreneurs (Dahlgren and Diderichsen 1989).

TABLE 18.9 Standardized mortality rate among Swedish men aged 25–64, 1976–80

	Age	
Occupational category	25–44	45–64
All men	100	100
Technical and scientific	71	85
Administrative and clerical	87	96
Commercial	90	100
Forestry and agriculture	103	82
Mining and stoneworks	168	128
Transport	110	108
Industry and construction	112	108
Service and domestic	118	112
Not economically active	204	245

Source: Dahlgren and Diderichsen (1989: Table 1).

In Norway research has demonstrated a clear relationship between health status and socio-economic status; occupation is the most powerful predictor of ill health – especially for men (Dahl 1991). While the standardized mortality rate (SMR) has declined in Norway in the last thirty years, there has been an increase in the differential between male socio-economic groups. However, while the age-specific SMR shows a decline in difference between socio-economic groups, it has increased for older men when comparing 1960–5 with 1980–5 (Dahl and Kjaersgaard 1993). In a sample of men aged 20–64 it was found that low status and low income were the best predictors of poor self-reported health (Dahl 1994). However, the research has not found a consistent relationship between women's occupational status and health status. In a further analysis Dahl (1991) found that the husband's socio-economic status had a significant impact on women's health. This is the reverse of British research, which has found husband's social class a weak predictor of women's health status (Arber 1990) and women's own occupation exerting a strong influence on self-assessed health (Macran *et al.* 1994).

A study comparing inequalities in health in Finland, Norway and Sweden (Lahelma *et al.* 1994) examined self-reported health in relation to educational level and found large differences in each country; low educational levels were associated with higher levels of reported ill health. The pattern was more distinct for men than for women, and the gap in illness between the highest- and lowest-educated groups was widest among Norwegian men and narrowest among Finnish women. The researchers also calculated the extent of inequalities in illness. Norwegian men had the highest level of inequality, but the differences between men in Sweden and in Finland were small. The extent of the inequality between women was smaller than for men – and smaller among Finnish and Norwegian than Swedish women.

In the United Kingdom, health inequalities and the 'health divide' have been extensively researched in the last two decades following the publication of the Black Report in 1979 (see Townsend and Davidson 1982). The Black Report indicated that there was a significant difference in health experience between the most affluent and the most impoverished in the United Kingdom. Indeed, despite thirty years of the welfare state and the National Health Service, the evidence suggested a widening of the gap in health experience between the professional and managerial groups and semi-skilled and unskilled workers – although all groups had improved overall. Since the publication of the Black Report, a number of studies have investigated health inequalities. At the same time they have moved away from using occupational social class as the sole indicator of social difference and examined a number of potential associations between social and material deprivation indicators and health indicators (see for example Abbott *et al.* 1992; Townsend *et al.* 1986; Whitehead 1987). A number of factors have been found to be associated with different levels of mortality and morbidity – occupational class, unemployment, income, car ownership, gender, race, age, marital status, area of residence, and so on. Studies have consistently found an association between material deprivation and ill health – indeed, deprivation measures are more highly associated with health status than is social class (Abbott *et al.* 1992; Townsend *et al.* 1986). While the research cannot demonstrate, beyond doubt, a causal link, it clearly supports the view that material deprivation is the major cause of the health divide: those who are materially advantaged, on average, experience the best health, and those who are materially most disadvantaged have the poorest health experience.

Wennemo (1993) examined the relationship between the infant mortality rate (IMR), public policy and inequality in eighteen industrialized countries. The research indicates that economic development has a strong but declining impact on IMR. Income inequality and relative poverty rates have a greater importance in explaining variation in IMR than differences in level of economic development between rich countries. Level of unemployment and social security benefit affect IMR – a combination of high unemployment and low benefit levels seems to be associated with relatively high IMR; a high level of family benefit is associated with a relatively low IMR. The research clearly indicates that the standard of living among the less affluent in a society is important in explaining the IMR, rather than the extent of inequalities *per se*.

The research on health inequalities, however, also raises another issue – the extent to which curative-orientated health services can actually bring about improvement in health or reduce the health divide. Arguably, most of the major 'killer diseases' and other causes of death in Western societies are due to non-medical factors – accidents, diet, pollution, cigarette smoking, and so on. A reduction in the health divide is more likely to result from improving the living conditions of the poorer members of society than from increased spending on curative health services. Indeed, some commentators have questioned the role that medicine has played in improving health, and others (for example Illich 1976) have argued that medical science has done more harm than good.

The power of medicine

We tend to take for granted the nature of healthcare as expressed in medical and health statistics; we have done so as authors, so far, in this chapter. In the

1960s and 1970s, however, concerns were expressed about the validity of the form that medical provision takes, and the relevance of doctor-centred, curative medicine came under question in what has come to be called 'the cultural critique of medicine'. Various critics raised questions about the competence of doctors, the appropriateness of a model of health which looked on the body as a machine to be serviced by experts, and the moral status of the way that the medical profession 'medicalizes' what it touches and claims hegemony over it.

The discussion so far in this chapter has equated 'health' with the provision of formal medical care, but the concept is potentially very much broader than this. Most of the healthcare decisions that are made and the healthcare which is undertaken belong not in the public sphere of doctors, hospitals and the state provision of medical care, but in the private sphere – done by people themselves or provided within families without help or advice. The claim of the medical profession to be responsible for the health of the nation is therefore open to question, as most of the nation's health decisions are not taken by the medical profession.

Looking back in history, it cannot be denied that health in Western European countries has improved a great deal over the years; in the late nineteenth and early twentieth century in Britain, for example, there was a very dramatic reduction in infant mortality and ill health generally. It is not clear, however, that this reduction was due to medical interventions such as the intervention of doctors in individual cases or even the provision of mass immunization programmes; more credit can reasonably be given to improved sanitation, the provision of clean drinking water and an improved standard of living coupled with better diet and housing (see Titmuss 1968). Thomas McKeown (for example 1976) charted the trends in death from infectious diseases since the early nineteenth century and demonstrated that in almost all cases the most rapid rate of improvement was already achieved before inoculation and the use of drugs became common (see Figure 18.5). For example, deaths from whooping cough were reduced by 1940 to a seventh of their 1850 level, deaths from tuberculosis to a sixth and deaths from measles to less than a tenth. In none of these cases did immunization become generally available till the 1950s at the earliest. Jane Lewis (1980) has argued, similarly, that the reduction in maternal mortality rates in the twentieth century is as much due to improved diet as to advances in medical science. There is also evidence that countries which have a high percentage of home deliveries in childbirth have entirely comparable infant mortality rates to those with a high percentage of hospital deliveries (see for example Himmelweit 1988).

The World Health Organization (1981), in *Global Strategy for Health for All by the Year 2000*, has explicitly recognized that the prime obstacle to achieving its objectives is inequality and has set specific targets to achieve reduction in health inequalities. It is now widely recognized that it is necessary to reduce social and economic inequalities in order to reduce health inequalities (World Bank 1993). The Healthy Cities Project proposed in Copenhagen in January 1986 explicitly recognizes the need for collective action to reduce health inequalities – activities targeted at whole populations, as nineteenth-century health measures were, rather than the individualistic self-help measures advocated by most

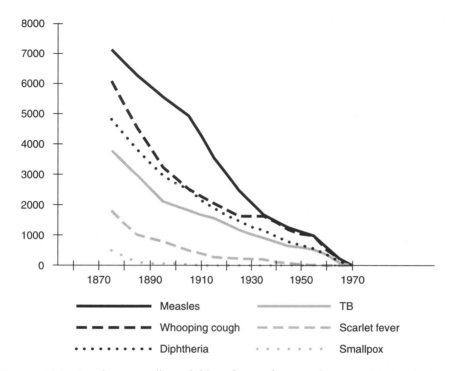

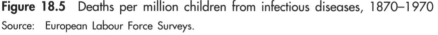

Figure 18.5 Deaths per million children from infectious diseases, 1870–1970

Source: European Labour Force Surveys.

Note: The bars represent the ratio of non-EU nationals that are unemployed for every EU national that is unemployed for four particular years. They also provide an indirect measure of the effect of racial discrimination on patterns of unemployment.

European governments (Ashton 1992). Towns and cities across Europe have adopted the WHO Health For All standards, and the thirty-eight European targets for 'Health for All by the Year 2000' have been written into local programmes. The underlying intention is to bring together the public, private and voluntary sectors to focus on improving health and to tackle health-related problems. The Scandinavian governments have introduced legislation intended to reinforce the shift towards primary healthcare and have commissioned reports focusing on Health for All. In Germany and Britain there has been more attention paid to the public health sector. However, there has been concern at the relative unwillingness of medical personnel to move towards a more social and less medical view of health; a move from curative to preventive medical models threatens the power of doctors.

The Healthy Cities Project is concerned to facilitate the development of action plans for health that will make collaboration possible between health-relevant agencies and bring about a reduction in health inequalities. The intention is to establish local strategies for improving health that go beyond educating individuals and address social issues such as poor housing, industrial pollution, traffic congestion and inadequate leisure facilities. There is an explicit recognition both of the wide range of factors that influence health and of the causes of ill health that are beyond the control of individuals. Liverpool in the United Kingdom is one of the poorest cities of Western Europe, but it has none the less developed a Healthy Cities Project. Liverpool has acknowledged the health inequalities which exist within its boundaries and has achieved a partnership between key city agencies, all committed to the Healthy Cities initiative. The objective is to achieve a measurable improvement, by the year 2000, in Liverpool's health relative to the UK and Europe and an even greater improvement within Liverpool's poorer districts. The city has a City Health Plan made up of six target blocks – health, lifestyles, the environment, appropriate care, research, development. The biggest project is the Croxteth Health Action Area, based on two poor council estates. In the early 1980s research indicated that poor housing was the biggest cause of ill health; subsequent improvements in housing have improved residents' health. The project aims to involve residents actively in other aspects of improving their physical and social environment.

Horsens in Denmark has built a Healthy Cities programme by recognizing that health is not created in the healthcare sector but in people's daily lives and looking at health, not disease. This moves the responsibility from medical knowledge and the curative health sector to politics, leadership and management (Bragh-Matzon and Holm 1992). Gothenburg in Sweden has adopted a plan for locally co-ordinated health promotion activities. The council has also put pressure on the central government for improved housing and a guarantee of work or further education for all school-leavers. The Gothenburg Health Promotion Committee sees health promotion as the identification of conditions which, if no counter-measures were taken, would result in illness or disability or would make it difficult to enjoy good health in the future, and taking appropriate measures against such conditions (Svensson 1992). Other cities in Europe that have adopted similar objectives include Camden in London, Sheffield, Oxford and Nottingham elsewhere in the UK, Eindhoven in the Netherlands (van der Kamp and Cosijn 1992), Barcelona in Spain (Costa 1992), Valencia in Spain (Alvarez-Dardet and Colomer 1992) and the Basque Country (Herrera and Mochales 1992).

While the Healthy Cities Project and the WHO initiative 'Health for All by the Year 2000' clearly move the focus from the medical model to a more socio-economic one and from curative to preventive medicine, attention often continues to be focused on the individual. Sociological research has clearly indicated, however, that the major cause of health inequalities is material deprivation – that individuals often do not have the financial and other resources to take the initiative in developing a healthy lifestyle. Healthy diets, for example, cost considerably more than the diet of many poor people. Indeed, Ashton and Seymour (1988) report that it was impossible to buy a healthy diet in the poorer districts of Liverpool at the time of their research. Health promotion aimed at changing the lifestyle of individuals will do little to reduce health inequalities in Western Europe until the material circumstances of the most deprived members of these societies are improved.

Reflection

The population of Western Europe as a whole has one of the highest standards of living in the world, and comparatively good health. The overall health of the population of the EU has improved dramatically in the last thirty years, as measured by mortality rates. The infant mortality rate was 34.8 per thousand live births in 1960 and had dropped to 8.1 by 1986 (EC 1992). The most dramatic reductions have occurred in Southern European countries; the rate has dropped by 85 per cent in Portugal and 80 per cent in Spain and Italy. Life expectancy has also increased dramatically, and only Japan has higher life expectancy than Europe. In 1991 average life expectancy was 72.9 years for men and 79.5 for women, compared with 67.3 for men and 72.7 for women in 1960. As with the IMR, the greatest increase in life expectancy has occurred in the poorer Southern European countries – for example, an improvement of 9 years for men in Portugal compared with 2.1 years in Denmark, and 10.6 for women compared with 3.6. Improvement in the general health of the population of Europe is more likely to come now from improving the standard of living of the poorer members of society than from increases in medical spending – although the role of medicine in alleviating the suffering of those with chronic health problems must not be ignored. On the other hand, Western governments are concerned to reform their healthcare systems and in particular to reduce the costs of healthcare – or at least, government contributions to them – at the same time as the age of the population and technological innovations require increased spending.

Summary

- The achievement of decreases in infant mortality, increases in life expectancy and improvements in standards of living.
- The contemporary requirement to reform healthcare systems and reduce the cost of state healthcare spending.
- The increasing scope and cost of medicine and medical technology and the increasing needs of ageing populations.

Further reading

Peter Townsend and Nick Davidson (eds) (1982) *Inequalities in Health: The Black Report (Sir Dougal Black et al.) and The Health Divide (Margaret Whitehead)*, Harmondsworth: Penguin. These are two classic British studies of health inequalities, first published a decade apart. The authors argue that the evidence indicates that material factors are the main determinants of health inequalities. *The Health Divide* summarizes the evidence accumulated in the years between its production and that of the original Black Report, which adds weight to the case for material deprivation as a major cause. Much of the research on health inequalities carried out in Europe is informed by the conclusions of these two reports.

John Ashton (ed.) (1992) *Healthy Cities*, Milton Keynes: Open University Press. This book provides a summary of the 'New Public Health' and case studies of the implementation of 'Healthy Cities' projects across Europe. It provides good examples of the ways in which the health policies in these cities take account of socio-economic factors.

Ivan Illich (1976) *Limits to Medicine*, Harmondsworth: Penguin. One of the major texts in what has come to be called 'the cultural critique of medicine'. Illich argues that medicine has done more harm than good – that is, that it is iatrogenic. He identifies three categories of iatrogenesis – medical, social and cultural.

Chapter 19

Crime and penal policy in Europe

Daniel Gilling and Will Hay

Introduction	380
Crime, criminology and the sociology of crime	380
A comparative tradition?	381
A rationale for comparative analysis	381
Information about crime	382
Comparing official statistics	383
Comparing victimization rates	386
Explaining and controlling crime	388
Criminal justice systems and penal sanctions	389
Comparative criminal justice systems	389
Sentencing	390
Competing paradigms	392
Imprisonment	393
Prison data	394
Recent trends	395
Summary	397
Further reading	397

Key concepts

- **Crime: a social construct of different reporting and recording practices**
- **Penality: the philosophical, ideological and practical context of penal policy**

Introduction

This chapter is organized around two main themes: firstly, the phenomenon of crime which, whilst varying in both form and incidence, is of a sufficiently broad nature to be discussed in its wider European context. The second part switches the focus to penality – the ideas and institutions around which punishment is built. In both sections we draw upon official sources of data which are not easily accessible. For this reason we include data on some countries which are not covered in the rest of this volume. However, as the text makes clear, the data presented cannot always be taken at face value.

It should be noted that criminal justice policy varies between the different countries within the United Kingdom. Here, when considering the United Kingdom, we confine our analysis in the main to England and Wales. Similarly, our discussion is confined to a comparison of the extent of crime and penal policies. There are many other issues of relevance to criminal justice within the European context, notably the policing implications of the removal of border controls in the European Union.

Crime, criminology and the sociology of crime

Crime attracts much interest. It features prominently in popular culture, and it makes 'good copy' for the print and news media. It is also a matter of political concern: in 1992/3 the government spent £9.4 billion on the police and other criminal justice institutions in England and Wales, although this has done little to stem the rising tide of recorded crime, which increased by 71.4 per cent between 1982 and 1992. Crime is a big issue for governments, and their apparent failure to control it can count against them – something the Labour Party found to its cost in the General Election of 1979.

Crime is also a big issue for individual citizens and communities. Fear of crime can have a debilitating effect on one's lifestyle, forcing one to stay indoors, to avoid certain places at certain times, and to invest heavily in a rapidly increasing market of security hardware. Crime incurs costs beyond those suffered by the victim; but there is another side to the coin, for most crime is petty in nature and few can deny that, at one time or another, they have committed an offence. Criminal activity can constitute a significant part of many people's livelihoods, so that for some crime can appear normal, and even justifiable, although the dominant view is that crime is harmful – a social problem which needs to be controlled.

This dominant view is largely taken for granted by the academic discipline of criminology, the main twentieth-century influences of which have been North American, although historically the lineage is European, ultimately traceable back to the eighteenth-century classical criminology of Beccaria from Italy and Bentham from England. In twentieth-century England, moreover, the discipline's rapid expansion owes a great deal to the contributions of a number of Central European migrants, such as Mannheim and Radzinowicz.

In general, criminologists are interested in determining the causes of crime and criminality, and proposing solutions to eliminate them. Causes thus identified have been physiological, psychological and social: so criminology draws on a broad church of disciplines: psychology, biology, anthropology, psychiatry, political philosophy and (more recently) economics. Some sociologists are also members of this church, but in more recent times many have preferred to see themselves as contributors to a sociology of crime and deviance. The distinction is important because it represents a more critical appraisal of the definition and meaning of crime itself. Sociologists of crime perceive of themselves as being less ready to accept official constructions of crime as a social problem, and are equally interested in turning the research spotlight on society and its criminal justice institutions, and how these produce crime as much as do the actions of individual 'criminals'.

A comparative tradition?

Europe has been a rich source of theories about crime and penality which are generally intended to be universally applicable, but the vast majority of applied criminological research has been restricted to individual countries. There is little in the way of a cross-national comparative European tradition in criminological research – although the survey of prison regimes and conditions in the eighteenth century by Howard is a notable exception (see Muncie and Sparks 1991).

There are several reasons for this lack of comparative tradition. Language is a barrier, which may explain the greater influence of North American criminology with which the British have a closer cultural affinity. Secondly, criminal justice institutions in Britain and Europe differ markedly regarding their base in law (English common law versus Roman law); in legal procedures (adversarial versus inquisitorial); and in policing (local unarmed 'bobbies' versus centralized, militarized state police). Such differences reflect and contribute to different conceptual frameworks, acting as barriers to mutual understanding.

Thirdly, academic inquiry ultimately depends on finance, the most important sources of which are domestic government departments such as the British Home Office. They have their own domestic priorities in discovering how much crime there is and how effective their own policies are, and comparative research understandably does not come high on the agenda. Fourthly, this inward-looking attitude has been reinforced by the findings of criminological research, which, as Levi and Maguire (1992) observe, have shown that crime patterns are locally variable, changing from area to area, thus questioning the purpose of research into broader national or international trends.

A rationale for comparative analysis

There are, however, at least three good reasons for comparing crime and penality in Europe. Firstly, as Heidensohn (1991) acknowledges, there has been an evolving commitment to striking closer comparative links between Britain and Europe since the mid-1980s. This growth has not come about as a result of the process of European integration fostered by the Treaty of Rome or the more recent Single European Act, because crime has never been a focal concern there. Rather, growing interest has had more to do with a recognition that some of the constituent elements of domestic crime problems have a cross-national dimension – notably drug trafficking, business crime, terrorism, football hooliganism and illegal immigration. As several writers observe (Levi and Maguire 1992), these mutual problems have prompted cross-border agreements by policing authorities, and such agreements have become more pressing, and more a cause for concern, as a result of the post-1992 removal of border controls.

Secondly, whilst cross-border communications have shown countries that they share specific crime problems, they have also shown that they share general crime problems. Crime rates have risen generally across Europe since the 1950s, and individual countries have increased expenditure on every aspect of criminal justice policy. Mutual awareness of problems has led to some sharing of solutions, hence both Graham (1987) and van Dijk (1991) demonstrate the general increase of interest in crime prevention policies across Europe.

Thirdly, and closely related to the above, there has been a slow recognition that countries within Europe have much to learn from each other's experiences. McClintock and Wikstrom make the point well:

> The potential value of cross-national comparisons lies in the possibility of identifying common and unique features of crime in different countries, and against this background evaluating existing theories and generating new ones. Cross-national comparisons are also of great value to public policy since they can provide a perspective on a country's crime problem (rates, patterns and so forth) and the ways in which similar problems are experienced and dealt with in other countries.
>
> (McClintock and Wikstrom 1992: 505)

So, comparative European analysis may have a number of practical benefits, which make it tempting to push ahead – to see if countries can learn from one another, to see whether any country has found a way of cracking the crime problem.

Information about crime

Before we get carried away with the practical benefits of comparative research, we must heed Vagg's (1993: 541) warning that 'comparisons between societies present problems'. Two of the problems he identifies are interpretation, 'where it is unclear what the data actually refer to or whether claimed similarities or differences actually exist', and context, 'where empirical findings have to be interpreted in very different lights in the societies under consideration'. Both must be borne in mind when considering the following data.

There are two main sources of data about crime. The first is official statistics – the information gained from official police records, or the records of other criminal justice institutions such as the courts. The second is the victimization survey, where randomly sampled individuals are asked about their experiences as victims of crime. Official statistics are more numerous and more easily obtainable because they are routinely produced, although that is not to say that all countries are equally willing to disclose such information. Victimization surveys are rarer because they are more expensive to produce and non-routine. There have, for example, been five official British Crime Surveys since the first in 1983, and two extensive international ones (van Dijk *et al.* 1991; Alvazzi del Frate *et al.* 1993) which included a number of European countries. Both sources, however, have their problems, and these are considered below.

In addition to official statistics and victim surveys there is one other source of information – the self-report study, in which individuals are asked to 'own up' to delinquent acts they have committed. Although there are some obvious drawbacks to such a research instrument, they have proved their usefulness, particularly in dispelling the myth that delinquency is predominantly a working-class phenomenon. Self-report studies would add a valuable dimension to the comparative analysis of crime in Europe, but whilst steps have been taken in this direction no widespread data are yet available.

Comparing official statistics

Official statistics are difficult to acquire in a form which facilitates direct comparison because different countries do not use the same categories when recording and counting crime – criminal laws, offence categories, and ages of criminal responsibility may all be different. Consequently, it is a major effort to standardize the information: that is why Interpol's most recent figures, as of December 1994, relate only to 1990.

Table 19.1 presents data on a selected range of offences for eighteen European countries, covering crimes of violence and against property. Although the raw numbers are included it is meaningless to compare these since they make no allowance for the different population sizes of each country; hence, the 'offences per 100,000 of the population' forms the main point of comparison, and the criterion by which countries are ranked into 'league tables'. Some observations can be made about these figures:

1   With some exceptions, there is fair consistency across offence categories, with the same countries appearing at the top, middle, and bottom of the league tables. Sweden, for example, only once drops out of the top two, whilst France's position varies only between seventh and ninth place.
2   There is a striking range of scores between highest and lowest ranked countries: the most crime-prone country in each category has approximately twenty-four times as many crimes overall, twenty-four times as many homicides, fifteen times as many rapes, twenty-two times as many thefts, and one hundred and forty times as many car thefts.

The range can, however, be a misleading measure of variance and we must ask how far it reflects real differences, or something else. Thus, before Scots and Swedes consider mass emigration, let us consider some important points.

TABLE 19.1 Figures, incidence rates and ranking of eighteen European countries for selected crime categories in 1990

	Total crime			Total theft			Homicide			Rape			Car theft		
	Number in thousands	Rate per 100,000 inhabitants	Rank	Number in thousands	Rate per 100,000 inhabitants	Rank	Number	Rate per 100,000 inhabitants	Rank	Number	Rate per 100,000 inhabitants	Rank	Number in thousands	Rate per 100,000 inhabitants	Rank
Scotland	959	18,800	1	359	7,000	3	471	9.2	3	494	9.7	2	36	708	3
Sweden	1,145	14,200	2	740	8,600	1	603	7.0	4	1,410	16.4	1	76	879	2
Denmark	527	10,300	3	430	8,400	2	234	4.6	6	483	9.5	3	30	576	5
England and Wales	4,544	9,000	4	3,417	6,800	4	1,145	2.3	13	3,391	6.7	11	494	977	1
Netherlands	1,134	7,600	5	827	5,600	5	2,206	14.8	2	1,321	8.9	5	27	182	11
West Germany	4,455	7,100	6	2,727	4,400	7	2,419	3.9	8	5,112	8.2	6	72	115	13
Luxembourg	24	6,600	7	15	3,900	10	8	2.2	15	28	7.5	9	0.5	131	12
France	3,493	6,200	8	2,275	4,000	9	2,526	4.5	7	4,582	8.1	7	294	520	7
Austria	458	6,000	9	226	2,900	11	178	2.3	13	533	7.0	10	2	27	16
Norway	236	5,600	10	176	4,100	8	111	2.6	11	383	9.0	4	26	609	4
Switzerland	356	5,300	11	310	4,600	6	214	3.2	9	428	6.3	12		n/a	
Italy	2,503	4,400	12	1,605	2,800	13	3,676	6.4	5	n/a			313	546	6
N. Ireland	57	3,600	13	46	2,900	11	307	19.5	1	125	7.9	8	3	193	10
Belgium	332	3,300	14	260	2,600	14	221	2.2	15	609	6.1	13	28	281	9
Greece	331	3,300	14	48	500	17	204	2.0	17	191	1.9	16	7	7	17
Spain	1,042	2,600	16	808	2,000	16	963	2.4	12	1,790	4.5	14	136	343	8
Eire	88	2,300	17	77	2,200	15	29	0.8	18	89	2.5	15	1	32	15
Portugal	83	800	18	45	400	18	287	2.8	10	117	1.1	17	5	48	14

Source: Official data collated by Interpol.

TABLE 19.2 Rates of change of officially recorded crime in sixteen European countries, 1987–92

	%		%
England & Wales	44	Norway	18
Belgium	32	Eire	12
Portugal	32	Netherlands	12
Austria	28	Sweden	11
Italy	28	Greece*	9
Finland	24	Denmark	8
Scotland	23	N. Ireland	6
France	21	W. Germany*	0

Source: Home Office Research and Statistics Department.

Notes: * Figures relate to period 1987–90.

The limitations of official statistics are well documented elsewhere: in brief, not all crimes are reported by the public to the police, and not all reported crimes are recorded by the police. The reasons for this are many and varied, but their combined effect is to under-represent crime in most but not all offence categories.

From a comparative angle, the problem is not under-representation *per se*, but rather the possibility that the degree of under-representation varies between countries: there may be cultural differences in the propensity to report and record crime, where for example countries which are less tolerant of a macho culture are more likely to report sexual offences; and they may stem from different pressures and traditions operating on law enforcement agencies, where for example countries with good police–community relations or more effective policing are likely to have higher reporting rates because there are higher levels of trust. These and many other variables must be taken into account when making cross-national comparisons.

The propensity to report and record may vary between countries, but also over time. Hence, whilst Table 19.2 eliminates some of the problems associated with 'snapshot' views by offering a deeper appreciation of rates of change, it cannot be known for certain whether some of the change is accounted for by changes in reporting and recording. Public awareness campaigns against domestic violence or child abuse might, for example, increase the propensity to report, as would an extension in insurance coverage, whilst closer official scrutiny of police practices might increase recording rates. It is very difficult to disentangle these sorts of changes from social ones such as improvements or declines in the socio-economic structure, changes in the pattern of drug misuse, or the increased availability of consumer goods.

An understanding of social contexts is an important part of any explanation for cross-national differences, and we need to consider how these social contexts might influence overall crime rates. Returning to the statistics, the following observations provide some explanatory force:

1   The exceptionally high rate of homicide in Northern Ireland can be explained by reference to the political and military conflict there. We should beware, however, of reading too much into crime rates based on low figures, because annual variations in the latter can make a big difference to the former. Thus we must be cautious about how we interpret the positions of smaller countries such as Northern Ireland and Luxembourg.

2   Countries with higher rates of crime are generally the most heavily urbanized, and most affluent. Cities are more crime-prone than rural areas, and richer countries provide more opportunities for crime than their poorer neighbours. Hence countries with lower rates of crime tend to be those which are least urbanized and least affluent.

3   One area about which we can speculate, and which Vagg (1993) considers an important issue, is the issue of community self-policing, where crime is 'managed' by the local community without recourse to official agencies. This is particularly likely where organized crime is well developed, for it is a paradox that organized crime co-exists with strong social control. The example Vagg draws upon is Japan, but it may equally apply to certain European countries, such as Italy, where the Mafia holds a strong influence, and Northern Ireland, where the paramilitaries perform a similar role. This could explain the relatively low position of such countries in Table 19.1.

4   It is a truism that law enforcement 'creates' crime in so far as the more formalized, developed and funded it is – assuming it is not also corrupt – the more crime it is likely to find and process, so we must also consider the different structures of law enforcement operating in each country.

Comparing victimization rates

Given the problems with official statistics, it is no surprise that alternative means of providing cross-national comparisons have been sought, notably victimization surveys which have a number of distinct advantages. They bypass the police, thereby eliminating problems of recording practices. They ask whether crimes have been reported, thus allowing a glimpse into cultural variations in reporting behaviour, which can be used to temper the picture gained from official statistics. They ask about victims' lifestyles, thereby facilitating a correlation between lifestyle (e.g. going out in the evening) and risk of victimization. Finally, they can distinguish between the overall *incidence* of crimes (the overall number of crimes) and *personal prevalence* rates, which show how many people suffered one or more of these crimes (the phenomenon of repeat or multiple victimization).

On the debit side, as van Dijk *et al.* (1991) admit, victimization surveys have limitations. Samples are relatively small, which when combined with low response rates increases the risk of unrepresentativeness, particularly when it comes to the rarer types of crime. Moreover, they cannot chart the extent of non-personal (i.e. where the victim may be an organization rather than an individual) or victimless crimes, or crimes against children, who are excluded from the sample population.

TABLE 19.3 Percentage of respondents victimized by crimes covered in the International Crime Survey in 1988

	%		%
Netherlands	26.4	Belgium	17.7
Spain	24.6	Norway	16.5
W. Germany	21.4	Finland	15.9
England & Wales	19.4	Switzerland	15.6
France	19.4	N. Ireland	15.0
Scotland	18.6		

Source: Adapted from van Dijk *et al.* (1991: 179, Table E6).

Victim surveys, furthermore, have to ask the same questions if they are to be used for cross-national comparisons – as the International Crime Surveys do, with a remarkable degree of consistency between their 1988 and 1992 findings (although the list of European countries covered in the surveys changes somewhat). So, what do they tell us?

Table 19.3 lists the overall percentage of people from the European countries in the first survey who were the victims of any crime in 1988. Comparing this with Table 19.1 (which draws data from 1990), a few interesting points arise. The tables may comprise slightly different lists of countries, but even so it is noticeable that Spain leaps from near the bottom of the table to near the top; Scotland acquires a more respectable mid-table position; and both the Netherlands and Germany leap-frog England and Wales. Significantly, the range of differences narrows sharply.

In order to explain this change we need other clues. Table 19.4 lists the reporting rate for all crimes in each of the countries surveyed, and makes possible a few hypotheses. Scotland's position in Table 19.1, for example, might be attributable to a high reporting rate, whilst Spain's ascendancy in Table 19.2 may be linked to its low reporting rate, which is half that of Scotland's. This may be, as van Dijk *et al.* (1991) observe, because Spanish rates of insurance coverage are low. Hence, when one looks at the reporting of car theft, one finds a 100 per cent reporting rate in 1988 for England and Wales, Scotland and the Netherlands,

TABLE 19.4 Percentage of crimes reported by victims to the police in 1988

	%		%
Scotland	62.3	W. Germany	47.9
France	60.2	N. Ireland	45.8
England & Wales	58.8	Norway	42.6
Switzerland	58.7	Finland	41.8
Netherlands	52.6	Spain	31.5
Belgium	48.6		

Source: Adapted from van Dijk *et al.* (1991).

but only a 76.9 per cent rate in Spain (1991: 177). These differences in reporting rates can have profound effects on the total volume of recorded crime, although we must not assume that all reported crimes are recorded.

Overall, the International Crime Surveys are important sources of data, although one needs additional background details before one can begin to explain differences in crime rates. For example, whilst the Netherlands has the highest rate of victimization in 1988, its position can largely be explained by the high levels of bicycle ownership and bicycle theft. Other factors which the International Crime Survey considers are a country's gross national product (GNP), rates of car ownership, type of housing, lifestyle patterns, and degrees of urbanization. Of these, degrees of urbanization and levels of car ownership appear to be positively correlated with criminal victimization rates.

Explaining and controlling crime

Whilst our limited knowledge of differences in reporting and recording rates means we must be cautious when forwarding explanations of cross-national variations, it does seem from the above that a knowledge of differences in social contexts can help considerably. Indeed, these social contexts vary not only between countries, but also within them, and provide valuable data for helping to explain regional variations too – something the International Surveys cannot easily cover given that their samples pick up a minimum of one adult in every 2,000 households.

These data lend themselves to social structural and environmental explanations of crime, as opposed to theories of individual or group criminality which have traditionally been the mainstay of criminology. These latter explanations require more detailed information about offending behaviour and offenders' circumstances – information which is not readily available in a cross-national self-report study format. Even if it were available, there are still many people who remain to be convinced of criminology's capacity to provide convincing explanations for criminality – especially those which could be used as a basis for an effective control strategy.

Social structural explanations have a limited appeal in policy terms because they draw attention to factors such as relative inequality about which countries are either unwilling or unable to do anything. By contrast, environmental explanations are more realistic as a basis for action, not least because they do not require prior knowledge of offenders, but only clues about opportunities for crime. The cross-national data shows these are greater in urbanized and wealthier countries (e.g. those with high car ownership rates). As van Dijk et al. (1991) point out, supply can generate its own demand here. The data also shows that opportunities appear to be higher against younger people, against men, those who are employed, those in higher income groups, and those who have already previously been victimized. The more specific these data can be made, the more useful it can be for preventive purposes.

The irony is that environmental explanations call forth preventive responses to crime which rely less and less on criminal justice agencies themselves, and more on the actions of the general public and other public or private agencies. The advantage of this is that it does not let the selective actions of law enforcement agencies set the agenda of the 'crime problem' (targeting some social groups and activities but not others). However, a disadvantage is that the consequent lack of interest in the offender's motivation gives us little with which to challenge a punitively minded penal system, which has so far manifestly failed to reduce crime.

Criminal justice systems and penal sanctions

We encounter an array of moral and practical dilemmas when we broach the subject of how best to deal with offenders, and it is scarcely surprising that the questions of justice and punishment have attracted the interest of philosophers and theologians down the ages as well as the modern-day interest of sociologists, psychologists and criminologists. Here we begin with an examination of the differences and similarities between European criminal justice systems before turning to the process of sentencing and the philosophies which underpin it.

Imprisonment features prominently in the criminological literature and is becoming of increasing interest in European social policy. The case against imprisonment can be made on a variety of grounds, including cost, the limited effect that prison has on the reduction of crime, and that offenders should, in any case, be dealt with in more humane and constructive ways. Consequently, we conclude with a discussion on the use of imprisonment as a penal sanction within Europe.

Comparative criminal justice systems

Only recently has there been any real interest in comparative data on European criminal justice procedures. We thus still lack a detailed knowledge and understanding of the ways in which other European countries approach penality, although it appears crime raises similar issues throughout Europe. States have also tended to share problems related to the smooth delivery of criminal justice policies: a lack of resources to tackle the issues that crime engenders; the complexity of legislation; increasing demands by the European Convention on Human Rights to increase the quality of criminal justice; miscarriages of justice and the general lack of confidence in criminal justice systems. At the same time, however, European criminal justice systems differ, not only in constitutional and structural terms but also in relation to such things as the age of criminal responsibility, attitudes to the victim(s), as well as the general principles concerning criminal procedure at all stages of the process from arrest and investigation, to detention, and the trial itself.

Perhaps the most marked difference is the 'adversarial' model of criminal justice practised in England and Wales and other English-speaking areas throughout the world and the 'inquisitorial' systems that form the basis for the delivery of criminal justice in other European states including France, Belgium and Luxembourg. In the adversarial (or accusatorial) model the tasks of prosecuting and defending the accused are separated. In English criminal law the case is tried, in the first instance, either by a judge in the Crown Court with a jury present, or a set of lay people in the Magistrates' Court. Proceedings and the range of sentences available to each type of court will differ accordingly. The accused is represented by a lawyer and the judge or the magistrates hear the evidence from the prosecution.

The main objective of the adversarial system is to establish whether there is enough evidence against the accused to warrant a conviction. In this regard, the trial represents a test of the evidence that is presented orally and publicly before the court. The court cannot call witnesses though the judge can ask questions of the witnesses within certain constraints. In contrast the inquisitorial system seeks to establish the 'truth' behind the accusation and everything is geared to this objective. Accordingly all participants engaged in the process from the point of arrest onwards are obliged to collect evidence both in favour of and against the accused. In Belgium, for example, 'Even the accused and his [*sic*] counsel are, to some extent, involved in this process of searching for the material truth: the defence is supposed to help the judge in finding the truth' (van den Wyngaert 1993: 19). Meanwhile, in Denmark the public prosecutor is not in 'opposition' to the accused, but rather 'intervenes in the interests of law and justice' (Greve 1993: 58) to find the *objective* truth. In this regard the prosecutor may further the interests of the accused.

It should be noted that the two systems are not always mutually exclusive. The pre-trial stage in Greece, for example, is characterized by some aspects of the inquisitorial process. However, during the trial, the characteristics of the adversarial process prevail. There is also an indication that some European states are beginning to reappraise their criminal justice systems in light of the criticisms that can be levelled against them. Such reappraisals that are occurring have, in some measure, been the result of constitutional pressures to comply with international rules concerning human rights. In Italy's case such pressures led, in 1988, to the abandonment of the key features of the inquisitorial system in favour of the adversarial process, whilst ironically in England miscarriages of justice have increased pressures for the adoption of some elements of the inquisitorial system.

Sentencing

Sentencing is an emotive issue, particularly when the crime committed has breached sensibilities in a pronounced way, such as offences involving children or particularly violent acts. It is also a complex process, entailing not only punitive notions of retribution, 'desert', deterrence and selective incapacitation on the grounds of dangerousness but also ideas of rehabilitation and reform and utilitarian concerns of deterrence. Any given penal measure entails a restriction of an individual's rights and liberties and, in this sense, intrinsically involves an element of coercion. One corollary of this is that penal sanctions need not only to be morally acceptable but also justifiable in terms of the purpose and aims of the measure in question. Sentencers cannot thus sentence according to whim or malice.

Unlike other European countries, where there is a closer link with penal policy, sentencing within England and Wales is regarded as being the ultimate preserve of the judiciary. It is difficult to overstate the importance of this separation, for as Harding and Koffman note:

> There are good reasons why judges should be impartial and enjoy protection from political interference ... this aspect of 'independence' is unquestionable. But does this same principle also justify a virtually unfettered discretion in matters of sentencing, which is not based on strictly legal criteria, but involves matters of social and penal policy, philosophy and economics?
>
> (Harding and Koffman 1988: 100)

Sentencing can never be apolitical or disembedded from the socio-economic context within which it occurs. Nor can it be reduced to mechanical applications of a set of legal strictures or rules, as each case must be taken on its individual merits. Nevertheless, despite individualized justice there is a need for consistency between courts, although in England research evidence demonstrates wider disparities of sentencing between court areas (see, for example, Moxon and Hedderman 1994). Many critics thus urge reform, especially for the need to limit the amount of discretion available to judges. This, in turn, would not only bring English judges more into line with their European counterparts but also make them more accountable. Some observers have argued for various middle ways which build upon the best of the existing principles and practices whilst improving the system overall. In particular this would entail providing sentencers with fuller and more consistent guidance than is presently the case. Yet another proposal is to introduce a Sentencing Council or Commission, a suggestion which has received widespread support among criminologists and organizations seeking penal reform. This option was given serious consideration in the Report of the Royal Commission on Criminal Justice (1993) but not acted upon. It should be noted that all of the suggestions for reform are profoundly controversial. They are thus likely to be the subject of debate for some time to come.

The sentencing process operates according to a ladder or tariff which fixes a proportional penalty in accordance with the offender's culpability and degree of harm engendered by the offence, after mitigating and aggravating circumstances have been taken into consideration. The range of penalties within Europe differ according to each country's tariff, and some countries may consider certain offences more seriously than others. Germany and the Netherlands, for example, have lower rates of incarceration for burglary than England and Wales, although those convicted of drink-driving offences are more likely to receive a custodial sentence in the Netherlands and Scandinavian countries than they are in Britain (Hudson 1993). Turning to offenders, there is some evidence that people appearing before courts in England and Wales may be differentially treated according to such factors as a person's gender, 'race' or psychological disposition. For instance, it is widely held that women are sent to prison for less serious offences than men (see Carlen 1990). People with mental health problems and the homeless are over-represented in the prison population, as are offenders from ethnic minorities, suggesting that widespread discrimination exists within the sentencing process.

In England and Wales, the tariff set out in the Criminal Justice Act 1991 ranges from a conditional or an absolute discharge, through to financial penalties, probation, forms of community service, and finally to suspended prison sentences and imprisonment itself with various combinations of these penalties in between. Whilst not being directly transferable – some countries do not have probation or community service, for example – this range of penalties is similar throughout Europe.

Competing paradigms

We have suggested that sentencing is a dynamic process, with conflicting purposes, values and beliefs. In the words of Garland (1990: 214) 'feelings of fear, hostility, aggression, and hatred compete with pity, compassion, and forgiveness to define the proper response to the law-breaker'. Those working within the system are entwined in an ideological conflict between two incompatible philosophies: welfare, and 'just deserts', which holds that punishment should be commensurate in severity to the crime. There is, however, a counter-argument to the latter which proclaims that a justification based on such principles is critically flawed, for the 'proportionality principle' ignores the (perhaps insurmountable) task of achieving a just desert in an unjust society. As one observer succinctly puts it:

> Most offenders committing common law crimes come from disadvantaged backgrounds, and disproportionately they come from minority groups. Arguments for a highly proportional system of deserved punishments evade the question of whether offenders from deeply deprived backgrounds deserve the same penalties as do other, less deprived, offenders.
>
> (Tonry 1994: 136–7)

This justice–welfare debate finds expression in an acute form when we confront the sentencing of juveniles.

The conflict between justice and welfare poses a dilemma which requires resolution. Ashworth (1994: 217) suggests one could give 'clear guidance to courts in cases where the aims conflict'. Alternatively, he argues, the tension can be accommodated by declaring 'a primary aim and then to delineate other classes of case in which different aims may prevail'. Ashworth cites the new Swedish sentencing law which (like the philosophy underpinning the Criminal Justice Act 1991) proclaims 'just deserts' as its leading aim, whilst at the same time allowing for other aims which are dependent upon specific offences and particular offenders. Other examples of this approach are also in evidence. Penalties in the former Western Germany, for instance, were essentially considered in desert and retributive terms, but they were also expected to serve rehabilitative purposes (Herrman 1987). Most European codes, however, remain ambivalent and ambiguous in this area.

Imprisonment

European prisons generally share a common heritage in terms of purpose and design, and they stand at the centre of European penal systems, although nowadays this deprivation of liberty is regarded by sentencers throughout Europe to be the last resort. Consequently, any comparison of criminal justice philosophy, policy and practice must include analysis of prison rates, which enables us to assess some fundamental issues. For example, what is the relation between imprisonment and other forms of penality? What do rates of imprisonment tell us about the penal climate of any given country in terms of, say, assessing the viability and commitment to reducing the prison population, an overt aim of many of the European states (see Muncie and Sparks 1991). Above all, what do European rates of imprisonment tell us about what Rutherford (1993) has termed the 'pursuit of decency' – the quest for a 'civilized', liberal and humanitarian penal system?

With the notable exception of David Downes's (1988) comparison between England and the Netherlands, little attention has been paid to such questions. Downes's interest in the Netherlands arose out of the Dutch achievement of a more substantial degree of decarceration than other European states during the post-war period. Reasons for this are many and varied. Part of the trend, Downes asserts, can be located in policy decisions emphasizing 'the principle of opportunity' whereby prosecutors are allowed the flexibility to waive prosecution on the grounds that it would not be in the wider public interest. Another explanation is that a 'culture of tolerance' exists in Dutch society which is unparalleled in other European states, with the possible exception of certain Scandinavian countries. Such 'politics of accommodation' helps to explain how those in positions of power have been able to implement their policies without eliciting fierce objections or public hostility. More widely still, Downes draws our attention to 'an unusually generous welfare state' which actively seeks the assimilation of minority groups, which in turn eases the task of justifying such measures. But, writes Downes:

> the main burden of accounting for the trends seems to fall ultimately on variables closely connected with the actual accomplishment of sentencing by the prosecutors and judges themselves; and here the manner of judicial training and socialisation, and the character and timing of the brief ascendancy of rehabilitative policies, seem to be crucial, in ways which have yet to be analysed at all adequately.
>
> (Downes 1991: 127)

The prison system thus connotes much about the kind of society that we inhabit. The increase in crime rates does not automatically mean an increase in the prison population. What, then, can data on prisons tell us about the kind of choices that European states make about its use?

Prison data

Data on prison rates (such as those presented in Table 19.5) need to be treated with some caution, not only because of the much-vaunted problem of comparing like with like in classificatory and numerical terms but also because imprisonment is part of a much wider *process* of sentencing practice. We cannot therefore look at prison rates in isolation from other factors. Many European countries in the last two decades have sought, for an amalgam of socio-economic, humanitarian and political reasons, to divert people from custody, or, via cautions and mediation schemes, from court altogether. Such trends have not progressed in a uniform or unitary way. West Germany, for instance, prosecuted fewer people than the Netherlands or Sweden (Rutherford 1993). Despite this, West Germany had a considerably higher rate of imprisonment per 100,000 head of population than the latter two countries (77.8 compared with 44.4 and 58.0 respectively).

The conventional way of establishing the number of prisoners held at any one time is to undertake a head count on a given day. Figures in Table 19.5 reveal wide variation between European states on a number of dimensions. Cyprus (38.0), Iceland (40.6) and the Netherlands (44.4) have the lowest detention rate

TABLE 19.5 European prison populations at 1 September 1990

	Total prison population	Detention rate per 100,000 inhabitants	Percentage of unconvicted prisoners	Pre-trial detention rate per 100,000 prisoners	Percentage of women prisoners	Percentage of foreign prisoners
Austria	6,231	82.0	31.5	25.8	4.6	17.7
Belgium	6,525	66.1	46.8	30.9	5.2	32.1
Cyprus	218	38.0	10.1	3.8	3.7	38.0
Denmark	3,243	63.0	26.5	16.7	4.8	11.7
Finland	3,106	62.2	11.6	7.2	3.0	0.6
France	47,449	82.2	40.7	33.4	4.2	28.7
FRG	48,792	77.8	26.4	20.6	4.3	14.5
Hungary	11,497	110.0	23.6	25.9	4.6	1.1
Iceland	104	40.6	3.8	1.6	6.7	0.0
Italy	32,588	56.6	40.6	23.0	5.2	11.6
Luxembourg	352	94.0	26.1	24.6	5.4	41.2
Netherlands	6,662	44.4	38.8	17.2	3.9	25.2
Norway	2,260	56.5	20.5	11.6	—	12.8
Portugal	9,059	87.0	32.2	28.1	5.4	7.9
Spain	32,902	85.5	39.5	33.8	7.6	16.4
Sweden	4,895	58.0	20.2	11.7	4.4	18.4
Switzerland	5,074	76.9	38.9	29.9	5.3	26.9
Turkey	46,357	82.1	37.4	30.7	2.6	0.6
England & Wales	45,659	90.3	22.1	20.0	3.5	1.5
N. Ireland	1,733	109.5	22.9	25.1	1.7	22.2

Source: Council of Europe 1992.

per head of population, with England and Wales (90.3), Luxembourg (94.0), Northern Ireland (109.5) and Hungary (110.0) heading the league table. The percentage of women prisoners varies from 1.7 per cent in Northern Ireland to 7.6 per cent in Spain. The percentage of women prisoners in England and Wales is 3.5 per cent of the total population.

Yet a note of caution needs to be sounded here. In addition to looking at the 'stock' of prisoners, we also need to look at the 'flow' rates of prisoners as they progress through the system. As Muncie and Sparks note:

> It is now generally agreed that the exceptionally large stock of prisoners in England and Wales results from the combination of rather (though not exceptionally) high rates of imprisonment with rather (though not exceptionally) long periods of detention. That is, the English flow is both strong and slow.
>
> (Muncie and Sparks 1991: 95–6)

In this respect the cases of Norway and the Netherlands have in the past presented a striking contrast with the English experience. The rate of detention in Norway in 1988, for example, was less than half that of England and Wales. At the same time its rate of imprisonment was unusually high, reflecting the fact that Norway was at that time among the countries with the lowest mean detention periods. The flow of prisoners was not only very high but also very fast.

Muncie and Sparks conclude that the English penal system is not only more extensive than other European country's, but also less likely to engage in diversionary strategies at an early stage in the penal process. However, it is important to note, they argue, that there is no prima facie case that the English penal system is more 'punitive' than other European systems.

Recent trends

Though it is difficult to arrive at adequate conclusions it is, nevertheless, possible to identify particular trends. As can be seen in Table 19.6 twelve European countries for which we have data experienced an upward trend in the previous year, with considerable variation in the size of the increase. At the same time, as Table 19.7 demonstrates, six states managed to achieve a slight decrease in their numbers of prisoners.

Such snapshots are subject to rapid change. In the case of England and Wales, for example, the decrease was to be short lived. At the time of writing the prison population in England and Wales stands just short of 55,000. This represents a rise of almost 10,000 in the prison population since 1990, with the bulk of the increase having occurred in the last two years or so. This increase has occurred despite the Woolf and Tumin Report (1991) recommendation to reduce the prison population following major disturbances at Strangeways and other English prisons in 1990, attributed in part to overcrowding.

Within the Council of Europe dialogue is beginning to take place as member states seek common standards and unified approaches to penal practice and

TABLE 19.6 Increases in prison rates

	Increase (%)		Increase (%)
Cyprus	14.1	France	5.2
Austria	8.0	Norway	4.1
Switzerland	7.6	Netherlands	3.1
Portugal	7.1	Sweden	2.1
Italy	6.5	Luxembourg	2.0
Spain	5.7	Finland	0.1

Source: Council of Europe (1992: 26).

TABLE 19.7 Decreases in prison rates

	Decrease (%)		Decrease (%)
Belgium	3.5	FRG	5.7
Denmark	4.0	England	5.8
Turkey	4.2	Iceland	8.0

Source: Council of Europe (1992: 26).

criminal justice based upon liberal ideals. The impetus for this movement is derived from two sources: the influence exerted by the European Convention of Human Rights, and the need for penal standards which enhance human dignity, sense of responsibility and self-respect, as embodied in the Council of Europe's European Prison Rules 1987. The need for conditions in prison life to be compatible with acceptable standards in the wider community is thus beginning to be examined in more detail, especially in the Scandinavian countries (Rentzmann 1992).

Neale (1992) argues that European penal philosophy is now more concerned with the social and penal prevention of crime and in the social rehabilitation of offenders than with retributive aspects of punishment. It is, however, difficult to reconcile this view with the penal policy emerging in England and Wales following the Criminal Justice Act 1991, with its overt emphasis on punishment as the guiding principle of penal policy, and recent Home Office pronouncements on the apparent effectiveness of imprisonment as a penal sanction. Moreover, as Mathiesen has argued, in the Western world 'there exists a persuasive and persistent *ideology of prison*' (1990: 137, italics in original). Despite the enormous costs this incurs, the current expansion of the prison system throughout Europe (including the Netherlands, Sweden and other 'liberal' states) suggests that there is much truth in Mathiesen's observation. The conceptual shift that is needed to alter European attitudes away from the ideology of punishment towards the 'culture of tolerance' is still some distance away.

Summary

- Crime rates reflect different reporting, recording and classification of offences.
- Crime patterns must be understood within an appreciation of different social contexts.
- Variations in sentencing between countries reflect different purposes, values and beliefs about the treatment of crime within the courts.
- Cross-national variations in imprisonment rates reflect different ideological commitments to imprisonment as a penal sanction despite profound humanitarian concerns, the immense financial costs involved, and evidence of its ineffectiveness in reducing crime rates.

Further reading

Jan van Dijk, Pat Mayhew and Martin Killias (1991) *Experiences of Crime across the World: Key Findings of the 1989 International Crime Survey*, Deventer, Netherlands: Kluwer. This is the first international crime survey.

Frances Heidensohn and Martin Farrell (eds) (1991) *Crime in Europe*, London: Routledge. This is an edited collection of chapters which cover a broad range of themes related both to crime and criminal justice policy within Europe.

C. van den Wyngaert (ed.) (1993) *Criminal Justice in the European Community*, London: Butterworth. This is an edited volume which covers a range of issues related to penality on a country-by-country basis.

John Muncie and Richard Sparks (eds) (1991) *Imprisonment: European Perspectives*, Hemel Hempstead: Harvester Wheatsheaf. This edited volume contains chapters on both the historical and contemporary use of imprisonment within Europe.

Guido Ruggiero, Michael Ryan and Joe Sim (eds) (1995) *Western European Penal Systems: A Critical Anatomy*, London: Sage. This edited collection highlights common trends in penal policy across Europe and seeks to assess the extent to which the commonalties are being generated by wider processes of political integration.

Looking forward: challenges facing Europe

PART FIVE concludes this book by looking at the future in terms of some of the challenges facing Europe. The issues that have been chosen for inclusion are the ones that strike us as particularly salient. Several others could of course have been included. The problem of the inner city is one that is common to all European countries. Urbanization and the transition to urban lifestyles has been central to the development of modern European culture, but the original industrial cities and some of the more recent ones too are no longer inhabited in the way that they were. Large areas, particularly central areas, have been abandoned by their former inhabitants and by the industries which employed them. The restructuring of industry in the face of the new international division of labour has devastated many cities and left them with often perplexing mixtures of enterprise and decay. Renewal is therefore constantly on the agenda of central and local government. Urbanization and industrialization were the cornerstones of European social development whilst the development of government has been in the form of the nation-state. This too has run into trouble. Not all of the people of Europe are content to be organized in the established state system. Peripheral nationalisms have emerged to challenge the authority of the nation-state. For instance, many Basques do not want to be a part of Spain, and some Italians want the prosperous north of that country to break away from its impoverished and Mafia-ridden south. As the European Union develops into a political as well as an economic union there appears to some the promise of more constitutional space for such alternative nationalistic entities to exist. The European Union is taking on more of the properties of a single state with many regions in order to survive in an increasingly competitive world with three politico-economic centres or cores, the so-called 'global triad'. This consists of North America, the European Union and East Asia led by Japan. The tendency is of enormous consequence for communication (the global 'super-highway'), international relations, global manufacturing and trade, and of course world order with its military ramifications. Some writers go as far as to predict a world dominated by the countries of the Pacific Rim with the Atlantic countries relegated to secondary importance.

Chapter 20

Urban change and urban problems

Eric Harrison

Introduction	403
The changing face of urbanism: expansion or decline?	403
Symptoms of urban illness: how and why to measure which ones?	409
Solutions	413
Summary	421
Further reading	422

Key concepts

● Decentralization and de-industrialization of urban areas
● Deprivation
● Regeneration policies

Introduction

Why do we have such a love–hate relationship with urban life? Many young people are attracted to cities in search of work; to the 'city lights', the concentration of leisure and night-life activities which urban settlements offer. Yet the following sentiments are typical of the anti-urban feelings which exist in most contemporary societies:

> Millions of people want to escape the noise, dirt and stress of cities for the peace of rural living, according to a survey published today. One in 10 city and suburban dwellers say they intend to move to the countryside in the next five years. Another one in five say they would if they could, but despair at being able to sell up and find work. The findings come from an NOP survey of 1,001 British adults commissioned by Mintel, the market research group. The most damning indictment of urban life the survey found is that the rich and the young are the most eager to leave it. Nearly 20 per cent of 15–34 year olds from the ABC1 social groupings said they wanted to escape cities. Of those wishing to move, 54 per cent said cities were too dirty and noisy, while nearly half yearned for the open space of the countryside. But less than 10 per cent said there was too much crime in cities or they feel safer in rural areas.
>
> (report from *The Guardian*, 2 November 1992)

Given this paradox, as sociologists it is important for us to recognize that many features of urban life which we view as problems may be the result of some remote and uncontrollable social forces, not of direct human action either by government or by individuals. Urban problems are thus both cause and consequence of our attitudes towards city life.

A second problem concerns just what one means by 'urban problems' in a European context. The UK's urbanization occurred so much earlier that it is almost a unique case among European nations. Britain's urban evolution, it can be argued, is at a more advanced stage than those of most of its neighbours, and has been more akin to that of the United States, even if on a much smaller scale. The so-called decline of cities is taking place in the context of an overall trend towards urban living generally. Table 20.1 shows how the total population of the EU countries living in urban areas has been rising for forty years and is set to rise still further well into the next century. We need therefore to distinguish firstly between areas of growth and areas of decline, and secondly between the decline of the city and the decline of the *inner* city. In the British case at least,

> If decline were a sufficient definition of the problem, then it could be said that it had been brought about, in part, by thirty years of policies, from 1945 to 1975, designed to disperse population and economic activity from the large conurbations to new towns and overspill areas.
>
> (Begg *et al.* 1985: 11)

TABLE 20.1 Proportion of the population resident in urban places, 1950–2010, for EC12 countries (percentages)

Country	1950	1970	1990	2010
Belgium	91.5	94.3	96.9	98.1
Denmark	68.0	79.7	86.4	90.4
Eire	41.1	51.7	59.1	69.3
France	56.2	71.0	74.1	79.9
Germany	71.9	78.7	84.6	87.3
Greece	37.3	52.5	62.6	72.8
Italy	54.3	64.3	68.6	76.2
Luxembourg	59.1	67.8	84.3	89.2
Netherlands	82.7	86.1	88.5	89.0
Portugal	19.3	26.2	33.3	46.7
Spain	51.9	66.0	78.4	85.5
UK	84.2	88.5	92.5	94.7
EC of 12	64.8	74.0	78.9	83.7

Source: Champion (1993).

Note: Figures refer to the twelve countries of the former European Community.

Post-war planners were concerned to reduce the overcrowding and slum conditions which were so widespread in industrial cities, and replace them with newly built housing developments surrounded by green fields. Some of these developments have now become problems in their own right.

The existence, then, of urban problems has long been recognized, but there is still much disagreement about the exact nature of those problems, and hence possible solutions. Much writing on cities uses medical metaphors – for instance, terms like 'urban ills' and 'policy remedies'. The medical practitioner, of course, is trained to distinguish the cause of illnesses from the symptoms which alert us to their presence. Policy-makers all too frequently seem to confuse the two and treat the latter rather than the former. In the short run of course, troublesome symptoms are a problem in their own right, and in practice we need to treat the symptoms and uncover the cause of the problem.

This chapter therefore has three main sections. The first looks at the background to debates about urban change in Europe, stressing two themes: (a) diversity of experience, and (b) inter-relationships between places. The second section examines the ways in which we measure and record the symptoms of urban decline or 'deprivation'. Here the key problems are (a) which indicators to use, and (b) what size of area to select for study and comparison. The third section surveys some past and current practice in policy-making in a number of locations. It concludes with an attempt to identify some trends for the future.

The changing face of urbanism: expansion or decline?

In the nineteenth century cities became both places to work (sites of production) and also places to find housing (sites of consumption). In order to flourish, then, cities need to be centres of population and centres of employment. However, both jobs and people are 'mobile'; that is to say that firms can shift their operations from place to place, and that individuals and/or households can migrate in search of particular types of work or particular types of housing. We saw earlier how the revolution in transport and communications in the nineteenth century led to the expansion of urban centres into 'metropolises'. These trends have been continued in recent years; indeed the expansion of car ownership and the extension of motorway networks means that it makes more sense to talk about 'city-regions', 'functional urban regions' or 'metropolitan regions', with people travelling often long distances between their place of residence and place of work. Society is now more fully urbanized than ever. On top of this, many European countries have strong traditions of regional identity, both economically and politically. This contrasts with the 'unitary state' of the UK (see Chapters 3 and 21) which has a more fragmented pattern of small counties and metropolitan boroughs. Suggestions to reform local government along the lines of the 'city-region' model were rejected by the Redcliffe–Maud Commission and the subsequent reorganization of local government in 1974.

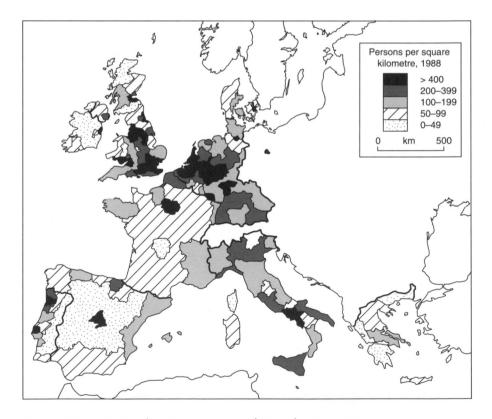

Figure 20.1 Regional variations in population density, 1988
Source: Champion, A.G. (1993: 26)

Legend:
- The Coffin or UK growth zone (after Taylor)
- Demographic centre (after Kormoss)
- National economic core areas
- Lotharingian axis
- Other national capital cities

0   km   400

Figure 20.2 The 'Manchester to Milan' growth axis of the EC

Source. Minshull, 1990.

Restructuring the European economy

If we take a look at the *overall* distribution of population within the EU countries, the picture is not so much one of urban decline but of a restructuring of population and economy. It is common to speak of a Europe divided into core and periphery, the former being densely populated and highly prosperous, the latter being underdeveloped, declining in population, and economically deprived. In other words, there are strong inequalities *between cities*. Figure 20.1 shows the diversity among a sample of European regions, while Figure 20.2 shows one version of the core–periphery model, with the core being concentrated in a corridor running from Manchester to Milan. Others have suggested a 'European megalopolis', a quadrilateral bounded by London, Lyons, Munich and Copenhagen. The concept of a core and periphery is used to illustrate the different paces at which European countries have urbanized, but it does not tell the whole story. Most of Europe's post-war urban growth was over by the 1960s, except for

Spain, Portugal, Greece and Ireland which continued to urbanize. Since the 1960s smaller cities have started to grow to match the large urban centres. In the past, European cities could be placed in a national rather than international context; that is to say, countries like Britain and France were dominated by London and Paris respectively. Germany, Italy and the Netherlands adopted a much more de-concentrated regional structure, with many independent urban centres (Parkinson *et al.* 1993).

Parkinson *et al.*'s report to the European Commission on the future of urban Europe suggested that a more accurate way of viewing Europe was in terms of a changing hierarchy of competitive cities rather than a simple core–periphery split. Instead they offer a three-way model comprising what they term the 'old core', the 'new core' and the periphery. The old core is represented by the trad-itional industrial cities such as Liverpool and other large Northern European centres. By contrast, the new core is moving slowly south, especially in the Mediterranean–Alpine–Southern Germany area, where smaller-scale enterprises involved in lighter industrial activities are based. Many of the larger industrial centres of Northern Europe still remain influential as established 'magnets' for investment. The peripheral regions are primarily agricultural and underdeveloped, and include parts of Greece, the south-west corner of Spain, and Portugal.

As markets have become more and more international, it is possible for employers to be increasingly mobile within Europe, leading to strong compet-ition between places to secure investment and the accompanying employment opportunities. In the Summer of 1993, in a much publicized case, the Hoover company held talks with unions at its plants in Dijon, France, and Cambuslang, Scotland. When the Scottish workers agreed a no-strike deal, Hoover announced its intention to cut 600 jobs in France and create up to 400 new jobs in Cambuslang, as labour costs were now relatively cheaper. It was argued by some at the time that countries which had weaker employment protection legislation and lower wage rates would effectively be poaching jobs from other localities. Given the importance of employment opportunities to the fortunes of cities, the stakes are clearly high. This is further illustrated by the fierce struggle which took place during 1993 between Plymouth and Rosyth to secure contracts to refit nuclear submarines at their respective dockyards. Late in 1994 Plymouth lost another 230 jobs when a large employer moved its operation to Mexico where labour costs were yet lower. Such competitive activity suggests that European regions may have to grow at the expense of others' decline.

Decentralization

Alongside this increased competition between urban regions, there has also been a trend within functional regions towards a decentralization or deconcentration of economic activity. The most common expression of this is the tendency for jobs and people to move away from the old cores of cities into surrounding 'rings' from where they commute into the cities. This process of *suburbanization* started in the nineteenth century with the development of the railways and has been further stimulated by the flexibility afforded to individuals by the car. In turn, many employers have now chosen to locate their businesses and factories in suburbs, away from the congestion of city centres and nearer to transport links such as motorway junctions and large trunk roads. This raises the possibility of what Wheeler (1974) calls 'reverse commuting' from a home in the city to a work-place in the suburbs. The last twenty years has seen the growing popularity of 'out-of-town' shopping developments such as superstores and hypermarkets, where an extensive range of goods can be offered under one roof, and extensive car parking offered adjacent to the store. Some retailers even run free bus services to entice those from further afield and the disabled to access their store. Out-of-town shopping then raises the demand for housing within easy reach of these facilities, thus encouraging builders to create new housing estates. In this way, the motor car has created a cycle of spatial change. This pattern of development also raises the possibility of a new kind of daily routine, where individuals avoid the city altogether, simply commuting from one out-of-town housing estate on the edge of town to a business park or industrial estate peripheral to the city but close to major transport routes. The UK's most obvious example is the M25 orbital motorway, where one can commute clockwise or anti-clockwise without ever reaching London; but other cities have been evolving this way. The various motorways circling Manchester are to be linked up to form a 'box' enclosing the city in a similar manner. All these patterns of development have implications for the older, more central areas of cities.

From the perspective of the town centre shop owner, this seems like a process of de-urbanization as s/he sees custom draining away; to rural dwellers it seems more like a process of advancing urban sprawl as they see the green fields at the bottom of the lane turn into executive homes and a superstore, and fears are raised about the destruction of the countryside. This example demon-strates an interesting sociological issue concerning urban life. As the tide of urbanization has swept over post-war Europe, sociologists have increasingly dismissed the idea of what they call an 'urban–rural continuum'; that is, any mean-ingful way of describing one style of life as more urban than another. However, what remains striking is how many people (including many of those sociologists!) aspire to a house in the country, to escape what they see as the negative features of urban life. The urban–rural contrast still exists today, both in the minds of individuals and in the expensive rural house prices which their demands help to create.

De-industrialization

In addition to the movement of existing jobs and population away from large urban centres, there has also been a large shift in the occupational structure (see Chapter 13) which has impacted disproportionately on certain established cities of the nineteenth century. Cheshire and Hay looked at two periods between 1974 and 1984 and concluded that 'if de-industrialization is defined in terms of falling employment rather than falling output, and long-term loss is accepted as a measure, then all EC countries except Ireland, Greece and Portugal are de-industrializing' (1989: 15). What these aggregative national data hide is the dramatic effects this can have on certain places. Since cities often grow in response to the expansion of one or two functions or products, the loss of those traditional industries can be devastating. Examples from the UK include the decline of Liverpool as an Atlantic-orientated port; the recent decline of Plymouth as a garrison town and dockyard; and the closure of Swan Hunter shipbuilders in Newcastle. As mentioned above, many of the new industries have located along arterial routes rather than in city centres, though many types of professional services, such as banking and law, continue to find city centre sites appealing and prestigious. During the 1980s Leeds became the second most important UK centre for legal services after London itself.

The inner city

While the relationships between cities become more complex and competitive, Parkinson and his colleagues (1993) point out that it is not possible simply to assume that a 'successful' city will necessary translate its wealth into high living standards for all its citizens. Cities in fact display high levels of inequality and segregation between areas or what are sometimes called 'quarters'. The problem of the inner cities is not simply their depopulation, but what we might call selective evacuation.

> Some types of economic activity have left the cities more quickly than others and some groups in the population have been able to leave the cities more easily than others. Specifically it is argued that it is the better-off groups in the population (those in higher income and social groups) which have been more inclined and better able to leave urban areas (while often continuing to commute daily into the cities to work), leaving the lower income and social groups concentrated in the inner cities.
>
> (Begg *et al.* 1985: 11)

In contemporary Europe, as in the nineteenth century, the city is extremely segregated in terms of social class (see Figure 20.3).

Most clearly, of course, this inequality is expressed through *residential* segregation, a feature common to all European cities but which takes different forms in each place. It is notable that in many Southern European cities the central areas are considered high status areas where the middle classes are over-represented. Northern Europe presents a more complex picture with many high status areas scattered across the whole of the city (White 1984: 163). In general, the following observations can be made:

1   Self-employed shopkeepers and business people play a much more significant part in the urban life of Southern Europe than in a country like Britain.
2   In general social class groupings are highly segregated, although inner city areas can be fairly mixed, due to the continuing desire of the European middle classes to have access to urban amenities.
3   There are not always direct relationships between social class and housing

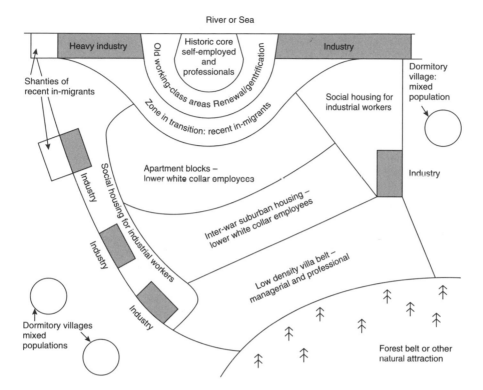

Figure 20.3 A model of the Western European city
Source: White, P. (1984: 188)

type or age. For instance, since the Second World War many new housing settlements have been constructed in peripheral areas in order to house working-class people.

4   Social areas are mostly distinctive for their social class composition, although the stage of the life-cycle which households have reached will also be influential, e.g. whether or not they have children (White 1984: 189–90).

Symptoms of urban illness: how and why to measure which ones?

We often use the term 'deprivation' to refer to the problems of inner city areas. It is important to realize that both individuals and areas can be deprived. A case of the former would be someone experiencing unemployment who also suffers from crime on the streets. Similarly, an area can be deprived in terms of its facilities, e.g. an inadequate public transport service or the absence of safe play areas for children. According to Robson (1994) there are four main dimensions of deprivation:

1   decaying physical environment;
2   lack of employment opportunities;
3   crime, both real and perceived;
4   poor quality housing.

These are some of the most oft-cited features, or indicators, of urban deprivation. But how do we select our definitions of deprivation? That is to say, how
do we decide which symptoms of urban ills are most in need of treatment? The
whole problem is extremely complex, and as so often in social science the terms
we use to describe what we do betray particular in-built perspectives. We have
already seen the diversity of experience in Europe, some countries experiencing
decline, others dealing with 'growing pains' and yet others still encouraging
growth. Even in the English case of decline, some talk of stress, others malaise,
or decay, decline, stagnation and so on. The blanket term 'deprivation' is most
commonly employed.

For those interested in specifying and quantifying urban problems (i.e.
where they are worst and how bad they are) there are two conceptual issues:

1   Which indicators do we choose?
2   What size of areas do we take as a unit of analysis?

The answers to these questions will reflect individual perspectives, and very
likely influence the conclusions drawn. Let us examine each of these problems
in turn. Indicators have to be constructed; they do not simply lie around waiting
to be discovered. The 'Creation of the Social Indicator' box neatly outlines the
process.

CREATION OF THE SOCIAL INDICATOR

observations
   organized systematically provide
data
   that contain basic information and can be ordered into
statistics
   either quantified on a scale or placed in an ordered ranking, further
   processed into
indicators
   designed to express
structure or change
   of phenomena related to
social and scientific concerns

(Horn 1993: 11)

The whole use of indicators has been criticized as 'empiricist'; that is, the
data are employed without any recourse to ideas about causal relationships. The
result, according to one observer,

has been a hotch-potch approach in which any variable deemed by the researcher to be even vaguely relevant to 'social stress', 'disadvantage', 'social need', 'social pathology' or 'social malaise', has been thrown into the statistical melting pot and those which emerged glued together by high correlation coefficients have been used as composite indices of urban deprivation.

(Edwards, quoted in Hamnett 1978)

These potential pitfalls make it essential that we clarify the nature and intent of our study approach. Hirschfield (1993) suggests four components of a research strategy which need to be clarified before commencing a successful project:

1   The concept under investigation (is it a housing problem, or one of poverty, few qualifications, high unemployment?).
2   The scale of analysis (see below).
3   The aim of the analysis (does it seek to simply measure and describe, is it looking at subsequent effects, i.e. impact evaluation, or does it actually seek to explain by correlations with other indicators?).
4   The perspective of the analysis (is it a snapshot or measuring change over time?).

The problem of choosing indicators becomes doubly important when we attempt to undertake *comparative* analysis. Certain indicators need interpreting; they do not speak for themselves. For example a commonly used indicator of deprivation is 'per cent households without a car'. This is likely to have a different significance in areas (like inner London) where there is frequent public transport than it does on a peripheral housing estate with no local shops or other amenities. Similarly, many studies have looked at the incidence of 'lone pensioner households'. The fact that an area has a large number of elderly people living alone says little about deprivation *per se*. They could indeed be isolated state pensioners, living in fear of crime and too poor to turn on their heating. They could equally well be inhabitants of a wealthy seaside retirement area, taking the morning air before driving down to the golf club in one of their household's two cars. In other words, as with all areas of social inquiry, we have to be sensitive to the need to interpret data appropriately.

Such are the variety of indicators available that it has become common practice to isolate areas or populations which display high scores on a number of measures; we then say that a place or community is 'multiply deprived'. Unfortunately, without detailed information about the experience of individual households, it cannot be assumed that the existence of multiple social problems in an area equates with the existence of multiple problems in particular households. This frequently unspoken assumption is known as the 'ecological fallacy'. In other words there may be two or more separate groups suffering in different ways, rather than a concentration of afflictions. Each of these situations would have rather different policy implications.

Questions of scale

We noted in the previous section that there are inequalities at a number of different levels:

- between regions;
- between cities within regions;
- between areas or 'quarters' of individual cities.

The problems posed by the ecological fallacy and the availability of particular kinds of data make the problem of scale much more significant than is often realized. What has made life especially difficult for policy-making is the fact that needs are often assessed within territorial units totally different from those through which resources are then allocated. For instance, unemployment rates are often provided for what we described earlier as 'functional regions' or 'local labour market areas' (LLMAs); in other words, a town or city and its neighbouring areas from where most of its workers commute. However, in a case like Manchester there are at least four separate borough authorities responsible for the geographical area which is the city's labour market. This makes the problem of co-ordination more difficult than in Europe where regional governments exist (see Chapter 15 on politics).

At what scales can we measure need or deprivation? The largest is the *region*. Eurostat produces comparative statistics across all the regions in the EU, the smallest of which equate with certain English counties. Within the standard English regions we do talk of sub-regions or LLMAs for the purpose of producing unemployment data. However, the most frequently made and published comparisons are between individual local authority areas, of which there are over 450 in Great Britain alone. Studies of this kind have revealed that the North of Britain has a greater tendency to suffer poverty, partly because of its industrial structure, and partly because it has more metropolitan areas than does the South. Comparison of local authority areas, however, can disguise very localized and concentrated pockets of deprivation, giving more attention to evenly spread problems. As we shall see, there can be important policy implications once again. Comparisons at the small area level in Europe remain extremely problematic because of the different bases on which data are collected and organized; they remain restricted to specific case studies.

Within local authorities themselves, it is common to compare conditions between smaller areas, such as electoral wards or the 'enumeration districts' used in the decennial census. This allows researchers to move beyond average 'deprivation scores' and look at the extent of inequalities within cities. This approach is useful because many so-called affluent cities have very deprived pockets which are often so concentrated that the visitor could be entirely unaware of them. A recent study for the Rowntree Foundation compared two British towns, Oldham and Oxford (Noble *et al.* 1994). Despite their contrasting images both have a similar 'poverty profile' in terms of numbers receiving benefits. The study showed that the gap between the most affluent and the most disadvantaged had widened between 1981 and 1991, and that they had become more geographically *polarized* too. Low-income households in Oldham had become increasingly concentrated on council estates. This was true to a lesser extent in Oxford. The extent of the differences also varied between the two towns when the research examined specific neighbourhoods. The most prosperous of these in Oldham had 2 to 3 per cent of residents in families dependent on income support, the poorest over 40 per cent. In Oxford the range between neighbourhoods stretched only from 5 per cent to 28 per cent.

Solutions

In discussing urban policy we need to be aware of the existence both of European-level policies for the regions and of national urban policies in member states. The European Union attempts to tackle regional inequalities through the structural funds (see Table 20.2). The funds offer support to designated areas to help alleviate specific problems such as long-term unemployment or the need for a better physical infrastructure. Since 1992 there have been a number of reforms to the structural funds and an increase in the resources devoted to them, largely designed to ease the introduction of the Single European Market in 1993 and to strengthen the cohesion of the EU as a whole. This approach has continued in the move towards closer economic and monetary union and has been supplemented by the establishment of a cohesion fund designed to aid the less well-off member states as they make the transition to EMU. Spain, Ireland, Greece and Portugal were the countries targeted.

In order to meet their goals, the structural funds focus on six priority objectives:

1   To promote the development and structural adjustment of underdeveloped regions, i.e. peripheral regions with relatively little industry or where industry is threatened, and whose per capita GDP is less than 75% of the

TABLE 20.2 Approximate breakdown by priority objective, billion ECU, 1994 prices

	1994	1995	1996	1997	1998	1999
Objective 1	12.9	13.9	14.9	16.0	17.4	18.8
Objective 2	2.2	2.3	2.4	2.5	2.6	2.8
Objectives 3 and 4	2.1	2.2	2.3	2.4	2.5	2.6
Objective 5a	1.2	1.1	0.9	0.9	0.9	0.9
Objective 5b	0.7	1.0	1.1	1.1	1.1	1.1
Total objectives	19.1	20.5	21.7	22.9	24.5	26.2
Community initiatives	1.9	2.0	2.2	2.3	2.4	2.6
Transitional and innovative measures	0.3	0.2	0.2	0.2	0.2	0.2
Total funds	21.3	22.7	24.1	15.4	27.2	29.0

Source: Eurostat (1996).

Note: In addition, ECU 4.7 billion (1995 prices) has been allocated to the three new member states for 1995–9.

EU average. Attention is focused on infrastructure, communications and water supply.

2   To redevelop regions or areas within regions (local labour markets or urban communities) seriously affected by industrial decline. In this case this means areas blighted by unemployment. Qualification criteria include above average unemployment, a disproportionate reliance on the industrial sector for employment, and signficant decline in such employment. Objective 2 status can be and is extended to other deserving areas with high unemployment or those affected by restructuring in the fishing industry. In all the above areas the intention is to develop industrial sites, improve links between research institutions and industry, and increase opportunities for training.

3   To combat long-term unemployment, to provide career prospects for young people (aged under 25) and to reintegrate persons at risk of being excluded from the labour market.

4   To facilitate the adaptation of workers to industrial change and developments in the production systems.

5a   To speed up the adaptation of production, processing and marketing structures in agriculture and forestry and to help modernize and restructure the fisheries and aquaculture sectors.

5b   To promote the development of rural areas.

6   Since the beginning of 1995, to promote the development of the northern regions in the new member states in Scandinavia (Finland and Sweden)

During the 1989–92 cycle of funding, the whole of Portugal and Ireland, large tracts of western Spain and the southern half of Italy qualified for Objective 1 funding which in total benefits 26.6% of the population of the EU. Since 1994 Merseyside has become the first part of England to join this grouping and be considered as a region of lagging development, putting it in the same category as the *Länder* of the former German Democratic Republic (East Germany). Many of the UK's old industrial centres met the Objective 2 criteria, as do pockets of industrial France, Italy and the Netherlands. Overall Objective 2 covers 16.8% of EU residents. France, Scotland and Wales have been the main beneficiaries of Objective 5b funding. In addition, more than ECU 4.7 billion is currently earmarked for the three new member states of Austria, Finland and Sweden.

In addition to European Commission programmes, some nation-states in Europe operate additional policies of one kind or another. However, the UK is unusual in perceiving urban decay as a major problem. Cheshire and Hay (1989: 180) remark 'there is, indeed, a crude coincidence between our diagnosis of when urban decline started and how bad it has been and the date and number of national policies introduced to relieve it'. Moreover, for a country like Greece, where urban growth is a comparatively recent phenomenon, it is too soon to worry about urban decline; peripherality from the core of Europe is a more pressing issue.

Another key problem in evaluating such policies in a UK context is to ask the question 'what is an urban or regional policy?'. Many government decisions have a spatial component or a spatial outcome, even if they do not carry an urban policy label, the battle of the dockyards being a classic example of this. The situation is complicated since almost alone among its European neighbours, the UK does not have a devolved tier of regional government (see p. 404). Central government has partially resolved this problem by running both a regional and (since 1968) an urban policy.

Regional policy in the period after the war was largely concerned with the problem of managing an orderly growth without threatening the Green Belt. The development of the New Towns, the programmes of slum clearance and the building of new public housing were all designed to aid 'dispersal' or, in the case of decaying municipal housing, 'decanting' from the cities. Since the 1960s, there has been more of a switch to the problem of decline, much of which was, in population terms, a direct and intended outcome of planning measures.

Critics of urban and regional policy complain of a lack of a consistent approach and of a lack of co-ordination between government spending departments – allegations which are not without some justification. For instance, the government's regional policy, administered by the Department for Trade and Industry (DTI) confers various levels of 'assisted area status' on localities in the UK. These designations have to be cleared with Brussels to ensure that they do not adversely affect free competition within Europe. Since August 1993, many parts of the South thought to be relatively prosperous have joined the list of assisted areas, including seaside towns such as Hastings in Sussex, Great Yarmouth in Norfolk and Weymouth in Dorset. During the same exercise, areas further north such as Accrington, Bradford, Darlington, Manchester and Telford all disappeared from the list, despite being in receipt of resources from various forms of policy.

Urban policy itself is believed to have been launched largely by accident, when Prime Minister Harold Wilson announced an urban programme in response to inflammatory remarks by Enoch Powell about racial tensions in Britain (the so-called 'Rivers of Blood' speech). There then followed six years of policy described by Lawless (1986) as a 'period of experimentation'. It could be argued that this epithet would apply equally well to the whole period from 1968 to the present day, with a constant switching of priorities, a renaming of programmes and the introduction of new instruments of policy. The Labour government's Inner Urban Areas Act of 1978 established local authorities as either Partnership or Programme authorities for receipt of Urban Programme resources. Partnership areas included Manchester/Salford, Newcastle/Gateshead, and Hackney/Islington. In addition to these several smaller authorities remained funded as Other Designated Districts (ODDs). In 1987 these designations were merged into one hierarchy of fifty-seven Urban Programme Areas (UPAs).

The Urban Programme has provided some continuity throughout this period, but perhaps the changes have been more significant. The Thatcher government elected in 1979 immediately pledged itself to a more free-market enterprise-driven strategy for economic recovery, based on the belief that wealth created in urban areas would 'trickle down' to the inhabitants of inner city areas. The emphasis of the Urban Programme turned from social to economic improvements, and the government experimented with the idea of Enterprise Zones, where businesses were given incentives to set up in a particular area. However, the high-water mark of inner city policy was in the Summer of 1981, when rioting broke out in some of Britain's urban areas, most famously Toxteth in Liverpool, Moss Side in Manchester, and the Brixton area of London. It was ironic that the immediate cause of all three disturbances was a breakdown of relations between police and black youth, since racial tension had been the catalyst for the development of urban policy. This time new developments were a response not to inflammatory words, but to a hail of inflammatory materials which destroyed large swathes of inner city communities. The Environment Minister Michael Heseltine made a now famous visit to Merseyside, promised action, and soon after was taking business leaders on bus tours of the area showing the need and opportunity for investment. The immediate outcome was the setting up of two new Urban Development Corporations, single-purpose agencies with extra planning powers which had a brief to develop specific geographical areas. The first of these were in Merseyside and in London Docklands; second and third waves of UDCs followed in 1987 and 1988. Most recently, Plymouth became the latest recipient when £45 million was made available to redevelop an ex-MOD site at Royal William Yard in the city's Stonehouse district.

Initiatives such as UDCs, Enterprise Zones, and the thirty-one City Challenge areas currently operating have raised questions over how government should best target its resources. We saw in the previous section that there are many methodological problems inherent in isolating the most deprived areas, most obviously those concerning our choice of indicators and our size of area. There is also the question of whether urban problems can ever be addressed *spatially* in any case, since they are largely the result of events beyond one geographical area. As long ago as the 1840s Friedrich Engels argued:

> The breeding places of disease, the infamous holes and cellars in which the capitalist mode of production confines our workers night after night, are not abolished; they are merely shifted elsewhere! The same economic necessity which produced them in the first place produces them in the next place also! As long as the capitalist mode of production continues to exist it is folly to hope for an isolated settlement of the housing question or of any other social question affecting the lot of the workers. The solution lies in the abolition of the capitalist mode of production.
>
> (quoted in Saunders 1986: 26)

In Britain spatial targeting of urban policy has taken two forms; firstly, there has been the designation of certain local authorities as Urban Programme Authorities, or 'Safer Cities' for example. Secondly, there has been increased pressure on authorities to target a small number of areas within their own boundaries. The issue of targeting has been controversial, but the evidence shows that in England targeting has been, if anything, too ambiguous or half-hearted. A recent government-sponsored report set out to examine expenditure patterns during the 1980s, looking in particular at programmes which were part of the Action for Cities (AfC) initiative after 1987/8. Table 20.3 shows the results of the analysis.

What these rankings show is that, even during the two-year period when AfC expenditure was officially targeted at the fifty-seven UPAs, and for which all

TABLE 20.3 Targeting of Action for Cities expenditure: ranking of the sample of 123 districts by per capita AfC expenditure, 1988/9 and 1989/90

Rank	District	Per capita	Designation (with main expenditure resource head for non-UPAs within the top 57)
1	Tower Hamlets	1,717.11	UPA
2	Newham	799.51	UPA
3	Scunthorpe	269.27	non-UPA (EZ)
4	Southwark	225.56	UPA
5	Gateshead	206.07	UPA
6	Corby	189.35	non-UPA (EZ and DLG)
7	Salford	183.26	UPA
8	Stockton on Tees	177.02	UPA
9	Hartlepool	170.82	UPA
10	Newcastle upon Tyne	148.63	UPA
11	Trafford	134.31	non-UPA (EZ and UDC)
12	Sandwell	132.40	UPA
13	Rochester-on-Medway	121.47	non-UPA (EZ and EE)
14	Middlesbrough	117.64	UPA
15	Liverpool	115.95	UPA
16	The Wrekin	105.86	UPA
17	Manchester	102.44	UPA
18	Dudley	98.58	UPA
19	Kingston upon Hull	98.06	UPA
20	Walsall	96.87	UPA
21	Islington	89.53	UPA
22	South Tyneside	89.10	UPA
23	Rochdale	87.38	UPA
24	Blackburn	86.18	UPA
25	Rossendale	85.86	non-UPA (EZ, DLG, EA and EE)
26	Wolverhampton	79.88	UPA
27	Burnley	79.75	UPA
28	Hyndburn	77.67	non-UPA (EZ, CG, DLG and EA)
29	Preston	71.23	UPA
30	Sunderland	70.83	UPA
31	Oldham	68.96	UPA
32	Coventry	68.44	UPA
33	Nottingham	65.65	UPA
34	Knowsley	65.54	UPA
35	Birmingham	61.10	UPA
36	St Helens	60.12	UPA
37	Sheffield	58.87	UPA
38	Wirral	57.66	UPA
39	Hackney	54.76	UPA
40	Leicester	52.82	UPA
41	Bradford	51.94	UPA
42	Rotherham	51.69	UPA
43	Lambeth	50.61	UPA
44	Halton	49.43	UPA

TABLE 20.3 continued

Rank	District	Per capita	Designation (with main expenditure resource head for non-UPAs within the top 57)
45	Haringey	49.06	UPA
46	Kensington/Chelsea	46.62	UPA
47	Greenwich	46.58	UPA
48	Bolton	43.58	UPA
49	Brent	43.58	UPA
50	Derwentside	43.40	non-UPA (DLG and EE)
51	Barnsley	42.80	UPA
52	Gravesham	42.69	non-UPA (EZ)
53	North Tyneside	41.85	UPA
54	Ellesmere	41.31	non-UPA (DLG and EE)
55	Doncaster	41.17	UPA
56	Wellingborough	39.64	non-UPA (EZ)
57	Langbaurgh	38.94	UPA
58	Derby	38.28	UPA
59	Barrow	34.60	
60	Wigan	33.89	UPA
61	Pendle	33.63	
62	Leeds	32.36	UPA
63	Hammersmith/Fulham	32.30	UPA
64	Ealing	27.89	
65	West Lancashire	26.39	
66	Wandsworth	25.23	UPA
67	Kirklees	24.53	UPA
68	Lewisham	23.33	UPA
69	Bristol	21.98	UPA
70	Wakefield	20.98	
71	Waltham Forest	20.92	
72	Easington	17.76	
73	Chester-le-Street	16.51	
74	Calderdale	15.45	
75	Stoke-on-Trent	12.05	
76	Sefton	11.00	UPA
77	Enfield	10.59	
78	Bury	10.40	
79	Plymouth	10.15	UPA

123

Source: Reproduced with the permission of the DoE from their report 'Assessing the Impact of Urban Policy' (1994).

Note: Details are shown for top 79 authorities so as to include all of the 57 UPAs.

Key: UPA – Urban Programme Authority; EZ – Enterprise Zone; DLG – area in receipt of Derelict Land Grant; EA – Estate Action Scheme area; EE – English Estates funding; CG – area in receipt of City Grant.

data was available, several unranked authorities appear very high up the list of beneficiaries. Similarly, many of the so-called '57' fall way outside the best-funded fifty-seven authorities in the country. What complicates this picture still further is the point made earlier about 'unlabelled' policy decisions having spatial outcomes and knock-on consequences for urban policy itself. In July 1993, fears were raised that due to a central government decision to cut their education funding to single parent families, metropolitan councils such as Bradford, Lambeth and Wolverhampton would lose out to wealthy shires like Oxfordshire and Surrey. We saw in the previous section how tricky the methodological problems of deprivation are; they can also have very real consequences for policy outcomes. Equally, government transport policy has overwhelmingly favoured private cars and road building schemes over public transport. This has a built-in anti-urban bias since it encourages the sorts of 'out-of-town' developments discussed on p. 407.

As the 1990s have progressed, 'policy remedies' have become increasingly holistic; that is to say, they have tried to cure the whole patient and not just a painful limb. Emphasis has been on the lasting and sustainable recovery of a city's economic base, rather than on tackling urban inequalities directly. The conflict bemoaned by Robson (1988) between the social and economic aims of policy has not been reconciled after all. Moreover, the central symbol of English urban policy, the Urban Programme, is being wound down and effectively the idea of a favoured fifty-seven urban areas with it. Intriguingly the government has set up integrated regional offices to manage a Single Regeneration Budget, suggesting a convergence between urban and regional policy similar to that of Europe. However, the important difference is that while the German *Länder* and the French *départements* have elected assemblies, the SRB is being run by what are effectively regional arms of Whitehall (Deas and Harrison 1994). Nevertheless, it demonstrates a degree of convergence in the European urban framework.

Increasingly it is the case that cities seek to solve their problems by redefining their roles in a world where heavy industry no longer dominates employment. This type of strategy is often referred to as 'cultural regeneration' (Bianchini and Parkinson 1993). In this way, a city's identity or image becomes very important in helping attract investment, population and tourist activity. Many administrations employ specialists in 'place marketing' to achieve these objectives, some with more success than others depending on their climate, resources and political clout. There are many examples of this being tried in Continental Europe.

Manchester has, since the 1970s, consolidated and expanded its role as a regional centre for the North of England. The area along and to the east of Oxford Road houses three universities and taken together forms the largest student 'campus' in Europe. Cultural attractions include the Hallé Orchestra and the Palace and Exchange theatres. A whole variety of bars, cafés and night-clubs make the city a huge draw for young people, whether studying or in paid employment. It has introduced a Light Rapid Transit (LRT) system which runs through the heart of the city and links north and south suburbs, encouraging the use of fast, clean public transport. Such initiatives represent an attempt to replace the productive activities of the nineteenth century (and associated images) with new ones based on leisure and consumerism. In addition, the city has made two bids to stage the Olympic Games which, though unsuccessful, have helped raise the

---

CASE STUDY: REBUILDING ROTTERDAM

Bombed flat in 1940 Rotterdam has spent most of the post-war period undergoing some sort of reconstruction or another. In its most recent form urban
regeneration has been concerned with the creation of a dynamic and 'interesting' urban environment in which people can live and work. In common with
many cities, after the Second World War Rotterdam was reconstructed along
'modernist' lines dominated by the Lijnbaan shopping area. The emphasis here
was on a practical urban environment where shoppers were able to move
freely and where areas were zoned into particular uses. During the two decades
after the war the urban population rose to its all-time high of 731,564, but fell
back during the late 1960s as planners sought consciously to move population
to the 'healthier' environment of the suburbs, though some new urban housing
was constructed during the period.

During the 1970s efforts were made to open up the city to greater public
use, to integrate the different uses of the central areas; in short to create a
'participative' city. This was the period when social objectives were at the fore-
front of policy. In recent years such ideals have had to take their place
alongside economic imperatives, as the city authorities have used cultural
regeneration techniques to address the needs and interests of the middle-class
white-collar workers it wished to attract. The so-called 'New Rotterdam' has
involved preserving the dynamism of the participatory period while moving
some way towards the resegregation of the city. Of particular interest here is
the area known as the Cultural Triangle. By attracting art galleries and other
'high cultural' activities to this sector the council hoped to create what we
might think of as an 'exclusive' or 'sophisticated' area. This has been made
more difficult by the continued existence of a more 'seamy' sub-culture well
known for illegal drugs and gambling, despite law and order legislation in that
direction. Thus the attempt to present urban living as dynamic and interesting
is by no means a straightforward task.

(derived from Hajer 1993)

---

city's international profile and attract government funding for a new cycling
stadium. Manchester has expressed the determination to attract the 2002
Commonwealth Games, although how far this has been damaged by the Arndale
Centre bomb in June 1996 is open to question.

The future of the city

We have stressed throughout this chapter that the whole question of urban life
is problematic, and that individual countries seem unsure how far to encourage
urban growth. Many of the policy solutions discussed here seem to assume that
cities are something we should want to maintain, and that wholesale urban decline
would be undesirable. As we have seen, there are essentially two sets of problems, one associated with the decline of the *city*, and another with deprivation

concentrated into certain areas often described as the *inner city*. They are largely related since it is the exodus of the most affluent groups into the countryside which helps undermine city economies and leads to decline for those left behind.

It is argued by many that urban life is a stimulating experience which allows one access to a whole host of economic and cultural facilities within easy travelling distance. The hustle and bustle, and the degree of anonymity which moving in a crowd gives us, provide an excellent human environment. Others take an ecological view; the city is the most *sustainable* form of living, avoiding the endless frustration and pollutants of automobile transport and protecting rural areas from needless new development while existing urbanized areas become ghost towns. In other words, for both population and planet, the city is the best hope for a civilized future.

However, the problems remain formidable, and will require not just specific policies carrying urban or even regional labels, but a re-think of the way human populations organize themselves. Only recently, a common perception of the city was given the backing of Britain's prime minister:

> Look at our suburbs and small towns and villages – where people, by and large, own their own homes. Here you will find networks of the voluntary associations which tie people into their neighbourhood, from Rotary Clubs to the active PTA to fund-raising and Meals on Wheels. The big problem lies elsewhere. It is from the inner cities, where the state is dominant, that businesses have fled. It is in the inner cities that vandalism is rife and property uncared-for.

Though some aspects of this analysis could be disputed there is no denying that such anti-urban attitudes strike a chord with many. In their eyes, inner city decay is not the outcome of social inequalities and the movements of competitive capital, but the cause. It is those who live in and rule the cities who have created the mess and who must be held accountable. These competing diagnoses of the chronic urban ills described in this chapter would seem to suggest that the nature of urban problems will continue to be hotly contested, and conflicting remedies prescribed.

Summary

- Urban 'problems' take many forms, both physical and attitudinal.
- There are many difficulties involved in measuring urban deprivation, including choice of indicator and choice of scale.
- Many approaches to urban policy have been tried, and these reflect the complexity of the causes of the original problems.

Further reading

Daniel Noin and Robert Woods (eds) (1993) *The Changing Population of Europe*, Oxford: Basil Blackwell. Chapters 3, 11 and 14 give a useful picture of what is happening to the population map of Europe, which areas are 'on the up' and which are in decline, by dealing with urbanization, employment and migration respectively.

Brian Robson (1988) *Those Inner Cities: Reconciling the Social and Economic Aims of Urban Policy*, Oxford: Oxford University Press. An accessible overview of urban problems in Britain and an assessment of some of the policy instruments employed by the Thatcher government in the 1980s. Particularly good on the relationship between regeneration and social justice, and is generally positive about the value of cities.

Franco Bianchini and Michael Parkinson (eds) (1993) *Cultural Policy and Urban Regeneration: The West European Experience*, Manchester: Manchester University Press. A useful collection of case studies demonstrating the value of the arts and culture more broadly in helping reshape cities and attract employment and investment.

Chapter 21

Peripheral nationalism in the European Union

Malcolm Williams

Introduction: contemporary challenges to the
   nation-state   424
The historical origins of peripheral nationalism   425
Peripherality and nationalism   426
The ethnic basis of national identity   427
The politics of peripheral nationalism   430
Conflict and violence at the periphery   431
A Europe of the peoples?   433
Summary   433
Further reading   434

Key concepts

- **Peripherality**
- **Identity, territory, ethnicity**
- **Civic and ethnic nationalisms**

Introduction: contemporary challenges to the nation-state

The European Union is a union of nation-states, of countries that often refer to themselves as 'nations'. Yet there is a very different kind of claim on the word 'nation' that comes from within the territories of virtually all of the member states of the European Union. 'Peripheral', or 'sub-state' nationalism is one of the most important social and political forces in the Union, and though the terms may not be familiar it is something which most people have encountered in one form or another. Images of violence in Northern Ireland or the Basque Country are commonplace on our TV screens, and though outside of the European Union the events in the former Yugoslavia illustrate the extremes of violence and degradation than can result from challenges to the existing order. Yet not all peripheral nationalism is violent. Much of it is about the assertion of identity based on territory and a distinct ethnic culture. This can take the form of movements for the promotion of languages such as Welsh, Breton, or Friesian. In other cases the challenges are political and may be in the form of constitutional parties such as the Scottish Nationalist Party, or single issue pressure groups. All of these challenges to the nation-state have one thing in common. They are an assertion of the rights of an indigenous ethnic group who live on a clearly identifiable territory. Most, but not all, claim some form of self-government based upon the territory. These claims to autonomy range from that of independence, in the case of Scotland, to simply aspirations to greater regional autonomy in (for example) Galicia, in northern Spain.

The territories of these 'ethnic communities' vary enormously in size from the tiny Isle of Man to Occitania, an area the size of England in the south of France. What is important politically and interesting for the sociologist is that peripheral nationalism takes such a variety of forms and levels of 'visibility'. For example, one could travel for some considerable period in the south of France and never really be aware of a separate Occitan identity (though more than 2 million people speak Occitan), yet half an hour in the Basque Country or Corsica is enough to realize there is a powerful sense of identity that is not Spanish or French.

Where have these – sometimes powerful – claims of identity come from? It is true that in recent years there has been a resurgence of peripheral nationalism in Europe, yet the themes and ideas that underlie it are somewhat older. Nations, whether they are France or Friesland require legitimation from their inhabitants to continue to exist. If suddenly (or even gradually) the people of France stopped believing in the concept of France, then France would cease to exist. The 'concept' of France, or Friesland, or Wales requires the recognition by a sufficient number of people of a shared identity, in particular the feeling of a common historical experience. This experience is expressed through things such as a separate language, music, art, literature, etc. Often these things are deliberately designed to win people's allegiance to the nation and can take the form of a national flag or anthem. In most cases and always in Europe, claims to nationality lie in the alleged antiquity of these cultural forms (see also Chapter 3 on nation, nationalism, nation-state in the emergence of the European state system).

Yet the idea of a 'nation', as we now understand the term, is not particularly old. Most of the nation-states that now comprise the European Union have existed for less than two centuries. Indeed many of the territories that have contemporary nationalist movements challenging the nation-states can claim an older pedigree. As Anthony Smith points out (1991: 58), both France and Spain emerged as identifiable nation-states only through annexation of culturally diverse territories, and in the latter case in particular this incorporation was never accepted by many Basques or Catalans. However whilst France and Spain 'absorbed' these quite separate territories it does not mean that these were fully formed nations in the way we understand them today. In some cases the 'absorbed' territories were no more than just ethnic communities who shared a common language and culture. Often the resistance to absorption was itself the mechanism through which a self-aware identity was established. Benedict Anderson maintains nationalism requires the imagination of a distinct community, with particular cultural and territorial characteristics (Anderson 1983).

What is important for nationalism is not so much an accurate representation of a group's history, but a shared belief in symbols that have come to represent that history. Not all of these have their origins in antiquity. For example, Scottish clan tartans are mostly traceable to the nineteenth century, and one of the cornerstones of Welsh identity, the Gorsedd, was 'invented' by the poet Iolo Morganwyg in the late nineteenth century (Williams 1985: 162).

The historical origins of peripheral nationalism

The idea of the 'nation' and 'nationalism' as political concepts is traceable only to the eighteenth century. Anthony Smith maintains that in countries such as France, Spain and Britain the 'state' existed before the nation, though this process was a complex one (Smith 1991: 60–1). He points to three sets of processes that were central in the creation of the state. The first was economic. The growth of capitalism increased trading networks in Europe and later the 'New World'; this in turn led to more efficient economies, the growth of the military and the need for more efficient administration. Secondly, the decline of the power of the Church was paralleled by a growing secular cultural elite. The new intellectual elite was itself recruited to serve the state. Thirdly, these processes allowed the newly powerful state to define the character and the boundaries of what were becoming national communities. This in turn brought more and more peripheral areas into the new 'nation-states'. However, this economic, administrative and cultural expansion led to the often unwilling absorption of cultures and territories that were quite different in character to that represented by the new nation-state. For example Basque culture and language were quite distinct from that of the Spanish state which claimed legitimacy over their lands. This claim accompanied a rapid industrialization in the north of the Basque Country – a process that involved Spanish capital and (mostly) Spanish workers. Until the nineteenth century the Basque Country was almost entirely rural and its contacts with the world limited – indeed it did not begin to think of itself in 'national' terms until after the process of absorption by Spain was well advanced (Sullivan 1988: 1).

Virtually all of the peripheral nationalist movements in the European Union of today have their origins in the late nineteenth century. Though all can point to moments of resistance to absorption into the nation-state the form that the nationalism subsequently took is a product of a cultural renaissance at the end of the last century. This renaissance, itself a reaction to the rationalism of the Enlightenment, placed great emphasis on the revival of language, in poetry, but most of all in the 'spiritual' value of the nation (Snyder 1954: 188–95) in opposition to the rationalizing tendencies of capitalism. The peripheral national movements we see today have their origins in both resistance to absorption into larger states and in a cultural reaction to the processes that created the nation-states themselves, and though the claims to separateness can be said to be based on an ethnic identity which may have a long history, an awareness of that identity and the symbols that have come to comprise that awareness may be relatively recent in origin.

Peripherality and nationalism

One important characteristic of the kind of nationalism we are discussing here is its basis in 'peripherality'. Like many terms in sociology its meaning is rather subtle. It can mean, and often does, that the territory of the ethnic group in question is geographically peripheral to the capital, or economic and cultural heartland of the nation-state it is within. For example, all of the territories where there are peripheral nationalist movements in Britain are a long way from London and the 'home' counties. Yet peripherality can and usually does mean other things. It is often claimed that a territory is economically peripheral in the policies of the nation-state. Nationalists in Scotland, for example, have long claimed that whilst Scotland makes a huge economic contribution to the United Kingdom it is treated as peripheral in economic development terms. It is claimed, in much the same way as in the developing countries, that Scotland provides cheap raw materials and labour but receives few economic benefits (see McCrone 1992). Empirical data does indeed support such assertions in Scotland and elsewhere. High unemployment, low wages and other forms of economic and social disadvantage have been historically common in the Celtic periphery of Britain, but whereas nationalist movements have arisen in Scotland, Wales and Cornwall they have not arisen in other deprived areas of economic peripherality, such as the North East or North West of England.

Economic arguments about peripherality are accompanied by cultural ones. The cultures of the groups described here are minority cultures within the wider nation-state and it is a nationalist claim that they are marginalized and trivialized. They are thus peripheral to the central cultural concerns of the majority of the nation-state. Correspondingly the 'nation-state' identity is said to be weaker. Oonagh O'Brien found that Catalans, in that part of Catalonia in the French state, whilst stressing the marginalization of their own culture by the French, also had a very weak 'French' identity concomitant with their distance from a French cultural 'heartland' (O'Brien 1993: 110).

Yet peripherality does not always indicate physical distance from a 'centre' or even clear-cut inequitable cultural or economic peripherality. Sometimes, as in the case of Belgium, two competing nationalisms (Flemish and Walloon) each claim disadvantage and discrimination allegedly imposed by the other group. In Northern Ireland peripherality takes quite a different form. Both 'Protestant' and 'Catholic' communities stress their feeling of distance from London. In the first case this is often a matter to be regretted, but in the latter geographic, economic and cultural distance are part of the argument for a desire for union with the Republic (Boyce 1991). Perhaps more importantly nationalists in the Catholic community will emphasize the 'distance' they feel from economic and political power within their own community.

The ethnic basis of national identity

Economic peripherality is not a sufficient condition for peripheral nationalism, whereas cultural factors are both a necessary and a sufficient condition. In other words nationalism is based in culture and not economy and moreover need not make any assertions about economic conditions. Almost all peripheral nationalism is, however, founded on a claim to a separate and distinct ethnic identity to that of the predominant group in the nation-state. But what is meant by 'ethnic' in this respect? Anthony Smith offers two extreme definitions (Smith 1986). The first is biological – that a group can trace biological descent to common origins. Ethnicity is exclusive and confined solely to those who can demonstrate biological descent. At the opposite extreme 'situational ethnicity' is seen simply as a matter of holding certain attitudes, perceptions and sentiments. This form of ethnicity is subject to change depending on circumstances. In Europe most claims to ethnic identity lie between these extremes. Nineteenth-century industrialization, wars and modern communications have had at least some impact everywhere in Europe and few communities could be defined in terms of unique biological character-istics. Conversely, situational ethnicity, though arguably important in the developing world, is rare in Europe. Smith (1991: 21) then, offers the following characteristics of an ethnic community:

1   a collective and proper name;
2   a myth of common ancestry;
3   shared historical memories;
4   one or more differentiating elements of common culture;
5   an association with a specific 'homeland';
6   a sense of solidarity for significant sectors of the population.

The presence of all of these characteristics might be said to correspond to a Weberian 'ideal type', though whilst such characteristics are present in most ethnic communities with nationalist movements in the EU, the extent to which they are present varies enormously and is often a characteristic which is not measurable. An example of how 'differentiating elements of common culture' may exert varying amounts of influence on an ethnic community is demonstrated through the use of the 'national' language. Virtually all peripheral nationalisms will make linguistic claims about their community, yet the role language plays in the day-to-day affairs of the ethnic community is quite a good barometer of the strength of identity.

Let us take some examples: in the Spanish region of Catalonia, Catalan is the language of the home, of commerce, of regional and local government. Simply using (what is for most) a first language is a continuous and everyday assertion of a differentiating aspect of common culture. Catalan is spoken across virtually the whole of Catalonia and even beyond in the neighbouring region of Valencia. Contrast this with Welsh or Breton. In both cases the 'ethnic' language is spoken by less than 25 per cent of the population and is mainly concentrated in quite small geographical areas. Now whilst these areas in Wales are the most 'nationalist' it is not the case in Brittany where a great deal of nationalist fervour is found in the cities where Breton is spoken by relatively few people. In some ethnic communities, such as Cornwall, the 'native' language has been revived after its effective death, but is nevertheless an important characteristic in claims to separate identity. What is important in the examples here is that language plays an important actual and symbolic role, even for non-speakers, but nevertheless can vary enormously in its importance in raising or maintaining a sense of identity (for a discussion of these issues, see MacDonald 1993).

Though most peripheral nationalisms rely on notions of separate ethnic identity this can give rise to quite different forms of nationalism. Some forms of nationalism have traditionally relied heavily on metaphors of kinship or blood, such as 'father/motherland', 'kith and kin', etc. These metaphors themselves serve as a delineation of who is part of the ethnic community and who is not. This delineation can take two main forms. The first might be described as 'exclusive'. In this case to belong to the ethnic community is a matter of demonstrating descent from that community, or by acceptance by the community. Either way the decision lies with other members of the community. The second can be described as 'inclusive', and whether or not one 'belongs' is a matter of individual choice. This form of nationalism can nevertheless be quite militant and is exemplified by ETA in the Basque Country. Jeremy MacClancy describes ETA's definition of being Basque:

> Members of ETA ignore people's surnames, do not look at the shape of their heads nor at the colour of their eyes, but stress the central importance of speaking Basque. To them, the Basque language is the main cultural prop, a besieged form of distinctiveness which must be maintained.
>
> (MacClancy 1993: 86)

ETA's brand of nationalism is suffused with particular views about class, but nevertheless can be seen as a form of territorial nationalism which stresses the oppression of those who inhabit a particular territory. Indeed, to be a Basque patriot – an *abertzales* – performance rather than birth is what is important. An *abertzales* is 'one who actively participates in the political struggle for an independent Basque nation with its own distinctive culture' (MacClancy 1993: 86). ETA, like the IRA, is a militant organization committed to armed struggle, yet 'inclusive' nationalisms which stress the civic nature of the ethnic community are common, and perhaps becoming more so, in the EU. For example the Scottish

National Party has long been committed to a civic nationalism which stresses equal citizenship for all who reside in a future independent Scotland. Civic forms of nationalism, whilst still stressing the importance of the ethnic community, have gradually replaced older more exclusive nationalisms in the EU.

THE ETHNIC AND CIVIC DIMENSIONS OF BRETON NATIONALISM

Brittany is located in North West France. Its population is just over 3 million, a third of which are concentrated in five large towns and cities. About 1 million people speak Breton. Most of these people live in the rural hinterland in the west of the province. Breton culture is Celtic and Breton nationalism has long stressed its cultural links with Wales, Cornwall and Ireland. Like most nationalisms mentioned in this chapter it has its origins in the romantic revival of the nineteenth century. Yet Breton nationalism has long stressed the importance of the antiquity of Breton culture and the independence of the Breton 'nation' up until the French Revolution. Breton nationalism up until after the Second World War was romantic, ethnic and exclusive in character. Indeed this form of nationalism reached its apotheosis during the Second World War when some nationalists in an organization called Breizh Atao (Brittany Forever) supported the Germans against the French, to the extent that specifically Breton units fought in the German army. Though an extreme group denounced by many Breton nationalists (who fought with the Resistance), there was nevertheless a consensus across the movement that the goal of Brittany for the Bretons was what Breton nationalism was about.

Yet in 1964 a very different form of nationalism emerged with the foundation of a new political party, the Breton Democratic Union (UDB). Whilst its founders were intellectuals, as was the case in Breton nationalism before, they were on the political left and were much influenced by contemporary anti-colonial struggles. In particular they saw parallels between the war against French rule in Algeria and the struggle for Breton autonomy. For UDB 'autonomy' came to replace 'nationalism' as a description of their aims. They did not claim to be a nationalist party as such, but a 'party of the Breton people'. The Breton people, in this case, were those who lived and worked in Brittany. The UDB was formed as a party of socialist autonomy and has attempted to build bridges between the traditional French Left and Breton nationalism. This has not always been popular with other nationalists and the participation of the party in the French Union of the Left in the early 1980s directly contributed to a waning of UDB fortunes. Yet arguably its brand of civic nationalism has left its mark. Whilst Breton nationalism has spanned a range of militancy, from the IRA-style Breton Liberation Front (FLB) to moderate cultural nationalists, the emphasis and style of Breton nationalism is nowadays inclusive. Its concern with environment and civil rights echoes the nationalisms of its Celtic neighbours in Cornwall and Wales. For further reading on Breton nationalism see McDonald (1990).

Recent anthropological and sociological studies of individuals in places such as Corsica, Wales and Catalonia (see for example O'Brien 1993) have shown the importance of the role of ethnic identity in one's personal identity. Brian Roberts's (1993) study of identity formation in an ex-coal-mining community in Wales, lays stress on the formation of new identities based on ethnic community as a survival strategy in the face of the collapse of older identities based on the economic community of mining. Welshness was seen as a positive characteristic with which individuals could self-identify. Indeed it is not just indigenous members of ethnic communities who wish to lay claim to particular ethnic identities. There is a small but increasing number of people who choose to move from the urban core – of Paris, London or Madrid, for example – to 'peripheral' ethnic communities in order to immerse themselves in the language, culture (and sometimes politics) of such communities. Two important points emerge from this. Firstly, the desire to self-identify with an ethnic community, whether or not one is native, seems to suggest an individual need for identity based on discernible geographic–cultural communities. Secondly, the dynamic nature of ethnic identity formation is evidence that the phenomenon of 'peripheral' identity and its emergent nationalism is not a historical hangover but a contemporary and vibrant phenomenon.

The politics of peripheral nationalism

One of the most important features of peripheral nationalism is the presence of political parties which organize only within the ethnic community itself. Virtually all of these parties make some form of claim to self-government, but the form this takes and the popularity it attracts vary enormously.

Though the peripheral nationalist political organizations campaign for autonomy, or self-government, and are thus opposed to the existing order, most are 'constitutional' – in other words they operate within the electoral framework of the nation-state. Many have been successful. Indeed in the Basque Country and Catalonia nationalist parties have controlled the regional governments for some time. In many other areas nationalist MPs or MEPs have been elected. What are the conditions necessary for the successful growth of peripheral nationalist political movements? James Kellas (1992) identifies a number of factors in the growth of Scottish nationalism and in particular the Scottish National Party (SNP). Firstly, whilst on some economic indicators Scotland is better off than many English regions (though very much worse off on others), there is nevertheless a sense of the South of England (in particular) being better off. The South of England is, of course, the seat of government of the British state. Thus there is a conflation of an economic dissatisfaction with a political one. Nevertheless these dissatisfactions would not be enough to lead to the development of nationalism. Moreover, Kellas notes that SNP membership is actually higher in the more prosperous rural North and lower in the relatively deprived South. This would suggest the importance of cultural factors in the growth of political nationalism. Kellas points to the existence of a separate literary tradition, education system and a number of 'national' institutions such as the National Trust for Scotland or the Scottish Arts Council. Though it does not follow that those associated with national culture will become nationalists it is certainly the case, in Scotland and elsewhere, that political expressions of nationalism are likely to have their origins amongst a native intelligentsia.

Indeed nationalism as a political and cultural doctrine has long been associated with the educated middle classes. Smith (1986) has suggested that nationalist movements originate with a rising intelligentsia where that group's cultural or economic ambitions become blocked. However, the nationalism of this bourgeoisie is tempered by its desire to maintain an ordered society and the possibility of making their demands known and accepted by the 'centre'.

Conflict and violence at the periphery

The question of why violence occurs in some ethnic communities and not others is complex and a question that is by no means uncontroversial. The way in which the politics of peripheral nationalisms develop is a function of a number of diverse factors, many of which are unique to particular states and ethnic communities. Violence is usually the result of a complex tangle of historical, cultural and political factors where the role of the nation-state and its relationships with the periphery can be crucial. Sustained campaigns of violence have been the hallmark of three peripheral nationalisms in the European Union. These have been in Northern Ireland, the Basque Country and Corsica. Each has a different character and history.

The conflict in Northern Ireland did not begin with the despatch of British troops to Belfast and Derry in 1968, but was the culmination of a history of conflict stretching back to the invasion of Ireland by Oliver Cromwell in the seventeenth century (Boyce 1991). The whole of Ireland was ruled from London until 1922 when the Treaty of Partition gave self-government to the South. The creation of the Irish Free State was the result of an armed struggle which had manifested itself in a number of risings over more than 150 years. The Treaty was an attempt by the British government to placate the Unionists in the North who were opposed to Irish home rule. The Unionists, who were passionately loyal to Britain, were the descendants of Protestant Scottish farmers settled by the British, mainly in the North, over two hundred years ago. The stance of the Unionists and the resulting partition was vigorously opposed by many of the nationalists and a brutal civil war ensued in which British troops (the 'Black and Tans') were deployed against the 'anti-treaty forces'. It is this historical baggage that underlies the more recent conflict. Without doubt the seeds of conflict lie in cultural identifications, which it might be argued have been reinforced by material deprivation.

The IRA has had a long history and unsurprisingly this has been mythologized by subsequent generations. Leaders of the 1916 Rising, such as James Connolly and Padraig Pearse, are not just the heroes of the militant nationalists of the present IRA but are legitimated as 'founders' of modern Ireland by the contemporary establishment in the Republic (Foley 1992). The modern IRA simply sees itself continuing the same struggle. However this 'struggle' would simply be an expression of romantic nationalism if the organization had not had a basis of popular support. Until comparatively recently Catholics in Northern Ireland did not enjoy the same civil rights as Protestants and, moreover, their access to jobs and good quality housing was poorer. This led to widespread resentment which erupted in the Civil Rights marches of 1968 and the subsequent despatch of British troops to Northern Ireland. Though the latter were initially there to protect the Catholic ghettos from Protestant mobs, their presence soon began to be resented and for many it was seen as the return of the 'Black and Tans'. (For a discussion of Ireland see Boyce 1991.)

The history of Corsica has been quite different to Ireland's. The island's position in the Mediterranean has historically given it strategic importance. Consequently it has been occupied by a succession of countries including Genoa, England and, since the nineteenth century, France. Corsican nationalism is both very ancient and yet in its present form comparatively recent. Its defining characteristic has been a continued resistance to foreigners. Thus a Corsican identity was forged early in opposition to (firstly) the Genoese. Yet ironically Corsican identity has been very diffused, partly as a result of the isolation of communities on this very mountainous island. Violent nationalism dates back only to the 1970s and was the culmination of growing anger at what was seen as French indifference to the plight of the island combined with an exploitation of its resources. Since the 1970s the Corsican National Liberation Front (FLNC) has sustained a campaign of bombings of (in particular) government buildings. This persistence and the fact that few of its members have been caught suggests a level of popular support that might be seen as the result of a long-held resentment of foreign domination. Corsica is perhaps atypical of peripheral nationalism in that whilst it has taken a very militant form it depends less on the uniting popular myths of nationalism, possibly because (compared to Brittany or Scotland for example) it was less fully absorbed into the nation-state. (For a discussion of Corsica see Ramsay 1987.)

Violence in the Basque Country emerged as a result of the oppressive dictatorship of General Franco. For a short period, during the Civil War of the 1930s, the Basque Country was nominally independent, but with the defeat of the Spanish Republican government the Basque Country became the scene of reprisals by the victorious Falangists. Though by the 1960s the Basques were a minority, as a result of large-scale immigration from Castille to the industrial north of the Basque Country, the ETA enjoyed popular support. As Sullivan (1988) notes, ETA were seen as less of a threat than the behaviour of the security forces, who in 1974 and 1975 alone killed twenty-two people. Yet since the death of Franco and the restoration of democracy ETA has continued its campaign, despite the granting of a large amount of autonomy to the Basque Country. As in Ireland this form of militant nationalism has continued to enjoy quite widespread popular support, though in both countries this has diminished somewhat of late. (For a discussion of the Basque Country see Sullivan 1988.)

The popular image of the IRA or ETA as a small group of ruthless criminals holding a population to ransom is a mistaken one. Rightly or wrongly both groups have received the necessary support to continue their activities. We must therefore conclude that these activities have been legitimated in the minds of a sizeable group in the population. This legitimation can only be understood in the context of specific 'national' histories and the nature of the emergence of nationalism. In each case material factors have been an important ingredient, but in each material conditions have not been sufficient.

A Europe of the peoples?

'Peripheral nationalism' is a complex phenomenon. Though its historical antecedents bear a similarity to those of 'state nationalisms', the title 'nationalism' for the former is perhaps unfortunate for it is a social phenomenon that is in opposition to state nationalism. John Coakley (1992: 213) has pointed out some of the pitfalls in attempting to define (and thus describe) such movements. Firstly, there is the problem of linguistic ambiguity. Those active in the movements often do not describe themselves as nationalist at all, but 'regionalist', 'autonomist', 'federalist', 'ethnic', etc. Thus it is quite possible the description 'nationalist' is inadequate and may actually lead us to poor, or wrong, descriptions. Secondly, this kind of ambiguity alerts us to the complexity of what is being studied. The temptation is to categorize, for example, the peripheral nationalism of Galicia, or Cornwall, as being the same kind of thing as that found in Northern Ireland, when actually they may well be distinct phenomena with quite different causes and quite different effects on their particular societies. Finally this complexity may lead sociologists to focus on particular aspects associated with these communities (such as the role of culture, or language for example).

That we may be dealing with a quite different kind of phenomenon in peripheral nationalism is perhaps exemplified by contrasting the new neo-Nazism of Germany with modern Welsh nationalism. The former is xenophobic, exclusive and inward looking. Its justification lies in an affirmation of biological descent, of the 'superior Aryan'. On the other hand the main Welsh nationalist party, Plaid Cymru, is overtly internationalist in its stance. Its vision of Wales has long been within a global 'community of communities' in which no one community imposes its will on another (Birch 1977: 126). Indeed, in Wales and other ethnic communities in the EU there has been a growing tendency toward common agendas with environmental groups.

To understand the political aims and agendas of peripheral nationalist movements we may have to see them in not just their local context but in a European and global one. If it is the case that the character of the nation-state is changing with power (in Europe in particular), becoming concentrated at a multinational level in the EU and at a local level through subsidiarity, then the phenomenon we have described as 'peripheral nationalism' is likely to become an important determinant in the Europe of the twenty-first century.

Summary

- Peripheral or sub-state nationalisms are an assertion of the rights of indigenous ethnic groups living in identifiable territories. They challenge the nation-state and are commonplace throughout the European Union.
- Whilst claims to separate identity are reinforced by perceived territorial

or economic peripherality all are grounded in claims to distinct ethnic identity.

- Peripheral nationalism rarely takes violent form and is often inclusive in its definition of membership of the nation. Indeed, many modern movements are overtly internationalist and pro-European. Though peripheral nationalism is difficult to categorize it takes very different forms to nationalisms associated with fascism.

Further reading

John Coakley (ed.) (1992) *The Social Origins of Nationalist Movements*, London: Sage. This is a collection of essays focusing both on theoretical issues surrounding an understanding of peripheral nationalism and contemporary nationalist movements. The essays on Brittany (Hervé Guillorel) and Scotland (James Kellas) are especially useful.

Montserrat Guibernau (1995) *Nationalisms – The Nation State and Nationalism in the 20th Century*, Cambridge: Polity Press. This text, through the use of examples, historically locates different kinds nationalism. Emphasis is upon the continued importance of nationalism and it is a convincing attempt to explain why such an important phenomenon has been given so little attention by social theorists. The book is written in a very approachable and engaging style.

Anthony D. Smith (1991) *National Identity*, Harmondsworth: Penguin. Smith's work is almost essential reading for those with an interest in nationalism. *National Identity* is a good introduction to Smith's work. The book examines why people feel loyalty to a 'nation' and the nature of the 'ethnic' roots of nationalism.

Chapter 22

Europe's changing role in the globalization process

Tony Spybey

Introduction	436
The rise of the West	436
The demise of European colonialism	438
Western culture as the world's first truly global culture	439
The post-war world	441
De-industrialization in Europe and throughout the West	443
The EEC becomes the EC becomes the EU	446
Globalization, the global 'triad' and the Pacific Rim	446
Summary	448
Further reading	448

Key concepts

- European civilization and Western institutions
- Colonialism and cultural imperialism
- Globalization and global culture

Introduction

This chapter seeks to trace the rise of European (Western) civilization and its impact upon the rest of the world. From the sixteenth century Europeans colonized other parts of the world until there was hardly anywhere in which they had not established a presence. Their activities involved the implantation of European cultural institutions in literacy and communication, politics and the nation-state, economy (trade and manufacturing), law and regulation. The implications of these influences are very broad and the result was that Western culture emerged as the world's first truly global culture. However, as more and more people were influenced by that culture they became involved in its reproduction. Consequently the outcome is increasingly in question and the global culture is no longer the sole property of Westerners.

The rise of the West

It was Europeans who created the world's first truly global culture. Between the late sixteenth and mid-twentieth centuries European countries maintained colonies throughout the world and within these European social institutions were, so to speak, implanted. Many peoples with many different social cultures became influenced by European culture even beyond the precise boundaries of the colonies. This was not just a process of coercion because, as Europe developed at a faster rate than other civilizations, its culture became attractive and European ways of doing things became persuasive to people in other parts of the world.

There are of course many cultural differences between the different European countries, but through the historical processes which we now call the Renaissance, the Enlightenment and the Industrial Revolution many aspects of these cultures were influenced by the European emphasis on *progress*. Thus it became possible to identify aspects of European culture with *modernization* and the twin social processes that go with it: *industrialization* and *urbanization* (see Chapters 1 and 2). Travel and communication were also important factors because it is through the communication of European culture that it became the world's first truly global culture. Together with the European model of state administration (the nation-state – see Chapter 3), industrialized production and urban living form the core to processes of globalization.

The beginnings of global communication

European colonialism established channels of global communication along which European institutions were transmitted. At first this was done by means of sailing ships, with improved means of navigation, with which Europeans accomplished the first successful oceanic explorations to be developed into something more – consolidated world trade. It was achieved through methods that are now completely unacceptable – colonialism and the slave trade. By the nineteenth century there were steamships and railways to intensify the European domination of world trade. Perhaps more significantly there were telegraph cables – the beginnings of modern communication. Messages could be transmitted for the first time in human history without the accompaniment of a human messenger and, of course, at much greater speed. Wireless transmissions (broadcasting) and air travel have been twentieth-century innovations and now at the turn of a new century multiple transmissions of information have become the norm. There are telephones and FAX messages; television by airwaves, cable and satellite; computer networks; and so on. The use of higher capacity satellites and optic-fibre cable networks are currently extending the potential.

European colonialism also involved the transplantation of European political institutions to other parts of the world. Generally speaking, the European countries ruled their colonial empires as mere appendages to the constitutional and political structures at home. Moreover, they did so as a collection of separate and independent states. There was never a European empire, as such, after the fall of Rome. This is an important factor which distinguishes European (Western) civilization from the others during the rise of the West. The successive caliphates of Islam which dominated the Middle East, or the dynasties of Imperial China, were unitary hierarchical structures with a single political focus, albeit at times a very unstable one.

Territorial transformations

The European pattern of separate sovereign states was qualitatively different and it was transmitted to the rest of the world through European colonialism. The result can be seen very clearly on the map of Africa which became a patchwork of colonies, mainly British and French but with German, Portuguese, Belgian, Spanish and Italian territories too. The legacy can be seen today because the modern map of Africa closely resembles that created by European colonialism, and virtually all educated Africans speak a European language as well as their own tribal language. English, French and some Portuguese are the languages of their colonial history and the pattern was similar across Asia, the Pacific and the Americas.

In some cases white settlers migrated in large numbers and this has resulted in what appear from a cultural perspective to be European countries in other parts of the world. In the British colonies of North America, Australia, New Zealand and in some Spanish and Portuguese colonies of Latin America, white people became the majority through conquest, emigration and the suppression of indigenous peoples. Their position since has therefore been dominant, although debates over the land rights of indigenous peoples have become much more vigorous during recent decades. Right across southern Africa, white minorities attempted to maintain their considerable advantages, ultimately with painful consequences, until the acceptance only rather recently of majority rule in Zimbabwe, Angola, Mozambique, Namibia and finally South Africa itself.

In Latin America there are various mixtures of descendants: those of the 'Indians' who lived there in the first place; those of the white settlers, both rich and poor, who subjugated and displaced them; and those of the black slaves who were transported from Africa to work on the colonial plantations. Brazilians speak Portuguese because the European colonists did, whilst the rest of the sub-continent speak predominantly Spanish for the same reason.

The white settler colonies first pressed for and gained constitutional independence from Europe during the eighteenth and nineteenth centuries. Yet all have maintained special relationships with European countries. The USA was the first and it seized its independence from Britain by force of arms in 1776. Nevertheless it has remained an English-speaking country and only now is its Spanish-speaking population challenging this, although so far the political power remains firmly with the descendants of settlers from north-western Europe. In fact the global importance of the USA has made English virtually a world language – and yet it is interesting to reflect that considering the substantial numbers of German-speaking people who settled there, the outcome might have been different.

The demise of European colonialism

During the twentieth century public opinion turned against colonialism generally, although there was resistance from fervent colonialists and from European governments which valued their colonies for political or economic reasons. Even the beginnings of change in public opinion, however, encouraged people subjected to European colonial systems to press their demands for constitutional independence. Ironically, the leaders of virtually all anti-colonial movements had been educated and socialized in European institutions. Thus even in their struggles against European colonial authority it was to European political and legal institutions that they turned for guidance. European culture propagated principles of human rights, equality before the law, freedom of the press, equality of opportunity, etc., for its own citizens and it should not be surprising therefore that anti-colonial movements should use the same principles for their arguments.

When independence was finally achieved, more often than not after long and violent struggles, it was the leaders of independence movements who subsequently won the first elections and attained political office, often moving straight from jail to the presidential palace. Nevertheless, as European colonial administrators handed over power, the new political leaders, socialized as they were in European institutions, ensured that European influences continued and the European pattern of the nation-state was adopted everywhere. Post-colonial countries for the most part maintained existing colonial borders and there was no official renewal of ethnic or tribal identities. The European model of the nation-state was adopted virtually in its entirety and people were encouraged to see themselves as 'citizens'. In Africa, old names were resurrected for some of its 'emergent nations' – Ghana and Zimbabwe for instance.

In formal terms, the familiar European state structure (as described in Chapter 3) became virtually universal in the former colonies:

- liberal democratic government guaranteeing rights of citizenship;
- bureaucratic administration ensuring impartiality;

- an independent judiciary dispensing justice;
- police and armed forces with a monopoly of legitimate violence.

The tragic thing was that the consistent maintenance of this model was even less likely than it had been in Europe. The economic resources which might have made the European pattern of citizenship a reality were always absent and for government and governed alike there was the ever-present alternative of tribal identity. There was some sense of legitimacy as each former colony duly took its seat at the United Nations and the world became a larger collection of constitutionally independent nation-states. At its foundation in 1945 the United Nations had fifty-one member states, now there are more than 180. But this was at most only a veneer and the reality for post-colonial Africa, Asia and Latin America has been endemic corruption, military coups as a ready alternative to civilian government, and not infrequently civil war or similar forms of strife. In the face of this, the most remarkable thing is the way that the former colonies have persevered with the Western model of the state and membership of the global nation-state system.

A separate word needs to be said about the powerful countries that did not succumb to European colonialism. The old empires of Russia, China and Japan were too big and powerful to be colonized but at the same time that does not mean that they escaped the influence of Europe's cultural ascendancy, particularly during the high point of European domination in the eighteenth and nineteenth centuries. They were forced into trade with Europe and became subjected to an increasing range of material influences. By the twentieth century these other great powers had been influenced to such an extent that they felt it necessary to adopt European institutions in order to participate in what has been described as a 'standard of civilization' (Gong 1984: 158). In order to gain access to the perceived benefits of the twentieth century – mass production, mass communication and mass consumption – they felt it necessary to take on some of the trappings of the West. At the beginning of the twentieth century there were explicit statements to this effect from Sun Yat-Sen upon the foundation of post-imperial republican China, and from Lenin upon the foundation of post-imperial Soviet Russia (Robertson 1992: 121). Meanwhile Japan began to emulate, it is said, German government and the British Navy as part of a combination of modernity and imperialism which was to bring it disaster in the Second World War.

Western culture as the world's first truly global culture

Concurrently with the *global political developments* which European colonialism introduced, the world was drawn into forms of *economic interdependence* which were increasingly centred upon Europe. These were the principal means by which aspects of broader Western culture were extended around the world.

Long-distance trade had of course existed long before European colonialism. There had been overland caravan routes across Asia and maritime trade in the Indian Ocean and China Sea for centuries. These were not however integrated forms of economic exchange, nor were they dominated consistently by any single culture. Rather, traders tended to exist as separate human groups, living a relatively nomadic or unsettled existence dependent upon their trade. During the sixteenth and seventeenth centuries this situation became increasingly over-shadowed by vigorous European maritime expansionism. The Portuguese made exploratory voyages around the coast of Africa throughout the fifteenth century and these culminated in Vasco da Gama's entry into the Indian Ocean during 1497–8. And of course there was Columbus's crossing of the Atlantic in 1492. Looking backwards in time each of these was a continuation of European Christian crusades against Islam. But looking forwards each was an attempt by Europeans to establish an independent trade route to India and China, circumventing the land blockade posed by Islam in the Middle East and North Africa. Indeed, many of the names that we apply to the areas of European exploration are names applied by Europeans which have subsequently been accepted into general usage – the West Indies and America after Columbus's voyage – the East Indies and Indo-China after Vasco da Gama's.

With these voyages and their consequences, European people became increasingly dependent upon the produce of other parts of the world and by the same token people there became accustomed to European products. As a result a *global economy* and an *international division of labour* came into being with Europe at its core. Immanuel Wallerstein (1974, 1979) has described this as the creation of a 'capitalist world-economy' with its focus first in Amsterdam during the seven-teenth and eighteenth centuries, then in London from the eighteenth to the early twentieth centuries, and subsequently in New York during the mid- to late twenti-eth century. His work has been tremendously influential, but he refers to this capitalist world-economy as 'the world-system', giving less attention to *global com-munications*, the *global nation-state system* and the *global military order*, each of which have been important conductors of European culture to the rest of the world.

Global military order

The European countries always backed up their quest for domination of the world with the use of considerable military force. The galleons which made oceanic exploration possible and enabled Europeans to establish colonies around the world also functioned as floating gun platforms to enforce European rule. When they turned up off the coast with the capacity to fire a 'broadside' from cannon, the effect was overwhelming. By the end of the fifteenth century European arma-ments had surpassed those of other civilizations and until the mid- to late twentieth century this enabled Europeans to do more or less as they pleased in the world. The military power of any European country was strongly linked with its colonial activities and by the nineteenth century Britain combined the most extensive colonial empire with the most powerful navy. The result has been referred to as the 'pax Britannica': extensive domination of world affairs. It was from this that contemporary ideas of world order emerged. They emerged from Europe to be imposed upon the rest of the world. As a part of this, the international relations and diplomacy of the European states became those of the world.

During the twentieth century the European countries exhausted much of their wealth and power in two devastating world wars and subsequently they relinquished their colonial empires. After 1945, therefore, it was the Americans (that is, Europeans who had settled in North America), who became the most powerful nation on Earth. Most significantly, the USA emerged from the Second World War as the only country with the economic resources to underwrite post-war reconstruction. In addition, at first reluctantly, it assumed the 'global policing' role. The subsequent period up to 1970 has sometimes been referred to as the 'pax Americana'.

Nevertheless, during the Second World War the global military order became complicated as a result of the Soviet Union's major role in the war. This had involved a huge military build-up and a national sacrifice of over 20 million dead in what the Soviet leadership propagated as 'the Great Patriotic War'. With victory in Europe came the acquisition of power over the Eastern European countries and, after 1945, the USSR as well as the USA attracted the label of 'super-power'. As a result, the period between 1945 and 1989 was one of 'cold war'. Military rivalry between the capitalist countries of the West and the state-socialist countries of the Soviet Union and Eastern Europe was held in stalemate by a balance of power in nuclear weapons. This was otherwise known as the 'nuclear deterrent' against a Third World War or as the strategy of 'mutually assured destruction' (MAD). World order was relatively clearly defined during this period around the military 'stand-off' between the USA and its allies in the North Atlantic Treaty Organization (NATO alliance) and the USSR and its allies in the Warsaw Pact. Thankfully this never came to full-scale military conflict, but countries throughout the world aligned themselves with either the USA or the USSR and the two powers entered battle by proxy in places such as Korea, Vietnam, Angola, etc. It was clearly a global conflict and yet in this context the terms 'West' and 'East' arose from the military division of Europe in 1945.

After 1989, with the sudden and unexpected collapse of the Soviet Union, all of this changed and the world order was thrown into a flux from which it has still not recovered. The USA remains the only surviving military super-power but it is an increasingly reluctant one. Whilst maintaining some aspects of its former foreign policy, it has insisted on sharing much of the politico-military burden – particularly through the United Nations Organization. Meanwhile, some commentators write of a 'triad' in the world. This refers to the three cores of social, political and economic activity in North America, Europe and East Asia. Alternatively, there is a concept of an emerging 'Pacific Rim' which links together East Asia, the west coast of North America and Australasia as areas of dynamic and potential economic development. This scenario threatens to supersede the Atlantic Rim as the future focus for global cultural, political and economic domination.

The post-war world

The 'decline of the West' is a notion that has existed roughly since the First World War. Although called a world war this was primarily a European war which demonstrated vividly the negative aspects to the rise of the West. The technological advances which had taken place between the eighteenth and early twentieth centuries had enabled the West to consolidate and maintain its leadership of a globalizing culture. But in this war industrialized production proved also to have an unprecedented capacity for destruction when applied to the supply of ever more terrifying weapons. Later on, the Second World War provided a second and even more comprehensive demonstration of the same destructive tendency. This time civilian casualties exceeded those of the armed forces, mainly through the widespread bombing of cities. There was also the Holocaust as an ultimate example of the application of perverted science and technology.

However, the Nazi menace to the world was overcome and additionally, on the credit side, the end of the war heralded an end to European colonialism. In 1941 the agreement between Britain and the USA, prior to the latter's entry into the war, involved the Atlantic Charter of which Clause 3 affirmed that both countries 'respect the right of all peoples to choose the form of government under which they will live; and [. . .] wish to see sovereign rights and self-government restored to those who have been forcibly deprived of them'. This was aimed primarily at Nazi-occupied Europe but it had equal relevance to Europe's colonies, a point not lost on the leaders of independence movements. It was followed in 1942 by a preliminary United Nations declaration which underlined the broader interpretation.

The Bretton Woods arrangements

Perhaps more significantly the USA wanted a post-war world that was open for trade and free of the colonial trading blocs that gave preference to European colonial powers. As the war had progressively destroyed much of Europe's industrial infrastructure, the burden of munitions production had been taken up by the USA. By 1945 it had become by far the world's biggest manufacturing nation. It has been estimated that at the end of the war the USA accounted for 40 per cent of the world's industrial output and also that it held 70 per cent of the world's gold and foreign exchange reserves (Brett 1985: 63). After 1945 the USA wanted to convert its military production capacity to civilian purposes and for this it needed open world markets.

The post-war period was therefore one of economic boom for the West sustained by the USA's underwriting of the global economy. This arrangement was formalized in 1945 with the drawing up of the 'Bretton Woods' financial institutions. These provided, amongst other things, a fixed international exchange-rate system. Stated simply, the value of the US dollar was tied to the value of gold whilst the rest of the world's currencies were given fixed exchange rates with the dollar. In practice this applied only to those 'hard' currencies which were dealt on international currency markets. Where necessary there were periodic adjustments to some exchange rates. Nevertheless, the Bretton Woods system meant that exchanges between currencies, for trade or for anything else, could be carried out on a predictable basis. Adjustments were planned by negotiation between the major economic powers.

The World Bank and the International Monetary Fund were the main institutions of the Bretton Woods arrangements and their prime function was to provide a stable basis on which Western capitalist industry and commerce could flourish. The World Bank gave loans for 'infrastructure' developments such as the building of roads, ports, etc. The intention was to facilitate economic development and encourage investment from the private sector. The IMF's task was to monitor international currencies and where necessary provide support in order to avoid the kind of currency collapses that had occurred after the First World War. There was also to have been an International Trade Organization (ITO) which would have monitored the international pricing of commodities. But the differences between European interventionist policies and American non-interventionism were too great and it never came into being. Instead there were periodic conferences to make decisions about General Agreements on Tariffs and Trade. Each series of GATT meetings went in a 'round', such as the Kennedy round of the 1960s and the Tokyo round of the 1970s. The Uruguay round of the 1980s was dogged by disagreement and did not end until 1995, by which time the decision had been taken at last to organize a permanent International Trade Organization.

The problem throughout was that the USA was opposed to interventionist economic policies. Its leaders felt that investment for economic development should come from the private sector. Therefore its contributions to the international agencies were consistently restricted to a level seen as 'pump-priming' for major private sector investment. During the initial meetings at Bretton Woods in 1944 the chief British representative was the economist John Maynard Keynes who wanted to establish the World Bank and the IMF on what have become known as 'Keynesian' interventionist principles. His American counterpart, however, was Harry Dexter White, an economist with entirely opposite ideas. Since the USA was the chief paymaster, non-interventionist policies prevailed. The World Bank therefore has always been funded at levels consistent with non-interventionist policy and has consequently often acted as an intermediary between private sector international banks and borrowing countries. It was not until the sweeping political changes of the 1980s that other countries came round to this way of thinking.

The Bretton Woods arrangements, as drawn up in 1944, remained in operation until 1970. By then the US government had accumulated a very large deficit on its balance of payments and it was decided that it could no longer support the arrangements as originally envisaged. The link between the dollar and the value of gold was terminated and exchange rates between currencies were left to float according to the fluctuations of international currency markets. Since then it has been necessary to consult the financial columns of newspapers on a daily basis in order to keep up with currency exchange values. The effects of these changes took hold during the 1970s when a succession of economic crises altered the nature of the West's relationship with the rest of the world both economically and politically.

De-industrialization in Europe and throughout the West

By 1970 the USA could no longer single-handedly underwrite the global economy because during the 1960s it had created for itself an enormous balance of payments problem. In simple terms, it had spent more than it had earned, relying upon the enormity of its economic power to ensure creditworthiness. Partially the imbalance was due to a lack of competitiveness in international markets, particularly with the industrial revival of Germany and Japan. Also, it was partially due to the huge cost of the Vietnam War caused by unprecedented levels of expenditure on equipment which was demanded to minimize the human cost to the young American conscripts involved. This reason, combined with increased anti-war feelings in American public opinion, meant that by 1970 the US government wanted to extricate itself from both its anti-communist crusade in Asia and the underwriting of the Bretton Woods arrangements. To this end, in 1970 the Nixon administration announced the end of dollar gold convertibility and, in 1971, a *détente* with China.

With the end of the Bretton Woods arrangements in their original form the world's currencies became subject to floating exchange rates. Since then the aggregated effects of exchange dealings and speculations in currency values have determined market prices. In Europe the Deutschmark has consistently been the strongest currency and elsewhere the Japanese Yen. In 1973 there was a further blow to the global economy when the Oil Producing and Exporting Countries (OPEC) restricted the supply of oil from the world's largest oil-fields in the Islamic countries of the Middle East. They did this in retaliation for Western support of Israel in the Arab–Israeli wars of 1967 and 1973. The restriction in supply of the world's leading energy resource meant that market prices quadrupled overnight. This had a knock-on effect for virtually all economic activity. For instance, all commodity prices fluctuated violently. Moreover, this took place concurrently with increasing industrial competition from Japan and East Asia, which had implications for both Europe and the USA. The economic growth of the 1960s turned into stagnation during the 1970s. It had become generally accepted that normal rates of inflation for Western European countries should be of the order of 2–3 per cent but in some cases they raced up to 20 per cent and beyond. The combination of economic stagnation and high inflation was reported in the press as 'stagflation' and unemployment rose sharply throughout Western countries, making a nonsense of post-war full-employment policies.

The re-structuring of the global economy

At first there was a tendency to consider this as merely a downturn in the economic fortunes of the West, from which it might recover as it had done on previous occasions. However, cycles of economic boom and slump proved to be only part of the explanation. Structural changes to the Western economies had taken place which would not be reversed by an upturn in the global economy. Many industries in Europe and North America were declining or even collapsing and disappearing completely. This was commonly attributed to a trend towards 'post-industrial society', neglecting the evidence that industries were disappearing in the West only because of their reappearance in other parts of the world. The role of the West as the world's leading industrial concentration was being challenged, particularly by Japan and other East Asian countries. Economists began to speak of 'newly industrializing countries' (NICs), especially when referring to parts of East Asia and Latin America where labour costs were much lower than in the West.

Textile manufacturing, the archetypal industry of the Industrial Revolution, was a case in point. People in many countries had learned the necessary skills, and the technology – which has been perfected by the end of the nineteenth century – was easily transferable. Therefore low wage countries could easily undercut the West and in time of economic difficulty it was the high wage sectors of the industry that tended to disappear. To a great extent the success of trade unions in raising wages and improving working conditions had rendered Western workers uncompetitive in what Folker Fröbel and his colleagues (1980) recognized as a 'new international division of labour'. Steel-making and shipbuilding, too, all but disappeared from Europe and North America in the face of competition from Japan and Korea.

The motor vehicle industry might be described as the touchstone of twentieth-century industrial growth. In this Japan developed new approaches to assembly-line production and mass marketing. They brought a more flexible approach to mass production which has become known as 'post-Fordism' to distinguish it from Henry Ford's pioneering techniques devised in the USA at the beginning of the twentieth century. These had been instrumental in presenting mass production and mass consumption to the world in the first place but they tended to be monolithic and inflexible. The Japanese have improved upon them often with ideas derived from the USA. For instance, the much admired 'just-in-time' component supply systems of Japanese manufacturing hinge upon the *kanban* stock card which was in fact copied from American supermarkets. The simple principle is the 'pulling out' of materials according to demand rather than their 'pushing out' according to supply. However, it is the commitment to its use in Japan's broader horizontal business networks, including external contract suppliers, through which the fullest advantage was achieved and indeed is now emulated in the West. Not that the West has always successfully emulated Japanese techniques. Quality circles, for example, originated in the United States but were more successfully used in Japan. However, their 'repatriated' use has nearly always failed to take into account the Japanese cultural inputs which made them so successful there.

A set of completely new manufacturing techniques has been built up around advances in electronics. This has proved to be the archetypal industry of the late twentieth century and as well as new products there are many new applications for older products. The transistor replaced the electrical valve and the microprocessor multiplied the implications of that technical breakthrough. Moreover, the electronics industry was established virtually from the beginning with large-scale participation from Japan and subsequently other East Asian countries. Overall, Japan invaded the West's global consumer markets and made a great success of it. The unemployment that had risen so starkly in the West was therefore structural unemployment and would not easily be reversed. Furthermore, the global economy did not recover from these traumas of the 1970s but instead entered the global recession of the early 1980s. This was reversed during the late 1980s only to be repeated again in the 1990s.

The EEC becomes the EC becomes the EU

The contemporary ideal of European union was born out of a perceived need to prevent the recurrence of two devastating world wars principally by unifying the interests of France and Germany. It was also of course a contribution to the economic recovery of Europe after the Second World War, in a world with a significantly altered balance of international trade. The Council of Europe was created in 1949 out of earlier ideas for a federal Europe. It had a broad membership but has never achieved its objective, which since the Maastricht Treaty has been taken over by the European Union. Also in 1949 the North Atlantic Treaty Organization (NATO) was formed to provide collective defence for Western Europe against the threat of Soviet Russian aggression. This also brought the USA back into a central military role after its partial withdrawal at the end of the Second World War.

The European Coal and Steel Community was formed in 1951 to provide a concrete example of Franco-German joint economic interest. It also involved Italy, Belgium, the Netherlands and Luxembourg. All of these were early manifestations of post-war European co-operation, but the Treaty of Rome in 1957 brought into being the European Economic Community with a broader remit to cover potentially all economic exchange. Britain decided not to join the EEC 'inner six' of France, Germany, Italy, the Netherlands, Belgium and Luxembourg. Instead it aligned itself with the 'outer seven' of Norway, Denmark, Austria, Sweden, Portugal and Switzerland in an alternative European Free Trade Association (EFTA).

Later, during the 1960s, Britain's entry into the EEC was prevented by France under the leadership of General de Gaulle and it was not until 1971 that Britain finally joined along with Ireland, Denmark and Norway. By then the EEC countries realized only too well that they needed mutual economic protection. To some extent they needed it to counter established North American dominance of the global economy, but this was actually diminishing. More importantly it was necessary to combat the rising threat of Japan and East Asia in global manufacturing. Later, during the 1980s, Spain, Portugal and Greece joined too and by then the EEC had broadened its objectives to become the European Community (EC).

However, it was the Maastricht Treaty signed in 1991 that took the agenda forward to involve EC countries in political as well as economic union, with the transition to the title of European Union (EU). Member countries were not all equally enthusiastic about this change and there has been much talk about different speeds of development and the principle of 'subsidiarity' to exclude certain issues. This debate continues, but there is determination amongst the more enthusiastic member countries to achieve a common currency and exchange rates before the end of the twentieth century.

Globalization, the global 'triad' and the Pacific Rim

These progressively federalist plans for European co-operation have clearly been formulated to provide protection against two politico-economic threats. Firstly, there is the outstanding economic success of Japan and other East Asian countries.

Secondly, there are currently attempts to revive the economic fortunes of the USA with increasing North American co-operation. The North American Free Trade Association (NAFTA) was extended in 1994 to include Mexico as well as the USA and Canada and plans are under consideration to admit other Latin American countries such as Chile. Such developments have tended to result in the formation of a triple core to the global economy, which also has political connotations. It has been referred to as a process of 'triadization'. The three cores are clearly apparent in all dimensions of global affairs.

In global communications, the concentration of optic fibre cabling in an expensive 'information super-highway' stretches principally between North America, Europe and East Asia. Other parts of the world tend to be neglected by this due to cost but, on the other hand, satellite communications can operate regardless of distance and location on the planet. In this there are the media 'empires', such as Rupert Murdoch's News International Corporation. NIC runs Fox cable TV in North America, the Sky satellite system in Europe and the Star satellite system which is based in Hong Kong but covers much of Asia (see Chapter 14).

The 'triad' is less apparent in global politics, with only the EU showing concrete signs of movement to political union. However, NAFTA clearly has political implications in that the USA, Canada and Mexico have set themselves apart from the rest of the American continent. Membership therefore becomes an aspiration for other Latin American countries, such as Chile. In East Asia, Japan has set in motion a number of initiatives which envisage its leadership of an Asian politico-economic bloc. For instance in 1991 Toshiki Kaifu, who was prime minister of Japan at the time, announced his 'Kaifu doctrine' for Asian co-operation and to that end embarked upon a comprehensive tour of Asian capitals. There has been much fluctuation in Japanese politics since then but this does not mean that the idea has disappeared

The 'triad' is of course extremely apparent in the global economy and the three areas dominate global mass production and mass consumption. At the same time less developed countries (LDCs) are utilized as reservoirs of disposable labour, particularly through the operation of export processing zones (EPZs). Labour intensive manufacturing processes are often contracted out from the West and from Japan to countries with extremely low wage rates. Swathes of territory are set aside as export processing zones with tax and customs duty exemptions. The less developed countries obtain jobs which they would not otherwise get for their under-employed populations. Foreign companies obtain cheap, trouble-free labour and tax 'holidays' too. This is often an extremely attractive proposition and it has added to the de-industrialization of the West.

Towards the end of the twentieth century, therefore, the European Union finds itself as part of a global 'triad' of politico-economic concentration. An alternative scenario however is a world dominated by the Pacific Rim. As mentioned earlier this would involve co-operation between the East Asian countries, the west coast of North America and Australasia. There are annual summit meetings of these Pacific Rim countries and, as an indication of how seriously they are taken, they are attended by the American president in person. The implication of this is a potential movement in the focus of the global economy from the Atlantic to the Pacific. Possibly this will be the most compelling argument in favour of further European co-operation and progression towards federalism.

Summary

- After the Second World War the European states began to disengage from external colonialism and co-operate internally, first as an economic community and now as the European Union.
- The consolidation of the European Union may be seen as a defensive strategy in a world dominated by three politico-economic 'cores': East Asia, Europe and North America (the 'global triad').
- The West created the world's first truly global culture but no longer controls it in the face of competition from countries of the Pacific Rim.

Further reading

Immanuel Wallerstein (1979) *The Capitalist World-Economy*, Cambridge: Cambridge University Press. This is Wallerstein's classic work on the creation by Europeans of a 'capitalist world-economy' from the sixteenth century. This involves a 'core' of economic activity in Europe and by the same token a 'periphery' embracing the rest of the world. The core moves initially from Southern Europe to North-western Europe, to North America during the twentieth century, and currently to Japan and East Asia.

Folker Fröbel, Jürgen Heinrichs and Otto Kreye (1980) *The New International Division of Labour* (translated by Peter Burgess), Cambridge: Cambridge University Press. This is the classic work on the restructuring of global manufacturing during the 1970s. Europe lost much of its manufacturing industry to other parts of the world with much lower labour costs. That meant that much of Europe's unemployment was structural and not merely due to economic downturn. It would not come back with the end of the recession.

Tony Spybey (1996) *Globalization and World Society*, Cambridge: Polity Press. This contemporary work examines the creation of a globalized world, but its main thrust is the analysis of the relationship between the individual and global institutions during the second half of the twentieth century. These are conceptualized in terms of the citizen in the nation-state system, the producer–consumer in the global economy, the viewer in the global communication system, the soldier in the world order and the development of global social movements.

Sources of data

The various agencies of the European Union regularly produce data that is relevant to the material in this book. Readers may find it useful to follow up the data presented in the chapters here by reference to original sources. This serves two purposes. Firstly, it constitutes an exercise in European data sourcing. Secondly, it will provide figures updated beyond the publication date of this book.

Note that the terminology can be confusing. The original European Economic Community changed its name to the European Community during the late 1980s and later to the European Union during the early 1990s. However, the supplementary term, 'European Communities', is also used in some contexts. Note also that reports and documents issued by one agency of the EU may also be distributed by its other agencies too.

The *Commission of the European Communities* (CEC), otherwise known as *The European Commission*, produces a number of publications through its offices in Brussels, Luxembourg and elsewhere, including London. Some of the most relevant are:

> Single European Market Factsheets – issued periodically.
> *Employment in Europe* – issued annually.

449

Reports of the European Commission Directorate-General for Employment, Industrial Relations and Social Affairs – issued periodically.

Reports of the Equal Opportunities Unit and its working groups – issued periodically.

Bulletins on Women and Employment in the EU – issued periodically.

Women of Europe Supplements – issued periodically.

Reports of the European Commission Child-care Network – issued periodically.

The Statistical Office of the European Communities in Luxembourg produces:

Europe in Figures ('Eurostat') – issued periodically.

The Eurostat Yearbook – issued annually.

Demographic Statistics – issued annually.

The *European Parliament*, through its Luxembourg administrative offices, issues:

Reports of the Consultative Committee on Civil Liberties and Internal Affairs (on subjects such as racism and xenophobia) – issued periodically.

Additionally, EURYDICE (The Education Information Network in the European Community) and CEDEFOP (European Centre for the Development of Vocational Training) issue various reports from Brussels on related subjects, including material from the Task Force on Human Resources, Education, Training and Youth.

These may well lead you to other useful sources.

Bibliography

Abbott, P. A. (forthcoming) 'Breaking the glass ceiling: promoting women's studies', in E. Olesky (ed.) *Problematyka Kobiet na Swiecie*, Lodz, Poland: Lodz University Press.

Abbott, P. A. and Sapsford, R. J. (1987) *Women and Social Class*, London: Tavistock.

Abbott, P. A. and Wallace, C. (1990) *An Introduction to Sociology: Feminist Perspectives*, London: Routledge.

Abbott, P. A. and Wallace, C. (1992) *The Family and the New Right*, London: Pluto Press.

Abbott, P. A. and Tyler, M. (1995) 'Ethnic variation in the female labour force: a research note', *British Journal of Sociology* 46, 1: 339–53.

Abbott, P. A., Bernie, J., Payne, G. and Sapsford, R. J. (1992) 'Health care and material deprivation in Plymouth', in P. A. Abbott and R. J. Sapsford (eds) *Research into Practice: A Reader for Nurses and the Caring Professions*, Buckingham: Open University Press.

Alber, J., Guillemard, A. M. and Walker, A. (1991) *The Impact of Social and Economic Policies on Older People in the European Community: An Initial Overview*, Brussels: EC Observatory on Older People.

Alcock, P. (1993) *Understanding Poverty*, London: Macmillan.

Allen, J., Braham, P. and Lewis, P. (eds) (1992) *Political and Economic Forms of Modernity*, Cambridge: Polity Press.

Almond, G. and Verba, S. (1965) *The Civic Culture*, Boston: Little, Brown.

Althusser, L. (1971) 'Ideology and ideological state apparatuses', in *Lenin and Philosophy and Other Essays*, London: New Left Books.

Alvarez-Dardet, C. and Colomer, C. (1992) 'Valencia', in J. Ashton (ed.) *Healthy Cities*, Buckingham: Open University Press.

Alvazzi del Frate, A., Zvikic, U. and van Dijk, J. (eds) (1993) *Understanding Crime: Experiences of Crime and Crime Control*, Rome: UNICRI.

Amin, A. and Tomaney, J. (eds) (1995) *Behind the Myth of the European Union*, London: Routledge.

Anderson, B. (1983) *Imagined Communities: Reflections on the Origin and Spread of Nationalism*, London: Verso.

Anderson, B. S. and Zinsser, J. P. (1990) *A History of Their Own: Women in Europe from Prehistory to the Present* (Vol. II), Harmondsworth: Penguin.

Anderson, P. (1979) *Lineages of the Absolutist State*, London: New Left Books.

Ang, I. (1985) *Watching 'Dallas': Soap Opera and the Melodramatic Imagination*, London: Methuen.

Appignenes, L. and Lawson, H. (eds) (1989) *Dismantling Truth: Reality in the Postmodern World*, London: Weidenfeld and Nicolson.

Arber, S. (1990) 'Opening the "black box": inequalities in women's health', in P. A. Abbott and G. Payne (eds) *New Directions in the Sociology of Health*, Basingstoke: Falmer Press.

Arber, S. and Ginn, J. (1991) *Gender and Later Life*, London: Sage.

Arber, S. and Ginn, J. (eds) (1995) *Connecting Gender and Ageing*, Buckingham: Open University Press.

Archer, M. and Giner, S. (1971) *Contemporary Europe*, London: Weidenfeld and Nicolson.

Ashford, S. and Timms, N. (1992) *What Europe Thinks: A Study of Western European Values*, Aldershot: Dartmouth.

Ashton, J. (1992) 'The origins of healthy cities', in J. Ashton (ed.) *Healthy Cities*, Milton Keynes: Open University Press.

Ashton, J. and Seymour, H. (1988) *The New Public Health*, Milton Keynes: Open University Press.

Ashworth, A. (1994) 'Criminal justice and deserved sentences', in N. Lacey (ed.) *Criminal Justice*, Oxford: Oxford University Press.

Aslund, A. (1990) 'Utbrytning ur Snedvandig', *Dagens Nyheter*, 25 May.

Atkinson, A. (1994) *Seeking to Explain the Distribution of Income*, WSP/106, Suntory-International Centre for Economics and Related Disciplines, London: LSE.

Avis, G. (ed.) (1987) *The Making of the Soviet Citizen: Character Formation and Civic Training in Soviet Education*, London: Croom Helm.

Aye Maung, N. and Mirrlees-Black, N. (1994) *Racially Motivated Crime: A British Crime Survey Analysis*, Paper 82, London: Home Office Research and Planning Unit.

Azria, R. (1994) 'Jews and Europe: historical realities and social identities', in J. Fulton and P. Gee (eds) *Religion in Contemporary Europe*, Lampeter: Edwin Mellen Press.

Ball, A. R. and Millard, F. (1986) *Pressure Politics in Industrial Societies: A Comparative Introduction*, Basingstoke: Macmillan Education.

Ball, S. J. (1993) 'Education, Majorism and "the Curriculum of the Dead" ', *Curriculum Studies* 1, 2: 195–214.

Barker, D., Halman, L. and Vloet, A. (1992) *The European Values Study 1981–1990. Summary Report*, London: Gordon Cook Foundation.

Barker, M. (1981) *The New Racism*, London: Junction Books.

Barnett, C. (1972) *The Collapse of British Power*, New York: William Morrow.

Basaglia, F. (ed.) (1968) *L'Instituzione Negate: Rapporto da un Ospedale Psichiatrico*, Turin: Einandi Editore.

Bauman, Z. (1991) *Modernity and Ambivalence*, Cambridge: Polity Press.

Bauman, Z. (1992) *Intimations of Postmodernity*, London: Routledge.

Bauman, Z. (1993) *Postmodern Ethics*, Oxford: Basil Blackwell.

Begg, I., Moore, B. and Rhodes, J. (1985) 'Economic and social change in urban Britain and the inner cities', in V. Hausner (ed.) *Critical Issues in Urban Economic Development* (Vol. I), Oxford: Oxford University Press.

Bejin, A. (1985) 'The extra-marital union today', in *Western Sexuality: Practice and Perception in Past and Present Time*, Oxford: Basil Blackwell.

Bell, D. (1973) *The Coming of Post-Industrial Society*, New York: Basic Books.

Bellerman, M. (1990) *Sozialpolitik*, Freiburg, Germany: Lambertus.

Ben David, J. (1971) *The Scientist's Role in Society: A Comparative Study*, New Jersey: Prentice-Hall.

Benevolo, L. (1980) *The History of the City*, Oxford: Basil Blackwell.

Benevolo, L. (1993) *The European City*, Oxford: Basil Blackwell.

Benigni, L. (1989) 'Italian women in research: status, aims and family organisation', Paper prepared for the European Network for Women's Studies Seminar 'The Interface of Work and Family', Brussels, September.

Benzeval, M., Judge, K., and Whitehead, M. (1995) *Tackling Inequalities in Health*, London: King's Fund.

Berger, P. L. and Luckmann, T. (1967) *The Social Construction of Reality*, London: Allen Lane.

Berger, P. L., Berger, B. and Gellner, H. (1974) *The Homeless Mind: Modernisation and Consciousness*, Harmondsworth: Penguin.

Berlanstein, L. R. (ed.) (1993) *The Industrial Revolution and Work in Nineteenth Century Europe*, London: Routledge.

Berlin, I. (1990) 'The apotheosis of the romantic will', in his *The Crooked Timber of Humanity: Chapters in the History of Ideas*, London: John Murray.

Bernal, M. (1987) *Black Athena: The Afroasiatic Roots of Classical Civilisation*, London: Free Association Books.

Beyer, P. (1994) *Religion and Globalisation*, London: Sage.

Bianchini, F. and Parkinson, M. (eds) (1993) *Cultural Policy and Urban Regeneration: The West European Experience*, Manchester: Manchester University Press.

Biggs, S. and Phillipson, C. (1995) *Elder Abuse in Perspective*, Buckingham: Open University Press.

Birch, A. H. (1977) *Political Integration and Disintegration in the British Isles*, London: George Allen and Unwin.

Black Women's Group (1974) 'Black women and nursing: a job like any other', *Race Today*, August: 226–30.

Blee, T. (1991) 'Health care in Finland', *Health Service Management*, February: 14–17.

Bodrova, V. and Anker, R. (1985) *Working Women in Socialist Countries: The Fertility Connection*, Geneva: International Labour Organisation.

Bogdanor, V. and Butler, D. (eds) (1983) *Democracy and Elections: Electoral Systems and their Political Consequences*, Cambridge: Cambridge University Press.

Borchurst, A. and Siim, B. (1987) 'Women and the advanced welfare state: a new kind of patriarchal power', in A. Showstack Sassoon (ed.) *Women and the State*, London: Hutchinson.

Bowles, S. and Gintis, H. (1976) *Schooling in Capitalist America*, London: Routledge and Kegan Paul.

Boyce, D. C. (1991) *Nationalism in Ireland*, London: Routledge.

Bradley, H. (1992) 'Class, gender and industrialization', in S. Hall and B. Gieben, *Formations of Modernity*, Cambridge: Polity.

Bragh-Matzon, K. and Holm, F. (1992) 'Horsens', in J. Ashton (ed.) *Healthy Cities*, Buckingham: Open University Press.

Braudel, F. (1981) *Civilization and Capitalism 15th to 18th Century: Volume 1 The Structures of Everyday Life*, London: Collins.

Braudel, F. (1984) *Civilization and Capitalism 15th to 18th Century: Volume 3 The Perspective of the World*, London: Collins.

Brauns, H. H. and Kramer, D. (eds) (1986) *Social Work Education in Europe*, Frankfurt am Main: Deutscher Verein für offentliche und private Fursorge.

Brearley, C. P. (1990) *Working in Residential Homes for Elderly People*, London: Routledge.

Brett, E. A. (1985) *The World Economy since the War: The Politics of Uneven Development*, London: Macmillan.

Brierley, P. (1991) *Christian England*, London: MARC Europe.

Briggs, A. (1959) *The Age of Improvement*, London: Longman.

Briggs, A. (1968) *Victorian Cities*, Harmondsworth: Penguin.

British Youth Council (1993) *Looking to the Future: Towards a Coherent Youth Policy*, London: British Youth Council.

Broberg, A. and Hwang, P. (1991) 'Day care for young children in Sweden', in E. Melhuish and P. Moss (eds) *Day Care for Young Children*, London: Routledge.

Brown, A. (ed.) (1984) *Political Culture and Communist Studies*, London: Macmillan.

Brown, P. (1990) *The Body and Society*, London: Faber and Faber.

Brown, P. and Crompton, R. (eds) (1994) *A New Europe?: Economic Restructuring and Social Exclusion*, London: UCL Press.

Bruce, S. (1986) *God Save Ulster: The Religion and Politics of Paisleyism*, Oxford: Clarendon Press.

Bruce, S. (1995) *Religion in Modern Britain*, Oxford: Oxford University Press.

Burgess, E. W. (ed.) (1960) *Ageing in Western Societies*, Chicago: University of Chicago Press.

Burke, P. (1986) 'City states', in J. A. Hall (ed.) *States in History*, Oxford: Basil Blackwell.

Butler, A. and Jeffries, A. (1994) 'Social work in crisis: a paradoxical learning opportunity', unpublished paper given at conference on Community Care and the Future for Social Work, University of Plymouth.

Butler, D. and Stokes, D. (1974) *Political Change in Britain: The Evolution of Electoral Choice* (2nd edn), London: Macmillan.

Button, G. (ed.) (1991) *Ethnomethodology and the Human Sciences*, Cambridge: Cambridge University Press.

Button, G. (ed.) (1993) *Technology in Working Order*, London: Routledge.

Bytheway, B. (1995) *Ageism*, Buckingham: Open University Press.

Cannan, C., Berry, L. and Lyons, K. (1992) *Social Work and Europe*, London: Macmillan.

Caplow, T. (1985) 'Contrasting trends in European and American religion', *Sociological Analysis* 46, 2: 101–8.

Carlen, P. (1990) *Alternatives to Women's Imprisonment*, Milton Keynes: Open University Press.

Castells, M. (1975) 'Immigrant workers and class struggles in advanced capitalism: the Western European experience', *Politics and Society* 5, 1: 33–66.

Castles, S., Booth, H. and Wallace, T. (1984) *Here for Good: Western Europe's New Ethnic Minorities*, London: Pluto.

Cavalli, A. and Galland, O. (eds) (1995) *Youth in Europe: Social Change in Western Europe*, London: Pinter.

CEC (Commission of the European Communities) (1991) *Women's Rights and Equal Opportunities, 1992: the Single European Market* (Factsheet No. 1), London: Commission of the European Communities in the UK.

CEC (Commission of the European Communities) (1992) *Legal Instruments to Combat Racism and Xenophobia*, Brussels/Luxembourg: Office for Official Publications of the European Communities.

CEC (Commission of the European Communities) (1993) *Employment in Europe: 1993*, Brussels/Luxembourg: Office for Official Publications of the European Communities.

CEC (Commission of the European Communities) (1995) *Women and Men in the European Communities*, Brussels/Luxembourg: Office for Official Publications of the European Communities.

Central Statistical Office (1994) *Social Trends 21*, London: HMSO.

Cesarani, D. (1987) 'Anti-alienism in England after the First World War', *Immigrants and Minorities* 6, 1: 5–29.

Champion, A. (1993) 'Geographical distribution and urbanization', in D. Noin and R. Woods (eds) *The Changing Population of Europe*, Oxford: Basil Blackwell.

Chandler, T. and Fox, G. (1974) *3000 Years of Urban Growth*, New York: Academic Press.

Cheetham, J. (1992) 'Evaluating the effectiveness of social work: its contribution to the development of a knowledge base', *Issues in Social Work Education* 12, 1: 52–68.

Cheshire, P. and Hay, D. (1989) *Urban Problems in Western Europe: An Economic Analysis*, London: Unwin Hyman.

Chisholm, L. (1992) 'A crazy quilt: education, training and social change in Europe', in J. Bailey (ed.) *Social Europe*, London: Longman.

Chisholm, L. (1993) 'Young people in the European Community: staking the terrain for European youth research', *Youth and Policy* 40, Spring: 49–61.

CIPFA (Chartered Institute of Public Finance and Accountancy) (1984) *Health in the UK 1984: An Economic, Social and Policy Audit*, London: CIPFA.

Coakley, J. (ed.) (1992) *The Social Origins of Nationalist Movements*, London: Sage.

Cochrane, A. (1993) 'Looking for a European welfare state', in A. Cochrane and J. Clarke (eds) *Comparing Welfare States: Britain in the International Context*, London: Sage.

Cochrane, A. and Clarke, J. (eds) (1993) *Comparing Welfare States: Britain in the International Context*, London: Sage.

Cohen, R. (1994) *Frontiers of Identity: The British and the Other*, London: Longman.

Cohen, S. (1985) 'Anti-Semitism, immigration controls and the welfare state', *Critical Social Policy*, 13, 5: 73–92.

Cole, A. (1994) 'The final respect', *The Guardian*, Nov. 30, Society Section: 2.

Coleman, J. and Hendry, L. (1990) *The Nature of Adolescence*, London: Routledge.

Coleman, J. and Warren-Adamson, C. (eds) (1992) *Youth Policy in the 1990s: The Way Forward*, London: Routledge.

Colletti, L. (1979) *Marxism and Hegel*, London: Verso.

Collins, R. (1977) 'Some comparative principles of educational stratification', *Harvard Educational Review* 47, 1: 1–27.

Collins, R. (1992) *Satellite Television in Western Europe*, London: John Libbey.

Collins, R., Garnham, N. and Locksley, G. (1987) *The Economics of Television*, London: Croom Helm.

Costa, J. (1992) 'Barcelona', in J. Ashton (ed.) *Healthy Cities*, Buckingham: Open University Press.

Council of Europe (1992) *Prison Statistics*.

CPA (Centre for Policy on Ageing) (1989) *World Directory of Old Age*, Harlow: Longman.

CPA (Centre for Policy in Ageing) (1993) *The European Directory of Older Age*, London: Centre for Policy on Ageing.

Crewe, I. and Denner, D. (eds) (1985) *Electoral Change in Western Democracies: Patterns and Sources of Electoral Volatility*, London: Croom Helm.

Crompton, R. (1993) *Class and Stratification*, Cambridge: Polity Press.

Crook, S. (1992) *Modernism and Social Theory*, London: Routledge.

Crook, S., Pakulski, J. and Waters, M. (1992) *Postmodernization: Change in Advanced Society*, London: Sage.

Cross, M. (1993) 'Generating the new poverty: a European comparison', in R. Simpson and R. Walker (eds) *Europe: For Richer or Poorer?*, London: Child Poverty Action Group.

Cummings, E. and Henry, W. (1961) *Growing Old: The Process of Disengagement*, New York: Basic Books.

Curran, J. (1996) 'Mass media and democracy revisited', in J. Curran and M. Gurevitch (eds) *Mass Media and Society* (2nd edn) London: Edward Arnold.

Curran, J. and Gurevitch, M. (eds) (1996) *Mass Media and Society* (2nd edn), London: Edward Arnold.

Curran, J. and Seaton, J. (1991) *Power without Responsibility*, London: Routledge.

D'Intignano, M. (1993) 'Financing of health care in Europe', in Artundo *et al.* (eds) *Health Care Reforms in Europe: Proceedings of the First Meeting of the Working Party on Health Care Reform in Europe*, Copenhagen: WHO Regional Office for Europe.

Daalder, H. (ed.) (1987) *Party Systems in Denmark, Austria, Switzerland, the Netherlands and Belgium*, London: Frances Pinter.

Daalder, H. and Mair, P. (eds) (1983) *Western European Party Systems: Continuity and Change*, London: Sage.

Dahl, E. (1991) *Inequalities in Health in Norway: A Review of the Evidence*, Oslo: National Institute of Public Health, Unit for Health Service Research, Working Paper 5/90.

Dahl, E. (1994) 'Inequalities in health and the class position of women: the Norwegian experience', *Sociology of Health and Illness* 13, 4: 492–505.

Dahl, E. and Kjaersgaard, P. (1993) 'Trends in socio-economic mortality differentials in post-war Norway: evidence and interpretation', *Sociology of Health and Illness* 15, 5: 587–611.

Dahl, R. (1961) *Who Governs? Democracy and Power in an American City*, New Haven: Yale University Press.

Dahlgren, G. and Diderichsen, F. (1989) 'Strategies for equity in health: report from Sweden', *International Journal of Health Services* 16, 4: 517–37.

Dahrendorf, R. (1959) *Class and Class Conflict in Industrial Society*, London: Routledge and Kegan Paul.

Dale, R. (1989) *The State and Education Policy*, Buckingham: Open University Press.

Davie, G. (1994a) 'The religious factor in the emergence of Europe as a global region', *Social Compass* 41, 1: 95–112.

Davie, G. (1994b) *Religion in Britain since 1945: Believing without Belonging*, Oxford: Basil Blackwell.

de Beauvoir, S. (1977) *Old Age*, Harmondsworth: Penguin.

de Vries, J. (1984) *European Urbanization*, London: Methuen.

Deas, I. and Harrison, E. (1994) 'Hopes left to crumble', *Local Government Chronicle*, 4 March: 13.

Deleeck, H., van den Bosch, K. and de Lathouwer, L. (1992) *Poverty and the Adequacy of Social Security in the EC*, Aldershot: Avebury.

Department of Employment (1991) 'Ethnic origins and the labour market', *Employment Gazette*, February: 59–72.

Derrida, J., quoted in G. Rose (1988) 'Architecture to philosophy – the post-modern complicity', *Theory, Culture and Society* 5, 2/3: 357–71.

Deshormes LaValle, F. (ed.) (1987) *Women and Men of Europe*, Women of Europe Supplements No 26, Brussels: Commission of the European Communities.

Deshormes LaValle, F. (ed.) (1991) *Equal Opportunities for Women and Men: The Third Medium-term Community Action Programme 1991–1995*, Women of Europe Supplements No. 34, Brussels: Commission of the European Communities.

Dickens, C. (1969) *Hard Times*, Harmondsworth: Penguin.

Dominelli, L. (1991) *Women across Continents*, Hemel Hempstead: Harvester Wheatsheaf.

Downes, D. (1988) *Contrasts in Tolerance: Post-war Penal Policy in the Netherlands and England and Wales*, Oxford: OUP.

Downes, D. (1991) 'The origins and consequences of Dutch penal policy since 1945', in J. Muncie and R. Sparks (eds) *Imprisonment: European Perspectives*, London: Harvester Wheatsheaf.

Dreyfus, H. C. and Hall, H. (eds) (1992) *Heidegger: A Critical Reader*, Oxford: Basil Blackwell.

Drury, E. (1993) *Age Discrimination against Older Workers in the EC*, London: Euro-Link Age.

Ducatel, K. (ed.) (1994) *Employment and Technical Change in Europe*, Aldershot: Edward Elgar.

Dunleavy, P. and O'Leary, B. (1987) *Theories of the State: The Politics of Liberal Democracy*, Basingstoke: Macmillan Education.

Dupaquier, J. and Jadin, L. (1972) 'Structure of household and family in Corsica', in J. Dupaquier, E. Helin, P. Laslett, M. M. Livi-Bacci and S. Sogner (eds) *Marriage and Remarriage in Populations of the Past*, London: Academic Press.

Duverger, M. (1964) *Political Parties: Their Organization and Activity in the Modern State* (3rd edn), London: Methuen.

The Economist (1993) *World in Figures*, London: Century Business.

Edgell, S. (1980) *Middle Class Couples*, London: Allen and Unwin.

Edwards, D. L. (1990) *Christians in a New Europe*, London/Glasgow: Collins.

Edwards, J. and McKie, L. (1993/4) 'The European Community: a vehicle for promoting equal opportunities in Britain?', *Critical Social Policy* 13, 3: 51–65.

Engels, F. (1976) *The Condition of the Working Class in England*, St Albans: Panther Books.

Enzensberger, H. M. (1994) *Civil War*, London: Granta.

Erikson, R. and Goldthorpe, J. (1992) *The Constant Flux*, Oxford: Clarendon Press.

Esping-Anderson, J. (1990) *The Three Worlds of Welfare Capitalism*, Cambridge: Polity Press.

EU (European Union) (1996) *Eurostat Yearbook 1995*, Luxembourg: Statistical Office of the European Union.

European Commission (1990) *Mothers, Fathers and Employment*, Brussels: Commission of the European Communities, European Commission Childcare Network.

European Commission (1992) 'The structural funds of the European Community and childcare with special reference to rural regions', Report of the Working Group on Structural Funds and Rural Childcare, Equal Opportunities Unit, DGV.

European Commission (1993) *Childcare Network Annual Report for 1992*, Brussels: Commission of the European Communities, European Commission Childcare Network.

European Commission (1994) *Bulletin on Women and Employment in the EU No. 5*, Brussels: European Commission Directorate-General for Employment, Industrial Relations and Social Affairs.

European Community (1992) *Europe in Figures (EUROSTAT)* (3rd edn), Luxembourg: Statistical Office of the European Communities.

European Parliament (1990) *Report Drawn up on Behalf of the Committee of Inquiry into Racism and Xenophobia*, Luxembourg: European Parliament.

European Parliament (1993) *Report of the Committee on Civil Liberties and Internal Affairs on the Resurgence of Racism and Xenophobia in Europe and the Danger of Right-wing Extremist Violence*, Luxembourg: European Parliament.

European Parliament (1995) Committee on Civil Liberties and Internal Affairs, *Consultative Commission on Racism and Xenophobia – Final Report*, DOC EN/CM/274/274586, Luxembourg: European Parliament.

Eurostat (1990) *Poverty in Figures: Europe in the Early 1980s,* Luxembourg: Office for Official Publications of the European Communities.

Eurostat (1991) *Demographic Statistics 1991*, Luxembourg: Office for Official Publications of the European Communities.

Eurostat (1992) *Europe in Figures* (3rd edn), Luxembourg: Office for Official Publications of the European Communities.

Eurostat (1995) *Demographic Statistics 1995*, Luxembourg: Office for Official Publications of the European Communities.

Eurostat (1996) *Europe in Figures* (4th edn), Luxembourg: Office for Official Publications of the European Communities.

EURYDICE and CEDEFOP (1991/1995) *Structures of the Education and Initial Training Systems in the Member States of the European Community*, prepared by EURYDICE (The Education Information Network in the European Community) and CEDEFOP (European Centre for the Development of Vocational Training) for the Commission of the European Communities Task Force on Human Resources, Education, Training and Youth, Brussels: EURYDICE.

Featherstone, M. (1991) *Consumer Culture and Postmodernism*, London: Sage.

Featherstone, M. and Hepworth, M. (1989) 'Ageing and old age: reflections on the postmodern life course', in B. Bytheway, T. Keil, P. Allatt and A. Bryman (eds) *Becoming and Being Old*, London: Sage.

Featherstone, M. and Wernick, A. (eds) (1995) *Images of Ageing*, London: Routledge.

Fejes, F. (1981) 'Media imperialism: an assessment', *Media, Culture and Society* 3, 3: 281–9.

Fenton, S. (1987) *Ageing Minorities*, London: Commission for Racial Equality.

Fernández-Armesto, F. (ed.) (1994) *The Peoples of Europe*, London: Times Books, HarperCollins.

Finch, J. (1990) 'Equal opportunities and welfare in the European Community: some questions and issues', in L. Hantrais, M. O'Brien and S. Mangen (eds) *Women, Equal Opportunities and Welfare*, Birmingham: Aston University Cross-National Research Papers.

Finch, J. and Mason, J. (1993) *Negotiating Family Responsibilities*, London: Routledge.

Finegold, D. and Soskis, D. (1990) 'The failure of training in Britain: analysis and prescription', in D. Gleeson (ed.) *Training and Its Alternatives*, Buckingham: Open University Press.

Finn, D. (1987) *Training without Jobs: New Deals and Broken Promises*, London: Macmillan.

Flamm, F. (1993) *The Social System and Welfare Work in the Federal Republic of Germany* (2nd English edn), Frankfurt: Deutsche Verein für Offentliche und Private Fursorge.

Fletcher, R. (1962) *The Family and Marriage in Europe*, Harmondsworth: Penguin.

Foley, C. (1992) *Legion of the Rearguard: The IRA and the Modern Irish State*, London: Pluto.

Forbes, I. and Mead, G. (1992) *Measure for Measure. A Comparative Analysis of Measures to Combat Racial Discrimination in the Member Countries of the European Community*, London: Employment Department.

Ford, G. (1992) *Fascist Europe: The Rise of Racism and Xenophobia*, London: Pluto Press.

Foucault, M. (1977) *Discipline and Punish*, London: Allen Lane

Foucault, M. (1984), see P. Rabinow (ed.) *The Foucault Reader*, London: Penguin.

Fraser, A. (1992) *The Gypsies*, Oxford: Basil Blackwell.

Fraser, W. H. (1981) *The Coming of the Mass Market, 1850–1914*, London: Macmillan.

Freire, P. (1972) *Pedagogy of the Oppressed*, London: Sheed and Ward.

Freire, P. (1985) *The Politics of Education*, South Hadley, Mass.: Bergin and Garvey Publishers Inc.

Fröbel, F., Heinrichs, J. and Kreye, O. (1980) *The New International Division of Labour* (translated by Peter Burgess), Cambridge: Cambridge University Press.

Fulton, J. and Gee, P. (1994) *Religion in Contemporary Europe*, Lampeter: Edward Mellen Press.

Gallagher, M., Laver, M. and Mair, P. (1995) *Representation in Modern Europe* (2nd edn), London: McGraw-Hill.

Garfinkel, H. (1984) *Studies in Ethnomethodology*, Cambridge: Polity Press.

Garland, D. (1990) *Punishment and Modern Society*, Oxford: Oxford University Press.

Gellner, E. (1987) *Culture, Identity and Politics*, Cambridge: Cambridge University Press.

Gellner, E. (1992) *Reason and Culture*, Oxford: Basil Blackwell.

Giarchi, G. G. (1987) *A Comparative Study of Very Old People in Europe*, Swindon: ESRC Report No. 90023 2397.

Giarchi, G. G. (1996) *Caring for Older Europeans*, Aldershot: Arena Books.

Gibbins, J. R. (ed.) (1989) *Contemporary Political Culture*, London: Sage.

Giddens, A. (1979) 'Positivism and its critics', in T. Bottomore and R. Nisbet (eds) *A History of Sociological Analysis*, London: Heinemann.

Giddens, A. (1981) *A Contemporary Critique of Historical Materialism: Vol. 1 Power, Property and the State*, London: Macmillan.

Giddens, A. (1985), *A Contemporary Critique of Historical Materialism: Vol. 2 The Nation-State and Violence*, Cambridge: Polity Press.

Giddens, A. (1990) *The Consequences of Modernity*, Cambridge: Polity Press.

Giddens, A. (1991) *Modernity and Self Identity*, Cambridge: Polity Press.

Gilloch, G. (1996) *Myth and Metropolis: Walter Benjamin and the City*, Cambridge: Polity Press.

Gilroy, P. (1987) *There Ain't No Black in the Union Jack*, London: Hutchinson.

Gittins, D. (1996) *The Family in Question* (2nd edn), Basingstoke: Macmillan.

Glasner, A. (1992) 'Gender and Europe: cultural and structural impediments to change', in J. Bailey (ed.) *Social Europe*, London: Longman.

Glover, J. (1993) 'Vesper scoots south for subsidy', *The Guardian*, 23 February: 13.

Golding, P. and Murdock, G. (1996) 'Culture, communication and political economy', in J. Curran and M. Gurevitch (eds) *Mass Media and Society* (2nd edn). London: Edward Arnold.

Goldthorpe, J. (1987) *Social Mobility and Class Structure in Modern Britain*, Oxford: Clarendon Press.

Gong, G. W. (1984) *The Standard of 'Civilization' in International Society*, Oxford: Clarendon Press.

Goody, J. (1983) *The Development of the Family and Marriage in Europe*, Cambridge: Cambridge University Press.

Gordon, P. (1989) *Fortress Europe? The Meaning of 1992*, London: Runnymede Trust.

Gorz, A. (1970) 'Immigrant labour', *New Left Review* 61: 28–30.

Gouldner, A. W. (1975) 'Romanticism and classicism: deep structures in social science', in his *For Sociology: Renewal and Critique in Sociology Today*, Harmondsworth: Penguin.

Graham, J. (1987) *Home Office Research and Planning Unit Research Bulletin Number 24: Special European Edition*, London: Home Office.

Gray, A. and Davey, B. (1993) 'International patterns of health care 1960 to 1990', in C. Webster (ed.) *Caring for Health: History and Diversity*, Buckingham: Open University Press.

Greaves, T. and Shaw, K. (1992) 'A new look in French teacher education?', *Cambridge Journal of Education* 22, 2: 201–14.

Green, A. (1990) *Education and State Formation*, London: Macmillan.

Greengross, S. (1988) *Results and Prospects: Elderly People and Poverty in Europe*, Brussels: Commission of the European Community.

Greve, V. (1993) 'Denmark', in C. van den Wyngaert (ed.) *Criminal Justice in the European Community*, London: Butterworth.

Griffin, C. (1985) *Typical Girls: Young Women from School to the Labour Market*, London: Routledge and Kegan Paul.

Griffin, C. (1993) *Representations of Youth: The Study of Youth and Adolescence in Britain and America*, Cambridge: Polity Press.

Grimler, G. and Roy, C. (1987) 'Les emplois du temps en France 1985–1986', *Collections de l'INSEE: Premiers Resultats*, No. 100, June, Paris: INSEE.

Guardian (1994) 'Dead alone', Sept. 22, Supplement: 3.

Gubrium, J. (1986) *Old Timers and Alzheimer's: The Descriptive Organization of Senility*, Greenwich, Conn.: JAI Press.

Guibernau, M. (1995) *Nationalisms – The Nation State and Nationalism in the 20th Century*, Cambridge: Polity Press.

Gurevitch, M. (1996) 'The globalization of electronic journalism', in J. Curran and M. Gurevitch (eds) *Mass Media and Society* (2nd edn), London: Edward Arnold.

Habermas, J. (1993) *Justification and Application: Remarks on Discourse Ethics*, Cambridge: Polity Press

Hajer, M. (1993) 'Rotterdam: redesigning the public domain', in F. Bianchini and M. Parkinson (eds) *Cultural Policy and Urban Regeneration: The West European Experience*, Manchester: Manchester University Press.

Hakim, C. (1979) 'Occupational segregation: a comparative study of the degree and patterns of differentiation between men's and women's work in Britain, the United States and other countries', Research Paper No. 9, London: Department of Employment.

Hall, J. (1986a) *Powers and Liberties: The Causes and Consequences of the Rise of the West*, Harmondsworth: Penguin.

Hall, J. (1986b) *States in History*, Oxford: Basil Blackwell.

Hall, S., Held, D. and McGrew, T. (eds) (1992) *Modernity and its Futures,* Cambridge: Polity Press.

Hammar, T. (ed.) (1984) *European Immigration Policy: A Comparative Study*, Cambridge: Cambridge University Press.

Hamnett, C. (1978) *Multiple Deprivation in the Inner City*, Unit 4, E361 Education and the Urban Environment, Buckingham: Open University Press.

Hantrais, L. (1990) *Managing Professional and Family Life: A Comparative Study of British and French Women*, Aldershot: Dartmouth.

Hantrais, L. (1993) 'Women, work and welfare in France', in J. Lewis (ed.) *Women and Social Policies in Europe: Work, Family and the State*, Aldershot: Edward Elgar.

Hantrais, L. (1995) *Social Policy in the European Union*, London: Macmillian.

Harding, C. and Koffman, L. (1988) *Sentencing and the Penal System: Text and Materials*, London: Sweet and Maxwell.

Harding, S. and Phillips, D., with Fogarty, M. (1986) *Contrasting Values in Western Europe: Unity, Diversity and Change*, London: Macmillan.

Harvey, D. (1990) *The Condition of Postmodernity*, Oxford: Basil Blackwell.

Hawes, D. and Perez, B. (1995) *The Gypsy and the State*, Bristol: SAUS Publications.

Hazekamp, J. and Popple, K. (eds) (1997) *Racism in Europe: A Challenge for Youth Policy and Youth Work*, London: UCL Press.

Heckman, S. J. (1986) *Hermeneutics and the Sociology of Knowledge*, Cambridge: Polity Press.

Heelas, P. (1988) 'Western Europe: self religions', in S. Sutherland and P. Clarke (eds) *The Study of Religion: Traditional and New Religion*, London: Routledge.

Heidensohn, F. (1991) 'Introduction: convergence, diversity and change', in F. Heidensohn and M. Farrell (eds) *Crime in Europe*, London: Routledge.

Held, D. and Thompson, J. B. (eds) (1989) *Social Theory of Modern Societies: Anthony Giddens and his Critics*, Cambridge: Cambridge University Press.

Hernes, H. (1987) 'Women and the welfare state: the transition from private to public dependence', in A. Showstack Sassoon (ed.) *Women and the State*, London: Hutchinson.

Herrera, R. G. and Mochales, G. A. (1992) 'The Basque Country', in J. Ashton (ed.) *Healthy Cities*, Buckingham: Open University Press.

Herrman, J. (1987) 'The Federal Republic of Germany', in G. Cole, S. Frankowski and M. G. Gertz (eds) *Major Criminal Justice Systems: A Comparative Survey*, London: Sage.

Hervieu-Leger, D. (1990) 'Religion and modernity in the French context: for a new approach to secularisation', *Sociological Analysis* 51, Spring: 15–25.

Hervieu-Leger, D. (1994) 'Religion, Europe and the Pope: and the experience of French youth', in J. Fulton and P. Gee (eds) *Religion in Contemporary Europe*, Lampeter: Edwin Mellen Press.

Herzog-Massing, H. (1986) 'Decoding Dallas', *Society* 24, 1, 74–7.

Hesse, B. (1993) 'Racism and spacism in Britain', in P. Francis and R. Matthews (eds) *Tackling Racial Attacks*, University of Leicester: Centre for the Study of Public Order.

Hills, J. (1995) *Income and Wealth: A Summary of the Evidence* (Vol. 2), York: Joseph Rowntree Foundation.

Himmelweit, S. (1988) 'In the beginning', Unit 1 of Open University course D211 *Social Problems and Social Welfare*, Milton Keynes: The Open University.

Hirsch, M. (1986) 'Tripartism in Luxembourg: the limits of social concertation', *West European Politics*, 9, 1: 54–66.

Hirschfield, A. (1993) 'Construction of social indicators, multiple variables and their interpretation', Paper presented to ESRC/UFC-ISC Workshop on the 1991 Census, University of Wales College of Cardiff, 26 March.

Hobsbawm, E. J. (1962) *The Age of Revolution*, London: Weidenfeld and Nicolson.

Hobsbawm, E. J. (1975) *The Age of Capital*, London: Weidenfeld and Nicolson.

Hobsbawm, E. J. (1983) *Industry and Empire* (reprint), Harmondsworth: Penguin.

Hobsbawm, E. J. (1985) *Industry and Empire: From 1750 to the Present Day*, Harmondsworth: Penguin.

Hobsbawm, E. J. (1987) *The Age of Empire*, London: Weidenfeld and Nicolson.

Hobsbawm, E. J. (1993) *Nations and Nationalism since 1780*, Cambridge: Canto.

Hobsbawm, E. J. (1994) *The Age of Extremes*, London: Penguin.

Hockey, J. and James, A. (1993) *Growing Up and Growing Old*, London: Sage.

Hohenberg, P. and Lees, L. H. (1985) *The Making of Urban Europe 1000–1950*, Cambridge, Mass: Harvard University Press.

Holden, B. (1993) *Understanding Liberal Democracy* (2nd edn), Brighton: Harvester Wheatsheaf.

Horn, R. (1993) *Statistical Indicators for the Economic and Social Sciences*, Cambridge: Cambridge University Press.

Hörning, K., Gerhard, A. and Michailow, M. (1995) *Time Pioneers: Flexible Working Time and New Lifestyles*, Cambridge: Polity Press.

Hornsby-Smith, M. (1987) *Roman Catholics in England*, Cambridge: Cambridge University Press.

House of Commons (1975) *Racial Discrimination*, Cmnd. 6234, London: HMSO.

House of Commons (1981) *Fifth Report from the Home Affairs Committee, Session 1980–81, Racial Disadvantage* (Vol. 1), London: HMSO.

House of Commons. (1994) *Racial Attacks and Harassment*, Home Affairs Committee, Third Report, Volume I.

Hudson, B. (1993) *Penal Policy and Social Justice*, London: Macmillan.

Hugman, R. (1994) *Ageing and the Care of Older People in Europe*, Basingstoke: Macmillan.

Hutchinson, S. and Brewster, C. (1994) *Flexibility at Work in Europe: Strategies and Practice*, London: Institute of Personnel and Development.

Hutson, S. and Liddiard, M. (1994) *Youth Homelessness: The Social Construction of a Social Issue*, Basingstoke: Macmillan.

Hyde, M. (1996) 'Fifty years of failure: employment services for disabled people in the UK', *Work, Employment and Society* 10, 683–700.

Hyde, M. and Armstrong, E. (1995) 'Underclass or underdogs? Britain's poor in the 1990s', *Public Policy Review* 3, 4: 44–6.

Hyman, R. and Ferner, A. (eds) (1994) *New Frontiers in European Industrial Relations*, Oxford: Blackwell.

Illich, I. (1976) *Limits to Medicine*, Harmondsworth: Penguin.

Inglehart, R. (1977) *The Silent Revolution: Changing Values and Political Styles among Western Publics*, Princeton: Princeton University Press.

Jacobs, S. (1985) 'Race, Empire and the welfare state: council housing and racism', *Critical Social Policy* 13, 5: 6–28.

Jamieson, A. (1990) 'Care of older people in the European Community', in L. Hantrais, S. Mangen and M. O'Brien (eds) *Caring and the Welfare State in the 1990s*, Aston University: Cross National Research Papers.

Jamieson, A. (1991) 'Community care for older people', in G. Room (ed.) *Toward a European Welfare State*, Bristol: School of Advanced Urban Studies.

Jeffries, A. (1992) 'The paradoxical strengths of British social work', Unpublished paper given at the 75th Jubilee Conference of the Fachhochschuler für Sozialwesen in Esslingen, Germany.

Jeffs, T. and Smith, M. (1994) 'Young people, youth work and the new authoritarianism', *Youth and Policy* 46, Autumn: 17–32.

Johnston, L. (1993) 'Post-punk nostalgia', *Youth and Policy* 40, Spring: 70–4.

Joll, J. (1990) *Europe since 1870* (3rd edn), London: Penguin.

Jones, G. (1973) *Rural Life: Patterns and Processes*, London: Longman.

Jones, G. and Miesen, B. M. L. (1992) *Care Giving in Dementia*, London: Routledge.

Jones, G. and Wallace, C. (1992) *Youth, Family and Citizenship*, Milton Keynes: Open University Press.

Jones, H. D. (1994) *International Centre Paper No. 2: 24*, London: National Institute of Social Work.

Jordan, A. G. (ed.) (1991) *The Commercial Lobbyists*, Aberdeen: Aberdeen University Press.

Joseph Rowntree Foundation (1995) *Inquiry into Income and Wealth* (Vol. 1), York: Joseph Rowntree Foundation.

Joshi, H. and Davies, H. (1994) 'Mothers' foregone earnings and child care: some cross-national assessments', in L. Hantrais and S. Mangen (eds) *Family Policy and the Welfare State*, Loughborough: Cross-National Research Paper No. 3.

Joshi, S. and Carter, B. (1985) 'The role of Labour in the creation of racist Britain', *Race and Class* 25: 53–70.

Jowell, R., Brook, L. and Dowds, L. (eds) (1993) *International Social Attitudes*, Aldershot: Dartmouth.

Jowell, R., Witherspoon, S. and Brook, L. (eds) (1989) *British Social Attitudes: Special International Report*, Aldershot: Gower.

Karger, C. (1992) Interview with Carmen Karger, psychologist-counsellor, Inkozentrum Arbeitslosenverbaud Deutschland e.v., Hellersdorf, East Berlin, 8 September, appears in M. Wilson, 'The German welfare state: a conservative regime in crisis', in A. Cochran and J. Clarke (eds) (1993) *Comparing Welfare States: Britain in the International Context*, London: Sage.

Katz, E. and Lazarsfeld, P. F. (1955) *Personal Influence: The Part Played by People in the Flow of Mass Communication*. Glencoe, Ill.: Free Press.

Kavanagh, D. (1972) *Political Culture*, London: Macmillan.

Kellas, J. G. (1992) 'The social origins of nationalism in Great Britain – the case of Scotland', in J. Coakley (ed.) *The Social Origins of Nationalist Movements*, London: Sage.

Kellerhals, J., Coenen-Huther, J. and Modak, M. (1990) 'Justice and the family, an exploratory analysis', *European Journal of Sociology* 31: 117–40.

Kemp, T. (1985) *Industrialization in Nineteenth Century Europe* (2nd edn), London: Longman.

Kennedy, P. (1989) *The Rise and Fall of the Great Powers*, London: Fontana.

Kirchheimer, O. (1966) 'The transformation of the Western European party systems', in J. LaPalombara and M. Weiner (eds) *Political Parties and Political Development*, Princeton: Princeton University Press.

Klapisch, C. (1972) 'Western Europe: household and family in Tuscany', in P. Laslett and R. Wall (eds) *Household and Family in Past Times*, Cambridge: Cambridge University Press.

Kokosalakis, N. (1992) 'The dynamics of religious change in modern Europe: a theoretical approach', Paper presented at the BSA Sociology of Religion Study Group, St Mary's College, Strawberry Hill, April.

Kumar, K. (1995) *From Post-Industrial to Postmodern Society*, Oxford: Basil Blackwell.

Kushner, T. (1994) 'Immigration and "race relations" in post-war British society', in P. Johnson (ed.) *20th Century Britain*, London: Longman.

Kuusela, K. (1993) 'A mosque of our own? Turkish migrants in Gothenburg facing the effects of a changing world', in S. Sutherland and P. Clarke (eds) *Religion and Ethnicity*, Kampen: Pharos.

Laczko, F. (1994) *Older People in Eastern and Central Europe*, London: HelpAge International.

Laczko, F. and Phillipson, C. (1991) *Changing Work and Retirement*, Milton Keynes: Open University Press.

Lahelma, E. and Valkonen, T. (1990) 'Health and social inequalities in Finland and elsewhere', *Social Science and Medicine* 31: 257–65.

Lahelma, E., Manderbacka, K., Rahkonen, O. and Karisto, A. (1994) 'Comparison of inequalities in health: evidence from national surveys in Finland, Norway and Sweden', *Social Science and Medicine* 38, 4: 517–24.

Langberg, K. (1994) 'Housework and childcare – from doing to sharing: a Danish example of how work in the family has changed', Working Paper, Graz University of Technology, Austria.

Lash, S. and Urry, J. (1987) *The End of Organised Capitalism*, Cambridge: Polity Press.

Lash, S. and Whimster, S. (eds) (1987) *Max Weber, Rationality and Modernity*, London: Allen and Unwin.

Laslett, P. (1972) 'The history of the family', in P. Laslett and R. Wall (eds) *Household and Family in Past Times*, Cambridge: Cambridge University Press.

Laslett, P. and Wall, R. (eds) (1972) *Household and Family in Past Times*, Cambridge: Cambridge University Press.

Lawless, P. (1986) *The Evolution of Spatial Policy*, London: Pion.

Le Magazine (1994) 'Open minds! Breaking invisible barriers', Editorial, Summer: 6 (Brussels: European Commission).

Le Play, F. (1855) *Les Ouvriers Européens*, Paris.

Leclerc, A., Lort, F. and Fabien, C. (1990) 'Differential morbidity: some comparisons between England and Wales, Finland and France based on inequality measures', *International Journal of Epidemiology* 19: 1001–10.

Lehmbruch, G. and Schmitter, P. C. (eds) (1982) *Patterns of Corporatist Policy-making*, London: Sage.

Leitner, H. (1987) 'Regulating migrants' lives: the dialect of migrant labour and the contradictions of regulatory and integration policies in the Federal Republic of Germany', in G. Glebe and J. O'Loughlin (eds) *Foreign Minorities in Continental European Cities*, Stuttgart: Steiner Verlag-Wiesbaden.

Leon, P. (1994) 'Fees back to square one', *Times Higher Education Supplement*, 7 January: 10.

Leslie, W. B. (1984) ' "Time, the subtle thief of youth": historians and youth', *Youth and Policy* 11, Winter: 49–51.

Leveau, R. (1988) 'The Islamic presence in France', in T. Gerholm and Y. G. Lithman (eds) *The New Islamic Presence in Western Europe*, London: Mansell.

Levi, M. and Maguire, M. (1992) 'Crime and cross-border policing in Europe', in J. Bailey (ed.) *Social Europe*, Harlow: Longman.

Lewis, J. (1980) *The Politics of Motherhood*, London: Croom Helm.

Lewis, J. (1992) 'Gender and the development of welfare regimes', *European Journal of Social Policy* 2, 2: 159–74.

Lewis, J. (ed.) (1993a) *Women and Social Policies in Europe: Work, Family and the State*, Aldershot: Edward Elgar.

Lewis, J. (1993b) 'Women, work, family and social policies in Europe', in J. Lewis (ed.) *Women and Social Policies in Europe: Work, Family and the State*, Aldershot: Edward Elgar.

Liebes, T. and Katz, E. (1993) *The Export of Meaning: Cross-cultural Readings of Dallas*, Cambridge: Polity Press.

Lijphart, A. (1968) *The Politics of Accommodation*, Berkeley: University of California Press.

Lijphart, A. (1969) 'Consociational democracy', *World Politics* XXI, October 1968–July 1969: 207–25.

Lipset, S. M. and Rokkan, S. (1967) 'Cleavage structures, party systems and voter alignments: an introduction', in S. M. Lipset and S. Rokkan (eds) *Party Systems and Voter Alignments: Cross-National Perspectives*, New York: The Free Press.

Locker, D. (1981) *Symptoms and Illness: The Cognitive Organisation of Disorder*, London: Tavistock.

Lorenz, W. (1994) *Social Work in a Changing Europe,* London: Routledge.

Lorwin, V. R. (1971) 'Segmented pluralism: ideological cleavages and political cohesion in the smaller European democracies', *Comparative Politics* 3: 141–175.

Lull, J. (1995) *Media, Communication, Culture: A Global Approach*, Cambridge: Polity Press.

Lustick, I. (1979) 'Stability in deeply divided societies: consociationalism versus control', *World Politics* XXXI, 3: 325–44.

Lynch, M. (1993) *Scientific Practice and Ordinary Action*, Oxford: Oxford University Press.

Lyon, D. (1994) *Postmodernity*, Milton Keynes: Open University Press.

Lyotard, J.-F. (1986) *The Postmodern Condition: A Report on Knowledge*, Manchester: Manchester University Press.

MacBride, S. (1980) *Many Voices, One World: Communication and Society Today and Tomorrow*, New York: UNESCO.

MacClancy, J. (1993) 'At play with identity in the Basque arena', in S. MacDonald (ed.) *Inside European Identities*, Oxford: Berg.

McClintock, F. and Wikstrom, P.-O. (1992) 'The comparative study of urban violence', *British Journal of Criminology* 3, 4: 505–20.

McCrone, D. (1992) *Understanding Scotland: The Sociology of a Stateless Nation*, London: Routledge.

MacDonald, S. (ed.) (1993) *Inside European Identities*, Oxford: Berg.

McDonald, M. (1990) *We Are not French: Language, Culture and Identity in Brittany*, London: Routledge.

McEwan, E. (1990) *The Unrecognised Discrimination*, London: Age Concern.

Macfarlane, A. (1978) *The Origins of English Individualism*, Oxford: Basil Blackwell.

Macfarlane, A. (1986) *Marriage and Love in England*, Oxford: Basil Blackwell.

McIntosh, M. (1984) 'The state and the family', Unit 9 of Open University course D209 The State and Society, Milton Keynes: The Open University.

MacIntyre, A. (1981) *After Virtue*, London: Duckworth.

Mack, J. and Lansley, S. (1985) *Poor Britain*, London: George Allen and Unwin.

Mackenback, J. P. (1992) 'Socio-economic health differences in the Netherlands: a review of recent empirical findings', *Social Science and Medicine* 34, 3: 213–26.

McKeown, T. (1976) *The Role of Medicine: Dream, Mirage or Nemesis*, London: Nuffield Hospitals Trust (2nd edn, 1989, Oxford: Basil Blackwell).

Maclean, M. and Kurczewski, J. (eds) (1994) *Families, Politics and the Law: Perspectives on East and West Europe*, Oxford: Clarendon Press.

McLean, M. (1990) *Britain and a Single Market Europe: Prospects for a Common School Curriculum*, London: Kogan Page, in association with The Institute of Education, University of London.

McLean, M. (1993) 'The politics of curriculum in European perspective', *Educational Review*, 45, 2: 125–35.

McNeill, R. (1963) *The Rise of the West*, Chicago: University of Chicago Press.

Macpherson, C. B. (1962) *The Political Theory of Possessive Individualism: Hobbes to Locke*, Oxford: Oxford University Press.

Macpherson, C. B. (1977) *The Life and Times of Liberal Democracy*, Oxford: Oxford University Press.

McQuail, D. (1991) *Mass Communication Theory: An Introduction*, London: Sage.

Macran, S., Clarke, L., Sloggett, A. and Bethune, A. (1994) 'Women's socio-economic status and self-assessed health: identifying some disadvantaged groups', *Sociology of Health and Illness* 16, 2: 182–208.

Macridis, R. (ed.) (1990) *Modern Political Systems: Europe* (7th edn), Englewood Cliffs: Prentice-Hall.

Mair, P. (ed.) (1990) *The West European Party System*, Oxford: Oxford University Press.

Mangen, S. P. (1985) *Mental Health Care in the EC*, London: Sage.

Mann, M. (1986) *The Sources of Social Power. Vol. 1: A History of Power from the Beginning to AD 1760*, Cambridge: Cambridge University Press.

Mansfield, P. and Collard, J. (1988) *The Beginning of the Rest of Your Life?*, Basingstoke: Macmillan.

Marchington, M. (1981) *Managing Industrial Relations*, London: McGraw-Hill.

Marcuse, H. (1968) 'Industrialisation and capitalism in Max Weber', in his *Negations*, London: Allen Lane.

Marshall, G., Rose, D., Newby, H. and Vogler, C. (1989) *Social Class in Modern Britain*, London: Unwin Hyman.

Marshall, T. H. (1950) *Citizenship and Social Class and Other Essays*, Cambridge: Cambridge University Press.

Martin, D. (1978) *A General Theory of Secularisation*, Oxford: Basil Blackwell.

Martin, D. (1991) 'The secularisation issue: prospect and retrospect', *British Journal of Sociology*, 42, 3: 465–74.

Martin, D. (1994) 'Religion in contemporary Europe', in J. Fulton and P. Gee (eds) *Religion in Contemporary Europe*, Lampeter: Edwin Mellen Press.

Martin, J. and Roberts, C. (1984) *Women and Employment: A Lifetime Perspective*, London: HMSO.

Martins, H. (1972) 'The Kuhnian revolution and its implication for sociology', in T. J. Nossiter *et al.* (eds) *Imagination and Precision in the Social Sciences*, London: Faber.

Maruani, M. (1992) *The Position of Women in the Labour Market: Trends and Developments in the Twelve Member States of the European Community 1983–1990*, Brussels: Commission of the European Communities.

Marullo, S. (ed.) (1995) *Comparison of Regulations on Part-Time and Temporary Employment in Europe: A Briefing Paper*, Employment Department Research Series No. 52, HMSO.

Marx, K (1959) *Capital* (Vol. 1), Moscow: Foreign Languages Publishing House.

Marx, K. and Engels, F. (1962) *On Britain* (2nd edn) Moscow: Foreign Languages Publishing House (Marx to S. Meyer and A. Vogt, London, 9 April 1870).

Mathias, P. (1969) *The First Industrial Nation: An Economic History of Britain 1700–1914*, London: Methuen.

Mathiesen T. (1990) *Prison on Trial*, London: Sage.

Maxwell, R. (1981) *Health and Wealth: An International Study of Health Care Spending*, Lexington, Mass.: Lexington Books

Mayhew, H. (1849) 'Jacob's Island', *Morning Chronicle*, 24 September.

Mayhew, H. (1864) *London Labour and London Poor* (four volumes 1851–62, revised 1967), London: Frank Cass.

Maynard, A. and Ludbrook, J. (1981) 'Thirty years of fruitless endeavour? An analysis of government intervention in the health care market', in J. van der Gaag and M. Perlman (eds) *Health, Economics and Health Economics*, Amsterdam: North-Holland.

Mazzoleni, G. and Palmer, M. (1992) 'The building of media empires', in K. Siune and W. Truetzschler (eds) *The Dynamics of Media Politics: Broadcast and Electronic Media in Western Europe*, London: Sage.

Meehan, E. (1993) *Citizenship and the European Community*, London: Sage.

Meny, Y. (1993) *Government and Politics in Western Europe: Britain, France, Italy and Germany* (2nd revised edn), Oxford: Oxford University Press.

Merchant, J. and MacDonald, R. (1994) 'Youth and the rave culture, Ecstasy and health', *Youth and Policy* 45, Summer: 16–38.

Michel, P. (1991) *Politics and Religion in Eastern Europe*, Cambridge: Polity Press.

Michel, P. (1994) 'Religion and democracy in Central Eastern Europe', in J. Fulton and P. Gee (eds) *Religion in Contemporary Europe*, Lampeter: Edwin Mellen Press.

Miles, R. (1993) *Racism after 'Race Relations'*, London: Routledge.

Miles, R. (1994) 'A rise of racism and fascism in contemporary Europe? Some sceptical reflections on its nature and extent', *New Community* 20, 4: 547–62.

Miller, J. (1990) *The Socio-economic Situation of Solo Women in Europe*, Brussels: Commission of the European Communities.

Minois, G. (1987) *History of Old Age*, Chicago: University of Chicago Press.

Minshull, G. (1990) *The New Europe: Into the 1990s*, London: Hodder and Stoughton.

Mitterauer, M. and Sieder, R. (1982) *The European Family. Patriarchy to Partnership from the Middle Ages to the Present*, Oxford: Basil Blackwell.

Modood, T. (1994) 'Ethno-religious minorities, secularism and the British state', *British Political Quarterly* 65: 53–73.

Moss, P. (1990) 'Childcare and equality of opportunity', in L. Hantrais, S. Mangen and M. O'Brien (eds) *Caring and the Welfare State in the 1990s*, Aston University: Cross National Research Papers.

Moxon, D. and Hedderman, C. (1994) 'Mode of trial: decisions and sentencing differentials between courts', *Howard Journal of Criminal Justice* 3, 2: 97–108.

Muncie, J. and Sparks, R. (eds) (1991) *Imprisonment: European Perspectives*, Hemel Hempstead: Harvester Wheatsheaf.

Murray, C. (1990) *The Emerging British Underclass*, London: Institute of Economic Affairs.

Nash, E. (1995) 'Family values soften impact of Spain's 22% unemployment', *The Independent on Sunday*, 29 October: 14.

Neale, K. (1992) *The Demosthenes Programme: A Penological Challenge*, Brussels: Council of Europe.

Needham, J. (1972) 'Mathematics and science in China and the West', in B. Barnes (ed.) *Sociology of Science*, Harmondsworth: Penguin.

Negrine, R. (1994) *Politics and the Mass Media in Britain*, London: Routledge.

Nikolinakos, M. (1973) 'Notes on an economic theory of racism', *Race* 14, 4: 365–81.

Nisbet, R. (1968) *The Sociological Tradition*, London: Heinemann.

Nitzova, P. (1994) 'Islam and Christianity in Central Eastern Europe', in J. Fulton and P. Gee (eds) *Religion in Contemporary Europe*, Lampeter: Edwin Mellen Press.

Noble, M., Smith, G., Avenell, D., Smith, T. and Sharland, E. (1994) *Changing Patterns of Income and Wealth in Oxford and Oldham*, Department of Applied Social Studies and Social Research, University of Oxford.

Noin, D. and Woods, R. (eds) 1993 *The Changing Population of Europe*, Oxford: Basil Blackwell.

Norman, A. (1985) *Triple Jeopardy: Growing Old in a Second Homeland* ('Policy Studies in Ageing', No. 3), London: Centre for Policy on Ageing.

Norris, H. T. (1993) *Islam in the Balkans*, London: Hurst.

O'Brien, O. (1993) 'Good to Be French? Conflicts of identity in North Catalonia', in S. MacDonald (ed.) *Inside European Identities*, Oxford: Berg.

O'Day, R. (1994) *The Family and Family Relationships, 1500–1900: England, France and the United States of America*, London: Macmillan.

O'Dwyer, T. (1994) 'The search for tomorrow's jobs', *Le Magazine*, Spring: 14 (Brussels: European Commission).

OECD (Organization for Economic Co-operation and Development) (1986) *Employment Outlook* (September), Paris: OECD.

OECD (Organization for Economic Co-operation and Development) (1991) *Human Development Report 1991*, CREDOC/OECD Paris/United Nations Development Programme, Oxford: Oxford University Press.

Offe, C. (1996) *Modernity and the State*, Cambridge: Polity Press.

Ogus, A. J. (1990) 'The Federal Republic as Sozialstaat: a British perspective', in H. Braun and M. Niehaus (eds) *Sozialstaat Bundesrepublik auf dem Weg nach Europa*, Frankfurt-am-Main: Campus.

Oliver, M. (1992) 'Changing the social relations of research production?', *Disability, Handicap and Society* 7, 2: 101–14.

Oppenheim, C. (1993) *Poverty: The Facts*, London: Child Poverty Action Group.

Ostner, I. (1994) 'The women and welfare debate', in L. Hantrais and S. Mangan (eds) *Family Policy and the Welfare of Women*, Loughborough: Cross National Research Papers.

Pahl, R. (1993) 'Does class analysis without class theory have a future?', *Sociology* 27, 2: 253–8.

Parker, R. A. (1988) 'An historic background', in I. Sinclair (ed.) *Residential Care: The Research Revisited*, London: HMSO.

Parkinson, M., Bianchini, F., Dawson, J., Evans, R. and Harding, A. (1993) *Urbanisation and the Functions of Cities in the European Community*, European Institute of Urban Affairs, Liverpool: John Moores University.

Parsons, T. (1951) *The Social System*, London: Routledge and Kegan Paul.

Parsons, T. (1959) 'The social structure of the family', in R. Anshen (ed.) *The Family: Its Functions and Destiny*, New York: Harper and Row.

Parsons, T. (1969) *Politics and Social Structure*, New York: Free Press.

Pateman, C. (1987) 'The patriarchal welfare state', in A. Gutman (ed.) *Democracy and the Welfare State*, Princeton: Princeton University Press.

Pateman, C. (1988) *The Sexual Contract*, Cambridge: Polity Press.

Paul, S. (1995) 'Does the community care?', *Professional Social Work* 5: 95.

Payne, G. (1989) 'Social mobility', in R. Burgess, *Investigating Society*, London: Longman.

467

Payne, G. and Abbott, P. A. (1990) 'Beyond male mobility models', in G. Payne and P. A. Abbott (eds) *The Social Mobility of Women: Beyond Male Mobility Models*, Basingstoke: Falmer Press.

Pearson, G. (1983) *Hooligan: A History of Respectable Fears*, Basingstoke: Macmillan.

PEP (1968) *Racial Discrimination*, London: Political and Economic Planning.

Perkin, H. (1969) *Origins of Modern English Society*, London: Routledge.

Perree, M. and Young, D. (1992) 'Two steps back for women: German unification, gender and university "reform"', Unpublished draft paper, Berlin Free University.

Pfaller, A., Gough, I. and Therborn, G. (eds) (1991) *Can the Welfare State Compete?*, London: Macmillan.

Phillips, A. and Taylor, B. (1980) 'Sex and skill: towards a feminist economics', *Feminist Review* 6: 79–88.

Philo, G. (1993) *Seeing and Believing*, London: Routledge.

Pilkington, E. (1994) 'Dead alone', *Guardian*, Thursday, 22 Sept.: 3.

Pillinger, J. (1992) *Feminising the Market: Women's Pay and Employment in the European Community*, London: Macmillan.

Platt, S. (1992) 'Race wars', *New Statesman and Society*, 28 February: 12–13.

Poggi, G. (1978) *The Development of the Modern State: A Sociological Introduction*, London: Hutchinson.

Popenhoe, D. (1987) 'Beyond the nuclear family; a statistical portrait of the changing family in Sweden', *Journal of Marriage and Family* 49: 173–83.

Popple, K. (1993) 'Young people in Europe: a *Youth and Policy* round table discussion', *Youth and Policy* 40, Spring: 62–8.

Potter, P. and Zill, G. (1992) 'Older households and their housing situation', in L. Davies (ed.) *The Coming of Age in Europe*, London: Age Concern.

Pounds, N. (1985) *An Historical Geography of Europe 1800–1914*, Cambridge: Cambridge University Press.

Power, B. (1980) *Old and Alone in Ireland*, Dublin: Society of St Vincent de Paul.

Ramdin, R. (1987) *The Making of the Black Working Class in Britain*, Aldershot: Wildwood House.

Ramprakash, D. (1994) 'Poverty in the countries of the European Union: a synthesis of Eurostat's statistical research on poverty', *Journal of European Social Policy* 4, 2: 117–28.

Ramsay, R. (1987) *The Corsican Timebomb*, Manchester: Manchester University Press.

Rappaport, R. and Moss, P. (1989) 'Exploring ways of integrating men and women as equals at work', Unpublished report to the Ford Foundation.

Rattansi, A. and Reeder, D. (eds) (1992) *Rethinking Radical Education*, London: Lawrence and Wishart.

Reid, I. (1989) *Social Class Differences in Britain* (3rd edn), London: Fontana.

Rentzmann, W. (1992) *Cornerstones in a Modern Treatment Philosophy: Normalisation, Openness and Responsibility*, Brussels: Council of Europe.

Richardson, J. J. and Jordan, A. G. (1985) *Governing under Pressure: The Policy Process in a Post-Parliamentary Democracy*, Oxford: Basil Blackwell.

Rifkin, J. (1996) *The End of Work*, New York: G. P. Putnam's Sons.

Roberts, B. (1993) 'The reconstruction of ethnic identity: the re-formation of "Welshness" in a valley community', Paper presented to the British Sociological Association Conference, University of Essex, 5–8 April.

Roberts, E. (1982) 'Working wives and their families', in T. Beuler and M. Drake (eds) *Population and Society in Britain 1850–1980*, London: Batsford.

Robertson, R. (1992) *Globalization: Social Theory and Global Culture*, London: Sage.

Robson, B. (1988), *Those Inner Cities: Reconciling the Social and Economic Aims of Urban Policy*, Oxford: Oxford University Press.

Robson, B. (1994) 'No city, no civilization', *Transactions of the Institute of British Geographers* 19, 2: 131–41.

Robson, B., Parkinson, M., Bradford, M., Deas, I., Garside, P., Hall, E., Harding, A. and Harrison, E. (1994) *Assessing the Impact of Urban Policy*, London: HMSO.

Roll, J. (1992) *Lone Parent Families in the European Community*, Luxembourg: Statistical Office of the European Communities.

Room, G. (ed.) (1995) *Beyond the Threshold*, Bristol: Policy Press.

Rose, M. (1991) *The Postmodern and the Post-Industrial: A Critical Analysis*, Cambridge: Cambridge University Press

Rose, R. (1991) *Bringing Freedom Back In*, Glasgow: University of Strathclyde.

Royal Commission on Criminal Justice (1993) *Report of the Royal Commission on Criminal Justice*, Cmnd. 2263, London: HMSO.

Ruggie, M. (1988) 'Gender, work and social progress', in T. Jenson and E. Hagen (eds) *The Feminisation of the Labour Force*, Cambridge: Polity Press.

Ruggiero, G., Ryan, M. and Sim, J. (eds) (1995) *Western European Penal Systems: A Critical Anatomy*, London: Sage.

Rundell, J. F. (1987) *Origins of Modernity: The Origins of Modern Social Theory from Kant to Hegel to Marx*, Cambridge: Polity Press.

Rutherford, A. (1993) *Criminal Justice and the Pursuit of Decency*, Oxford: Oxford University Press.

Sainsbury, D. (1996) *Gendering Welfare States*, London: Sage.

Saunders, P. (1986) *Social Theory and the Urban Question*, London: Unwin Hyman.

Saunders, P. (1990) *Social Class and Stratification*, London: Routledge.

Saunders, P. (1996) *Unequal but Fair?*, London: IEA Health and Welfare Unit.

Sayer, J. (1986) 'Ideology: the bridge between theory and practice', *Community Development Journal* 21, 4: 294–303.

Schiffauer, W. (1988) 'Migration and religiousness', in T. Gerholm and Y. G. Lithman (eds) *The New Islamic Presence in Western Europe*, London: Mansell.

Schiller, H. (1985) 'Electronic information flows: new basis for global domination?', in P. Drummond and R. Paterson (eds) *Television in Transition,* London: BFI.

Schmitter, P. C. and Lehmbruch, G. (eds) (1979) *Trends toward Corporatist Intermediation*, Beverly Hills: Sage Publications.

Schultheis, F. (1988) *Sozialgeschichte der französischer Familienpolitik*, Frankfurt: Campus.

Scott, R. A. (1991) *The Making of Blind Men: A Study of Adult Socialization*, New Brunswick: Transaction Books.

Scott, S. and Morgan, D. (1993) *Body Matters*, London: Falmer Press.

Scriven, J. (1984) 'Women at work in Sweden', in M. Davidson and C. Cooper (eds) *Women at Work*, Chichester: Wiley.

Segalen, M. (1980) 'The family cycle and household structure: five generations in a French village', in R. Wheaton and T. Hareven, *Family and Sexuality in French History*, Philadelphia.

Seidman, S. and Wagner, D. G. (eds) (1992) *Postmodernism and Social Theory*, Oxford: Basil Blackwell.

Senftleben, P. (1992) 'Bericht zur Abteilung fur Sozialwesen', *Geschaftsbericht 1990–1991*, 44–87, Berlin: Bezirksamt Tiergarten.

Sennett, R. (1993) *The Fall of Public Man*, London: Faber.

Sharpe, K. (1992) 'Educational homogeneity in French primary education: a double case study', *British Journal of Sociology of Education* 13, 3: 329–48.

Shulman, L. (1993) 'Developing and testing a practice theory: an interactional perspective', *Social Work* 38, 1: 91–7.

Siim, B. (1987) 'The Scandinavian welfare states: towards sexual equality or a new kind of dominance?', *Acta Sociologica* 30, 3/4: 255–70.

Simmel, G. (1971) 'The metropolis and mental life' in D. N. Levine (ed.) *On Individuality and Social Structure*, Chicago: University of Chicago.

Sinclair, I. (1992) 'Social work research: its relevance to social work and social work education', *Issues in Social Work Education* 11, 2: 65–80.

Sivanandan, A. (1988) 'The new racism', *New Statesman and Society*, November.

Sjerps, M. (1988) 'Indirect discrimination in social security in the Netherlands: demands of the Dutch Women's Movement', in M. Buckly and M. Anderson (eds) *Women, Equality and Europe*, Basingstoke: Macmillan.

Skinner, Q. (ed.) (1990) *The Return to Grand Theory in the Human Sciences*, Cambridge: Cambridge University Press.

Skocpol, T. (1979) *States and Social Revolutions: Comparative Analysis of France, Russia and China*, Cambridge: Cambridge University Press.

Slattery, M. (1985) *Urban Sociology*. Ormskirk, Lancashire: Causeway Press.

Smigielska, J. and Czynczyk, A. (1994) 'What do family members and friends expect from one another at the transition to democracy?', in M. Maclean and J. Kurczewski (eds) *Families, Politics and the Law: Perspectives on East and West Europe*, Oxford: Clarendon Press.

Smith, A. (1987) 'The fading industrial age', in J. Curran, H. Smith, and P. Wingate (eds) *Impacts and Influences*, London: Routledge.

Smith, A. D. (1986) *The Ethnic Origin of Nations*, Oxford: Basil Blackwell.

Smith, A. D. (1991) *National Identity*, Harmondsworth: Penguin.

Smith, D. (1987) *Social Work and the Sociology of Organisations*, London: Routledge.

Smith, D. J. (1977) *Racial Disadvantage in Britain: The PEP Report*, Harmondsworth: Penguin.

Snyder, L. L. (1954) *The Meaning of Nationalism*, Westport, Conn.: Greenwood Press.

Sohn-Rethel, A. (1978) *Intellectual and Manual Labour: A Critique of Epistemology*, London: Macmillan.

Solomos, J. (1989) *Race and Racism in Contemporary Britain*, Basingstoke: Macmillan.

Springhall, J. (1983) 'Sure and steadfast: re-assessing the history of the Boy's Brigade', *Youth and Policy* 2, 1 (Summer): 19–21.

Spybey, T. (1992) *Social Change, Development and Dependency*, Cambridge: Polity Press.

Spybey, T. (1996) *Globalization and World Society*, Cambridge: Polity Press.

Squires, A. (ed.) (1991) *Multi-Cultural Health Care and Rehabilitation*, London: Edward Arnold.

Sreberny-Mohammadi, A. (1996) 'The global and the local in international communications', in J. Curran and M. Gurevitch (eds) *Mass Media and Society* (2nd edn), London: Edward Arnold.

Stacey, B. (1978) *Political Socialization in Western Society*, London: Edward Arnold.

Stedman-Jones, G. (1992) *Outcast London: A Study of the Relationship between Classes in Victorian Society*, London: Penguin.

Steed, M. (1986) 'The core–periphery dimension of British politics', *Political Geography Quarterly*, Supplement to 5, 4: S91–S103.

Stevens, O. (1982) *Children Talking Politics: Political Learning in Childhood*, Oxford: Robertson.

Stevenson, G. (1993) *Third Party Politics since 1945*, Oxford: Blackwell.

Sulkunen, P. (1992) *The European New Middle Class*, Aldershot: Avebury.

Sullivan, J. L. (1988) *ETA and Basque Nationalism: The Fight for Euskadi 1890–1986*, London: Routledge.

Sutherland, M. (1990) 'General report', Paper prepared for ENWS Seminar, The Interface of Work and Family, Brussels, September.

Svensson, I. (1992) 'Gothenburg', in J. Ashton (ed.) *Healthy Cities*, Buckingham: Open University Press.

Symes, V. (1995) *Unemployment in Europe*, London: Routledge.

Task Force Human Resources Education, Training and Youth (1991) *Memorandum on Higher Education in the European Community*, Brussels: Communication from the Commission to the Council.

te Maarssen, A. and Janssen, L. (1994) 'Reforming health care in the Netherlands', *Health Services Management*, January: 19–21.

Thoma-Venske, H (1988) 'The religious life of Muslims in Berlin', in T. Gerholm and Y. G. Lithman (eds) *The New Islamic Presence in Western Europe*, London: Mansell.

Thomas, K. (1978) *Religion and the Decline of Magic*, Harmondsworth: Peregrine.

Thompson. E. P. (1968) *The Making of the English Working Class*, Harmondsworth: Penguin.

Thompson, J. (1991) 'East Europe's dark dawn', *National Geographic* 179, 6, June: 37–68.

Thompson, J. (1992) *Ideology and Modern Culture*, Cambridge: Polity Press.

Thränhardt, D. (1995) 'Germany: an undeclared immigration country', *New Community* 21, 1: 19–36.

Tilly, C. (1975) 'Reflections on the history of European state-making', in C. Tilly (ed.) *The Formation of National States in Western Europe*, Princeton, N.J.: Princeton University Press.

Tilly, C. (1992) *Coercion, Capital and European States AD 990–1992*, Oxford: Basil Blackwell.

Tilly, C. and Blockmans, W. P. (1994) *Cities and the Rise of States in Europe, AD 1000 to 1800*, Oxford: Westview Press.

Tilly, L. and Scott, J. (1978) *Women, Work and the Family*. London: Holt, Rhinehart and Winston.

Titmuss, R. (1968) *Commitment to Welfare*, London: Allen and Unwin.

Toffler, A. (1970) *Future Shock*, London: The Bodley Head.

Toffler, A. (1980) *The Third Wave*, London: William Collins.

Tonry, M. (1994) 'Proportionality, parsimony, and interchangeability of punishments', in A. Duff and D. Garland (eds) *A Reader on Punishment*, Oxford: Oxford University Press.

Towers, B. (1992) 'From AIDS to Alzheimer's', in J. Bailey (ed.) *Social Europe*, London: Longman.

Townsend, P. (1979) *Poverty in the UK*, Harmondsworth: Penguin.

Townsend, P. (1993) *The International Analysis of Poverty*, Brighton: Harvester Wheatsheaf.

Townsend, P. and Davidson, N. (eds) (1982) *Inequalities in Health: The Black Report (Sir Dougal Black et al.) and The Health Divide (Margaret Whitehead)*, Harmondsworth: Penguin.

Townsend, P., Phillimore, P. and Beattie, A. (1986) *Inequalities in Health in the Northern Region*, Northern Regional Health Authority.

Traynor, I. (1996) 'Welcome to the leisure zone', *The Guardian International*, 14 September: 10.

Tudor Hart, J. (1971) 'The inverse care law', *Lancet* 1: 405.

Tunstall, J. and Palmer, M. (eds) (1993) *Media Moguls*, London: Routledge.

Turner, B. (ed.) (1990) *Theories of Modernity and Postmodernity*, London: Sage.

Turner, B. (1992) *Regulating Bodies*, London: Routledge.

UN (1986) *World Population Prospects*, New York: United Nations.

UN (1991) *Demographic Yearbook 1989*, New York: United Nations.

UN (1994) *The Sex and Age Distribution of the World Populations*, New York: United Nations.

Unemployment Unit (1990) *Creative Counting*, London: Unemployment Unit.

Vagero, D. and Lundberg, O. (1989) 'Health inequalities in Britain and Sweden', *Lancet*, 2: 35–6.

Vagg, J. (1993) 'Context and linkage: Reflections on comparative research and "internationalism" in criminology', *British Journal of Criminology* 33, 4: 541–53.

van de Woude, A. M. (1972) 'Variations in the size and structure of the household in the United Provinces of the Netherlands in the seventeenth and eighteenth centuries', in P. Laslett and R. Wall (eds) *Household and Family in Past Times*, Cambridge: Cambridge University Press.

van den Wyngaert, C. (ed.) (1993) *Criminal Justice in the European Community*, London: Butterworth.

van der Kamp, J. and Cosijn, J. (1992) 'Eindhoven', in J. Ashton (ed.) *Healthy Cities*, Buckingham: Open University Press.

van Dijk, J. (1991) 'More than a matter of security: trends in crime prevention in Europe', in F. Heidensohn and M. Farrell, *Crime in Europe*, London: Routledge.

van Dijk, J., Mayhew, P. and Killias, M. (1991) *Experiences of Crime across the World: Key Findings of the 1989 International Crime Survey*, Deventer, Netherlands: Kluwer.

Vattimo, G. (1988) *The End of Modernity: Nihilism and Hermeneutics in Postmodern Culture*, Cambridge: Polity Press.

Vogel, T. (1987) 'The victims of unemployment: labour market policy and the burden of unemployment', in Z. Gerge and S. Miller (eds) *The Dynamics of Deprivation*, Aldershot: Gower.

von Waldersee, K. (1995) 'Volkswagen hit by strikes in trial of strength as union rejects longer working week', *The Guardian*, August 30.

Walby, S. (1990) *Theorizing Patriarchy*, Oxford: Basil Blackwell.

Walker, A. (1993) *Older People in Europe: Social Integration*, Brussels: Commission of the European Communities.

Walker, A. and Maltby, T. (1996) *Ageing Europe*, Buckingham: Open University Press.

Walker, A. and van Craeynest, D. (1993) 'Two barometer surveys: Europeans' attitudes towards ageing and older people', in *Social Europe*, 1/93, Brussels: Commission of the European Communities, 33–40.

Walker, A., Alber, J. and Guillemard, A.-M. (1993) *Older People in Europe: Social and Economic Policies*, Brussels: Commission of the European Communities.

Wall, R. (1989) 'The residence patterns of the elderly in Europe in the 1980s', in E. Grebenik, C. Hohn, and R. Mackensen (eds) *Later Phases of the Family Circle: Demographic Aspects*, Oxford: Clarendon Press.

Wallerstein, I. (1974) *The Modern World System*, New York: Academic Press.

Wallerstein, I. (1979) *The Capitalist World-Economy*, Cambridge: Cambridge University Press.

Ward, A. (1975) 'European capitalism's reserve army', *Monthly Review*, November, 17–32.

Weber, M. (1958) *The Protestant Ethic and the Spirit of Capitalism*, New York: Scribner's.

Weber, M. (1978) *Economy and Society* (2 vols), Berkeley, Calif.: University of California Press.

Wennemo, I. (1993) 'Infant mortality: public policy and inequality – a comparison of eighteen industrialised countries 1950–1985', *Sociology of Health and Illness* 15, 4: 429–46.

Whale, J. (1977) *The Politics of the Media*, London: Fontana.

Wheeler, J. (1974) *The Urban Circulation Noose*, Belmont: Wadsworth.

White, P. (1984) *The West European City: A Social Geography*, London: Longman.

Whiteford, P. and Kennedy, S. (1995) *Incomes and Living Standards of Older People*, London: HMS0.

Whitehead, M. (1987) *The Health Divide: Inequalities in Health in the 1980s*, London: Health Education Council.

Whitty, G. (1992) 'Education, economy and national culture', in R. Bocock and K.

Thompson (eds) *Social and Cultural Forms of Modernity*. Cambridge: Polity Press, in association with The Open University.

Wiener, M. (1981) *English Culture and the Decline of the Industrial Spirit 1850–1980*, Cambridge: Cambridge University Press.

Wilkinson, R. (1992) 'Income distribution and life expectancy', *British Medical Journal* 306: 165.

Willaime, J.-P. (1994) 'Protestant approaches to European unification', in J. Fulton and P. Gee (eds) *Religion in Contemporary Europe*, Lampeter: Edwin Mellen Press.

Williams, G. (1985) *When Was Wales?* Harmondsworth: Penguin.

Williams, O. F. and Houck, J. W. (eds) (1993) *Catholic Social Thought and the New World Order: Building on One Hundred Years*, Notre Dame: Notre Dame University Press.

Willis, P. (1977) *Learning to Labour: How Working Class Kids Get Working Class Jobs*, Aldershot: Saxon House.

Wilson, B. (1985) 'Secularisation: the inherited model', in P. E. Hammond (ed.) *The Sacred in a Secular Age*, London: University of California.

Wilson, C. (1965) *England's Apprenticeship 1603–1763*, London: Longman.

Wilson, E. (1977) *Women and the Welfare State*, London: Tavistock.

Wilson, G. (1987) 'Money: patterns of responsibility and irresponsibility in marriage', in J. Brannen and G. Wilson (eds) *Give and Take in Families: Studies in Resource Distribution*, London: Allen and Unwin.

Wilson, M. J. (1993) 'The German welfare state: a conservative regime in crisis', in A. Cochrane and J. Clarke (eds) *Comparing Welfare States: Britain in International Context*, London: Sage.

Winch, P. (1987) 'Ethical relativism', in his *Trying to Make Sense*, Oxford: Basil Blackwell.

Winter, J. (1986) *The Great War and the British People*, London: Macmillan.

Winther-Jensen, T. (1994) 'Denmark', in C. Brock and W. Tulasiewicz (eds) *Education in a Single Europe*, London: Routledge.

Witte, E. (1992) 'Belgian federalism: towards complexity and asymmetry', *West European Politics* 15, 4: 95–117.

Wolin, R. (1992) *The Terms of Cultural Criticism: The Frankfurt School, Existentialism, Poststructuralism*, New York: Columbia University Press.

Woods, B. (1993) *Communication, Technology and the Development of People*, London: Routledge.

Woods, R. T. (1989) *Alzheimer's Disease*, London: Souvenir Press.

Woolf, H. and Tumin, S. (1991) *Prison Disturbances April 1990*, Cmnd. 1456, London: HMSO.

Woolgar, S. (1988) *Science: The Very Idea*, London: Tavistock.

World Bank (1993) *World Development Report 1993: Investing for Health*, Oxford: Oxford University Press.

World Health Organization (1981) *Global Strategy for Health for All by the Year 2000*, Geneva: WHO.

Wrench, J. and Solomos, J. (1993) *Racism and Migration in Western Europe*, Oxford: Berg.

Youngs, G. (1994) 'Fighting talk', *The Guardian*, 16 March: 12.

Zaller, R. (1984) *Europe in Transition, 1660–1815*, Lanham, Md.: University Press of America.

Index

absolutist states: administration 58–9; development 56–9; diplomatic relations 61; military power 60–1; power hierarchy 57
Action for Cities (AfC) 416–19
adolescence 163
adversarial criminal justice 389–90
advertising 18–19, 289
AfC *see* Action for Cities
Africa: colonialism 32–3; European colonialism 437
ageism: definition 174; historical 177–84
agriculture: Common Agricultural Policy 353–4; decline 261; employment 103–4; mechanization 62; occupational transition 114–15; surplus production 73; working hours 102, 266
AIDS, mortality rates 368, 370
Albania: elderly 195; religion 245
Althusser, Louis 276
Americanization 281, 289
Amsterdam: city-state 54, 62; history 31–2
Antwerp, city-state 54
Aristotle, cities 27, 29

armies, absolutist states 57, 60–1
Austria: consociationalism 310, 311; elderly 189
Austro-Hungarian Empire 57
autonomous metropoles 34

Babylon 29
Balkans, religion 245, 246
bargaining metropoles 34
Basque Country: conflict 432; ETA 428, 432; nationalism 63, 424, 425
Belgium: child-care 139; consociationalism 311; criminal justice system 390; divorce 215; education 224, 226, 231; elderly 184, 188; infant mortality 367; migrant labour 152; nationalism 427; parental leave 139; political parties 305; poverty 348; religion 247; television 282; women 127, 130; youth 166
Benjamin, Walter 48
Berlin, political activity 43
Berlusconi, Silvio 278
Bertelsmann Group 287
Beyer, P. 242
bias, mass media 274–5
Black Death 31

Black Report 372–3
Black Women's Group 154
BNP *see* British National Party
Bochum, political activity 43
Bosnia 160
bourgeoisie 35, 37, 41, 43, 97
Bretton Woods arrangements 442–3, 444
Britain: assisted area status 415; child-care 139, 140; children 216; class attitudes 103–4; constitutional structure 315; crime 387; criminal justice system 389–90; criminal sentencing 391–2; de-industrialization 261, 407–8; divorce 215; education 224, 226, 227–9, 232, 236; EEC membership 3, 446; elderly 184, 187; employment 260, 266, 267; families 205, 212, 213, 214, 216; global power 85–6; health inequalities 371, 372–3; Health Service workers 154–5; healthcare expenditure 363, 364, 365; Healthy Cities Project 376; immigrants 149, 153, 154; income inequality 108–9; industrialization 12–16; Jewish immigrants 150; mass media 279; meritocracy 117–18; migrant labour 149, 154–5; Muslims 253; nation-state development 62; peripheral nationalism 426; political parties 305; poverty 346, 356–7; prisons 395; racism 156–7, 158, 159; religion 247, 248, 249, 250; social cleavages 315; social services provision 330, 331; social welfare policy 319, 321–4; social work examples 339–40; social workers 325–9, 334–5; television 282; unemployment 166; urban decline 402–3; urban policy 414–20; women 127, 130, 131, 134, 136; youth culture 167, 168–9; youth inequalities 165–6
British National Party (BNP) 157, 170–1
British Social Attitudes Reports 110, 112
Brittain, Leon 3
Brittany: Breton language 428; Breton nationalism 429
Bruges, city-state 54
Bulgaria: elderly 190; fertility rates 215
Burke, Peter 53–4

Callaghan, James 226
cancer, mortality rates 368–70
CAP *see* Common Agricultural Policy

capitalism: development 103; industrialism relationship 13, 27; Marxist view 97–8; migrant labour 151–5; organized 17–18
cardiovascular disease, mortality rates 368, 369
Castells, M. 152
Catalonia 426, 428
Central Council for the Education and Training of Social Workers 326
child-care, state provision 127, 139–40
children: child labour 206–7; mothers' employment 134–6; number in family 214–15, 216; outside marriage 215–16
China: European influence 439; European rationality comparison 72–3; state socialism 66; trade 54
Christianity: Balkans 246; historical spread 244–5; *see also* Church, the
Church, the: family roles 209; medieval period 56; modernity role 74; monarchy relationship 56, 58; state relationship 250–2
cities 402–22; assistance policies 413–20; categories 34–5; city-regions 404; city-states 52–5; crime rates 386; cultural regeneration 419; de-industrialization 407–8; decentralization 406–7; deprivation 409–13; early history 27–31; future 420–1; growth 30–2, 33; health 376; industrial 36–9; inner cities 408–9; medieval period 31–2; Mediterranean 27; metropolis development 43–8; modernity 47–8; personality types 46–7; political activity 43; population 402–4; problems 402–3; rioting 416; Roman Empire 27, 28; social conditions 39–43; social segregation 408–9; transport development 44–5; *see also* urbanization
citizenship rights 64–5
city-states 52–5
civilization, Western 70–6
Clarke, Kenneth 227–8
class system: analysis 119–20; attitudes 110–13; cities 42–3; definition 96; fragmentation 103–4; health inequalities 108; inequalities 106–10; Marxism 97–9; occupational differentiation 104–6; occupational transition 113–16; origins 15–16; political parties 305; Registrar-General's classification 105–6; service sector 19; social

mobility 113, 116–18; underclass 121,
349–50; war effects 21; Weber's view
99–100
CNN global news channel 287–8
Coca-Cola 289
Colbert, Jean-Baptiste 58
cold war 440
colonialism 32–4, 436, 437–8; demise
438–9
Common Agricultural Policy (CAP)
353–4
communication 6; global 436–7, 447; *see
also* mass media
communism, religion abolition 245
Community Charter of the Fundamental
Social Rights of Workers (1989) 144
community workers 325–6, 334–5
commuting 44–5; reverse 407
competition, employment opportunities
406
computers, post-modernism 87
conflicts, nationalism 431–3
consociationalism, political participation
310–12
Constantinople 34
constitutional structures 314–16
consumer goods, mass market 18–19
consumption sector 121
core–periphery model 405
corporatism, political participation 308–10
Corsica: conflict 432; families 206
cotton industry 13, 14
Council of Europe 446
Council of Ministers 3
craft-based industry 36, 37
crime 7, 380–97; comparative analysis
381–2; data sources 382–3; explaining
and controlling 388–9; official
statistics 383–6; penal policy 389–96;
self-policing 386; victimization surveys
382–3, 386–8
criminal justice systems 389–90;
sentencing 390–2
criminology 380–1
crusades 54
cultural imperialism 288–92
cultural reproduction 235
culture, global 439–40
culture industry 81
Curran, J. 277
customs duty 59
Cyprus, elderly 196
Czech Republic: elderly 191; television
283

Czechoslovakia: fertility rates 215;
religion 251

Dahrendorf, R. 114–15
Dallas 290
de Gaulle, Charles 3, 446
de-alignment 305–6
de-industrialization 407–8, 443–5
Denmark: child-care 139; children
215–16; criminal justice system 390;
divorce 215; education 224, 225,
229–30; elderly 184, 185; families 214;
Healthy Cities programme 376;
parental leave 137–9; racist violence
157; social workers 325–6; women
127, 129, 134, 136–7
deprivation: comparisons 412–13;
indicators 410–11
Descartes, René 70
Dickens, Charles, *Hard Times* 38, 41, 81
diplomacy, absolutist states 61
disabled people, poverty 349
diseases, death rates 374–5
division of labour, origins 14
divorce 215; rate comparison 217
Downes, David 393
Durkheim, E. 240

earnings *see* income
Eastern Europe, urbanization 27
EC *see* European Community
Economic and Monetary Union (EMU),
employment 258
economy: sectoral model 260; state
intervention 19–20; *see also* global
economy; market economy
education 6, 220–37; comprehensive
schools 228–9; curriculum 224–5, 226;
encyclopaedism 221, 222, 230;
European standardization 235–6;
female employment 134; folk schools
230; health relationship 372; higher
231–3; historical developments 220–3;
humanism 221, 222, 225, 228;
language teaching 225–6; National
Curriculum 226, 227, 236; naturalism
222, 224–5, 228; political repertoires
222–3; pre-school 223–4; primary
223–8; secondary 228–31; social
workers 326–9; sociological interpretations 233–5; vocational training 231;
vocationalism 221–2
EEC *see* European Economic
Community

EFTA *see* European Free Trade
Association
Eire *see* Ireland
elderly 174–98; Central Europe 189–90;
Eastern Europe 190–2; families 216;
living standards 184–96; loneliness
183–4; medicalization 180–1; Northern
Europe 184–6; post-modernism 181–4;
poverty 348; proportion of population
175–6; racism 184; Southern Europe
192–6; state provision 127; welfare
provision 175–7; Western Europe
186–8; *see also* ageism
electoral systems 312–14, 315–16
employment 6, 258–71; flexibility 262–5;
gender pay gap 132; industrial
relations 267–9; industrialization
effects 40–1; labour market segmentation 131–4; occupational transition
113–16; part-time 131, 132, 134, 264,
267, 268; sectoral structure 260–2;
service sector 261–2; socio-economic
groups 105–6; women 120, 128–40;
working hours 265–7; *see also* migrant
labour; unemployment
EMU *see* Economic and Monetary
Union
encyclopaedism, education 221, 222,
230
Engels, Friedrich 37–8, 416
Enlightenment 72, 76
epidemics 39
equality 5–6
Erasmus programme 163–4, 234
ERDF *see* European Regional
Development Fund
ESF *see* European Social Fund
ethics, global 88
ethnic groups: inequalities 120–1;
poverty 348–9; unemployment 166;
see also racism
ethnic identity: language 427–8; nationalism 427–30
ethnic origins 64
EU *see* European Union
Europe, definition 2
European Commission 3; equal opportunities 143–4
European Community (EC) 4, 446;
higher education 233, 234; structural
funds 413–14; youth programmes
163–5; *see also* European Union
European Economic Community (EEC)
446; formation 3; organization 3–4

European Free Trade Association
(EFTA) 446
European Parliament 3–4
European Regional Development Fund
(ERDF) 353–4
European Social Fund (ESF) 353
European Union (EU) 446; equal pay
legislation 142–3, 353; formation 2–4;
gender equality 142–4; migrant
workers legislation 353; poverty
programmes 354; racism policy 158–9;
Social Chapter 322, 355; social policy
352–6; television policy 292
European Values Systems Study Group
(EVSSG) 110, 112–13; families 211,
216–17; marriage 210; religion 245–50
Eurotechnet programme 234
EVSSG *see* European Values Systems
Study Group

factory system, origins 14–15
families 6, 202–18; accommodation 211;
definitions 202–3; economic aspects
210, 211–12; extended 203; gender
roles 208–9, 211–12; industrialization
relationship 41–2, 204–9; labour
206–7; nuclear 202–3, 204–5; political
dimension 212–13; size 204–6, 214;
social reproduction 203–4; structure
changes 213–16; values 216–17; *see
also* children; marriage
fascism 170–1
fertility rates 214–15
feudalism 56; decline 101–3; origins
100–1
film industry, globalization 288–9
Finland: education 224, 225–6; elderly
186; health inequalities 371–2; infant
mortality 366
First World War 20–1
Fletcher, R. 206
Florence 32, 35
Force programme 234
Ford, G. 169–70
Fordism 180, 280, 281, 286
Foucault, M. 180
France: child-care 139, 140; children
216; education 224, 226–7, 230;
elderly 183, 184, 188; families 212,
213, 214; formation 57; health
inequalities 371; healthcare expenditure 363, 364; industrial relations
268–9; migrant labour 149–50, 152;
Muslims 253; nation-state 62; parental

leave 139; patriarchal control 208;
  racist violence 157; religion 247, 248,
  250–1; social mobility 117; social
  workers 325; television 282; women
  127, 130, 131, 134, 136; youth 166
Frankfurt School 80–1
Friedrich the Great 58
functionalist theory of stratification
  118–19

Galileo 70
Gama, Vasco da 54, 55
GATT *see* General Agreements on
  Tarrifs and Trade
GDP *see* Gross Domestic Product
gender inequalities 126–45
gender roles, families 208–9, 211–12
General Agreements on Tarrifs and
  Trade (GATT) 443
generation gap, historical 162–3
Genoa, city-state 54
Germany: constitutional structure 315;
  education 224–5, 230, 231, 233;
  elderly 184, 189; employment 260,
  262, 266; Fachhochschulen 326, 328;
  families 213, 214, 217; fertility rates
  214; healthcare expenditure 364; local
  government 324; migrant labour
  148–9, 150, 152; Muslims 253, 254;
  organized capitalism 18; poverty 346;
  prisons 394; racism 155–6, 158;
  refugees 329; religion 247, 251; social
  identity 332; social mobility 117;
  social services provision 329–31;
  social support legislation 323; social
  welfare policy 319, 321–4; social
  workers 325; sociology views 79;
  Sozialpolitik 321; television 282;
  urbanization 44; women 127, 130, 131,
  134, 136, 140–1; youth 166, 168
Ghent, city-state 54
Gini coefficient 108
Gittins, D. 205
global economy 67, 442–5; European
  power 85–6; nineteenth century
  16–17; origins 74; triadization 2, 447
global military order 440–1
globalization: European role 436–48;
  mass media 286–92; religion 242;
  social impacts 331
Gordon, P. 160
Gorz, A. 152
governments, acceptable behaviour 299
Greece: ageism 178; children 216; city-

states 53; criminal justice system 390;
  divorce 215; education 225; elderly
  183, 184, 195; employment 260–1,
  266–7; families 214; healthcare
  expenditure 364; infant mortality 366;
  women 130, 134, 136; youth 166, 167
Greenwich Mean Time (GMT) 62
Gross Domestic Product (GDP), health
  expenditure relationship 364–5
gypsies 148, 154

Habermas, Jürgen 81–2
Handy, C. 265
Haussmann, George 45–6
health 360–78; education relationship
  372; healthcare expenditure relationship 365–6; industrial cities 39;
  inequalities 108, 360–2, 371–3;
  medical profession 373–6; socio-
  economic status relationship 372
healthcare: elderly 180–1; European
  systems 363–5; expenditure 362,
  363–5; expenditure/infant mortality
  relationship 366–7
Healthy Cities Project 374–6
Henry VIII 58
Heseltine, Michael 416
Hill, R. 170–1
Hobsbawm, E. J. 13, 16, 33, 148
Hollywood globalization 288–9
Holy Roman Empire 57
homosexuals, families 216
Hoover, employment competition 351,
  406
household, definition 203
housework, gender roles 211–12
humanism, education 221, 222, 225, 228
Hungary: death rate 177; elderly 191;
  fertility rates 215; religion 251; social
  mobility 117; television 283

Iceland, elderly 186
Ideological State Apparatuses 276
ideology, mass media 275–6
IMF *see* International Monetary Fund
immigration: European policy 158–60;
  see also migrant labour
imperialism 16
income: inadequate 345; inequalities
  106–10, 111
India: colonialism 33; television 291–2;
  trade 54
industrial relations 267–9
Industrial Revolution 12, 62

industrial transition 113–16
industrialism, capitalism relationship 13
industrialization 5, 12–23; ageism 180;
    Britain 12–16; cotton 13, 14; de-
    industrialization 407–8, 443–5;
    definitions 13, 27; Europe 16–20;
    family effects 204–9; iron production
    14; nation-state development 62–3;
    newly industrializing countries 444–5;
    origins 12–16, 102–3; proto-industrial
    period 34–6, 37; Soviet Union 21–2;
    steam power 14; urbanization relation-
    ship 26–7, 34–9; war 20–2; women
    41–2
industry: craft-based 36, 37; mass
    production 280–1; nationalized 66
inequalities: attitudes 110–13; employ-
    ment 120; ethnic groups 120–1; health
    108, 360–2, 371–3; income 106–10,
    111; pay rates 142–3; significance
    118–19; social 94–5; women 126–45;
    youth 165–7
infant mortality 360, 366–7; healthcare
    expenditure relationship 362; standard
    of living effects 373
information super-highway 286
information technology, post-modernism
    87
inquisitorial criminal justice 389–90
interest groups, political mediation
    306–12
International Bank for Reconstruction
    and Development see World Bank
International Crime Surveys 387–8
International Monetary Fund (IMF) 67,
    442–3
International Trade Organization (ITO)
    443
Ireland: child-care 139; EC funding 414;
    education 224; elderly 183, 184, 187;
    employment 260–1; families 126, 217;
    fertility rates 214; healthcare expendi-
    ture 364; infant mortality 367; social
    mobility 117; women 130, 134, 136,
    137; see also Northern Ireland
Iris programme 234
Irish, Britain's labour force 149, 150,
    151
iron industry 14
Islam: Balkans 246; European position
    244, 245, 252–4; trade blockade 54, 60
Italy: children 216; city-states 53; crime
    386; criminal justice system 390;
    divorce 215; EC funding 414; educa-

tion 228, 230–1; elderly 183, 184,
    193–4; families 206; infant mortality
    367; marginalization 35; mass media
    278; racist violence 157; religion 251;
    television 282; unemployment 269;
    women 130, 134, 136; youth 166
ITO see International Trade
    Organization

Japan: European influence 439; industri-
    alization 445; infant mortality 366;
    mass production 281
Jews: anti-Semitism 148, 155; Britain
    149, 150; European identity 244–5;
    migration 148; urban population 43
Johnston, L. 168
Jones, Gwyn 48
Joseph, Keith 350

Kay, J. P. 15
Kellerhals, J. 212–13
Kemp, T. 13
Keynes, John Maynard 443
kingdoms see sovereign states
Kinnock, Neil 3
kinship see families
Kokosalakis, N. 251

labour force: children 206–7; migrant
    labour 148–55; women 128–31
labour market: changes 350–1; women
    353
language: colonialism influence 437–8;
    ethnic identity 427–8; teaching 225–6
Laslett, P. 205
law, absolutist state 59
Le Play, Frederic 204–5
legislation, social support services
    323
Lenin, V. I. 16
Leonardo programme 163, 234
liberal democracy 65
liberal pluralism, mass media 277
life expectancy 360, 361
Lille 36
Lingua programme 234
Lipset, S. M. 303
Liverpool: health 376; overcrowding 39
local government, social welfare role
    324
London: cholera epidemic 39; financial
    centre 13; growth 34; political activity
    43; suburban development 44
Louis XIV 58

Luxembourg: corporatism 309; divorce 215; education 224, 225; elderly 184, 188; fertility rates 214; infant mortality 367; maternal mortality 367; parental leave 139; television 282; women 130, 136, 137; youth 166
Lyotard, J.-F. 87

Maastricht Treaty 4, 144, 446; Social Chapter 355
MacDonald, R. 169
McDonald's, mass production 280–1
Macfarlane, A. 205
Malta, elderly 194
Manchester: cultural regeneration 419–20; industrial growth 37
Marcuse, Herbert 80–1
market economy, emergence 73
market forces, inequalities formation 119
marriage: definition 202; divorce 215; divorce rate 217; expectations 210; homosexual 216; trends 215; see also families
Marseilles, foundation 27
Marshall, T. H. 65
Marx, Karl: class theory 15, 97–9; families 204; ideology 276; Irish workers 151; modernity 78–9; social mobility 117
mass communication 281
mass consumption 280–1
mass media 274–93; audience response 290–1; bias 274–5; cultural imperialism 288–92; future developments 284–6; globalization 286–92, 447; hypodermic model 280; ideology 275–6; liberal pluralism 277; mass-manipulative model 278–9; moguls 278–9; state collusion 278–9; television 282–4; transnational corporations 286–8; uses and gratifications approach 280; video cassette recorders 284, 285
mass production 280–1
mass society theory 279–80
maternal mortality 367, 368
maternity leave 137–8
Maxwell Communication Corporation 287
media see mass media
medicine, healthcare role 373–6
medieval period: ageism 178–9; cities 31–2; kingdoms 55–6

Mediterranean, cities 27
mercantilism 26, 31–2, 59, 75
Merchant, J. 169
meritocracy, Britain 117–18
Merseyside 414, 416
Mesopotamia, city-states 52–3
Methodenstreit 79
metropolis, development 43–8
migrant labour 148–55; discrimination 154–5; economic importance 152; racism 155–8; rights 353–4; welfare needs 153–4
migration, rural–urban 104
Milan 32
military order, global 440–1
military technology, absolutist states 60–1
modernity 70–90; certainty 83–6; cities 47–8; definition 72; post-modernism 86–9
Monaco, television 282
monarchy, Church relationship 56, 58
Monnet, Jean 3
mortality rates 206, 360, 361; causes 367–70; nineteenth century 39; Sweden 371–2; see also infant mortality; maternal mortality
Murdoch, Rupert 278–9, 286–7
Murray, C. 349–50

NAFTA see North American Free Trade Association
Naples, foundation 27
nation-states 5, 7; citizenship 64–5; development 61–3; global adoption 66–7
National Curriculum 226, 227, 236
national identity 7, 424–5
nationalism: conflicts 431–3; definition 64; ethnic identity 427–30; peripheral 7, 424–34; politics 430–1; youth 169–71
nationalization, industry 66
NATO see North Atlantic Treaty Organization
naturalism, education 222, 224–5, 228
navies, development 61
neo-conservatism, education 223
neo-liberalism, education 223
Netherlands: child-care 139; consociationalism 310, 311; crime 387, 388; education 224, 231, 233; elderly 184, 187; families 206, 217; health inequalities 371; healthcare expenditure 363;

Healthy Cities Project 376; migrant labour 149–50; political parties 305; prison system 393; religion 247, 248, 251; social workers 325; television 282; unemployment 269–70; urban regeneration 420; women 127, 130, 134; youth 166, 168
newly industrializing countries (NICs) 445
news agencies, global 286–9
news stories, bias 275
Nice, foundation 27
NICs *see* newly industrializing countries
Nietzsche, F. W. 84–5
Nigeria, nationalism 64
nihilism 85
North American Free Trade Association (NAFTA) 2, 447
North Atlantic Treaty Organization (NATO) 446
Northern Ireland: conflict 431–2; crime 386; peripherality 427; religion 249, 251
Norway: elderly 185; health inequalities 372; maternal mortality 367; prisons 395; television 282; women 127
Nuffield Mobility Study 117

Occitania 424
occupational differentiation, class system 104–6
occupational transition 113–16
Oil Producing and Exporting Countries (OPEC) 444
old age, definition 174
old people *see* elderly
Oldham 412–13
OPEC *see* Oil Producing and Exporting Countries
Oxford 412–13

Pacific Rim, domination 447–8
Pahl, R. 119–20
Paris: growth 35; Haussmann's redevelopment 45–6; modernity 47; political activity 43; suburban development 44
Parsons, T. 203–4
paternity leave 137–9
penal policy 389–96
pensions, elderly 184–96
peripherality 426–7
Perkin, H. 13, 15, 19–20
Plaid Cymru 304, 305
pluralism, political participation 307–8

plurality 313
Poggi, Gianfranco 58
Poland: death rate 177; elderly 191; families 210–11, 213; religion 245, 251, 252; social mobility 117; television 283
political activity, cities 43
political culture 298–300
political institutions 312–16
political participation 7, 298–316; education 222–3; electoral systems 312–14, 315–16; interest group mediation 306–12; peripheral nationalism 430–1
political parties 312–14; social cleavage 303–5, 306
political socialization 302–3
population: regional variations 404, 405–6; urban areas 402–3
Portugal: EC funding 414; education 228, 233; elderly 183, 184, 193; employment 260–1, 267; families 214; healthcare expenditure 364; infant mortality 366; maternal mortality 367; parental leave 139; poverty 346; women 129, 134, 136; youth 166
positivism 77–82
post-Fordism 281, 445
post-industrial economy 260
post-materialism 306
post-modernism 86–9; elderly 181–4
poverty 344–58; causes 349–52; definitions 344–5; disabled people 349; elderly 348; ethnic minorities 348–9; European Union programmes 354; explanations 349–52; health relationship 373; incidence 345–9; international comparisons 345–7; women 347–8
Powell, Enoch 415
prisons 393–6; women 395
progress, sociology 77
proletariat 41, 43, 97
property ownership, class system 99
proportional representation 313
proto-industrial period 34–6, 37
Prussia, bureaucracy 58
punishment 7

racism: cultural 158, 159; elderly 184; European policy 158–60; violence 155–8; youth 169–71
railways, European growth 17
rationality 71; China comparison 72–3

reason, modernity role 70
reconstructive sciences 82
Reformation 74–5
refugees, welfare provision 329
Registrar-General: social classes 105–6; socio-economic groups 105–6
relativism, post-modernism 88
religion 6, 240–55; abolition 245; Balkans 246; Britain 249; Christianity spread 244–5; church attendance 247–50; decline 246; definitions 240–1; European divisions 242–5; globalization 242; Islam 252–4; orthodox beliefs 248; Poland 252; privatization 241–2; secularization 241, 250; Sweden 254; unorthodox 250; *see also* Church, the
Renaissance 74; city-states 53–4
repressive tolerance 81
Rokkan, S. 303
Roman Empire: ageism 178; Christianity 244; cities 27, 28
Romania: elderly 192; families 213
Romanticism 77–8
Rome 29
Rotterdam, regeneration 420
rural–urban migration *see* migration
Russia: elderly 192; European influence 439; *see also* Soviet Union

Saunders, P. 117–18
Scandinavia: health inequalities 371–2; religion 248; women 127, 131
Schuman, Robert 3
science: debunking 88; modernity role 75–6; nineteenth century 17
scientific rationalism 47–8
Scotland: crime 383, 387; education 226; nationalism 424, 425, 428–9, 430–1; peripherality 426
Scottish National Party (SNP) 304, 305, 430
secularization 241
SEGs *see* socio-economic groups
sentencing, criminals 390–2
Serbia, television 283
service sector 261–2; origins 19; women 132–4
shanty towns 39
Sheffield, political activity 43
Simmel, Georg 46–7, 79
Single Market 4
single transferable votes 313
slave trade 33, 151

Slovakia, elderly 191
Smith, Adam 14
SNP *see* Scottish National Party
social class *see* class system
social cleavages: de-alignment 305–6; political behaviour 303–5; post-materialism 306
social dumping 351, 356, 357
social hierarchy, European cities 35
social indicators 410
social inequalities 94–5, 118–19
social mobility 113, 116–18
social pedagogues 325
social policy: Britain/Germany comparison 321–4; scope 320
social reformism, education 223
social reproduction 203–4, 235
social stratification 94–123; definition 95
social transformation, education 223
social values: formation 300–1; political culture 298–300
social welfare: comparisons 319; policy framework 321–4; provision 329–31; retrenchment 351–2
social work 318–42; analysis 332–3; paradoxes 336–40; partnership ideology 338; practice examples 339–40; practice/theory gap 333–4; praxis 337–9
social workers: education 326–9; management/practitioner gulf 328; policy implementation 331–41; role 325–6
socialization, political 302–3
society, origins 75–6
socio-economic groups (SEGs) 105–6; occupational transition 114–16
sociology, development 76–82
Socrates programme 163, 234
sovereign states 55–6; absolutist 56–61
Soviet Union: industrialization 21–2; state socialism 66; USA relationship 441; *see also* Russia
Spain: crime 387, 388; EC funding 414; education 228, 231; elderly 183, 184, 193; employment 261, 265; families 214; formation 57; healthcare expenditure 364; Healthy Cities Project 376; infant mortality 367; television 282; women 130, 134, 136; youth 166
Stalin, J. 21–2
standardization 280–1
state intervention, economy 19–20
state socialism 66

state, the 52–68; absolutist 56–61; Church relationship 250–2; city-states 52–5; creation 425; mass media collusion 278–9; nation-states 61–6; origins 52–3; sovereign state 55–61
statistics, crime 383–6
status groups 99
steam power 14
Structural Functionalism 118
structural funds 413–14
students: debt 232–3; Erasmus programme 163–4
subordinated metropoles 34–5
suburbs 44, 406–7
surveys, attitudes 110–13
Sweden: education 224; elderly 185; healthcare expenditure 363; Healthy Cities Project 376; infant mortality 366; mortality rates 371–2; parental leave 126, 137–9; religion 254; social mobility 117; television 282; women 127, 141–2
Switzerland: consociationalism 310, 311; elderly 190; families 212–13; healthcare expenditure 363; migrant labour 149, 150, 152; television 282

technology, mass media 282–6
television, cable and satellite 282–4
Tempus programme 234
tertiary sector see service sector
textile industry: craft-based 36; mechanization 14
Thatcherism: youth culture 167, 168–9; youth effects 165–6
Thirty Years War 60–1
Thompson, J. 276
Thränhardt, D. 156, 158
time, work regulation 62, 102
Tocqueville, A. de 250, 251
total war 20–1
trade: city-states 54–5; modernity role 75
trade unions 267–8
transnational corporations, mass media 286–8
transport, cities 44
triadization 447
Turkey: elderly 196; religion 251
Tuscany, families 206

UDCs see Urban Development Corporations
UK see Britain

UN see United Nations Organization
underclass 121, 349–50
unemployment 269–70; non-EU nationals 349; youth 166–7
United Nations Organization (UN), formation 66–7
United States of Europe 2, 4
unmarried mothers 349–50
UPAs see Urban Programme Areas
urban areas see cities
Urban Development Corporations (UDCs) 416
Urban Programme Areas (UPAs) 415–18
urban renewal 7
urbanization 26–49; behavioural 27; core–periphery model 405–6; definitions 26–7; industrialization relationship 26–7, 34–9; structural 26; see also cities
Uruk 53
USA: Declaration of Independence 63; global economy 67, 442–4; healthcare system 362; religion 251; Soviet Union relationship 441

values, political 300–1
Venice 35, 54–5
victimization surveys 382–3, 386–8
video cassette recorders 284, 285
Vienna 35
vocationalism, education 221–2
voting 312–14

Wales: ethnic identity 430; nationalism 424, 425, 433; Welsh language 428
war: industrialization effects 20–2; social effects 21
Weber, Max 59, 79–80; class system 99–100
welfare provision, elderly 175–7
welfare state 7; women 126–8, 137–40; see also social welfare
Westphalia Congress 61
Wilson, Harold 415
women 126–45; children 134–6; employment 120, 128–40; equality 142–4, 353; factory work 15; family role 208–9; family situation 208, 211; health 372; maternity leave 137–8; men's attitudes 136–7; migrant labour 154; nineteenth century 41–2; poverty 347–8; prisoners 395; service sector employment 19; welfare state 126–8, 137–40

work *see* employment
working class, industrial cities 37–8
working conditions, nineteenth century
  40–1
World Bank 67, 442–3
world economy *see* global economy
World Wars, social effects 21

young people *see* youth
youth 162–72; cultural exchange 164;
cultural life 167–9; historical attitudes
162–3; inequalities 165–7; nationalism
169–71; racism 169–71; student
mobility 163–4; unemployment
166–7
Youth for Europe programmes 163,
  164–5
Yugoslavia: elderly 194–5; religion 245

zadruggas 203